D1253857

EMPIRE

EMPIRE

The Russian Empire and Its Rivals

DOMINIC LIEVEN

Yale University Press

New Haven and London

*For my great-uncles Colonel Prince Anatol Lieven,
Regiment of Chevaliers Gardes, Imperial Russian Army, and
Lieutenant Thomas Kennedy, Royal Artillery, British Army,
and for my great-aunt Marjory Taylor (née Kennedy),
children of empire and its victims*

First published in Great Britain in 2000
by John Murray (Publishers) Ltd.
Published in the United States in 2001
by Yale University Press.

A catalogue record for this book is available from the British Library
Listed by the Library of Congress
ISBN 0-300-088590

Typeset in 10/12 Monotype Bembo by Servis Filmsetting Ltd, Manchester
Printed and bound in the United States of America

10 9 8 7 6 5 4 3 2 1

Contents

Maps

Preface

I have been interested in empires for a long time, but it has been a furtive and guilty interest. I am really a historian of tsarist Russia. For years, in bookshops, I would peep at works on other empires. Occasionally temptation would prove too strong and I would snatch a volume on the Habsburg monarchy or the Spanish empire in South America. But I never had the time to read widely or think systematically about empires.

Salvation came from an unexpected quarter. The appointment to a lectureship in politics, at the London School of Economics, of a young, rather nervous student who had just completed his PhD on tsarist history was bizarre. I had never read any work of political science, or indeed of any of the social sciences. The sum total of my knowledge of Soviet history was based on work done for one weekly essay written at Cambridge as an undergraduate. Living in the Soviet Union while researching for my thesis, I had regarded Soviet society and government above all as a tiresome obstacle between my archive and myself.

Then Mikhail Gorbachev became leader of the Soviet Union. By early 1988 I was very interested in current Soviet events and convinced that I was beginning to understand what was going on. By early 1989 the feeling stole upon me that I actually understood what was happening rather better than many professional Sovietologists. As the great issues of Russian history returned to the agenda in the Gorbachev era, the historian found little difficulty in orientating himself. The basic dilemma of the Gorbachev leadership was only too familiar to historians of the tsars. The competition for external power, status and security made it imperative for the empire's rulers to modernize its economy and society quickly. But rapid modernization imposed from above had the potential easily to run out of control, destroying regime and empire alike. In Russian history 'modernization' generally meant importing alien political and economic principles from the richer and more powerful West. Could an authoritarian empire rooted in very different principles import these alien conceptions and survive?

Nor were judgements on the Soviet Union's future just a question of drawing correct parallels with tsarist experience. Psychologically it was easier for a historian than for a Sovietologist to contemplate the thought that the Soviet Union might actually disappear. Historians have – or at least ought to have – long memories and broad horizons. They are attuned to dramatic changes. The Sovietological imagination was narrower, its memory stretching back to 1917 at most, and often not much beyond 1953, the year of Stalin's death. Nor is it at all easy to devote a lifetime to studying the elephant alive and on the hoof, only then to have to contemplate the extinction of the species.

As the Gorbachev era drew to its close, I decided to write a book on dilemmas of empire in Russian history. Above all, I conceived this as a study of nationalism and of international power politics. By studying questions of ethnicity and nationalism I would educate myself, since I had been shamefully remiss in concentrating on history at the centre and rather ignoring the problems of the tsarist and Soviet non-Russian peoples. By concentrating on power politics I might give a little nudge to my historian-colleagues, who for decades had been obsessed by the revolution of 1917 and who tended to regard attention to questions of power, strategy and diplomacy not merely as politically incorrect but also as an unfair intrusion into the all-consuming battles within the Western academic intelligentsia as to the rights and wrongs of the various ideological camps in 1917.

A fundamental purpose of this book is therefore to put the history of Russia within its international context. The demands of international power politics and of membership of the European and then global system of great powers were of overwhelming importance in Russian history. More probably than any other single factor they determined the history of modern Russia. This view is unpalatable to many Russians and is deeply unfashionable in Western, and especially American, academia. To a great extent, however, the English, the French and the Americans have been the subjects of global history in the last four centuries. To an increasing degree it has been their power, their values and ideologies that have imposed themselves on the other peoples of the world. Like most of these peoples the Russians have been the objects of this power – whether expressed in military, economic, ideological or cultural forms.

The Russians, even less than most other peoples, have certainly not been inert objects of West European and North American power. They have struggled with immense courage, brutality and perseverance to carve out an authentic, independent and distinct niche for themselves within modernity. But their whole modern history has been crucially influenced by the fact of their relative weakness, a fact that their geographical proximity to the heartlands of European power made evident to their rulers well before this reality imposed itself on most other non-Western peoples. The powerful can, up to a point and temporarily, afford to forget the realities of power. This is never an option for the weak. One partial way of looking at this book is therefore to see it as a study of relative weakness. At its heart is an analysis of Russia's position within the international system, of that system's dynamics, and of its impact on Russian history.

In the last years of the Soviet regime my thoughts wandered naturally if unsystematically towards comparisons with the decline and fall of great empires of the past, and I decided to look into empire as a concept and write a history comparing Russia and the Soviet Union to the great empires of the past. Colleagues who had muttered about my obsession with the nineteenth century would watch in surprise as I looked further beyond the nineteenth century to the eras of the Ottomans and the early Han. In comparing the Soviet Union to Rome and the early Han Empire I would be acceptably contemporary but also happily ancient. Thus was this book conceived.

My aim in writing it has been to see what the history of empire has to teach a scholar knowledgeable about Russia and what a Russianist can contribute to the overall history of empire. Initially I was overwhelmed by how much the Russianist had to learn. It remains the case that one of the great joys of working on this subject is that I have been able to read many superb books by other historians. In time, however, I did come to a modest confidence that the Russianist also had something to offer. No one has ever tried to write a study of empire from a Russian perspective. Most historians of empire steer well clear of Russia, which they see as an uncharted swamp patrolled by fierce and slightly weird academic guard dogs. To include the Soviet Union in a study of empire before 1991 was not just intellectually daunting but also politically suspect. For very many Western historians of Russia the country's uniqueness is a matter of faith. For many Russians it is the core of true religion itself. In comparing Russia to other societies it is by no means my intention to deny the uniqueness of Russian culture and history. If all histories and cultures are unique, Russia's are unique in more ways than most. That is no reason to keep Russia to itself in a box: after all, comparison is actually a good means of seeing what is truly unique in a people's history and culture. Moreover, precisely because a Russianist by definition comes to the study of empire from a strange angle, he or she may say something genuinely unusual and interesting.

An attempt to span the divide between history and political science, such as is made in this book, is even more difficult now that it would have been twenty years ago. The adherents of the powerful 'Rational Choice' school of political scientists, to whom the study of politics through history appears worthless, have pulled the study of politics in a positivist direction, taking supposedly 'hard' and 'scientific' economics as their model. Meanwhile the study of history has tended to move in the opposite direction, towards literary studies, narrative and postmodernism.

Even outside the Rational Choice school, many political scientists are not interested in anything that occurred more than fifty years ago. Dominated by the Americans, and to a lesser extent the British and the French, political science can be politically very correct. This book is certainly not an apologia for empire, but even an attempt to understand an empire's dilemmas and to compare some of its achievements not unfavourably with democratic nationalism will raise hackles.

Above all, however, the book's methodology will have its critics. Political science is concerned with concepts, and especially with concepts that are sharply defined, all-encompassing, and applicable to the politics of today's world. I have benefited greatly from precise and wide-ranging debates among my colleagues about concepts such as nationalism, legitimacy and power. I am myself very interested in the history and meanings of the word 'empire' and in this book I use the idea of empire as a central organizing principle and a means of comparison between a number of great imperial polities. But it is absolutely not my intention to set up empire as some sharply precise, all-encompassing concept through which to comprehend present-day polities. In fact, quite the opposite: in this book I go to great lengths to show that empire is a rich and imprecise concept full of ideological traps and very dangerous when applied in current political debate. I do not believe that it is possible to advance a useful general theory about the nature and fate of empire: certainly I have no intention of trying to do so in this work.

Time matters greatly to historians, and time is an easy victim of a book of this scale, with its insistent need to compress, to compare and to hurry. Academic works of history generally focus on rather narrow subjects, at least in comparison to the present topic. For a number of historians the whole idea of comparative history is nonsense: to them history is a seamless web, societies and events are unique, and the sort of comparisons attempted in the present work have no validity. Above all, concern for original sources and their correct interpretation is at the core of the historian's trade. A book on the scale of this one cannot be much concerned with original sources, faces all the dangers of dependence on other scholars' interpretations, and therefore has inevitable weaknesses.

Nevertheless, a book of this scale and ambition seemed to me opportune. Empire is a crucial subject, with a lot to say about the nature of power today and the moral and historical foundations of our world. These questions are also vital to Russia's history and its future. Formers of Western public opinion and Western policy-makers will think more clearly about Russia if they compare its past and present to those of other empires.

For Russia and Russians are the core of this book, of its subject and even its intended readership. This is a difficult but important moment in Russian history, when the country's identity and its future are being redefined. Given empire's overwhelming role in Russian history, coming to terms with empire is absolutely central to this redefinition. To make an impact on this debate, it is essential to look at empire in the round and comparatively, stressing Russia's place in the shifting European and global constellation of power. Given the tremendous constraints under which scholars operated, it is remarkable how much good history was written in the Soviet Union. Nevertheless, it is hard to deny that the cutting edge of scholarship during the Soviet period was usually Western, and above all North American. It is in no way a criticism of this often splendid work to state the obvious fact that historians are inevitably influenced by the ideology and values of their own society, and by the problems and issues which appear of paramount concern to that society at any given time. It is high time for Russians to regain the lead in the writing of their own history. The process has great possibilities and great dangers. The subject of empire comes high on the list under both headings. Hence the potential usefulness of a book such as this.

Whole pages have passed in which I have talked about empire without defining what I mean by the term. My definition of empire is actually very simple and unsophisticated. In this book all I mean by empire is, first and foremost, a very great power that has left its mark on the international relations of an era. I also mean a polity that rules over wide territories and many peoples, since the management of space and multi-ethnicity is one of the great perennial dilemmas of empire. For me, an empire is by definition not a democracy, in other words not a polity ruled with the explicit consent of its peoples. Since very few societies indeed before the nineteenth century were democratic in this sense, this distinction only acquires salience in modern times. Even then, to say that empire is undemocratic does not necessarily mean that it is illegitimate or unpopular in the eyes of most of its subjects. To these definitions I would add that the most interesting and important empires have been those liked to some great religion and high culture, thereby leaving a major impact on the history of world civilisation.

It seems to me that these criteria do differentiate an empire rather clearly from both a nation state and a multi-ethnic polity, but I would be the last to claim that the distinction is entirely clear-cut. How and when a people signifies its consent to government, for example, is a thorny question. And again, many states share some but not all of empire's characteristics. By a process of assimilation of peoples and democratization of institutions empires can transform themselves into multi-national federations or even nation states. It is, for example, one of this book's aims to ask whether and in what senses the European Union, the United States and a number of other contemporary states can usefully be described as empires. On the other hand, it is certainly not my intention, by defining the Soviet Union as an empire, to imply that it was necessarily doomed to disintegration.

It is important to make clear also what I do not mean by empire, since my definition of the term is not the one most current among scholars. The more usual definition sees empire as the political and cultural domination, and the economic exploitation, of the colonial periphery by the metropolitan state and nation. This definition owes most to twentieth-century Marxist scholarship. It has flourished because of its political salience. Arguments about empire defined in these terms went to the heart of Cold War polemics. This definition also fits another crucial contemporary political debate about the origins and causes of the huge disparity of wealth and power between the First and Third worlds. The models for this understanding of empire are the modern West European maritime empires in which a very clear distinction existed between their rich, White metropolitan core nations, which enjoyed democratic political rights, and their much poorer, non-White, colonies beyond the oceans which were subject to some form of authoritarian rule. This conception assumes the existence of metropolitan nations, by which I mean countries united not just by cultural and ethnic solidarity, but also by a conception of citizenship and civic equality. Particularly where the British, French and Dutch empires are concerned, this assumption of metropolitan nationhood is largely correct.

In some cases pre-modern empires were also created by nations: Rome is the obvious example. More often, however, they were the creation of some variety of aristocratic, warrior elite whose sense of solidarity with subordinates even of similar ethic origin could be anything from weak to non-existent. On the other hand these elites might well accept, assimilate or cooperate with the aristocracies of the initially peripheral regions of the empires. Many aristocratic empires exploited the population of their core territories more ruthlessly than the peripheral regions because it was politically safer and logistically easier to do so. A further traditional variation on the theme of empire is seen in regimes linked to great universal proselytizing religions. Such polities could become enormous empires in which distinctions between centre and periphery were weakened by common religious allegiance and by relatively open recruitment into the elite of people from diverse ethnic and regional backgrounds.

It is one of the main themes of this book that the student of contemporary politics cannot afford to ignore the experience of these empires. Certainly no student of Russian history and politics can afford to do so. Most of these empires were great homogeneous land masses, ruled over by monarchs who in principle at least wielded absolute power, embodying some great universalist religion and high culture, and dominated by an elite which in culture, sympathy and identity was divorced to varying degrees from all plebeian elements in the population. The parallels between this and key aspects of the tsarist and Soviet empires are too obvious to need much emphasis. On the other hand, both the pre- and post-1917 Russian empires had major similarities too with modern European maritime empires. From the eighteenth century the ideologies that sustained, legitimized and partly motivated the Russian and Soviet empires were largely Western European in origin. So too were most of the techniques and technologies that enabled Russia to expand so successfully. The subjects of empire, often non-Christian and sometimes nomadic, were frequently similar in the Western European and Russian cases, as was the timespan of the Russian Empire's rise and fall between the sixteenth and twentieth centuries. Above all perhaps, the key dilemma of modern empire was similar – how to square the demands of power, which required a state of continental scale, with the challenge presented by ethnic nationalism.

Empires have existed since ancient times. They are one of the commonest forms of state in history. To write the history of empire would be close to writing the history of mankind. No one can be a true expert on so huge a subject. The history of empire cannot be 'merely' political, military and diplomatic. Economics is crucial and so too is culture. In the long run the strength and attractiveness of an empire's culture will contribute greatly to its longevity and its influence. Imperial ideologies are both fascinating in themselves and vital to empire's survival. The rise and fall of empires has much to do with the history of ideas: it is very far from being the mere story of power defined in crudely material terms. The history of the word 'empire' stretches back two millennia to the Latin *imperium*. So ancient a word and concept has acquired many meanings and connotations even in English, let alone when translated across languages and cultures. Many of these meanings are highly polemical. To unravel the theme of empire, these many meanings have to be detected and explored. Above all, empires are by definition huge and varied polities. Generalizing about their many provinces and colonies can be perilous. To be significant, empires must survive over long periods, during which they always evolve and sometimes change radically. An empire is a kaleidoscope moving through space and time. Comparing kaleidoscopes is never easy and nor certainly is the comparative history of empire. When that comparative history is merged with an attempt to analyse Russia's place within the international system of states, matters get still more complicated. My own imperfect method for surmounting this challenge is organized in the following way.

First (Part One, 'Empire') I introduce the concept of empire and explain the international context in which the Russian state had to survive. In Part Two, 'Empires', I consider in some detail the rise and fall of three empires which were contemporaries and rivals of the Russian Empire – the British, the Ottoman and the Habsburg. Part Three, 'Russia', is devoted to a study of the Russian Empire from its sixteenth-century origins to its demise in 1917 and of the succeeding Soviet Empire. Part Four, 'After Empire', compares the results of empire's collapse in the former Soviet Union with the earlier experience of the Ottoman, Habsburg and British empires.

In the first of the two chapters of Part One I look at the many meanings of the word 'empire' over the millennia, at the way it has travelled across languages and cultures, and at the polemics that have surrounded the term. To understand empires some grasp of the word's importance, of the politically charged connotations it has acquired, and of the richness of the word's history, is vital. One reason for writing this chapter has been to warn the reader about the many hidden traps the word possesses for the unwary. Another is to show that empire is actually a much more interesting idea than contemporary polemics about imperialism might suggest. In one sense the aim of the chapter is not at all to clarify the concept of empire in the reader's mind: indeed, quite the opposite. Far from attempting a single, dogmatic, all-encompassing definition against which all empires might be measured, this chapter shows how various, contradictory and important the meanings of 'empire' have been.

Chapter 2 has a number of crucial purposes. Its opening section compares the ancient Roman Empire with imperial China. It seeks too to explain why a tradition of imperial universalism has on the whole prevailed in China, whereas since the fall of the Roman Empire, Europe has been a continent divided into many centres of power, which in time became sovereign and even nation states. The aim of this section is to introduce the reader to key aspects of empire (e.g. direct and indirect rule, aristocratic and bureaucratic empire, the roles of culture and assimilation) which will be recurring themes of this book. This section also attempts to explain the survival of empire in China and its demise in Europe by invoking key sources of power[1] (geopolitical, demographic, military, political, economic and ideological-cultural) to which I return on many later occasions when discussing the power of empires and the reasons for their rise and fall.

In explaining the origins of the European state system, this opening section of Chapter 2 introduces the context in which the Russian state operated, a context which was of crucial importance to Russia and is at the centre of this book. The rise and fall of the Russian and Soviet empires was determined to a great extent by geopolitics, by the nature of the European (and later global) system of states, and by the strengths and weaknesses of Russia's rivals. Most of Chapter 2 – all of its central sections – is devoted to explanation of these issues. These sections are designed to illustrate the various sources of power of the major European states, the dilemmas of power and empire from the seventeenth to the twentieth century, and the shifting relations between Europe's great powers. The nature of power and the balance between its elements (e.g. military, economic, ideological) to some extent shifted between the pre-industrial and industrial eras, and again in the late twentieth-century era of the computer and the microchip. This had big implications for the rise and fall of Russian and Soviet empire but so too did the shifting relationships between Russia's rivals.

The final section of Chapter 2 takes up the theme of the present global order by looking at a number of polities from the perspective of empire. One purpose of this is to see how the sources of power in today's world are changing. Another is to measure the strengths and weaknesses of the 'new world order' which exists under the hegemony of the United States. Russia's future will depend enormously on the nature and the stability of this global order, meaning above all the benefits, constraints and temptations which it will offer to a weak and defeated Russia. But the last section of Chapter 2 has another purpose which links it to Chapter I and to a key aim of this book as a whole. The concept of empire is dangerous: to European and American eyes it has a built-in teleology. Empire is redundant, wicked and doomed. The fall of the dynastic empires in 1917-18, confirmed by the collapse of first the European colonial empires and then the Soviet Union, underlines the power of nations and history's verdict against empire. In fact matters are not so clear-cut. The nation state itself, empire's nemesis, now also faces a major challenge. Witness the impact of multi-culturalism and globalization, or the emergence of the European Union. Meanwhile the three greatest states in Asia — India, Indonesia and China, though they are not empires, bear many of empire's marks and face many of its dilemmas. One aim of this section is therefore to stress the point that the history of empire and of twentieth-century international relations is not just a simple morality play in which evil empire is overthrown by the democratic nation state, harbinger of progress.

In Part Two, 'Empires', systematic comparison of empires begins. Tsarist Russia's three main rivals, the British, Austrian and Ottoman empires, are here covered. These were very different in many ways both from each other and from Russia. They differed in their relative power and in the balance of the elements (military, political, economic, geographical, demographic, cultural and ideological) by which imperial power is constituted. They varied too in the cultures and political traditions from which they sprang, in the number and variety of the peoples they ruled and in other crucial ways. In the nineteenth century Britain was the world's leading industrial power, the Ottoman realm was becoming a backward periphery of Europe, and Austria like Russia was a hybrid, in some respects modern and capitalist, in others a military, dynastic, land empire based on very traditional principles. These three imperial polities therefore provide a very wide range of variations on the theme of empire against which Russia can be compared. But the comparison is made more pointed and revealing by the fact that these polities competed with Russia in the same era and international system of states, thereby sharing key dilemmas of empire.

In Part Three, 'Russia', Chapter 6 concentrates on the geopolitics of empire in Northern Eurasia, on the significance of Russia's peripheral position in Europe and the global economy, and on the very different types of empire that existed in Russia's various borderlands. Chapter 7 investigates the origins of Russian statehood and national identity before empire began in the sixteenth century, and the way in which tsarist political traditions, originating before empire began, influenced the whole subsequent nature and development of the Russian Empire. Chapter 8 studies the rise and fall of tsarist empire. Above all, it explores how and why the rulers of tsarist Russia responded in specific, and often unique, ways to the general dilemmas of empire which I discussed in Chapter 2. Chapter 9 is in no sense a general history of the Soviet Union, or even a narrative of Soviet empire. Rather, it compares the Soviet Union above all to the tsarist, British, Ottoman and Habsburg empires, the aim being to show both the imperial quality of the Soviet regime and its many peculiarities when compared to other empires. The chapter on the Soviet Union is also designed to bring together general themes discussed in earlier chapters and in particular to show how the USSR combined many unique features with elements very familiar to historians both of modern West European maritime empires and some of the great empires of antiquity and Islam.

Part Four, 'After Empire', consists of only one chapter, though a long one. I looks first at the aftermath of British, Ottoman and Habsburg empires in the twentieth century. It seeks to show the consequences of empire's collapse for its former 'colonies', for the 'ruling' imperial people and their state, and for the international order, and then, in rather more detail, examines the aftermath of Soviet power in Northern Eurasia. Above all, its aim is a comparison of the consequences of Soviet empire and its collapse in the 1990s with what happened after the fall of the Ottoman, Habsburg and British empires.

The history of empire is far too important to be value-free. The rise and fall of empires to a great extent determines which values and ideologies will dominate an era. The study of empire says much about the contemporary global order, its origins, its moral and political bases, and the manner in which it may evolve. It is important to study empire in as many-sided, objective and 'sympathetic' a way as one can manage. It is neither possible nor desirable to be neutral about its history. In this subject neutrality would be equivalent to indifference to the fate of the human race. Judgements are inevitably influenced by who one is and by the dominant perspectives and values of the time at which one is writing. The descendent of a West Indian slave may have a rather different perspective on the British Empire from that of a European liberated from Nazi rule by British and imperial armies. It is certainly possible to condemn outright the hideous suffering of those subjected to Stalin's rule but idle to pretend that history would not have mitigated this condemnation had the society he created endured for generations and resulted ultimately in ever higher levels of material prosperity, Soviet global power, and even some degree of individual freedom. In writing this book I have done my best to be objective and to present as rounded a picture of empire as possible.

Narrative is back in fashion. Historians are in the business not just of establishing truths but also of telling stories, often of how individuals and communities perceive themselves. Perhaps therefore I can be forgiven for telling part of the story of empire as it relates to my own family and the lives of the three people to whom this book is dedicated, children of empire and its victims. To do so is to say something of the ambivalence of power and empire, and of the lives and identities which are associated with them.

At first glance my grandfather's brother, (Prince) Anatol Lieven, might seem an unlikely victim of anything. The son of Alexander II's Lord Chamberlain and himself a great landowner, he lived at the summit of tsarist Russia's aristocratic society. He commanded the Escort (i.e. First) Squadron of the regiment of Chevaliers Gardes, the senior cavalry unit of the Russian Imperial Guard. Since the time in the late eighteenth century when his great-grandmother had been a close friend of Maria Fyodorovna, Paul I's empress, and the governess of her children, the Lievens had been very close to the Romanov family. Though supposedly descended through his mother from Peter I, Anatol Lieven was neither ethnically Russian nor Orthodox in religion; though he was much more Russian in sympathy and Petersburg in culture than the overwhelming majority of the Baltic German landowning nobility, the class from which his family sprang. For many centuries before 1750 the Lievens had been rather typical members of the German warrior and landowning class which dominated most of the coastlands of the Baltic Sea from Denmark to Estonia.

But it was always the family's belief that ultimately they were not of German origin, being instead descended from the Liv chieftain who had collaborated with invading German knights and converted to Christianity at the end of the twelfth century. In a Gothic gesture Anatol Lieven's father had bought back the area from which his ultimate Liv ancestor derived, building a fine Palladian house with splendid views over a Romantic landscape of valley, river and forest. True or not, the family's story about its origins shaped Anatol Lieven's identity and actions amidst the conflicts between Russians, Germans and Latvians that dominated much of his homeland's politics during his lifetime – a lifetime in which the old dynastic and aristocratic world was largely displaced by the voices of communism and nationalism. After fighting with courage and distinction in the Chevaliers Gardes in the First World War, he commanded a section of Yudenich's White army in the

Russian Civil War, being severely wounded in the cause of preserving the empire ('Russia – one, great and indivisible'), the goal for which the White movement stood. Subsequently he refused to support efforts to use his force in a coup to stop the progress toward majority rule in Latvia, though the republic's domination by the ethnic Latvian majority would inevitably doom not merely his family's traditional position of leadership but also their landowning wealth.

In nineteenth-century Ireland my mother's family, Gaelic Catholics who provided two Chief Justices of Ireland for the crown, to some extent duplicated the Lievens' equivocal position within empire, though one rung lower in the social ladder, at the point where the landowning gentry and the top of the professional middle class intersected.

My mother's father was a judge in the (British) Indian Civil Service. Her sense of British identity was consolidated by her experience as an ambulance-driver in the Second World War, attached first to General Huntziger's Second French Army at Sedan in 1939–40 and then to the British Eighth Army in North Africa. But her family's Britishness was never unequivocal. She herself was largely educated at home by a governess at a time when her parents were still on service in India. She was never taught any English or Irish history since this caused quarrels between her loyalist uncle and her republican aunt. Instead she was taught Chinese and Byzantine history, and the French, German and Italian languages. Entrusted to the English for two final years of school in a Cambridge convent, she was then dispatched to the great Catholic capitals of Europe for the next four years: one year apiece in Rome and Vienna, and two in Paris, where her family had close French relations (the other great Catholic capital, Madrid, was not an option in the late 1930s). A memory lingered of a time when Gaelic Ireland served with pride in the armies of royal and Catholic France.

Most interesting of all, though also most tragic, was the experience of my only truly middle-class great-grandfather, a successful Scottish barrister in late-Victorian India, two of whose children, Marjory and Thomas Kennedy, figure in this book's dedication. After the death of his first wife their father, Pringle Kennedy, married an Indian woman, at that time something which required considerable moral and social courage. Marjory and Thomas were the children of that second marriage. In 1908 their mother and one of their half-sisters were assassinated by Indian nationalists, who mistook their carriage for that of an unpopular British official and threw a bomb into it. In no British or Indian history book that I have seen is it mentioned that in this incident, the only politically motivated killing of White women in India between the 1857 rebellion and the end of the Raj, one of the victims was actually an Indian. Thomas Kennedy, a lieutenant in the Royal Artillery, was killed at Ypres in 1915, aged nineteen. His sister Marjory lived to the age of ninety, worked for a time for Arnold Toynbee and was a woman of exceptional courage and intelligence, unbowed either by family tragedy or by the taint of mixed blood in a world shot through with racial prejudice. Far too proud and independent to consider herself a victim of anything, she was very much a child of the British Empire.

I leave it to the reader to decide what influence this mixed heritage has had on my judgements in this book. For myself I am conscious both of an acute inherited interest in empire and a great dislike for the fashions and academic camps that sometimes distort its study.

Acknowledgements

Many people and institutions have helped me to produce this book. The British Academy and the Nuffield Foundation both gave me fellowships, and I was also awarded a one-year fellowship by the Economic and Social Research Council, though in the end I was not in a position to take up the offer. My deep thanks go to all three institutions. My publishers, Grant McIntyre and Tsuneo Taguchi, have been patient with a work which grew bigger in ambition and scale with every passing month. Antony Wood had to cope with readers' comments arriving in the midst of the copyediting, with only ten months to go before the deadline for publication imposed by the Research Assessment Exercise. I am very grateful to him for his patience.

A number of people read all or part of the manuscript for me. I owe a great debt to Professor Christopher Bayly, of Cambridge University's History Faculty, and Professor Geoffrey Hosking, of the History Department of the School of Slavonic and East European Studies, University of London. My brother, Anatol Lieven, read most of it, often at times when he himself was extremely overworked. My colleagues, Dr James Hughes and Dr Gwendolyn Sasse, also read the final section at short notice and corrected a number of errors. I am very grateful to all of them. For two years I taught an MSc programme on empires at the London School of Economics with Dr Christopher Binns, from whom I learned a great deal, above all about the Roman Empire. Professor Michael Leifer, of LSE's Department of International Relations, gave me sound advice about Indonesian history and politics. A word of thanks is also in order to the battered British community of scholars of Russia and the former Soviet Union. Given the strain under which so many colleagues have been working, their combination of constructive criticism, charity and benevolent despair at the ramblings of an obsessive imperialist has been admirable and much appreciated.

During my research for this book I found myself reading about subjects

I had not thought about since my undergraduate or even school days. In so doing I was sometimes reminded of how fortunate I had been in my history teachers from an early age. Desmond Gregory at Downside was the original source of my interest in the American Civil War period. For this and for many other reasons I owe him a great debt. Memories returned too of seminars on American history at Cambridge with Dr Jonathan Steinberg, as well as sessions on British history with Professor Henry Pelling and Dr Neil McKendrick, and on modern European history with Professors Simon Schama and Norman Stone. Any scholarship of any value that I produce always carries the mark of the superviser of my PhD, Professor Hugh Seton-Watson, and of my former colleagues at LSE, Professors Leonard Schapiro and Peter Reddaway. Of these only Peter Reddaway is still alive: his record in being proved right both as regards the vulnerability of the Soviet regime and as regards the moral and political bankruptcy of much of the strategy pursued by the Yeltsin government is almost unique in the profession.

My students have also often been a source of renewed enthusiasm and support as I struggled to write this book. If fifty-plus postgraduate tutees simultaneously might sometimes be described as a bit too much of a good thing, nevertheless teaching the history of Russia and the comparative history of empires to interested, intelligent and very cosmopolitan graduate students at LSE has been a privilege. Above all, my PhD students, many now fled the nest and secure in academic posts, have been a great source of support and friendship. To list them all would not be possible, but those whose subjects came closest to this book include: Philip Boobbyer, Elisa Chait, Sally Cummings, Mark Galleotti, Michael Hughes, Nicole Jackson, Dejan Jovic, Razmik Panossian, Gudrun Persson, Zhand Shakibi, Carolina Vendil and Andrew Wilson.

The sheer scale of this book has inevitably made annotation a difficult matter. The attempt to note the sources for all the facts, ideas and interpretations it contains would have resulted in hundreds of pages of notes, some of them requiring detailed assessments of scholarly debates on specific issues: I have confined myself to noting direct quotations, key statistics and occasions when I am conscious of having borrowed an idea in its entirety from another scholar. My discursive bibliography, which must be regarded as short, sets out a few of the key works that introduced me to this book's many themes; my deep thanks go to all the scholars represented in it and my apologies to anyone whom I have inadvertently omitted.

During the period when this book was being researched and written I was very fortunate indeed to have four extremely hard-working and conscientious heads of department, deeply committed to encouraging first-class scholarship. In any British university today the job of head of department is miserable, ungrateful and very frustrating. I feel a great sense of gratitude to Brian Barry and Alan Beattie, who worked immensely hard to adapt the Department of Government at LSE to modern British academic realities, and to Christopher Hood, who was the most efficient, the fairest and the most conscientious convenor that I have ever encountered in any university. Fairer, more generous with his own time and effort, and more efficient than Christopher it is not actually possible for any head of department to be. My current convenor, Brendan O'Leary, convinced me, for the first time in a career spanning over twenty years at LSE, that a rather idiosyncratic historian like myself actually belonged in comparative politics and in the Government Department: for this too enormous thanks.

Last but definitely not least comes my family. My son Maxie was really the biggest victim of my enthusiasm for empires. Overexcited by the fall of the Berlin Wall, and by the liberation and re-emergence of Central Europe, I christened him Maximilian Leopold. He has survived and his books and videos on intergalactic empires have provided a new angle on my studies. My daughter Aleka has had to put up with an exhausted and frequently hysterical father, trying to cope with life and empire simultaneously. My wife, Mikiko, has coped with the hectic life of an investment banker and a husband who wakes up at all hours of the night ranting about Napoleon and ancient Chinese emperors. Our house high on a hill in Japan, with its face to Mount Fuji and its back to the Pacific Ocean, is a good vantage-point from which to view empire, Russia and the sometimes Gogolian world of the contemporary British university.

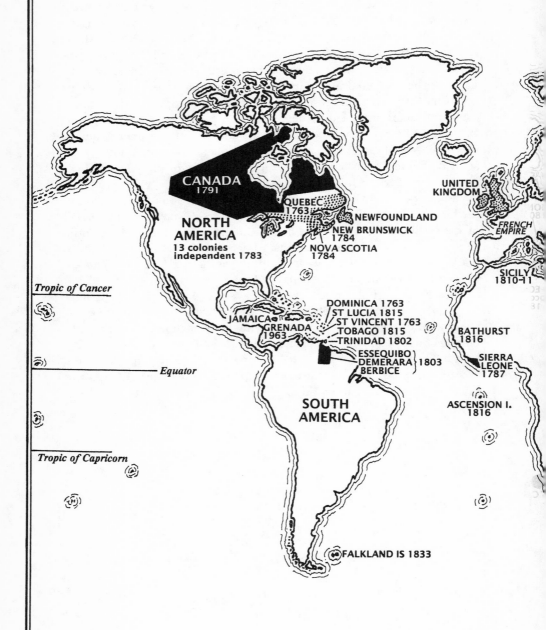

1. EXPANSION OF THE BRITISH

CANADA
1791

QUEBEC
1763

NEWFOUNDLAND

NEW BRUNSWICK
1784

NORTH
AMERICA
13 colonies
independent 1783

NOVA SCOTIA
1784

UNITED
KINGDOM

FRENCH
EMPIRE

SICILY
1810-11

Tropic of Cancer

DOMINICA 1763
ST LUCIA 1815
ST VINCENT 1763
TOBAGO 1815
TRINIDAD 1802

JAMAICA
GRENADA
1963

BATHURST
1816

ESSEQUIBO
DEMERARA } 1803
BERBICE

SIERRA
LEONE
1787

Equator

SOUTH
AMERICA

ASCENSION I.
1816

Tropic of Capricorn

FALKLAND IS 1833

MC

EMPIRE, 1750–1830

RUSSIAN EMPIRE

IONIA
1809-14

OTTOMAN
& EMPIRE
MALTA
1800

CHINA

JAPAN

EGYPT
occupied
1801

SINDH
1838

BENGAL
1765

ASSAM
1826

East India Co.
factory at Canton

ADEN
1829

INDIA
Bombay 1798–
1818

ARAKAN
1826

Calcutta
Madras

TENASSERIM
1826

AFRICA

CEYLON
1797–1818

PENANG
1786

SINGAPORE
1819

JAVA
1811–16

MAURITIUS
1810

AUSTRALIA

NATAL 1824

SWAN RIVER
1829

NEW
SOUTH WALES
1778-1830

CAPE COLONY
1795-1806

TASMANIA
1825

 Occupied by 1765

Occupied 1765–1830

Dates of acquisition are given for territories
acquired between 1750 and 1830

2. THE BRITISH EMPIRE AT

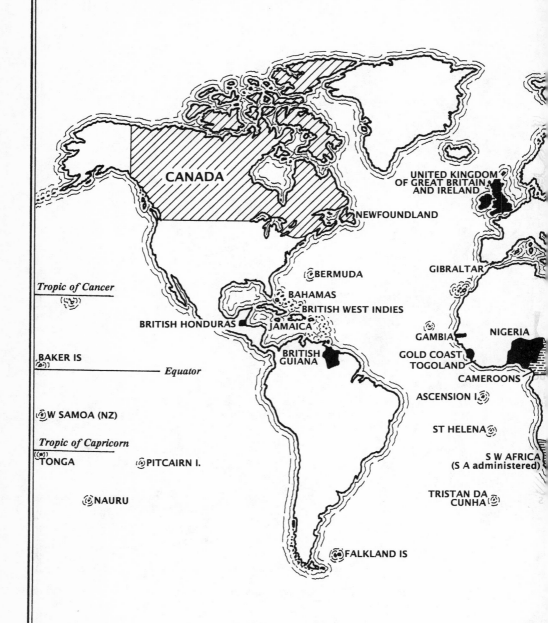

CANADA

NEWFOUNDLAND

UNITED KINGDOM
OF GREAT BRITAIN
AND IRELAND

GIBRALTAR

Tropic of Cancer

BERMUDA

BAHAMAS

BRITISH WEST INDIES

BRITISH HONDURAS

JAMAICA

NIGERIA

GAMBIA

GOLD COAST
TOGOLAND

CAMEROONS

BAKER IS

Equator

BRITISH
GUIANA

ASCENSION I.

ST HELENA

W SAMOA (NZ)

Tropic of Capricorn

TONGA

PITCAIRN I.

S W AFRICA
(S A administered)

NAURU

TRISTAN DA
CUNHA

FALKLAND IS

MC

ITS GREATEST EXTENT, 1920

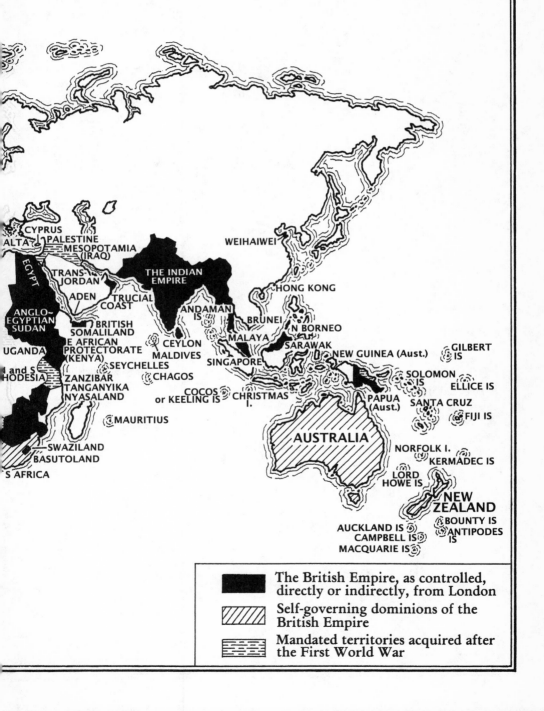

CYPRUS
MALTA
PALESTINE
MESOPOTAMIA
(IRAQ)
WEIHAIWEI
TRANS-
JORDAN
EGYPT
ADEN
TRUCIAL
COAST
THE INDIAN
EMPIRE
HONG KONG
ANGLO-
EGYPTIAN
SUDAN
BRITISH
SOMALILAND
E AFRICAN
PROTECTORATE
(KENYA)
ANDAMAN
IS
BRUNEI
N BORNEO
UGANDA
CEYLON
MALDIVES
MALAYA
SARAWAK
SINGAPORE
NEW GUINEA (Aust.)
GILBERT
IS
N and S
RHODESIA
SEYCHELLES
ZANZIBAR
TANGANYIKA
NYASALAND
CHAGOS
COCOS
or KEELING IS
CHRISTMAS
I.
PAPUA
(Aust.)
SOLOMON
IS
SANTA CRUZ
ELLICE IS
FIJI IS
MAURITIUS
AUSTRALIA
SWAZILAND
BASUTOLAND
S AFRICA
NORFOLK I.
KERMADEC IS
LORD
HOWE IS
NEW
ZEALAND
AUCKLAND IS
CAMPBELL IS
MACQUARIE IS
BOUNTY IS
ANTIPODES
IS

The British Empire, as controlled, directly or indirectly, from London

Self-governing dominions of the British Empire

Mandated territories acquired after the First World War

AUSTRIA

Vienna

Czernowitz
BESSARABIA

Budapest
HUNGARY
MOLDAVIA

Venice
Mohacs
TRAN-
SYLVANIA
Odessa

Karlowitz
Akkerman

CROATIA
ROMANIA

Belgrade
Bucharest
Kuchuk
Kainardji

Sarajevo
R. Danube
Ruse

Scutari
SERBIA
BULGARIA

Skopje

Monastir
Salonika
Plovdiv
Constantinople

Ioannina
San Stefano

CORFU
GREECE
Chanak
Mudania

Lepanto
Brusa

Athens
Smyrna
Eskisehir

MALTA
SAMOS

Navarino
Antalya

Adriatic Sea

ITALY

RHODES

Mediterranean Sea

Tripoli
CRETE

TRIPOLITANIA

Benghazi
CYRENAICA

Alexandria
SUEZ CANAL

Cairo

EGYPT

R. Nile

BALKAN BOUNDARIES, 1913–1914

AUSTRIA-HUNGARY

TRAN-
SYLVANIA
MOLDAVIA

BANAT

BOSNIA
WALLACHIA

SERBIA
ROMANIA

MONTE-
NEGRO
BULGARIA

ALBANIA
EASTERN
ROUMELIA

MACEDONIA
Constantinople

EPIRUS

THESSALY

GREECE
DODECANESE

PELOPONNESE

3. THE OTTOMAN EMPIRE, 1683; THE REPUBLIC OF TURKEY, 1923

RUSSIA

R. Dnieper

Kherson

Azov

CRIMEA

Sebastopol

Caspian Sea

Black Sea

Sinope

Batum

Samsun

Kars

GEORGIA

Trebizond

Yerevan

Erzerum

Ankara

ARMENIA

Konya

Diyarbekir

Teheran

Mosul

Alexandretta

Kirkuk

Aleppo

R. Tigris

SYRIA

YPRUS

LEBANON

R. Euphrates

Baghdad

Beirut

Damascus

Kut-el-Amara

Jaffa

Amman

Jerusalem

Basra

Gaza

Kuwait

uez

Persian Gulf

Red Sea

Medina

HEJAZ

Jeddah

Mecca

	Boundary of the Ottoman Empire, 1683
▨	Turkey after the Treaty of Lausanne, 1923

miles 0   100   200   300   400   500

kms 0   200   400   600   800

GERMANY

Reichenberg

R. Elbe

Troppa

Prague

SILESIA

BOHEMIA

MORAVIA

R. Vltava (Moldau)

Brunn (Brno) Trencsen

R. Danube

T

S

UPPER
AUSTRIA

LOWER

Linz

AUSTRIA

Vienna

Pressburg
(Bratislava

R.
Leitha

Bregenz

SWITZER-
LAND

VORARLBERG

U

Salzburg

A

STYRIA

Graz

H

Innsbruck

SALZBURG

TYROL

CARINTHIA

Klagenfurt

Trento

Laibach
(Ljubljana)

R. Drava (Drau)

Görz
(Gorizia)

CARNIOLA

Agram
(Zagreb)

Trieste

AUSTRIAN
Parenzo

ISTRIA

Fiume

CROATIA

SLAVONIA

R. Sava

LITTORAL

ITALY

Adriatic Sea

D
A
L
M
A
T
I
A

Zara

BOSNIA

Sarajevo

HERZE

Mostar

GOVINA

JMC

OF AUSTRIA-HUNGARY c.1900

R U S S I A

R I A

R. *Vistula*

Cracow

G A L I C I A

Lemberg
(Lwow)

R. *Dniester*

Munkacs

Czernowitz
(Cernauti)

R. *Theiss*

R. *Pruth*

BUKOVINA

Budapest

N G A R Y

R. *Tisza*

Klausenburg
(Kolozsvár)

T R A N S Y L V A N I A

R O M A N I A

Szegedin

R. *Maros*

Kronstadt
(Brasso)

Esseg
(Osijek)

Hermannstadt
(Nagy Szeben)

Temesvar

R. *Danube*

Belgrade

SERBIA

BULGARIA

R. *Drina*

R. *Danube*

MONTENEGRO

Names of crownland capitals and
one-time capitals of historico-political
units are italicized

miles 0 — 100 — 200
kms   0 — 100 — 200 — 300

North Sea

DENMARK

NORWAY

SWEDEN

Stockholm

Baltic Sea

Barents Sea

NOVAYA ZEMLYA

Kara Sea

Riga

LIVONIA

L. Ladoga

L. Onega

Archangel

W. Dvina

PRUSSIA

Warsaw

R. Vistula

POLAND

Smolensk

R. Dniester

LITHUANIA

R. Dnieper

BELO-RUSSIA

Kiev

UKRAINE

R U S S I A

N. Dvina

Ural Mountains

R. Ob

R. Volga

Yaroslavl

Moscow

R. Oka

R. Kama

Voronezh

Kazan

R. Ob

R. Don

Saratov

Ufa

Tobolsk

Sibir

R. Volga

R. Tobol

Tara

Azov

Tsaritsyn

Tomsk

Black Sea

Astrakhan

R. Irtysh

OTTOMAN EMPIRE

Caucasus Mts

Caspian Sea

Aral Sea

PERSIA

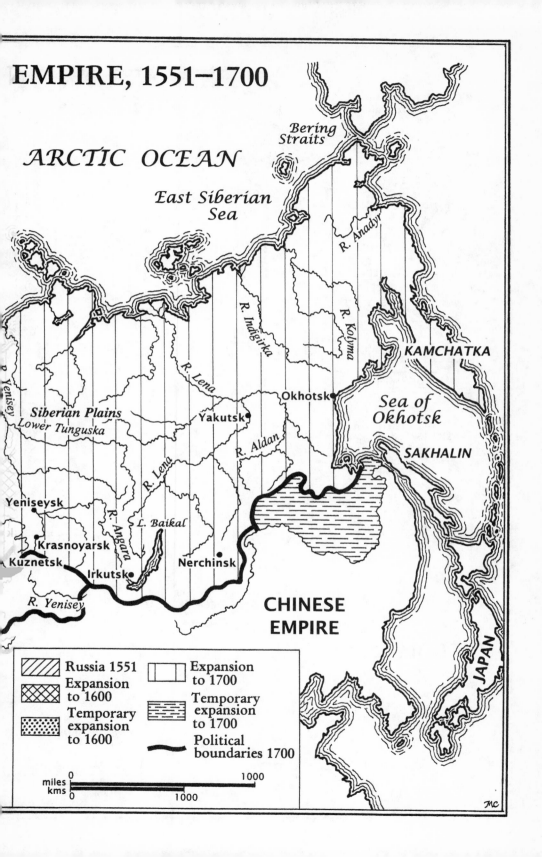

EMPIRE, 1551–1700

ARCTIC OCEAN

Bering Straits

East Siberian Sea

R. Anadyr

R. Indigirka

R. Kolyma

KAMCHATKA

R. Lena

Okhotsk•

Sea of Okhotsk

Siberian Plains
Lower Tunguska

Yakutsk•

R. Aldan

SAKHALIN

Yeniseysk•

R. Lena

R. Angara

L. Baikal

•Krasnoyarsk

Kuznetsk•

Irkutsk•

Nerchinsk•

R. Yenisey

CHINESE EMPIRE

JAPAN

▨ Russia 1551	▭ Expansion to 1700	
▧ Expansion to 1600		
⁙ Temporary expansion to 1600	▤ Temporary expansion to 1700	
	━ Political boundaries 1700	

miles 0   1000
kms 0   1000

MC

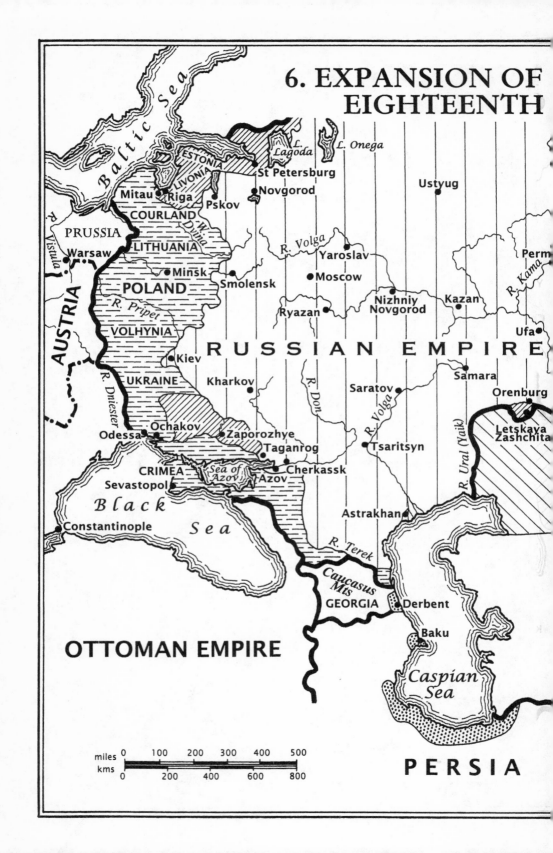

6. EXPANSION OF
EIGHTEENTH

Baltic Sea

L. Lagoda *L. Onega*

St Petersburg
Novgorod Ustyug

ESTONIA
LIVONIA
Mitau Riga
Pskov
COURLAND

R. Volga

Yaroslav Perm

LITHUANIA

PRUSSIA
Warsaw
Minsk Smolensk Moscow Kazan R. Kama

POLAND

Nizhniy
Novgorod

AUSTRIA

R. Pripet
Ryazan Ufa

VOLHYNIA

R U S S I A N   E M P I R E

Kiev Samara

UKRAINE Kharkov Saratov Orenburg

R. Don

Odessa Ochakov
Zaporozhye Letskaya
Zashchita
Taganrog Tsaritsyn
R. Volga

CRIMEA *Sea of
Azov* Azov Cherkassk

Sevastopol

Black Astrakhan

Constantinople *Sea*

R. Terek

R. Ural (Yaik)

*Caucasus
Mts*

GEORGIA Derbent

OTTOMAN EMPIRE Baku

*Caspian
Sea*

R. Dniester

R. Vistula

R. Dvina

miles | 0 100 200 300 400 500
kms | 0 200 400 600 800

PERSIA

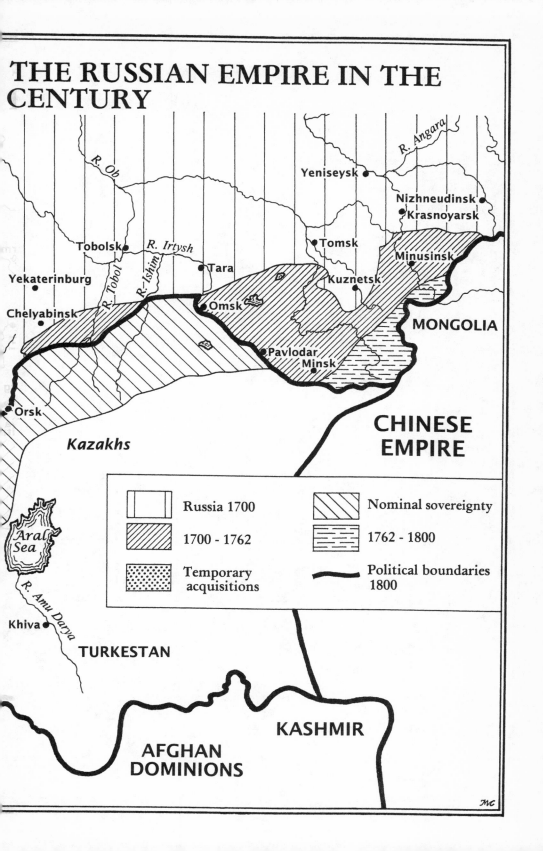

THE RUSSIAN EMPIRE IN THE CENTURY

R. Angara

Yeniseysk

Nizhneudinsk
Krasnoyarsk

R. Ob

Tobolsk
R. Irtysh
Tomsk
Minusinsk

Yekaterinburg
R. Tobol
R. Ishim
Tara
Kuznetsk

Chelyabinsk
Omsk
MONGOLIA

Pavlodar
Minsk

Orsk

CHINESE
EMPIRE

Kazakhs

	Russia 1700		Nominal sovereignty
	1700 - 1762		1762 - 1800
	Temporary acquisitions	—	Political boundaries 1800

Aral Sea

R. Amu Darya

Khiva

TURKESTAN

KASHMIR

AFGHAN
DOMINIONS

JVC

7. THE RUSSIAN EMPIRE AT EXTENT, 1914

North Sea

NORWAY

SWEDEN

Barents Sea

NOVAYA ZEMLYA

Kara Sea

Stockholm

Berlin

Baltic Sea

Riga

L. Ladoga

St Petersburg

L. Onega

Archangel

N. Dvina

Vienna

R. Vistula

Warsaw

W. Dvina

R. Volga

Ural Mountains

R. Ob

Budapest

Smolensk

Yaroslavl

R. Dnieper

Moscow

R. Oka

R. Kama

R. Dniester

Kiev

Voronezh

Kazan

Ufa

Tobolsk

Sibir

R. Ob

Bucharest

Odessa

R. Don

Saratov

R. Volga

R. Tobol

Tara

Tomsk

Constantinople

Azov

Tsaritsyn

Black Sea

Astrakhan

Caucasus Mts

KAZAKH LANDS

R. Irtysh

OTTOMAN EMPIRE

Caspian Sea

Aral Sea

TURKESTAN

Tehran

PERSIA

AFGHANISTAN

Kabul

INDIA

miles 0 — 1000
kms 0 — 1000

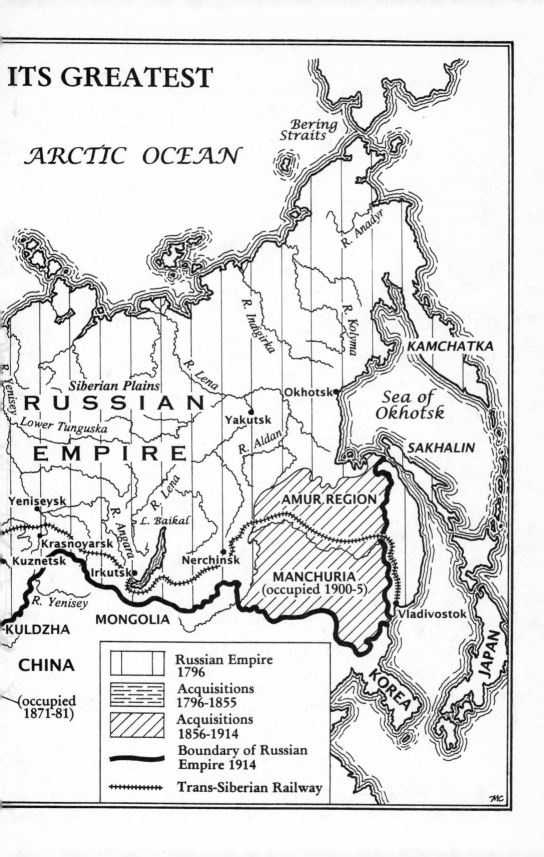

ITS GREATEST

ARCTIC OCEAN

Bering Straits

R. Anadyr

R. Kolyma

R. Indigirka

R. Lena

KAMCHATKA

Siberian Plains

RUSSIAN

Okhotsk

Sea of Okhotsk

Lower Tunguska

Yakutsk

EMPIRE

R. Aldan

SAKHALIN

Yeniseysk

R. Lena

AMUR REGION

R. Yenisey

R. Angara

L. Baikal

Krasnoyarsk

Kuznetsk

Irkutsk

Nerchinsk

MANCHURIA
(occupied 1900-5)

Vladivostok

R. Yenisey

MONGOLIA

KULDZHA

CHINA

(occupied
1871-81)

KOREA

JAPAN

| | Russian Empire 1796 |
| Acquisitions 1796-1855 |
| Acquisitions 1856-1914 |
| Boundary of Russian Empire 1914 |
| Trans-Siberian Railway |

MC

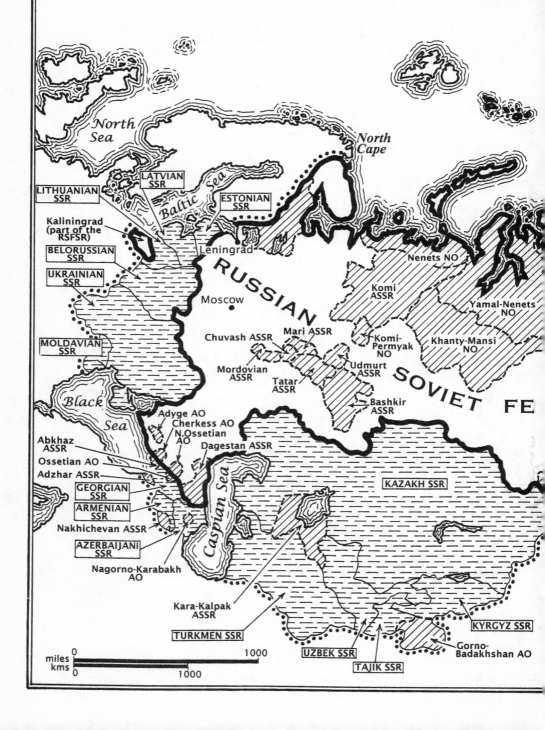

8. REPUBLICS AND AUTONO
OF THE SOVIET UNION,

North Sea

North Cape

LATVIAN SSR

LITHUANIAN SSR

Baltic Sea

ESTONIAN SSR

Kaliningrad (part of the RSFSR)

BELORUSSIAN SSR

Leningrad

Nenets NO

UKRAINIAN SSR

RUSSIAN

Komi ASSR

Yamal-Nenets NO

Moscow

MOLDAVIAN SSR

Chuvash ASSR

Mari ASSR

Komi-Permyak NO

Khanty-Mansi NO

Mordovian ASSR

Tatar ASSR

Udmurt ASSR

SOVIET FE

Black Sea

Bashkir ASSR

Adyge AO
Cherkess AO
N.Ossetian AO

Abkhaz ASSR

Dagestan ASSR

Ossetian AO

Adzhar ASSR

Caspian Sea

KAZAKH SSR

GEORGIAN SSR

ARMENIAN SSR

Nakhichevan ASSR

AZERBAIJANI SSR

Nagorno-Karabakh AO

Kara-Kalpak ASSR

KYRGYZ SSR

TURKMEN SSR

Gorno-Badakhshan AO

UZBEK SSR

TAJIK SSR

miles 0   1000
kms 0
    1000

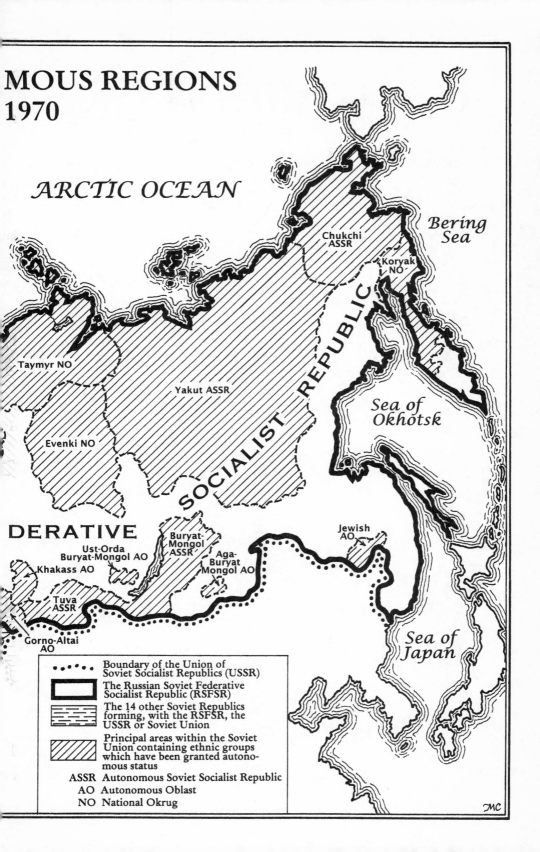

MOUS REGIONS
1970

ARCTIC OCEAN

*Bering
Sea*

Chukchi
ASSR

Koryak
NO

Taymyr NO

Yakut ASSR

SOCIALIST REPUBLIC

*Sea of
Okhotsk*

Evenki NO

DERATIVE

Jewish
AO

Buryat-
Mongol
ASSR

Ust-Orda
Buryat-Mongol AO

Aga-
Buryat
Mongol AO

Khakass AO

Tuva
ASSR

*Sea of
Japan*

Gorno-Altai
AO

• • • • •	Boundary of the Union of Soviet Socialist Republics (USSR)
▭	The Russian Soviet Federative Socialist Republic (RSFSR)
≣	The 14 other Soviet Republics forming, with the RSFSR, the USSR or Soviet Union
⧄	Principal areas within the Soviet Union containing ethnic groups which have been granted autonomous status
ASSR	Autonomous Soviet Socialist Republic
AO	Autonomous Oblast
NO	National Okrug

JMC

Part One

EMPIRE

I

Empire: A Word and its Meanings

MINEFIELDS, POLITICAL AND CULTURAL

Over the last two millennia the word 'empire' has meant many different things to different people from different countries at different times. Indeed it has often had different meanings to people from the same country at the same time. Statesmen and political thinkers have on occasion noted the word's ambiguity, themselves deliberately using it in different contexts to convey a variety of meanings.

It greatly complicates matters that use of the term 'empire' has often been highly polemical. To call any polity an empire was at various times instantly to label, praise or condemn it. In the Cold War the Soviet Union denounced its Western enemies as imperialists. They responded by labelling the Soviet Union an empire. Scholars debating these terms were therefore sucked into the polemics of the Cold War, becoming part of the almost universal ideological and geopolitical struggle that dominated the postwar decades. Though the terms of the debate and the specific context differed from anything that had gone before, politically charged confrontations over the meaning and legitimacy of the concept of empire were not new. In the eighteenth century empire, though often given another name, was frequently condemned and debated in not entirely dissimilar terms to those current in contemporary discussions of imperialism. In medieval Europe pope and emperor clashed furiously over conflicting doctrines of empire, which embodied rival claims to leadership within Western Christendom and different conceptions of the role of church and king in a Christian society.

In contrast to the late twentieth and (more equivocally) the eighteenth centuries, in medieval Europe the concept of empire enjoyed almost universal approval. It had connotations of unity within Christendom, as well as of peace and justice within the Christian community of kings and their subjects. Similarly, in the late nineteenth and early twentieth centuries, for most Europeans (except some of those themselves subject to empires) the concept of empire was a positive one. To be an empire was to be powerful, in an era when the gulf between strong and weak states was growing ever wider, and when the weak seemed doomed to marginalization or extinction. Empires were in the van of progress and civilization, bringing all the benefits of Western values and technology to the benighted 'lesser races', and ensuring that the world of the future would carry the stamp of the imperial people's own culture and history.

A century subsequently, 'empire' has once again become a dirty word. Embodying externally imposed and authoritarian rule over a society, it clashes head-on with democracy, the dominant ideology of the modern world. Implying the domination of the Third World by Western political, economic and cultural power, it arouses the wrath not only of the Third World's intelligentsia but also of groups within Western society who feel themselves to have been the victims of the class, sex and value systems that have dominated and set the tone of European and North American civilization over the last two centuries.

Whether or not one defines a polity as 'imperial' therefore has major political implications. Britain and France provide clear examples of this. By the standard of most empires in history it is rather easy to distinguish on the one hand the British and French metropolitan polities, and on the other hand their overseas colonies. The British and French nation states were distinct from their peripheral empires, over which they exercised unequivocal domination. The two great anomalies within these empires were, however, Ireland and Algeria, which in constitutional terms were defined as part of the metropolitan polity itself.

Because Ireland after 1801 was part of the United Kingdom, historians of the British Empire have usually considered it beyond their remit. Yet sixteenth-century Ireland was where many of the key principles that underlay British imperial rule were first established. These included the ideology of a civilizing mission, a deep and generally contemptuous sense of cultural superiority over the native peoples, and the doctrine of *terra nullius* – the idea that land (and by implication other economic resources) not effectively utilized by the indigenous peoples could legitimately be expropriated and developed by a superior invading nation more competent to do so. Although eighteenth-century Ireland is now increasingly studied by historians in a colonial or North Atlantic context (in other words as part of an imperial system that included the American Colonies, the West Indies and Scotland), in studies of Britain after the Act of Union which defined Ireland as British, such comparisons tend to cease. In the nineteenth century Britons stopped seeing Ireland in a colonial context, and so largely did historians.

In late nineteenth and early twentieth-century Britain this definition mattered hugely. Already by the 1860s it was implicitly accepted in London that the White Dominions were self-governing communities which had the right ultimately to determine their political future for themselves. In 1870 Earl Russell, the former prime minister, was stating a platitude when he commented that 'once the majority in any of our dependencies declares by the vote of its representatives that it wishes to separate from us, no attempt will be made to hold on to it. The mistakes made by G. Grenville, Ch. Townshend and Lord North will not be repeated.'[1] No such indulgence was accorded to Ireland. Forty years later home rule for Ireland encountered huge opposition in London and to avoid the risk of Irish independence much of the British elite was willing to encourage gross violation of the British constitution and even civil war. Of course the determination to treat Ireland very differently from the White Dominions was far more than a mere question of definitions. Nevertheless, the latter did matter greatly as a weapon for holding Ireland within the empire and as a means of shaping public consciousness of the Irish issue. In very similar terms, whether one defined Algeria as a colonial possession or as 'l'Algérie Française' determined whether one saw Algerian independence as a legitimate and inevitable part of the decolonizing process or, on the contrary, as a violation of the sacred unity and territory of France.

Never has the definition of empire been more important and more contentious than in contemporary Russia. A post-communist Russia has to determine for itself a new sense of identity and purpose, and to do so has to come to terms with its tsarist and Soviet past. Especially given the Marxist-Leninist simplicities in which most Russians have been educated, to define the Soviet Union as an empire is to condemn it outright, in the process despatching much of the lives of Russia's older generations to the rubbish bin, or even damning them as morally tainted. If the Soviet Union was an empire then not merely was it illegitimate, it was also fated to disappear in a modern world in which empire is taken to be redundant. In the contemporary global village where markets are open and ideas flow freely across the Internet, any attempt to reconstitute an empire would be quixotic, reactionary and hopeless. If on the other hand the Soviet Union was not an empire but a supranational community with a strong sense of common identity, worth and purpose, then its destruction was certainly a mistake and possibly a crime. The desire to reconstitute part or even all of it is neither necessarily wicked nor hopeless. Since much of the Russian population has not yet come to terms with the post-Soviet order and will not do so definitively for at least a generation, the question of empire and its definition remains extremely important and politically contentious.

In 1902 the English scholar J.A. Hobson began his book on imperialism with an attempt to define the concept. He commented that 'where meanings shift so quickly and so subtly, not only following changes of thought, but often manipulated artificially by political practitioners so as to obscure, expand or distort, it is idle to demand the same rigour as is expected in the exact sciences.'[2] Empire is a much older, more complicated and more diffuse concept than imperialism, which indeed the word 'empire' itself to a great extent encompasses. Nevertheless, unless this book is to lose all clarity of structure and argument, it is essential that the reader has some grasp of the many meanings of the word 'empire', of the contexts in which they have been used, and the manner in which they have evolved.

The laziest approach to the concept of empire is simply to accept a state's right to call itself whatever it chooses. Bokassa's polity was an empire because he chose to call it one. The Soviet Union was not an empire because its rulers vigorously rejected the term. This approach will not yield many rewards.

It is much more interesting to consider what images and value judgements the word 'empire' conjures up in the everyday (i.e. non-academic) English-speaking world. To the older British generation 'empire' is associated above all with a specific imperial polity, namely the British Empire. It conjures up memories of a time when the British felt themselves to be the world's most powerful, most civilized and most envied nation. A sense of solidarity with kith and kin across the oceans is also evoked. So too is remembrance of a time in 1940 when Britain stood isolated, heroic and vulnerable, and when volunteer imperial forces came to her assistance. Contemporary Britain still possesses many concrete leftovers from empire, ranging from 'Tales of the Raj' Indian restaurants up to its rather top-heavy post-imperial monarchy, perhaps even slower to come to terms with shrunken post-imperial status than is the nation it symbolizes and represents.

For the youngest generation, even in Britain, let alone in North America, 'empire' has different connotations rooted in inter-galactic conflict and science fiction. Children's books and videos embody the dominant modern judgement of empire, especially in North America. Their heroes struggle to free themselves from the dominion of evil empires whose authoritarian rule is rooted in ruthless coercion and trickery, whose greed is insatiable, whose minions look like spaceman versions of Nazi storm-troops, and whose leaders have the faces and voices of English upper-class colonial governors or Prussian aristocrats. Books and videos that stretch children's imaginations by projecting them into a far-distant, inter-galactic future also, rather appropriately, pick names from an almost equally imaginary and far-distant imperial past. Sargon I, ruler of ancient Akkad and perhaps the world's first emperor, lives again in inter-galactic imperial guise. Such visions shape the thinking not just of the broad public but even of some political leaders. Ronald Reagan's depiction of the Soviet Union as an evil empire surely owed something to science fiction and certainly struck a chord with a people used to its terminology. Which is by no means necessarily to say that Reagan's view of the post-Stalinist polity was wholly wrong.

To understand the many meanings and nuances of the word 'empire' it is essential to trace the evolution of the word over the millennia. Nevertheless, this approach does have its dangers. 'Empire' derives from the Latin word *imperium*, the meaning of which is best defined as legitimate authority or dominion. Other key words such as 'emperor' (*imperator*), 'colonialism' and 'colonization' (*colonia*) also have Latin roots. Over the centuries these words evolved within the Latin Christian tradition and were used, by a constant process of analogy, to mean things somewhat far removed from the initial Latin conception. Nevertheless, it is possible to see a thread of evolutionary logic running through the uses of the term 'empire' in the Western tradition.

But the term has also been applied not merely by scholars but also by Western society in general to political systems well outside the Latin tradition. In many cases the analogies are rather clear and the use of the term 'empire' is justified and fruitful. Nevertheless, a little caution is required. Even where laws, institutions and political systems seem very similar, they cannot avoid reflecting in part the cultures and civilizations in which they are rooted. Institutions may be disarmingly similar but the mentalities and assumptions of those who people them alarmingly different. The same word used in a different cultural context may give a wholly illusory sense of common reality.

The term 'emperor', for instance, in its initial Roman context meant a successful general. Though even in Roman times the word came to denote the monarch, it always retained its strong military connotations. Roman emperors always remained, first and foremost, military commanders-in-chief. Over the millennia, within the Western tradition, the term 'emperor' came to have other connotations too but the military ones never died and, from the eighteenth century, gained renewed strength. The last German and Russian emperors were seldom pictured out of uniform. Often their favourite image was as commander of the most prestigious regiments of their armies, namely the heavy cavalry of the Guards, their helmets crowned with eagles which symbolized their direct descent from military Rome.

When Meiji–era Japan decided to westernize itself sufficiently to join the club of 'civilized' great powers, it chose these powers as its models. Logically enough, Imperial Germany was its preferred role–model. The Japanese monarch called himself an emperor, for to be anything less would be an admission of a status inferior to that of the leading European rulers – after all, even the British queen proclaimed herself an empress (of India) in 1876. The Japanese emperor dressed in modern–style military uniform and reviewed his troops, whose supreme commander he was proclaimed to be, just as he was also – constitutionally – head of state and supreme director of the polity. None of these roles had been performed traditionally by the *Tenno*, who was closer to a high-priest than a monarch in the Western tradition. Not even after the Meiji Restoration did the Japanese monarch adjudicate between ministers or determine policy in a way that European emperors were supposed to do and still to some extent did. But the Emperor Hirohito, reviewing his victorious troops on a white horse, acted out the imperial play which the Western concept of emperorship had established in Japan, and in the process demonized himself in the eyes of much of Western public opinion, which inevitably understood symbolism imported from Europe in Western terms. It is not a complete exaggeration to say that the Japanese monarchy fell victim to the transfer of words and concepts into alien cultural milieux, where they took on a different meaning camouflaged by similar terminology and symbolism.

ROMAN CONCEPTIONS OF EMPIRE

Forewarned about the pitfalls and suitably modest about the inherent limits of the project, let us continue to explore the word 'empire' and its evolution. The *imperium* of a Roman magistrate was his right to give orders and exact obedience from those legally subject to his authority. In time this concept was extended by analogy to mean Rome's right to command obedience from the peoples it had subjected. As one might expect of the Romans, the initial concept of empire was well–defined, legal and political. To some extent it remained that way both in Western history and among Western historians. Certainly it is safer to use the concept of empire if one can keep it straitjacketed in tight legal and political definitions. In this sense empire is a specific polity with a clearly demarcated territory exercising sovereign authority over its subjects who are, to varying degrees, under its direct administrative supervision. It is not mere hegemony or predominant political influence, still less is it the magnetic appeal of a great culture or the power of some shadowy global economic system. Least of all is it merely any form of alien and imposed authority and influence.

But although it is more convenient to confine empire to a narrow political definition, it may at times prove both difficult and limiting to do so. Michael Mann[3] has convincingly shown that politics, armed force, economics, culture and religion are all factors of power, their relative weight differing from era to era. At the beginning of the twenty-first century as economic and cultural power occupies the foreground, does this mean that empire is dead or merely that it requires redefinition in terms more appropriate to the contemporary constellation of power? At its most significant and interesting, after all, empire has always tended to be the political face of a great civilization or at least of a culture of far more than purely local significance. The civilization itself has often been, in part anyway, the embodiment of some great religion.

In Roman eyes, the Roman Empire was a universal monarchy: it encompassed the whole globe, or at least all of it that was worth bothering about. The barbarians beyond the empire's wall they regarded in terms somewhat similar to nineteenth-century European colonists' view of 'natives'. Their only imperial neighbour, the Parthian Empire, was considered by the Romans to be 'an oriental despotism, a barbarian, braggart and motley nation'.[4] As in every other aspect of their culture, the Roman sense of universalism owed much to the Greeks. Alexander had conquered virtually the whole of the known world and although his empire was very short-lived the spread of Hellenistic culture was not. 'The Greek philosophers, in particular the Stoics, stressed the notion that all mankind formed one community, partaking of universal reason . . . it was, indeed, the Greeks who from the second century BC had regarded the Roman Empire and the universe (*oikoumene*) as one . . . Ideas such as these made a deep impression on the minds of the political and intellectual elite of Rome, and through their influence the two notions of *orbis terrarum* and *imperium* came to be regarded in the first century as identical: from then on no distinction was ever made between them.'[5]

The adoption in the fourth century of Christianity, a world religion which recognized no ethnic or cultural borders, could only increase the

Roman imperial sense of universalism. In time Christian clergy under-took evangelizing missions outside their polities' borders, converting whole peoples to their religion and therefore, in the end, also to a great extent to their culture. This the rulers of imperial Rome had never con-ceived of. The combination of a universalist imperial tradition with a monotheistic world religion created a somewhat new type of empire, a type which was to include many of the most significant polities that have existed until today. Compared to the syncretic, polytheistic empires of the past, the 'doctrinal rigidity' of Judaic monotheism could be a source of both solidarity and division. Common religion could contribute to shared culture and even nationality. But 'we should consider the possibil-ity,' writes Garth Fowden, 'that monotheism itself may, under certain circumstances, have divisive effects. For where polytheism diffuses divin-ity and defuses the consequences, if not always the intensity, of debate about its nature by providing a range of options, monotheism tends to focus divinity and ignite debate by forcing all the faithful, with their potentially infinite varieties of religious thought and behaviour, into the same mould, which sooner or later must break.'[6]

HEIRS OF ROME

Roman, Christian monotheistic empire had three heirs: Byzantium, Islam and Western Christendom. In the seventh century the onslaught of Islam hugely weakened the Byzantine Empire and dramatically reshaped its culture, society and institutions of government. Until then, however, Byzantium was not really Rome's heir but simply the Roman Empire continued. Gaul, Spain and Britain had always figured among Imperial Rome's less important and wealthy provinces. The heartlands of the Mediterranean empire's culture and economy were to an increasing extent on the sea's southern and eastern shores, and it was here that the Roman Empire consolidated itself in the fifth century. A century later, under Justinian, the Byzantines recaptured most of Italy. After the seventh century Byzantium differed from Western Christendom in many crucial respects. Where empire is concerned, the biggest single difference was that the Byzantine emperor controlled the patriarch of Constantinople and the Eastern Church much more fully than it was possible for any emperor in the West to command the pope. In addition, Western Christendom came to be dominated by the hereditary territorial aristoc-racy. The latter put strong constraints on royal and imperial power not only *de facto* but also by law. The feudal contract was a mutually binding agreement whose infringement by the monarch legitimized resistance by his vassals. As with every autocratic monarchy in history, the theoretically absolute power of the Byzantine emperor was in practice constrained by many factors. But it was not limited by law or conceived as a contract, and therein lay a key distinction between East and West in Europe.

In 1453 the Byzantine Empire collapsed, leaving no direct heirs. Though tsarist Russia inherited some aspects of Byzantine imperial ideology and symbolism, the tsarist polity was very different indeed from Byzantium in most respects. Still less can one draw any line from Rome to the Soviet Union through Byzantium and tsarist Russia. All such genealogies are wholly fanciful. Nevertheless, in one important respect the Soviet Union could be considered to stand in the Roman Christian tradition of empire, combining great power and territory with a would-be universalist and monotheistic world religion. International communism in time suffered a fate similar in some respects to earlier monotheistic universal empire: rival centres of power emerged, grouped around political factions but legitimized by different interpretations of doctrine. These new polities rejected the control of the religious and imperial centre, and over time came to absorb much in the traditions and culture of the regions from which they sprang. Such comparisons, beloved of Arnold Toynbee, have sufficient merit to be worth considering when we come to study the Soviet polity in the context of empire.[7]

Islam was not so directly Rome's heir as had been the case with Christian Byzantium. The emperor did not convert to Islam, nor did the Roman-Byzantine elite become the spiritual and secular leaders of the Islamic community, bringing to it (as had been the case with the Christian Roman and Byzantine empire) their values, ideas and traditions. The empire of the early caliphate was above all founded on a new religion, around which formed a distinctly new civilization.

Yet in an important sense the early caliphate of the Abbasids and Umayyads *was* Rome's heir. The new religion was monotheistic and universalist in the tradition established by Christian Rome. Islam accepted its descent from Christianity and showed considerable tolerance to 'people of the Book'. The caliphate occupied many of the heartlands of the Roman Empire but its dominion extended well beyond them, stretching across the whole Fertile Crescent, the Persian plateau and into Northern India. To a degree that no other empire ever matched, the caliphate controlled almost the whole of the ancient world, in other words Egypt and what we nowadays describe as the Middle or Near East. In time this empire fell victim not just to the huge strains of governing so vast a territory with pre-modern communications but also to the doctrinal disputes that monotheism invited.

In its wake the caliphate left behind what Garth Fowden calls a commonwealth: 'a group of politically discrete but related polities collectively distinguishable from other polities or commonwealths by a shared culture and history.'[8] The French historian A. Miquel describes what it meant to live in this community, even after its political unity had cracked. It meant 'being able to discuss theology or law, from one end of a gigantic territory to the other, according to one vocabulary and one code accepted throughout; to debate the claims of tradition or of personal judgement; to be moved at the tomb of a holy person, venerated since one's childhood in Palestine and buried thousands of kilometres from there; to recognise the observation of the same rites and common membership of the same school of legal thought; to share the same timetable divided by the five daily prayers; to cite an author known and celebrated throughout; to engage everywhere in the controversy over the legitimacy of the Umayyads; to be understood in Arabic almost everywhere; in every Mosque the place indicating the direction of Mecca; in brief to share a history, a culture, features of everyday life and a common sensibility'.[9]

In time this commonwealth was to spread far beyond even the wide borders of the former caliphate. Muslim warriors and, above all, traders carried it to parts of East Africa, to India and Central Asia, and beyond them to Java, Sumatra and even China. In many of these areas Islam was to penetrate native culture and overcome native religion much more successfully than generations of later Christian empire. Even amidst the very powerful and assimilationist forces of Chinese culture the sense of Islamic identity among the ethnically Han Muslim minority (the Hui) was so strong that, despite the fact that they lacked a territorial base, largely spoke Chinese languages and looked like Han Chinese, they were officially recognized as a separate nationality by the communist regime – a unique recognition of identity rooted in religion and one that flatly contradicted the official Chinese definition, derived initially from Stalin, that saw nationality as a product solely of language, territory, economic life and common culture.[10]

In the fifteenth and sixteenth centuries much of the old caliphate was restored as a single polity – an empire – by the Turkish dynasty of the Ottomans. Unlike the Umayyads and Abbasids, the Ottomans were not descendants of the Prophet and made no claim to be. They never controlled Spain or Northern India, nor for any meaningful period did they dominate the Persian plateau. On the other hand, also unlike the early caliphate, they did conquer the Christian Balkans and, above all, Constantinople – the imperial city, the Roman Christian capital, of whose capture Islam had dreamed for so long. If, obviously and above all, the Ottoman sultans and caliphs were the heirs to universal Islamic empire, they were also to some extent the heirs to Byzantium and Rome. Calling themselves the Sultans of Rum (i.e. Rome) and installed in the 'Roman' capital, they very definitely saw themselves as the legitimate successors to Rome in particular, but more generally to the Mediterranean and Near Eastern tradition of empire. Particularly in the first century after Constantinople's capture, one aspect of this imperial legacy was the haven of relative peace, security and tolerance which the Ottomans offered not just to Muslims but also to Christian and Jewish subjects of their would-be universal empire.

EARLY EUROPEAN CONCEPTS OF EMPIRE AND THEIR LINEAGE

The third heir of Imperial Rome, namely Western Christendom, was for many centuries the least impressive. Nothing in medieval Europe equalled the splendour or power of Byzantium, let alone the caliphate, at their peak. Nevertheless, in the end it was to be the descendants of medieval Latin Christendom and the political concepts they supported that were to dominate the globe. For that reason particular care has to be devoted to the evolution of the word 'empire' (i.e. *imperium*) in the Latin Middle Ages.

Although 'empire' had a number of different, albeit overlapping, meanings in the medieval era, three were to be of long-term historical importance. The first may be called 'German'. Empire in this context meant a specific polity, the 'Holy Roman Empire (*Reich*) of the German nation', and the institutions, ideals, interests and memories associated with it. Although this polity had the tenth-century Saxon dynasty and even Charlemagne among its ancestors, in its early modern and narrowly German sense it dates back to the fourteenth century. It was in this period that the empire devised its own constitution, increasingly free of papal interference and Italian entanglements. Even subsequently the Reich was never wholly German, including for instance the Czech and Dutch peoples. Nevertheless, the empire was overwhelmingly German in its population, culture and preoccupations and it encompassed the great majority of Europe's German-speaking communities.

In the nineteenth and twentieth centuries, which German tradition and which political camp was the true heir to the old Reich became a cause of hot debate. In reality the Reich had been a loose confederation of multiple and overlapping sovereignties, preserving the maximum autonomy for local communities and princelings, but sometimes capable of uniting against an external threat to the region and its people. Those Germans who spoke out against a centralized nationalist German state in the name of the old Reich certainly had true history on their side. But the second half of the nineteenth century witnessed the simultaneous flowering of the modern 'scientific' study of history and of German nationalism. The German Empire created by Bismarck called itself a renewed Reich, heir to the old Holy Roman Empire, and could mobilize in defence of this claim not merely the usual crowd of propagandists anxious to sign up in the camp of the victorious but also much of Germany's academic elite. The old Reich from which they claimed descent was above all that of the Saxon and Hohenstaufen dynasties, whose heroic efforts to create a German national and imperial state between the tenth and thirteenth centuries were thwarted above all, in the view of these overwhelmingly Protestant historians, by the machinations of the pope.

The Nazi Third Reich endorsed this view of history, defining the German nation in the narrowest biological terms and claiming, in Hitler's words, 'one blood demands one Reich ... It must be a greater honour to be a street-cleaner and citizen of this Reich than a king in a foreign state.' But although Hitler's empire was a complete perversion of the traditions of the old 'Holy Roman Empire of the German Nation', it cannot so easily be dismissed as irrelevant to the concept of empire as a whole. In late nineteenth- and early twentieth-century Europe it was increasingly believed that multi-ethnic, polyglot empires were extremely fragile in the age of nationalism, and that only a large territory encompassing a homogeneous nation could survive and impose its will on the international scene. This was why champions of empire in Britain at that time called for the creation of a 'Greater Britain', in other words a federation of the White Dominions. In tune with such thinking, Hitler's Greater Germany (*Grossdeutschland*) or Greater German Empire (*Grossdeutsches Reich*) was to be 'a nation of a hundred million people', a homogeneous racial community, as well as a great world empire, though of course it was to embody none of the liberal principles on which British imperialists prided themselves and saw as the essence of Englishness.[11]

The second major concept of empire in medieval Christendom one might call European or perhaps Carolingian. The founder of this tradition was Charlemagne, king of the Franks and first monarch (AD 800) of the 'restored' (Holy) Roman Empire. The borders of Charlemagne's empire were those of the Frankish kingdom. He saw himself always as first and foremost the king of the Franks. His imperial title contributed to his prestige and marked him out as the pre-eminent monarch in

Christendom and the chief defender of the Latin Christian church. But Charlemagne was never prey to universalist ambitions and illusions. He never claimed sovereignty over the English or Iberian kingdoms. Nor had he any wish to enter into conflicts with the Byzantines over his imperial title or over hegemony in the Mediterranean region. Charlemagne's kingdom encompassed most of what we would now describe as France, Germany and Italy. These were the territories too of Napoleon's empire; Napoleon was greatly interested in Charlemagne and introduced Carolingian titles and symbols into his court. These countries were also the founder-members and core of the European Union. If contemporary Europe as a concept is much wider than Carolingian, the 'European idea' still retains its strongest hold in this region.

Adherents of European union invoke Charlemagne and the Holy Roman Empire not just because of the territories that were controlled but also because of these polities' constitutions. Even Charlemagne's state, let alone the Reich of later centuries, was not a bureaucratic, centralized empire. Even at its most unified, the Reich was a feudal kingdom, with maximum devolution of power. Its overlapping institutions and power-holders were constrained by feudal law, historical custom and the moral order of Latin Christendom. If the later Holy Roman Empire was more truly German than European, the same could not be said of the dynasty that provided the great majority of its monarchs in its last half millennium. For the Habsburgs were not only Holy Roman Emperors of the German nation, but also rulers of a swathe of Hungarians, Slavs, Italians and Romanians (to name only the major groups) as well. If any family in modern Europe embodied the supranational European imperial idea, it was these descendants of Charles V.

Appropriately therefore the heir to this heritage, Dr Otto von Habsburg, is a member of the European Parliament and an advocate of a 'European Union, which we want to make a supranational lawful polity in the sense of the old *Reich*'. Dr von Habsburg is, however, quick to point out that the Reich he is recalling has nothing in common with the nation state created by Bismarck and perverted by Hitler. Indeed, 'in the 1860s, with the victory of nationalism in the German region began Europe's decline, and the German people betrayed their vocation.' Like the old Holy Roman Empire, Habsburg argues, the new European Union must be a confederation of mixed and overlapping sovereignties, with legal authority fixed at the level most appropriate for the specific tasks in hand, and with a strong stress on preserving the maximum of local identity and autonomy. Lest the word empire (i.e. *Reich*) prove a source of confusion, he comments that 'Empire meant for the French a centralized polity which is a great power (*zentralistischer Machtstaat*). This is much more similar to the Roman Empire, a territorially sovereign polity with defined borders, than to the Holy Roman Empire of the Middle Ages, that wanted to be and was something completely different. In distinction to the French the English have an equivalent to the German word "*Reich*", namely commonwealth.' Once again, this time with unusual clarity, one is faced with conflicting definitions of empire, rooted partly in political disagreements about what an empire ought to be and what role a specific empire played in history, but also caused in part by the need to translate terms into foreign languages whose own conception of a word is rooted in a different historical memory and culture.[12]

The third and 'purest' concept of empire[13] in medieval Christendom could be labelled 'universal' or 'papal'. Twelfth- and thirteenth-century advocates of papal dominion recognized no territorial boundaries, unlike Charlemagne or the later Holy Roman emperors. The pope's writ ran throughout Latin Christendom. His right to legitimize the authority of Christian monarchs and to depose those who offended Christ's church and its doctrines made the pope, in principle, the supreme ruler of Latin Christendom. Moreover, although reality forced the papacy to confine most of its activities to this region, Christianity remained not only in principle but also to some extent in practice an evangelizing and universalist religion. The papacy sought to convert the pagan and the Muslim in the Mediterranean region, in Eastern Europe and later in the Americas. To this end it also launched crusades. In its more optimistic or desperate moods it sent emissaries to find the legendary Prester John or to convert the descendants of Genghis Khan to Christianity.

By the fourteenth century all hope of empire in Western Christendom seemed dead. Its remaining advocates, of whom Dante was the most famous, operated in the realm of utopia, not of practical politics. Having destroyed any chance of the Holy Roman Empire exercising hegemony in Christendom, the papacy had itself been mastered by the French king. With empire dead, the triumph of the separate kingdoms of Europe appeared irreversible. In the sixteenth century, however, empire's fortunes revived for a time. The Emperor Charles V accumulated more territories than any European monarch since the fall of the Roman Empire. As king of Castile he was heir to the Aztec and Inca empires and ruler of the Americas. His motto, '*plus ultra*', symbolized his wish not just to equal the Romans but to surpass them, for they had never possessed huge realms on both sides of the great ocean.

For other Europeans, and particularly Protestants, Habsburg power was all the more alarming because it was sustained by American silver and allied to the Catholic Counter-Reformation. Not just political independence but also religious freedom was at stake. In response the Habsburgs' enemies had recourse to the doctrine that 'the king is emperor in his own realm', first devised by French lawyers in the early fourteenth century to defend the absolute sovereignty of their royal master from the claims of Holy Roman emperor, pope or too independent vassals. To the modern mind this concept of empire runs counter to the usual understanding of the word, yet it was the meaning most widespread in the sixteenth century.

For the next two hundred years the word 'empire' retained this meaning but had many other senses as well. 'The Empire' still meant the Holy Roman Empire ruled over by the Habsburgs, a situation only marginally confused by the acceptance of the Russian Empire as a fully-fledged great power after 1763. 'Empire' in English eighteenth-century parlance could mean great power, or even simply state, but in some cases it signified all the king's possessions, European and colonial, including England itself. Increasingly the word was used to mean 'extended empire'; in the words of Sir William Temple, 'a nation extended over vast tracts of land and numbers of people arrives in time at the ancient name of kingdom or modern of empire'.[14] Only in the nineteenth century, however, did empire come to have this meaning alone and not until the 1860s did it acquire definitively the sense in which it is commonly understood today, namely the overseas possessions of the crown as distinct from the British metropolitan polity.

EMPIRE AND IMPERIALISM: THE MODERN DEBATE

All this was despite the fact that in the seventeenth and eighteenth centuries the European maritime powers built up a colonial system embodying most of the principles a later era would define as imperial, or indeed imperialist. These included autarchy, protectionism and the unblushing and consistent exploitation of the colonial economy in the cause of metropolitan prosperity and power. Perhaps it was because the colonies were viewed as commercial rather than territorial assets that they were so often not seen as empire properly speaking. Edward Gibbon, a fierce enemy of empire, saw no inconsistency in supporting all Britain's efforts to suppress the American Revolution.[15] Alexander Hamilton, who fought against the British in this war, also felt no constraint in proclaiming the United States to be 'an empire in many respects the most interesting in the world'.[16]

Nevertheless, although they may have called it by different names, the leading figures in the late Enlightenment understood what a later age would define as empire and imperialism, and roundly condemned it. This was for two main reasons. In the first place empire was taken to mean extensive territory and imperialism to place insuperable obstacles in the way of self-government. Rome had been a self-governing republican polis: territorial expansion inevitably turned it into a despotic empire. For Montesquieu empire was an essentially Asiatic concept suitable to the continent's vast plains and to its peoples' subservient spirit. In his view, 'a great empire necessarily requires a despotic authority for him who governs, since it is essential that decisions are taken promptly to make up for the remoteness of the places to which they are conveyed, that fear puts a check on the distant governor and magistrate, and that the law springs from a single head, capable of never-ceasing adjustments in accordance with the chance events which always multiply in the state in proportion to its dimensions. Without this there would be a dismemberment of the Monarchy into its separate parts and the diverse peoples, released from a domination which they regard as foreign, would begin to live under their own laws.'[17]

The second line of attack was on the colonial system. In part this was for the same reasons that Montesquieu had attacked universal monarchy. Colonial empires spread over wide territories could not be governed democratically. In addition, the colonial economy, rooted in slave labour, was denounced on moral grounds. Above all, however, mercantilism's presumption that international trade and economic development was a zero–sum–game was denied. The bible of anti-mercantilism was Adam Smith's *The Wealth of Nations*[18] in which he argued that free trade and the international division of labour were of universal benefit, and that mercantilism not only reduced the general wealth but also entailed the expense and suffering of armaments and war. These arguments, loudly proclaimed by English Victorian liberals, could be described as the official ideology of liberal capitalism, of the IMF and today's other multilaterals and indeed of the contemporary world economic order.

In the last three decades of the nineteenth century neo–mercantilism and protection again raised their heads. Their popularity was linked to the renewed strength of the imperial idea, which stressed the advantages to any state of direct political control over non-European land, labour, raw materials and targets for secure and profitable investment. Empire was also invoked as a cause which could not only enrich a metropolitan people but also unite it spiritually, providing all sections of the community with an uplifted ideal of their country's grandeur, its civilizing mission and its assured future place in world affairs.

In the face of this challenge, liberal and radical theorists reasserted the old free trade arguments. They stressed that protectionism reduced economies' efficiency and the global accumulation of wealth. Autarchy bred enmity between states and fed the interests of pre-modern aristocratic and militarist elites, who were now sometimes in league, in the view of John Hobson, with financiers and arms manufacturers who had an interest in expanding empire and extolling war. It was partly in these terms that Hobson explained the Boer War. For Hobson it was self-evident that 'the intricate and ever-growing industrial cooperation of the civilised nations through trade does not permit any nation to keep to herself the gain of any market she may hold.' 'Protection is the natural ally of imperialism' and both were irrational. 'Our most profitable and progressive trade is with rival industrial nations.'[19]

Joseph Schumpeter was equally convinced that protection, war, territorial expansion and imperialism were all connected and all equally irrational in the conditions of a modern economy. 'A purely capitalist world therefore can offer no fertile soil to imperialist impulses.' Whereas 'imperialism ... is atavistic in nature', capitalism encourages 'the progressive rationalisation of life and mind'. He added, 'it does not matter, assuming free trade, which of the "civilised" nations undertakes the task of colonization. Dominion of the seas, in such a case, means little more than a maritime traffic police.' The continued existence of imperialism could be explained in Schumpeter's view only by the existence of military aristocratic ruling classes and redundant war machines in the European states. 'Whoever seeks to understand Europe must not overlook that even today its life, its ideology, its politics are greatly under the influence of the feudal "substance", that while the bourgeoisie can assert its interest everywhere, it "rules" only in exceptional circumstances, and then only briefly.'[20]

Leading British advocates of empire would probably have felt that, in Britain's case, the criticisms of Hobson and Schumpeter largely missed the mark. Of course Britain was the foremost imperial power and had secured the lion's share (Egypt, 'Nigeria', the Boer Republics) in the partition of Africa between 1880 and 1914. In this period London took a growing interest in the exploitation and development of her non-White tropical and subtropical empire. As the arch-imperialist Lord Milner put it in 1910, with the single exception of the West Indian sugar industry – of which Britain had no reason to feel proud – 'our stepmotherly neglect of these colonies in the past has been one of the least honourable pages in our history.' Now this neglect must end. The non-White colonies 'are enormous in extent; they are lands of immense fertility ... and we have so far only scratched the surface of their natural resources.'[21]

Like most but by no means all British imperialists, Milner was also a protectionist. At times his speeches took a strongly neo-mercantilist tone, rejoicing at the empire's potential for autarchy in a world of competing imperialist economic blocs and of a potential shortage of commodities. 'It is no small advantage at any time, and it may under given circumstances be vital, for a great industrial country to have the raw materials, upon which its principal industries depend, produced within regions that are under its own control.'[22]

Yet even for Milner and his allies, protection was less an end in itself than a means to other greater goals. Above all, it was a means to stop the gradual drifting apart of the White Dominions and to consolidate them into an imperial federation. For British imperialists at the time, this was by far their greatest priority, and it was something to which anti-imperialists such as Schumpeter had no objections, so long as the empire did not become a closed economic bloc. The overriding reason why imperialists wanted federation – and this takes us to the core of empire's meaning – was not economic but political: it was a question of power. John Seeley, professor of history at Cambridge and prophet of imperialism, made the point squarely in 1885. 'If the United States and Russia hold together for another half century, they will at the end of that time completely dwarf such old European states as France and Germany, and depress them into a second class. They will do the same to England, if at the end of that time England still thinks of herself as simply a European state, as the old United Kingdom of Great Britain and Ireland, such as Pitt left her.' The only alternative was to think imperially, by which Seeley meant to concentrate on the White Dominions, not on non-White colonies which could never be brought into a true federation with Britain. 'The other alternative is, that England may prove able to do what the United States does so easily, that is, hold together in a federal union countries very remote from each other. In that case England will take rank with Russia and the United States in the first rank of states, measured by population and area, and in a higher rank than the states of the Continent.'[23]

Would such a federation be an empire? Neither Seeley nor most other imperialists were sure. Lord Rosebery commented that he knew of no other word than empire which 'adequately expresses a number of states of vast size under a single sovereign' but, undoubtedly, 'our Empire is not founded on the precedents associated with that name.'[24] Seeley himself wrote that 'our Empire is not an Empire at all in the ordinary sense of the word ... the English Empire is on the whole free from that weakness which has brought down most empires, the weakness of being a mere mechanical forced union of alien nationalities ... when the State advances beyond the limits of the nationality, its power becomes precarious and artificial.' The British Empire was not really an empire but rather 'a vast English nation, only a nation so widely dispersed that before the age of steam and electricity its strong natural bonds of race and religion seemed practically dissolved by distance.'[25]

But what about the rest of the empire, in other words the non-White colonies? Milner commented that 'I often wish that, when speaking of the British Empire ... we could have two generally recognised appellations by which to distinguish the two widely different and indeed contrasted types of state of which that Empire is composed.' Milner himself to some extent supplied the answer as to what linked the two empires together in the eyes of imperialists. It was British civilization and the power required to spread and sustain it. 'Empire and imperialism are words which lend themselves to much abuse. It is only when stripped of tawdry accessories that the ideas which they imperfectly express can be seen in their real grandeur ... we wish the kindred peoples under the British flag to remain one united family for ever. And we believe that it is only by such union that they can attain their highest individual development, and exercise a decisive influence for peace, and for the maintenance of that type of civilisation which they all have in common, in the future history of the human race.'[26] Rosebery's vision of empire was if anything even more uplifted. The British Empire was 'the greatest secular agency for good known in the world' and its progress was, though 'not without the taint and reproach incidental to all human work ... constructed on the whole with pure and splendid purpose. Human, and not yet wholly human, for the most heedless and the most cynical must see the finger of the divine.'[27]

God and imperialism were the two greatest enemies of the new world order which revolutionary Marxism sought to create in the twentieth century. Marx himself was equivocal on the subject of European overseas empire. He regretted European capitalism's devastation of the native peoples' economies but saw it nevertheless as a force for progress, awakening the natives from their 'undignified, stagnatory and vegetative life' and their 'brutalising worship of nature',[28] and enabling them in the long run to aspire to a truly human and rational existence. On the other hand, he did believe that Irish economic backwardness owed much to the fact that the Irish nation lacked the power to impose a tariff on the British industrial goods which were flooding their market.

Lenin was by no means the most interesting or sophisticated Marxist thinker on imperialism even in his own time but because of his later fame, his *Imperialism: the Highest Stage of Capitalism*[29] became the most important work written on the subject from a Marxist perspective. Lenin denied any connection between pre-capitalist empire and the imperialism of the contemporary European great powers. The latter was derived exclusively from the nature of the modern capitalist economy, which was now monopolistic and dominated by finance capital. Denied sufficient profits in its domestic markets, capitalism sought new markets for trade and investment, new sources of cheap labour and raw materials in the colonial world. 'Monopoly finance capital' and government had fused in the leading imperialist states. The latter were in ferocious competition to divide up the world which was, in Lenin's view, why the First World War occurred. The huge profits generated by exploitation of the non-White colonies had enabled capitalism to buy off sections of the working class, subverting the latter's unity and radicalism, and demonstrating just why the workers' revolution predicted by Marx seemed even further away than in his lifetime. But once the workers understood that the price of capitalist bribery was never-ending wars between the imperialist powers, revolution would return to the agenda. These wars would be inevitable since every shift in power between the leading capitalist states would ignite conflicts to redivide the colonial pie. Lenin's attention was always concentrated on Europe and the European revolution, though there were signs that in the very last months of his active life, as hopes of a European revolution again faded, he was beginning to pay increasing attention to the colonial world and its potential for the future socialist world order. Especially after Stalin's death, Soviet writing concentrated on developing this theme. Nevertheless, if Adam Smith was the leading saint of the Western camp in the Cold War, and still more of the post-Cold-War global political economy, Lenin was his equivalent on the Communist side of the barricades.

In the second half of the twentieth century the notion of 'empire' disappeared from the contemporary political debate and became the property of historians. Partly because the Marxists had shifted its focus from politics to economics (and thereby allowed it to outlive the collapse of formal empire), 'imperialism' not only survived as a concept but flourished. The immense passion stirred up by the debate on imperialism was a measure of its political importance. Not merely did the debate go to the heart of the ideological struggle between the Soviet Union and the West during the Cold War. It was also a crucial element in the argument about the causes of Third World poverty and the widening gap between the globe's rich 'North' and its beleaguered 'South'.

Much debate centred around the idea of 'neo-colonialism', in other words indirect control over the Third World by the West's invisible economic and financial power. So-called 'dependency theory', whose leading scholar was Immanuel Wallerstein,[30] was the most interesting strand in this line of thought for the historian of empire. Though Wallerstein's ideas were much more interesting and sophisticated than those expressed in Lenin's *Imperialism*, the two shared many of the same premises. Wallerstein saw the world as having been dominated since the sixteenth century by a group of European (and later American) capitalist powers who had achieved immense wealth for themselves by fixing the international terms of trade in their favour, by looting and exploiting the Third World, and by locking it into a position of hopeless dependency within the world economy from which it was impossible to escape. One element in this dependency were native 'comprador' elites, who shared their countries' wealth with Western imperialist capital, whose agents they were and after whose luxuries and lifestyles they lusted. By importing Western luxury goods for themselves and transferring much of their wealth abroad, these elites squandered their countries' resources and wrecked their balance of trade. These ideas were particularly popular among some South American scholars in the 1960s and 1970s, who used them to explain the failure of Latin America to join the First World of advanced capitalist democracies. If liberal economic ideology and globalization fail to result in economic advance in the Third World, then new variants of dependency theory may regain a following. Unless Russia's economy recovers vigorously from the disasters of the 1990s, then many adherents of the 'new dependency movement' will be found there.

By the 1990s probably the most fashionable strand in the scholarly debate on imperialism concentrated on the cultural sphere. During the period of decolonization (and more specifically during the Algerian war of independence) Franz Fanon had become famous for his denunciation of colonialism's impact on the culture, the psyche and the self-respect of the native peoples it ruled. The key text in the 1990s debate was, however, Edward Said's *Orientalism*.[31] This is a subtle work, not easily summed up in a paragraph. Among its arguments is the claim that Western scholars specializing in non-European societies and cultures served as handmaidens and legitimizers of colonial rule. In addition, the West constructed and popularized a view of the non-Western world that stereotyped it as irredeemably backward and exotic, in the process justifying the global domination of Western power, interests, ideologies and values. It is not at all hard for a historian of Russia to sympathize with part of this argument, faced by a Western public for which the whole history of pre-Soviet Russia appears to be summed up by the story of Rasputin and the Grand Duchess Anastasia, mixed in with tales about the Russians' insatiable appetite for territorial expansion. The Russians, so it seems – now, then and always – are congenitally corrupt and inescapably imperialist. As always with such caricatures, the fact that they contain some element of historical truth makes them all the more dangerous when swallowed wholesale and used to explain contemporary politics. The Russian people's failure to absorb and appreciate a particularly vicious lesson in dogmatic, corrupt and unregulated liberal capitalism in the 1990s, and their resentment at the lesson, are thereby easily cited as irrefutable evidence of the Russians' hopeless genes.

But the disciples of 'Orientalism', more actually than Said himself, are inclined to take the argument much too far, as well as often to wrap it in a numbing, imprecise and inherently very elitist jargon. 'Orientalist' scholarship in Europe (including Russia) has been much more than just a handmaiden of imperialism. It was and is often driven by a deep respect for the societies and cultures it studies. Its greatest early figures were in fact very often Germans, who never had an empire in the Muslim world (Said's main concern) and only briefly ruled a rather miserable empire anywhere outside Europe. Not merely many scholars but even some of the practitioners of empire actually far preferred the 'Orient' to the modern West, whose philistine, materialist, egalitarian mass culture and politics they often despised. Unequivocal old reactionaries and the contemporary left are not always as far apart as either would find comfortable. Moreover, there are dangers in mixing up traditional political analysis of empire and imperialism, which are the concern of this book, with discussion of cultural politics in the contemporary world. Equating the attacks on cultural imperialism with 'protests against the spread of (capitalist) modernity', John Tomlinson complains quite rightly that 'these protests are often formulated in an inappropriate language of domination, a language of cultural imposition which draws its imagery from the age of high imperialism and colonialism' and is a cause of muddle when applied to the different world of globalization and post-modernity.[32]

In conclusion, something must be said of present-day scholarship on empire. Since this book ends with a bibliographical essay on the subject, only the bare outlines will be set out here. Most current scholarship is on specific empires of the past. It is not much concerned with concepts and definitions. Among scholars who do try to define and compare empires, two main schools stand out. The first takes its basis in the modern European maritime empires. It therefore defines empire as the relationship between metropolitan core and colonial periphery, usually viewed in terms of economic exploitation and cultural aggression, and always in terms of political domination. Michael Doyle[33] is the most widely read current scholar in this tradition. In the other camp stand those whose interests lie mainly in the great military and absolutist land empires, often linked to universalist religions, which existed from antiquity into the twentieth century. Samuel Eisenstadt[34] and Maurice Duverger are contemporary scholars who study and define empire largely from this perspective.

Interest in what causes the rise and fall of empires is of course very old indeed. The ancient Chinese theory of Heaven's Mandate is an early attempt to come to grips with this issue. In tune with Chinese philosophy and 'religion', it linked the rise and fall of empire to various natural phenomena and cosmic patterns, as well as to the moral behaviour of emperors whose greatest duty was to conduct their lives in strict harmony with the Confucian conception of natural order. The great ancestor of modern Western scholarship on empire is Edward Gibbon.[35] Contemporary classical scholars such as Ramsay Macmullan[36] and A.H.M. Jones[37] develop his theme of the role of ideology and corruption in the decay and collapse of great empires.

Most contemporary scholarship on the rise and fall of empires is, however, concerned with power, defined above all in economic and military terms. Shifts in the balance of economic power are seen as the main determinant in the rise and fall of empires. In the university world departments of international relations form the core of such studies, though the scholar in this field best known to the public is in fact a historian, Paul Kennedy.[38] While students of international relations concentrate on power, often defining it very narrowly in economic and military terms, problems of nationalism obsess many political scientists. From the 1950s to the 1970s it was widely assumed that modernity would create a global village in which nationalism was redundant. By the 1990s the continuing hold of nationalism even in modern Western Europe, together with its role in the collapse of the Soviet Union, had confounded such expectations and was inspiring an avalanche of literature on questions of ethnicity and nationhood.

It is one of the great advantages of looking at empire in the Russian and Soviet context that one is forced to bring together literature from a range of fields whose authors usually live on separate academic planets. Power – 'military and economic' – is obviously central to the rise and fall of empire in Russia and the Soviet Union. So is nationalism, both Russian and non-Russian. But no sensible observer of the rise and decay of the Soviet empire could deny the significance of corruption and ideology in this process. To make only one obvious point: the Soviet economic system was the product neither of circumstances nor of Russian history – it was the creation of Marxist-Leninist ideology. The failure of this economic system was therefore above all else the failure of an ideology, and was generally perceived as such both within the Soviet Union and abroad. Very obviously, however, the collapse of the Soviet Union was not just a product of long-term impersonal forces. It owed a huge amount to circumstances, chance and personalities – above all to the personality of Mikhail Gorbachev. In this book an attempt is made to balance all these factors in studying and comparing the rise and fall of empires.

2

Power and Empire in the Global Context

ROME AND CHINA: SOURCES OF POWER, FOUNDATIONS OF EMPIRE

Two thousand years ago two great empires dominated both ends of Eurasia. In the west there was Rome, in the east the Chinese Han Empire. Both these great polities were empires in every sense of the word. Even by modern standards they covered a huge area. Given the communications of that time their extent is miraculous. Like most empire-builders, their rulers lavished resources on creating an effective road system across which armies could march and messages fly at maximum speed. Roman roads are still famous in Europe. The first Chinese emperor built so-called 'speedways'[1] to link his newly amalgamated dominions.

These two empires were not only vast but also multi-ethnic and very powerful. They dominated their regions of the earth. Those peoples who lived beyond their frontiers were regarded as barbarians, unworthy of respect. Neither empire had any conception of equality within a society of independent states; each was the world, or at least its centre. These empires had inherited rather than created great civilizations. Their high culture, philosophies and arts had matured in the centuries before empire. But empire did play a role in reshaping these cultures and, even more, in spreading and preserving them. It was after all under the empire that Rome and Christianity merged, subsequently spreading across Europe and defining it as a unique and separate civilization.

Some empires seek to assimilate conquered peoples or at least their elites. Others hold themselves aloof, for instance shunning intermarriage. On the whole the modern Western (especially Protestant) maritime empires belonged to the latter category, attaching great significance to purity of blood and whiteness of skin. By contrast, the Roman and

Chinese empires were more assimilationist. What mattered were culture, behaviour and lifestyles. Those who adopted Roman or Chinese culture and manners were accepted even into the empires' elite. By the early third century AD even Italians, let alone Romans, were no longer in a majority either in the Senate or in the equestrian order.[2] Increasingly, emperors themselves were to come from outside Italy. No prejudice seems to have existed against Black Africans. Over the centuries too the Chinese proved willing to assimilate barbarians, including barbarian conquerors of China itself. On occasion this willingness slipped, above all when Chinese self-confidence was rocked by foreign conquest or domestic chaos. At such moments xenophobia and ethnic pride were to the fore.[3] But on the whole culture defined being Chinese. The huge prestige and attraction not just of Chinese high culture but also of China's technology, for instance its agricultural techniques, were a great source of both pride and power for the Chinese and their empire. Conquered peoples often assimilated willingly over time, bowing to the superiority of their rulers' civilization. Much the same was true of Roman rule in Western Europe.

In both the Roman and Han empires, willingness to assimilate and transform conquered peoples went along with great cultural arrogance. The latter is indeed usually one of the hallmarks of empire. The Romans did acknowledge a deep debt to Greek culture, indeed even the latter's superiority. In cultural terms the empire was a Roman-Greek amalgam, and Rome made little effort to impose its own culture or language on its Greek territories. The Chinese case was always more self-confident. From the Han era until today few Chinese have ever doubted the absolute superiority of their culture to all others in the region. One contemporary expert on China's minority peoples speaks of 'an innate, almost visceral Han sense of superiority'.[4] Certainly communism did nothing to weaken this sense, in fact quite the opposite. What it did do was to rigidify and add 'scientific' legitimacy to age-old assumptions of superiority. Even in the sixteenth century the Chinese made clear distinctions between the civilized (themselves) and various levels of 'cooked' (i.e. semi-savage) and 'uncooked' (i.e. wholly savage) barbarians. Marxism-Leninism has sanitized such assumptions, or rather the jargon in which they are expressed, by invoking scientifically proven stages of unilinear historical development in which, miraculously, the Chinese stand at the top of the ladder with the minorities climbing dutifully in their wake. Such ideologies and visions still justify the colonization, development and spoliation of minority land not just in Xinjiang or Tibet but in regions too of southern China.[5] As is the case with modern European empires, some assumptions made by the Chinese as to the superiority of their civilization look rather dubious to modern eyes. Like many European imperialists, the Chinese have always tended to shudder at the lasciviousness of 'native', in other words minority, women: the Chinese saw the refusal of native cultures to follow the Han custom of crippling women by binding their feet as children as a clear mark of cultural inferiority.[6]

There were a number of crucial differences between the Roman and Chinese empires. In the long run, what matters most are the divergences between the civilizations these empires sustained and extended. From the perspective of AD 2000 the crucial elements in Roman culture were the rationalist and logical way of arguing inherited from the Greeks, the Roman system of law, the Greek stress on the individual and on existential tragedy, and the Graeco-Roman tradition of self-government. To these one must add the impact of the Christian drama of Christ's life and resurrection; belief in the individual soul, its sinfulness and redemption; and the importance of monotheism and the exclusionary and dogmatic mindset it fosters. Most of these elements are alien to China's Confucian tradition, to Chinese Legalism and to later Buddhist influences on Chinese civilization. The Chinese tradition holds fundamentally different views of the role of the individual in society and the cosmos, the relationship between heaven and earth, and the proper forms of political order, less interest in belief, dogma and logic, and a correspondingly greater stress on behaviour and ritual. No doubt these distinctions are too black and white. Human beings share much in common, as do most civilizations, systems of government and empires. Nevertheless, distinctions between Roman and Chinese civilization that crystallized in the late Roman and early Chinese dynastic empires were fundamental and remain so in today's world.

Important differences may also be seen on a more down-to-earth political level. Empires tend to choose between direct and indirect methods of rule. In the latter case much power is devolved to usually established local rulers and elites, with the corollary that great freedom is allowed to traditional cultures and methods of rule. Direct imperial rule entails the creation of appointed agents of the central power in the regions and localities. It therefore implies the existence of a considerable bureaucracy through which, in principle, the ruler can implement his policies. In reality, especially in pre-modern empires, the distinction between direct and indirect rule was not clear-cut. Problems of size and communications made every empire dependent in the long run on the collaboration of local elites. The resources never existed to create a huge salaried bureaucracy capable of exercising all the functions of government in modern style. Even had they done so, such a bureaucracy could not have been controlled by the centre given primitive communications. Among pre-modern empires the Chinese came closest to creating such a bureaucracy and experiencing the nightmare of trying to control it. Chinese government, though still ultimately dependent on local landowners' collaboration, was far more direct, centralized and bureaucratic than the Roman even in the first and second centuries, let alone subsequently under the Song and Ming dynasties. Writing on the period 27 BC to AD 235, one authority on Roman government comments that 'the Roman empire remained undergoverned, certainly by comparison with the Chinese empire, which employed, proportionately, perhaps twenty times the number of functionaries.'[7] Even after the dramatic increase in bureaucracy and centralization under Diocletian in the next century, the late Roman Empire still had only one-quarter of the Chinese level of bureaucrats. In the empire's heyday the emperor was commander-in-chief of the army and supreme judge but his role as chief executive officer of an administration was very limited. 'The secret of government without bureaucracy was the Roman system of cities which were self-governing and could provide for the needs of the empire', to quote the above authority once more, and another historian concurs that 'Roman government would have been impossible without immense delegation of administration.'[8]

Many Chinese emperors lived a life surrounded by bureaucrats and bureaucracy. Like almost all ancient and many modern empires China was in theory an autocracy. Reality, in China as elsewhere, was usually very different. Existing in the world's greatest and most long-lasting tradition of bureaucratic empire, Chinese monarchs developed virtually all the conceivable techniques an emperor might use to control the bureaucratic machine. The only exceptions were some of the mechanisms considered essential in present-day democracies – namely elected parliaments, a free press and an independent judiciary.

Some Chinese monarchs resorted to terror to control their bureaucrats, sometimes (especially under the Ming dynasty) on a grand scale. They developed a system of procurators, the so-called 'censorate', to act as an independent watchdog over bureaucratic wrongdoing. Monarchs created one form or another of personal secretariat – the 'inner court' – in order to receive reliable information, cut through lengthy procedures, and impose their own priorities on government. They cultivated unofficial informers and correspondents in the bureaucracy, sought out loyal and trustworthy agents, and despatched personal confidants on secret missions into the provinces. As in most monarchies, emperors tended to be very suspicious of their own male relatives, who were usually the only conceivable rivals for their office and were the natural focus for factions and conspiracies. But a wife's relatives were no such threat and might be a very loyal and dependable group at the heart of government. So too might non-Chinese groups, particularly if, like the Manchus, they were of the same nationality as the dynasty itself. For a Chinese dynasty, one alternative such group to non-Chinese might be eunuchs. Alone among males they could work in the inner palace, where the emperor spent most of his days. They were usually loyal to the monarch, whom they had helped to look after in his childhood: they were also dependent upon him. Their position as non-men sharply isolated them in Chinese society and they were usually loathed and despised by the bureaucracy, which lessened the chances of a common front against imperial power.

The emperor's dilemma was partly due to the fact that China and its bureaucracy was vastly larger and more sophisticated than was the case with any European state before the nineteenth century. In addition, Chinese bureaucrats had a unique *esprit de corps*. Most bureaucracies worship their procedures and precedents but few see them as guarantees of cosmic harmony and the moral order of society. The Chinese did, largely because the Confucian bureaucrat filled the roles that in Europe were divided between royal official and priest. Many monarchs, and in particular many modern European ones, have felt deeply frustrated and alienated by the bureaucratic machinery through which they have been forced to rule. China provided stark precedents for this. In the late sixteenth century, for instance, the Ming emperor Wanli refused for many years to appoint new officials, conduct business or meet his ministers. 'As an emperor who actually carried on a strike against his own bureaucrats over a long period of time, Wanli has come down in history without any close parallel.'[9] Chinese history taught another crucial, albeit commonsensical, lesson about emperors' relations with great bureaucratic machines. The ruler who sought to dominate his government must devote his life to this task. In her brilliant account of the reign of Emperor Yongzheng (1723–35), one of China's most effective monarchs, Beatrice Bartlett comments that his system of rule required a monarch who 'threw his energies into the hurley-burley of governing, his long days and half his nights consecrated to his mission of ruling.' Most hereditary monarchs were neither willing nor able to make this sacrifice, particularly over the span of a long reign. Yongzheng himself commented that 'one man's strength is not sufficient to run the Empire' and died after twelve years on the throne.[10]

★

The status and power of its civilian bureaucrats marked China off sharply not just from Rome but also from subsequent European polities. Rome's elite for most of its history was a military aristocracy which thirsted for military glory as a source of status, wealth and political office. This thirst was a key reason for Rome's territorial expansion. All later European empires shared this characteristic to a great, albeit varying degree. In none of them were civilians and their values nearly as dominant as in China. Even the British Empire, sometimes described as an essentially commercial and financial enterprise, accorded far greater prestige and power to soldiers than was the case in China. Not until nineteenth-century Prussia did any European mandarinate enjoy a prestige remotely comparable to that of the Chinese elite bureaucracy. But even in Prussia mandarins had to defer in status and sometimes power to the army and its officers, a group on which Chinese elite society usually looked with contempt.

The differing traditions of civil-military relations in Chinese and European civilization had important consequences. In most polities in history, controlling military force has posed problems. Armies are essential for external security and expansion, but often dangerous to a ruler and the domestic political order. This dilemma is bound to be particularly acute in empires, for which expansion is often a *raison d'être* and security on distant borders an inevitable burden. Great armies forced to operate autonomously many hundreds or even thousands of miles from an emperor's capital were bound to pose a potential threat to the throne. The Romans never found a solution to this problem, countless military rebellions greatly contributing to the empire's disorder and vulnerability in its later centuries. Preserving a large professional army also strained the empire's tax base beyond endurance, which contributed to military revolts and an increasing lack of civilian loyalty to the empire and its rulers. The Chinese faced similar financial and political dilemmas. Overall the Chinese suffered fewer military revolts than the Romans, but the civilian elite's contempt for and meanness towards the army weakened the empire's defences, as did the bureaucrats' policy of dividing military commands and undermining the prestige of any generals who were too successful. Towards the end of the Ming dynasty, for example, this policy not merely undermined military effectiveness but persuaded a number of key generals that the regime was not worth defending. In comparison with China, let alone Rome, later European empires were usually more successful in squaring the circle of military power and obedience. The sacredness of the royal bloodline and of the monarch appointed by God – who also happened to be the uniformed descendant of the feudal warlord – was crucial in securing military loyalty to European dynasties.

The collapse of the Roman Empire was a great trauma for Europe and its elites. Much energy and passion has been expended in explaining the causes of this collapse. The comparison with China suggests that part of this effort may have been misplaced. The Han Empire also collapsed, and did so for reasons that were sometimes similar to the causes of Rome's demise. The significant point is that subsequently empire reimposed itself in East Asia as the predominant form of polity, whereas in Europe a very different and largely non-imperial tradition came out on top. To ask why this was the case is important for a number of reasons. In the first place the predominance of empire in East Asia but not in Western Europe was of huge significance for subsequent world politics and created the context in which Russia's historical development occurred. Secondly, contemplating this issue tells one much about the sources of imperial power and the factors that contribute to the rise, fall and longevity of empire.

In looking comparatively at two millennia of Chinese and European history, as indeed at any other long-term historical process, there is a strong temptation to forget the impact of personalities, circumstances and sheer chance. The story is often told as if its dénouement is inevitable, with great impersonal forces moving in inexorable patterns. Particularly where politics and international relations are concerned, this is a great mistake. In the first place, history written in this way tends to deepen the already very strong instinct of its readers, particularly if American or English, that their values and assumptions are the inevitable culmination of historical progress. In the second place, the story told in this way simply isn't true.

Certainly there was nothing inevitable about the predominance of empire in East Asia over the last two millennia. Nature in many ways pulled hard in the opposite direction, not merely because of China's unmanageable size but also because of the rivers and mountains that divide so much of southern China into semi-enclosed regions with separate economies, cultures and languages. A polity whose core, Han (that is, ethnic Chinese) population even today speaks a range of first languages almost as diverse as the major languages of Europe could easily be seen as ripe for division into nation states. For much of China's history, separate states did in fact exist. In the long run the preservation of a single written script understood and venerated by all educated Chinese as the medium of high culture and of government was crucial to China's unity. In the centuries immediately before China's unification in 221 BC, however, this script was beginning to diverge from one polity to another. The same era witnessed a 'proliferation of local literatures'. It was the supreme achievement of the 'First Emperor', Qinshihuangdi, to reverse this process irrevocably by reimposing a standardized Chinese script. 'Without the Ch'in reform, it is conceivable that several regionally different orthographies might have come into permanent existence. And had this happened, it is inconceivable that China's political unity could long have survived.'[11] In his vast and scholarly history of world government, Sam Finer comments that the First Emperor, in 'his short, barbarous, but prodigiously energetic reign irrevocably shaped the entire subsequent history of the Chinese state. His reign was decisive and irreversible.' No other individual has ever 'left so great and so indelible a mark on the character of government at any time or in any place of the world.'[12]

One can certainly imagine a Chinese-style scenario in which empire might have reasserted itself in Europe and an imperial language and high culture – perhaps Roman-Latin or perhaps Arabic and Muslim – not merely united the continent's elites but in time seeped down into the rest of the population and obliterated or superimposed itself on their tribal allegiances. For centuries the Roman Catholic clergy provided a common language and educated elite for all Western Christendom. Just as Chinese civilization defined itself against the barbarians of the northern steppe, so in time the 'other' against which Christian civilization above all defined itself came to be Islam. A sense of common danger and external threat is often a crucial factor in the consolidation of empires. As regards Islam, Christians had good reason to feel this danger. For most of the first millennium of Christian-Muslim relations it was Christendom that was on the defensive. The Crusades, Christendom's main counterattack, were only briefly successful in recapturing the Holy Land. On the other hand, in the fourteenth and fifteenth centuries Islam destroyed the remnants of Byzantium, the centuries-old bulwark of Christianity, and conquered the Balkans. Even more glittering prospects opened up with the conversion to Islam of most of the heirs of Genghis Khan and their dominions. In the sixteenth century the Habsburg ambassador to the Ottoman sultan, Ghislaine de Bubesq, had seemingly good reason to predict that only disaster could come from the confrontation between a united Islamic Ottoman Empire and a Christendom divided into a number of warring states.

Nor is it inconceivable, at least in the seventh to ninth centuries, that Islam itself could have provided the basis for an imperial unity spanning Europe, the whole Mediterranean world and Persia too. Though in time, as often happens with neighbours and relations, Christianity and Islam defined themselves against each other in hostile fashion, they were in fact very similar religions within the tradition of Mediterranean culture and Judaic monotheism. Islam's history certainly reminds any historian of empire never to underestimate the power of religion and ideology. The arrival on the scene of Islam in the seventh century transformed forever the geopolitics and the history of Europe and the Middle East. Until the seventh century it is perfectly possible to argue that the Roman Empire was not dead: it had merely retreated into those provinces ruled from Byzantium which already in the fourth century had been its economic, demographic and even military core. These included Syria, Egypt, Asia Minor and parts of Greece. From this power-base in the sixth century Justinian reconquered much of Italy and Spain. At a later time a renewed effort towards imperial reunification might have succeeded: there were after all Chinese parallels for 'resurgence from the south'. It was the wholly unpredictable and revolutionary upsurge of a new ideology, its formidable expansionist energy, and then the division of the Mediterranean between Christianity and Islam that undermined this possibility of empire renewed.

By the eighteenth century the idea of universal empire in Europe appeared a chimera and an impossibility. Though European culture was still hugely influenced by the heritage of classical antiquity, for the first time European elites were beginning to feel that their civilization had advanced beyond its Roman limits. Montesquieu wrote a famous book claiming that universal monarchy in Europe was now unthinkable. Not merely were geography and the spirit of the European peoples opposed to it, but so too were the technology and the culture of contemporary European warfare. In former days armies and peoples had lived off plunder and conquest, but nowadays Europe was too civilized to operate in this way and wars cost more than they were worth. 'The Romans carried to Rome in their triumphs all the riches of conquered nations. Nowadays victory yields nothing but unfruitful laurels.'[13]

Montesquieu was quite right to argue that after well over a millennium of separation, the peoples of Europe would not easily be united under a single empire. Nevertheless, within decades Montesquieu's own country under Napoleon's rule came closer to imposing universal empire on Europe than any other polity since Charlemagne's era. In the short run at least, France and its armies made empire pay handsomely. Under Napoleon the Frenchman paid one-third of the taxes of his British enemy. In 1803 the Frenchman contributed 15.2 francs in taxes, the citizen of conquered Holland 64.3 francs. In the 1806–7 campaign against Prussia France netted one-third of its annual revenues from the tribute it imposed on conquered territory. Nor do these sums include the benefits of quartering troops on foreign soil, allowing them to live off plunder, or conscripting hundreds of thousands of non-Frenchmen into the armies of Napoleon and his satellites. 'Who was Attila's Chancellor of the Exchequer?' retorted William Wilberforce when his political opponents argued that Britain's superior financial resources and management would ultimately guarantee Napoleon's defeat.[14] Napoleon operated according to the traditional logic of empire but his work was sustained, as is often the case with empire-builders, by more than mere power. For all the compromises Napoleon made with Ancien Régime traditions, he retained enough of the reformist baggage of 1789 to win considerable support for his empire outside France as well.

Although the course of European and Chinese history was not fore-ordained and chance and personality played a big role, there were certain underlying reasons why a tradition of empire was more likely to sustain itself in East Asia than in Western Europe. The monotheist, universalist religious culture of Europe and the Middle East was much more likely to spawn ideological explosions than a Confucian political culture with its stress on behaviour rather than belief and its willingness to welcome regional cults and deities into the imperial pantheon.

Also crucial was the fact that Christendom was threatened not just by steppe nomads from Central Asia but also along a huge southern front that stretched across North Africa to Persia and provided a geographical base from which Islam could challenge Europe. China faced no real threat on its southern or coastal fronts until the Western 'barbarians' arrived in the nineteenth century. On the contrary, the vast population of southern China – based on intensive rice farming and therefore far more numer-ous and dense than its European rural equivalent – could be used to restock a northern China sometimes devastated by invasion, civil war and natural catastrophes. China's population density contributed to both political and economic integration. The rural surplus could also flood out into the rest of today's 'Greater China', colonizing new territories and displacing the indigenous population and culture by sheer weight of numbers, as well as by the economic and cultural skills that Chinese migrants brought with them. The process continues to this day. Xinjiang was only incorporated into the Chinese empire in the 1750s, in other words two and a half centuries after Europeans first arrived in the Americas. It only became a regular Chinese province in 1884, while even in 1949 a mere 6.7 per cent of its population were Han Chinese. By 1990 this figure had grown to 37.6 per cent.[15] The indigenous Muslim peoples of Xinjiang were at increasing risk of being swamped, a fate that had long since occurred in the homelands of most of China's other minorities.

Geopolitics also to some extent favoured empire's cause in East Asia, at least in comparison to Europe: 'The north China plain remained throughout by far the largest *single* region in terms of numbers. This meant that whoever controlled the plain was bound to have an advantage over political rivals who disposed only of the more limited resources of one of the southern or western regions.'[16] The Asian steppe grasslands were the world's leading habitat for nomadic warrior societies whose military superiority to sedentary civilizations was a fundamental strategic fact for more than a millennium before AD 1500. North China was much closer and more vulnerable to these cavalrymen than the heartlands of West European civilization. The Mongols conquered Song China, at that time by far the richest and most advanced society in the world. Western Europe lay just, but only just, beyond their grasp. Ironically, vulnerability to nomadic invasion worked on the whole to empire's advantage. Disunited for much of the millennium that followed the fall of the Han dynasty in the third century AD, China was reunited by the Mongols and has remained united ever since. Between the 1640s and 1912 it was ruled by the Manchus, in other words a new wave of 'barbarian' semi-nomads from the north. On the whole nomadic conquerors were prepared to assimilate Chinese culture and to accept the Chinese imperial tradition. What they brought to China was the military means to enforce imperial political unity. In addition, a dynasty drawn from outside China could use soldiers and officials from its own native people as an independent power-base, which helped monarchs to preserve a degree of independence from China's own many regional and bureaucratic interests and factions. As beneficiaries of imperial unity, a nomadic dynasty was usually only too happy to support the Confucian ideology of 'one ruler under heaven' which sustained their great empire.

The Confucian scholar-official elite was under most dynasties the dominant group in Chinese politics, society and culture. It was this group that largely defined Chinese conceptions of political legitimacy and correct order. For these scholar-officials the only legitimate polity was the all-imperial one, encompassing all China. Regrettably, de facto division into a number of polities might occur, but such divisions could never be legitimate or more than temporary. Not only the ideals but also the interests of officialdom were of course linked to the existence of the imperial state, whose chief bureaucrats were often not only the most admired but also among the richest subjects of the emperor. These men formed the elite of China's upper class, whose families invested great hopes and resources in training their more talented members for the examinations that allowed entry into the higher reaches of the civil service. The examination system thereby became an additional, formidable weapon with which the imperial state and its officials could define and homogenize the values and aspirations of Chinese society, meaning above all its landowning elite.

Nothing remotely like this existed in Christendom. The most basic political fact about Christian society was that secular and religious authority were divided. The aristocratic warrior-cum-landowner and the royal official were not priests: nor even was the king himself. For largely practical reasons the split between royal and priestly power was more real traditionally in Latin Christendom than in Orthodox realms. The Orthodox patriarch in Constantinople lived closely under the eye of the Byzantine emperor. Subsequently the same was true of the Orthodox hierarchy in Russia. But the papacy, once the Roman Empire had fallen, was forced to adopt a more independent stance. No great monarch ruled its city or region. The popes became independent territorial princes but also wielded a huge spiritual prestige as the religious leaders of Western Christendom. The clergy were also overwhelmingly the most educated and literate sections of medieval European society.

When an imperial monarchy did re-emerge in Latin Christendom in the ninth century, the papacy was crucial in limiting its power. This in turn aided the emergence of independent princes and power centres in Latin Christendom, the most important of which were the kingdoms of France and England. These princes were legitimate Christian rulers in their own right by the Grace of God. They were powerful enough to shrug off any claim by the papacy, let alone the emperor, that they ruled by his authority or as his lieutenants. Around these princes there formed separate feudal military aristocracies. These enjoyed considerable autonomy not merely de facto but also according to the feudal law that united king and aristocracy by mutually binding contract and was the basis of the medieval European polity. A polity in which power was divided between king, church and aristocracy allowed space for autonomous towns to develop as havens for corporate self-government and civil rights. Aristocracies, royal courts and the officials they created spoke a vernacular language and in the Middle Ages began to generate a vernacular literature. They acquired a distinct identity which might well gain a hold on wider sections of society. These dynastic polities fought each other and to some extent defined themselves against each other. English armies trampling across France during the Hundred Years' War might leave many humble people with the strong sense that they certainly were not English. On the contrary, they were subjects of the king of France, descendant of Saint Louis and protégé of Joan of Arc. The arrival of Protestantism in sixteenth-century Europe encouraged the development of national consciousness in parts at least of Europe. Catholic and Protestant peoples and polities could measure themselves against each other, especially if they were neighbours. By encouraging the reading of the Bible, Protestantism hugely encouraged the spread of mass literacy and the vernacular languages. In Protestant realms, royal and ecclesiastical power were merged but not, Chinese-style, on a pan-European imperial basis but in separate states which in some cases – England, the Netherlands, Sweden – were well on the way to being nations by 1600. Some Protestant churches operated on the principle of parochial self-government and therefore invested the sense of religious-national community with a strong element of egalitarianism and even citizenship. The Bible itself held up as a model to all that most national of ancient polities, the people of Israel.[17]

China was an empire: its rulers' overriding preoccupation therefore was the preservation of empire. Europe became a world of many polities, in constant competition with each other for survival, power and pre-eminence. By the eighteenth century all Europe formed a single community of states: no major state could be indifferent to shifts in power in any part of the continent. From this reality sprang the practice and theory of balance of power: all major states could agree that it was in none of their interests that a single dominant polity should emerge. Against this background emerged, after 1648, the basic concept of European inter-state relations, namely that polities were sovereign, in one sense legally equal, and that these sovereign states enjoyed unlimited authority within their own borders. Because the major states were in constant competition, any policy that enhanced the power of one was certain to be copied by others. In general, by the eighteenth century the competition for power was sidelining considerations of ideology or social conservatism. Europeans have usually contrasted the inherently dynamic and progressive impact of this competition with empire's tendency to impose ideological conformity, social conservatism and political centralization on its subjects. Mao Zedong might well have agreed. He once commented that 'one good thing about Europe is that all its countries are independent. Each of them does its own thing, which makes it possible for the economy of Europe to develop at a fast pace. Ever since China became an empire after the Qin dynasty, our country has been for the most part unified. One of its defects has been bureaucratisation, and excessively tight control. The localities could not develop independently.'[18]

THE EUROPEAN SYSTEM OF STATES

For European dynamism, however, a price was paid in terms of constant insecurity and frequent war. By the twentieth century the wars that sprang partly from the absence of empire in Europe not merely devastated the continent and much of the rest of the globe, but also lost Europeans their position of worldwide dominance. After 1945 not just Europe's regeneration but the very survival and worldwide pre-eminence of its values were owed above all to the United States. Ironically, American ability to sustain this role depended greatly on the fact that the United States was in one sense an empire, or at least a polity of continental scale which dominated an entire hemisphere.

When compared to East Asia or the Islamic Middle East, the various types of polity that have existed in Europe in the last millennium share many common characteristics. Within Europe there has been, however, great diversity — much greater than one finds in any other part of the world. There were city states and even a few republics such as Venice and the Netherlands which extended well beyond the confines of a single city. There were feudal monarchies which might or might not make the transition to absolutist or constitutional monarchies in the eighteenth century and to nation states in the nineteenth. There were the multi-ethnic dynastic empires of the Habsburgs and the Romanovs, which covered huge territories. Inevitably too there were many unique or anomalous cases such as Sweden, which had for instance never passed through a genuinely feudal stage before becoming a constitutional monarchy and a nation state. By the twentieth century it appeared to be the nation state that alone enjoyed legitimacy and could flourish in Europe. As Charles Tilly remarks, however, 'only late in the millennium did national states exercise clear superiority over city states, empires and other common European forms of state.'[19] If present-day attempts at European federation succeed, the triumph of the nation state may prove brief.

By the eighteenth century there had emerged from the plethora of European states a small group of great powers. At one point Spain, the Netherlands, Poland and Sweden all belonged to this group. From the mid-eighteenth century down to 1914, however, there were only five true great powers. These were the United Kingdom and Prussia, both of which were predominantly Protestant realms; France and the multi-ethnic and predominantly Catholic empire of the Austrian Habsburgs; and, last but not least, Russia – another multi-ethnic, aristocratic empire, whose core population and ruling dynasty were Orthodox.

What made a state a great power was, first and foremost, the resources it could mobilize for war. Armies and fleets were the essence of power. To sustain them required adequate manpower, which Sweden, to take one example of a failed great power, barely possessed. In modern war, however, manpower was useless unless it was trained and properly officered. Fleets were technically more complicated than armies and their officers and men therefore needed even higher levels of professionalism. To compete, a great power required sufficient numbers of educated subjects of its own or the ability to attract and use foreigners. The further east one went in eighteenth-century Europe, the more important the foreign element was likely to be in the state's military and administrative elite.

No modern military machine could be sustained without an adequate administration. Soldiers had to be conscripted or recruited. Without pay, weapons and supplies armies and fleets would disintegrate, ceasing to be an effective tool in the ruler's hands and turning instead into a threat to domestic order and security. Taxes were crucial: a great power required a viable fiscal administration, though if it also had the mechanisms to raise large and cheap loans its staying power in wartime would be enhanced greatly. The provision of adequate manpower, officers, taxes and equipment was not just a technical matter: politics was crucial too. Above all else, to meet the needs of power a state required an effective alliance between the state and the social elites. Poland was the great example of a polity destroyed by the weakness of the monarchy and an over-mighty and irresponsible aristocracy. By contrast, Prussia showed how an effective royal administration fused with a landowning gentry committed to the dynastic state could mobilize sufficient resources and skill to create a great power out of a relatively small population and territory in a geopolitically unfavourable location. Prussia's rise also showed the supreme importance of intelligent, coordinated and single-minded leadership, which in early modern Europe could seldom be divorced from the quality of the monarchs that the competing dynasties produced. In the Great Elector, Frederick William I and Frederick II the Hohenzollerns provided Prussia with exceptionally effective, albeit personally unattractive, leaders.

Britain and the Netherlands are often viewed as a distinct subgroup within the European community of states. Both were Protestant polities which early developed representative institutions and which were the centres of European, and subsequently world, commerce and finance. Modern capitalist systems of credit and finance need to be managed in a way that is open to the trust and scrutiny of bankers and investors. The connection between financial power and representative institutions was not fortuitous. In Poland aristocratic liberty destroyed the state. In Britain representative institutions dominated by the aristocracy on the whole enhanced the state's might, and not merely because of their role in financial management. Unlike the case of the continental dynastic states, leadership was not so dependent on biological chance. The British and Dutch polities are widely studied because they are seen to have represented the wave of the future. They played the great initial role in the creation of the contemporary integrated global economic and financial system. They also, so it is said, set the precedent of striving for wealth and economic power rather than territory and military vainglory. They are seen as the first great modern models of political and economic liberalism, the founders of the contemporary world in which democratic institutions, a dynamic liberal capitalism and immense global power are fused in the major states, and above all in the United States.

The picture is true up to a point but is sometimes overemphasized. The present is too uncritically read into the distant past. In the Anglo–Dutch case this leads to exaggeration of these polities' power vis-à-vis their major continental rivals in the eighteenth and nineteenth centuries. It takes their ultimate triumph as inevitable and foreordained, and ignores the more traditional geopolitical and military factors which, alongside financial and commercial strength, also contributed to the power of Britain and the Dutch Republic. The Dutch have been described both as the world's leading power in the seventeenth century and as essentially pacific.[20] Since the Dutch secured and defended their dominance of world trade to a considerable extent by military means, 'pacific' is a rather strange way to describe them. Moreover, although the Dutch overseas enterprise was initially seen as purely commercial, in time it created a great territorial empire in the East Indies. Very similar was the experience of the British, whose East India Company turned into a traditional territorial empire, governed autocratically, resting on a land tax, and contributing hugely to Britain's geopolitical power and status. In the seventeenth century the Dutch were certainly powerful, but whether they were actually more powerful than a Qing Empire ruling over hundreds of millions of subjects is dubious. In 1662, at the zenith of Dutch power, the local warlord in Taiwan – a very small part of Greater China – had little difficulty in expelling the Dutch forces.[21] The Dutch homeland itself was acutely vulnerable to French pressure, which it could hope to counter only with the help of foreign allies.

The shift in power from the Netherlands to Britain in the eighteenth century was owed initially not to Britain's commercial or financial superiority but to her geopolitical position and greater military and demographic resources. The same was true when Britain was replaced as the world's leading power by the United States in the twentieth century. The American economy was stronger than the British, but what really counted was that the United States was a continental fortress with not just economic but also demographic and military resources to match its scale. Quite unlike the British and Dutch, its continental size provided a vast domestic market and allowed a somewhat autarchic policy of economic development. Continental scale and hankerings after autarchy are very typical attributes of empire.

In addition, it is important to remember the limits of British power even at its zenith. Ultimately it was not the British who overthrew Napoleon but the fact that in 1813–14, for the first time since 1793, Russia, Prussia and Austria united against France and put overwhelming forces in the field against her. When the wars of 1864–71 brought German unification and heralded the next great challenge to the continental balance of power, the British could only stand and watch. Bismarck commented that if the British army landed on the continent he would send the Prussian police force to arrest it. Though the British did recruit a considerable army in India, metropolitan Britain provides a fine example of how wealthy states are not always willing or able to turn economic into military power, and of the possible impact of this unwillingness on international power politics.

Of the major continental states France was by far the likeliest hegemon between 1648 and 1815. At the zenith of its power in 1803–12 it offered a Europe united under the banner of Napoleon's compromise between the 'principles of 1793' and the requirements of order and property. On their own the Austrian Habsburgs were never powerful enough to threaten to dominate Europe but before 1648, in alliance with their Spanish cousins, they could do so. The imperial vision they offered the continent was of universal Catholicism's restoration in the form of the Counter-Reformation and under the protection of overwhelming Spanish power. Tsarist Russia was actually never strong enough to dominate Europe, though the British feared its power before 1854 and the Germans launched the First World War in 1914 partly because Russia's rapid economic and military development made it look like a possible future hegemon unless it was checked. But Russia reached the apogee of its power in the Soviet era, offering Europe and indeed the whole world an imperial order based on its own version of socialism.

In the century after 1850, however, the country likeliest to dominate Europe was Prussia-Germany. Prussia had some resemblance to the ancient state of Qin whose ruler had united China in 221 BC. Like Qin, Prussia existed on the periphery of the civilization to which it belonged – in its case, on the eastern European plains conquered by crusading knights in the medieval era. Like Qin, and like many states that founded empires, it combined the rugged military virtues of a borderland with access to the technology and culture of a civilization's core. Like Qin, Prussia was regarded as a touch barbaric and uncompromisingly militarist. The two states also had the most efficient administration in their region, whose overriding purpose was the mobilization of resources for war.

In 1864–71 Prussia conquered and united Germany. As the Industrial Revolution moved from Western to Central Europe in the second half of the nineteenth century Germany became its heartland. By 1914 it had the largest and most dynamic economy in Europe, in particular leading in 'new industries' such as chemicals, electrics and precision engineering. Its entrepreneurial dynamism was second to none; it had the best schools, universities and research institutes in Europe; it led too as regards the quality of its administration. Here in other words was economic and military power combined. The 'German model' was not yet clearly defined in 1914. Its economic system was basically similar to Britain's though better rooted in scientific research, somewhat more influenced by the banks, and with a rather more authoritarian style of management. Its political system was distinctly more authoritarian and militarist, though one aspect of its 'Old Prussian' authoritarian character was reflected in Europe's earliest and most effective system of social insurance for workers. Illiberal in this as in most other ways, Germany was also the heartland of European socialism and the home of its largest party. Arnold Toynbee commented that in the twentieth century Germany had made 'a strenuous attempt to provide our society with its universal state' – in other words to create a European empire on the German model. Elements of that model included 'how to raise a whole population to a standard of unprecedented social efficiency by a system of compulsory education and of unprecedented social security by a system of compulsory health and unemployment insurance.'[22]

Quite how the German model would have evolved in the event of victory in the 1914–18 war and hegemony in Europe it is difficult to say. Victory would have encouraged German arrogance vis-à-vis Slavs and Latins. The populist and nationalist right would have been strengthened, at least in the short run. On the other hand victory and the task of actually ruling the many peoples of Eastern and Central Europe might have sobered and softened the Hohenzollerns, as it had the Habsburg regime. To keep such an empire stable, prosperous and secure would have required more than arrogance and military power. Europe would have been integrated on German terms but it would almost certainly have avoided anything as nasty as Hitler or Stalin. Perhaps we would have seen the triumph of the 'Asian Capitalist' model, albeit with a strong militarist twist, two generations before the virtues of Asian Capitalism began to be trumpeted by leaders in Singapore and Malaysia in the 1980s. Here in other words was a possible model for a modern global capitalism which was more authoritarian and disciplined than the American version that dominated the twentieth century and was much less tolerant of individualism or of cultural and sexual pluralism than late twentieth-century American liberal capitalism turned out to be. In the context of a history of empire, however, the important point to note is that the German 'Asiatic model' was not eclipsed because it was less modern or economically less efficient than the American one. It was overthrown by military defeat, caused above all by American intervention in the struggle for mastery in Europe.

DILEMMAS OF MODERN EMPIRE

Europe's expansion into other continents took off in the sixteenth century. The Islamic enemy, which blocked direct expansion to the south, was outflanked by European seapower. The whole world was increasingly drawn into a single commercial network. Because Europe itself was divided there was never any chance of a single European overseas empire. The various European motherlands stamped their own identity on their overseas empires. So too, however, did local conditions. Colonies might have rich mines or agricultural lands with large native populations to exploit them. They might have abundant land in temperate regions with little available indigenous labour. They might be settled by White colonist small farmers or by imported African slaves. They might be territorially very small and essentially commercial enterprises, which themselves might, or might not, subsequently turn into great territorial empires. These colonies might be governed by bureaucrats or soldiers sent out from Europe in the monarch's name. They might have relatively democratic elected assemblies or be run by narrow Creole elites. Whatever form they took, all these colonies contributed to Europeans' eventual domination of most of the globe and their expropriation of much of it from the original American or Australasian inhabitants, or sometimes from Africans and Asians.

The process went in stages. The Americas were quite quickly conquered and colonized, but even in 1700 European merchants and envoys still trod very humbly in the court of the Great Mogul, let alone in the domains of the Chinese emperor or the Japanese shogun. In the eighteenth century European military and economic power grew greatly, but China and Japan were still to a large extent able to hold themselves aloof. The Industrial Revolution, however, transformed the balance of power and wealth between Europe and the rest of the world. One result was the extreme cultural arrogance that came to dominate European thinking about other races and civilizations in the decades before 1914. Another was the crescendo of territorial annexations which reached its high-point between 1876 and 1915, during which period one-quarter of the world's land surface changed hands.

In itself annexation was nothing new for Europe's great powers. As was most graphically illustrated by Poland's disappearance from the map, the European powers were happy to grab additional territory within Europe whenever it was available. But annexation within Europe was difficult. All states watched with acute jealousy any territorial aggrandisement of a rival. Hostile coalitions would mobilize to oppose annexations and could usually bring their power to bear effectively given Europe's confined space and the relatively equal strength of its leading states. It was Bismarck's peculiar genius to unite Germany in two successful wars without bringing a European coalition down on Prussia's head.

Outside Europe annexation was far easier. There was initially enough territory for all the major rivals to gorge themselves. The acquisition of specific territories was not so easily seen as a matter of life and death by a rival when these lands were far from a European state's metropolitan core. Moreover, it was often much more difficult for hostile coalitions to block annexations in faraway lands than in Europe. As European military technology improved, the costs of victorious colonial war lessened. Not only military but also improved medical technology made the penetration and domination of non-European colonies easier. The conquest of malaria in the nineteenth century was the essential prerequisite for the annexation of tropical Africa. The railway and the steamship made it not just easier to conquer new lands but also potentially far more profitable. The railway could open up continents to agriculture and mining. Together with the refrigerated cargo steamship this, for instance, allowed the meat of Argentina and Australia to be exported at great profit to European markets. The rapid advance of technology, including that of surveying and exploration, meant that lands long considered barren might suddenly acquire great value. By 1900 the discovery of gold and diamonds in the Transvaal, together with the development of deep-mining technology, had turned this backwoods into the economic and geopolitical core of southern Africa. British administrators kicked themselves for allowing this jewel to slip from their grasp. In 1899 they started a war to win it back.

Changes in the European balance of power had a big impact on the acquisition of territory outside Europe. Already by the 1820s Friedrich List was arguing that unless Germany created its own modern industry behind protective tariffs it would be doomed to ever-greater inferiority to Britain in terms of both wealth and power. Alexander Hamilton had long since made the same point about the United States and Russian statesmen were later to espouse the same doctrines. By the last quarter of the nineteenth century both industrial and agricultural protection were the norm in most great powers. Protectionism and autarchy inevitably put a heavy value on direct control over the maximum of territory and raw materials, if only to stop rival powers grabbing colonies and excluding others from their markets. By the end of the nineteenth century it was widely assumed that colonies were a key source of present wealth and future power. The French imperialist Paul Leroy-Beaulieu was uttering a commonplace when he noted that 'the nation which has the most colonies is the pre-eminent people; if it isn't today it will be tomorrow.'[23] Joseph Chamberlain in Britain, Heinrich von Treitschke in Germany and Alfred Mahan in the United States would all have agreed that a European power that lacked colonies was doomed to second-class status in the twentieth-century world. In the first decades of the nineteenth century de Tocqueville and List had both prophesied that, a century hence, the continental scale of the USA and Russia would make them superpowers. As List put it in 1828, 'Russia and the United State in one hundred years will be the two most populous empires on earth' and would uphold sharply antagonistic imperial ideologies.[24]

Creating a worldwide empire was seen as the only way to stay in the American and Russian league. Hence the growing stress on naval power, which was essential in any competition to acquire and hold territories divided from Europe by the oceans. In 1897 Captain Baron von Luttwitz of the Prussian General Staff wrote: 'in the last century we were too late to partake of the general partition. But a second partition is forthcoming. We need only consider the fall of the Ottoman Empire, the isolation of China, the unstable condition of so many South American states, to see what rich opportunities await us ... In order not to miss

these opportunities this time we require a fleet.'[25] Geopolitical realities at
the end of the nineteenth century seemed therefore to point to a future
in which the world would be partitioned between a small group of
powerful empires. Yet there was a dangerous weakness in this prophecy.
The modern Europe that had created the race for overseas empires had
also given birth to their nemesis, nationalism. In late Victorian England
Sir Arthur Seeley was the arch-prophet of imperialism and of Greater
Britain. But he was also aware of the vulnerability of empires: 'when the
state advances beyond the limits of the nationality, its power becomes precarious and artificial.'[26]

As we have seen, nations already existed in some parts of Europe even in
the sixteenth century, albeit at varying stages of development. But the
doctrine of nationalism dates from the French Revolution of 1789. Its
basic teaching was that sovereignty belonged to the nation, in other words
to the community of citizens. The revolutionary nationalist doctrine of
1789 was both absolute and abstract. It demanded a far higher level of
commitment to the state than was the case in a traditional monarchy. In
fact the nation became almost an object of worship. No allowances were
made for ethnic, regional or historical divisions within the population.
All must participate enthusiastically in the nation of citizens. Even in an
ancient and relatively speaking homogeneous polity like the kingdom of
France this was to court disaster. The demands of the new centralizing
republican nation sparked off huge resistance in the west of France to
which the republic responded savagely. 'The guerilla war in the Vendée,
in particular,' one historian has recently noted, 'became notorious for the
government's near genocidal collective punishments against entire communities, regardless of age, sex or actual counter-revolutionary activity.
A total of at least 250,000 were killed in this area, and some modern commentators put the true figure as high as a million.'[27] When the principle
of revolutionary nationalism was applied subsequently to communities
far less homogeneous than France, the results were much more catastrophic even than this. Moreover, although in principle Jacobinism
defined the nation in civic and political, not in ethnic terms, in reality, as
became very clear in France after 1789, no community exists in abstrac-
tion and without ethnic markers and inherited characteristics. The citizens of 1789 were also Frenchmen, spoke the French language, and held
a number of deeply rooted assumptions, one of which was that the
French were the most progressive and most cultured people of Europe.
The national revolution of 1789 brought mass terror to the royalist

provinces of western France and twenty-three years of nearly uninterrupted war in Europe, whose fundamental cause was the existence in
France of an army and polity which lived off the proceeds of territorial
expansion and the plunder of foreign peoples.

One effect of French imperialism was to encourage the development
of nationalism in areas of Europe subjected to French armies and tax collectors. More important in the long run were the nationalist doctrines
developed at this time above all by the German Romantics. These put a
heavy stress on ethnicity, and above all language, as the essential defining
elements in communal identity. Initially cultural rather than political in
their thrust, these doctrines were never necessarily democratic. Solidarity
not constitutional democracy was seen as the nation's requirement.
Nevertheless, ethnic nationalism was inherently populist: the true bearer
of authentic national culture was a peasantry that had retained its
customs, folk music and languages, in other words its unique individual-
ity. Merging with the heritage of 1789, these doctrines contributed to
the growing belief that the nation ethnically defined was the supreme
focus for an individual's identity and loyalty, and that fully to realize its
potential a nation must enjoy individual statehood.

For empire this was a fatal and alarming doctrine. Every king and aristocrat was threatened by the theory of popular sovereignty. But the ruler
of an ethnically homogeneous state had far better chances to compromise
with nationalism, retain his throne and keep his kingdom undivided. Nor
was this the sole difficulty. An autocrat or even an aristocracy could rule
over ethnically different peoples citing the same justifications of divine
appointment, prescription or superior culture that they used to legitimize
their governing of peoples of their own ethnicity. But a sovereign democratic nation could only justify its rule over other peoples in the long run
by doctrines of innate racial superiority. Of course in the short run the
imperial power could argue that it was fulfilling an educational mission
for backward peoples as yet unfit to govern themselves. But in the longer
term this argument could not be sustained, particularly if the empire did
actually take seriously its mission to educate subject peoples. The
dilemma was worsened by the fact that Britain, France and the
Netherlands were both the leading democracies of Europe and among
the greatest colonial powers. In two world wars they defined their cause
as defence of democracy and, in 1939–45, the rejection of racism. There
is truth in James Mayall's comment that 'the Achilles' heel of liberal
empire was ... the cognitive scheme and political values on which liberalism itself was based. In other words, all they could do was play for
time.'[28]

49

For a time the rulers of these empires could persuade themselves that the nationalist doctrines and movements that threatened empire in Europe would not strike a chord in alien cultures. Even in 1897, however, Alfred Mahan, for all his sympathy for British imperialism, had begun to see the writing on the wall for British rule in India. 'In India, though there be no probability of the old mutinies reviving, there are signs enough of the awakening of political intelligence, restlessness under foreign subjection, however beneficent, desire for greater play for its own individualities; a movement which, because intellectual and appreciative of the advantages of Western material and political civilisation, is less immediately threatening than the former revolt, but much more ominous of great future changes.'[29]

Within Europe in the nineteenth century nationalism was increasingly adopted in most polities by conservative elites and right-wing parties. Bismarck and Disraeli were in the forefront of this process. In part nationalism served as a popular doctrine with which to challenge the potential hold on the masses of radical and socialist ideologies. In part too it was a natural response of leaders trying to retain a sense of solidarity and purpose in a community whose traditional values and identities had been transformed by urbanization, mass education and work in the factory. The old dynastic, religious and local loyalties which might suffice for a peasant needed to be fused with something broader and more inclusive for his newspaper-reading, city-dwelling children. An additional incentive to encourage nationalism was that Britain, France and Germany, all of which were perceived as nation states, were the most successful and powerful polities in Europe. By contrast the polyglot Habsburg and Ottoman empires appeared unsuccessful, backward and doomed to decline.

Military factors reinforced political imperatives. The victories of the Prussian conscript army in 1866 and 1870 forced every continental great power to abandon the old model of a long-service, professional military. Meanwhile modern firearms made open order tactics essential and doomed attacking infantry to horrendous casualties as they crossed an ever deeper zone of fire. How were short-service conscripts drawn from civilian life and no longer packed in close-order columns under their officers' eyes to be motivated to fight in these conditions? Foreign observers in 1904–05 were hugely impressed by the patriotism of the Japanese infantry and their willingness to absorb tremendous casualties in attacks. But Japan was the most ethnically homogeneous nation on earth. If continental scale was a necessity for the great power of the future, how could the peoples living in such a state be inspired with a patriotism to equal Japan's national army?

This was the great dilemma for all empires in the century following 1850. What solutions a specific polity adopted depended on circumstances and on its political institutions and values. One solution, the most radical and ambitious, was to seek some new supra-ethnic identity perhaps linked, as had sometimes been the case in the past history of empires, with a universal religion of salvation. The Soviet Union took this path. Alternatively, the rulers of an empire could seek to sustain and foster one of the old universal religions: the Ottomans attempted this with Islam and the Habsburgs with Catholicism, though in the Austrian case, raison d'état and the impact of secular, liberal values made heavy inroads on the foundations of the old confessional state in the eighteenth and nineteenth centuries. A further possibility was to seek to consolidate as much as possible of an empire's people into a core nationality, ethnically defined. This was the logic of British efforts at imperial federation, which would unite the White colonies into some version of Greater Britain. Geopolitical realities and Britain's political traditions ensured that London would attempt to pursue this policy by means of compromise and persuasion. In tsarist Russia and Hungary more forceful methods were used in the effort to consolidate the largest possible core nationality at the heart of empire. The most extreme and terrible strategy was to use genocide as a means to destroy a people who threatened an empire's homogeneity and thereby its survival. Before 1918 only the Ottomans had used this policy, in their case against the Armenians. At the opposite end of the spectrum an attempt was made in the Austrian half of the Habsburg empire to move in the direction of multi-ethnic federation, in which all nationalities would enjoy not just the traditional peace and security of empire but also constitutionally guaranteed equal rights and opportunities.

THE AMERICAN CIVIL WAR

Ironically, the first country after 1850 to face this modern dilemma of empire in acute form was not a European empire but the United States. In its continental scale the United States was imperial. So in a sense were the core values that defined being an American and underlay the political system. The United States was conceived as a radically new society and polity, a break with mankind's abysmal past, a laboratory of progress. Its values were seen as universal, though most mid-century Americans would have believed that they were only truly applicable to Whites, and the United States government had made it clear early on that sympathy for universal values of freedom and equality did not imply any desire to intervene in foreign lands to ensure their triumph. From the start isolationism vied with the American instinct that their country offered a mirror to all mankind's future. On the other hand, within North America the United States displayed expansionist claims and energies worthy of any empire. Americans believed they had a right to occupy an entire continent and must exercise this right to fulfil their nation's potential and its historic destiny. These were the values of nineteenth-century nationalist and imperialist geopolitics, whose logic ultimately led to Hitler's doctrine of *Lebensraum*.[30] In the American case too *Lebensraum* was crucial to the creation of a state of continental scale and power, but one whose values differed sharply from those of Hitler and whose power was to be crucial to the survival of liberal and democratic values worldwide in the twentieth century.

It is true that it was much easier to create a homogeneous nation on a continental scale in North America than in Europe. This new nation was based on English institutions and values, and around an initially British ethnic core. Even in the mid-nineteenth century it was still a mostly Protestant community of British origin. But in this vast land with a state that imposed few demands on its citizens, people of many origins could find a niche without great difficulty. Unlike the multi-ethnic subjects of a European monarch, these people were not taxed and conscripted by an emperor who ruled their ancestral homeland by right of conquest or fortunate marriage. By themselves deciding to emigrate to America, they had consented in a meaningful way to rule from Washington – to the extent that Washington could be said to rule Americans.

Whatever their British origins, American concepts of law, liberty, progress and populism were of universal appeal and could form the basis of a community not rooted in ethnic solidarity. Above all, in their American context these ideals and institutions seemed to work. Most emigrants to the United States, and certainly most of their children, had no doubt that their lives were superior to anything available to them in their homelands. The American dream worked, partly because of the principles on which it was founded and partly because of the immense untapped resources of the continent that Americans had occupied. As tends to be the case with great experiments in progress, social mobility and the creation of new civilizations, the fate of the victims of this progress – in this case the indigenous Americans – caused little concern to the victors. In time the United States combined continental scale, economic dynamism and national homogeneity more effectively than any of its would-be rivals. This was the basis for its world-wide hegemony at the end of the second millennium. Before the United States could aspire to global leadership, however, it had to survive the great challenge of the 1860s.

In the British tradition of political thought, which the Americans shared and inherited, the greatest problem with empire was that its scale – and perhaps the barbarian peoples it had absorbed – made self-government impossible. Republican Rome had sacrificed political freedom in empire's cause, in other words on the altar of power. The federal system was, however, seen as a means by which the United States could square the requirements of power and continental scale on the one hand and republican self-government on the other. In the Civil War of 1861–5 this federalist solution to democratic empire's dilemma met its great crisis. The individual states had a historical legitimacy and identity, constitutional rights and powers, and a strong hold on the loyalty of a population whose horizons were inevitably far more local than in a later era of constant mobility and bombardment by all-American mass media.

In 1861 the great question was whether the Southern states would succeed in creating a Confederate nation. Many American historians believe that the weakness of Confederate nationalism was a key reason, perhaps even the key reason, why they failed to do so. The experience of the Vietnam War had some influence on this analysis. Its lesson seemed to be that no degree of inferiority in weaponry, numbers or economic power could defeat a nation truly committed to its independence. It is in fact quite true that by many historical comparisons Confederate nationalism was weak. In the late eighteenth century, for example, Poland disappeared off the map. Rousseau told the Poles, 'You may not prevent [your enemies] from swallowing you up [but] if you see to it that no Pole can ever become a Russian, I guarantee that Russia will not subjugate Poland.'[31] Rousseau proved to be right. Poland disappeared off the map for more than a century but because the Polish elites retained their sense of national identity and in time inculcated this sense into the masses, a Polish nation state did finally emerge in the twentieth century. By Polish standards, however, nationalism in any White colony in the New World was likely to seem very weak in the nineteenth century. The Polish state had a centuries-old and glorious history with which Polish elites identified. They had their own distinct high culture and vernacular literature long before their state disappeared into neighbouring empires. Russia in the east and Prussia in the west were states rooted in very different cultures, wholly separate languages, and religions which were not merely distinct from Polish Catholicism but were its ancestral enemies.

A far more realistic comparison is between Confederate nationalism and nationalism in Britain's White anglophone colonies. By this standard the Confederacy scores quite strongly, even if the measure is Australasian or Canadian nationalism in 1900 rather than 1860. It is quite true that geography and distance supported the idea of Australasian or Canadian national identities separate from Britain in a way that was certainly not true for a Confederacy which bordered directly on the United States. Even more important, for most of the nineteenth century most metropolitan Britons did not think of overseas colonies as forming part of the British nation. Virtually all Americans did see the South as an integral element in a nation whose identity was defined partly by the Declaration of Independence and by its Manifest Destiny to fill and unite a continent. That is the most basic reason why hundreds of thousands of Northern men were willing to die in order to deny the South its independence. It is also true that in the South identities were still confused in the 1860s, with state and Confederate loyalties partly in conflict with each other and even, in a minority of cases, with American nationalism.

Even in 1914, however, Canadian and Australasian national identity was by no means clear-cut and overlapped both with provincial loyalties and with a powerful British imperial patriotism. Canadians and Australians had no one, and above all no neighbour, to hate and against which to define themselves. This tends to be a crucial weakness in the formation of national identity and nationalist ideology. Certainly no anglophone Canadian or Australasian hated Britain in 1914 in a way that many Southerners had come to hate the Yankee by 1860. Slavery provided a burning issue to divide North and South. It also helped to make the South with its plantation-owning elite a very different society from that of most of the Northern states. The fact that Southern propagandists were probably quite wrong to imagine themselves to be the heirs of Cavalier gentlemen[32] and Yankees to be the descendants of mechanics is not really to the point. As Benedict Anderson[33] reminds us, with particular relevance to colonial nationalism, the nation is to a considerable degree a product of the imagination, and myths are usually more important in its creation than historical truth. It is quite true not merely that the Confederate nation excluded the Black population but also that Southern White nationalism defined itself against it. Nationalism in the British White colonies was not, however, much different as regards aboriginals and Asian immigrants.[34]

258,000 Confederate soldiers died in the Civil War, one out of every three who served in the armed forces. Between 75 per cent and 85 per cent of all White men of military age fought in the army, an incredibly high percentage for that or any other time. A far smaller percentage of Northern men served and died. Confederate percentages of men mobilized and killed are vastly higher than American losses and participation in any other war, including the War of Independence.[35] There are of course many reasons why soldiers serve and die in a war which have little to do with nationalism. Nevertheless, these statistics suggest that Southerners' commitment to their new nation was impressive. Certainly the outcome of the war was not foreordained. There were no modern precedents for the subjugation of so vast a territory as the Confederacy in the face of determined resistance. Without the steamship and the railway, both recently invented, the logistics of conquering the South would probably have proved impossible. Even with this technology the issue was close-run. Of all human activities war is the most confused and uncertain: civil war is particularly so because of the political issues involved. The one point that appears certain is that, if the South had won, a Confederate nation would have lived forever. Wars create nations. They generate memories and myths which contribute enormously to a sense of shared history and of solidarity. The immense commitment and suffering invested in Confederate victory would have set national independence in stone for generations and defined the parameters of national politics.

Imagining the dissolution of the United States and the creation of a Confederate nation is not easy. For Americans it offends patriotic instincts and flies in the face of the myths and historical narratives by which any nation – but in particular a new nation in a New World – is constructed. The fact that Confederates could fight with such immense courage and self-sacrifice for a cause tightly linked to the defence of slavery upsets modern values and assumptions. Everyman is one's ancestor as well as oneself. Everyman is also the sovereign in contemporary democracies. The inherent virtue of the sovereign is a basic principle of most political orders but particularly of ones where the sovereign is oneself, at least in collective form. If the Confederacy was a nation then perhaps its suppression was morally dubious: the right of a people to self-determination is after all enshrined firmly in the Declaration of Independence, was the cornerstone of Woodrow Wilson's thinking and is the basis of modern democratic ideology. The idea that a Confederate nation was destroyed by a massive and timely use of force offends contemporary sensibilities. Still worse in a way is the thought that this vast application of force was hugely successful and of vital and beneficial importance to the world. The idea that the Union was consolidated after the war partly by handing local power back to Confederate elites and largely allowing them to run race relations as they chose is also unpalatable.

Above all, however, the dissolution of the United States is hard to imagine because many of the core values of contemporary politics and culture that are taken for granted or assumed to be inherent in modernity in fact exist because of American pre-eminence in the twentieth-century world. Even more than the British, the Americans dislike geopolitics and prefer it sweetened and well wrapped in tales of moral certainty. But had the United States and its ability to project its power worldwide been critically weakened in the 1860s the twentieth-century world would have been a very different and probably much nastier place. It is of course impossible to speak with any certainty of the long-range consequences of Confederate victory. But the emergence on North American soil of a nation rooted in populist racialism and ruled by an agrarian semi-aristocracy might well have changed the whole balance of geopolitical and ideological forces in the world. It might, for example, have impeded the construction of the Anglo-American alliance. A consequence of Confederate independence could also easily have been an attempt by the North to seize Canada to make up for the loss of the Confederacy. Even without this, lasting Anglo-American enmity could have resulted from the manner in which Confederate independence was gained and internationally recognized, or indeed from the way in which the break-up of the Union encouraged London to pursue its traditional policy of trying to maintain a balance of power in North America rather than – as actually happened after 1865 – accepting the hegemony of the United States in its hemisphere and appeasing American leaders. Since Anglo-American solidarity was crucial to the victory of democracy in the twentieth century, the possibility that it could have been compromised by the long-term consequences of the American Civil War is of great significance.

THE TWO WORLD WARS

In 1917 and 1941 American intervention in two world wars was of decisive importance. The outcome of the First World War was to a great extent decided in the winter of 1916–17. By that time the war had to some extent resolved itself into a competition as to whose home front collapsed first. In the event Russia lost this competition. It disintegrated not as a result of military defeat but because the February 1917 Revolution led to the collapse both of the home front and of discipline and morale in the army. In the winter of 1916–17 German leaders did not, however, predict this collapse. They were acutely aware both of allied preponderance in soldiers and resources, and of growing strains on the home front in Germany and Austria. They decided that defeat could be averted only by rapidly knocking Britain, the heart of the enemy coalition, out of the war. The only method to hand was unrestricted submarine warfare, which was adopted despite the near-certainty that it would bring the United States into the struggle against Germany. The great irony is that this decision was taken only a matter of weeks before the Russian Revolution began the process of disintegration in Russia, thereby creating the probability of German victory in the First World War.

Without Russia and without American intervention allied victory over Germany would have been impossible. By the winter of 1916 the allies were facing major difficulties as regards financing their crucial purchase of war supplies from the United States, though historians differ as to how easily these could have been surmounted.[36] American intervention solved this crisis. Much more important, without American military reinforcements the British and French would have lacked the means and the will to defeat Germany on the Western front. It is probably also true, though less certain, that even with the reinforcements they could bring from the East the Germans would not have succeeded in defeating the Western allies. But to win the First World War this was not necessary. All that was required was stalemate in the West and the consequences of Russia's disintegration in the East. These consequences were the Treaty of Brest-Litovsk of February 1918, German domination of Eastern and Central Europe, and therefore the accumulation of power on such a scale that Germany would inevitably be the dominant empire in the continent as a whole.

The Treaty of Brest-Litovsk confirmed the breakup of the Russian Empire. All Russia's western borderlands from Finland in the north to the Trans-Caucasus in the south became independent, which meant inevitably that they came under German domination and protection. Above all, Ukraine became an independent state. In 1914 this region had been the heart of Russian agriculture, and of much of the empire's metallurgical and mining industry. Without it, at least until the Urals and Siberia could be developed, Russia would cease to be a great power. The Russia that survived after Brest-Litovsk had been reduced to her borders before Peter I made her a European great power, in other words more or less to her borders in AD 2000. In addition, the Revolution had devastated her economy and society, and she was on the brink of civil war.

Throughout the twentieth century Germany and Russia have been, at least potentially, continental Europe's most powerful states. They alone have had the resources to allow them the possibility of dominating the entire continent. In alliance, as they briefly were in 1939–41, their position was impregnable. In competition, the fall of one inevitably led to the rise of the other. The British scholar Halford Mackinder was among those who first understood this reality most sharply. In 1919 he reminded a public not much inclined to geopolitics that the state that dominated the resources of Northern Eurasia and East-Central Europe must be the master of the whole continent. He understood that Brest-Litovsk had opened up this possibility for Germany and that, without American intervention, Britain and France would have been unable to challenge the reality. 'West Europe had to call in the help of America, for West Europe alone would not have been able to reverse the decision in the East ... Had Germany elected to stand on the defensive on her short frontier towards France, and had she thrown her main strength against Russia, it is not improbable that the world would be nominally at peace today, but overshadowed by a German East Europe in command of all the heartland [i.e. Northern Eurasia]. The British and American insular peoples would not have realised the strategical danger until too late.'[37]

The events of 1916–17 confirm the role of chance even in such large long-term processes as the rise and decline of empires, and the domination of continents by specific states and the values and ideologies they sustain. Had the Russian Revolution come a few weeks earlier or the decision on the U-boats been postponed until only a few weeks later even Ludendorff might have hesitated before launching a policy that brought America into the war. More important, the decisions that led to the U-boat campaign tell us something fundamental about the nature of empire and power. These decisions were irrational, reckless, and unrealistic. They did not properly balance the political, diplomatic, military, economic and even psychological factors linked to American involvement in the war. Nor did they realistically calculate the German submarines' chances of victory. This owed much to the interests and mindsets of German ruling elites, to the pre-eminence of the military in decision-making, and to the absence of individuals and institutions that could coordinate policy, bring ends and means into harmony, and balance conflicting political, military and diplomatic priorities and pressures. Very much the same could be said about the initial decision to launch the war in 1914. In fact, German policy in the two decades before the war embodied most of these failings too. A policy that simultaneously alienated the British and the Russians was a danger to German security, interests and international influence. In any drive to dominate Europe it was obvious folly.

The failure to determine priorities, define goals and coordinate policies obviously owed much to the mistakes of those individuals who ran the German state but it was also rooted in that state's constitution. Because the Prusso–German elites despised democracy and saw it, on the whole wrongly, as incompatible with their interests, they were unwilling to accept the principle of popular sovereignty. The only alternative principle by which to legitimate the state was the historical, monarchical one. Huge power remained with Prussia's king, who was now also Germany's emperor. In the end only he, or a deputy to whom he gave unwavering support, could impose unity and coherence on German foreign, domestic and military policy. Under William II no one ever succeeded in doing this in Bismarckian style.[38] This was by no means the only reason for Germany's wayward and self-destructive foreign policy. Increasingly radical pressure from below made it harder to run a rational foreign policy than had been the case in Bismarck's day. But personal and institutional weaknesses at the summit of the political system were very important. They are a reminder of the obvious but sometimes neglected fact that in the rise and fall of empires power is seldom enough. However strong a state, it requires institutions and leaders that can pursue coherent and realistic strategies, measuring a state's goals against its resources, controlling wayward and destructive domestic pressures, and using the opportunities that exist in the international arena to maximize its power.

Germany's failure in 1900–18 is a classic example of these weaknesses. So too was the Japanese record between 1930 and 1941. The Japanese borrowed their constitution from imperial Germany and experienced its inherent problems. In principle only the emperor had the constitutional right to coordinate foreign policy, domestic political and economic policy, the army and the navy. The Japanese imperial dynasty did not even, however, have the Hohenzollerns' tradition of exercising real and effective power as chief executive officers of their government. Once the elder statesmen (Genro) inherited from the nineteenth century had disappeared from the scene, no one effectively coordinated policy. By the 1930s no one was effectively measuring ends against means, or ensuring that grand strategy and diplomacy were in harmony either with each other or with a realistic grasp of the international balance of forces. The result was that Japan blundered into devastating wars which she had little ultimate chance of winning.

Thanks to American intervention the allies won the First World War. Liberal democratic states sprang up across most of Europe and flourished briefly. But the European order created by the Versailles Treaty was never likely to last. By a series of coincidences Germany and Russia, though fighting on opposite sides in the war, had both ended in the ranks of the defeated. The post-war settlement treated them as such. The peace was imposed on Germany, not negotiated with it. She lost considerable territory and was burdened with large reparations and a formal acceptance of responsibility for having started the war. Reduced to a tiny rump state, the Austrian Germans were denied their wish to unite with the new German Republic to the north. Russia lost Finland and the Baltic republics and had to accept a pro-Western, independent Poland whose borders extended well into Belorussian and Ukrainian-majority territory. In any case, as the world's first communist state, the Soviet Union by definition had to be opposed to the existing European order. Meanwhile no sizeable part of German public opinion and no conceivable German government regarded the Versailles settlement as just or permanent.

Although defeated, Germany and Russia remained Europe's most powerful states, at least potentially. Crucially, Russia regained Ukraine. German defeat meant the end of the German protectorate over Russia's western borderlands and without German protection no Ukrainian state at that time could have avoided reincorporation into one form or another of Russian empire. Germany itself was disarmed to a great extent but not fundamentally weakened. No effort was made by the allies to reverse the result of the wars of 1866–71 and break Germany up into a number of smaller states. A territorial settlement to which both the continent's leading powers were opposed was not likely to last, though it did not necessarily need to collapse in the devastating manner that actually occurred in the 1930s. Territorial revision was inevitable, Hitler was not. The economic depression of the 1930s and its catastrophic impact on the legitimacy of both liberal democracy and the Anglo-American version of capitalism must take much of the blame for his entry upon the scene.

When Hitler pushed, the Versailles order in Europe collapsed with little resistance. Given irreconcilable differences between nationalities in East-Central Europe over territory, any settlement in 1919 was bound to make many enemies. The winners in that region from the post-war settlement – Poland, Czechoslovakia, Yugoslavia, Romania – were too weak and too disunited to stand up to Germany. In the areas of Eastern and Central Europe previously ruled by the Romanov, Habsburg and Ottoman empires there was a power vacuum into which Germany found it easy to advance.

The only force that could have stopped this process were the allied great powers who had dominated the Versailles settlement and created the postwar European order. But they proved unwilling or unable to do so. This order would never have come into existence without American intervention in Europe. When the United States retreated into isolation after 1919, the postwar settlement lost one of its key bulwarks. Of the two other victor great powers, Britain (even without counting her dominions) was stronger than France. But Britain faced the task of defending a world-wide empire with resources which – relatively to those of her potential enemies – were much fewer by the 1930s than had been the case a half-century before. Even in alliance with France, she could expect to be hard-pressed to survive a simultaneous challenge by Japan, Italy and Germany in three continents. In any case, the British had always evaded major military commitments on the European continent. The break with this tradition in 1914–18 had cost them dearly and they did not intend to repeat the experience. They felt little commitment to the territorial settlement in East-Central Europe and less inclination to defend it by force of arms against a German challenge. They were willing to make many concessions, at the local peoples' expense, to win German acquiescence in this settlement. Doubts about the morality of the 'Versailles Order' were combined with horror at the prospect of any return to the Somme and with an emphasis on imperial rather than European priorities and commitments. The result was that when Hitler's challenge was finally faced in September 1939, Britain's initial contribution to the Western front was tiny: two not very impressive divisions.

The French were left holding the baby. The basic point was that, on her own, France never had the means to sustain the Versailles settlement for long. In the 1920s there were twice as many Germans in Europe as Frenchmen. German industry was much stronger than France's. Even before 1914 France had little chance of standing up to Germany, let alone Germany and Austria, on her own. This was the logic behind the Franco-Russian alliance of 1894. Russia's revolution and disintegration in 1917 was a catastrophe for France and for the European balance of power. It is true that when Germany re-emerged as a threat in the 1930s, tentative efforts were made to recreate the alliance with Russia. But the *cordon sanitaire* of usually very anti-communist states created in Eastern Europe in 1919 made it difficult for the Soviet Union to intervene directly against Germany. More important was the ideological split between Soviet communism and Anglo-French liberal capitalism. Much of British and French public opinion loathed the idea of alliance with communist Russia. Whatever the rhetoric of the Popular Front era, London and Paris knew that Soviet commitment to the existing European order was purely temporary and tactical. Stalin's purges both increased repugnance at his regime and convinced Western governments that a polity that massacred its own military and political elites was unlikely to perform effectively in war.

For their part, the Soviet leadership reciprocated Anglo-French dislike and distrust. They interpreted the Munich agreement as Anglo-French encouragement of Germany to expand eastwards at Soviet expense. The Soviet government had very good reason to believe that in any war with Germany they would have to do most of the fighting. The French had built the Maginot Line and clearly intended to shelter behind it. Their psychology and strategic doctrines were defensive, above all in reaction to the huge losses incurred on the offensive during the previous war. Meanwhile, the state of the British army made it self-evident that Britain would be of little use on land in anything but a very lengthy European war. All these factors contributed to the inability of the French, British and Russians to forge a solid front against Germany. The result was that Hitler nearly succeeded in imposing a German imperial order in Europe, this time in Nazi form.

Hitler's Reich was in many ways a model empire. Its top priority was power and expansion, above all territorial expansion by military means. The First World War convinced its victors that war could not pay. The subsequent development of military technology, above all the bomber, reinforced this assumption. Hitler despised the humanitarian ideals of the French and British. In addition, however, his strategy of blitzkrieg was designed to win victory on the cheap and thereby to make war once again a plausible means to achieve a state's aims. In 1940 France was destroyed in six weeks at a cost to Germany which was, in First World War terms, minimal. Subsequently conquered areas in West and Central Europe were exploited in traditional imperial style. A limited but sufficient terror was allied to the advantages modern technology provided to an occupying power. By 1938 the German economy was seriously overheating. Hitler saved his economic policy by conquering, looting and exploiting most of Europe: 'Nazi Germany succeeded dramatically in mobilising Western Europe for its war effort against the Allies. Germany used more than a third of Western European economic potential and absconded with much loot and foreign labour besides.'[39] The French used roughly 23 per cent of their national income for war in 1939, the Germans about 33 per cent of the national income of conquered Western Europe. A ruthless imperial conqueror can squeeze hard. Moreover, occupation cost Germans very little as regards troops and police. Conquered peoples and their administrations to a great extent policed and exploited themselves in a context of fear, resignation, and the need to get on with the business of living.

Hitler fully absorbed the modern logic of national empire. His Reich was to be wholly German. To be sure, non-German elites would continue to run a number of protectorates and satellites. But in the areas of Slav Eastern Europe slated for annexation, no concession whatever would be made to the non-Germans. Their elites would be massacred and their masses reduced to servile status and denied the possibility of anything but the most elementary of educations. There would be no question of assimilating Slavs into a racially pure German people. There were some parallels between this and European overseas empires, where racialism and horror at racial intermarriage were common, and the education of the indigenous population often anything but a priority.[40] But Hitler's Reich combined all the worst aspects of European colonial empire since its inception, turned them into a policy, and carried them to their logical extreme.

The Nazi regime and its Reich were, however, much more than mere empire, even in its nastiest form. This regime went far beyond empire's calculation of power or profit. With its exclusive racial and nationalist ideology, Nazi totalitarianism could not match the great universal salvation religions or their modern socialist equivalent. The Nazis' illogicality from the perspective of empire is shown by the greatest of their crimes, the extermination of the Jews. There were, it is true, precedents of a sort. As Hitler noted, the Ottoman regime had got away with genocide of the Armenians. But Ottoman policy, evil though it was, had a geopolitical and imperial logic. The destruction of the Armenian people was designed to end the risk that the Turks would ultimately be deprived of part of their ethnic homeland by a combination of Armenian nationalism and European intervention. It was also designed to create a homogeneous nation at the Ottoman Empire's core, and perhaps to build a solidly Turkish empire all the way from Constantinople to the Caucasus. No such logic lay behind Hitler's extermination of the Jews, which was rooted not only in evil but also in lunacy. The Jews of Eastern and Central Europe would in fact have been loyal allies of a German empire in which they were offered freedom and opportunity. Not just in Europe but also in the Middle East, the Jews' record in supporting empire was second to none. They had good reason to look back on the Habsburg and Hohenzollern realms as countries where Jews were far better treated than in most of the Slav lands to their east and south. As with other aspects of Hitler's Reich, the Holocaust was a product of modern pathology, not of traditional imperial thinking.

THE COLD WAR

Its part in getting rid of Hitler was the best thing the British Empire ever did, but Hitler's war speeded up the collapse of the British Empire by a generation at least, and did fatal damage to the overall cause of empire. Racialism and authoritarianism were disgraced. Colour-blind democracy became the only respectable ideology in the West. The two superpowers that emerged from the Second World War were both declared enemies of empire. In time the Soviet Union provided arms for some national liberation movements and rhetorically supported anti-imperialism in the United Nations. But for the European empires the American position was more important. The United States was born in a struggle against British empire. The Irish-Americans in particular loathed this empire, but most Americans regarded 'imperialism' with distrust. Dislike of closed imperial trading blocs which frustrated American exporters was a factor in this. More important after 1945 was the view that Third World elites, usually nationalist in sympathy, were Americans' natural and essential allies in the war against communism. Support for European imperialism antagonized them. The struggle against communism meant that in most cases the Americans would tolerate and even sustain European colonial policies and administrations in the short run. In some cases, however, American intervention was crucial in weakening the position of European empire. This was most notable in US opposition to Dutch efforts to rebuild empire in postwar Indonesia and in the undermining of Anglo-French policy at Suez in 1956. The basic American position was that in anything but the short run formal empire was redundant, its only safe function being to arrange the peaceful and stable transfer of power to those Third World elites who could be trusted to pursue pro-Western policies. By the 1950s this to a great degree was the British view too. In that decade, for instance, the British fought and won a war against communism in Malaysia. But they well understood that the political precondition for victory was the confidence of Malay elites and nationalist leaders that independence would quickly follow the war's end. Malcolm Macdonald, the British 'viceroy' in South-East Asia, commented that 'if we were to resist the pace of change, we should lose the support of Asian leaders.'[41]

The Second World War destroyed the German and Italian empires. It also eliminated the empire of Japan. But the Japanese did nevertheless largely achieve their proclaimed goal of driving European imperialism out of Asia. Japanese victories in 1941–2 did great damage to European empire's prestige throughout South-East Asia. Under Japanese rule indigenous anti-imperialist forces were able to organize themselves and, particularly in 1945, to acquire arms. The Dutch and French never fully regained control in Indonesia or Indochina.

By the late 1930s Britain's ability to hold India for much longer was already doubtful. The war undermined her means or will to resist independence. To do so by 1945–7 was to court anarchy and the dangerous radicalization of Indian politics. It was far safer to hand over power to basically pro-Western elites in both India and Pakistan while they still existed and could maintain stability. To hold on to power even in the short run would have demanded a big investment of British military and economic resources, which in the context of postwar Britain was politically and economically inconceivable. It was also by no means evident what benefits the British could derive from these enormous costs. For many years before independence the price of ruling India in the face of growing pressure from Indian elites and nationalists had been the dismantling of most of the economic, financial and military arrangements that had made the Indian empire so worthwhile to Britain. By 1939, to take only one example, it was no longer the case that the Indian taxpayer sustained an army that played a key role in maintaining British global power. On the contrary, the mechanization of the Indian army and its preparation for the Second World War, together with all its overseas operations, were now paid for by London. Given postwar Britain's reduced needs, hiring Gurkhas from the independent kingdom of Nepal was a less costly and politically dangerous alternative, and one that London has pursued to this day. In abandoning formal empire the British undoubtedly often had illusions that great influence could long be retained by informal means. But they were certainly right in believing, first in India, but by 1960 also in the rest of Asia and Africa, that in terms of costs and benefits explicit, formal empire was no longer worthwhile.

This was partly because of the way in which the international economy developed after 1945. Empire always made most economic sense in eras of protection and closed trading blocs. In eras of free trade, when access to non-European commodities, markets and labour existed, it was less valuable. To the extent that the American-dominated world economy after 1945 made free trade a reality, it contributed to empire's redundance. More important was the fact that in the 1950s and 1960s Western Europe and Japan, together with North America, were much the most economically dynamic regions of the world. Even in purely economic terms, let alone in terms of political costs and benefits, it made far more sense by the late 1950s to join the EEC than to fight to retain a territorial empire overseas and direct control over its commodities. Indeed, in the longer run, success in maintaining an empire might have proved a great deal more problematic for the metropolitan nation than failure. As an American observer noted in the mid-1950s, 'the term "colony" has become unfashionable, and designations such as Overseas France or

Overseas Portugal have replaced it.'[42] The long-term logic of 'Overseas France' or 'Algérie française', however, was likely to be the integration of former colonies into the metropolitan nation. The price paid in terms of non-White immigration or non-White power in metropolitan electoral politics would have been totally unacceptable to the French, as to most European metropolitan peoples.

Traumatic and important though it was, the end of empire was to a great extent subsumed in the broader and grander drama of the Cold War. Whether or not one chooses to define the United States and the Soviet Union as empires, their conflict was truly imperial. For the first time, two great powers were locked in a competition that encompassed the whole globe and was simultaneously military, economic and ideological. American liberalism and Soviet socialism were sister ideologies. Both had their roots in the European eighteenth-century Enlightenment and in nineteenth-century British political economy. Both believed that history was a tale of human progress and would continue to be so. Both took it for granted that happiness would result from science, the conquest of nature and the creation of great material wealth. But there were sufficient differences in the ideologies, in their practical applications, and in the historical cultures and societies in which they took root, to describe the Cold War as a clash of civilizations.

Very fortunately, no latter-day Hitler came forward with believable new tactics or technologies to make nuclear war winnable, cost-effective and therefore 'rational'. Though brinkmanship, miscalculation and accident might have brought catastrophe, in fact they didn't. In the absence of all-out military conflict, the West was always likely to win the Cold War. American resources were much greater than those of the Soviet Union. Its economic power in particular was an enormous asset in winning allies, wooing clients and providing a vision of the 'good life' which had mass appeal abroad and at home. Apart from North America, the traditionally and potentially richest regions of the world were Western Europe and Japan. Both were within the postwar American sphere of influence. Forced to choose between the United States and the Soviet Union, their elites would always opt for the former. In some of these countries, in the chaotic aftermath of war-time devastation, the position of the mass electorate was less certain. But the Americans had the resources, the will and the intelligence to subsidize rapid economic recovery in these regions and their populations' natural dynamism, education and skill did the rest. Once economic recovery had occurred, the West European and Japanese electorates were not likely to opt for the Soviet model.

The combined resources of North America, Western Europe and Japan were immense. It helped too that the United States was unequivocally and unchallengeably the leader of the 'Western' coalition but that its allies believed they benefited from the alliance and also had some input into its policies. NATO and the American commitment to European security owed their origins, after all, to European demand at least as much as to American willingness to play the imperial role. In contrast the Soviet Union had much less to offer in economic terms, and a much greater instinct – and no doubt need – to coerce. Its main ally, China, was even in the medium term as powerful potentially as the Soviet Union and had long-standing grievances against the Russians.

There were probably three ways in which the West could have lost the Cold War. First, socialism could have proved as superior to capitalism in the creation and distribution of wealth as its supporters believed. This faith sustained Nikita Khrushchev and infused his policies and his 1961 Party Programme. There were many intelligent and idealistic people outside the Soviet Union in the 1950s, and even 1960s, to whom this faith did not seem incredible. Not did it necessarily entail belief in the miraculous potential of central planning and state ownership of the means of production. In international relations power, wealth and status are always relative. Had the global capitalist economy suffered another disaster like the 1930s, even a half-way successful socialism would have looked good. Instead the decades after 1945 saw an unprecedented increase in the wealth of the Soviet Union's main capitalist rivals.

The wealth and relative unity of its enemies confounded the second main possibility of Soviet victory in the Cold War. Lenin's thinking on imperialism was the source of much Soviet theory about the nature of international relations. It taught the inevitability of war between the major capitalist states over markets, labour and territories suitable for the investment of capital. More broadly, as the balance of power shifted between the capitalist empires, the newly strong would fight in order to redistribute the world's resources and territories in their own favour.

This analysis seemed to make sense in terms of Soviet history. If the great capitalist powers had not been locked in war, there could have been no successful Bolshevik revolution in Russia. Had the Bolsheviks come to power as a result of the revolution of 1905, for example, the result would have been European intervention spearheaded by the German army. Russia was far too important both geopolitically and economically for the peace-time European great powers to allow it to secede from their community, repudiate its debts and set off alone in pursuit of socialist Utopia. United and unweakened by war, great power intervention, which would have had many allies within Russia, would undoubtedly have succeeded.

After initial euphoria in 1917–19 when it appeared that European capitalism might collapse, the Bolsheviks under Stalin accepted the reality that they must consolidate their power in their Soviet base and wait for developments in the global capitalist economy to bear out Lenin's predictions. In the 1930s they appeared to do so. The 'have-not' capitalist powers (Germany, Italy, Japan) attempted to displace rivals who had grabbed much larger territories in an earlier era (Britain, France, the Netherlands, the United States). The resulting war hugely weakened the global capitalist system. The Soviet Union's relative power and international status grew dramatically in 1941–5. Eastern Europe and China joined the socialist camp. The next task, it might seem, was to wait for the capitalists to renew their civil war. After 1945, however, this did not happen. The transition from British to American global leadership was managed peacefully and, by historical standards, with astonishing amity. The existence of a common Soviet threat helped this process. In comparison to the pre-1914 world or the 1930s, the capitalist powers under American leadership showed great solidarity and cooperation. To put matters in terms familiar to Marxists, Karl Kautsky's prediction about cooperation between the great capitalist powers seemed finally to have come true, with disastrous consequences for the Soviet Union's international position.

There remained perhaps one other possibility of Soviet victory in the Cold War. Looking back on the events of the 1930s and 1940s, a Russian general commented that 'the Third Reich's Nazi ideology and dictatorial, autocratic regime achieved superiority over Western bourgeois democracies; but in the East it met with a similar, perhaps even better organised regime, and fascism could not withstand the trial by fire ... Democratic institutions of power, no matter how attractive they may be to most peoples, cannot withstand the test when confronted by despotic dictatorial regimes in open armed conflict.'[43]

But perhaps the real test of democracy would come not in the unequivocal context of actual war but in the lengthy, subtle and partly hidden geopolitical and ideological competition between the Soviet Union and the West which dominated the postwar decades. British, French and American democracy had not reacted effectively when faced by Hitler's challenge in the 1930s. By its very nature democracy excludes the possibility of rulers' ruthless exploitation and sacrifice of their own people in the cause of imperial power. The American constitution in particular was not designed to manage the foreign policy of a great power. Secrecy was difficult to secure, the executive power had constantly to placate powerful independent barons in Congress and their domestic lobbies; above all the sovereign – in other words the American people – knew little about foreign affairs, suffered isolationist moods, was inclined to apply its own domestic moral and political assumptions to the outside world, and was patently incapable of the cold geopolitical reasoning and tactical shifts of a Hitler, a Stalin or even of traditional European statesmen such as Palmerston or Bismarck. In the event, however, the post-1953 Soviet leadership showed itself to be the heir of neither Hitler nor Stalin. Its management of Soviet foreign policy was less successfully Machiavellian and the running of American policy less democratically naïve than pessimist hawks in the West often imagined in the decades of Cold War.

AMERICAN EMPIRE?

The Cold War ended not, as many had expected, in stalemate, nor in convergence between the capitalist and socialist systems. It was not overshadowed or subsumed by new challenges or some new configuration in global politics. Instead it concluded with the collapse of Soviet communism and of the international communist movement, and the disintegration of the Soviet Union. If the USSR had been defeated in a great war its peoples would have suffered far more than they did in the 1990s. But the Russian state, shorn of almost all its acquisitions since the 1650s and rudely demoted in international power and status, could barely have suffered a worse fate.

Russia's collapse left the United States as the only superpower. In terms of a whole range of factors of power – military, economic, political, ideological and cultural – no country has ever come as close as the present-day United States to global dominion. In military terms American preponderance is now enormous, though the ways this can be used to bolster American interests are less clear. In the near future an increasing number of second- and even third-rate powers will possess nuclear, chemical or biological weapons and the missiles to deliver them. Even the degree of leverage that the United States currently possesses as regards a Yugoslavia or an Iraq will be diminished. In the era of nationalism, the Kalashnikov and the anti-tank grenade committing ground forces to combat can be very costly, particularly for a country as averse to seeing its soldiers killed as America. All this limits the application of American military power to sustain the present global order, without of course making US armed might unimportant or dispensable.

In economic terms the situation is also not entirely clear. Obviously the United States has the world's largest and richest economy. In the 1980s, however, the relative decline of American technology, innovation and productivity was an obsession of one school of thought in the USA, which predicted a Pax Nipponica for the twenty-first century. At the beginning of that century, the American 'goldilocks economy' shares the planet with a Japan in deep recession and a Germany struggling to come to terms inter alia with reunification. A mood of euphoria equal to that of the 1920s reigns again on Wall Street. Should it be followed by another 1929 then once again predictions as to which economy will lead mankind in the twenty-first century will presumably be modified. Making any such predictions on the basis of a few years' statistics of economic performance has inherent difficulties. Comparisons with the past are not only easier but often more fruitful.

In comparison to the decade following the Second World War, the United States appears to be militarily somewhat more dominant today (i.e. there is no Soviet competitor and no recently 'lost' China) and economically somewhat less so. This has an impact on its policy towards Russia. For most of the first half of the twentieth century the United States was both isolationist in political terms and in its economic policy protectionist and tight-fistedly orthodox. 'By 1947, however, Americans began to perceive not only the economic weakness of Europe, but also the growing threat of Soviet expansion ... Subsequently, the United States stopped insisting on convertibility; eased its pressure on the Dutch, French, and British for decolonisation and dismantlement of colonial trade preferences; promoted European integration; and accepted discrimination against the dollar.'[44]

In that era the United States had an enormous economic margin over all other countries and could afford generosity. It also feared communist power and therefore had an incentive to be generous. Neither side of the equation holds true today. Short-term US (or European Union) economic interests or liberal economic ideology have been sacrificed far less to accommodate the post-communist countries' needs than was the case with post-war Europe or Japan. From this perspective contemporary Russia's interests lie in the emergence of a major Chinese geopolitical threat in East and South-East Asia, or a genuine Islamic threat to Western interests which would include the overthrow of pro-Western regimes in the centres of the Middle Eastern oil economy. In the face of such a crisis the price of Russian oil and gas would soar, and Russia's indispensability to the West would give her greater leverage in Washington and Brussels.

Economic and political power are intertwined. To America's considerable benefit the dollar is the world's reserve currency. The institutions that to some extent regulate the world economy, above all the IMF and the World Bank, were largely created by the United States and are still dominated by it. They have the power to reward those countries that run their economies according to Western liberal principles and to punish those that do not. The same is also true of the international capital markets, in which American banks are the biggest players. As a mechanism for conducting grand strategy the American system of government is very imperfect. It is even so a miracle of efficiency and coordination by the standards of 'Europe', in other words Brussels and the various European states' governments. Meanwhile European and Japanese military dependence on America inevitably gives the latter some political leverage.

The dominance of democratic ideas in politics and liberal capitalist ones in economics is a hugely important factor in American global power. Since it is more difficult to coerce other peoples than used to be the case, converting them to one's own values becomes correspondingly more important in a world where peoples, states and economies are much more interdependent than in former times. Francis Fukuyama[45] was much mocked for predicting the end of history but he is quite right to stress the absence of any universalist ideological rival to American liberalism now that both communism and fascism have been defeated. Even in an unlikely worst-case scenario in which global finance and trade repeated the collapse of the 1930s, there would still not be a communist Russia or fascist Italy or Germany waiting to exploit liberalism's crisis, armed with fresh universalist ideologies enjoying real credibility and public support, and already established in government in two great powers before the crisis began.

The connection between American ideological and cultural power is obvious. As Zbigniew Brzezinski argues, the American mass entertainment industry spreads US values across the world in a popular and accessible form. CNN gives an American slant to the selection and interpretation of newsworthy events. The American language not merely has its own inbuilt values and assumptions but also, as the language of international communication, draws the would-be elite of all societies to American universities, where they absorb American values. The United States looks out to both Atlantic and Pacific, it has a population of immigrants drawn from all over the globe, and its identity is built around ideas and values which are of universal appeal, not around ethnicity. For all these reasons, as well as because of its enviable wealth and power, the United States is, to use Toynbee's term, the universal state for today's global civilization.[46]

Americans themselves, including the country's most eminent professors of international relations, are divided on the extent of their country's global cultural influence. In contrast to Brzezinski, Professor Samuel Huntington of Harvard is contemporary America's equivalent to Oswald Spengler or Arnold Toynbee, though by their standards he remains an optimist. Cultural pessimism is after all inimical to American traditions, nor has an American yet the same reason for pessimism as a twentieth-century Englishman or German. Like Spengler and Toynbee, however, Huntington represents a society and civilization whose relative influence he feels to be in decline.[47] In his view American cultural influence is shallow and largely confined to elites, whose legitimacy in their own civilizations is limited. Technology and even capitalism need not necessarily embody American values and culture. The Internet, for example, is a matter of techniques not values, and ultimately can as easily be used against the West as for it. The American dream appals members of some civilizations because of the values it embodies, and angers others because it remains so unobtainable for themselves.

Given this book's theme, it is interesting to ask to what extent American power is imperial, in other words similar to the manner in which power was created and applied by the great empires of the past. In its internal affairs the United States is clearly not an empire. The American president does not rule without consent over vast conquered territories and their populations. In part this is because the original indigenous peoples of North America have been swamped, submerged and even in certain cases exterminated. Not just in America but often elsewhere, the historical origins of present-day democratic nations can often be bloodier and more terrible than those of empires. This does not alter the fact that the contemporary United States is a democratic nation state and not an empire.

The interesting point is that it is a nation – a New World nation of very diverse ethnic origins – subjected to the strains and divisions of contemporary multi-culturalism. Cultural communities defend their own identity and demand a degree of autonomy to make this defence effective. The nation becomes less homogeneous, its claim to the exclusive loyalty of its citizens less legitimate and less real. The search begins for a common sense of civic and political citizenship which transcends ethnic, 'tribal' cultural identities. The pursuit of an agreed and effective foreign policy becomes more difficult than ever for a democratic superpower. Even the multi-cultural nation is not an empire and does not face all of empire's dilemmas. Blacks and even Hispanics lack a clear territorial base and are unlikely to secede from the United States. But the multi-cultural super-power does confront some of the key problems previously faced by modern empire. Moreover, the nation is not only empire's nemesis but also the basis of modern notions of legitimate statehood and international order. As the nation state weakens, the possibility grows that power will form and be legitimized according to different models in the twenty-first century. This is very far from saying that one of these models will be imperial.

As regards the United States' international role, this also is less than imperial. As is the case in American domestic affairs, not to be an empire is not always and necessarily a mark of virtue. It is arguable that a Western community that really took seriously its duty to impose a regime of human rights – economic as well as legal – on the rest of the world would be more imperialist and more virtuous. Indifference can impose costs as high or even conceivably higher than empire.

As Professor Finer puts it, empire 'always carries the connotation of domination.'[48] The emperor does not merely exercise influence over his subjects and his legitimacy is definitely not founded on their consent. He always has the right to command and, where it really matters to him, usually also possesses the means to enforce his decrees. It makes little sense to apply this model to America's relationship with its allies in NATO and the G7. Nor are the IMF or World Bank imperial institutions, though they no doubt often seem that way to the weak and poor states that come to them for assistance. We do not live in the age of Lord Palmerston and Commodore Perry. States that choose economic autarchy and isolation today will not have their ports opened by Western gunboats, nor does any sane American believe that territorial expansion will enhance his or her country's wealth or security. The key point, however, is simply that autarchy seems to guarantee impoverishment and that participation in the global capitalist economy appears the only path to prosperity. Those who join the global capitalist system, however, have to abide by its rules. Inevitably these rules have been made largely by and therefore for its rich founder members, who dominate the institutions that enforce them. Even these members, however, are to some extent subject to global economic forces – such as the money markets – which are beyond the control even of Washington.

In a number of key areas the term 'global empire' greatly exaggerates American strength. No emperor has ever been truly unlimited in his power, but even a very modest autocrat would expect to stop any subject from creating military might sufficient to challenge his writ. The United States, however, is in fact unlikely to be able to contain the spread of weapons of mass destruction or ballistic missiles. It is unable to impose the peace of empire as yet even in areas such as the Middle East which it considers crucial to its interests. The significance of direct political control over territory and population – in other words true 'imperial' power – is confirmed by a comparison between a post-war Japan and Germany in which reconstruction along liberal and democratic lines was sustained by American military occupation, and the efforts of the IMF and the United States to encourage the creation of a capitalist economy and liberal polity in post-Soviet Russia through the medium of a politically independent local oligarchy.

How stable and long-lasting will the present-day global order, the American Age, prove to be? Given the speed with which technology is transforming all aspects of human existence, such predictions are even more difficult now than in the past. Technology will not, however, quickly change the fact that individuals live very brief lives and are specks in the face of the cosmos: it has undermined the old religions which related speck to cosmos in a comprehensible and comforting fashion. That remains a long-term potential source of weakness in Western civilization.

In more down-to-earth terms, the combination of Western ideology and global ecological pressures may threaten the long-term stability of the contemporary global order. Ecological constraints may well mean that the bulk of mankind can never hope to live the Western good life. Meanwhile television brings images of this life even into poverty-stricken villages in Africa. Western influence undermines the belief systems that traditionally sustained inequality and resignation. The official values and ideology of the world's dominant states are democratic and egalitarian, but the present-day world is actually more unequal than it was in 1500. Never have political ideology and reality been more contradictory. It is hard to imagine that this has no implications for international political stability.

In one sense contemporary global politics has something in common with the politics of the most advanced European states in the 1850s. The political nation comprised an upper- and middle-class electorate who shared relatively high levels of education and a considerable stake in the existing order. The bulk of the community was disenfranchised. The transition from this political order to mass democracy depended in part on creating sufficient wealth both to satisfy the have-nots and to reassure the haves that their essential interests were not in jeopardy. It also depended on creating political institutions and values that allowed conflict to be resolved through negotiation and compromise, something much more easily achieved when the polity concerned in ethnic and cultural terms was relatively homogeneous. Managing a similar transition on a global scale will certainly not be rapid or without violence, and may be impossible. Until it is achieved, however, it will be difficult to talk about a stable American global order or the deep penetration of the world's masses by American values.

EMPIRE IN EUROPE AND ASIA

In the contemporary world American power far outstrips that of any other state. According to definition and taste the United States may or may not be an empire: no other state can be so in terms of empire's most fundamental essence, which is power. Nor are there in today's world obvious equivalents of the Ottoman Empire in 1900, in other words old empires long in decline but still clinging to life. What do exist in the Third World are a number of huge, multi-ethnic states which in these terms are very reminiscent of empire. It will be worth giving some attention to these states whose existence, and seeming viability, calls into question current Western assumptions about the enormous and seemingly all-conquering power of ethnic nationalism. These assumptions have drawn strength from the collapse of the Soviet Union and the challenge of minority ethnic nationalism even in Britain, France and Spain, in other words Western Europe's oldest and seemingly most stable 'nation states'.

Faced with the continuing existence of an India or an Indonesia one might conclude that Europe is unique and that Asian culture and political traditions make the survival of huge multi-ethnic states easier than is the case in the West. Alternatively, one could argue that Asia is simply more backward and that patterns of political development pioneered in Europe will spread in time to the Asian continent. Since India already has a middle class of 200 million and almost every Indonesian child by now has access to primary education, presumably the day of reckoning is not far away, for nationalism in nineteenth-century Europe began its destructive career when its peoples were less advanced than this. Should this interpretation prove accurate, then twenty-first-century Asia will be a zone of chaos, its enormous population offering potential blood sacrifices to ethnic nationalism which will put even the sufferings of nineteenth- and twentieth-century Europe in the shade. Another, and in my view truer, view is that the triumph of ethnic nationalism is by no means inevitable and depends greatly on circumstances. Nor in any case does nationalism mean precisely the same thing across the globe. In both India and Indonesia, for example, anti-colonial nationalism was not ethnic. Its goal was the expulsion of European rulers, power to indigenous communities, and the rapid modernization of economy and society. A nationalism based on ethnicity or religion was anathema to the independence movements because it would enable the colonial power to exploit divisions within indigenous society, and because it was a sure pledge of separatism and chaos after independence.

Neither India nor Indonesia is a true empire. Indonesia is potentially the pre-eminent country in South-East Asia and India much the most powerful one in South Asia. Neither state can exercise much power beyond its own region. Nor does either country embody some great and potentially universal ideology or religion which would allow it to assume a role of global leadership. Both India and Indonesia are, however, enormous countries in terms of territory and population. Indonesia contains over 200 million people, India almost one billion. With the collapse of the Soviet Union, Indonesia is far bigger in population than any European country, while India is on a scale entirely different from Europe. As regards language, ethnicity and history, both India and Indonesia are very diverse. Except for a few chaotic years in the 1950s and the current experiment after Suharto's fall, Indonesia has never been ruled by democratic means. The Indian case is more complicated. Democracy and democratic federalism were not merely part of Congress's programme at independence, they were also crucial elements of the modern, secular Indian identity with which Nehru and the Congress leadership wished to surmount the traditional ethnic and religious divisions of Indian history. To a considerable extent they succeeded. The new India was not conquered and ruled in typical imperial manner. Bargaining, cooption and the counting of votes are at the core of Delhi's relationship with the various regions and peoples of India. Nevertheless, the state's considerable coercive power is seldom far in the background. President's Rule, the heir to Section 93 of the old (British) Government of India Act of 1935,[49] is very frequently[50] invoked by Delhi to overturn democratically elected state governments. Potentially secessionist provinces, above all Kashmir, are denied self-determination and where necessary military repression is used unsparingly to keep them in line.

It was external imperial power, first Muslim and then British, that created today's enormous India. Domestic Indian forces would probably never have sufficed or been sufficiently united to build and sustain such an immense territory under one state. As elsewhere in the Third World, post-colonial elites struggle to consolidate countries initially created by external forces. The two Asian giants, India and China, were both to some extent united by semi-nomadic military dynasties which invaded over their northern borders. India differed from China, however, in that these dynasties never truly controlled the whole Indian subcontinent and regional centres of power quickly reasserted themselves. Above all, in the 500 years before British rule India's invading military dynasts were Muslims. Unlike their counterparts in China, the conquerors did not adopt the local religion and civilization. Not did they convert the major-ity of their subjects to Islam. In the twentieth century, when religious and communal identities became politicized and sharply defined, this was to prove very important. In an era of mass politics and inter-communal polarization the native princely states on which the British increasingly relied for support in the twentieth century usually lacked the legitimacy of the Middle Eastern or Malayan monarchies, where at least ruler and ruled generally shared the same faith. As British rule neared its end, Muslims were between one-quarter and one-third of India's popula-tion.[51]

In very typical post-colonial fashion, the end of empire in India aroused acute anxiety in the minds of sections of the minority as regards their future in a Hindu-dominated independent state. Competitive party politics encouraged the mobilization of these fears and of deeply entrenched religious and communal identities. In 1947–8 inter-commu-nal violence and the subsequent partition of India resulted in somewhere between 500,000 and one million deaths, and the movement of eleven million refugees across the new border between India and (West) Pakistan.[52] The current rise of Hindu nationalism, largely Hindi-speak-ing and rooted in northern India, carries the risk of encouraging further tension between India's many ethnic and religious communities.

For the student of empire many of India's problems are very familiar. Not merely is the country hugely diverse in ethnicity and language but ethno-nationalism has become a more powerful and more dangerous force in Indian politics than it was in the years immediately after inde-pendence. In part this is because the Congress Party and its ruling anglo-phone elite have lost much of the prestige they gained in the anti-imperial struggle. The Congress Party has atrophied and its local cadres' struggle for office at any cost has sometimes undermined a stable balance between Delhi and the non-Congress state governments. Democracy, literacy and the tremendous appeal of state employment in a poor country with a large and interventionist bureaucracy have all sharpened the conflict between ethnic groups for power and jobs. As was true in Europe, ethno-nationalism can usually draw on linguistic, cultural and historical identities which appeal much more deeply to the emotions than loyalty to the supra-ethnic, bureaucratic and in this case basically anglophone central state. Tamil Nadu, for example, is larger in size and population than most contemporary European states. There is a big 'contrast between the immensely richer emotional reserves and symbolic imagination of Tamil nationalism, and the relatively limited imagination of the supra-national state'.[53] Nevertheless, ethno-nationalism is not usually secessionist in contemporary India. At present, for example, it is not so in Tamil Nadu. But ethnic nationalism, mobilized by the various regional elites in their struggle for influence and advantage both in their home areas and in Delhi, makes all government in India difficult, and coherent government devoted to far-reaching programmes of all-Indian modernization particularly so. In Kashmir, exceptionally, ethno-nationalism is sometimes secessionist and draws strong support from neighbours fearful of Indian power and in some cases ambitious to expand at her expense.

Contemporary Indian politics has something of a late-Habsburg smell. In both cases domestic minority nationalism is actually or potentially sometimes linked to irredentism in neighbouring countries, causing acute concern for the multi-ethnic state's security. Domestic politics combines compromise, negotiation and attempts at cooption with periodic reassertion of the state's authoritarian power. In very Habsburg fashion, when President's Rule replaces party government in Indian states the appointed state governors and the bureaucracy administer public affairs and the police are quite willing and able to repress disorder. When Czech-German wrangling paralysed party politics in late nineteenth-century Bohemia, much the same happened. The combination of everyday politics poisoned by petty party and ethnic conflict, and an impressive all-imperial elite high culture is also reminiscent of old Austria. Salman Rushdie, a product of this anglophone elite, commented in 1987 in very Austrian style that 'India regularly confounds its critics by its resilience, its survival in spite of everything. I don't believe in the Balkanisation of India ... It's my guess that the old functioning anarchy will, somehow or other, keep on functioning for another forty years, and another forty years after that. But don't ask me how.'[54]

Of course, there are great differences between pre-1914 Catholic

Austria and contemporary Hindu India. Politics in India is more democratic and much more violent than was the case in Austria. The bulk of
the population is even now still poorer and more primitive, though the
gap should not be exaggerated. India has no Habsburgs, though the later
members of the Nehru dynasty might have played a more useful role as
all-Indian monarchical symbols than as party politicians.

India certainly has advantages that Austria-Hungary lacked. Its use of
English gives its elite a unity that was never possible in a Habsburg empire
divided between Austrian-Germans and Hungarians. By now it has a
large middle class which, for all its ethnic diversity, is committed to Indian
unity, from which it derives significant economic advantages. For the
moment at least, it has no great-power enemy as powerful or hostile as
Russia in 1914, and the whole crucial international context remains
much less dangerous than great-power rivalry in Europe under the old
regime. In Hindu nationalism India has a force capable of mobilizing a
much wider section of the population than any single nationalist movement in Austria-Hungary did, though at the expense of infuriating not
just Muslims and Sikhs but also possibly, and very dangerously, the non-
Hindi-speaking peoples of the Dravidian south. If the Indian political
system looks ramshackle and conflict-ridden, that is partly because it is
flexible and operates through bargaining and compromise. In thoroughly
un-Jacobin style, it accepts ethnic and religious diversity. It lacks the
apparent but often brittle solidity of an authoritarian state though it possesses much of an authoritarian state's backbone in the shape of military,
bureaucratic and police cadres and institutions largely inherited from the
British. It has on its side inertia, a much underrated force in politics, and
particularly the international sentiment that opposes any changes in state
borders. It ought also to have fear on its side. No observer of politics in
South Asia over the last fifty years could imagine peaceful divorces of
peoples or 'velvet revolutions' in this region of the world.

Indonesia has even less ethnic, religious, linguistic or historical legitimacy than India. It lacks a multi-ethnic middle class on an Indian scale,
whose interests are intertwined with the preservation of the Indonesian
state. It contains many potential ethnically defined nations. 'Many societies in the archipelago fulfil the classic definition of a nation, possessing
unique languages, cultures, and historical traditions, and some developed
nationalist activity based on these characteristics.'[55] The main centres of
Malay population and culture are Sumatra and the Malayan peninsula.
The Dutch ruled the former, the British the latter, and the colonial
border still prevails. In pre-colonial days Indonesia was never a single
country. Even the main island, Java, was historically divided between

inland and coastal states. There was no all-Indonesian equivalent of India's Mogul Empire. The Dutch arrived in the East Indies at roughly the same time that England's East India Company began to trade in India. A century before independence, however, almost all of today's India was under British rule. By contrast, Dutch rule in much of present-day Indonesia was only established at the beginning of the twentieth century. This was true not just in the outer islands, Bali for instance, but even in northern Sumatra, where the historic sultanate of Aceh was only finally conquered by the Dutch in 1904 and was never reconciled to colonial rule. After the war of independence against the Dutch not only Aceh but also a number of other regions resorted to armed rebellion against the new, Javanese-dominated central government. With roughly 60 per cent of Indonesia's population living in Java and almost half of the total population Javanese, the other islands' fear of Javanese hegemony is inevitable.[56] In the brief period of democracy between the end of the war of independence and Sukarno's imposition of authoritarian rule in 1957 most parties had distinct ethno-regional or religious constituencies. Often the two were intertwined. With the collapse of General Suharto's authoritarian regime in 1998, the threat of ethno-nationalist separatism again raised its head.

A sense of Indonesian identity and Indonesian nationalism is a creation purely of the twentieth century and of Dutch rule. It emerged in the inter-war years among a narrow, native elite who were educated in high schools and colleges founded by or with the permission of the Dutch. This Indonesian nationalism was political not ethnic. It united Indonesians by defining their identity as a colonized people and against their Dutch masters. As in the Soviet case, the new Indonesian identity was consciously linked to progress and modernity, while the old regional, ethnic identities were defined as part of a backward, poor, weak and obscurantist past. The new Indonesia would hold its own in the modern world and would be a country with which modern people could identify with pride. In Indonesia 'careers and educational opportunities exploded with independence and have continued to expand since.'[57] Apart from gaining independence and then holding Indonesia together for fifty years the nationalists' greatest feat was the creation of a widely accepted all-Indonesian literary as well as everyday language based not on Javanese but on a Malay dialect. In 1971 40.8 per cent of the population were literate in this language, by 1980 61.4 per cent. The creation of Bahasa Indonesia (i.e. the modern Indonesian language) is 'one of the great success stories of cultural integration, both among ethnic groups and between elite and mass, in the Third World'.[58]

In the twentieth century the British raj allowed much more scope for constitutional nationalism and electoral politics than was the case in the Dutch East Indies. The Congress Party was forced to mobilize mass electoral support to lever the British out of India and it acquired decades of experience in semi-democratic politics. Dutch rule was overthrown in a war of independence. This war created national pride and important national myths, not to mention an army deeply committed to keeping Indonesia together. Neither the war nor the colonial era that preceded it created much of a basis for parliamentary democracy, however. The acute conflict between ideologies, parties and interests in the early 1960s was settled by the imposition of military dictatorship and the massacre of 500,000 or more civilians, most of them communists.[59] Suharto's regime then sought to legitimize its rule by anti-communism and by the stability and tremendous economic growth that occurred in the 1970s and 1980s. Gross corruption, economic crisis and then Suharto's fall potentially threaten not just a regime but the Indonesian state itself.

Nevertheless, until 1999 most Western experts were confident that support for separatism was much less widespread than a simple application of European assumptions to Indonesia would lead one to expect. Given real freedom to choose, they believed that a strong probability of East Timor's secession existed and a real possibility that Irian Jaya would go the same way. Neither province is typical of Indonesia, however, since East Timor never belonged to the Dutch East Indies and was only acquired in 1975, while Dutch rule in Irian Jaya continued until 1963. A lesser though still real possibility of secession was seen to exist in Aceh. 'Beyond these three regions, separatism is not likely to be an issue at all. The ties of Indonesian nationalism, rooted in the (independence) movement and revolutionary years, appear to remain strong. They have been fortified for the elite and for an increasingly educated citizenry by common experiences in school, the spread and growth of modern Bahasa Indonesia and the all-Indonesia culture whose values and struggles that language expresses and shapes, and by a pervasive political-economic network of institutions.'[60]

The events of 1999, however, cast some doubt on these optimistic forecasts and open up the possibility that Indonesia might suffer the same fate as the Soviet Union. The failure, albeit maybe temporary, of Suharto's strategy to modernize Indonesia's economy and society could delegitimize not just a regime and ruling clique but the Indonesian state itself. Since this state still to a considerable extent depends for its existence on the army, any weakening of the latter imperils Indonesia's survival. Unfortunately for Indonesia's generals, after the end of the Cold War the international climate is less friendly towards a state that seeks to hold its territories together by force, especially if this state requires financial assistance from the West. The one point that appears certain in any comparison between Indonesia and the Soviet Union is that if Indonesia did disintegrate, it would be most unlikely to do so in the almost bloodless fashion of the Soviet Union.

A chapter that began by looking at the history of empire in Eastern and Western Eurasia might neatly and briefly conclude by contemplating the salience of empire in these two regions today. At first glance empire and its aftermath might seem of less obvious significance in Europe and China than in the former Soviet space, in the ex-Ottoman Middle East, and in former British South Asia. From a broad historical perspective, however, this is not the case. In a sense the European and Chinese are grappling with the same problem though they are approaching it from diametrically opposite directions given the predominance of an imperial tradition in China and its absence in Western Europe. In China's case the problem is to maintain a polity of continental scale while allowing the regional initiative and individual enterprise that empire's needs and ideology have traditionally constrained. In Europe's case it is to square a tradition of national sovereignty and democratic self-government with an attempt to create a polity of continental scale in order to achieve goals which are beyond the power of the nation state.

In China the most obvious legacies of empire are Tibet and Xinjiang. Non-Han minorities may comprise only 6 per cent of China's population but they predominate in half of China's territory, which includes most of the country's raw materials and sources of energy. The legacy of empire is also not entirely dead in the Han regions. Empire typically has problems with coming to terms with rapid economic development at the periphery but not the centre. A traditionally centralized, bureaucratic imperial regime struggles to accommodate dynamic economic regions and elites far from its core. Losing control over regional elites and taxes can be followed by great tension and conflict as the centre struggles to regain its ground. This was a problem, for example, that occurred in both British and Spanish America in the eighteenth century. In the late Soviet era Gorbachev's efforts to reassert in Central Asia, by a massive anti-corruption drive, a control over local elites and revenues that Brezhnev had allowed to lapse caused acute tension. There are some parallels in contemporary China as regards Beijing's relations with the southern coastal regions, which diverge from the capital not just in their economic profile but also to some extent in culture, language and history. Nevertheless, the basic political reality in present-day China seems to be that it has achieved what most nineteenth-century empires came to see as their greatest goal and ambition. It has consolidated a national identity and a commitment to national unity in the core of its empire and the overwhelming majority of its people, 94 per cent of whom are defined as Han Chinese. It is possible to imagine serious conflicts over decentralization and federalism in the core of China, even conceivably temporary disintegration as in the warlord era. But the sense of national identity among the Han Chinese by now seems much too firmly entrenched to allow any legitimate long-term division of China into a complex of separate states (Taiwan possibly apart). The transition from the old imperial concept of 'one centre under heaven' to modern nationalism appears to have been achieved. As a result of this largely successful transition from empire to nation, China is the natural future hegemon in East and South-East Asia.

Europe's case is more complicated. In one sense the project of building the European Union and its dilemmas are quintessentially imperial. Continental scale and resources are still crucial if a polity is to be a great power and thereby to have an effective voice on the world scene. At least in economic terms, being a great power and having a voice is part of the EU's *raison d'être*. A faint whiff exists of autarchy, of protected imperial economic space, and this might become much stronger in the event of some 1930s-style catastrophe in the global free trading economy or of Europeans' growing unwillingness to put up with the pressures of uninhibited economic globalization. As with the empires that existed in 1900, the basic dilemma for the EU will be to reconcile the continental scale required for external power with a sense of solidarity and of the polity's legitimacy among its multinational citizens.

It is true that the dilemma of empire in Western Europe is not as acute at the beginning of the twenty-first century as it was a hundred years ago. Multi-culturalism, consumerism and the resurgence of some of the continent's historic regions have done something to reduce the hold of the nation on popular imaginations and loyalties. Unlike the empires that existed in 1900, the EU does not require a legitimacy sufficiently deep to keep millions of conscript soldiers loyal to the polity during years of total war. For the moment economics is the core of power and military strength to a considerable extent its spin-off. Moreover, conscript armies are redundant in the First World. The conscript lacks the time to master modern military technology. The values he brings to the army from European consumer society are the antithesis of the traditional military virtues still often required at the sharp end of war. The conscript is in any case generally unusable save in direct defence of the nation's territory and existence. Present-day technology, politics and culture – at least in the First World – have conspired to restore the pre-eminence of the professional army, which was in fact always a more trustworthy servant of empire than the male community in arms.

Acceptance of the rule of a European central bank or of the EU Commission demands a lesser order of commitment and legitimacy than death in the trenches. Nevertheless, the absorption of East-Central Europe into the EU and the consolidation of economic and monetary union require the creation of more powerful and effective federal political institutions. In today's Europe these cannot operate without some degree of popular legitimacy and consent. The dilemmas of empire exist in watered-down form; they have not disappeared.

To speak of the EU in the context of empire raises many hackles and insecurities, particularly if 'empire' is translated into the German equivalent, which is *Reich*. The view of the EU as a new vehicle for German domination of Europe is particularly strong in England, though by no means confined to that country. Germany's size, economic weight and geographical position make probable its pre-eminence within any configuration of Europe and therefore also within the EU. The basic laws of European geopolitics operated once again in the late twentieth century. Germany and Russia remained the continent's potentially most powerful states. As one fell, the other rose. At Brest-Litovsk in 1918 Russia's defeat and disintegration gave Germany its best chance this century to dominate Europe. In 1945 Soviet victory and the division of Germany led to a Soviet empire's establishment in Eastern and Central Europe. The collapse of Soviet power led to the reunification of Germany, its pre-eminence in its continent, and the creation of a geopolitical no man's land in much of East-Central Europe. The absence of empire in this region is one reason why the conflict in the Balkans has raged so destructively and for so long.

The events of 1985–91 have thus reopened some of the great questions of modern European history. How is Germany's power to be mobilized for the continent's peace and prosperity? How is stability to be secured in East-Central Europe, in the region stretching from Sarajevo to Danzig where two world wars began? For 45 years Germany was divided, East-Central Europe lay quiet under Soviet rule, and the Americans took responsibility for the great military and geopolitical challenges confronting the West. The collapse of the Soviet Union has changed this situation radically, in the process undermining the case for a major American military presence in Europe.

Potentially the EU offers answers to some of these new and old realities. If Europe is indeed to become a pillar of order and stability in the world, it can do so only by mobilizing German power under a European flag. Traditional balance of power tactics in Europe at nation state level make no sense and are a waste of the continent's resources and its potential. The present German Federal Republic is very different indeed from the Wilhelmine Reich and about as far from the Nazi empire as it is possible for any polity to be. In a Europe still shadowed by American global hegemony, such balance of power tactics are doubly foolish. But within the European Union there may be the potential for German power to be both mobilized effectively and constrained. This corresponds to the fundamental reality that French elites value the EU partly because they have a historical fear of the Germans, and Germans – at least of Helmut Kohl's generation – value it because they have a historical fear of themselves and of German power.

In an increasingly interdependent world part of the logic of European integration has always been that it would give Europeans a major say in key global issues that will determine the continent's fate. The EU already possesses such a say as regards international trade. If the Euro is successful, it will reduce the dollar's monopoly as the international reserve currency. If ecological issues become truly crucial, a united Europe will certainly have a louder voice than a string of small independent states, and might well develop a policy which diverges usefully from that of Washington. A clearly separate line on questions of global poverty is also conceivable.

There is no point in dreaming of a global role, however, so long as Europe continues to be unable to take the leading role in guaranteeing peace and stability even in its own region. Refugees from the Balkans will arrive in the EU, not in Middle America. So will most of the effects of anarchy or economic collapse throughout the former communist bloc. It is absurd that a rich EU should look to the United States to take the major role in ensuring stability in the area. It is not after all as if many European troops will bale out the Americans in the event of a major crisis in Korea or even Kuwait. A willingness to take on real responsibility and pay a real price to defuse potential instability from the Baltic republics through Ukraine to Albania and the Maghreb will be a first step towards playing a genuine international political role. That will require effective, professional military forces and a much more coordinated foreign policy. Behind this there will need to lie a greater sense of common purpose than currently exists.

The events in the Balkans were both warning and incentive. If

Europeans in the end did begin to make, by their standards, a considerable military and political effort to solve the crisis in Kosovo, that was
partly owed to their sense that what might happen elsewhere in the world
was not permissible in their continent. There is both a smug feeling of
superiority and considerable self-interest in this sense, attitudes which are
usually an important ingredient in the creation of any form of political
community. On these it might be possible to build. The European Union
is not, never could be and never should be an empire. In a curious way
it might become a Reich, not in the sense of the Third Reich which
obsesses many of United Europe's enemies but of the older Reich that
disappeared in 1806. That Reich, like the EU, was a wholly *sui generis*
political community made up of overlapping jurisdictions and sovereignties. But even in its last centuries it retained a considerable cultural
and ethical solidarity, a number of quite effective legal and consultative
institutions, and an ability to mobilize resources against some external
threats. Despite the anguish caused by the word 'Reich' to the English
imagination, it is actually both more comforting and more realistic to
think of a Europe built around a modernized version of this very specific
imperial tradition than of pan-European statehood in the conventional
modern sense.[61]

Part Two

EMPIRES

3

The British Empire

FORMS OF IMPERIAL RULE

Empires are by definition large and diverse. Their diversity makes generalization about any one empire difficult. But the British ruled over much the largest and most diverse empire the world had ever known. It extended over every one of the world's climatic zones, over every inhabited continent, and across all the world's major religions and civilizations. It included some of the world's richest countries, some of its poorest, and some that were in between.

The British Empire varied hugely not only over space but also over time. As empires go, it was not enormously long-lived. Less than four centuries separated the founding of the first English colonies in America and the empire's demise. By contrast, Byzantium lived for a thousand years, and indeed far longer if one considers it merely an extension of Rome's *imperium*. But during the last four hundred years the world has changed at unique speed. Mentalities, expectations and ideologies have altered dramatically since the Tudor era. The Industrial Revolution has transformed economies, armies and communications. No people has been immune to these changes but the British have been at their forefront. Inevitably their empire changed hugely in response to shifts both in the outside world and in Britain's own political system, economy, culture and values.

By most imperial standards the British Empire was extremely decentralized and heterogeneous in its system of government. The empire never enjoyed anything approaching a single law or administration. The Kingdom of England was, and always remained, the empire's core. Its resources were the empire's mainstay, its capital city the empire's centre. By 1900 the whole Gaelic fringe of the British Isles had, however, been merged into a single, unitary British state. Exactly the opposite development had occurred in the White overseas colonies, which by 1900 were unequivocally not part of the United Kingdom. Like Britain these White Colonies were parliamentary democracies. Unlike it, some of them were federations.

In complete contrast, Britain's largest non-White possession, India, was an authoritarian, centralized, bureaucratic state with much more in common in constitutional terms with traditional continental European enlightened despotism than with Anglo-Saxon concepts of liberty and representative government. India itself, however, was not governed in a uniform manner. Roughly two-thirds of the continent was administered directly by the mostly White Indian Civil Service, one-third being ruled indirectly through Indian princes. No non-White colony in 1900 enjoyed self-government and all were governed by authoritarian regimes but some other parts of the non-White empire were also ruled indirectly. Although in constitutional terms the difference between direct and indirect rule was significant, and the relative advantages of the two systems of rule were much debated, in reality British rule in all the non-White territories depended enormously on native collaborators. Indirect rule through native princes simply allowed these collaborators greater autonomy and status, while signifying that Britain's main allies were a territory's traditional ruling elite rather than the new semi-Westernized middle classes which had grown up often under imperial rule and which provided most of the junior and middle-ranking cadres (but never the top ranks) of Britain's colonial bureaucracies. Just beyond the boundaries of formal empire were protectorates, whose rulers were theoretically sovereign but whose foreign policies were to varying degrees controlled by Britain. In the twentieth century, for instance, both Egypt and Iraq were in this position for many years.

Beyond even the protectorates there were at times large areas of the world where Britain exercised very great influence because of its economic and financial power, and because of the might of the Royal Navy. Of all the world's continents South America was the one in which Britain's territory (Guyana and a few offshore islands) was by far the smallest. On the other hand, for most of the nineteenth century and part of the twentieth British influence in most of this continent was so great that formal empire seemed barely necessary. Just how great British power in the region truly was remains a cause of dispute;[1] but in the mid-nineteenth century when Britain's industrial and commercial supremacy reached its apogee, it seemed to many observers that she had no need to exercise formal control in most areas of the globe since her overwhelming power ensured the triumph of her interests and her civilization regardless of whether territories flew the Union Jack or not.

By 1900, however, the viability of 'informal empire' was less certain than it had been fifty years before. The ability of the Royal Navy to control strategic maritime communications across the globe was being challenged. So too was British exports' ability to compete with European and American goods in open markets. In some cases, where major interests were at stake, the response to these challenges might be to turn informal empire into formal. Even before the late nineteenth century brought European challengers into the field, however, informal empire was always vulnerable to the internal political dynamics of the territories in question. The empire itself might easily undermine the indigenous clients on whom informal empire rested. If these clients were nomadic chieftains who had traditionally lived from raiding their sedentary neighbours, then the peace proclaimed by empire might easily rob them of their revenues and their legitimacy. The same could result from the sudden abolition of the slave trade or shifts in global demand for the products on which a client's revenues and power depended.

In Britain's colonies, where the Union Jack did fly, almost the only common principle that applied at all times and in all places was allegiance to the crown. Monarchy and empire were crucial to each other. In one sense, as other props fell away, the monarchy's importance for imperial unity grew greater than ever in the twentieth century. This helps to explain why a relatively trivial issue, Edward VIII's marital problems, could take on real importance in 1936. At a time of growing international danger British security depended crucially on the voluntary assistance which the Dominions might provide in war-time. Any weakening of the monarchy's prestige or of its hold on colonial loyalty was therefore dangerous. The extent to which the crown did in fact have a hold on the loyalty and imagination of its overseas subjects seems astonishing. Governor-General Lord Northcote commented on Australians' equivocal attitude to Britain and its empire in 1904 but also on their extraordinary affection for a monarch whom virtually none of them had ever seen.[2] Indian soldiers, sometimes indifferent and even equivocal about their officers, appear to have felt genuine loyalty to the monarch and great enthusiasm when rewarded or addressed by the king-emperor in person.[3]

In both 1600 and 1939 the monarchy was a source of legitimacy and a focus for loyalty across the crown's dominions. By 1939, however, the power actually exercised by the monarch as an individual had shrunk enormously. In the seventeenth century, to state that Ireland was subordinate to the king but not to the English parliament was to make an important distinction. The king personally chose Ireland's Lord Lieutenant and supervised his activities, just as he issued charters (and could revoke them) to the trading and plantation companies which spearheaded England's creation of an empire in both Asia and the Americas. As parliament grew in power in the eighteenth century, Irish and American claims of subordination to the king but not to the legislature became increasingly anachronistic, though they remained a useful tactic on occasion. Not until the 1840s, however, did British political practice or constitutional theory reflect the principle that the monarch's ministers, in other words the executive power, were actually responsible to the elected legislature. No longer did the monarch personally choose his ministers and play a significant role in the making of policy. The steep decline in royal patronage as a result of early nineteenth-century administrative reforms, together with the extension of the electorate after the 1832 Act and the growth of political parties, all sharply reduced the monarch's room for manoeuvre. Henceforth governments and their policies would be determined by general elections and party allegiance, with the monarch retreating to the margins of politics. This change was crucial not merely to Britain but to the empire as a whole, opening the way both to parliamentary democracy and to the devolution of power from London to self-governing colonies. Once the basic principle of ministerial responsibility to parliament had been conceded in Britain itself, it became far easier for British ministers to accept that elected governments should rule in the White colonies rather than the monarch's representative, in other words, the governor. Accepting this principle was the crucial step in the rapid development of colonial self-government in the mid-nineteenth century.[4] First to move in this direction were the provinces of British North America, some of which had witnessed increasingly sharp conflict in the 1830s between governors and elected assemblies.

VARYING MOTIVES FOR EMPIRE

The various territories of the British Empire were acquired and valued for a variety of reasons, some very traditional but others unique to European empires in the modern era. Most traditional empires were dominated by some version of a military aristocracy which seized its neighbours' land and levied tribute on the peasants who worked it. Sometimes, as in feudal Europe, these aristocrats themselves settled in the countryside and directly exploited the peasantry. In other empires a monarch levied tribute and distributed its proceeds among his courtiers and warriors.

Ireland is the clearest example of this first type of dominion in the British Empire, though settlers in twentieth-century Kenya ruled in something of the same style. Anglo-Norman aristocrats arrived in twelfth-century Ireland to conquer and exploit land and people, as their ancestors had done in England itself only one century before. In the sixteenth and seventeenth centuries the seizure of land was renewed but in more systematic and devastating form. By the early eighteenth century the old Catholic upper class – Gaelic and Anglo-Norman – owned only 5 per cent of the land. The Penal Laws existed to ensure that it could not stage a recovery. The near-monopolization of land and power by a carpet-bagging new Protestant aristocracy has to be seen within the context of the religious conflicts that devastated sixteenth- and seventeenth-century Europe. A parallel with Ireland is Bohemia, where the triumph of the Habsburgs and Catholicism resulted in the expulsion of much of the old aristocracy and its replacement by a uniformly Catholic and usually imported ruling class of very varied ethnic origin. In Bohemia, however, as elsewhere usually in Europe, the victorious monarch successfully imposed religious uniformity not just on the aristocracy but also on the rest of the population. Ireland was unusual in combining an overwhelming Protestant aristocracy with a peasantry who in their great majority remained Catholics.[5] At the same time in many regions, and especially Ulster, there was sufficient immigration of Protestant farmers to enrage their Catholic neighbours and deepen resentment at the loss of ancestral land.[6] These factors helped to make British rule in nineteenth-century Ireland uniquely vulnerable. Nationalism and socio-economic resentments were easily, indeed almost naturally, combined. This enabled nationalist intellectuals to mobilize mass support easily for their cause. By the end of the nineteenth century the British were attempting to break this link by buying out the Protestant landed class and seeking a *modus vivendi* with the richer sections of the Catholic peasantry. But by then the land issue had helped nationalism to sink roots deep into the population.

The British conquest of India was to a considerable extent an Asian variation on the traditional theme of territorial conquest by a rapacious military elite. Although the East India Company started as a commercial operation, by the late eighteenth century it had become a state in Bengal, and moreover a state whose priorities and methods in many ways conformed to Indian tradition. Eighteenth-century India did not know absolute property rights in the European sense. The Mogul emperor granted to his lieutenants not land but the right to raise revenues from specific territories, keeping a cut for themselves and passing the rest to him. With the empire in full decline, the East India Company acquired this right[7] for Bengal from 1765. Its officers made huge fortunes in the process and Bengal, the subcontinent's richest region, became the geopolitical base for conquering the rest of India. The company's large army, the most formidable army in Asia at that time, provided the means of territorial expansion and its officers were among the main beneficiaries. Territories were conquered above all to secure the land revenues, which then – in very traditional Indian fashion – were used to sustain the victorious army. Some of those who directed this expansion, notably Lord Wellesley, came from the military aristocracy of Britain's Gaelic fringe. They did not need to adapt family traditions very greatly in order to accommodate themselves to Indian imperial opportunities.

In the Americas Britain also sought land to conquer and exploit. A plantation economy was established in the southern colonies of the American mainland and in the West Indies. It was dominated by a landowning elite which took its cultural and political models from the English landed gentry. These plantation colonies, however, diverged from the traditional pattern of aristocratic imperialism in crucial ways. From the middle of the seventeenth century their workforce was overwhelmingly African. Between the late sixteenth and the nineteenth centuries eight million[8] Blacks were forcibly transported across the ocean to the Americas. Though the mines and plantations of Portuguese-ruled Brazil were their largest single destination, millions also went to the plantations of the British West Indies and North America. These plantations were created to supply Europe with products, above all sugar and tobacco, which it could not grow for itself. Slave-produced commodities and the slave trade itself were much the most significant element in Atlantic commerce between 1650 and 1800.[9] They were the first example in history of the massive movement of labour and commodities across the oceans. The immense wealth they generated for British planters, merchants and seamen made the West Indies the jewel in the crown of the British Empire of the eighteenth century. In other words, slavery was crucial to the development both of Britain's empire and of the modern integrated global economy. Its costs to the slaves were very high. Since prevailing winds made the voyage from Africa to the West Indies twice as long as that to Brazil, mortality rates on board were 30–50 per cent higher.[10] West Indian planters reckoned, at least until the 1760s, that it was more profitable to use up their labour supply and buy new slaves from Africa than to create conditions which would encourage breeding.

To do the Europeans justice, they did not create either slavery or the slave trade in Africa. Both existed before the Europeans arrived, and could not have been expanded to meet increased European demand without enthusiastic African collaboration. Nevertheless, in any comparative study of empires which seeks to assess relative costs and benefits, the major role played by a particularly ruthless version of slavery in early European, and British, imperialism cannot be forgotten.

In this book's context, the obvious comparison is between New World slavery on the one hand and Russian serfdom on the other. The difference that most clearly distinguishes Russian from West European empire is that no slaves were White Britons whereas most serfs were Great Russians. Black slavery was a much harsher form of exploitation than Russian serfdom, which itself was probably the most arbitrary and oppressive form of serfdom in eighteenth-century Europe. A large percentage of the Russian peasantry, more than half by the time of emancipation in 1861, were not serfs but so-called state peasants, who paid a money rent to the state for their land. Many serfs also actually paid a money rent to their masters, often working off their owners' estates as artisans or labourers in the towns. The groups most comparable to Black slaves were the serfs who worked as servants in noble households, and above all those employed as agricultural labourers. Even among the latter, the great majority were essentially farmers on their own plots, who also had to labour in their masters' fields. Unlike most slaves, they were not basically landless agricultural labourers. Nor were their lives nearly so controlled by their owners as was the case with Black slaves. Russian magnates owned far more serfs than the slave force even of the richest planter. These peasants had their own village communal institutions and showed a much greater sense of solidarity than was usually found among Blacks on a plantation. Custom played a bigger role in regulating most nobles' relations with their serfs than was the case on plantations in the West Indies or North America. Russian peasants had not been ripped out of their own cultural milieu: to a great extent peasant culture dominated the countryside, with often absentee landlords and their bailiffs floating on its surface. There was no Russian equivalent of West Indian planters' policy of simply using up their labour force and importing new slaves from Africa to fill the gaps, nor indeed of the trans-Atlantic voyage itself. Perhaps the closest tsarist Russia came to this was the brutal and arbitrary system of military conscription in force from Peter I's reign to 1874. But the morale, heroism and sense of identification with their leaders shown over the generations by peasant soldiers of the tsar's army would have been inconceivable in an army of colonial slaves.[11]

Land and its resources were coveted and seized not just by British aristocrats and planters but also by farmer-settlers. The latter went overwhelmingly to temperate zones of the empire where European animals could live and European agriculture could be practised. In most of these regions the indigenous populations were also far smaller than in the Asian colonies, partly because they were hugely reduced in number by the diseases which the British brought with them. Large-scale colonization by farmers took a number of forms. Sometimes the state was involved. Because it considered major strategic and political interests to be engaged, the crown directed many plantations in Ireland, and above all in Ulster. In the nineteenth century it assisted mass emigration to the New World, above all to clear 'excess population' from the Scottish Highlands and parts of Ireland. In a manner very typical of empires it also helped to colonize remote territories by transporting criminals there. Having lost its American dumping ground in the 1770s, it created penal colonies in Australia from 1788 to fill the gap.

Many free individuals emigrated to the White colonies, sometimes establishing themselves as farmers. The most famous and important group of free farmer-colonists were the New England Puritans. The exceptional growth of this community in the seventeenth century was owed above all to the uniquely high percentage of Puritan women who emigrated. Religious commitment also helped these communities to flourish in the rugged conditions of early colonial subsistence farming. New England was, however, unique among early settlements because its backers were motivated by religious not commercial considerations. Small-scale agriculture did not generate the commodities and profits which commercial backers sought as a return on the considerable investments required to establish and sustain colonies in seventeenth-century conditions.

In contemporary White consciousness aristocratic imperialists and, still more, slave-owners enjoy little sympathy. By contrast, the farmer-settler, Everyman's ancestor, is admired and even romanticized. From the point of view of the subjected indigenous peoples this makes little sense. An imported aristocratic ruling class was generally either assimilated by the native culture (as in England) or ultimately marginalized or expelled (as in Ireland). Indigenous society and culture was much more likely to be destroyed in the long run by a mass of alien colonists, particularly if its land was expropriated. In traditional Old World empires mass migration into alien lands by conquering peoples might occur but usually did not. Rule by aristocratic military elites was more common. When mass migration did occur it would usually entail great bloodshed but the final result would often be a merging of peoples and cultures. Over the centuries, for example, Celtic, Saxon and Viking invaders of England merged into a single English people. This never happened in Britain's overseas colonies. The cultural gap between immigrant and native was too great. Aboriginal non-White peoples were despised and regarded as irredeemably inferior both in America and Australia. Intermarriage with these natives was anathema. Until the late eighteenth century very little effort was put into converting them to Christianity. Together with disease and the sheer scale of White immigration, this resulted in the near-obliteration of native society and culture. Unlike the case of land empires which colonized contiguous areas, the British overseas colonies in time acquired separate statehood and separate identities. But these were rooted almost entirely in the White immigrant population. Where, as in Southern Africa, large non-White populations did continue to exist alongside White ones they were subjected to a regime of extreme racial discrimination. In Africa as in Australia and North America, the ordinary White working-class colonist saw a non-European as a threat to his status and to the value of his labour.

Acquiring land was a very traditional motive for empire and one which the English shared. Some other traditional causes of imperial expansion mattered much less in their case. The only important overseas possession acquired by the English through dynastic marriage was Bombay, which was part of Catherine of Braganza's dowry in 1661. At the empire's core, however, the crucial Anglo-Scottish alliance stemmed initially from the pure biological chance that Scotland's king became legitimate heir to England's throne. Such dynastic unions were not uncommon in early modern Europe and sometimes led in time to the creation of consolidated states and even nations. Because of the United Kingdom's crucial role in world history, the Anglo-Scottish union of 1707 was the most important example of this process.

In one sense, religion was a relatively unimportant factor in Britain's empire. From the seventh and eighth centuries, for instance, Muslim conquerors converted the Near East and the southern Mediterranean to Islam, in the process changing forever identities and geopolitics in a vast region. Religion was also very important in the Spanish conquest of the Americas, great effort being put into subsequent conversion of the indigenous population. Though Elizabethan imperialists sometimes talked the language of religious mission, in reality little effort went into converting indigenous peoples to Christianity in the seventeenth and eighteenth centuries. Until 1813 the East India Company strictly limited missionary activity in India. Only with the onset of the Evangelical Movement in the late eighteenth century did missionaries begin to play a role of any significance in the British Empire. Even subsequently, however, missionaries never converted large communities and when compared to the activities of the Islamic or Spanish empires, their impact was very small.

From another angle, Protestantism was vital to the whole English sense of imperial mission. From the sixteenth to the twentieth century, most Englishmen believed that the Protestant conscience was at the core of all progress. They were convinced that the Protestant had a sense of individual responsibility and a strong motivation to better himself and succeed in life. He was self-disciplined, purposeful and based his life on firm moral principles, which he derived for himself by reading the Bible and struggling to define his own path to salvation. Eighteenth-century Enlightenment and nineteenth-century liberalism had no doubt of their descent from the Protestant tradition even if they had sometimes lost faith in a personal god. By contrast, Catholics were seen to be the slaves of sentiment, tradition, ritual and ignorance. Muslims were worse, and Hindus and Buddhists worst of all. Racial stereotypes of Africans in the late nineteenth century were very familiar from sixteenth-century Ireland: the natives were shifty, immoral and idle, and needed for their own good to be forced to work.[12] Nor had English attitudes to Catholics in general or the Irish in particular necessarily changed much over the previous 300 years. In 1882 the Regius Professor of History at Oxford University commented that 'the Celts of Ireland are as yet unfit for parliamentary government ... Left to themselves, without what they call English misrule, they would almost certainly be ... the willing slaves of some hereditary despot, the representative of their old coshering chiefs, with a priesthood as absolute and as obscurantist as the Druids.'[13]

Such views explain the English imperialist's powerful sense of cultural superiority and civilizing mission among indigenous populations. They explain too the doctrine of *terra nullius*, first proclaimed in sixteenth-century Ireland, which justified the expropriation and exploitation by a more civilized invading people of human and natural resources which a backward native society was wasting. Armed with this doctrine, one could easily justify the expropriation of indigenous peoples' land and the eradication of indigenous culture in the name of progress. One could even at a pinch justify turning the lazy African into a productive slave or forcing the Chinese government to allow the import of opium, since these were essential to the development of the British-led international economy and the latter was the driving wheel of progress.

Whether Catholics, Muslims and pagans could actually be converted to English Protestant virtues and, if so, how quickly the task could be accomplished was a moot point. As one might expect, the Enlightenment and its early Victorian heirs were optimistic. Some Enlightened eighteenth-century observers expected the conversion of Irish Catholics to 'rationality', in other words to the culture of the Protestant elite but with God largely removed. In the 1830s it was widely believed that consistent government policy, particularly as regards education, would lead to Anglicization first of India's elites and then of the whole population. In the reformers' minds there was no doubt that this would be wholly to Indians' advantage, their belief in mankind's perfectibility being matched only by their utter contempt for non-European cultural and intellectual traditions. As Charles Trevelyan put matters, 'trained by us to happiness and independence, and endowed with our learning and political institutions, India will remain the proudest monument of British benevolence.'[14] In these first pristine years of Victorian liberal optimism some Englishmen had a faith in rapid progress to rationality along unilinear paths foreordained by history which was subsequently equalled by Lenin's.

In the British imperial context this vision always had its doubters. They included pragmatists conscious of the social disruption and political danger liberal policy might create; financial officials aware that Westminster would insist on India living on its own revenues, and that the latter barely sufficed to pay for army, police and administration – let alone 'luxuries' like education. More ideological opposition to liberalism also existed. This encompassed an increasing tide of late Victorian racialism, which stressed the innate biological inferiority of non-Whites. It included too romantics and, later, anthropologists, who gloried in native culture and proclaimed the need to preserve its unique traditions.

But the British Empire could never give up its basic, albeit stuttering commitment to progress and enlightenment, since these were essential to its British elite's understanding of history, their perception of themselves and of the legitimacy of Britain's empire. Clearly, British liberal values and ideology did convert growing sections of the indigenous elite, firstly in India and then elsewhere: it was precisely in the name of these values that self-government and independence from Britain were demanded. But in this as in so much else formal empire was only one element in a much broader process of change and Westernization. In empire's aftermath the television, the market economy and the Americanization of global youth culture have had a deeper impact on native society than the scattered district officers and teachers of Britain's empire ever achieved.

The British Empire did have an important ideological dimension. It was also a powerful instrument for territorial aggrandisement and for creating British communities across the globe. In its first two centuries –

outside Ireland – it was above all, however, an empire of trade. When the English first established themselves in the West Indies their aim was to raid Spanish trade and smuggle their own goods into Spanish America. Subsequently the West Indies were valued above the vastly larger mainland colonies because of the huge contribution they made to Britain's global trade and thereby to the state's revenues. The East India Company was established as a purely trading enterprise and largely fulfilled this role during its first century. Designed initially to cut out middlemen and secure uninterrupted access to the Asian spice trade, it became in time a key element in Britain's global trading network which linked Europe, the Americas, Africa, India and even China for the first time in history. It was a fixed principle of British policy from the 1650s to the 1840s to maintain this trading network as a closed imperial system from which outsiders were excluded. All trade within this system was to be carried by vessels flying the Union Jack and no colony was normally to trade with foreign countries, unless it did so through British ports. Much reviled by Adam Smith and his followers, this system actually made good sense for most of the period during which it operated. In the era before the Industrial Revolution began the seemingly never-ending increase in global wealth and productivity, it was not irrational to see demand as inelastic and one country's gain as another's loss. Still more to the point, given the ferocious competition for trade between the European states, there was no realistic alternative to creating closed imperial trading systems and defending them sword in hand. When in the 1930s the global trading system collapsed and ferocious neo-mercantilist competition between nations returned, the British themselves reverted to earlier principles and recreated a semi-closed autarchic trading bloc. This was crucial to sustaining Britain during the Second World War and its aftermath. Ironically, on the eve of the empire's demise its reality as a commercial entity was greater than at any time for a century.

The 1840s to the 1930s were decades of Britain's 'free trade empire'. Until the 1890s the doctrines of Adam Smith and his followers totally dominated British thinking about economics, commerce and, to a considerable extent, international relations. Although from the 1890s protectionism began to regain intellectual respectability, it remained the intellectual and electoral underdog until the slump of the 1930s. For Victorian liberals the vast expansion of wealth and productivity created before their eyes by the Industrial Revolution seemed almost self-evident proof that the old mercantilist conception of trade as a zero-sum competition for a limited cake was false. Over the decades, as Britain's free trade economy and empire matured, powerful vested interests developed which subsequently defended this system against the early twentieth-century protectionist challenge. 'The import economy of the south which generated so much of the mercantile, financial, rentier and professional incomes shared a free trade outlook with the textiles, metal and machinery export industries of the north, with the shipowners of the great ports and the ship builders of the Tyne, the Mersey and the Clyde. Large imperial, military and naval interests relied indirectly on free trade, and investment in primary production and transport overseas were the mainstay of the late Victorian stock exchange. Working-class electors stood firm against any attempt to exclude foreign grain.'[15]

Continental critics were not slow to point out that free trade doctrines were one more example of British hypocrisy. High-minded preaching of the benefits of free trade for international peace and prosperity came, so it was said, rather easily from a nation whose industrial supremacy enabled it to out-compete any other country in 'free' and 'fair' markets. By the late nineteenth century a minority of British intellectuals were accepting that this criticism was at least partially true. Halford Mackinder wrote in 1902 that 'it is difficult to see how foreign governments, concerned for the maintenance of poorer and continental peoples, can resist the pressure put upon them for protection against a trading nation which has insular security and a long lead in the race.' Given international free trade, 'such a nation would almost inevitably increase its lead, and might ultimately reduce the whole world to economic subjection.'[16]

'Free trade,' wrote Mackinder, 'is the policy of the strong ... Did Lancashire realise that it was by force that the free import was imposed on India?'[17] Writing in the 1880s, Seeley made the same point about India as MacKinder. Unlike most imperial rulers of earlier eras, he argued, Britain drew no direct tribute from India. No revenues flowed from its taxpayers to the king in London and his treasury. The British gave India peace and security, in return receiving the benefits of an open, unprotected market. 'We have here a great foreign trade, which may grow to be enormous, and this trade is secured to us so long as we are masters of the Government of India.'[18] In the White Dominions, by the 1880s Britain was no longer master in the Indian sense. Nevertheless, even in the free trade era it would be naïve to imagine that British industry and commerce did not derive significant advantages from the existence of colonies inhabited by English-speaking peoples with strong political, economic and cultural links to the motherland.

Finance was a key element in British power. In the great struggle for empire waged between Britain and France from the 1690s to 1815 'overwhelming financial superiority' was among the greatest causes of British victory.[19] Even before the Industrial Revolution eighteenth-century Britain was a relatively rich country with an economy that was advanced for its time. But France was much bigger and more populous: even in the 1760s its government revenues were 30 per cent higher than Britain's. The British fiscal and credit systems were, however, far more effective in tapping the country's wealth. Already the most heavily taxed people in Europe in 1789, by the Napoleonic era the average Briton was paying three times the taxes of his French equivalent. In the Hanoverian era 60 per cent of revenue came from indirect taxes, the excise covering 100,000 businesses by the 1780s. Even more important was the system of public credit. In the eighteenth century Britain could borrow more than France at far lower rates of interest. The key to this was investors' confidence in the institutions established in the 1690s, including the Bank of England, and above all in the system of parliamentary control over finance. The moneyed classes felt comfortable about lending their wealth to a state controlled by people like themselves whose financial system was methodical, transparent and efficient. By contrast, lending money to kings had always been extremely risky, high premiums being the inevitable result. The British strategy of subsidizing continental allies to tie down French resources in land warfare was effective, reaching its apogee in 1813–14, when huge sums helped to keep the Russian, Prussian and Austrian armies in the field until the final defeat of Napoleon. During the majority of the wars between the 1700s and 1815 British trade actually increased, as French commerce and shipping were destroyed and lucrative colonies and their trade conquered. Inevitably, growing wealth and a string of victories helped to legitimate and consolidate the parliamentary constitution and the British ruling class.[20]

The core of this class was an aristocracy which already in 1800 was the richest in Europe. During the eighteenth century the financial and commercial elite of the City of London emerged as the aristocracy's main, though still junior, ally. By the end of the nineteenth century the landed classes as a whole had suffered a relative decline in power and wealth, though the process was by no means complete. A core of aristocratic magnates usually with big interests in urban property or coal remained at the heart of the new plutocracy, whose other largest component were men who had made fortunes in the city. Virtually no industrialist could match the immense wealth of the richest aristocrats and financiers. In the nature of things close links tend to exist between government and finance. In the British case, where finance was a key component in the state's strategy and power, these links were particularly strong. The fact that government and finance lived side-by-side in London, and that aristocratic and financial elites increasingly intermarried and shared the same values and lifestyles, strengthened the tendency. Around this plutocratic core there formed a much broader elite rooted in the professions, government, the gentry, the armed forces, the colonial services and certain sectors of trade and even industry. The geographical base of the entire elite was south-eastern England and its homogeneity was ensured, above all, by the public schools. This elite was sufficiently open and its rule sufficiently successful to ensure it great legitimacy.

Much less visible than government and its panoply, financial bonds were important for integrating the empire. Victorian Britain generated huge savings which the British economy proved unwilling or unable to absorb. The City channelled these savings overseas, where they earned higher returns for investors and helped to develop a number of non-European territories. British overseas investment was in no way confined to the empire: by 1913, for instance, one-quarter of all publicly issued British overseas assets were in South America.[21] Nevertheless, by the 1890s British colonies had preferential access to London money markets and enjoyed considerable trust among the British public. Colonial governments put a high priority on sustaining this confidence by orthodox financial policies on which the City of London put its stamp of approval. No British colony ever would or could default on its debts. The need to return to the London markets to raise future loans made this policy imperative but in any event for most middle- and upper-class Britons, whether in the colonies or in the United Kingdom itself, sound money was not just an essential ingredient of economic progress but also a moral principle. Debauching the currency and building up unsustainable debts was merely one of the many ways in which Latins, Slavs and other lesser breeds typically failed to match the Protestant Briton's unique capacity for disciplined self-restraint. At times when the value of colonial exports sank, the burden of debt repayments to London seemed especially heavy. Particularly in Australia, the White electorate in the colonies sometimes chafed under these burdens and resented dependence on the London financial oligarchy. On the whole, however, the White colonies benefited enormously from British investment, which helped them to grow at great speed and in the twentieth century to become some of the richest and most developed countries in the world.

The British Empire is probably best conceived of as a worldwide system of power and influence, sustaining a particular civilization and its values. Many elements fed into this power – finance, ideology and territory are merely three of the most obvious ones. The importance of specific territories to the Empire waxed and waned. The West Indies were Britain's most important overseas possession in 1750 but an economic and strategic backwater by 1900. India was of much more economic value to the British in 1890 than in 1939, by which time political pressures within India had forced the Raj to accept tariffs against British imports and to use British taxes to pay for the Indian army's modernization and its use outside the subcontinent. A particular colony's value depended not just on its internal development but on changes in the international context and the challenge they presented to Britain. In the mid-nineteenth century the abolition of the closed imperial economic bloc and the granting of self-government to the White Colonies certainly did not mean that the British government was indifferent to empire or wished its demise. Even so, London valued Canada, Australia and New Zealand more in 1900 than it had in 1850. In part this was because all three countries had grown greatly in population, wealth and resources in the second half of the nineteenth century. It was also because Britain itself was, relatively speaking, weaker and more vulnerable than in the early Victorian era. In many key industries she now trailed well behind the United States and Germany. Her exports were now barred from many foreign markets not just by fierce competition but also by protective tariffs. The rise of other aggressive imperialist powers posed a major potential threat to her worldwide territories and interests. Colonial support was therefore increasingly vital. When threat became reality in 1914 the colonial contribution to Britain's victory was huge, both in economic terms and in particular on the battlefield. In the First World War over 2.5 million men from Britain's overseas empire served in the armed forces, of whom almost one in ten were killed.[22] By 1918 on the crucial Western front the Australian, New Zealand and Canadian forces were probably the best formations in the British army.[23]

DEFENDING THE EMPIRE

The main line of defence of a maritime empire was inevitably, however, the Royal Navy. Its main role was to defend the British Isles, the Empire's political and economic heartland, against invasion. Britain's island position gave it crucial advantages against its main European rivals, first France and then Germany. So long as its navy remained pre-eminent Britain did not need to commit anything like the same level of resources to its army as a continental power. When mounting a challenge to Britain at sea, neither France nor Germany could afford to forget their acute vulnerability on land to other powers. It was partly for this reason that in the great naval race before 1914 Britain could outspend and outbuild the Germans, in the same way that she had previously defeated the French.

Nevertheless, Britain could not afford to be more than semi-detached from Europe. Any other state that dominated the continent would control coastlines very close to the United Kingdom and command resources which would make Britain potentially indefensible. The traditional British response to this danger was to pursue a balance of power policy on the continent, which contrasted rather sharply with Britons' belief in the universal benefits of their own maritime imperial hegemony. Above all, the British sought to mobilize support among continental states against any European country that approached a position of pre-eminence. In the eighteenth and nineteenth centuries this policy worked well and did so at relatively small cost to Britain. In the twentieth century the price escalated sharply. Huge British land forces had to be committed to Europe in two world wars to defeat Germany. Having greatly weakened the German counterweight to Russia in 1945, the British were for the first time then forced permanently to commit large land forces to the continent to provide security against a possible Soviet threat to dominate Europe. This inevitably limited the resources they could deploy to preserve and develop their empire.[24]

The navy ensured that foreign powers could not intervene in Britain's colonies. Rebellions would receive no external support – a crucial consideration for any empire. British rulers of eighteenth-century Ireland knew their regime was illegitimate in Catholic eyes but believed that repression, inertia and the near-elimination of the Catholic landed class made them invulnerable so long as Ireland was not invaded by French armies. Should this happen and the spell of British power be broken, they expected mass rebellion.[25] In the Boer War Britain was isolated and very unpopular in Europe but so long as the Royal Navy controlled the oceans British reinforcements could pour in to overwhelm the Boers and no effective foreign intervention was possible.

The Royal Navy's relationship with British commerce was symbiotic. By protecting British trade and conquering new markets for it, the eighteenth-century navy boosted government revenues, the merchant marine and the shipbuilding industry. All three were crucial for naval power. To survive in war-time the Royal Navy needed to draw on large reserves of trained seamen. In the sailing navy and, still more, in the armoured battlefleet, the warship embodied the ultimate in contemporary technology. The navy also played an important role in domestic politics. The army was not just expensive – as of course the navy was too.

An atavistic memory of Cromwell and James II lurked in the minds of eighteenth-century Englishmen. The army might prove a foe to the people's liberty. It might be deployed to promote royal obsessions with European power politics or, still worse, Hanoverian interests. Press gangs apart, the Royal Navy by definition could pose no threat to constitutional government. It protected Britain from foreign invasion and despotism, and defended British trade with formidable success. The merchant community's support for a state dominated by aristocrats was enhanced by the belief that this state was an effective defender of commercial interests. Popular celebrations of naval heroes and martyrs also contributed to the legitimacy of state and ruling class alike. In the late Victorian and Edwardian eras popular nationalism and its close ally, imperialism, could feed on the stark symbolism of power and majesty offered by the great battleships of the Royal Navy. Britain might be slipping in some other respects but its navy was still supreme: it is usually easier to glory in a battleship, or indeed a king, than in a machine-tool.

To some extent the symbolism of power was power itself. A great naval review, a royal ceremonial or the fine buildings of Lutyens's Rajpath in New Delhi were designed to show the invincible power and dignity of British rule, as well as in Lutyens's case its rootedness and legitimacy within the Indian political tradition. The British tended to see their non-White subjects as immature, even child-like, and definitely more impressed by appeals to emotion, symbolism and force than to reason. They tailored their own behaviour accordingly. A degree of cool, dignified but sometimes stern aloofness was often seen as essential to the prestige of imperial rulers vastly outnumbered in a sea of natives whose culture was totally different from their own. Insecurity bred insistence that authority must never be humiliated or the White Man's superiority shaken. How much all of this was really a conscious tactical show and how much simply the British behaving naturally is debatable. In their homeland where there were no natives to impress, the British revelled in imperial pageantry. Behaving so as to sustain the White Man's Burden had a suspicious resemblance to the natural habits and attitudes of the public schoolboy. The often cold and aloof arrogance of imperial rulers was a characteristic of the English upper class often noted by foreign visitors to Britain itself.[26]

Where legitimacy was concerned, perhaps the British worried too much. One of their Indian subjects commented that 'whoever could conquer a country was accepted as its legitimate ruler ... the British had no more and no less right to rob or rule India than all the other rulers who had held the country by force before them.'[27] Not just in India but in many other parts of the non-White empire, the mass of the population had low expectations of government and were inured to the rule of outsiders in some shape or form. So long as these outsiders did not impinge on local life too greatly or exploit too gratuitously they would be tolerated. Their tyranny was unlikely to equal that of nature, to whose cycles and arbitrary cruelties the mass of the population was enslaved. Probably too in the village there would be exploiters and predators whose impact on the peasant mass would be far greater than that of a distant imperial ruler and his officials. So long as power existed and was strong it would generally be obeyed. In the British Empire the authorities were quite willing and able to show strength when required. In India the Mutiny was suppressed ruthlessly, the 1930–4 civil disobedience movement was countered by police repression and the war-time Quit India movement was crushed by the British army. Even in its last two decades the Raj could defend itself quite adequately when challenged. The police and army imposed the Raj's authority on strikers, demonstrators and rioters far more violently than would ever have been accepted in twentieth-century Britain.[28] Force was an imperial response to what was perceived as a primitive society's potential for anarchy. It was also a substitute for genuine legitimacy at a time when Indian society was changing quickly and the old resigned acquiescence in alien rule could no longer be taken for granted among wide sections of society.

The ultimate weapon of the Raj, namely the Indian Army, was used very often 'in support of the civil power' in the twentieth century. Use of firearms was frequent. The troops' loyalty on almost all occasions was exemplary. For this there were many reasons. India was a poor country and the secure, relatively well-paid employment offered by government was a huge attraction. The army was a professional long-service force, its soldiers to some extent apart from civilian society and bred in an intense *esprit de corps*. Above all, the Indian Army was recruited overwhelmingly (by 1900) from so-called martial races – Sikhs, Pathans, Gurkhas and suchlike – which (at least in the British view) had very little in common with the bulk of the Indian population. Even within the martial races' regions recruitment was primarily in backward rural areas where literacy was very low and comprehension of nationalist slogans and politics nonexistent. Such an army might find it difficult to adapt itself to fighting the Germans or Japanese, though in time it did so in the Second World War with considerable success. But it was a perfect internal security force for the colonial state.

As with the army, so with India as a whole. In a poor society desperate for jobs and patrons the government could find many clients. Above all, India was deeply divided between language groups, religions, regions and castes. Like their predecessors, the Moguls, the British had come to rule India through exploiting these divisions. In India, as indeed in any colonial society, if a genuine sense of nationalism emerged to unite indigenous elites, let alone broader strata of the population, imperial rule would quickly prove impossible.

Intelligent British observers always knew this. Professor J.R. Seeley of Cambridge wrote the imperialists' bible, *The Expansion of England*, in the 1880s, a time when Britain's empire and its power seemed very solid to outside observers. One might have expected considerable, if restrained, self-congratulation and self-confidence. In fact Seeley's emphasis is very different. He commented that 'our Western civilisation is perhaps not absolutely the glorious thing we like to imagine it.' Europeans were not cleverer than Hindus and certainly did not possess richer or broader minds. In comparison to Roman imperialism 'the light we bring is not less real, but it is probably less attractive and received with less gratitude.' The key to Britain's rule in India was that 'there is . . . no Indian nationality, though there are some germs out of which we can conceive an Indian nationality developing itself.' 'Nationality is compounded of several elements, of which a sense of kindred is only one. The sense of a common interest and the habit of forming a single political whole constitute another element.' British rule was established in large part owing to Indian disunity and 'the mutiny was in great measure put down by turning the races of India against each other.' India was still very far indeed from being a nation but British rule was doing more than any previous Indian polity to turn it into one. If India should ever develop a nationalist movement comparable to the Italian nationalism of the 1850s, then British rule would disintegrate overnight. The Habsburgs could not hold Italy though Austria was a military empire and garrisoned Italy with troops from outside the region. India was a colony garrisoned largely by Indian troops and left to its own financial devices without subsidy from London. If the British ever had to rule India as conquerors without local allies and mass acquiescence, 'we should assuredly be ruined financially by the mere attempt.' In reality Britain would quickly withdraw since the military and financial commitment she was willing to make to hold India had always been very limited. 'It is a condition of our Indian Empire that it should be held without any great effort.'[29]

VULNERABILITIES OF EMPIRE

Seeley's comments are not the last word on attitudes to empire and India in late Victorian Britain. By the standards of some of his contemporaries he was distinctly liberal and 'wet'.[30] Nevertheless, these comments are a useful introduction to the inherent weaknesses of the British Empire. Of these, the most basic was strategic over-extension. By 1900 Britain was a maritime power with crucial commercial interests in the Americas, South Africa, the Indian Ocean, Australasia and the Far East. The Industrial Revolution and free trade doctrines increased its global commitments by making it very dependent on imported food and raw materials. In addition to defending all the world's major sea lanes, Britain also had to worry about the land defences of its empire. In the first three-quarters of the nineteenth century, defence of the long Canadian frontier against American expansion was a major concern. The United States invaded Canada in 1812 and for many decades subsequently some politicians in Washington harboured the ambition to swallow all North America.

In the late nineteenth century, as fears for Canadian security waned, the British became increasingly obsessed with the Russian threat to the north-west frontier of India. Russian railways in Central Asia seemed to be bringing the threat closer with every year and British strategists frequently reminded themselves that India had often been invaded and conquered across its north-west frontier. Realistic planners conceded that a modern European army like Russia's would find it far harder than the cavalry forces of earlier conquerors to cross Afghanistan's rugged terrain. In 1904 George Clarke, the Secretary to the Committee of Imperial Defence, called it 'sheer lunacy' to imagine that Russia could sustain large forces in Afghanistan: 'the great factors of war – supply and communications – are either ignored or absolutely miscalculated.' The real fear, however, was not so much of a successful Russian invasion as of the strain that conflict with Russia would place on a Raj which its own rulers perceived to be fragile. In the event of war 'any check to our arms, or any long pause, after offensive action had once begun, would tend to excite Native Society.'[31] Defeat would wreck the Raj's prestige and Indian acquiescence in British rule. Moreover, war would dangerously stretch Indian revenues, which could not safely be increased without a serious risk of political unrest. In retrospect British fears seem exaggerated, but it is in the nature of military planners to contemplate worst-case scenarios. It is also in the nature of those who rule without consent over alien peoples to be very jealous of their reputation for invincible power and fearful of any outside shocks which might stir those subjected to their rule from their inert acceptance of its inevitability.

So long as Britain enjoyed overwhelming economic superiority as the world's only true industrial nation, these strategic burdens might be carried successfully. By the 1880s, however, other states had developed powerful industrial economies and Britain's strategic position was becoming vulnerable. The Franco-Russian alliance of 1894 also encouraged the British to strengthen their navy in order to guarantee maritime supremacy in European waters. When the much more formidable Germans embarked on rapid naval expansion in order to challenge Britain, this concern became acute. Meanwhile the growth of the American and Japanese economies and navies threatened Britain's previous naval supremacy in the Western hemisphere and the Pacific. The British government responded to this challenge with an intelligent, cool calculation of relative threats, costs and benefits which contrasted very sharply with German inability to adjust ends to means or to define priorities. In 1902 an alliance with Japan was signed. In the quarter-century before the First World War a consistent policy was pursued of appeasing Washington and avoiding anything that might inspire American resentment. Under American pressure London backed away from collaborating with Berlin to enforce European investors' rights in Venezuela, in contrast to its earlier attitude, for instance, towards bondholders' rights in Egypt. Britain also conceded the Americans' right to build and control the Panama Canal, which she could justifiably have contested on the basis of earlier treaties. British defences in Canada and the West Indies were run down. American domination in the Western hemisphere was conceded. Better to hold Singapore and Canada with the consent respectively of Tokyo and Washington than make London's security dependent on the erratic goodwill of the Kaiser's Germany.

On the whole in the twentieth century British statesmen and the British public, if forced to choose and given the option, preferred the American alliance to any other. Where the statesmen were concerned this was mostly a cool calculation of strategic options and risks. The United States was uniquely powerful. Its interests were seen as, in general, congruent with Britain's. Even for British leaders, let alone for public opinion, a sense of shared language, culture and political values was also very important. British public opinion, granted the luxury of the Channel as a defensive moat and strongly influenced by Protestant and liberal values, always preferred to view foreign policy, British power and the British Empire in moral rather than starkly geopolitical terms. The British Empire was made legitimate in British eyes as a bulwark of world peace, a liberal international economic and political order, and Anglo-Saxon civilization – which was almost universally perceived as superior to anything else on offer. Alliance with the United States, even ultimately the transfer of world-wide pre-eminence to the Americans, was widely seen as sustaining the goals for which British power and empire existed.

In the century following American independence matters had often been very different. The aristocratic oligarchy that ruled Britain for much of the nineteenth century had tended to view American democracy as an ideological challenge to British social and political values, as well as a threat to Britain's position in the Western hemisphere. America's rancorously nationalistic public opinion was also seen as inherently aggressive, unstable and expansionist. Lord Palmerston, the most important figure in British foreign policy from the 1830s to the 1860s, embodied all these attitudes and, left free to pursue his own policy, might well have intervened in the American Civil War in order to secure the independence of the Confederacy and permanently weaken a potential threat to Britain's world position. By 1900 matters had changed greatly even among the conservative and aristocratic section of Britain's leadership. For Arthur Balfour, wealthy aristocrat, Tory prime minister and key figure in British foreign policy over four decades, Anglo-American relations were 'the greatest enthusiasm of his political life'. For Balfour, institutions and treaties were always less important than shared sympathies, cultures and values. Balfour had no doubt about the total superiority of Anglo-Saxon civilization to any other. 'The cause of ordered freedom' in the world depended on the Anglo-Saxons because they alone possessed the virtue of 'reasonable moderation'. Ultimately, the United States and Britain were allies in sustaining worldwide progress, order and civilization because 'if you scratched the American you found the Briton.'[32]

The American alliance, carefully cultivated since the 1890s, saved Britain in two world wars and created an international order more acceptable to the British than any other possible grand strategic alternative. Nevertheless, dependence on the Americans had its costs. In the immediate aftermath of the First World War desire to avoid confrontation with the USA and to avert a competition for naval pre-eminence contributed to the ending of the Anglo-Japanese alliance, of which the United States strongly disapproved. Since the Americans offered no equivalent guarantee of Britain's territories and interests in the Far East, this increased the empire's vulnerability. The influence of Irish-American and Jewish-American lobbies constrained British policy in Ireland and Palestine. After 1945 American attitudes towards the British Empire were equivocal. On the one hand they helped to sustain their leading ally and its pro-Western clients in the struggle against international communism. On the other hand, in some parts of the world Washington perceived the empire as an obstacle to an international free-trading order and as a red rag to Third World nationalists, whose sympathies would otherwise – so it was believed – naturally support an anti-imperialist and democratic America in its containment of Soviet totalitarianism. Born out of a struggle against imperial rule, American ideology could never easily support empire. The dominance of American values in the 'free world' after 1945 weakened the ideological defences of British empire. As Suez showed, British strategic and economic dependence on the United States made any major unilateral initiative to reassert British power very hazardous unless approved by Washington.

The American alliance also had important implications for Britain's relationship with the White Dominions. Defence is generally a key justification for empire. Even communities which have little natural affection for their imperial rulers may welcome the protection of empire's power as a source of security in a dangerous international environment. Though the Dominions' contribution to imperial defence in peacetime was very limited, in the two World Wars it was immense and crucial. Britain became involved in these wars above all because of fears for its own security, which were caused by threats to the European balance of power. For Canadians and Australasians these were bound to seem rather distant issues. The only conceivable threat to Canada came from the United States. By 1900, however, almost no one could imagine the Americans invading Canada and absolutely no one of any sense could conceive of the British defending the colony against the United States should the unthinkable happen.

The Australasian position was different. Isolated and relatively small White communities at the far end of the earth, they did want Britain to defend them against rival European powers and, above all, Japan. Colonies whose prosperity rested in part on dispossession of indigenous non-Whites and rigid exclusion of immigrant Asian labour had particular reason to fear the rise of the world's only non-White great Power. Australia had been one of the main agents in the refusal of the Versailles Peace Conference to accede to the Japanese call to enshrine a declaration of racial equality in the peace settlement. The Singapore naval base, constructed between the wars, was intended as both symbol and nerve-centre of Britain's defence commitment to its Australasian and Asian empire. Its dramatic and humiliating loss in 1942 exposed the hollowness of this commitment and resulted in Australasian dependence on the United States for security. Moreover, to the extent that peace, the consolidation of White control in the New World, and the worldwide pre-eminence of Anglo-Saxon civilization had been among the great attractions of the British Empire to Australasians, these would not be threatened by the shift in global hegemony to the United States.

Even as regards defence and foreign policy – the core of empire – simple geography ensured that British and Dominion perspectives were bound to conflict. Overall defence priorities as perceived from London meant that the aircraft squadrons that might have saved Singapore from the Japanese were instead deployed in Russia and the Middle East. In the 1930s British awareness that the Dominions were strongly opposed to military involvement in Europe was a factor, though not the most important one, in London's anxiety to appease Germany even beyond the limits of prudence. New societies growing up in new environments were bound to have different perspectives and priorities from those of the metropolis. Land, immigration, tariffs and treatment of the indigenous population were just some of the main areas of divergence. Mindful of the tensions behind the American Revolution, the British largely left these issues in colonial hands after the 1840s, rightly fearing that the White colonies were reaching a level of development and population that would make attempts by London to impose its wishes in these matters increasingly fruitless and dangerous. By the 1840s, for instance, the White population of the future Canada had reached the level attained by the American colonies on the eve of independence.

In the seventeenth and eighteenth centuries, 'crossing "that frightful ocean" [was] an experience that etched itself deep into the consciousness of generations of European migrants.'[33] In the mid-nineteenth century the weeks aboard an immigrant ship racing through the huge seas of the Southern Ocean were likely to be a major formative experience for the migrants to Australasia and a bond between them. In the New World the colonist would be confronted with animals and plants exotically different from those of the homeland. Before the twentieth century the overwhelming majority of those who emigrated from Britain never saw their homeland again. In the era before the aeroplane, the television and the telephone, retaining traditional identities across the oceans was much more difficult. So too was the political integration of metropolitan and colonial elites. In the 1770s Adam Smith had seen the only alternative to the separation of the American colonies as being the integration of their political elites into Westminster and Whitehall, where the power, perks and patronage available to those standing at the helm of a great empire might woo them away from particularism and secession.[34] In the 1770s, even had Britain's aristocratic oligarchy been willing to share power with flea-ridden colonials, distance and pre-modern communications would have made the scheme impractical. By 1900 the invention of the steamship, the railway and the telegraph made such proposals more feasible in technical terms, but by then the Dominions had long possessed self-governing democratic institutions and, partly as a result, a growing sense of separate identity.

Democracy was an important factor in the collapse of the British Empire. As regards the White Dominions, it is true that much more than politics went into the creation of new national identities in the former colonies. In Canada and South Africa much of the White population was French or Dutch. Initially brought into the empire by conquest, these people retained strong, distinct identities and no inherited affection for Britain. The Dutch and French Canadians might – or might not – be willing to cohabit with British colonists in new nations but they would never accept the subordination of these nations to a greater British empire and its purposes, or the dwarfing of local non-British minorities that any scheme of imperial federation would entail. In anything but the short run London after the 1840s was unwilling to bear the cost or the odium of ruling Frenchmen or Dutchmen by authoritarian means, but the granting of democratic self-government to Canada and South Africa inevitably increased their political weight.

In Australasia the overwhelming majority of the population in 1900 was of British origin. By mixing together English, Scots, Welsh and Irish it was in one sense more British than the United Kingdom itself. To some extent the English social hierarchy and its values were left behind in Europe and a more egalitarian, populist and rugged New Britain emerged on the other side of the world. Not only did colonial interests and perspectives diverge from metropolitan ones, but a separate sense of identity emerged by defining itself against the British. The heightened emotions and sufferings of war help to create nations, as do the myths that wars produce. Encountering Old England in a particularly atavistic and hierarchical military form, a populist Australian identity could readily be defined against the sometimes arrogant and incompetent British generals who commanded the empire's armies at Gallipoli and elsewhere in 1914–18. Above all, however, political institutions gave shape to these separate identities, interests and perspectives. To do the British justice, far from playing at divide-and-rule among the provinces of their White colonies, they sought to federate them in viable nation states. The politicians who ran these democratic communities existed to articulate and defend their interests and identities. They were also very unlikely to want to surrender the power, patronage and status gained by self-government into the hands of superior imperial bodies.

Even more striking was the impact of democracy in Ireland. In 1801 the formerly separate Kingdom of Ireland was integrated into the United Kingdom, above all to avert further threats to security and British rule such as had occurred during the 1798 rebellion. In many other empires, the Russian one included, essentially colonial territories were often integrated into the unitary, metropolitan imperial state. Ireland is the only similar example in the British case and illustrates some of the pitfalls of such a policy when the metropolis is a liberal and ultimately democratic country. The main support for the British connection was the Protestant community which, outside Ulster, constituted a small elite minority dominated by landowners and members of the professional classes. Democracy undermined their position at Westminster and in local government, shifting power into the hands of the new Catholic middle class of shopkeepers, priests, farmers and professional men. These dominated not just politics but also mass education and, increasingly, cultural life. The Irish identity they fostered was resolutely Catholic and was to a considerable degree defined against the English in terms of historical wrongs committed under British rule. In response to the rise of Catholic Irish nationalism, the Ulster Protestant majority also availed itself of the opportunities of democracy to mobilize in opposition to demands in Dublin for all-Irish autonomy from Britain. By 1914 civil war loomed. Democracy weakened London's ability to control the 'two Irelands' in many ways, largely because it allowed an inchoate public opinion to be articulated, organized and channelled. On occasion it also allowed Irish representatives to hold the balance of power in Westminster and impose their agenda on British politics. As one governor-general of Canada put matters, 'the existence of 72 votes in the House of Commons always on the watch how to impair the Empire' was a source of alarm to all patriots.[35]

Nineteenth-century Irish radicals had long hoped that a major European war would open the path to Irish independence. Forced to mobilize all available resources for war, empires have on a number of occasions sparked off rebellion by imposing unprecedented and unpopular burdens on outlying provinces whose loyalty to the centre is equivocal. Confronted by dire need for manpower on the Western front in the face of the German 1918 offensive, Lloyd George resorted to conscription in Ireland, in the process putting the final nail in the coffin of constitutional nationalism. The armed struggle that followed was small-scale by the standards of many twentieth-century anti-colonial wars. Even in 1919–21, however, the brutal and arbitrary tactics used by the authorities in the course of the counter-insurgency campaign stuck in the gullets of the British public. The far more draconian measures advocated to crush the rebellion by 1921 could not have been tolerated for long, particularly since even 'victory' was very unlikely to result in lasting stability or Irish acquiescence in British rule. As the unionist leader Edward Carson commented, however, if the British were unprepared to bear the political and other costs of crushing rebellion only twenty miles from England's coasts, they were unlikely to put up much of a fight for other less significant territories when seriously challenged.[36]

Democracy in Britain put limits on the use of repression to sustain the empire in the twentieth century. As information from the colonies proved harder to suppress and public opinion shifted against empire, these limits grew. The British public's sense of shame, its benevolent and liberal image of itself and its empire, all counted in this context. So too did a strong disinclination to pay the price of empire in blood or treasure. Many empires have rested on the ruling elite's ability to exploit the metropolitan poor ruthlessly in their defence. Democracy ensured that this would be impossible in the British case. In the decades before the First World War when democracy took root, its implications for British strategy and power were a cause of worry to many statesmen. It was blamed for spiralling welfare budgets, which put sound finance and adequate defence expenditure in jeopardy. Lord Roberts, Britain's senior soldier, lamented the electoral impossibility of conscription, in his view an absolutely essential preparation for the major European war he saw looming on the horizon. Still more frustrated were Tory leaders, for whom some version of economic protection seemed crucial to integrating the White empire and ensuring that Britain remained a great power in an era of continental-scale polities. Both before and after the First World War all calls for imperial preference proved electorally fatal, for fear above all of increased consumer prices. 'The foolish and vacillating individual, the man in the street' was also no friend to the mandarins who ran British foreign and imperial policy, though opinions that had been expressed openly in parliament before 1867 were now muttered in clubs or confidential and private letters. Lord Hardinge would still have got away in public with the comment that 'foreign policy based on sentiment can only end in disaster' but Sir William Tyrrell's view that 'our horizon is confined to Westminster and it is almost on the sly that now and then we can pursue a statesmanlike policy' was by 1914 clearly subversive.[37]

Of course the conservative and traditional elite who regretted the impact of democracy on Britain's power had their own axe to grind. Democracy threatened their own status within the United Kingdom. To the limited extent that the British electorate in the twentieth century made a conscious choice for democracy over empire, it is hard to deny that they acted wisely. Certainly their refusal to allow their sons to be conscripted to defend alien rule in British colonies showed sound political instincts. These were less in evidence when, for instance, deterring Hitler's Germany came on the agenda in the 1930s. In that context the old mandarinate's dismay at public opinion's sentimental incapacity for *Realpolitik* seems justified.

As regards the non-White colonies, the British concept of democracy was deeply subversive. A monarch could rule over all his subjects by some form of divine sanction. An aristocracy might rule by prescription and a bureaucratic elite by denying the capacity of the mass of humanity for self-government. But a country which proclaimed itself to be the heartland of democracy was bound in the long run to find it difficult to justify ruling without consent over hundreds of millions of subjects. One could delay matters by arguing that these subjects were not yet ready for self-government and must be educated in its disciplines. But having conceded democracy to the British masses, including Irish Catholic peasants, the only way that authoritarian rule in the empire could be justified in the long run and in principle was by overt racialist principles. A sense of racial superiority had always existed among the British overseas, though in seventeenth- and eighteenth-century India it was qualified by respect for the power and culture of Indian rulers. By the second half of the nineteenth century the arrogance of overwhelming power and the advance of pseudo-scientific racialist doctrines had lowered British respect for Indians. On the eve of the First World War most Britons would have agreed with Sir Charles Lucas that 'the qualities, character and upbringing of most coloured men are not those which are in demand for a ruling race, and are not, except in rare individual cases, eliminated by education on the White man's lines.[38]

But there were always powerful counter-currents to such views. The British ruling elite was a shrewd and politically sophisticated class. By the twentieth century its basic orientation could best be described as Whig or liberal-conservative. In the nineteenth century it had conceded increasing advances of democracy while retaining much of its own power and status. It was capable of recognizing hopeless positions and had a tradition of political management rather than of ruthless, repressive authoritarianism. The British saw their own nineteenth-century history as a heroic example of peaceful reform, in which order and change were balanced.

In India, and later in other non-White colonies, the British rulers always understood the need for indigenous collaborators and were generally capable of recognizing the importance of the new educated

Westernized class and trying to co-opt it, or at least its more malleable and 'moderate' members. To an extent, they even misapplied nineteenth-century Whig interpretations of British history and misunderstood colonial realities. 'With hindsight it appears that the makers of British policy towards India in the first three decades of the twentieth century were guided by a fallacious belief that reforms could bring complete and lasting political peace to India.'[39]

Even had they realized that Whig policies would ultimately lead to their own ejection from India, the British had little alternative to pursuing them. Even as it was, the increasingly illegitimate twentieth-century Raj, with its growing reliance on the police and emergency powers, was coming to look embarrassingly like tsarist Russia. But the British liberal self-image had to convince itself that its Raj lived 'on an incomparably higher moral plane than that of the Russian empire'. In any case tsarism was prepared to commit resources to sustain authoritarian rule on a scale that the British could never equal in a colony. Even in 1881 the Viceroy, Lord Dufferin, was determined 'to govern more and more by means of, and in accordance with, the growing public opinion, which is beginning to show itself throughout the country.'[40]

Probably the most important step towards realizing this policy was that of the Morley-Minto reforms of 1911, which 'vastly extended the range of Indian participation in the governance of their country'[41] and, more importantly, established the principle that Indians were not congenitally incapable of such participation. The authors of the 1911 reforms did not expect them to lead quickly, or perhaps ever, to full-scale democracy and independence. Nor, however, did the Whig politicians who introduced the 1832 Reform Act in Britain expect or desire it to lead to universal suffrage. In both cases, once the principle of reform and increased participation had been accepted, its further extension had a momentum and logic of its own. Neither in nineteenth-century Britain nor in the twentieth-century British Empire would further change have come simply of its own accord. Pressure from below was essential. In both cases, however, such pressure was also in time inevitable.

By 1900 race was one of the British Empire's main problems. The majority of the queen's subjects were non-White. In India, and especially Bengal, the British had created a native intelligentsia which spoke English and had sometimes acquired great sophistication as regards grasp of European civilization and its ideas. These people inevitably felt frustrated when denied access to positions of power and status in the government of their country. They felt humiliated by the crude racialist arrogance of Whites in India, let alone Britain's White self-governing dominions: experience of British Africa, for instance, was a factor in turning Gandhi against empire. In Canada, Australia and New Zealand, White power and prosperity was based on the expropriation of native land and the rigid exclusion of immigrant Asian labour. The populist and egalitarian White colonial culture was racialist through and through. Self-government left questions of land, immigration and policy towards the indigenous population in local hands. London had little power or inclination to intervene. Consolidating the White empire was seen as crucial to Britain's future as a great power, and this could be achieved only by sacrificing 'the native' and cultivating a British Imperial White consciousness and solidarity, which in the circumstances was bound to be shot through with racialism. Nevertheless, some members of the British ruling class were uncomfortable with this reality. Not just viceroys but also prime ministers and monarchs were appalled by the insulting treatment of Indians and the prejudices shown against them in India and the colonies. In Britain itself, where non-Whites were as yet very scarce and represented no threat to anyone's job or status, the White population was far more tolerant, though basically no less convinced of its superiority to all other peoples, let alone non-Whites. As some more sensitive members of the British elite realized, however, colonial treatment of non-Whites was a dangerous affront to Britain's claims to moral and economic leadership in the world. In 1908 Alfred Lyttelton, a former colonial secretary, acknowledged the dangerous hypocrisy of Britain's position on international trade and migration of labour. ' "Free competition in your land; monopoly in ours" – that was the doctrine, and he quite agreed . . . that such a principle could only be maintained and asserted by force.'[42] In 1885 Lord Blatchford had sought to deflate grandiose rhetoric about the worldwide civilizing impact of a British imperial federation, exercising global hegemony in alliance with the United States. 'The notion of an Anglo-Saxon alliance will degenerate into an unsuccessful contrivance for bullying the rest of the world. To contend for such an alliance that Anglo-Saxons – the great exterminators of aborigines in the temperate zone – would, when confederated, set a new and exceptional example of justice and humanity seems to me a somewhat transcendental explanation.'[43] Such views were relatively rare in Britain, but much less so in the public opinions of continental Europe.

The only empire that the British liked to compare with their own was that of ancient Rome. They recognized, however, that race and assimilation were areas in which the two empires differed fundamentally. As

Charles Lucas noted,[44] the Romans were largely colour blind and they created a genuine sense of universal imperial citizenship, something the British never achieved. Even if the British had been colour blind assimilationists, however, they would never have succeeded in implanting their culture and values in most of their subjects. Both numbers and time were against them. The great majority of imperial subjects were peasants from cultures as remote from that of Britain's metropolitan elites as it was possible to be. Cultural borrowing would require centuries. Geopolitics ensured that the British Empire did not have centuries at its disposal. The conquest of mainland East Asia for Chinese values and high culture was the product not merely of millennia but also of that high culture's dominance within a huge but rather isolated region. Britain was not isolated from the rest of Europe. Its culture was a branch of a broader European culture and, for most of its history, certainly not the main branch. The factors that went into the dramatic growth of British power in the eighteenth and nineteenth centuries were largely common to Western Europe and could be transplanted without too much difficulty. The nature of early modern Europe's economy and society meant that ideas and technologies travelled easily across state boundaries. The sharp competition between European states ensured that governments would quickly borrow from their competitors anything that contributed to enhancing their power. Britain's unequivocal pre-eminence in Europe lasted from 1815 to the 1890s. Even then she never had the army, the population or the will to turn pre-eminence into dominance. The level of cultural impact which China made on a huge region over the millennia could not be replicated in a few decades, even with all the advantages of modern technology and communications.

COMPARISONS BETWEEN THE BRITISH AND RUSSIAN EMPIRES

Probably one of the few points on which most historians of the British Empire would agree is that Britain's empire was very different from Russia's. Some would stress the contrast between autocracy and liberalism, others the distinction between a financial and industrial superpower at the core of the global economy and a much more underdeveloped agrarian society towards its periphery. For other scholars the main difference is between an empire which maintains a clear distinction between its metropolis and its colonies, and one which absorbs conquered and dependent territory into a centralized, homogeneous imperial state. This latter emphasis merges easily with a geopolitical perspective, for which the contrast between maritime and continental power is most significant. Since a comparison between Russia and other empires is at the heart of this book, it will be worthwhile to conclude this chapter with a few comments on these distinctions, inasmuch as they concern the British Empire.

Little needs to be added to what has already been said in this chapter about Britain as a liberal empire, though it is important to note that pre-1914 liberalism had far more in common with the ideas of Reagan and Thatcher than with the cultural pluralism, moral relativism and timid welfarism usually associated with the term in contemporary North America. On the whole, Britain's empire was liberal in the traditional meaning of the word, though its progress in this direction was less unequivocal, inevitable and teleological than British myth has suggested.

Britain's American and West Indian colonies were never subjected to the close bureaucratic supervision that the Habsburgs imposed on sixteenth- and seventeenth-century Latin America. Without gold and silver, the English colonies were seen as far less worthy of the crown's attention and were initially much less able to fund the costs of an imperial bureaucratic machine. Differences between the systems of government of the metropolitan states were also very important. In medieval times both the Spanish and English kingdoms were feudal realms in which royal power was relatively weak. In the sixteenth and seventeenth centuries, however, when the Spanish kings created an 'absolute' monarchy, the English ones failed to do so. Had the Stuarts succeeded in their struggles with parliament, they would undoubtedly have attempted to consolidate royal power in the colonies too. Indeed, James II was beginning to move in this direction in the 1680s. The process was stopped by the Glorious Revolution. In a manner typical of the fall of empires, when the imperial centre in the 1760s attempted to reassert the power it had allowed to slip away into colonial hands over the previous century, it sparked off the American revolt. London's response to American independence was to tighten administrative and financial controls over its remaining colonies. Even so, in 1791 representative assemblies were granted to Upper and Lower Canada. Great respect was still paid to the rights of the elected legislatures of the West Indian colonies. The imposition on sizeable British communities of pure, authoritarian military or bureaucratic rule was deemed unacceptable. From this position to full colonial self-government in the 1840s was a considerable step but scarcely a complete transformation. In the end the right of White Protestant males to self-government was extended to all subjects of the crown.

The contrast between backward and peripheral Russia and mighty

Britain, at the core of the modern global economy, is also valid. The history of the British Empire is both less and more than the story of Britain's industrial and financial power: nevertheless, the two are closely connected and the rise and fall of Britain's empire has to be seen within the context of the emergence of the modern, global, capitalist economy. To argue that, within this context, Russia was an undeveloped and purely peripheral country is to put things too strongly. The sharp distinction made since 1945 between First and Third World must be applied very cautiously to pre-1914 Europe. In the Victorian era much of the European continent is best described as Second World. This group of lands included not merely most of Southern, Eastern and Central Europe, but also Scandinavia and Ireland. Russia was one of the poorest (the people) and most powerful (the state) members of this group.

Nevertheless, although Russia in most sectors of its economy was more developed than British India, for example, it is true that in some respects tsarist Russia can be more easily compared to British India than to Britain itself. In both cases a European elite ruled over a peasant mass whose culture was alien and partly incomprehensible, and whose potential for disorder and 'barbarism' the elites feared. Tough police regimes, not always much concerned with the niceties of law, were one consequence. But so too, quite often, was the romanticization and idealization of the simple peasant. Western man, while enjoying the benefits of modernity, has always harboured some doubts about the world he has created and, above all, about his own condition. Projecting these doubts on to a some-times idyllic vision of the noble savage has been to find an outlet for such doubts, which does not necessarily mean that the doubts were not well founded or that admiration for the simple peasant or warrior and his world-view was not genuine and human.

In this as in most other respects, however, British India was a pale reflection of tsarist Russia. The admiration which the British officer might feel for his Indian troops was less deep and less complex than a Russian nobleman's idealization of peasants of the same ethnic and reli-gious stock as himself, whose glorification combined powerful elements of anti-modernism, Russian nationalism, and personal insecurity and injured pride. Inevitably, in every way, the Russian elite was much more committed to its own country than the British ever could be to India. Even the British administrator or army officer ultimately had a pension and a retirement house waiting for him in Cheltenham. For most of their time in India the British would sustain a relatively small professional army, drawn from 'martial races' and ideally suited to purposes of inter-nal repression (during the two World Wars, however, the British did recruit massive additional forces in India). Forced to mobilize their native resources to meet the challenge of the world's leading powers, the tsars from 1874 created a conscript army, with all the threats to domestic order this inevitably entailed. Above all, the different levels of commitment were reflected in economic policy. The British built railways and an impressive canal and irrigation system, but their contribution to the development of Indian heavy industry was unimpressive, and fell far below even eighteenth-century tsarist standards. Even in the 1930s the Maharajah of Mysore did more for the development of the Indian aircraft industry than the British. 'Japan invested more capital in Manchukuo in a decade than Britain had invested in India in two centuries of imperial rule,'[45] though whether Indian nationalists who criticized Britain's lack of an industrial policy would have welcomed the price of Japanese-style colonial development is debatable.

The contrast between a Russian empire in which metropolis and colony were merged, and a British one in which they were kept sharply separate, seems obvious and indisputable. The oceans and, as regards the non-White empire, clear differences of race and culture separated Britain from its overseas possessions. For most of the empire's history, Britain's constitutional laws also made a sharp division between the United Kingdom and the crown's overseas possessions. From early days of empire the English were wary of Roman precedents: merging a self-governing metropolis with its conquered territories may have consolidated the empire but – so it was universally believed in eighteenth-century England – it had led to the Roman metropolitan people's corruption and loss of liberty. To avoid the temptations of empire, despotism, oriental luxury and corruption, England would keep its own government sharply distinct from that of its overseas possessions.

From another perspective, that of Seeley and his disciples, the history of England and that of its empire cannot be so sharply divided. The core of English power was found in south-eastern England, whence it had spread first through the British Isles and then throughout the world. The Anglo-Saxon kingdom had united England and, in a process very familiar to historians of Russia, had achieved this partly by squeezing and enserfing much of the peasantry in the cause of royal and aristocratic power and partly by territorial expansion. This kingdom had then been taken over by a Franco-Norman aristocracy, which itself began the conquest of Ireland in the twelfth century. For a time much of Ireland became part of an empire whose geopolitical centre was the Kingdom of England and whose ruler was England's king. It was scarcely part of an English empire in the modern British understanding of the word since the English were themselves subjects of an alien, cosmopolitan aristo-cratic elite. To Russians, once again, all this is very familiar. For many centuries their empire's geopolitical centre was Great Russia and its ruler this territory's monarch. But Russia's own people, the majority of whom were serfs, can scarcely be described as a ruling, dominant or privileged nation. The distinction between *rossiyskiy* (Russian – of the state and ruler) and *russkiy* (Russian – of the people and culture) has its equivalent in English history if one searches far enough into the past.

Only in the sixteenth century could one talk of the English, elite and mass, being forged into a nation by common Protestant values, shared enmity towards Catholic Spain, widespread literacy, and the deliberate propaganda and policies of the Tudor regime.[46] In the seventeenth century an English empire in the modern sense of the word did come into being and it is important to remember that empire in the form of American colonies and the East India Company preceded the creation of Great Britain, in other words the Union of England and Scotland, by many decades. The 1707 union was the product of cool calculation by English and Scottish elites. By absorbing Scotland the English increased their relative power in the European balance and avoided the risk that France would acquire a Stuart-ruled client kingdom on England's north-ern border. The Scottish elites in time gained access to power and profit not just in London but throughout England's empire. As was always true in this era, neither the English nor the Scottish masses were asked their opinion on this deal. It took until the mid-eighteenth century for Glasgow to boom on the proceeds of imperial trade, and for Scottish aris-tocratic and professional elites to harvest rich pickings at Westminster and in colonial government. In time, however, the Union proved a huge success, becoming the richest and most powerful country in the world. Shared Protestantism helped to consolidate the Union, and victory and wealth reinforced the assumption of English and Scottish Protestants that God was on Britain's side, and that its liberal constitutional institutions were the key to human progress. The main victim of this progress was the Gaelic world of northern and western Scotland, whose society and culture were obliterated by the power of the Lowlands' political union with England, but even more so by the impact of the Industrial Revolution in Lowland Scotland on its Highland periphery. As also occurred in some overseas colonies (especially in Latin America), having obliterated Gaeldom and its threat, the new Scotland then appropriated some of its external features as markers of Scottish separate identity.

In 1801 an even more hard-headed deal was struck between British and Irish elites. Ireland was absorbed into the United Kingdom. So long as politics was confined to elites this project was viable. But modern mass nationalism is often defined by religion and against a hostile neighbour or historical oppressor. As literacy spread and politics became democratic, the emergence of anti-English and strongly Catholic Irish nationalism is therefore unsurprising. In 1914 the Irish were much richer than they had been in 1801: on a level with the Spanish, Italians or Finns; much wealthier than the Greeks, Portuguese or Hungarians. Unlike Scotland, however, Ireland had not become one of the richest industrial countries in the world. Living within the Union, Irishmen compared their wealth with England, not with Spain. In these terms, unlike Scotland, the Union had not been legitimized by dramatic economic success. Moreover, nineteenth-century Ireland had witnessed the terrible famine of 1845–8 and very high levels of subsequent emigration. Though there is probably not much reason to think that an independent Irish government would have mitigated these economic disasters to any great extent, they were inevitably blamed on the Union, though more in subsequent nationalist retrospect than at the time of the Great Hunger itself. Geography also played its role in the Union's weakness. Situated at Europe's western extreme and cut off from the continent by the Royal Navy, Ireland could have no other oppressor than the English. In contrast, Polish loathing of Russia, for example, was always likely to be mitigated by fear of Germany. The Irish in the nineteenth century had only England against which to define themselves, all the more so since their imperial neighbour also possessed the world's most dynamic economy and culture. The fact that, unlike the Poles, Ireland did not become a battleground between rival powers was a benefit of empire for which the Irish, like most modern imperial subjects, showed little gratitude. On the other hand, the reality of Britain's enormous power made the chances of independence from London seem remote to many Irishmen before 1914, even among those who desired such independence.[47]

In the 1880s it was possible to imagine many future Britains with hugely different borders. An abject pessimist, of whom there were virtually none at the time, could have conceived of a Britain reduced to England and Wales. In fact, at that time the great majority of Englishmen believed that even the union with Ireland was an irreversible *fait accompli*, though a minority were prepared to concede a limited autonomy to the Irish. Some Englishmen believed that their country's future lay in a Greater British Federation encompassing the White overseas colonies. From the vantage-point of the shrunken England of 2000 such assumptions and perspectives seem fanciful but they were shared by many intelligent contemporaries and must not simply be dismissed with the arrogance of historical retrospect. Geography and distance were always against the creation of a Greater Britain, as was the unwillingness of the English to tamper with their own domestic constitution in order to adapt it to the needs of empire. But one should also not underestimate the crucial significance of the colonial self-government granted in the 1840s for establishing wholly separate governments and increasingly separate identities in the colonies. When the principle of self-government was established, the steamship and telegraph had not yet shrunk distance and made some version of imperial federation technically feasible. A Britain at the pinnacle of its political and economic domination had limited need for colonial support. Had the issue of self-government not emerged until the 1880s, when both technology and Britain's relative international position had changed greatly, it is hard to imagine that Westminster would not have attempted to combine democracy in the colonies with the creation of some version of over-arching, albeit restricted, all-imperial institutions. Whether under the pressures of the twentieth century such institutions would ultimately have evolved any differently from the existing British Commonwealth is debatable. But such imperial institutions, if created, would certainly have left their mark on the later history of Britain and its White colonies.

Finally, one comes to the most basic difference of all between British and Russian empire: on the one hand a power that is insular and maritime, on the other a great continental land empire. This distinction needs no labouring. There is virtually no aspect of England and British history which was uninfluenced by the country's insular position. Maritime power, whether in the age of sail, coal or oil, has a mobility and flexibility which is both its great strength and its great source of vulnerability.

In one key sense, however, geography made England and Russia very alike. In European terms both are peripheral lands and powers. Much flowed from this, including much of their empires' history. In an era when Europe's might grew enormously relatively to other continents, it was Europe's peripheral states who could most easily bring this power to bear outside Europe's borders. It was therefore no coincidence that in the nineteenth century Russia and Britain possessed Europe's greatest non-European empires. During the nineteenth century, as they spread across the globe, these two empires became each other's major rivals. One result was the famous 'great game' in Inner Asia. But although the great peripheral empires proved rivals outside Europe, within that continent, where their most crucial interests lay, they were natural allies against the possible hegemony of any continental power. This natural alliance was the crucial factor in the defeat of Napoleon. In the twentieth century it re-emerged in the face of possible German domination of Europe. The English Channel and Russia's vast spaces were both huge obstacles to any power that sought to dominate Europe from a Franco-German base. In addition, Britain and Russia could both mobilize the resources not just of relatively secure geopolitical heartlands but also of non-European imperial peripheries against any power that threatened to dominate the continent. These were facts of decisive importance in the history of twentieth-century Europe.

Both in Russia and in Britain there were always influential voices urging isolationism. Sometimes these voices welcomed the idea that their rival on Europe's opposite periphery would be dragged into the continent's conflicts while they would be able to flourish in peaceful isolation. Kutuzov saw Russia as pulling England's chestnuts out of the fire in the struggle against Napoleon. In 1939 Stalin did what some conservative British historians believe London should have done at this time, in other words abstained from involvement in continental conflict in the hope that Hitler and his enemy on Europe's other periphery would wear each other down in years of struggle. In 1940 as in 1811, however, Russia found the consequences of a single power's domination of the European continent devastating for its security. In the end British policy-makers always came to the conclusion that the same would be true for a United Kingdom that stayed outside continental conflicts. On balance, the Channel, the Royal Navy and the empire usually gave peripheral Britain somewhat greater room for manoeuvre than peripheral Russia but, in the eyes of British policy-makers, not much. A foreign state that controlled the Channel ports and could mobilize all Europe's resources against the United Kingdom was seen as an intolerable danger to British security, almost regardless of any such state's protestations of peacefulness and friendship towards Britain. This was the most basic reason for Britain's intervention against Germany in two world wars in this century.

4

The Ottoman Empire

In their origins, the Russian and Ottoman empires had many similarities. The initial homelands of the Muscovite and Ottoman dynasties were on the margins of the great territories and cultures that they were subsequently to dominate. Moscow was an outpost of Kievan Rus, itself one of the last and most remote 'conquests' of Byzantine Christianity and civilization. The Turks of Central Asia, whence the Ottomans ultimately derived, were at least as remote from the heartlands of Islam. Like the Russian, the Turkish conversion to Islam commenced in the tenth century. The Turks' influx into Anatolia began in earnest after the Byzantines' defeat at Manzikert in 1071; in the same period Slav immigrants began to pour into north-eastern Rus, the future Muscovite heartland. In medieval times the religion of the ordinary Ottoman or Muscovite subject was rather far removed from the creed proclaimed by city-based religious leaders of Eastern Orthodoxy and Islam. The peasantry of north-eastern Russia was only very spottily Christian until the fourteenth century. Ottoman folk religion at this time was an amalgam of Muslim, Christian and pagan elements, as was perhaps to be expected in a border region newly invaded by alien Turkish elements but subject for centuries to a variety of cultures, civilizations and rulers.

Osman, the founder of the Ottoman dynasty, married the daughter of an influential Dervish sheikh. His son married the daughter of a Christian lord. The early Ottoman rulers, like their Muscovite counterparts, were tough, pragmatic military leaders of warrior bands. Much of their legitimacy was rooted in military success: their leadership provided followers with booty, land and prestige, as well as a sense of fulfilling religious duty in wars against the Christian. In the Ottomans' case, a crucial stepping-stone to empire was their control of the strategic emirate of Gallipoli, through which Turkish raiders passed from Anatolia into Thrace and the Balkans. Very important in the rise of both dynasties in the fourteenth century was the fact that each family's lands were inherited by a single heir. In the Ottomans' case this was a matter of principle, in the Muscovites' of happy biological accident. In time both families evolved from being warrior leaders of military bands to being monarchs ruling over states. They created institutions which sustained their dynasties for centuries. At this point the Ottomans and Russians diverged, since the institutions of the Ottoman state were rooted in a Middle Eastern and Islamic tradition of government which had no influence in Russia. Nevertheless, for a time some similarities remained. Even in the sixteenth century the bulk of both the Russian and Ottoman armies was made up of cavalrymen who received land from the monarch in return for military service. These cavalrymen were much more closely controlled and regulated by the ruler than was the case with the knighthood of feudal Europe. Failure to answer the call to service in the sixteenth century led to certain and speedy loss of lands. Not merely, however, did many Russian warrior-nobles also hold other land originally as outright private property, but in time they were also much more successful than the Ottomans in turning their service-linked estates into private property too.

Both the Muscovites and the Ottomans grew up in the shadow of the Mongols, and in regions indirectly controlled by successor states to the Great Khan. As the Mongol Empire receded, the Muscovites and Ottomans moved into the space it left behind. The Ottomans, for instance, annexed and dominated the Black Sea and its northern shore. From the mid-sixteenth century the Muscovite push southwards into the steppe collided with the Ottomans and, above all, with the Ottomans' client, the Crimean Khan. At this point the previously distant but amicable relations between the two states turned sour. During the eighteenth, nineteenth and early twentieth centuries Russia was to be the greatest enemy and major grave-digger of the Ottoman Empire. In this era Russian victory over the Ottomans was owed to many factors, of which geopolitics was one. After Russia had destroyed the Muslim khanates on the River Volga in the 1550s, her path to the east lay open. In territorial terms she was to be the leading heir of the Mongol horde.

By contrast, in the sixteenth century to the Ottomans' east a powerful new state was established by the Safavids in the Iranian core of the former Mongol Ilkhanate. This state blocked Ottoman expansion eastwards. It also cut the Ottomans off from their homeland and traditional recruiting ground in Central Asia. This was a factor in one of the major long-term weaknesses of the Ottoman Empire, namely the relatively small size of its Turkish population, which limited its ability to colonize conquered regions. More immediately, Safavid Iran ensured that the Ottomans would always need to contemplate war on two fronts, against not just the Christians to the north but also an equally hostile power in their rear. The fact that the Safavids were Shiites, an Islamic 'heresy' supported by many of the Ottoman sultan's own subjects in the sixteenth century, increased the danger. In the sixteenth and seventeenth centuries, when a fragmented Christian Europe stood face-to-face with a united Ottoman Empire stretching from Algeria to Crimea, Christians took comfort in the Ottomans' need to divert huge resources and time to their troublesome eastern front.

In the Ottoman case it makes little sense to talk of metropolis and periphery, still less of the rule of imperial nations over subject colonies. Constantinople was unequivocally an empire's capital with unrivalled prestige and traditions which placed it far above any other city in the empire. Its palaces, mosques and public buildings had all the grandeur, scale and confidence of empire. By far the biggest city in Europe at the empire's apogee in the sixteenth century, Constantinople remained a great cosmopolitan centre of cultures and peoples right down to the empire's demise. But Constantinople stood by itself and for the empire as a whole. It never belonged to any specific region or people. Even in the 1850s Muslims constituted only 44 per cent of its population, and ethnic Turks an even smaller percentage.[1]

In no meaningful sense was Anatolia the empire's metropolis. This might seem strange to Europeans, who are and always were much inclined to use the words Ottoman and Turkish interchangeably when describing the empire. Anatolia was where the Ottoman state originated. It was the only major region of the empire the majority of whose population was Turkish. It was the territory of the main successor state to the Ottoman Empire, namely the Turkish Republic. But, until the Balkans were lost, Anatolia was never the strategic, economic, political or fiscal core of the empire. At the beginning of the fifteenth century, when the Ottomans almost lost control of Anatolia, they regained the province by mobilizing their Balkan power-base for a campaign of reconquest. At the empire's peak in the late 1520s the revenues from all of Asia Minor were only three-quarters of the take from the Balkans, and not much more than receipts from Egypt alone. Anatolia was always one of the poorer and less developed regions of the empire. In 1800 population density in Anatolia was between one-half and one-third of that in the empire's

Balkan provinces. A century later, per capita incomes were five times greater in (now independent) Bulgaria, Serbia and Greece than in the Ottomans' non-European provinces. In Romania they were seven times greater.[2] For most of the empire's history the Anatolian Turks were at least spared having to pay the poll tax, which was imposed on non-Moslems only. As always, however, the Ottomans thought in religious not ethnic terms: Muslim Arabs too avoided the tax. Unlike the Turks, however, many Arabs also avoided compulsory military service in the empire's last decades. Colmar von der Goltz, Germany's leading military adviser to the Ottomans, commented at the end of the nineteenth century that the Turks were the only ethnic group that made any real contribution to the empire's military power: 'the Hejaz and the Holy Places live at the expense of the rest of the empire and the remaining Arabian and African provinces contribute little or nothing.'[3]

Muslims were never more than one-third of the population of the Ottoman Balkans. Roughly half of them were the descendants of immigrants, the other half of converts. Except for the relatively small percentage of Balkan boys conscripted for service in the janizary corps and the sultan's household (the famous *devsirme*), the Ottomans did not force conversion to Islam and were not great proselytizers. The Prophet had commanded his followers to show tolerance to 'people of the Book' (i.e. Jews and Christians) and there were also sound fiscal reasons not to convert the Christian population, whose poll tax contributed greatly to the empire's treasury. Only in much of Albania and parts of Bosnia and Bulgaria did mass (voluntary) conversion of Christians occur. Large Muslim populations were concentrated in a core of Balkan provinces closest to Constantinople. Above all, this meant Thrace, Bulgaria, Macedonia and parts of present-day Greece. Elsewhere sizeable Muslim communities existed only in towns, though Muslim cavalrymen (*sipahis*) held land on conditional military tenure and lived in the countryside when not on campaign. An outer ring of Christian territories were ruled indirectly by the Ottomans through native leaders. Of these, Moldavia and Wallachia (present-day Romania) paid a heavy tribute to Constantinople, while Ragusa (Dubrovnik) benefited greatly from Ottoman protection and from its position as privileged middleman between the Ottoman and European economies.

The Balkans were the empire's geopolitical centre not just because of their relative wealth but also because they commanded the approaches to the empire's capital. In the sixteenth and seventeenth centuries the army far preferred the Balkans to Iran as a field of campaign because the booty was richer, communications were better and the terrain and distances were not so formidable. In the last three centuries of its existence the main threat to the empire came from the north, initially from the Austrians and later from the Russians. In the face of this threat the fact that Muslims were a minority in the Ottoman Balkans was a great weakness and danger. In the end the Ottomans were to have the worst of both worlds in the Balkans. Empires that rule over indigenous peoples without colonizing their lands almost always in the end lose the territories in question but they tend to do so relatively easily and bloodlessly. On the other hand, empires that swamp conquered land with colonists tend to absorb them forever if they are in contiguous territory, or to create new nations of their own culture if they are overseas. Half-hearted colonization which leaves the imperial people a distinct but sizeable minority causes the worst long-term problems, above all for the colonists themselves. Certainly this was to be true in the case of the Muslim communities in Europe.

The Ottoman Empire can be divided relatively neatly into three territorial blocs. The first to be acquired was Anatolia, by 1500 mostly Turkish and Muslim. The second was the mostly Christian Balkans. The third was the mostly Muslim and Arab provinces of Asia and Africa, whose acquisition really began under Selim I between 1512 and 1520. These provinces were never colonized by the Turks. Even if spare Turks had existed as potential colonists, which was not the case, the relatively small areas of the Arab provinces that were fertile or urban were already densely populated when conquered by the Ottomans. Nevertheless, the acquisition of the Arab lands radically changed the empire's character. At the end of the fifteenth century, and for more than a century before that, the empire's territory was split more or less equally between Europe and Asia. Between 1481 and 1566, however, the European provinces declined from slightly less than one-half of the empire's territory to slightly more than one-quarter.[4] The overwhelming majority of Arabs were Muslims and the Arab provinces included Islam's Holy Places and, in Jerusalem, Damascus and Cairo, some of its most famous cities. Inevitably, the empire became more Islamic in character.

The difficulties of governing and defending such a vast territory increased enormously. The Ottoman army, whose bases and area of concentration lay around Constantinople, already for logistical reasons found it hard to operate effectively north of the Balkans and of Crimea, and on the Iranian plateau. Now the Ottomans also needed to defend the North African shore against Christian forces in Italy and Iberia, and to control the crucial sealanes which were the main link between Constantinople and its African provinces. It also had to defend the pilgrims' routes to the Holy Land and to guard trade routes across the Indian

Ocean against the Christian navies. These burdens could only have been sustainable if the Arab provinces in the long run had brought great military and fiscal benefits to the imperial treasury. In fact, within a century of their conquest, they were failing to do so. As with all empires, the Ottomans found it exceptionally difficult to control and exploit far-flung and heavily populated provinces at the end of long and vulnerable lines of communication. By the eighteenth century North Africa was Ottoman in name alone.

ISLAMIC OR TURKISH EMPIRE?

The Ottoman Empire was never dominated by the Turkish nation for the good reason that no such nation existed in imperial times. In the fifteenth century the dynasty did still celebrate its Central Asian ancestry. It was from this source that the Ottomans drew their belief in the sacredness and unique legitimacy of the royal bloodline, an idea alien to classical Islam. With the conquest first of Constantinople and then of the great centres of Islam, the Ottoman elite became ever more imperial and less Turkish. In terms of blood the dynasty and the elite were in fact scarcely Turkish anyway. The imperial harem was packed largely with concubines of Christian descent, and for two centuries the *devsirme* ensured that the sultan's top advisers and officials were his household slaves, and usually therefore also of Christian origin. More importantly, Ottoman elite culture owed as much to Persian, Arab and even European sources as to Turkish ones. Court Ottoman was incomprehensible to the ordinary Turk. The Ottoman elite did not think of themselves as Turkish: to them the term 'Turk' was one of disparagement, signifying a yokel from the Anatolian primitive backwoods. Nor indeed did the inhabitants of this backwoods think of themselves as a nation. Their loyalties and sense of identity were linked to village and tribe on the one hand, and to the great community of Islam on the other.

When a Turkish nationalist sentiment, and later a movement, did begin to emerge in the empire's last decades it faced many difficulties in defining what was the Turkish nation and where its borders ended. Turks were a majority in Anatolia but perhaps one-third of the population was not Muslim, and some of the Muslims were not ethnic Turks. On the other hand, many Turks lived in the empire's Balkan provinces. Virtually no Turkish nationalists before 1914 were willing to abandon the Arab provinces, with all this would entail for the Turks' pride and international status. Promoting the nation and preserving the empire were, as is generally the case, not easily combined.

An extra complicating factor was that millions of Turks lived outside the Ottoman Empire, most of whom were subjects of the Russian tsar. Many of the most influential Turkish nationalist publicists were in fact refugees from Russia, where they had developed their doctrines partly in imitation of Russian nationalism and partly in response to Russian discrimination against Turkish institutions and culture. For such people the Turkish nation was bound to extend well beyond Anatolia. From the perspective of the beginning of the twenty-first century the idea of a Greater Turkey may seem a chimera but for many of the empire's key leaders in 1914 it was real and influential. In that year the Ottoman declaration of war stated that 'the ideal of our nation and our people leads us towards the destruction of our Muscovite enemy, in order to obtain thereby a natural frontier to our Empire, which should include and unite all branches of our race.'[5] During the war the vision of a Greater Turkish empire in the east, racially homogeneous and therefore supposedly much stronger than the lost empire in the Balkans, was partly responsible for the Ottomans' excessive stress on the Russian front at the expense of the defence of the Arab provinces against the British. Literally days before the collapse of the Central Powers, Enver Pasha was urging his armies forward beyond Baku and towards the Northern Caucasus. He was to pursue his own personal dream of a Greater Turkish empire until it led him to his death in action against Soviet forces in Central Asia in 1922.

Enver Pasha was a member of the tiny, and largely Turkish, inner core of the so-called Committee of Union and Progress, usually known to Europeans as the 'Young Turks'. After the revolution of 1908 this group dominated Turkish politics until 1918. It provided most of the ideas and cadres on which Kemal Atatürk's later republican movement was based. The Young Turks were the products of the Western-style schools and colleges created by the Ottoman regime from the mid-nineteenth century onwards. The movement's core often consisted of army officers but included many civilian professionals as well. They had many similarities both with Russian revolutionaries of their time and with later Third World radicalism. Their great enemy was their country's backwardness, which they blamed on the Ottoman regime and, usually, on religion, which they saw as the main cause of the people's ignorance, sloth and conservatism. Their own creed was a rather crude belief in science and materialism, combined with a linguistic and ethnic Turkish nationalism based on European models. They were populists but also great Jacobin elitists, convinced that it was the new Westernized elite's duty to lead the nation to prosperity and power. They were seldom themselves of traditional upper-class origin, and their radicalism owed much to the sense that their own professional merit went unnoticed by a regime whose rulers promoted clients on the basis of personal connection and political loyalty. The initial base of the Young Turk movement was Macedonia, where its rank and file developed a powerful sense of Turkish solidarity and nationalism in response to pressure by Bulgarian nationalist bands on the Muslim population. The development of mass Turkish nationalism in the Anatolian heartland came later: it was partly a product of the Greek invasion of Anatolia in 1920 and partly the creation of the schools and propaganda of Atatürk's republican regime of the 1920s and 1930s. In this pattern whereby mass nationalism spread from the borderlands to a people's core territories, the Turkish experience was relatively common. It was in the borderlands that a people often had most cause to meet and clash with foreigners, and it was here too that insecurity and disputes over frontiers had most resonance.

Once in power, the Young Turks' official policies and pronouncements were imperial and Ottoman: in other words, they stressed their loyalty to the supranational empire, the Islamic faith and the bonds that united Turk and Arab in common loyalty to dynasty and religion. In their private conversations and plans, however, Turkish nationalism was a more dominant theme. The Young Turks in reality looked down on the Arabs as backward, poor fighters and potential traitors to the empire, quite unlike non-Turkish Balkan Muslims (e.g. Albanians) whom the Turks in general respected and trusted, seeing them indeed as potential members of the Turkish national community.[6]

These views were no secret to many Arab leaders and caused great distrust. The Young Turk regime was committed to military power, centralization and efficiency. In pursuit of these goals it sought a near-monopoly of power. Its leaders hoped to extend the centre's control over the provinces, to increase and equalize military and fiscal burdens, and to spread the Turkish language and a common, basically Turkish, imperial patriotism. Imperial realities quickly persuaded them, however, that some concessions to Arab notables' determination to control their own provinces were essential; otherwise these notables, especially in Syria, would swing overwhelmingly to the camp of Arab nationalism, which in some regions was already beginning to emerge as a threat by 1914. The result was the grant of considerable autonomy to the Arab provinces in 1913. Whether in reality a peacetime Young Turk regime in Constantinople would have been willing and able to maintain a *modus vivendi* with Arab provincial elites remains uncertain, since the war and the empire's collapse came before the new policy had time to take effect.

The Young Turks' great enemy, Sultan Abdulhamid II (1876–1909), was also enmeshed in his own dilemmas of empire. The professional military and civil cadres who were the Young Turks' greatest supporters had been created by the Ottoman regime itself. By the second half of the nineteenth century any ruler of the Ottoman Empire knew that modernization was essential to the survival of empire and dynasty. The state had to respond to the challenge of European military and economic power. But Western technology and professional skills could not be imported without Western values. An Ottoman sultan had good reason to be fearful of the loyalty of his new professional military officers. For two centuries after the overthrow of Osman II in 1622 many sultans had been deposed and murdered by their janizaries. The dynasty may have been held sacred but the lives of individual sultans certainly were not. The old janizary army had been a formidable element in factional politics at court, usually supporting opponents of reform and Westernization. The new professional army could easily prove as formidable, though this time on the side of radical reforms and Turkish nationalism.

The civil bureaucracy was at least as serious a threat. By tradition senior officials were the slaves of the sultan, on whose whims not merely their careers but also their lives and property depended. In the so-called Tanzimat era of reforms in the mid-nineteenth century all this changed. The government was in fact controlled by senior bureaucrats who now enjoyed security of life and property, who oversaw the reform programme, and who pushed the sultan to the margin of politics. Abdulhamid's aim was to reassert the monarch's central role against a bureaucracy growing in size, self-confidence and professional skills. His ambition, and the struggles that resulted, had many parallels in other supposedly absolute monarchies both in his own day and in earlier eras. The sultan concentrated power in his personal chancellery, cultivated a network of personal clients and informers in the administration, and ran a large secret police network which created an atmosphere of fear and distrust in the political world. In the Ottoman official yearbook of 1908 officials attached to the sultan's person and palace cover forty pages, the ruler's aides-de-camp sixteen more.[7] Colmar von der Goltz, the distinguished Prussian adviser to the Ottoman army, commented that Abdulhamid's system of personal rule was similar to royal absolutism in eighteenth-century Prussia, except for the fact that the sultan's intensely suspicious nature spread division and distrust even within his personal secretariat, while the greatly expanded scale and complexity of government would in any case have doomed old-fashioned arbitrary rule by a monarch to inefficiency and frustration.[8] Inevitably, Abdulhamid's personal rule was condemned both by much of the Ottoman elite and in Europe.

Nevertheless, it is to some extent possible to sympathize with Abdulhamid's strategy, and not merely because it was rooted in well-justified fears for his own throne and life. The sultan saw himself as the standard-bearer of Islamic empire. In this he was true to the tradition of his house and its historical *raison d'être* as the champion of a great world civilization against the challenge of the West. Abdulhamid rightly understood that Islam meant far more to the overwhelming majority of his subjects than any version of modern secular nationalism, whether Turkish or Arab. He shared his Muslim subjects' resentment at reforms and values modelled on Europe and imposed on the empire by European pressure. 'Sultan Abdulhamid seems to have been of the belief that his two predecessors ... the sultans of the Tanzimat period, neglected to create links with the common people especially in the Arab provinces.'[9] The sultan took every opportunity to stress the dynasty's Islamic identity and his own position as caliph and spiritual leader of all Muslims. In doing so he enhanced the monarch's legitimacy and raised his status far above that of mere secular politicians. He also tried to appeal to Muslims worldwide to support the only remaining Islamic empire against Christian pressure. In this he had some success: both the Russians and the British had reason to fear the caliph's hold on the loyalties of their Muslim subjects. In the immediate aftermath of the First World War, British treatment of the Ottoman dynasty caused great indignation among some Indian Muslims, the Khalifat movement even serving for a time to unite the Muslims with the Hindu-dominated Congress in opposition to the Raj. In the nineteenth century European intervention in Ottoman domestic affairs became ever more overt and humiliating. Resurrecting the caliphate and stressing its international role was a means of paying back the European empires in their own coin.

The main purpose of the caliphate, however, was domestic. Between 1876 and 1913, as the Ottoman Empire in the Balkans shrank and finally almost disappeared, the state's survival and its international role depended ever more obviously on its ability to reconcile its Turkish and Arabic subjects. Islam might achieve this but no form of nationalism could do so. Nor indeed did Abdulhamid confine his empire-saving strategy to the realm of ideology. To an extent unprecedented by his predecessors or successors, he sought to bring Arabs into his court and administration in Constantinople. When the Young Turks subsequently purged these Arab placemen in the name of progressive politics and administrative efficiency they contributed greatly to growing distrust of the new regime in the

Arab provinces. Whether 'reactionary' sultans or 'progressive' Young Turks, twentieth-century Ottoman rulers confronted the dilemmas of empire in particularly sharp form. This was because the international context was so threatening, domestic (Christian) nationalism an obvious danger, and the Ottoman Empire so weak when compared to its enemies. One key problem revolved around ideology. Islam was seen as essential to empire's survival by some, an insurmountable obstacle to modernity by others. Could this circle be squared? A great dilemma also surrounded the issue of centralized or devolved power. Constantinople needed soldiers and revenues as never before, but it also faced subjects increasingly conscious of their ethnic separateness, and provincial Arab leaders determined to preserve their power and status. Although these problems were acute, they were scarcely new, however. In fact these two issues run as a thread through much of Ottoman history and, above all, through the debate about the decline of the Ottoman Empire after its golden age in the fifteenth and sixteenth centuries.

THE DEBATE ON OTTOMAN DECLINE: RUSSIAN COMPARISONS

Traditionally, historians took the Ottomans' decline as an established fact and merely investigated its causes. Economic decline was put down to the impact on the Ottoman Empire of a global economy dominated by the capitalist great powers. The story began with the European capture of the luxury long-distance sea trade between Asia and Europe. This started in the sixteenth century when the Portuguese rounded the Cape and conquered the Indian Ocean – thereby depriving Islamic merchants and the Ottoman Empire of their lucrative position as intermediaries between Asia and Europe. It culminated in the supposedly complete domination of Ottoman markets and finance by Europe in the Victorian era. In military matters Ottoman decline was dated from the end of the sixteenth-century Golden Age when the armies of Suleiman the Magnificent were the terror of Europe. Thence the trajectory was seen as inexorably downwards, passing through a string of defeats by Russia and Austria in the seventeenth and eighteenth centuries to the final disaster of 1918. In government, the traditional story is of helpless and inept sultans, prisoners of the harem, who allowed corruption and factionalism to ruin effective administration. Not until the mid-nineteenth century, the so-called Tanzimat reform era, did the centre begin to put its house in order and by then it was too late. This picture of relentless decline seemed to be confirmed by Ottoman statesmen and scholars throughout the post-1600 period, lamenting the fall in their empire's power and virtue.

In the last generation, however, some historians have challenged the whole idea of Ottoman decline during this period. The new history has made some convincing corrections to traditional views of the Ottoman Empire in the last three centuries of its existence. All was not as consistently black as it has been portrayed. Moaning about decline turned out to be an Ottoman genre much in evidence even in the Golden Age. The economy of the eighteenth-, let alone seventeenth-century Ottoman Empire now appears to have been still overwhelmingly in local hands. The European impact was limited. The political crisis of the early seventeenth century was surmounted under the mid-century Köprülü grand viziers and a stable relationship between the centre and most provincial elites was restored for a time. The Ottoman resurgence in the second half of the century brought them within an inch of taking Vienna in 1683. Although the next 35 years saw major defeats against the Austrians, these were largely reversed in the 1730s when the Ottomans regained most of the territory they had lost in the century's first two decades. In 1711 even Peter I with Russia's new model European army was forced into a humiliating capitulation by the Ottoman forces.

Nevertheless, it is important not to go too far. Between 1550 and 1800 Ottoman power and prestige did decline dramatically in relation to the Turks' main foreign enemies. In 1550 the Ottoman Empire was the most formidable state in Europe. Its disciplined, highly motivated and well-armed janizaries were the largest and most feared professional force of infantry on the continent. Ottoman military technology and leadership were second to none. The sultan's territories and revenues were greater than those of any of his Christian rivals. By 1800 the picture had changed completely. In the recent wars against Russia Ottoman military and naval forces had proved themselves to be hopelessly inferior in discipline, training, technology and leadership. The previously effective fiscal and administrative system had crumbled. In the mid-sixteenth century, to take only one example, Egypt had been a major contributor to Ottoman power. By the late eighteenth century Cairo contributed virtually no revenue to the central treasury and, at best, tiny military contingents whose vicious indiscipline made them far more of a threat to the friendly civilian population than to any enemy.

A state's power can to some extent be measured by the size of its revenues and the efficiency with which they are raised. In 1789 Ottoman revenues were estimated at £3.75 million, British at £16.8 million and French at £24 million.[10] Among the European great powers Russia was much the most fiscally inefficient, if efficiency is measured by the percentage of revenue that is sacrificed to costs of collection. Only 75 per cent of Russian revenue actually reached the treasury.[11] In the Ottoman case the corresponding figure was 18.75 per cent, more than four-fifths of the state's revenue in one way or another sticking to the fingers of those who collected it.[12] Since in all countries at that time central government revenues were spent largely on preparing and fighting wars or paying the loans incurred by past conflicts, these statistics are comparable. They are also a rather obvious mark of the Ottoman state's failure in the business of empire. It is nowadays sometimes fashionable to play down the importance of this business. Kings and battles often seem remote from the lives of the masses. But the consequences of the Ottoman Empire's failure to sustain an adequate military and fiscal machine were in no way remote from the everyday lives of the sultan's subjects. In time these consequences were to be devastating for the Muslim masses in Anatolia and, even more, in the empire's outlying regions. They were also to have a huge impact on political stability in the Middle East into and throughout the twentieth century, contributing greatly to the whole region falling under the domination of the European powers.

Ottoman decline has usually been viewed in the context of Western Europe's rise to global dominance. The stress here is generally put on the impact of the Industrial Revolution and global trading patterns on the Middle East. By the early nineteenth century this was very important and in the last century of its existence the Ottoman Empire became a weak and dependent element in an international economy dominated by Europe. Nevertheless, historians have frequently been too obsessed by the impact of economics and the view from Western Europe. Well before European capitalism came to dominate key areas of the Ottoman economy, the Ottoman state had failed to match the military, fiscal, administrative and cultural transformation that had turned eighteenth-century Russia into a European great power. It is interesting to compare the Ottoman Empire to Russia. Both states dwelt on Europe's periphery. Both were ruled by supposedly autocratic monarchs. Neither had a European feudal nobility with powerful traditions of corporate rights and self-government. The Russians and Ottomans faced the challenge of European power in the seventeenth and eighteenth centuries, and major domestic obstacles to meeting that challenge. But the conservative alliance of traditional military units (*streltsy*), religious sectarians and urban artisans which Peter I overcame in the 1690s was still blocking reform in the Ottoman Empire until Mahmud II's destruction of the janizaries in 1826. Partly for that reason, whereas the Ottomans had been much more powerful than the Russians in 1500, they were far inferior three centuries later.

Some reasons for the Ottomans' relative failure in comparison to Russia are rather down-to-earth and have already been mentioned briefly. Geopolitics was crucial. By the seventeenth century the Ottomans had reached the natural limits of their expansion. Even had military factors allowed further conquests, demographic weakness meant that new territories could not be settled or consolidated under Ottoman rule. It was in any case impossible to keep armies in the field north of Hungary or on the Iranian plateau for logistical reasons. Although the Ottomans nearly captured Vienna in the 1520s and 1680s, in the end they found the heartlands of Habsburg power too distant to be conquered. When Ottoman artillery and supplies finally arrived at Vienna from the south too little time remained to take the city. Campaigning over the winter this far from Ottoman bases was logistically and politically dangerous, and would have destroyed the army. In time Habsburg power built up in the north and presented the Ottomans with an increasingly formidable threat, particularly in the late seventeenth century when Constantinople was faced with a ring of allied Christian powers, and in the 1710s when the brilliant Prince Eugene of Savoy inflicted devastating defeats on the sultan's armies. Meanwhile, ironically, the closing down of the former western front against Spain in the seventeenth and eighteenth centuries also to some extent worked to the Ottomans' detriment. In the sixteenth century the North African Muslims had welcomed and invited Ottoman rule in order to check the advance of Habsburg Spain across the Mediterranean into their territory. When this threat subsequently receded, the *raison d'être* of Ottoman rule in this region for the local population to a great extent disappeared.

Meanwhile in the north-east geopolitics favoured Russia's expansion into Ukraine, the Steppe and Siberia, thereby greatly enhancing her power. The Russian army conquered these areas and from the eighteenth century the Russian population grew hugely, allowing them to be developed. From the 1450s the Black Sea had been an exclusively Ottoman lake. In the last quarter of the eighteenth century, however, under Catherine II Russia seized the Crimea (previously an Ottoman protectorate) and rapidly consolidated its power on the Black Sea's north shore. As the economy of south Russia grew enormously in the nineteenth century, so too did her commerce on the Black Sea. Her exports had to pass through the Straits and were therefore very vulnerable to Ottoman blockade. The security of Russia's Black Sea ports and coast was also under permanent potential threat from British or other navies which the Ottomans could allow into the Black Sea at any time. For these and other reasons control, or at least dominant influence, at Constantinople became a Russian dream, and sometimes a Russian policy. The famous 'Eastern Question', which occupied Europe's statesmen in the nineteenth century, was born. For the first time in centuries the core and capital of the Ottoman Empire was under threat.

In part the Ottomans' very success was the cause of their subsequent failure. They were loath to question methods that had served them so well. The fact that, before the defeats at Russia's hands in 1768–74, Ottoman decline had been neither abrupt nor continuous blinded them to its reality. Russia's failure to match its European rivals in the sixteenth century was clear. In the early seventeenth century key provinces were lost and Moscow itself occupied by foreign enemies. Nothing so drastic happened to the Ottomans. There were, it is true, serious problems in the early seventeenth century but the Köprülü grand viziers appeared to have solved these by the 1650s by rooting out corruption and returning to the principles of statecraft that had ruled in the Golden Age. Given the possibility of solving problems by tried and traditional methods, most states will prefer this course to adopting foreign models with destabilizing potential.

Obviously, personalities also mattered greatly. The seventeenth- and eighteenth-century Ottoman dynasty never produced rulers comparable to Peter I and Catherine II. This, however, was more than just a question of biological chance. As a boy and young man Peter had been free to roam the foreign quarter in Moscow. Here he found large numbers of Protestants from Northern Europe, much the most dynamic area of the continent as regards new ideas and technologies. Some of these men occupied important positions in his father's service.

No Ottoman prince could conceivably have enjoyed such freedom. Part of the problem was the succession to the throne, always a question of huge sensitivity and importance in any dynastic polity. In the fifteenth century the sultan's sons were established in autonomous governorships and allowed the luxury of civil war to decide the succession. The consequences for the empire's stability were devastating and by the late sixteenth century an alternative system of succession was practised: a sultan backed one son as his heir, who, on coming to the throne, massacred all his brothers. This proved deeply unpopular in Constantinople and in the early seventeenth century almost resulted in the dynasty's extinction. As a result new conventions emerged. Younger brothers survived but all were virtually confined to the harem until they succeeded an elder brother on the throne. This was deemed the only way to limit the threat they represented to the reigning monarch. If male siblings were a threat to rulers in most monarchies this was particularly so in the Ottoman Empire. Sultans after the sixteenth century did not marry. No lady in the harem was allowed to bear the sultan more than one son. If he succeeded to the throne, her position and that of her faction was secure. If he did not, her status and even life were threatened. The complete lack of solidarity between half-brothers made court politics a zero sum game.

To allow heirs to the Ottoman throne to roam the streets and bazaars of Constantinople was therefore unthinkable. Nor in any case was a large community of Northern Europeans to be found in important positions in the sultan's military and administrative service, which in the seventeenth and eighteenth centuries were dominated exclusively by his Muslim subjects. Here one finds a crucial difference between the Ottomans and Russians: even in the seventeenth century, let alone in the eighteenth, Russian society was far more open to European technology, immigrants and ideas. The most spectacular example of this was Catherine II herself, a ruler of great skill and intelligence whose reign (1762–96) covered precisely the period when Russia began to draw far ahead of the Ottomans in terms both of power and of economic and cultural modernization. Very obviously no woman and no German could have sat on the Ottoman throne.

At first blush Russia's great advantage over the Ottomans in this respect might seem unsurprising, almost indeed self-evident. Russia was after all a Christian and European country. In fact matters are not nearly so simple. In the fifteenth century the Ottomans occupied large territories which Europeans saw as far more intrinsic to Christendom than Moscow. Moreover, in 1500 the Ottomans were very open to European technologies and the skilled Christians who taught them. The Ottomans readily adopted Western military technology, and created a fleet to rival that of the Venetians in record time despite having no naval traditions. Subsequently, Ottoman openness to outside influences declined greatly. This remained true even at the beginning of the nineteenth century, as Selim III found to his cost when he tried to introduce Western-style military units into the Ottoman army. The sultan's efforts to reform his army and state in the wake of disastrous defeats by Russia led to his overthrow and murder.

One explanation for this has to be the changing role of Islam in the intervening centuries of the Ottoman Empire's existence, centuries during which Europe established its lead in science, technology and administration. In the sixteenth century the old somewhat heterodox border realm became Islam's greatest empire, and its champion against the infidel. The centres of traditional Sunni orthodoxy were incorporated into the empire in the first half of the sixteenth century. The Ottomans initially had ruled a peripheral border realm whose culture was eclectic and rather shallow. Certainly Central Asian Turks such as the Ottomans did not bring to empire a large and sophisticated cultural baggage of their own. That is one reason why they – like the Mongols and many other nomadic conquerors before them – tended rapidly to adopt the high culture of the sedentary societies they conquered.

By the time Mecca and Medina fell to the Ottomans in the early sixteenth century, Islam had existed for almost a millennium. It had therefore put down very deep roots. It had also absorbed much of the region's pre-Muslim high culture. The Islamic world-view and values permeated every aspect of the region's life and its rich culture. Preserving religion and the way of life it permeated was the highest ideal for ruler and subject alike. Having absorbed Islamic high culture and become the world's leading Islamic empire and champion, the Ottomans were bound to find it harder to accept and impose European innovations, especially since so many of them did ultimately challenge Islam's core beliefs and values. Since Islam was to some extent defined against the Christian West, open borrowing was even more difficult.

The confrontation with Safavid Shia Iran which began in the sixteenth century and, still worse, the challenge of widespread Shia dissidence within the empire were also reasons to identify the empire strongly with traditional Sunni Islam, and to look with suspicion at any deviation from its norms. 'The ideological need to portray the Safavids as "infidels" produced a corresponding need to portray the Ottoman sultans as pious Orthodox Muslims, and the only defenders of true orthodoxy against such infidelity. This need arose at a time when the ulema had come to dominate the intellectual life of the empire, and the result was a reformulation of Ottoman claims to legitimacy in terms of orthodox, canonical Islam.'[13]

Also at the root of the Ottoman long-term failure to match Russia was the crucial relationship between the central government and regional elites. Within the limits that distance and pre-modern communications allowed, Constantinople's control over its provinces was tight in the fifteenth and sixteenth centuries. In comparison to the Christian monarchs of his day, the sultan was very successful in drawing soldiers, supplies and revenues from his subjects. But the fiscal and administrative system worked in a manner that was usually orderly, predictable and relatively moderate in its demands. This enhanced its legitimacy among the mass of the population. There is good reason to believe that Christian peasants in the Balkans preferred the peace and order of Ottoman rule in its first two centuries to the war and disorder among Christian princes and nobles that had preceded it. Above all, in comparison to Christian feudal kingdoms, the Ottoman regime controlled local elites and limited the dues they could squeeze from the peasant. Unlike the European aristocrat, the Ottoman cavalryman (*sipahi*) possessed no judicial powers over the peasantry on 'his' land. In any event the land was not 'his' in the European sense, since the *sipahi* was assigned different holdings in the course of a lifetime and did not put down strong local roots, let alone bequeath estates to his heirs. The tight regulation of peasant dues and services, not to mention the existence of an independent state-run judiciary, were features of the early sixteenth-century Ottoman Empire which the Habsburgs had not yet achieved in 1750 and which Nicholas I was still struggling to create in mid-nineteenth century Russia.

Unfortunately, by 1800 these were also no longer features of Ottoman life either. Sustaining the complicated bureaucratic machinery of the Ottoman state over the generations was difficult, as indeed was the case with the even larger and more sophisticated bureaucratic machine of imperial China. The Russian alliance between tsar and serf-owner was cruder, less just but probably in the long run more durable. In most provinces by the mid-eighteenth century the centre's power to coerce or tax was very limited or even non-existent. Local notables farmed the taxes and raised small armies to enforce their collection. By the end of the century these tax farms were held by lifetime, or even semi-hereditary tenure. Governors appointed by the centre might or might not be rejected by the local notables. Even if they were accepted, they had no loyal troops and few other resources through which to command obedience. The Ottoman garrisons had long since asserted their autonomy and found local means to acquire the pay which the sultan had failed to provide. Since governors' terms of office were very brief and the bribes to secure appointment increasingly exorbitant, the office-holders' main concern was to secure a good return on their investment. Sometimes the local population lived well enough under the rule of local notables. They might even prefer the light hand of notional Ottoman rule to the more efficient tax-collectors of Venice or nineteenth-century Egypt.[14]

The rule of local notables could even benefit the centre. In Ottoman Iraq, for instance, the local regime remitted an almost notional tribute to Constantinople but it did at least protect the vulnerable border with Iran at its own expense. The long domination of local politics in Baghdad by a single military family preserved a degree of stability and order. In some regions, however, the collapse of central power allowed local notables unlimited exploitation of the peasantry. Anarchical struggles for power between local factions and armed bands sometimes devastated the countryside. It was in an effort to curb the mayhem caused by conflicting local Ottoman elites that the Serb rebellion began in 1804. This was to be the first of the many Balkan revolts in the nineteenth century. Only towards the middle of the nineteenth century did the Ottoman state recreate an effective centralized army and administration. At this point it could reassert its authority in a number of provinces. By then however many key areas – Greece, Serbia, Hungary, Egypt and most of North Africa for instance – had been lost for good.

A number of explanations exist for the declining effectiveness of Ottoman central government in the seventeenth and still more, eighteenth century. As noted earlier, Ottoman failure was in part the result of earlier success. In the sixteenth century the Ottoman Empire had been much more minutely, efficiently and justly administered than most of early modern Europe, let alone Russia. As in other bureaucratic empires, however, maintaining the administration's efficiency over the generations was very difficult given pre-modern communications, vast distances, and the absence of modern checks on the bureaucracy such as a free press and a truly autonomous legal system. A huge amount depended on the ability of rulers chosen by heredity. Memories of a golden age inhibited reforms.

In its earliest centuries the Ottoman state had been in large part a mechanism for making war and acquiring booty, land and revenue. Success legitimized the polity, bound ruler and provincial elite together, and enriched both. But even by 1600 the age of booty and territorial expansion was almost over. The state would now have to fund its war machine entirely on its own resources. It would also need to find new means to ensure the loyalty of provincial elites.

The nature of war was also changing, to the Ottomans' disadvantage. Professional, disciplined, expensive infantry was now becoming the core of the modern army, the *sipahi* cavalryman was becoming redundant. Since the *sipahi* had been not just a soldier but also a key figure in rural police and order, this was a serious matter. In Europe too the noble cavalryman became partly redundant but he transformed himself into the officer in his monarch's army, adding a powerful material and emotional bond to the alliance between ruler and provincial landowning nobility which was the basis of the polity both in eighteenth-century Russia and elsewhere in Europe. The Ottomans failed to create so stable and fruitful an alliance between centre and provincial elite. This provincial elite was not a well-rooted, hereditary landowning aristocracy. Its ownership of property was very insecure. The sons of Ottoman provincial notables did not become loyal and efficient servants of the state's military power. Instead, if they survived local power-struggles they became autonomous warlords, usually acknowledging the sultan's legitimate authority but doing little to make it effective. Meanwhile the infantry units raised in ever larger numbers for modern war strained the exchequer beyond endurance. Unpaid garrisons, often forced to take up civilian employment or banditry in order to survive, posed a major threat to public order and to the authority of the state. More often than not provincial high politics became a battle for spoils between and within free-floating garrison troops and one species or another of local notable.

The centre's ability to impose its will on these groups was not helped by the dramatic decline in the quality of rulers after 1600: with all possible male heirs confined to the harem until the moment they ascended the throne, a balanced training in government or human relations was barely possible. A strong vizier might take the sultan's place – as the Köprülüs did – but only if the ruler and the palace factions allowed him to do so. In any event one was no longer dealing with a ruling elite of slaves of the sultan, recruited through the *devsirme* and to some extent divorced from society. Instead the empire's elite officials were recruited from the households and families of the capital's grandees, some of whom were themselves married to the sultan's sisters and daughters. The pursuit of office was increasingly frantic, the time spent in office increasingly brief, the resources expended on factional struggles increasingly great.

Whatever the reasons for the decline in Ottoman power, its results were disastrous for the dynasty's legitimacy and for political stability within the empire. Power breeds respect. An emperor must be a figure of power and authority. It is difficult to preserve rulers' prestige and their hold on their subjects' loyalty if the state they govern is seen as weaker, poorer and less effective than its foreign competitors. History and fortune are perceived to have abandoned the regime. In this sense the Mandate of Heaven is not a merely Chinese phenomenon. As important, without power the Ottomans could not legitimize themselves in the eyes of their Muslim subjects by defending the land of Islam against its Christian rivals. In the early sixteenth century Muslim North Africa had called in the Ottomans to defend them against Christian invasion. The Ottomans had responded effectively and successfully.[15] They had taken over defence of the Holy Places from the faltering Mamluks of Egypt in the 1510s and had driven the Portuguese back from the northern shores of the Indian Ocean. But by the late eighteenth century they were too weak to stop the Russians from seizing the Muslim Crimea. By the 1820s they were unable even to try to help the Algerians in the struggle against French invasion. Even in the early twentieth century most Arabs would have loyally supported a Muslim empire that could protect their land against Christian invasion and annexation. But already strong Arab doubts on this score were confirmed in the First World War. If the Ottomans could not protect them and offer them that security which is the *raison d'être* of empire, the Arab notables would have little alternative but to shift for themselves.[16]

THE OTTOMANS AND MINORITIES

For the Christian population of the Balkans the impact of declining Ottoman power was even more fundamental and came earlier. This was partly because the Balkans were in the front line as regards the Ottomans' rivalry with the Christian powers. Weakness was quickly felt as the Austrian and Russian armies invaded the empire's Balkan territories. In addition, the Christian populations inevitably felt limited loyalty to the cause of Islamic empire. As the empire weakened, its hold on the Christian provinces began to crumble. A yoke that had been tolerable partly because it seemed inevitable looked very different to many Christian subjects when powerful Christian armies defeated the Ottomans, invaded the Balkans and proclaimed the cause of liberation.

Which is not to assert that Ottoman rule in the Balkans rested solely on conquest, inertia and the awareness of overwhelming imperial power – crucial as these factors were (and usually are in the case of empire). Though no one ever asked their opinion, no doubt the Christian peasantry of the Balkans welcomed the law, peace and order that Ottoman rule brought in its first two centuries. Even subsequently, thousands of Bessarabian peasants fled 'liberation' by Christian but serf-owning tsarist Russia when their province was annexed in 1812. Ottoman rule seemed much preferable, even at the expense of abandoning their farms.[17] More important, key Christian elites had good reason to welcome and support Ottoman rule, of which they were major beneficiaries. These included Ragusan merchants, the 'Phanariot' Greek ruling class of the Romanian principalities, and the hierarchy of the Greek Orthodox Church. The latter in particular exercised great authority under Ottoman licence over the whole Orthodox population, whether ethnically Greek, Slav or Arab. Under Ottoman rule they in fact recovered a power over Slav Orthodox churches that they had never possessed in the last centuries of Byzantine rule. Often allied to the ecclesiastical hierarchy, both Greek and Armenian, were wealthy merchants and, in the Armenian case, financiers. Until well into the nineteenth century their property and even lives were never wholly secure against arbitrary attack by the Ottoman authorities. In this, however, their position was little different from that of wealthy Muslims. Most of the Greek and Armenian business elite supported the empire, saw it as the heir to Byzantium, and wished to improve their position within the Ottoman realm, not to break it up. As Western concepts of nationalism penetrated the Christian community and a secular, radical and populist intelligentsia grew up, both the Greeks and the Armenians experienced bitter conflict between this new intelligentsia on the one hand and the old religious and merchant elite on the other.

Ottoman treatment of the Christians and Jews followed the traditions of Mahomed and the early caliphate, as well as of pre-Islamic empire in the Middle East. So long as other religious communities paid their taxes and were politically loyal, they were allowed autonomy and toleration as regards religious and cultural affairs. A far harsher line was traditionally taken towards schismatics and heretics within the empire's dominant religion, particularly if their cause had outside support from rival foreign powers. In the early Ottoman centuries, much the most ruthless treatment of religious minorities occurred under Selim I (1512–20) and was directed against the Shia population of Anatolia. On both sides of the Ottoman-Safavid political and religious frontier the rival regimes resorted to large-scale massacre, expulsion and forced conversion of Muslim communities considered heterodox and politically subversive by Sunni and Shia rulers.

Eastern Anatolia and the Trans-Caucasus were never subsequently to escape this tradition in which competition between empires became connected to savage conflict between local Sunni, Shia and Christian communities, resulting on all sides in large-scale massacre and expulsion of populations. As we shall see, the Russian Empire was to fall prey to this regional tradition as well. Both the Russian and the Ottoman authorities feared that a minority sharing the same religion as an external enemy would become the latter's trojan horse. By the early twentieth century Ottoman attitudes to the Armenian population of eastern Anatolia were influenced by this fear. To do the Ottomans justice, the previous alliances between Christian minorities and the great powers had provided excellent reason for this anxiety. The Armenian genocide, though incomparable in its scale and horror, must to some extent be seen within the context of this regional tradition.

There was, however, a huge gap between the experience of ethnic conflict and massacre in the empire's last terrible decades and the far more tolerant behaviour of Ottoman rulers in earlier centuries. 'It is easier to be tolerant when one feels strong than when one feels weak and endangered.'[18] Ottoman treatment of Christians and Jews in fact fitted logically into the overall picture of religion's place in Ottoman society. Though in its classical age the Ottoman regime regulated some aspects of economic and cultural life, in general the role of the political authorities in Islamic society was a strictly limited one. Most of everyday life was ruled by religious law, the *sharia*. The latter not merely determined most family, cultural and educational affairs but also had a considerable influence on economic and even political behaviour, broadly defined. It was therefore logical for the Ottoman authorities to leave questions of family, culture, education and social life to the minority religious communities too, demanding in return that these communities obeyed the law, paid taxes and showed loyalty to the sultan. This was the essence of the so-called *millet* system, by which the Ottoman regime's relations with the empire's non-Muslims were regulated. Although the term itself is strictly speaking an anachronism when applied before the nineteenth century,[19] it remains nevertheless a useful shorthand to encapsulate a type of imperial inter-ethnic relations which guaranteed political loyalty to rulers and cultural autonomy to the many ethnic and religious groups over which they ruled.

In some ways the millet system has a curiously modern echo. Cultural pluralism was combined with political loyalty in a state that allowed great autonomy to society in most spheres of life. In some ways this prefigures modern multi-culturalism. In the long run, however, the millet had serious disadvantages from the Ottomans' own perspective. Neither expelled, exterminated nor assimilated, minorities retained their identity, and once nationalism came on the intellectual and political agenda, they became serious threats to the Ottoman regime. In the nineteenth century the long tradition of autonomy was stoutly defended by Christian communities determined to defeat Ottoman efforts to centralize and to create a common sense of Ottoman citizenship and loyalty. Nevertheless, the millet's organization and institutions were not usually well suited to nationalist aspirations, at least before the reforms of 1856. In the case of the Jews the millet's religiously defined borders did coincide with those of the nation. But of all the Ottoman minorities, the Jews were the most satisfied and the most loyal. The core of the Jewish community were Sephardis who fled Christian persecution in fifteenth- and sixteenth-century Iberia and had good reason to be grateful for Ottoman tolerance and protection. Though in the nineteenth century they were no longer as prosperous as in their first generations under Ottoman rule, their loyalty was unshaken. Awareness of pogroms in Russia and the Christian Balkans, not to mention conflicts with the Greeks within the Ottoman Empire, served to strengthen this loyalty. Moreover, with the exception of a tiny minority of Zionists, Jews saw no conceivable alternative to empire in the form of a nation state that they could make their own. They had every reason to fear Arab and, even more, Christian ethnic nationalism, one of whose prime targets they were likely to be. The logic that made most Jews loyal subjects of the Habsburgs and subsequently attracted many of them to internationalist marxism worked also in favour of the Ottomans.

Where the Christian, and especially the Greek Orthodox, millet was concerned matters were rather different. The Greeks were not refugees from persecution but a conquered people who had been the core of a great Christian empire. A memory of Byzantium and a hope for its resurrection lurked in Greek mass consciousness. The Orthodox millet before the nineteenth century was defined by religion, not by ethnicity. In the eighteenth century its Greek ecclesiastical elite sought to use their powers within the millet to hellenize part of the Slav community. Since in most ways the millet authorities had more impact on their lives than the Ottoman ones, Christian Slav and Arab nationalism was often at least as anti-Greek as it was anti-Turk. In common with the Armenian churches and indeed with the Ottoman conservative religious and political elites, the religious leadership of the Greek millet had good reason to dislike the emerging secular intelligentsia and their nationalist creed. The Ottoman reforms of the millet structure in the mid-nineteenth century in fact facilitated the growing influence of this new class and their nationalist creed within the non-Muslim community, in the process weakening the regime's conservative allies.

It is important not to romanticize the millet system. Under its terms non-Muslims were unequivocally second-class subjects. They paid a special tax and were subject to discrimination by laws (e.g. on what they wore and how they travelled) which could be humiliating. Though the millet's religious leaders possessed honour and power within the Ottoman regime, the latter's ruling core was almost exclusively Muslim, even indeed after the 1856 reform in principle opened high office to subjects of any faith. Nevertheless, by the standards of many empires and most Christian states in history the millet system does stand out for its tolerance of religious and ethnic diversity.

THE LAST CENTURY: SURVIVAL AND COLLAPSE

But the relative peace and tolerance sometimes created by empire is always rooted in power. It survives as long as imperial power is generally regarded as invincible. The Ottoman Empire was unequivocally a Muslim land in which Muslims were the superior, ruling community. Universal recognition of this fact underlay the millet system, as did the acknowledgement on all sides that the Ottoman state had the means and the will to crush any revolt or any questioning of the system's premises. In the nineteenth century the increasing wealth and confidence of the Ottoman Christians, and the power of their foreign allies, undermined the premises on which the millet system rested and unleashed horrific inter-ethnic conflict.

The Ottoman Christians were bound to be affected by the worldwide advance of Christian civilization and of the Christian powers in the nineteenth century. The Islamic world community was being assailed, undermined and conquered in every continent where it had taken root. Christianity, progress and power seemed irrevocably linked, Islam in headlong retreat. Apart from imbuing educated Ottoman Christians with increased self-confidence, Western example also pointed to nationalism and popular sovereignty as the wave of the future and the principles on which a legitimate polity should be built.

The intervention of powerful European states had an immediate and obvious impact in the Balkans. A string of crushing Russian military victories over the Ottomans in the late eighteenth and nineteenth centuries was the most important cause of Greek, Serbian, Romanian and Bulgarian independence. Russia was a particular threat to the Ottomans not merely because of its power but also because it shared the Orthodox religion with most of their Christian subjects. This both drew it into Balkan affairs and increased its appeal to Ottoman Christians. Russia was the most serious threat but not the only one. The French conquered Algeria, the British took Egypt and Cyprus, and the Austrians seized Bosnia. The concert of great powers, which dominated international relations between 1815 and 1914, was made up exclusively of Christian states. The sultan's Christian subjects could usually expect a sympathetic hearing from the powers. Christian revolts could expect and might receive direct military support by Russia or, in the Greek case, even Britain. By the second half of the nineteenth century, even if the Ottomans defeated a revolt, the means they used to do so would bring the wrath of the Christian powers down on their heads, and with it the prospect of outside intervention to enforce the protection of the

Christian community concerned. By the 1890s this pattern was well established: Armenian revolutionaries could confidently plan revolts and terrorist attacks in the belief that the Ottoman response would provoke European intervention.[20]

Russian victories and successful Balkan revolts caused massive bloodshed and emigration among the Muslim population of the lost provinces. The first Muslim region to be conquered by a Christian power was Crimea, from which roughly 100,000 Tatars fled to the Ottoman Empire in the late eighteenth century. In 1854–6 when Ottoman, French and British forces invaded Crimea, the loyalty of the Tatar population was suspect in Russian eyes and many villages were ravaged by Cossacks. Subsequently some 300,000 more Tatars emigrated to the Ottoman Empire, many thousands dying in the process. The Russian conquest of the Caucasian mountaineers also resulted in massive emigration, in part forced: 'of the 1.2 million Circassians and Abkhazians who departed their lands,' it has been estimated, 'only two-thirds survived'; and together, the mid-nineteenth-century 'refugees from the Crimea and the Caucasus were equal to about 10 per cent of the population of Ottoman Anatolia.'[21] Ultimately, however, refugees from Black Sea territories conquered by Russia were to be outnumbered by the Muslim exodus from the Balkans. The final result of the Ottoman Empire's decline and fall was that the overwhelming majority of the Muslim population of the Balkans had been expelled or killed by 1923, as had all but a very small minority of the Christian population of Anatolia.[22]

Inevitably, a flood of Muslim immigrant refugees exacerbated inter-ethnic tensions in the remaining provinces of the Ottoman Empire but other factors were also very important. In the nineteenth century much of the Ottoman economy was dominated unequivocally by Europeans and by Ottoman Christians. In the seventeenth century foreign trade had still been mostly with other parts of Asia. Now it was overwhelmingly with Europe, and the Ottoman Christians were best placed through their languages, culture and contacts to be its middlemen. On the eve of the First World War all 40 private bankers in Constantinople were non-Muslim, as were all the stockbrokers. 'One-third of the Ottoman Chambers of Commerce consisted of Greek firms and organizations'.[23] Even in areas such as agriculture and handicrafts, where one might have expected continued Muslim domination, foreigners played a big role. Carpet production in western Anatolia, for instance, was now dominated by six British large firms. 'Whereas the Muslims accounted for the bulk of the traditional grain crops, the millets developed and controlled the more valuable cash crops exported to foreign markets.'[24]

Christian domination of the Ottoman economy was sustained, though not directly caused, by the policies of the European powers. In 1838, when the Ottomans were totally dependent on the great powers for protection against Mohammed Ali's Egyptian army, the British forced a free trade convention on Constantinople. Subsequently a similar policy was forced on the Egyptians, though their very expensive and inefficient protectionist strategy of boosting domestic industry would probably have come to grief even without European interference. Ottoman state bankruptcy in the late 1870s led to the formation of the foreign-controlled Public Debt Administration in 1881. By 1912–13 it employed more officials than the finance ministry. As far back as the sixteenth century the sultan had agreed the so-called Capitulations with foreign powers, granting them the right to trade in the empire and to be judged by their own consuls. At the time this was in no sense a concession born of weakness but simply an extension (revocable at any time) of the principle that non-Muslims should manage their own affairs. By the nineteenth century, however, not merely were the Capitulations being interpreted as a binding international agreement, they were also being used as a means to provide thousands of Ottoman Christians with foreign passports and the protection of consular courts for their business activities. An additional privilege that came with foreign citizenship was exemption from Ottoman taxation.

For a Muslim society that had long taken for granted its superior status and its domination of the empire, these developments were an outrage. The 1856 reform designed to create a single equal Ottoman citizenry was unacceptable both to Christians determined to preserve their autonomy and to Muslims insulted by demotion to the same level as infidels. Since foreign and Christian competition simultaneously hit some local crafts and businesses, the indignation was all the greater. Pogroms against the Christians resulted. The Ottoman central government did not usually welcome, let alone incite, these pogroms but its control over popular outrage, especially in the provinces, was limited. The first great pogroms occurred in Lebanon and Syria in 1856–60, and were directed against the Christian Maronite community, whose wealth and confidence had been growing in recent years. After almost 40,000 lives had been lost French troops intervened to impose a new form of government for the region. In 1861 Lebanon was turned into an autonomous region with a Christian governor and a council on which all communities were represented. The settlement was guaranteed by the great powers and could not therefore be touched by the Ottoman government. On the one hand this settlement was an early, interesting and relatively successful example of the use of devolved authority, power-sharing and a number of other mechanisms for ensuring that hostile communities could live together in the same territory without bloodshed, insecurity or the domination of one group by another. But 'power sharing on a communal basis' had the inevitable 'corollary of a very limited role for government.' The local communities could not agree on sufficient levels of tax and conscription to sustain basic order and public services. Lebanon therefore depended on an Ottoman subsidy. Since the semi-bankrupt Ottoman government was not itself allowed to tax or conscript in the Lebanon it is not at all surprising that Constantinople viewed these arrangements without enthusiasm.[25] In a manner typical of empires, compromises that benefited the cause of domestic inter-ethnic accord did so at the cost of weakening the state's ability to mobilize resources in the cause of defence against external threats.

By 1900 the Ottoman Empire was the 'sick man of Europe'. All the problems that beset other empires were present here in exaggerated form. If a ruler of empire wished to see nightmarish possibilities for his own empire's future, he needed only to look at the Ottoman present. In this period, for instance, tensions frequently existed in Europe between monarchs anxious to use their traditional powers and bureaucracies growing in size and sophistication which claimed, often *sotto voce*, an increasing right to determine policy. Only in Abdulhamid's realm, however, did the monarch set up a large semi-private secret police whose boss was a psychopath who used his home for purposes of torture and rape.[26] Nor on the other hand did senior officials in other realms conspire with émigré revolutionaries to depose their own sovereign. Every empire feared decline, the loss of territory, the inability to compete with foreign powers, and consequent loss of control over ethnic minorities within the empire. Nowhere had this process gone so far among European empires as in the Ottoman case.

Even in 1700 the Ottoman population was much greater than Russia's. By 1914 the Ottoman sultan ruled perhaps 33 million subjects, the Russian tsar 170 million. Despite successful attempts to reform their army and administration in the nineteenth century, the Ottomans were no longer masters of their own fate. Their future was now the one dreaded by every empire: dominated economically by foreigners, their survival depended on the inability of potential predators to divide up the cake between them. Because no great power wished the Ottomans to be strong but each of them feared lest one of its rivals were to be the beneficiary of the empire's collapse, 'they had every interest in keeping the Ottoman state weak, though not so weak as to bring about its demise. Such a fine balance could not be maintained indefinitely.'[27] By 1914 it was generally accepted that polyglot, multi-ethnic empires were acutely vulnerable to the threat of nationalism. Almost everywhere, rulers of empire sought to turn as much as possible of their territory into a consolidated nation. Probably no European would have doubted that of all empires the Ottoman one was the most fragile. The final Ottoman response to this threat during the First World War was also the most extreme, taking the form in 1915–16 of the genocide[28] of the Armenians, designed to ensure that the combination of foreign invasion and Christian nationalism which had driven Muslims out of the Balkans amidst vast suffering and death did not now repeat itself in the Turks' sole remaining Anatolian homeland.

Yet ironically, if on the one hand the Ottoman Empire was acutely vulnerable in 1914, from another perspective its chances of survival were rather better than those of some of its seemingly more powerful rivals. As Colmar von der Goltz had noted in 1897, the loss of the Christian provinces had its beneficial sides. Given the Turks' lack of numbers, the strength of nationalism and the influence of the Christian great powers, it was inconceivable that the Ottomans could long sustain their rule in the Balkans. Left with an empire consisting only of Turks and Arabs, however, they possessed in Islam what every empire craved, namely a supranational ideology of sufficient power and attractiveness to compete successfully with secular ethnic nationalism. In 1914 there was good reason to believe that domestic political stability and the loyalty of the bulk of the population to the caliph and his empire could be preserved.

Von der Goltz, however, left two factors out of the equation. An empire's survival depends crucially on its relationship with the core, majority population. If the latter's elites begin to adopt a narrow ethnic nationalism rather than a broader imperial patriotism, then the empire's stability will be undermined. In the late Ottoman Empire imperial patriotism and emergent Turkish nationalism had to be squared. Ahmed Cevdet Pasha, one of the most intelligent of the late Ottoman statesmen, commented that 'the only thing uniting Arab, Kurd, Albanian and Bosnian is the unity of Islam. Yet the real strength of the Sublime State lies with the Turks.'[29] It is clear that the Young Turks were by nature much better Turkish nationalists and Jacobins than imperial patriots and that, to preserve the empire, they would have to control this instinct and enter into a genuine imperial and Islamic partnership with the Arabs.

Much more important was the grim logic of geopolitics and international power, which was and always had been empire's basic currency. The Ottomans had simply shrunk to too small a territory and population to defend themselves against predators. The weak could not survive forever by playing the predators off against one another, particularly in the context of a European war in which both sides would pressure Constantinople to commit itself to their cause. In 1914 the Ottomans chose the side that lost. Given the ambitions and priorities of the Entente powers, it is probable that the empire would not have survived even had it attempted to remain neutral or chosen the side that eventually won.

5

The Habsburg Empire

A Peripheral, Aristocratic Empire

The Austrian and Russian empires had many similarities. Both were great land empires covering huge territories and ruling over many different peoples. These were quintessentially continental, military and – in their last centuries – bureaucratic empires. Commerce and the oceans were of secondary importance. It is only a slight exaggeration to say that the Russian state possessed no fleet before the reign of Peter I (1689–1725). Between Peter's death and 1917 some Russian rulers did devote considerable resources and attention to the navy, but it was always very much the army's younger brother. The Austrian case was if anything even more extreme. The Habsburgs' only major port was Trieste. Not until 1766 did the Habsburg navy build its first major warship. Attempts to create a Habsburg company for the East Indies quickly came to naught. In Alaska Russia possessed one (rather insignificant) overseas colony. Uniquely among the European powers, Austria never possessed a colony outside Europe. The Emperor Francis Joseph, who ruled from 1848 to 1916, was never seen in naval uniform.

The Russian and Austrian empires had almost precisely the same lifespan. Russia became an empire in the 1550s. In the Austrian case 1526 might be an appropriate choice for the empire's year of birth. In that year, Ferdinand of Austria became king of Bohemia and Hungary, thereby uniting the crowns and territories that were to remain the Habsburg Empire's core throughout its history. Another possible year of birth is 1556, when the Habsburg inheritance was split definitively between the family's 'Spanish' and 'Austrian' branches. Both the Romanov and Habsburg empires were destroyed by the First World War, only twenty months separating the Russian Revolution of March 1917 and the flight of Emperor Charles I, Austria-Hungary's last ruler.

Austria became a genuinely great power between 1683 and 1719. For much of this period her armies were commanded by Prince Eugene of Savoy, probably Europe's finest general in that era. In 1683 Ottoman armies came very close to capturing Vienna. Had they done so and gone on to ravage the core of the dynasty's dominions, Habsburg resources, power and prestige would have plummeted. By 1719 the Ottomans had been smashed, all Hungary and Transylvania and even part of Serbia conquered. Austria also emerged much enlarged and on the whole victorious from the wars against Louis XIV's France, at the time Europe's most powerful country. It was in the same period that Peter I defeated the Swedes, replacing them as the leading power in the Baltic and North-Eastern Europe. For neither Russia nor Austria was their status as European great powers fully secure by 1720. Both, for instance, still lagged some way behind France in this respect. In 1740 the death of the last male Habsburg, Charles VI, unleashed a war which could easily have resulted in the dismemberment of the Habsburg dominions. But by the end of the Seven Years' War in 1763 no one could doubt that Russia and Austria were unequivocally great powers, the equals of France. From that date until the First World War these two empires remained members of the exclusive club of great powers which dominated – even to some extent regulated – the affairs of Europe.

For both the Habsburgs and the Romanovs, being a European great power was hugely important. It was in fact the single overriding priority of both dynasties. The rulers' sense of pride, self-image and legitimacy was linked absolutely and inescapably to the great power status of their dynastic empires. If the dynasty ceased to rule over a great power then the preservation of its throne was barely worthwhile in its monarchs' eyes, and could in any case easily prove impossible in an international environment in which weak states tended to go to the wall. To the extent that Habsburg and Romanov rulers could control the political systems, societies and economies of their empires, they subordinated, shaped and manipulated them to meet the overriding priority of military might and great power status.

The Austrian Monarchy only truly became a state, as distinct from a conglomerate of separate territories, under Maria Theresa (1740–80). Becoming a state meant creating institutions in Vienna which could coordinate policy, together with a hierarchy of offices stretching down to provincial and local levels which could raise revenues sufficient to sustain the army, the bureaucracy, and the communications and supplies on which they depended for their effectiveness. The near-catastrophe of the 1740s, when the Prussians, Bavarians and French almost destroyed the

Monarchy, made this development self-evidently essential. After seizing Silesia from the Habsburgs in the 1740s, King Frederick II of Prussia was immediately able to increase provincial revenue by 50 per cent while actually lessening the tax burden on the population.[1] The key was administrative rationality and efficiency. If Austria was to survive it had to follow the Prussian road. Under Count Haugwitz, Maria Theresa's leading minister in the 1740s and 1750s, it began this process. Maria Theresa's overriding aim in supporting Haugwitz's reform was to create a military and fiscal machine capable of defeating the Prussians and regaining Silesia. Acting in parallel with Haugwitz, Maria Theresa's wily foreign minister, Prince Kaunitz, drew Russia and France into an anti-Prussian coalition which fought Frederick from 1756 to 1762. Despite the military and administrative reforms undertaken from the 1740s, and despite the coalition's great preponderance in numbers and wealth, Prussia survived. One result was a further, more radical round of reforms in Austria, designed to increase the empire's power. Among these reforms was the expropriation of much of the property of the Catholic church and its redirection to the task of mass education. The roots of power were now more fully and intelligently understood than had previously been the case. The failings of the existing education system were seen (correctly) as a key reason why Austria was lagging behind the Protestant powers in administrative efficiency and economic dynamism.

In the nineteenth century Habsburg (and Romanov) rulers continued to subordinate domestic political and economic policies to the requirements of military power and international prestige. The Emperor Francis Joseph came to the throne in 1848. In the first decade of his reign Austria's great objective was the reassertion of its international power and prestige after the humiliating, and indeed almost fatal, weakness revealed during the revolution of 1848–9. The means to achieve this end were, domestically, extreme authoritarian centralization and (supposedly) rationalization of inherited administrative and economic laws and patterns of behaviour: in foreign affairs, a ruthless *Realpolitik*. Defeat against France in 1859 and Prussia in 1866 showed the bankruptcy of these policies and forced a major rethinking.

In the famous Compromise of 1867, Francis Joseph divided his empire in two for most purposes. He handed over to the Magyar elite almost complete control over the internal affairs of the Kingdom of Hungary, more than half of whose population were not ethnic Hungarians. In return the emperor secured the – albeit equivocal – support of the Magyar elite for his empire, a considerable Hungarian contribution to sustain the imperial armed forces, and recognition that foreign and defence policy would remain the almost exclusive concern of the monarch and those officials to whom he chose to turn for advice. The 1867 Compromise was the decisive event in late Habsburg history. It determined much of the empire's domestic policy and some of its foreign policy down to the Monarchy's demise in 1918. Cold and, in the long run, dubious calculations of power drove the emperor to adopt the Compromise. As he wrote to his daughter, 'I do not conceal from myself that the Slav peoples of the monarchy may look on the new policies with distrust, but the government will never be able to satisfy every national group. This is why we must rely on those which are the strongest ... that is, the Germans and the Hungarians.'[2] Relying on 'the strongest' would bring domestic political stability, at least in the short run. Above all, it would allow the emperor the time and resources to renew his challenge to the Prussians, which would make it possible to reverse Austria's humiliating defeat at Königgrätz in 1866 and to ensure that the independent South German states did not fall under Prussian rule. Only with Prussia's defeat of France in 1870–71 and her absorption of the remaining German states did Austria's hopes of revenge disappear.

With Italy united under the House of Savoy and Germany under the Hohenzollerns the Habsburgs' international role was much reduced. The dynasty's traditional claim to status – indeed pre-eminence – in Europe had been its position as provider of the Holy Roman Emperors of the German Nation. For almost four centuries before 1866 in fact as well as in principle it had been the leading dynasty in Germany. For 150 years it had ruled or dominated much of Italy. Now the only field in which it could operate as a great power was the depressingly narrow one of the Balkans. Unlike the other great powers, including even the Italians, the Habsburgs did not have overseas colonies about which they could gloat and around which the peoples of the Austrian and Hungarian halves of the Monarchy might unite in pride and self-interest. Even in Belgium, Walloons and Flemings could share pride and interest in the exploitation of overseas empire. In Austria-Hungary no overseas empire existed to divert attention from rivalry between the nations under the Habsburgs' sceptre or to make up for a sense that the Monarchy's power and status were in decline.

But although the dynasty's role had declined, its basic thinking about power and status had not. To act, and to be seen to act, as a European great power remained Francis Joseph's overriding objective. No doubt the emperor would have believed that failure to act in this way would have doomed the empire to extinction at the hands of foreign predators and their potential allies among the Monarchy's subject peoples. Given the ruthless world of imperialist power politics, Francis Joseph may have been right. Certainly, consciousness of his empire's declining might and prestige helped to convince him that Serbia must be destroyed in 1914. Failure to respond to the Serbian challenge and to the humiliation of Francis Ferdinand's assassination would be to confirm the world's growing assumption that Austria-Hungary had become too weak and pusillanimous to defend its interests or the great power status of its dynasty.

In June 1914 Conrad von Hötzendorf, the Chief of the General Staff, wrote that the coming war might well prove a 'hopeless struggle, but even so it must be, because such an ancient monarchy and such an ancient army cannot perish ingloriously.'[3] This was an echo of the attitudes that had prevailed in ruling circles throughout Francis Joseph's reign. In 1866 it was considered dishonourable to sell or cede Venetia to the House of Savoy without a war but acceptable to do so once thousands of soldiers' lives had been sacrificed in its victorious but politically hopeless defence.[4] At the very outset of his reign in 1848 Francis Joseph had declared that 'we owe it to our honour, to our country, and to our position in Europe as a whole' to fight rather than to compromise and cede territory to the Piedmontese enemy.[5] Here to some extent spoke the logic of great power politics. Prestige, which required a reputation for might and courage, was essential to the defence of one's interests against the predators who roamed the international jungle, and prestige could be earned only by a willingness to defend one's honour sword in hand.

But honour, a concept so dear to Francis Joseph, also reflected the values and mentality of the male, dynastic, aristocratic and military elite that ruled both Habsburg Austria-Hungary and Romanov Russia. In 1914 Austria-Hungary's rulers believed that not just their great power status but also their honour would be undermined if they failed to respond manfully to the Serbian affront. Russian elites believed the same should their Serbian client be abandoned in the face of Austro-Hungarian threats. On both sides there prevailed the ethic of the duel, in which the nobleman defended his honour without concern for the personal risks involved. In the duel between empires, however, it was very much more than the lives of the noble principals that was at risk.

It is of course not at all surprising that Austrian and Russian imperial elites shared similar values and conceptions. They came from the same social and cultural milieux, and had pursued similar lifestyles and 'careers'. They lived within a single pan-European world as regards currents of opinion and accepted norms of behaviour. Even in their earliest origins the two elites had much in common. Both were the descendants of hereditary cavalrymen and landowners, whose original status had been owed to military prowess and to the favour of princes. Before the eighteenth century the isolated, inward-looking, Orthodox warrior-cum-courtier of Muscovy lived in a different world from that of the Austrian magnates with their feudal traditions and their baroque Counter-Reformation culture. But from the 1700s the two elites were subject to the influences of the Enlightenment and Romanticism, and to the challenges of revolution, liberalism, democracy and nationalism. They read the same books, dressed in similar clothes, shared common amusements, and conversed easily with each other in the French language in fashionable salons and spas across the continent. In addition, both elites had to come to terms with the inescapable consequences of the growth of the modern bureaucratic state, and with the competitive logic of the great power rivalry which was the essence of international relations in Europe.

Moreover, the Austrian and Russian empires were not just both European great powers, but also East European. That meant that in both the eighteenth and the nineteenth centuries they were remote from the main centres of European finance, industry and trade. To be sure, Austria was never as remote as Russia in cultural, historical or geographical terms. In the early sixteenth century, when Russia was still largely a world apart, cultured Viennese were part of 'a sort of educated freemasonry stretching from London to the Ottoman frontier.'[6] By the mid-sixteenth century most of the Habsburgs' Czech and German subjects were Protestants. It was the rise of the Atlantic trade routes on the one hand and the triumph of the Counter-Reformation in the Habsburg lands on the other that created a sharp divide between Austria and the countries of Northern and North-Western Europe.

Even in 1700 this divide was not as wide as the gap between Moscow and cities such as Amsterdam or London. Eighteenth-century Austria was much more literate and urbanized than Russia. 'By the end of Maria Theresa's reign the monarchy boasted well over 6,000 schools and 200,000 students.'[7] Largely for this reason, Maria Theresa (1740–80) and Joseph II (1780–90) were able to create an effective provincial bureaucracy which enabled them to put some check on arbitrary noble treatment of the peasantry in the German and Czech provinces. The Russian administration was barely capable of doing this even in the mid-nineteenth century. By that time because the Industrial Revolution's impact had so far been deeply felt only in Britain, Belgium and to some extent northern Germany, the Austrian and Russian empires in relative terms were more backward than had been the case in 1750. By 1914 both empires were catching up again but levels of prosperity, literacy, industry and urbanization in the German and Czech provinces of the Habsburg Empire were far superior to any major region in Russia.

Nevertheless, the basic point is that between 1700 and 1914 both Russia and Austria were poorer and less developed than their great power rivals in North-Western Europe. In the eighteenth century, in Austria as in Russia, ideas, techniques and people were borrowed from Protestant Europe (and to a lesser extent France) in order to close the gap. The rulers of both empires regarded their native languages, German and Russian, as vulgar and somewhat barbaric. French predominated at the Habsburg and Romanov courts, as indeed was the case in Berlin. In the 1740s and 1750s Crown Prince Joseph, heir not only to the Habsburg lands but also to the Holy Roman Empire of the German Nation, was taught Latin, French and Italian. 'The fact that Joseph received no systematic instruction in German literature, and little in German language, is symptomatic of the contempt in which they were held at this period by the upper classes.'[8]

If Vienna and Bohemia might seem very Central European, Galicia, much of Hungary and most of the South Slav provinces looked more like Russia. The historian of Maria Theresa's army wrote that in Hungary's southern borderlands 'the heat, the vegetation, and the vast horizon are a world removed from Western Europe.'[9] Here indeed was to be felt the pull of that endless steppe which dominated so much of Russian life and stretched from Hungary to Mongolia. In nineteenth-century Hungary, as in Russia, the familiar trademarks of backwardness were also evident: the urge to modernize, the shame and resentment of inferiority, the conflicts – often within one and the same person – between an exaggerated cosmopolitanism and an equally exaggerated chauvinism and celebration of simple native virtues. In Hungary, more than in Austria or even Russia, the financial, commercial and industrial bourgeoisie was of alien – usually Jewish or German – origin. Little of the Austrian Empire and almost no part of the Russian Empire (save perhaps Petersburg and the Baltic provinces) was truly 'First World', to use a modern term anachronistically. Both empires were really 'Second World', meaning that they belonged to the less developed eastern, southern and south-western periphery of Europe's economic heartland. Most of the Russian Empire in 1914 was towards the bottom of the Second World in terms of wealth, literacy and industry. More of Hungary and most of Austria was towards the top. But in power-political terms Austria-Hungary could not match Russia's huge natural and human resources, nor the ability of the Russian state to mobilize these resources in the cause of its military might and international status.

In comparison with Russia, the Habsburg Empire had limited room for expansion. Another way of saying the same thing is to note that for most of its history the empire was surrounded by states which were individually of equal or greater power than itself, and which also on occasions formed formidable anti-Habsburg coalitions. Until well into the seventeenth century the Austrian Habsburgs could not easily match the Ottoman Empire on their southern border without the assistance of allied states. By the end of the seventeenth century this was no longer the case, and in the following decades the Habsburgs reconquered and recolonized all of Hungary and Transylvania. Important though it was, this acquisition could never hope to match the vast potential resources that Russia acquired through its annexation of Siberia, Ukraine and the huge Eurasian steppe. Although in principle Ottoman decline made further advance to the south possible, in fact the only major acquisition of Balkan territory after 1750 was Bosnia-Herzegovina. This restraint is explained by the considerations that Balkan land and resources were not in general very valuable, that their acquisition carried the near-certainty of antagonizing Russia, and that bringing ever more Orthodox South Slavs into the empire did not seem sensible to the German and, still less, Magyar elites that dominated the Monarchy.

Once Poland had been removed from the map by the late eighteenth-century partitions Austria bordered directly on Russia. At no time between 1800 and 1914 could the Habsburgs have expected realistically to emerge victorious from a war without allies against the Romanovs. To the west lay France: in the seventeenth, eighteenth and early nineteenth centuries Habsburg and French armies clashed frequently in Italy and southern Germany. The struggle was not an equal one. Not until the eve of the revolution of 1789 did the Monarchy's population almost equal France's, and even then it was on average considerably poorer. Between 1792 and 1814 the balance was further tilted in France's favour by annexations in the Rhineland and Italy. By 1812 the imbalance was again so great that it was approaching the position of 1700, when the Habsburg monarch ruled over less than half as many subjects as the French king. On the eve of the War of the Spanish Succession (i.e. 1700) Habsburg revenues were one-eighth of France's, though failure to measure respective costs can make such direct comparisons a little misleading.[10]

To the north Austria's great rival from the 1740s to the 1870s was Prussia. For all this period Prussian potential resources and revenues were much inferior to those of the Habsburgs. In 1788, for example, Vienna had double Berlin's revenues and 50 per cent more soldiers. In the nineteenth century, however, the north German economy industrialized more quickly than the Austrian one. More important, the Prussians usually mobilized and utilized their military and fiscal resources more efficiently, ruthlessly and intelligently than the Austrians. Between 1500 and 1914 the Ottomans besieged Vienna twice, the French captured it twice, and the Prussians came within range of doing so both in the mid-eighteenth century and in 1866. The Austrians never reached Constantinople or Berlin, and only got to Paris in 1814 in alliance with the Russians, Prussians and British.

Austria's geopolitical position and relative weakness therefore made alliances essential for most of its history. Before the mid-seventeenth century its great ally was the senior branch of the Habsburg family, enthroned in Madrid and ruling over a vast empire both in Europe and across the oceans. With the decline of Spain and of the family alliance after 1648 the position of the Austrian Habsburgs became critical. An isolated Monarchy was now the main bulwark against the westward expansion of France and the northward expansion of the Ottoman Empire. To make matters worse, a loose informal alliance linked Paris to Constantinople. When 100,000 Ottoman troops and a horde of auxiliaries advanced on Vienna in 1683 they swept aside the 36,000 soldiers which were all the Habsburgs could place in their path. Besieged Vienna was saved in the nick of time by a Christian army only one-third of which was made up of the Habsburgs' own troops. German and Polish forces rallied to the emperor's support in order to defend Christian civilization and keep the Ottomans out of Central Europe. Neither for the first nor for the last time Austria prospered by convincing other powers that its survival served both their interests and pan-European needs and values. Charles Ingrao rightly comments that 'patterns of Habsburg statecraft that later became associated with Clemens von Metternich, such as coalition and balance of power diplomacy and the maintenance of legitimate frontiers, were already evident by the seventeenth century.'[11]

In the war against France during the first half of the eighteenth century Austria relearned both the necessity and the frustrations of coalition warfare. Victory over Louis XIV in the War of the Spanish Succession would have been inconceivable without English and Dutch support, which was given generously since both powers feared French domination of Europe. Without this backing in the 1730s War of the Polish Succession Austria was defeated by France and its allies. In the 1740s

Maria Theresa's British and Dutch paymasters did come to her rescue but at the price of imposing on her their priorities (war against France) rather than allowing her to pursue her major interest and goal, namely the recovery of Silesia from the king of Prussia. Austrian coalition diplomacy was never more brilliant than in the 1750s when it succeeded in luring Petersburg and Paris into a war of extermination against Prussia that served Austria's interests much better than those of Russia, let alone France. But a coalition rooted in this reality had difficulty sustaining unity and commitment under the strains of war. At least as important, and very typically, Austria's own armies lacked the Prussian-style ruthlessness to drive home their advantage against the outnumbered and cornered forces of Frederick II.

Joseph II, who shared power with his mother from 1765 and ruled alone from 1780, greatly admired Frederick and tried to emulate his methods. As was usually the case, however, Habsburg efforts to abandon conservative principles and pursue a policy of Machiavellian *Realpolitik* rebounded to their disadvantage. Most of the independent princes of the Holy Roman Empire allied with Frederick II against Joseph because they feared the latter's expansionist ambitions and because they knew that the reforms carried out since 1740 had made Austria potentially a good deal more powerful than much smaller and less populous Prussia. In 1793–1814 this judgement was shown to be correct. Austria fought for twice as long against revolutionary and Napoleonic France as either Prussia or Russia. In 1809 the Archduke Charles won the first clear-cut victory of a continental power over Napoleon. Ultimate defeat in successive wars against France in this period bankrupted Austria and deprived her of important territory. But after the single crushing defeat of 1806–7 Prussia ceased to be a great power and risked being wiped from the map. Nevertheless, the wars also made evident Austria's inferiority to Russia. Far more easily and for far longer than the Austrian emperor, the Russian tsar could afford to stand aside as the French advanced into Italy and even western Germany. When forced to fight he could use his empire's vast territory as a defensive weapon. Napoleon reached Vienna twice, shortly thereafter destroying the main Austrian army. He reached Moscow once and annihilated his own army in the process.

Austria emerged as one of the key victors in 1813–14, regaining her lost territory and becoming the dominant power in Italy and the predominant one in Germany. But the extent of her commitments now exceeded her resources. This was particularly true because Austrian finances had been devastated by two decades of war and because in the period 1815–48 the Austrian economy lagged seriously behind not just industrialized Britain but also an industrializing northern Germany. The key guarantor of Austria's status and territory was Russia, which Metternich kept loyal to the Austrian alliance partly by persuading Russian rulers of this alliance's crucial importance in sustaining peace and conservative stability against the threat of Jacobin revolution and the international anarchy which would surely follow, as it had in the two decades of war after 1792. In 1848–50 the value of this Russian guarantee was made clear. Russian armies intervened against the Hungarian revolution. Russian pressure forced Berlin to retreat from any challenge to Austrian pre-eminence in Germany.

Unfortunately, the lesson that the new young emperor, Francis Joseph, and his advisers preferred to learn from 1848 was that the dynasty had been saved by its army. A policy of *Realpolitik* and of reliance on military force would therefore serve best to defend the empire's status and restore its shaken prestige in foreign affairs. In 1853 when Russian troops occupied much of present-day Romania in order to put pressure on the Ottoman Sultan, Vienna was in a difficult situation. The Danube was a key Austrian commercial artery and, in addition, any major increase in Russian influence in the Balkans would reduce Austria's hold on the peoples and governments who lived just on the other side of its own southern frontier. Nevertheless, Austrian policy during the Crimean War of 1854–6 was one of catastrophic stupidity. By siding aggressively with Britain and France, and threatening the tsar with war, Vienna destroyed its alliance with Russia and made Petersburg Austria's unremitting enemy for the following twenty years, during which crucial changes occurred in European power politics, all of them to the Habsburgs' disadvantage. Austria threatened war in 1854–6 but in the end did not fight on the allied side, which won her the dislike of London and Paris. In fact, however, nothing that Austria could have done in the Crimean War would have secured a British or French guarantee of Austria's pre-eminence in Germany and Italy. In 1859 and 1866 she fought without any great power allies against first France then Prussia and lost. In 1870, when given the opportunity to ally with France to revenge herself on Prussia, awareness that Austrian involvement would almost certainly bring Russian intervention on Prussia's side was a major disincentive to action.

To do it justice, Austria's military leadership was appalled by Vienna's diplomacy in 1854–6. 'The policy which the Austrian government pursued during the Crimean War was flatly contrary to the opinion of the army and led precisely to the result which they had so feared – namely to the Danube Monarchy's isolation in foreign affairs. The army's faith in Austrian foreign policy was minimal.'[12] It was only a pity that Francis

Joseph's faith in the military leadership and in the army's effectiveness was not equally low. In the war against Napoleon III and the kingdom of Piedmont in 1858–9, the Austrian infantry was better armed than the French but failed to train its soldiers in the tactics appropriate to its weapons, 'believing it all but impossible to teach uneducated peasant recruits to measure ranges and aim fire at moving targets.' After 1859 the Austrians might have been expected to learn the lessons of modern warfare better than the Prussians, who had not fought a great power since 1814. In addition, in 1866 Francis Joseph ruled over 34 million subjects, his Prussian rival over 19 million. Almost all the other German states fought on Austria's side though admittedly, with the exception of Saxony, they did so with great inefficiency. Inadequate finance was certainly not the problem. Because after 1848 the army was the regime's favourite and no parliamentary bodies existed to check the emperor's budgetary priorities, the 1850s was 'a decade of unprecedently heavy military spending.'[13]

But a military bureaucracy uncontrolled from outside spent money foolishly and, in part, on itself. Tactical training was neglected and out-of-date, strategic railways were not built, and – above all – senior commanders and their staff officers were not forced to think intelligently about the ways in which increased numbers and better educated soldiers, new weapons and new communications technology were transforming contemporary warfare. The Prussians won in 1866 not because their country was economically more developed or more effectively embodied German nationalist principles but because their officers – and above all their staff officers – were encouraged to think harder about their profession. For this Francis Joseph himself must bear some of the blame. It was after all he who had written that 'the strength of an army lies less in educated officers than in loyal and chivalrous ones.'[14]

Isolated and without great power allies from 1856 until the 1870s, in 1879 Austria found security in its alliance with Europe's greatest military power, namely its old foe Prussia-Germany. Once again the Austrians succeeded in persuading a more powerful state that their well-being was in its essential interests. As had often been the case in the past, the basic reason why they could pull off this feat was because their arguments were correct. The German government realized that the collapse of the Habsburgs would create a huge vacuum in Central Europe which would threaten the whole European balance of power. It would also inevitably lead to bloodshed between the many peoples, mostly Slav or German, of the former empire. For both geopolitical and domestic political reasons Germany and Russia were almost certain to be dragged into the conflict on opposite sides. Given French enmity towards Germany since 1871,

Paris was equally certain to join in a Russo-German war on Petersburg's side. In any case the French could not afford the risk that German defeat of Russia would make Berlin the invincible hegemon of all continental Europe. Even if Germany emerged victorious from such a conflict, the results of victory might well turn to ashes in its rulers' hands. The last thing that Prussian elites desired would be the almost certain result of such a victory – namely, union with millions of Catholic Austrian-Germans and the creation of a Catholic majority in the Hohenzollerns' empire.

Although some of these factors counted only in Berlin, most European statesmen (including even most Russian diplomats) understood the appalling consequences for peace and stability of the Habsburg Empire's demise, and did not desire it. This did not of course stop the Russian and Italian governments in particular from often pursuing policies which were dangerous for Austrian interests. Moreover, precisely because Vienna was linked to Berlin by domestic political and cultural ties, the British increasingly saw it as a mere appendage to Germany, and to the German threat to dominate Europe. By 1914 a combination of factors, both international and domestic, were inclining Austria's rulers away from caution and convervatism and towards a renewed appeal to force and *Realpolitik* to assert their power within the empire and their prestige and influence outside it. As was usually the case with Austria, the radical appeal to aggression and force proved a disaster. The army's leaders bungled operations in 1914 and proved incapable of fulfilling their promises of quick victory. A war on three fronts ensued, which ended in the empire's disintegration.

A CONGLOMERATE OF CROWNLANDS

To make any sense of Austria's international position or foreign policy, however, it is essential to see both within the context of the Monarchy's domestic politics. The basic fact about the Habsburg Empire was that it was a conglomerate of separate territorial units, most of which had deep-rooted and powerful individual indentities. Many of these identities were very ancient. The two most important territories ruled by the Habsburgs were the Kingdom of Hungary (Crown of St Stephen) and the Kingdom of Bohemia (Crown of St Wenceslas). The Kingdom of Hungary was vital because by the nineteenth century it included almost half of the empire. The Kingdom of Bohemia was smaller but it had always been – and remained to the end – the most economically advanced region of the empire and the greatest source of state revenue. Without Bohemia or

Hungary a Habsburg Empire could not exist and could never have existed. But when the Habsburgs acquired these two kingdoms in 1526 both of them already had a history which stretched back over half a millennium. Their institutions and their identity were very well established both in fact and in the minds of the two kingdoms' elites. Hungary for instance had its Magna Carta, the Aurea Bulla of 1222. In Stephen Werboczy's *Tripartium*, published in 1517, it had its definitive interpretation and exegesis of the ancient constitution, to which Hungarian elites accorded near-biblical status. It had boundaries 'relatively unchanged for centuries' before the Ottoman sixteenth-century conquests.[15] It had representative estates, in other words a parliament, which were dominated by the nobility (itself almost 5 per cent of the population) and which played a more crucial role in governing the realm than the king. Even in the sixteenth century, let alone subsequently, the Hungarian parliament was more powerful than any of the equivalent estates in other Habsburg lands. But as often happens in empires, all the territories tended to draw inspiration from the one whose autonomy vis-à-vis the centre was greatest. 'The autonomy of the Hungarian diet was always a model for the other estates in the Habsburg lands.'[16]

The separate kingdoms, duchies and counties ('crownlands') over which the Habsburgs ruled were originally feudal polities. Within such polities royal power was anything but absolute. Below the central level almost all authority was exercised by feudal landowning nobles, by the church, and by semi-autonomous towns, to the extent that the latter existed. King and noble were linked by a mutually binding contract. A right of resistance to an unjust and arbitrary ruler might or might not be written into the fundamental law – as it was in Hungary – but it was always implicit. New laws and all taxes required the consent of the estates, whose power would be all the greater if their monarch ruled over many such polities and was necessarily an absentee in most of them. To a great extent the estates, together with the king, were the polity. They defined its borders and its identity. This identity was a political one. In its traditional and now anachronistic sense the 'nation' in this region meant those groups represented in the estates, and therefore above all the nobility: the Hungarian 'nation', for example, really meant little more than the nobility.

Neither in Hungary nor in Bohemia did language or ethnicity have much to do with this definition. In the eighteenth century many Hungarian nobles were not ethnic Magyars and did not speak the Magyar language. Latin was the language of parliament and government. But the nobility's commitment to their kingdom's ancient constitution and territorial integrity, of which they of course were the chief beneficiaries, was total and remained so until 1918 and beyond. By the nineteenth century the Bohemian aristocracy was less formidable an obstacle to the Habsburgs than its Hungarian counterpart, partly because it was almost entirely made up of wealthy magnates, by tradition closely linked to the Habsburg court and without the long history of fierce antagonism to Vienna which marked much of the Hungarian lesser nobility, whose more formidable autonomist representatives were often Protestants. Nevertheless the Bohemian magnates were very committed to the territorial integrity and historical rights of the Kingdom of St Wenceslas, with which the traditions of their own families were intertwined.

In the nineteenth century, for the first time, the concept of the 'nation' came unequivocally to mean the entire people and to define itself in ethnic and linguistic terms. The conflicts between such nations became the greatest domestic problem for the Habsburg Empire. The existence of the ancient crownlands, with their historic borders and identities, greatly complicated this problem. A crownland's borders, even historically, were very seldom those of an ethnically defined nation. In the nineteenth century massive migration caused by urbanization and industrialization further muddied the picture in the Austrian crownlands. In Hungary matters were also confused by large-scale Slav colonization of the kingdom's depopulated southern regions after their reconquest from the Ottomans in the early eighteenth century. Historical and ethnic claims to territory clashed, while partition was ruled out by the elites' commitment to the territorial integrity of the crownland. Nor by the late nineteenth century was this commitment confined to the traditional elites alone. For all nationalists, here as elsewhere in the world, all the lands within the historical boundaries of the kingdom became sacred national soil. This sentiment was particularly strong among Hungarians and Czechs because, in their minds, historical, ethnic and linguistic identities and borders could easily merge. The kingdoms of St Stephen and St Wenceslas had always been associated with Magyar and Czech culture and tradition. These crownlands were the only ancestral home of the two peoples. Particularly for the Hungarians, there was no broader national identity into which loyalty to the crownland could be subsumed. But even where this was the case, as in the German-speaking crownlands, provincial identity could sometimes be intense right down to 1918. After the Monarchy's collapse, for example, the Tyrolese parliament preferred the preservation of provincial unity even at the price of absorption into much-despised Italy to its only alternative, which was partition between Italy and the new Austrian Republic.[17]

Before the seventeenth century the Habsburgs themselves regarded their crownlands as basically separate entities. The dynasty's patrimony was divided up among the ruler's sons. Only biological chance resulted in the reunification of all the crownlands in the person of Archduke Ferdinand of Styria (Ferdinand II) in the early seventeenth century. More important, most of the Habsburg crownlands came to the dynasty by marriage and inheritance, not by conquest. They therefore came with all their historic constitutions and privileges intact. When monarchs were elected, as was initially the case in both Bohemia and Hungary, the constraints on royal power went ever deeper. By the eighteenth century, even in Hungary, the principle of heredity was accepted but no Magyar regarded a Habsburg as his true king until he had been crowned in Budapest. The coronation service embodied oaths that bound the ruler to the ancient constitution and territorial integrity of St Stephen's Kingdom.

On a number of occasions the Habsburgs seized the opportunity offered by unsuccessful rebellions to declare crownlands conquered territory and to abrogate their inherited constitutions. This happened after the defeat of the Bohemians at the Battle of White Mountain in 1618 and after the crushing of the Hungarian rebellions of the 1660s and 1848–9. These revolts were followed by Habsburg efforts to unify and homogenize the whole Monarchy.

In the seventeenth century the great force for homogenization was the Catholic Counter-Reformation. By the 1580s, the majority both of the aristocracy and of the mass of the population in most crownlands were Protestants. In an astonishingly successful counter-offensive spearheaded by the dynasty, the church and the Jesuits, first the magnate class and then the masses were won back for Catholicism. In an era and region in which religion mattered more than language or ethnicity, the Habsburg Counter-Reformation created a distinct and separate identity for the Monarchy. This identity encompassed a specific education and mentality, a very un-Protestant attitude towards the intellect and the senses, and a distinct, original and superb style in baroque art, architecture and music which clearly labelled the separate cultural world of the Austrian Habsburgs. But there was one vital, albeit partial, exception to the triumph of the Counter-Reformation and this was Hungary. Though almost all the Hungarian magnates and the bulk of the population were reconverted to Catholicism, fierce armed resistance forced the Habsburgs to recognize and tolerate Magyar Protestantism, which was particularly strong among the county gentry (i.e. lesser nobility) of the eastern provinces and Transylvania.

In the eighteenth and nineteenth centuries homogenization and unification took more secular and administrative forms. The process began under Maria Theresa with the creation of a single, centralized system of rule and a single bureaucracy for the Austrian and Czech crownlands. Caution and, perhaps, a lingering recognition of Magyar loyalty in the dynasty's crisis of 1741–2 held the empress back from imposing this system on Hungary. Her son, Joseph II, proved less reticent. In the 1780s he abolished the historic self-governing counties, divided Hungary into 'rational' administrative districts, and imposed rule from Vienna by officials appointed by the crown, whose efforts at radical reform of noble-peasant relations infuriated the Hungarian elites. In a way that was later to be echoed by many colonial oligarchies, the Magyar nobility used the democratic rhetoric of the American and French revolutions to defend its own privileges, its oppression of the Hungarian peasantry, and its monopoly of power. The strength of Hungarian resistance forced Joseph's successor, Leopold II, to withdraw his brother's reforms but after the 1848 rebellion there came a renewed drive to centralize government in Vienna and to impose all-imperial principles of rule on the Hungarians. No regime that governed in the teeth of the ancient constitution could be legitimate in the Hungarian elite's eyes, however, and true political stability in the kingdom was impossible in the face of the Magyar nobility's opposition. This was particularly the case since the emperor wished to concentrate his attention and his armed forces on the struggle with Prussia for influence in Germany, and since the Habsburg regime proved unwilling or unable to mobilize the Slav and Romanian minorities of the Hungarian Kingdom against its Magyar social elite. The result was Francis Joseph's compromise with the Magyar elite in 1867 and his agreement to be crowned as constitutional king of Hungary, with all the constraints on royal power that this entailed.

Hungary's unique position within the Monarchy, its successful defence of its autonomy, was owed not just to the formidable powers of resistance of the Magyar nobility but also to external geopolitical factors. Every empire has its rebellious provinces. Revolt is often sparked by the centre's need to control outlying provinces more fully and to exploit their resources more effectively in the cause of the empire's military power. A province's ability to resist such pressure will depend crucially on the existence or otherwise of outside support. In this respect the Hungarians were fortunate. The Habsburg Empire was surrounded by powerful rivals happy to exploit its domestic problems. In the seventeenth century Vienna knew that Hungarian rebels could count on the support of the Ottomans, whose empire at that time included most of historic Hungary and the autonomous, Hungarian-ruled principality of Transylvania. In

1790 and in the 1860s armed Prussian support could be guaranteed for Hungarian opponents of Habsburg centralization. Both in 1790 and in 1867 Vienna's concessions to the Magyars owed much to awareness of this danger.

THE PEOPLES AND THE STATE

The 1867 Compromise reconciled most of the Magyar elite to the Habsburg Empire, even if their loyalty was pragmatic and tactical rather than heartfelt. As regards other nationalities, however, the last decades of the Monarchy saw increasing danger that domestic opponents of Habsburg rule would link up with the empire's foreign enemies. The links between domestic and foreign policy became even tighter and more dangerous than in the past. Among the Habsburgs' subjects foreign policy became a more divisive issue than had previously been the case, partly because of the growing hold of nationalism on the population and partly too because, as education spread, more people took an interest in politics in general and foreign policy in particular. Many politicians saw a close connection, at least potentially, between the empire's foreign policy and their own nationality's position within the Monarchy.

For the Hungarians, hostility to Russia was the empire's main *raison d'être*. In 1870 Count Andrassy, Hungary's leading statesman and the Monarchy's future foreign minister, commented that 'like everyone else in Hungary, I consider collision between Austria-Hungary and Russia to be an inevitable event.'[18] The Hungarians had not forgiven Russian intervention to suppress their revolution in 1849. Much more to the point, Magyars made up roughly only half the population of the Kingdom of Hungary and were greatly outnumbered by Slavs in East-Central Europe as a whole. They were acutely aware of the fact that behind these Slavs might stand Russia, a Slav great power whose population and resources were infinitely greater than Hungary's. Unloved and irksome though the Habsburg Empire might be to most Hungarians, their leaders believed it was a geopolitical necessity if Magyars were to survive in a hostile world. Only with the revolutions of 1917 and Russia's seeming extinction as a great power did this key reason for Hungarian elites' allegiance to the Habsburgs lose its strength.

Budapest saw the Germans, and in particular German liberals, as its main allies within the Monarchy. German liberals too viewed tsarist Russia as the chief external threat to German interests and European liberal values. Just as Magyars dominated the Kingdom of St Stephen, so Germans were the leading people in the Monarchy's other half in terms of wealth, culture, power and status. There was little affection between the German and Hungarian peoples of the empire but many of their leaders believed that only in unison could they preserve their pre-eminence within the Habsburg Monarchy. They also tended to see the 'Dual Alliance' with Germany, first signed in 1879, as the essential guarantee of this pre-eminence throughout East-Central Europe against Russia and the Slavs. For the Austrian Germans the Dual Alliance also satisfied their sense of cultural and ethnic solidarity with their German cousins in the Hohenzollern Reich. Just as the twentieth-century Anglo-American alliance was based on cultural solidarity as well as geopolitical interest, so too was the Dual Alliance between Vienna and Berlin. Indeed, for those of the Habsburgs' subjects who inclined towards German nationalism, the Dual Alliance was an inadequate but nevertheless important compensation for their exclusion from the German national Reich that Bismarck had constructed in 1871.

For many of the Monarchy's Slavs such views were anathema. As far back as 1848 Czech leaders had stressed that the Monarchy's main purpose was to preserve East-Central Europe from either German or Russian domination. As a small people, the Czechs knew that they stood no chance of preserving their independence alone against the two potential master-peoples of Europe. They needed the Habsburgs to protect them. But this protection was only truly valuable if it allowed the Czechs to preserve their culture and live in equality with the other peoples of the Habsburg empire. Conflicts with Germans within the Monarchy helped to incline the Czechs towards sympathy with Russia. The same was even more true of many of the South Slavs who lived under Hungarian rule. As this rule became more oppressive in the Monarchy's last decades and Pan-Slav sympathies therefore inevitably grew, so the vicious circle reinforced itself and Hungarian hostility to Russia was encouraged.

In these circumstances a genuinely popular foreign policy which would unite the peoples of the Monarchy was impossible. In everyday terms, and above all in peacetime, this mattered little. Foreign policy was made by the emperor and a tiny circle of advisers. The day-to-day impact of public opinion on policy-making was minimal. However, given the power of the Germans and Magyars within the empire, major long-term constraints on foreign policy did exist. The abandonment of the Dual Alliance and the pursuit of a consistently pro-Russian orientation was inconceivable. But for much of the period 1873–1908 a policy of cautious compromise with Russia prevailed, relatively friendly relations with Petersburg having the added advantage of reducing Vienna's dependence on Berlin. In any case, in normal circumstances foreign policy impinged very little on the life of the ordinary citizen. Conflict over the language of instruction in local schools was far more likely to inspire nationalist passions.

The secret workings of great power diplomacy always entailed the danger of war, however. At that point foreign policy and alliance systems would impinge hugely on the lives of ordinary people. The strains of modern war might, if conflict was prolonged, demand a level of public unity and commitment which would not come easily to the Habsburg Empire. The Dual Alliance ensured that all the Habsburgs' subjects would fight alongside Germany in an all-European war whose outcome would probably decide whether the German Reich would dominate the continent. If victory in such a war did not come quickly and its participants were given time for reflection, many of them might easily conclude that they had little interest in such an outcome, especially since the victory of the Hohenzollern Reich must inevitably strengthen the position of Germans and Magyars within the Habsburg Monarchy.

In 1914–18 these issues became extremely important. Before the war they loomed much less large, though the government was worried about the prospects of wartime disaffection among the Slavs and Romanians, and indeed rather exaggerated its likely dimensions. In the last peacetime decades of Austria-Hungary's existence these fears were linked to the so-called 'irredentist' problem, the existence outside the Monarchy of a number of nations that might act as a magnet to their fellow-nationals within Austria, drawing their loyalty away from the Habsburgs.

It was a fundamental weakness of the Habsburg Empire that, of its eleven major peoples in 1914, only five lived exclusively within the empire's borders. In each of the other six cases (Germans, Italians, Poles, Romanians, Ruthenes and Serbs), the majority of the people concerned actually lived outside the Monarchy. Of these six peoples neither the Poles nor the Ruthenes had an independent state of their own and neither showed any inclination to leave the Monarchy, though their conflict over language, education, jobs and power in Galicia added an extra twist to the Austrian nationalities problem.

The Italians did have a nation state to which to look and most Italians would no doubt have voted to join it if given the option. Since this was obviously not a possibility, save as a result of a European war, most Italians got on with more pressing daily business, which on the Adriatic coast included defence of their traditional pre-eminence in economics, culture and local politics against the Slovenes and the Croats. As the latter became more educated and migrated into towns and industry, the Italians' position was threatened in a manner very similar to what was happening to German urban and elite minorities in Slav-majority crownlands further east. Meanwhile in the Alpine region, and above all Tyrol, Germans and Italians were in direct conflict over the issues of language, jobs, education and power – in other words the usual sources of national discord in the Monarchy at the time. Because the Italian districts of the Monarchy were the obvious targets for the Italian nation state's future expansionist ambitions they were a complicating factor in Austria's foreign policy. Despite the Triple Alliance (Germany–Austria–Italy), Vienna did not trust Rome and, sensibly as it turned out, made plans to defend itself against Italian attack. When this attack came in 1915, however, it was not an unmitigated disaster for Vienna. Though it further strained already overstretched Austrian resources, it provided the empire with an enemy whom most of its peoples could loathe for their wartime betrayal, and which the Austrian army could defeat now as surely as it had done in 1866 and 1848, thereby contributing to military morale. In addition, well-publicized Italian annexationist aims were a reminder to the Slovenes and even Croats that there were much worse fates than being a Habsburg subject.

The Serb and Romanian problems were in some respects similar. In the last decades of the nineteenth century Serbia and Romania had been allies, and in the Serbian case clients, of Vienna. In the twentieth century the growing strength of nationalism in both countries made this difficult to sustain. Serb and Romanian victory in the Balkan Wars of 1912–13 increased the territory, resources, self-confidence and ambitions of the two kingdoms. The Romanian and Serb lands within the Monarchy were their obvious next target for expansion. In 1914 the Romanian state was less unequivocally hostile to Vienna than was the case with Serbia, because Romania resented Russian rule in Romanian-majority Bessarabia as much as Hungarian rule in Romanian-majority Transylvania. In addition, the majority of the Romanian population in Transylvania were Uniates with a strong sense of provincial identity and a certain feeling of distance therefore from the Romanian kingdom.[19]

Among the Serbians attitudes were much less equivocal. The Karageorgević regime, in power since 1903, was strongly pro-Russian. Serbia, or at least some key Serbian officers, sustained a terrorist movement in (Austrian) Bosnia-Herzegovina whose most famous victim was the Archduke Francis Ferdinand. Strong Hungarian discrimination against Slavs and Romanians over jobs, language and education helped to poison relations. Given the power of nationalism, probably no policy pursued by the Monarchy would have stopped Serbs or many Romanians wanting to unite with their own nation-state on the other side of the border. But perhaps had Hungarian discrimination been less extreme, so also might have been Slav and Romanian antagonism. Certainly, only foolish policies in Budapest and Vienna could have induced the Catholic and traditionally loyal Croats to look with some favour on the possibility of a South Slav federation with the Orthodox Serbs. Meanwhile the mere existence of the independent Romanian and Serb kingdoms ensured the survival of the two peoples' high culture and made the goal of Magyarizing the Monarchy's Romanian and Serb subjects even more difficult than would otherwise have been the case. The growing strength and self-confidence of these two kingdoms also inevitably had an impact on their fellow-nationals in Hungary.

But the most interesting and potentially the most important irredenta was the German. The Germans were the largest, much the richest, and historically the leading people in the Monarchy. They tended to take German economic and cultural domination within the Monarchy for granted. They regarded the Habsburg state as largely their own creation and as existing, in part, to bring German culture and German-style modernity to the more backward peoples of the region. Before 1866 the Habsburgs' German subjects had no doubt that they belonged to the German nation. Except for the relatively small minority of Germans who lived in the Hungarian Kingdom (1.95 million in 1880),[20] they were citizens of the German Confederation, created in 1815 as successor to the old Holy Roman Empire of the German Nation. To be sure, the Confederation like the former Empire was a rather insubstantial creation but it was the only all-German political entity in existence and the Austrian German was as much its member as the Saxon or the Prussian. Indeed, since his monarch was the president of this Confederation he was perhaps its senior member.

In 1866–71 all this changed. Bismarck created a new German Reich from which the Austrian Germans were excluded. After the victories of 1866–71 this Reich was bathed in military glory. Between 1871 and 1914 it became the pre-eminent economic power in Europe. Clearly the new Reich was the dominant German community in Europe and hopes for the Germans' future global influence were pinned on it. Moreover, after 1866 Austrian Germans suffered a number of other blows to their traditional identity and self-esteem. In 1867 half the Monarchy was handed over to the unchecked domination of the Magyar nobility. The German community in Hungary, abandoned to its fate by the imperial government, was one of the major victims of Magyarization, even if in some cases its assimilation of Hungarian language and culture was voluntary. By 1900–14 even the absolute number of Germans in Hungary was in decline owing to assimilation and emigration. Meanwhile, in the non-Hungarian half of the Monarchy (usually referred to by the shorthand name Cisleithenia) the Germans were also under pressure. They were still much the richest group in the region. On the eve of the First World War they comprised 35.8 per cent of Cisleithenia's population and paid 63 per cent of its direct taxes.[21] But they were losing, or had lost, control over many towns and even whole crownlands which they had traditionally dominated. Prague was a good case in point. Traditionally a German town in language, appearance and culture, it was increasingly swamped by Czech immigrants in the second half of the nineteenth century. By 1910 there was not a single German left on the city council.[22] Not surprisingly, the German community's politics, especially in mixed nationality crownlands, was often an unlovely combination of traditional cultural arrogance with hysteria about the threat to its identity and status offered by Slav numbers, migration and increasing self-confidence.

Not at all surprisingly, many Austrian Germans were enthusiastic about the new German Reich. In 1871, noting this fact, Count Andrassy warned Francis Joseph that it would be fatal to pursue internal policies in Cisleithenia which further antagonized the Austrian Germans. If this were done, 'the Austro-Germans would then turn to the forces of German democracy, which would tear the national banner out of the hands of Prince Bismarck and carry it forward until the whole German race was united.'[23] Andrassy's comments were not those of a neutral observer. The Magyar elite, of which he was a leading representative, saw German domination of Cisleithenia as essential to keeping the Monarchy's Slavs in their place. In particular, plans for 'trialism', in other words for giving the Crown of St Wenceslas (i.e. Bohemia and Moravia) the same sort of autonomy as the Crown of St Stephen, were anathema to the Hungarians since they would dilute their influence in Vienna (one out of three territories rather than one out of two) and would set very dangerous precedents for the Hungarian Kingdom's Slav minority. Nevertheless, in the end Andrassy's prediction, a logical one in a nationalist and increasingly democratic era, was to come true in Hitlerian form, and it is important to ask why this prophecy remained unfulfilled before 1914.

One key reason, already mentioned, was that the Protestant, Prussian and anti-democratic elites who dominated the Second Reich loathed the prospect of incorporating the Austrian Germans. Another reason was that the absorption of the Austrian Germans into the Reich, which would have transformed the European balance of power, was most unlikely to occur in peacetime and without the support of one or more of the great powers. But a third reason, at least as important, was that the Austrian Germans were a divided community with many conflicting loyalties and identities. Most of them were by no means ready to abandon the Habsburg Empire.

To make any sense of the very complicated roles and identities of the Austrian Germans, two basic points have to be remembered. Firstly, on the eve of the Great War they comprised only 23.4 per cent of the Monarchy's population. Secondly, they were in no sense a nation, let alone a ruling nation.

Demography is crucial to the history of modern empire. In 1900 the German Empire was overwhelming German in ethnic composition. It was in fact a nation state. It was not entirely unrealistic for Englishmen to believe that imperial federation could turn the White empire into a Great British nation, nor for Russian elites to hope to transform their empire's core into a Russian nation state. No one could imagine, however, that a Habsburg Empire less than one quarter of whose population was German could be transformed into any form or version of a nation. Nor was it possible by the second half of the nineteenth century to rule the Habsburg Empire by resting on the support only of the 23 per cent of the population who were German, let alone the much smaller percentage who belonged to the German elites.

At first glance this might seem a strange statement since many empires in history, including for instance British rule in India, have rested on a much narrower base than this. But these empires were populated overwhelmingly by peasant communities from which alien rulers extracted a tribute partly by playing divide-and-rule among local elites. The Habsburgs certainly were no strangers to divide-and-rule, but by the last third of the nineteenth century their empire was increasingly literate and urbanized: some of its peoples were already on the way to becoming nations in the full meaning of the word. In particular the formidable Magyar elite – united, large, politically astute and self-confident – was not easily gainsaid. The need to co-opt this elite was the logic behind the Compromise of 1867. By adding the 10 million (in 1910) Magyars to the 12 million Germans as 'satisfied', 'ruling' peoples, the Habsburg Empire was based, in principle, on the support of 44 per cent of the population, which was almost precisely the percentage of Great Russians in the tsarist Empire.

Nevertheless, to base an empire even on 44 per cent of the population, potentially dooming 56 per cent to second-class status, was no guarantee of political stability. In any case two dominant peoples were less easily managed than one, particularly given Magyar intransigence, suspicion and chauvinism. Budapest's relationship with Vienna even after 1867 was very difficult and did much to weaken the empire. Moreover, even within post-1867 Cisleithenia, where they were 35 per cent of the population, the Germans found it difficult to sustain their traditional dominance. The main problem here was the Czechs, who made up 23 per cent of Cisleithenia's population. Numbers were, however, only part of the problem. By 1900 Czech society was actually more literate than Austrian-German and its pattern of employment was only slightly more traditional. The large Czech middle class was challenging the Germans in the economy, in culture and in public office and was creating a range of conflicts and tensions in the process.[24]

The Czech-German struggle in the crownlands of St Wenceslas, i.e. Bohemia and Moravia, was the most important national conflict in Cisleithenia and probably in the whole Monarchy. This was partly because these Czech crownlands were the geopolitical and economic core of the empire, which could not survive their secession. It was also because these conflicts, in the empire's most advanced region, created models and set the tone for other disputes elsewhere. Because of its size, wealth and history, Bohemia rather than Moravia was the area of the fiercest and most intransigent struggles.

The two sides' interpretation of history clashed. For the Czechs, history made the crownlands of St Wenceslas uniquely theirs. These crownlands were not merely the historic but also the only cultural home of the Czechs. The Germans by contrast had a secure cultural base elsewhere. Though by 1900 they had already settled parts of the crownlands for half a millennium or more, they were defined by Czech nationalists as 'newcomers', the Czechs having been there first. As the Czech leader František Palacký put matters, 'all the Germans now living in Bohemia are latecomers, colonists and guests in this land.'[25] The German view was very different. The two crownlands had always been part of the Holy Roman Empire of the German Nation. Therefore they were German in the political sense.

On the whole, however, questions of ancient history and constitutional law were less significant than issues of language, culture and socio-economic development. In this sense the conflict was 'modern' and 'middle-class' rather than historical and aristocratic both in its emphases and in its rhetoric. The bearers of Czech nationalism were the new middle class, not, as in Hungary, a nobility obsessed with history and legalism.

The social, economic and political overall context in which the Czech–German confrontation occurred influenced it greatly. Urbanization and industrialization were very rapid. In 1850 Prague's population was 157,000: in 1900 already 514,000. Migration forced the two peoples to live more closely together. New relationships of power at work and in the neighbourhood almost always had an ethnic content. As society became more modern, the state bureaucracy grew enormously in its size and the roles it played. It therefore became much more rewarding and much more important to capture it for one's own nationality, whose sons it could employ in droves and whose interests and culture it could promote. Issues of language and education came immediately to the fore. In what language should administration be conducted? Traditionally the Habsburg administration had used German – for reasons of convenience rather than nationalism – in its internal workings, though it had always sought to communicate with its subjects in their own tongue. Now it was said that the use of German in the Czechs' homeland discriminated against them, even insulted them.

By the last decades of the nineteenth century the Habsburg authorities themselves were prepared to accept bilingualism but the Germans were not. The 1897 ordinances of Prime Minister Count Badeni making bilingualism compulsory for officials in the crownlands brought widespread rioting and chaos in the Bohemian parliament. The basic problem was that the German lower middle class who targeted most of the provincial bureaucracy's jobs were too arrogant and too stupid to learn Czech: this was the milieu from which Adolf Hitler sprang. For these people German was a world language of high culture, Czech a mere provincial patois, useless to them in everyday life and despised as inferior. German sneering at the new Czech literary culture touched a raw nerve among the Czechs, who inevitably felt sensitive as their new literature and their music struggled against centuries-old and universally recognized German competition. Still worse were the battles surrounding education, a key source of cultural and national identity, and a gateway to future jobs. Should all communities, including immigrant ones, be taught in their own language? Should they be taught the language of the other provincial community as well, something to which the Germans strongly and short-sightedly objected? Violent conflicts erupted over such issues and over control of the local school boards. By 1900 most of local public life had long been controlled by democratically elected commune councils. Since 1867 electorates for provincial and central parliaments had been widened until in 1907 universal suffrage was introduced for the Reichsrat in Vienna. Electoral politics mobilized the rival communities for battles of power and status – both of which were involved in the control of public office. German calls to partition Bohemia on ethnic lines were rejected furiously by the Czechs, for whom the crownlands of St Wenceslas were sacred national soil and who – in the German view – were also determined not to lose the revenue which the rich German-majority districts paid to the crownland treasury.

The Habsburg authorities after 1867 genuinely tried to be neutral in these disputes, as in similar later conflicts in other crownlands. The context in which they operated was Article 19 of the December 1867 'Constitution' of Cisleithenia. This guaranteed equality and protection for all nationalities and languages, specifying that all children could be educated in their own language and that all languages customary in a crownland could be used in administration and public life. Subsequently, more detailed regulations attempted to ensure the realization of these constitutional principles in everyday life. In 1869, for instance, the Imperial Public School Law made it obligatory to establish a school teaching in the appropriate language whenever 40 children lived within one hour's walking distance and were more than four kilometres from an alternative school. The point about these constitutional promises and administrative regulations was that Cisleithenia was a state based firmly on the rule of law. The Supreme Court and the Supreme Administrative Court were appealed to frequently on the basis of Article 19 and other equal rights legislation; they defended the legal rights of minorities strongly and effectively. In this Cisleithenia was unique in the great empires of its day. No constraints were permitted on the movement of racial minorities, for instance, which allowed often poverty-stricken Galician Jews to migrate to Vienna in large numbers. It was inconceivable for the Habsburg authorities to connive at pogroms or activities of racialist lynch mobs. This distinguished Austria-Hungary from Russia, which in any case had no equivalent to Article 19, from the United States, but also from the British Empire, in whose White colonies non-White subjects were often denied civil rights (e.g. freedom of movement, freedom to form trade unions, secure property rights) and were almost always denied any political rights.

The Habsburg regime developed a number of laws and practices which were later taken up by other civilized societies facing the challenges of multi-ethnicity and conflict between races and nationalities. Article 302 of the Penal Code made it an offence to incite hostility against other nationalities and religions. As early as 1873 separate Czech and German school boards were established in mixed-nationality districts. Subsequently, other cultural matters were also devolved at local and crownland level to separate national organizations. Separate national electoral rolls were established in some crownlands to reduce political conflict and ensure a political voice for minorities. By the 1880s the prime minister, Count Taaffe, was proclaiming the principle that where sensitive national issues such as language were concerned, policy should be made by consensus between the communities, not by majority vote or administrative fiat. But the Habsburg administration also made a major contribution to managing ethnic conflict simply by its existence. National conflicts could paralyse the crownlands' parliaments, even force their almost indefinite suspension. But much of public life continued unaffected under the supervision of the elected local communes, themselves subject to the law and to some oversight by the imperial administration. The judiciary was imperial and crownland governors appointed by the monarch could administer provinces despite ethnic conflicts and in the absence of parliaments. In the last resort the army was loyal to the emperor alone, and was more than capable of overawing rioting crowds. Moreover, the Habsburg culture developed through the rule of law, civil rights and representation had its impact on political practice. Nationalists might riot and scream abuse. They might indulge in a never-ending round of petty obstructionism. But they would not yet shoot each other or engage in guerrilla warfare.

As their handling of the nationalities issue suggests, the elites who dominated the Habsburg regime were German, if at all, only in a very muted and limited sense. The Habsburgs were German in ultimate origin and Francis Joseph liked to stress that he was a German prince when competing with the Prussians in the 1860s for the loyalty of other Germans. But of course the emperor was in no sense a German nationalist, partly no doubt because his own empire would have been the first victim of German nationalism carried to its logical conclusion. In any case the secular, populist and modern core of German nationalist thinking was totally alien to Francis Joseph's hierarchical, Catholic and dynastic mindset and values. The product of Metternich's era, he viewed all his peoples with equal benevolence and distrust, and probably doubted the capacity of any of them to govern themselves, let alone the hugely complicated Habsburg Empire as a whole. After 1867 Francis Joseph would have been quite prepared to grant the Crown of St Wenceslas, i.e. Bohemia and Moravia, the same autonomy that he had allowed to the Crown of St Stephen. The resistance of the Austrian Germans, the Magyars and Berlin stopped him from doing so.

In 1867 the emperor abandoned the German community in Hungary to the Magyar elite with no qualms once geopolitical and dynastic priorities made this necessary. A comparison of the fate of the German Hungarians and the Ulster Protestants tells one a good deal about the British and Austrian empires in these decades. To be sure, the two communities were not strictly comparable. The Germans in Hungary were much more diverse, were scattered over a greater area, and lacked an aristocracy or even rich bourgeoisie of their own. They were more easily imposed on by the state than was the case with Ulster's Protestants. But different political systems also mattered greatly. In pre-1867 Austria the Hungarian Germans had few opportunities to mobilize and unite politically, to choose leaders, adopt programmes and defend their own interests. Nor could they look for the support in Vienna that the Ulstermen found in London. Not merely was it the case that the British in 1867 were much more of a nation than the Habsburg Empire's Germans, they were also ruled by a parliament. By contrast, the 1867 compromise with Hungary was made not by 'Austria', whatever that might mean, but by its monarch, whose power in this context was close to absolute.

The aristocratic and bureaucratic elites who were Francis Joseph's main ally in government shared most of his views. Unlike the case in Hungary or Prussia, the landowning class in Cisleithenia had a very small lesser gentry element and was dominated by great magnates owning huge estates, above all in Bohemia and Moravia. The Habsburg Empire had been built on these magnates' alliance with the dynasty. Despite the massive confiscation of lands in the 1620s after the suppression of the Bohemian estates' rebellion, many of these families were actually of ancient Czech origin. Much more to the point, in their political sympathies they were loyal to the Habsburgs, Catholic, and determined to uphold the integrity and autonomy of the traditional crownlands. Most of them loathed all forms of populist nationalism, which threatened their power, their values and very possibly their property as well. The Habsburg administrative elite was more ethnically German than the magnates, more Viennese, and more likely to be consciously and proudly German in language and culture. It did associate progress in East-Central Europe with German culture and language. But the high bureaucracy was above all imperial and Habsburg in sympathy, and its overriding concern was to manage domestic conflicts so that the state could continue to function and could maintain its international status and self-esteem.

Since they did not elect the empire's leaders or control their policies the Austrian Germans were scarcely a ruling nation, although even in 1914 they were still pre-eminent in the empire's economy and culture. The most that one could say is that no ruler of the Habsburg Empire who valued its political stability and long-term survival could scorn the interests, prejudices and values of the German middle classes and, increasingly, the mass electorate too.

In fact, the Austrian Germans were not a nation at all in any meaningful sense of the word. The community was very diverse, as was its sense of identity and the main focuses of its political loyalty. The latter might include the dynasty and the Monarchy as a whole, an individual's crownland or city. These could easily overlap and be combined. Some Austrian Germans felt loyalty above all to the entire German nation, whose political centre was now Berlin. These were, however, a relatively small minority. Most German Austrians were Catholics, and the Church was very loyal to the Monarchy and suspicious, if not downright hostile, to the Hohenzollern Reich. The latter's 'Cultural War' against Catholicism in the 1870s and 1880s strengthened this hostility. The one group to which almost no Austrian German would feel an overriding loyalty was the community of Habsburg German subjects, for the very good reason that no such community existed either in fact or in anyone's imagination.

In general the Austrian-German peasantry remained strongly Catholic, provincial and monarchist in its sympathies. So too did lower-middle-class Vienna. Nationalism, which did not necessarily include a desire for secession from the empire, was strongest in Bohemia and in other regions where Germans lived side by side with other peoples. The Viennese upper bourgeoisie, which provided economic and cultural leadership for much of Cisleithenia, was very strongly influenced by its Jewish element, who played a huge role in finance and a big one in business, the professions and culture.

Jewish identities were themselves very fluid and confused. At a time when most peoples of the empire were gaining a secure national identity, many Jews were abandoning all or part of their traditional culture in order to assimilate into Christian society. Whereas the bulk of Galician Jewry was still very 'East European' – which in Jewish terms meant unassimilated, traditionalist and religious – most of Viennese Jewry had followed the North-West European pattern of assimilation into local Christian society. Nevertheless, even in Vienna, few Jews shed all aspects of their traditional culture and identity, which included for example a formidable respect for learning. In any case the experience and the strains of transition from a closed Orthodox Jewish world to a cosmopolitan, secular and (in tradition) Christian one left their mark and themselves shaped identity. Clearly there was something special in the Jews' background or they could not have made a contribution to the Austrian economy, intellectual life and the arts out of all proportion to their numbers. Total Jewish assimilation in Vienna would in any case have been a rather strange concept. To lose one's own identity, one has to assimilate into a society with a strong fixed identity of its own. Since no clear Austrian identity existed, and since the Jews were actually a crucial constituent element in the creation of the Viennese haute bourgeoisie, the complete submergence of the Jews in an anonymous wider society was impossible. The old Austrian aristocracy of great land-owning magnates was almost impenetrable to members of the bourgeoisie, whatever their wealth and ethnic origin. This enhanced the impact of wealthy Jews on the haute bourgeoisie, the so-called 'second society' of Vienna. This elite was liberal in its politics and German in culture, since the Jews associated enlightenment, civic equality and the spread of the capitalist economy with German mid-century liberalism. But the Jewish elite was also solidly imperial and dynastic in its loyalty. Under the Habsburgs it had been not only tolerated but also honoured and allowed to become rich. Even less than the Habsburgs did it have anything to gain from the break-up of the empire as a single economic unity and the triumph of any version of populist nationalism, whether German or Slav.

The Jews' great prominence in Austrian finance and the Vienna stock exchange made them obvious targets for those who had suffered from the onset of rapid capitalist economic development since 1850, who disliked its values or merely envied its beneficiaries. After the crash of 1873 dented capitalism's prestige and wiped out many people's savings, these feelings became more acute, particularly among the Christian lower middle class of Vienna. The latter's insecurities and resentment added a vicious element to Austrian politics. The Christian Social Party, overtly anti-Semitic, tapped these feelings. Francis Joseph disliked many aspects of Christian Social politics, including its demagogic anti-Semitism, and twice prevented its leader, Karl Lueger, from becoming mayor of Vienna. He finally gave way in 1897 because Lueger clearly was the popular choice and since he was deemed more amenable than either the socialists or the German nationalists, the obvious alternatives as mass parties. The government's calculations proved correct. In office the Christian Socials proved effective in administration, totally loyal to empire and dynasty, and happy to work with established elites, the Jewish banking oligarchy included.

The Austrian strategy of tolerance, respect for law and co-option also worked with the Social Democrats. Although in principle still a revolutionary party, in reality they not only accepted but even to a considerable degree (albeit rather surreptitiously) supported the Habsburg regime in a way that would have been impossible in the much more oppressive Hohenzollern Reich and totally inconceivable in Russia. 'The socialists assumed that they could count on a minimal level of respect from these agencies (i.e. the government and bureaucracy) based on the proceduralism of the Austrian administrative service, on the modulation implicit in the ethos of the centralistic Josephist state of law, and, ironically, on the slow but perceptible acknowledgement by the socialists of Francis Joseph's equitable style of governance.'[26] The Austrian Social Democrats were not without their share of German patriotism and belief in German cultural leadership in Central Europe. Ernest Pernersdorfer, the leader of their parliamentary faction, commented for instance that 'we Germans can certainly draw a degree of self-confidence from the fact that modern socialism originated from within the German people.'[27] As in Britain, socialists' support for the empire to some extent reflected pride in their country's historical pre-eminence, cultural mission and embodiment of progressive political principles. In the Austrian case, however, it also reflected the correct perception that nationalism was a threat to the unity of the party and working class. In marxist terms the large imperial market was a force for economic development and was therefore deemed progressive. Meanwhile Karl Renner, the leading socialist authority on the nationalities issue, shared the belief of de Tocqueville, Seeley and others that the future belonged to great powers of continental scale, not to nation states. For Renner, the idea that every nation needed independent statehood was a false conception 'grounded in the dogma of sovereignty rooted in the French Revolution, and was thus a thoroughly bourgeois form of nationalism which had nothing in common with proletarian internationalism.'[28] In more down to earth terms Renner also saw the principle of national statehood, if applied to East-Central Europe, as a certain recipe for economic decline and anarchic struggles between the region's peoples.

It was in fact Renner and his socialist colleague, Otto Bauer, who produced the best-known strategy for solving national conflicts within the Monarchy in the early twentieth century. Although complicated in its details, the basic plan was relatively simple. The historic crownlands should be broken up and replaced by provinces whose borders should be determined by economic and geographical rationality. These provinces should then be divided into districts, which would as far as possible be ethnically homogeneous. Where this could not be achieved, jobs in the administration would be distributed in proportion to the size of the various communities. All issues concerning culture, education and national identity should be hived off from these regular organs of territorial administration. 'We must organise the population twice, once nationally and once according to administrative requirements.'[29] The model for these national organizations should be the churches, to which individuals belonged voluntarily, which traditionally handled most educational and cultural affairs, and which in some cases were crucial too to the preservation of national identities. Renner's aim was to guarantee individuals' national identity wherever they might migrate, and to take the struggle for territory and its symbols out of politics. In many ways the Austro-Marxists were offering a modernized version of the millet system. But there were major difficulties in adapting this type of solution to ethnic issues in an early twentieth-century context. The Ottoman bureaucracy was much smaller and less intrusive than that of a modern European state, with its system of conscription, its welfare services and its economic role. Divorcing national-cultural and territorial administration would not be easy. Nor would it by any means necessarily appease the desire of nations for their own territory and statehood, or end bitter quarrels between neighbouring peoples which by 1900 had been raging for decades.

EMPIRE'S DILEMMAS: AUSTRIAN SOLUTIONS

To say that the Austro-Marxists' proposals were not going to solve the Habsburg Monarchy's nationalities problem is not, however, to say very much. Given the strength of nationalism and the empire's ethnic mix, no 'solution' to the nationalities question was conceivable, at least in the twentieth century, after decades of inter-communal tension and conflict. It is sometimes argued by historians that these tensions were in large part caused by the Habsburg authorities themselves, who played nation against nation in order to keep power in the hands of the emperor and his officials. In particular Francis Joseph is blamed for tearing up the so-called Kremsier Constitution of 1849, over which German and Czech democratic nationalists had worked together and which embodied compromises on a number of points that were later to be great sources of contention. There is something in this line of argument but not much. In the first place, Francis Joseph, victorious over the 1848 revolution, could not be expected to accept a constitution embodying the principles of popular sovereignty, the disestablishment of the Church, the separation of Austria and Hungary as constitutional entities and the abolition of all noble titles. Once the absolutist enemy was gone, moreover, unity between Czechs and Germans would have been more difficult to sustain. In 1849 the enormous strains that industrialization, mass politics and the changing balance of power and settlement put on inter-communal relations were still to come. To give only three examples, the Kremsier Constitution would not have stopped Czech resentment at German arrogance, German insecurity at being displaced as the natural rulers of Bohemia or the Viennese lower middle class's visceral anti-Semitism. To argue that more rather than less democracy would have cured the problems of the Habsburg Monarchy is an act of faith. It fits contemporary assumptions, power relations and ideology. The people are sovereign and inherently virtuous. If conflicts occur, wicked elites are probably to blame. In particular, emperors are born with horns on their head. Applied to struggles between nations, such democratic self-congratulation can be naively complacent.

Certainly by the last quarter of the nineteenth century the most that could be hoped for was, in Count Taaffe's famous words, bearable dissatisfaction. Managing this empire was a nightmare. Vladimir Beck commented that, as prime minister, he was responsible for 'eight nations, seventeen countries, twenty Parliamentarian bodies, twenty-seven Parliamentarian parties, two complicated world views, the intricate relations with Hungary and the cultural differences of eight and a half degrees of latitude and longitude.'[30] National conflict seeped into the pores of this empire and created situations little short of bizarre. Ferocious battles between rival national communities over the nationally correct title of a railway station could be solved only by a compromise which left no place-signs on the platforms at all. The bewildered traveller from abroad had a sharp introduction to the Kafkaesque world of irony and fantasy which was the old Austria. At the time many observers saw the Monarchy as moribund, weak, pathetic and very possibly doomed. From the perspective of the twenty-first century matters look a little different. We are more used to the cacophony of pluralism, multiculturalism and democracy: less enamoured of the methods by which nation states were created, made homogeneous and praised for their virility in the crude, brutal and Darwinian intellectual climate of the early twentieth century. Above all we have seen East-Central Europe's history under Hitler and under Soviet rule. In this comparison the Habsburg era appears bathed in golden light.

It is easy to see in Cisleithenia the forerunner of today's European Union, in both the Kafkaesque and the positive sense. Stopping the clock in Brussels is the closest modern European equivalent to a world in which railway stations have no names in order not to offend national sensibilities. Ponderous multi-lingual bureaucracy links the two eras. If Cisleithenia was scarcely a perfect democracy, the same might well be said of the rule of the Commission and the European Central Bank, or the backroom deals between national governments and pressure groups which represent the reality of power in contemporary Brussels. Of course, Cisleithenia was explicitly not a democracy, in a way that is not true of the European Union. In principle, sovereignty remained in the emperor's hands. In a poorer, more primitive and more politically dangerous world than today's Western Europe there were, however, far greater justifications for keeping ultimate power out of the hands of the peoples. To take one crucial example: a lifetime of bitter experience divides Germans in today's Federal Republic from the German nationalism which spawned Hitler in late nineteenth-century Bohemia and Vienna.

The Habsburg Empire possessed common legitimate institutions and symbols to an extent still beyond the dreams of contemporary European federalists. The empire was in a sense both archaic and ahead of its time in 1914. The archaism is obvious. But the pettiness and cynicism of late Austrian nationalist politics, the cacophony of voices and interests, the resigned acceptance that bearable dissatisfaction is the best to be expected of any politics – all this is familiar in contemporary democracy. Old Austria was a very inefficient great power in the age of nationalism and imperialism, of Social Darwinism and the mass conscript army. It would have suited much better a world in which economic power counted for more than military might, multi-national capitalism and multi-cultural politics were in the ascendant, and conscript armies were redundant.

Nor is it fair to judge the empire mostly by its handling of the nation-alities issue. At best this could be only a holding operation, the least bad solution to an intractable problem. As an economic unit, however, the empire flourished in its last decades. Even the Hungarians, who complained incessantly about dependence and exploitation, in fact benefited greatly from the existence of the Monarchy and its single market. Hungary more or less avoided the post-1873 Great Depression and, at a very conservative estimate, its economy grew at 3.8 per cent p.a. between 1870 and 1913, a high rate in that era. Not merely did the rest of the Monarchy provide an excellent and maybe irreplaceable market for Hungarian exports, 'to a large extent Hungary's ability to industrialize was contingent on unencumbered access to Austria's capital markets.'[31]

In parallel with economic development which was closing the gap with the French and British, Austria also enjoyed unprecedented significance as a centre of world culture. At the turn of the century Vienna's contribution to science, music and the arts was immense. The Habsburg regime did not directly create or foster this new culture, as it had for instance created the baroque Counter-Reformation centuries earlier. It is not, however, the business of liberal regimes in pluralist societies to determine culture. At most they can allow and facilitate. This the Habsburg regime did. The cultural richness of Vienna would have been inconceivable without the empire and set merely in one of the region's rather small nation states. To the very considerable extent that this culture was Jewish, it owed a debt to the protection and tolerance granted by the imperial authorities to the Jews, which compared very favourably to the practices of the Habsburgs' Russian rival, of most of the empire's successor states, and even of Prussia and France.

To a unique extent Austria-Hungary by 1900 was beginning to transcend the historical definition of empire and was moving in the direction of a democratic multi-national federation, able to offer its peoples the economic benefits of a huge market, legally protected equality in status, and the security that was empire's traditional boon. It is quite true that the process was by no means complete and was attended by much hatred and conflict. Given the context, however, the Austrian achievement was impressive. Not merely was Vienna forced to cope with the various nationalisms in their naïve, brutal and selfish adolescence. It also had to master the effects on social stability and mass consciousness of rapid industrialization, urbanization and vast-scale migration. Simultaneously there occurred a great expansion of the state's role in society as regulator and provider of services, an inevitable cause of increased struggles to control the bureaucratic machine by diverse peoples and interests. In the midst of this came too the introduction of democracy and the advent of mass political parties. To expect all these trends to have occurred simultaneously and not caused major conflict would be very unrealistic.

To set against this positive judgement, however, one needs also to take into account the management of the Hungarian Kingdom between 1867 and 1918, and a foreign and military policy which in 1914 resulted in Austria pulling down over its head the European civilization of which it had been a worthy pillar.

The Hungarian Kingdom in the Monarchy's last decades was a strong contrast to Cisleithenia. By 1910 54 per cent of the population were

Magyars and there was no equivalent of the Czechs in Hungary – economically advanced and with a big middle class – to challenge them. Their elites were homogeneous, self-confident, politically skilful and, above all, national. The Hungarian aristocracy shared many of the values and assumptions of its Cisleithenian peers and indeed of Francis Joseph himself. This eased the 1867 Compromise and to some extent protected it against dramatic appeals by Vienna to the Hungarian masses and the non-Hungarian minorities against the Magyar elite. This elite, drawn mostly from the old nobility, totally controlled the state. It excluded the great majority of the adult male population from the franchise and nevertheless gerrymandered the electoral process. It justified this by claiming, not necessarily incorrectly, that any approximation to democracy would threaten the interests of property and the chances of turning the Kingdom of St Stephen into a genuinely Hungarian nation state. Koloman Tisza, the long-serving prime minister, commented that in the event of universal suffrage 'entire regions of the country would be lost to the national cause and fall easy prey to anti-Magyar subversion coloured by socialism; 200–300 Magyar deputies would face 150–200 non-Magyars, and a certain part of the former bloc would be controlled by the agents of the international socialist movement. The rural constituencies would be swept by demagoguery of the worst kind. The serious, responsible representatives of the national policy would be reduced to a handful.'[32] By the early twentieth century this was closer to the reasoning of a Russian statesman than of an Austrian. But, as its leaders so fiercely insisted, Hungary was not Austria.

In 1867 Francis Joseph resigned control over the kingdom's internal affairs to the Magyar elite. So long as they did not challenge his control over the army and foreign policy he made little effort to interfere in Hungarian domestic politics for the rest of his reign. In other words he basically abandoned the non-Hungarians to their fate. Not for the first time, for example, the loyal soldier-colonists of the southern border (Grenzer) region, formerly administered directly from Vienna, were sacrificed when this suited the Habsburgs' need to do deals with the Hungarian elite. In 1867, however, there were some justifications for the Compromise, even leaving aside Francis Joseph's impatience to shore up stability in Hungary so that he could return to the struggle with Prussia in southern Germany. The Croats had gained nothing from the era of absolutism since 1849 and were relatively content with the autonomy initially granted by Budapest after 1867. The other national leaders were unhappy, but on paper and in its first years the implementation of the Hungarian government's nationalities legislation and policy was much less oppressive than it had become by 1900. It was Vienna's failure to use its chances to intervene in later decades that was truly blameworthy, and in particular its unwillingness to force a large extension of the franchise on the Hungarian oligarchy during the crisis which erupted in 1905–6 over the status of the imperial army. It may well be that, faced with constant mayhem caused by inter-communal conflict in Cisleithenia, Francis Joseph welcomed Hungary's surface calm. Perhaps he simply believed that the Magyar elite was too powerful to oppose and that no stable order in Hungary could be built without accepting its hegemony. It certainly is the case that to move sharply towards democracy in Hungary had much more radical implications than in Austria. This was an altogether poorer society with a history of violence and fewer traditions of compromise. The radical agrarian, Slav nationalist and socialist parties which would come to the fore would be far harder to handle than Karl Lueger's Christian Socials or Karl Renner's Social Democrats in Austria. Nevertheless, simply to abandon the Croats, the Grenzer and the Romanian peasants of Transylvania to the increasing oppression and chicanery of the Hungarian government was a poor reward for past loyalty to the Habsburgs and was likely to increase political instability in the long run, whatever its short-term convenience.

The Hungarian elite took the centralizing, homogenizing French nation state as their model. Their slogan was the words of the Comte de Clermont-Tonnerre in the National Assembly of 1789: 'There cannot be a nation within a nation.'[33] The Magyars did accept that the Croat kingdom had a historical right to autonomy, although by the twentieth century they were beginning to infringe on this autonomy. Members of other nationalities possessed civil rights, however, but no recognition of separate national status, let alone territorial autonomy. The Magyar nobility dominated official jobs, persecuted those who objected to its rule, and used government power and patronage, together with the educational system, to Magyarize the population. To be fair to the Hungarians, they did not use the methods of twentieth-century dictatorship. There were no mass deportations or secret executions. The rule of law was abused but not totally subverted. Private property was secure for minorities as well as Hungarians. The considerable respect allowed to the Orthodox and Uniate churches permitted the Serbs and, still more, the Romanians the freedom to run many of their own schools. By 1914 the latter had to teach Hungarian to a high standard but they were nevertheless an important obstacle to Magyarization, which made considerable headway among urban Germans and Jews but very little in the South Slav territories or among the Romanians.

The basic point, however, is that in attempting to turn the Kingdom of St Stephen into a Hungarian nation state the Magyar elite was facing a much more difficult task than the French with fewer resources at its disposal. To Magyarize the Orthodox, or even Uniate, Romanian and Serbian peasantry was to cross one of the great divides in European civilization. The Magyar language had nothing in common with Slavic or Romanian linguistic roots. No one could pretend these languages were mere dialects. The new Serb and Romanian intelligentsia, in universal nineteenth-century fashion, saw them therefore as the basis of nationhood and eventual statehood. Serbian and Romanian nation states existed on the other side of the border to sustain the dream. Even the older elites in Croatia, Transylvania and the border region were linked by history and sympathy to Vienna, not to Budapest. There were very powerful objective reasons why Brittany could never be more than a region in early twentieth-century Europe. Local elites, new and old, understood this reality. Brittany had belonged to France for centuries. Its elites spoke French and had long merged their ambitions with those of the French state. The Bretons, like the French, were Catholics, and there was no independent Brittany on the other side of an artificial political border to lure them towards an alternative destiny. The situation in Hungary was very different, and by refusing to accept this reality the Magyar elite both stored up unnecessarily great long-term problems for themselves and created immediate and grave additional problems for the empire's foreign policy and its influence in the Balkans. It was indeed to be foreign policy and war that ultimately destroyed the Hungarian Kingdom. Whatever its internal tensions in 1914, it was in no danger of succumbing either to domestic nationalist opposition or to social revolution.

The greatest sin of the Hungarians was that at the same time as they were weakening the Monarchy's foreign policy and international position, they were also drastically undermining its armed forces. Because the Habsburg army was dynastic and imperial rather than national, the Hungarians disliked it, feared (not entirely unrealistically) that it might be used against them, and consistently starved it of funds in an effort to squeeze concessions out of Francis Joseph. 'Between the 1850s and 1914, the military budget of Austria-Hungary was proportionately the smallest of all the European great powers, far below the financial capacity of the monarchy's economy ... The Hungarian parliament and government consistently sabotaged military expenditures, at least until 1912, when it was too late.'[34] The weakness of the army contributed greatly to the pessimism of the empire's rulers and the hopes of its enemies. In an era that celebrated 'national egoism' as life-sustaining virility, the weak army confirmed a sense of crisis and malaise which the disputes between the nationalities had aroused. Drawn from the old social elites, the Monarchy's rulers were bound to suspect that modernity was their enemy and that the future might be bleak. All these factors strengthened the sense that power must be reasserted and the gathering circle of foreign and domestic enemies overawed if long-term disaster was to be avoided. All these sentiments fed into the attack on Serbia in 1914.

So too, however, did a problem common to empires. Independent Serbia was a magnet for all Serbs, perhaps all South Slavs, within the Monarchy. To destroy it would restore one of empire's great bulwarks, namely its subjects' sense of its invincible power and the immutability of the order it represented. But how could a state such as Serbia be destroyed? Annexation might exacerbate the problem by increasing the number of South Slavs within the Monarchy at a time when the authoritarian but not ruthlessly dictatorial Hungarian state was already having considerable trouble in controlling its existing minorities. But if Serbia was not annexed, by what means short of permanent, and very expensive, military occupation would it be possible to sustain in power a national elite willing to do Vienna's bidding? As was the case with many empires, indirect rule might prove impossible and annexation unpalatable.

After the Second World War the Soviet leadership was to face a similar problem with the western Ukraine (consisting mostly of Galicia). Their misunderstanding and mishandling of this problem was to cost them dear. Meanwhile in the 1890s the British too had confronted a similar dilemma in southern Africa. Gold and diamonds had made the independent Transvaal and Orange Free State the economic and geopolitical core of the whole region. More than half the Cape Colony's population was Boer. Would they not inevitably gravitate towards their fellow Boers in the independent republics to their north? In the 1890s the British tried a variety of experiments, up to and including connivance at an armed unofficial invasion led by Dr Jameson, all of them designed to secure indirect control over the republics. When all else failed, Joseph Chamberlain and Lord Milner went to war to secure British control of southern Africa. Having won the war, they lost the peace. Though prepared to herd the Boer civilian population into concentration camps on the grounds of wartime necessity, in peacetime London lacked the means and the ruthlessness to transform demographic realities in the conquered region by deporting the Boers or forcibly transplanting British colonists. After incorporating the two republics in British southern Africa, it then conceded democracy to the Whites it had conquered, ultimately giving them control over the entire region. In 1899 and 1914 British and Austrian dilemmas of empire were not so different. Nor in one sense was there much moral difference between the actions they took to secure their imperial interests. A key distinction was that the British were more powerful and were therefore able to get away with unilateral aggressive defence of their interests. More important still, great powers could behave outside Europe in ways that would not be tolerated within the continent. When the Austrians failed to observe this rule, they brought about the crippling of European civilization and the beginning of the end of European global dominance.

Part Three

RUSSIA

6

The Russian Empire: Regions, Peoples, Geopolitics

Arnold Toynbee believed that empires were bred in cold climates and on poor soils; that a people toughened itself for the burdens of empire by struggling initially to overcome a harsh and hostile environment. 'The Capuan Campagna was as kindly to man as the Roman Campagna was dour; and while the Romans went forth from their forbidding country to conquer one neighbour after another, the Capuans stayed at home and allowed one neighbour after another to conquer them.' But for Toynbee, Rome was merely a particularly striking example of the general 'truth that ease is inimical to civilization'.[1]

In making these claims for the bracing influence of an adverse environment Toynbee was echoing, among others, Montesquieu. The great eighteenth-century Frenchman was a firm believer in the environment's influence on mentalities and levels of civilization, and in particular in the superior temperament of peoples bred in cold and rugged climates.[2] To some extent both men were searching for scientific explanations for one of the most crucial developments of the modern era – namely the increasing and unprecedented domination of the globe by peoples originating in Northern and North-Western Europe, far from the traditional centres of civilization. No doubt Toynbee was also touched by the ethos of the English public school, with its stress on character-building and its fear lest an imperial ruling class become soft and effeminate.

Halford Mackinder, early twentieth-century Britain's most famous geographer, had a rather different view on the links between empire and environment. According to him, the great empires of Antiquity originated in fertile soils with good water communications and warm climates. Thus in ancient Egypt 'all the essential physical advantages were combined for men to work upon. On the one hand were a rich soil, abundant water, and a powerful sunshine; hence fertility for the support of a population in affluence'. The Mediterranean region as a whole shared these basic characteristics: a single waterway was surrounded by 'fertile shorelands with winter rains and harvest sunshine'. Rome had benefited immeasurably by short and easy access by river to the sea and by possession of the fertile plain of Latium. If in the end, despite many vicissitudes, the European civilization whose origins lay in Greece and Rome had defeated the great Islamic threat to its survival, this owed much to the geographical base from which Islam had been forced to mount its challenge. Mackinder saw the explosion of Islamic power from the seventh century as representing, much more truly than either Alexander of Macedon or even Rome, a bid for world domination. This bid was 'vitiated by one fatal defect; it lacked in its Arabian base the necessary manpower to make it good.' Only briefly did a single Islamic state control the resources both of the Persian plateau east of the River Euphrates and the Fertile Crescent to its west. Neither region could in fact sustain big populations but the area west of the Euphrates from which the main challenge to Europe was mounted was particularly lacking in this respect. North Africa, Syria and even Asia Minor did not possess 'inexhaustible manpower', that great resource of empire, 'for they were based on arid and semi-arid deserts and steppes, and on comparatively small oasis lands.'[3]

If Toynbee and Montesquieu were right, the Russians ought to have been the greatest of imperial peoples, for the environment from which they sprang was uniquely hostile. Among modern nations only Canada shares the same latitudes and continental scale as Russia. But the main regions of Canadian agriculture lie along the same latitude as Kiev, not as the Muscovite heartland to which the Russian state was confined until the seventeenth and eighteenth centuries. Moscow is very remote from the great core areas of empire, both ancient and modern. The fertile river valleys of the Nile, Tigris, Euphrates and Yellow rivers – cradles of ancient empire and civilization – lie far to the south. The Atlantic trade routes, control of which was the essence of modern European maritime empire, are equally far to the west and south. In the thirteenth and fourteenth centuries, during which the Muscovite state was born, world civilization revolved around China, the Islamic Middle East and – very definitely in third place – Latin Christendom. A recent book on global history in this era allows Russia one paragraph, which is devoted to the place of the fur trade in the international economy.[4]

Geography is one reason why Russia stands somewhat alone and isolated in the history of empires. Other empires fit to varying degrees into families, sharing a common lineage and characteristics. This is most obvious in East Asia where one Chinese dynasty after another asserted its loyalty to a common imperial tradition. In the Middle East lines of descent are more blurred but nevertheless real. A line runs from ancient Persian and Hellenistic empire through Rome and Byzantium into the Islamic imperial tradition which culminated with the Ottomans. To some extent modern European maritime empires shared a common Roman heritage: more to the point, all of them were oceanic and partly commercial enterprises.

For two hundred years Russia was part of a Mongol empire. Even those historians who stress Russia's Mongol inheritance would, however, be hard-pressed to argue that this provided any form of common identity or heritage with other former Mongol territories such as China or Persia. Far more significant was Russia's debt to Byzantium, from which it drew its religion and most of its pre-modern high culture. But even Kievan Rus was on the outer margins of the Byzantine commonwealth, with Moscow still more remote and different. Of course, imperial traditions and cultures can travel far from their original homelands while retaining a powerful hold. In some ways sixteenth-century Russia's position was comparable to that of Scandinavia. Both regions were poor and peripheral in European eyes, and both Scandinavian and Russian elites came in time to feel this backwardness and to hanker for recognition as equals by the rest of Europe.[5] But as Latin Christians Scandinavians were peripheral to a vibrant civilization which came to dominate first Europe and then much of the world. The Russians were not simply more peripheral in geographical terms but were also – culturally – on the edges not of Latin Christendom but of Byzantium, which disappeared in the fifteenth century. In time Russia would come to share many of the characteristics of modern European empire, but its medieval pre-imperial heritage and its geographical position ensured that it would never fit snugly into a common European pattern.

As many Europeans have pointed out, Russia's geography is typically Asian rather than European. Europe is a continent of many sharply differing regions, divided from each other by mountains and rivers. It has a long warm-water coastline, much of it Atlantic. The vast, low-lying Russian plain, its rivers flowing into inland or frozen seas, is a total contrast to Europe's geography. On the other hand, the fact that Russia is on Europe's borders, is indeed part of Europe by most definitions, sharply differentiates it from other flatlands of continental Asia.

In most respects the Russian land was a poor natural base for empire. The thick forests and relatively infertile soils of most of the Muscovite heartland could not sustain a great population. This heartland was also remote from the major international trade routes, not only the maritime and Atlantic ones, but also the main land routes along which Asia's commerce with Europe traditionally flowed. International trade created towns, revenues and relatively large literate populations. The tsarist state was weak in all these respects. A vast country with a small and scattered population was difficult and expensive to govern and defend. Very low levels of literacy and urbanization meant that Russia could not create a true civil service until well into the nineteenth century. In 1763 the government employed 16,500 officials. Prussia, 1 per cent of Russia's size, employed 14,000.[6] At a time when much of a German state's middle and higher bureaucracy would expect to have a university education, Russia possessed only one university, in Moscow, which opened only in 1755. Miraculously, tsarist Russia succeeded in creating a formidably effective military and fiscal machine, the essential basis of any great power's might in early modern Europe. Even in 1914, however, the state was still far from being able to provide adequate, modern medical, educational and welfare services to an enormous, largely peasant population scattered thinly across by far the largest country in the world. Maintaining an adequate communications system is essential for far-flung empires but always difficult given pre-modern communications. In Russia truly vast distances, inadequate labour, and spring and autumn climate conspired to make land communications a nightmare for much of the year. As the empire expanded, the problem of deploying troops to cover its many vulnerable frontiers worsened. In the eighteenth century the foundation of St Petersburg and the opening up of Ukraine's wheatfields and the Black Sea export trade were hugely important stages in the growth of Russian wealth and power. But a capital city on the sea and the increasing dependence of Russia's exports and balance of payments on secure exit through the Bosphorus made Russia far more vulnerable to enemy seapower than had previously been the case. In general, the country's size and climate imposed an immense value added tax on almost any activity. Empire in Russia usually had to be built against nature, against the odds and on the cheap.

Nevertheless, the picture was not entirely a bleak one. At least Russia's ferocious winters kept it immune from the tropical diseases which devastated life in some other parts of the globe. The northern Russian forests were rich in animals, for whose furs there was great international demand. They were also rich in the timber on which pre-modern wooden navies depended for their existence. The forests provided some defensive cover even against highly mobile nomadic raiders. Slower and more heavily equipped modern European armies found Russia's immense distances, poor communications and inadequate supplies of food much more of an obstacle. Freezing winters, blisteringly hot summers, and seas of mud in spring and autumn further contributed to their woes. The vast marshlands of Belorussia provided some cover for Russia's north-western frontier and forced invading armies to follow relatively narrow and predictable lines of advance.

Russia is blessed with a dense and viable network of rivers, a huge asset in the pre-railway era when goods travelled far more easily and cheaply on water than on land. Though central Russia, the Muscovite heartland, is far from the sea, it is well connected to it by rivers. The Volkhov, Narva, Neva and Western Dvina flow into the Baltic, the Northern Dvina into the White Sea, the Volga into the Caspian, and the Don and the Dnieper into the Black Sea. Because these rivers meander slowly over flat country they are for the most part easily navigable. Though the greatest rivers flow from north to south, their many tributaries create a dense net throughout European Russia, portages between the main river systems being for the most part short and easy. One reason for this is that most of the great rivers originate in a relatively small region of north-western Russia. Only in Russia do so many great rivers originate in a flat and habitable region, and this fact undoubtedly contributed greatly to the Russians' ability to dominate and colonize the enormous plain that stretches from Central Europe to the Urals. The British geographer William Parker comments that 'dispersal of mighty streams from a habitable zone occurs only in central Russia, and thus the conditions favouring the rise and expansion of Muscovy were unique. Its growth would be unintelligible without reference to the river system.'[7] Undoubtedly a plain criss-crossed by navigable rivers not merely made for easy, albeit slow, movement of goods and people but also facilitated political unity. Geography – above all mountains – contributes greatly to the diversity of languages, customs and people in much of Europe and China. By contrast the Russian plain's bias is towards homogeneity and unity.

The river system both aided Russian expansion and determined some of its axes. Siberia could be crossed and conquered within a few decades because its rivers allowed rapid and relatively easy movement of people and goods. The Urals could become the world's leading iron-producing region in the eighteenth century despite its remoteness because its produce could flow down the Kama to the Volga, and thence by river and canal to St Petersburg and to European export markets.

In more general terms, any state as dependent for its prosperity on rivers as was the case with early modern Russia was almost certain to seek control of the whole extent of these rivers and their exits to the sea. To do otherwise was to allow foreign, and very probably hostile, states to tax and interdict one's trade at will. 'Inevitably the power that gained control of these riverheads came to dominate the whole country, each river offering a direction for expansion.'[8] The Russians achieved control over the Volga and access to the Caspian Sea in the 1550s, conquest of the Baltic and Black Sea coastlines in the eighteenth century. In time these acquisitions made a huge impact on Russian trade and economic development, and on the wealth and power of the Russian state. Nevertheless, all three seas were either landlocked (the Caspian) or approached the ocean through narrow exits (in the Baltic the Sound, in the Black Sea the Straits at Constantinople) easily blocked by foreign fleets. Russia's position as a maritime and commercial power was always under threat because of this basic geographical fact.

THE MANY RUSSIAN EMPIRES

Not only the river but also other aspects of Russian geography crucially influenced the axes of Russian expansion and the growth of the Russian Empire. The Moscow region lies within a broad belt of vegetation running east–west across Eurasia which is dominated by forests but whose soil makes agriculture possible, if not usually very productive. North of this huge zone coniferous forests spread over many millions of square kilometres, while the most northern region of all is largely made up of frozen swampland. Within these vast areas the human population is very sparse since agriculture is usually impossible. But the cold climate and abundant vegetation breed a range of animals whose furs made a crucial contribution to Russian exports and revenues until the early eighteenth century. It was these furs that lured Russians into the bleak expanses of the far north-east and thence, from the mid-sixteenth century, across Siberia. They moved so quickly across the huge Siberian region because they rapidly depleted stocks of precious furs in any area they penetrated, which forced them ever onwards in pursuit of the sable, the arctic fox, the beaver and the marten. Historians usually speak of imperial expansion in terms of 'push' and 'pull'. The former means those factors in the metropolis that encouraged states and peoples to expand and colonize. In Siberia the 'push' was fur. In a sense there was no 'pull' factor. There was, for instance, no vacuum, no anarchy, no threat that sucked the Russians into a region which they were loath to conquer. On the other hand there was very little resistance to their advance. In part this was because of political factors. The collapse of the Mongol Empire and of its Muslim successor Khanates left a power vacuum to Moscow's east. At least as important, however, was geography. The rich Siberian fur-bearing regions sustained too small and primitive a population to offer effective resistance to the Russian advance.

In the steppe grasslands well to Moscow's south the situation was very different. The plain that stretches from the Carpathians to Mongolia is the greatest area of open grassland on earth. It was quintessentially the home of the nomadic pastoralist and warrior. From the seventh century BC to the seventeenth century AD, nomadic peoples ruled supreme in this vast area, terrifying the sedentary societies north and south of the steppe. A nomadic people could mobilize all its adult males for war. Indeed, no such thing as a male civilian existed. The skills and tactics of war were bred from childhood and were in any case similar to those of the pastoralist and hunter's horse-centred life The nomad was a light cavalryman, exceptionally mobile and formidably armed. 'The standard compound bow of the steppes . . . was made of layers of horn and sinew on a wooden frame. This bow required a pull much stiffer than the English longbow, even though it was fired from horseback. It had impressive range and power of penetration. It was a very long time indeed before the hand gun could match the compound bow in range, penetration or rate of fire.'[9] Sedentary societies could seldom match these nomadic armies. Conscript militias would be outmanoeuvred and outfought on the battlefield, and could in any case not be kept permanently concentrated and away from their agricultural tasks. Professional military forces of a size and calibre to match the nomads were ruinously expensive and often politically unreliable. Until the eighteenth century the Chinese were far more powerful, economically advanced and wealthy than the Russians. Even they, however, had no lasting answer to the nomadic threat. For most of the period between the fall of the Han dynasty (third century AD) and the collapse of China's last dynasty, the Qing (Manchu) in 1911, all or most of China was ruled by nomadic invaders and their descendants.

Only from the mid-sixteenth century, and even then only precariously, could the Russian advance into the steppe begin. Not until the late eighteenth century was the whole region controlled by Russia and freed from nomadic raiding parties in search of plunder and slaves. So long as the Russians were confined to the forest regions and poor soils well north of the steppe they could not generate the population or wealth to make true empire possible. In this their situation was very different from that of the Chinese. The latter could expand southwards, away from the steppe, into vast and hugely fertile regions beyond the Yangtzse. The Russians had only the frozen taiga and tundra to their north. Even in the mid-eighteenth century the Russian population remained smaller than that of France. The Russia which is familiar to every European – with a huge population, powerful, and controlling the whole region between the Baltic and Black seas – is a recent phenomenon.

The geography of Northern Eurasia's various regions – meaning both their location and their natural and human resources – to a considerable extent determined both the reasons for their annexation and the roles they played within the Russian economic and even political system of empire. The 6000 kilometres of steppe grassland that stretched along Russia's southern border in Europe and Asia were the Russians' New World. Here were the equivalents of the vast regions of the Americas, Australasia and Africa which West European immigrants colonized and turned over to farming from the sixteenth to the twentieth centuries. In Northern Eurasia as elsewhere mass colonization was the most effective way to consolidate control over a region and thereby to change the balance between peoples and civilizations across the globe. Colonization was one of the key elements in the expansion of Europe and it usually, though not always, implied ethnic cleansing on a grand scale. This was true in Russia as elsewhere. If large areas of what is now southern and eastern Ukraine – above all, the region of the Zaporozhye Cossacks[10] – were largely empty because of Tatar raids for slaves and plunder, in parts of Europe and almost all of southern Siberia the advance of agriculture and the colonist was at the expense of the nomadic peoples and culture that had previously dominated the steppe.

In the Russian new world too, colonization was justified as the development of regions previously unexploited or 'wasted' by nomadic herders. Agriculture was seen as a step above nomadism in civilization's ladder. Russians like Anglo-Saxons celebrated the courage and back-breaking labour of the farmer-colonist struggling in a hostile wilderness against an unfamiliar climate in order to bring improvement and civilization to vast 'empty' regions of the earth. As was sometimes true with West European colonization, the new societies established by the Slav colonists differed. In Asia colonization was entirely peasant. In Siberia there were virtually no nobles and big landowning estates. In so-called New Russia (what we now call southern and south-eastern Ukraine), on the other hand, about half the land in the mid-nineteenth century was held as large estates, and mostly by nobles.[11] Nevertheless, even in New Russia, let alone in Siberia, the newly colonized regions were very different from tsarist Russia's heartland. In New Russia for instance serfdom never made much headway, most peasant colonists were actually Ukrainians, and the booming south coast cities were an incredible ethnic mix. Jews were welcomed as colonists in New Russia at a time when most of them were banned from settling in the Russian heartland. Odessa contained one of the largest and richest Jewish communities in the world, along with large colonies of Greeks, Italians and Armenians. The city's site was selected in 1794. By 1823 Odessa had a population of 30,000, by 1914 630,000. Here was a new world city like Sydney or New York. Mark Twain commented that Odessa 'looked just like an American city.'[12]

The 'front line' in the nomads' confrontation with Russian colonization was manned by the Nogais in the steppe north of the Black Sea, by the semi-nomadic Bashkirs in the region of the southern Urals and by the Buddhist Kalmyks in between. Russian expansion into their regions aimed in part to reach the cities and trade routes that lay beyond the lands the nomads controlled. It was designed too to enhance the security of the areas settled by the Russians. Moscow itself was burned by Tatars and Nogais in 1571 and raids deep into the Russian heartland continued well into the seventeenth century. The lines of forts pushed out into the steppe protected both this heartland and the advancing waves of farmer-colonists. But the land itself was the main target for Russian expansion, all the more so since it was generally much more fertile than the farmland of old Muscovy. Ultimately, in the modern battle between the nomad and the colonizing European (and therefore also Russian) farmer there could be only one victor. The Bashkirs were conquered by the 1740s, and most of the Kalmyks and Nogais fled beyond Russia's borders in the last decades of the eighteenth century in order to escape the onrush of farmer-colonists into the steppe and the growing controls over nomadic society imposed by the tsarist state. Of the 150,000 Kalmyks who set off in 1771 on the long trek eastwards to Mongolia perhaps 50,000 survived, though cold, starvation and their old nomadic enemies, the Kazakhs, were the immediate cause of disaster rather than the Russians.[13]

Beyond the Kalmyks and the Bashkirs Russia encountered the main body of West Asian nomads, whom we now call the Kazakhs but whom the Russians in tsarist times referred to as 'Kirghiz'. These peoples' resistance was largely broken by 1850, after which colonization began in their region too. The tempo of colonization of the Kazakh steppe sharply increased in the 1890s and grew even more rapid after the 1905 Revolution. The mass colonization of the 'empty' Kazakh steppe was perceived by the regime in the early twentieth century as a crucial element of its programme to relieve peasant poverty and overcrowding in parts of

European Russia and Ukraine, and thereby to counter increasingly dangerous peasant discontent against the tsarist agrarian order. In the decade before 1914 three million Slav immigrants poured into the Kazakhs' region. The so-called Steppe Statute of 1891 had opened the way to the nomads' dispossession by allowing the indigenous population the equivalent of only 40 acres per head, far less than what was needed to preserve a nomadic way of life.[14] The result was the native rising of 1916, whose other cause was the regime's attempt to conscript Kazakhs for labour service at the front. The rising was crushed, with over 200,000 Kazakhs killed and many others fleeing over the border to the more backward Chinese Turkestan, where colonists were not yet so much of a problem.

The Kazakhs' fate in the Soviet era was in the short run to be much worse even than in tsarist days. The huge famine created by the collectivization campaign killed a third of the indigenous population in 1932–3 and Khrushchev's 'Virgin Lands' policy of the 1950s deprived the Kazakhs of much of their ancestral land in the north of Kazakhstan. In the last three decades of Soviet rule the Kazakhs, however, staged both a demographic and political recovery. By 1991 they were once again the largest people in their republic, with every prospect of becoming its majority in the near future. Kazakhs dominated top positions in late Soviet Kazakhstan, let alone after independence. Unlike many of the nomadic peoples who had stood in the path of European colonization, they now controlled a huge independent state, blessed by immense mineral wealth and defined as the homeland of ethnic Kazakhs.

Beyond the Asian steppe lay the old urban and agrarian communities of Central Asia, which by the mid-nineteenth century were divided between the khanates of Khiva and Kokand and the emirate of Bokhara. Russia conquered Central Asia between the 1850s and 1880s partly in order to increase and protect its trade with the region. Long before the conquest Peter I had dreamed of opening up and monopolizing a major international trade route between Western Europe, Central Asia and the Asian lands beyond. Subsequently, Sergey Witte, Nicholas II's finance minister, dreamed that the Trans-Siberian railway would also make Russia a key intermediary and carrier in east-west trade. As regards the actual conquest of Central Asia, however, geopolitics was a more important spur than commerce. From the 1830s to the 1900s Russia's major rival was Britain. Britain fought the Crimean War in 1854–6 in order to reduce Russian power, Lord Palmerston planning to roll Russia back from the Black Sea and the Caucasus and to deprive her of most of the territory she had gained since the mid-eighteenth century. Britain lacked the armies to attain this goal on her own and Napoleon III was unwilling to make the colossal military effort that would have been necessary to achieve such grandiose war aims.[15] Nevertheless, the 1856 Treaty of Paris denied Russia the right to protect her Black Sea coast and river mouths either by a fleet or by adequate fortifications, thereby making her very vulnerable to subsequent attack by the Royal Navy. The Russian response was to move forward in Central Asia, partly as a means of regaining prestige and partly in order to create an equivalent threat to the frontiers of British India. In reality, at least until the 1880s, the Royal Navy was a much greater threat to Russia's Black Sea ports than the Russian army was to India, but acute British sensitivity about the Raj's vulnerability made the supposed threat from Central Asia a useful card in Russia's hands.

Central Asia's role within the Russian imperial economy was totally different from that of the steppe grasslands. There was no room for colonists in the Fergana Valley or the other densely populated oases of Central Asia. The rapid expansion of cotton-growing under tsarist rule, however, by 1914 meant that half of Russian industry's demand for cotton was now being met from Central Asia, thus saving considerable foreign currency and securing access to a strategic resource.[16] Already in 1914 much of Central Asia was becoming a food-deficit region because of its concentration on cotton. In the Soviet era this process was to be greatly worsened, the all-out drive for maximum production ultimately having dramatic ecological consequences because of excessive use of pesticides and incompetent irrigation policies. Both in tsarist and Soviet times, the bulk of the cotton crop was exported to factories in Central Russia, providing an obvious parallel to economic relationships between metropolis and periphery in the European colonial empires. Nevertheless, particularly in the tsarist era, there were important differences between cotton-growing in Central Asia and the plantation economy of a typical West European colony. In Central Asia most cotton was grown by indigenous small farmers, who were not driven off their land and replaced by immigrant indentured or slave labour. In the first decades of Russian rule the growth of cotton production provided many benefits to Central Asia and certainly enriched a growing indigenous middle class. In this and other ways the tsarist-era cotton economy of Central Asia had most in common with the nineteenth-century Egyptian cotton industry, developed initially under Mohammed Ali and subsequently extended under British rule.

★

In the Trans-Caucasus we meet another face of Russian empire. In many ways geography ought to have kept the Russians out of the Trans-Caucasus. The immense Caucasus mountain range was Russia's obvious southern natural frontier. It divided the world of the steppe from the quite different peoples and lands to their south. It provided formidable natural defences. Tsarist Russia first intervened in the North Caucasus after its conquest of the whole length of the Volga in the 1550s. The Russia of Ivan IV overstretched itself, however, both on its Southern Caucasian front and by attempting to seize the Baltic provinces. It took well over a century from Ivan IV's death for Russia, under Peter I's inspired leadership, to conquer Livonia and Estland. A further half-century was then required before Catherine's Russia could decisively defeat the Ottomans and annex Crimea and the huge empty steppe to its north. Only when these gains were secured by the final annexation of Crimea in 1783 did Russia move on to the conquest of the Caucasus. To do so required bases on the Black Sea, secure river communications back to central Russia, and a settled agricultural population in New Russia from which to draw supplies. The exceptionally rapid development of New Russia under Prince Potemkin and a succession of later very able viceroys created a formidable new centre of Russian power in the Black Sea region from which the further advance against the Ottomans in the Caucasus and elsewhere could be developed.

To some extent the Russians were pulled into the Trans-Caucasus – in other words across the mountains – by appeals for support from the Georgians, a fellow Orthodox people. Georgia was too weak to defend itself against increasing pressure from both the Ottomans and the Persians. Georgia had good reason to seek the protection of empire and to escape the anarchy, economic devastation and loss of population that had resulted from existing in an insecure borderland. In the mid-thirteenth century there were five million Georgians, by 1770 barely 500,000.[17] In the last decades of the eighteenth century Petersburg wavered as to whether it was worthwhile to take on the burden of defending and ruling Georgia. In the end what mattered most were strategic and geopolitical considerations. Given both traditional hostility to the Ottomans and growing rivalry with Napoleonic France and Britain in Persia and the Ottoman Empire, it was decided to annex Georgia as Russia's base and centre of power beyond the Caucasus. Once established in the region, however, the Russians to some extent had to obey the laws of local geopolitics. This entailed, for example, conquering the land and sea communications between the Trans-Caucasus and Russia. Subduing the mountain peoples of the North Caucasus proved a hugely expensive and time-consuming struggle, not concluded until the 1860s. In Shamil, the leader of Chechen and Dagestani resistance to Russia from the 1830s, the North Caucasus provided one of the most striking and famous figures in the history of the struggle of indigenous peoples (in this case Muslim) against the expansion of Europe.

The Caucasus had always been a border region between empires. It was sufficiently far from empires' core and sufficiently mountainous to be hard to control. On the other hand the roads that crossed the region were too important both strategically and commercially for neighbouring empires to ignore. By 1800 the three great imperial rivals were the Russians to the north, the Persians to the south-east and the Ottomans to the south-west. It complicated matters that each of these empires had co-religionists in the Caucasus. The Turkic Shia Muslim peoples of the Eastern Trans-Caucasus (who in the twentieth century came to call themselves Azeris) at least neighboured on Shia Persia, their natural ally and protector in an era when religion was far more significant than vernacular language or ethnicity as a focus of loyalty and identity. Christian Georgians and Armenians by contrast were cut off from Russia by the largely Sunni Muslim North Caucasian mountain peoples, who from the Russian perspective were dangerous enemies well to the rear of the Russo-Ottoman front line. In wartime co-religionists frequently constituted a fifth column in the enemy's rear, which left them open to accusations of treason and to massacre. The awful results of this Caucasian tradition, including the Armenian genocide, have been described in Chapter 4.

The Russians too, however, participated in the Caucasian tradition of mass deportation, ethnic cleansing and massacre. When the North Caucasus was finally conquered in the 1860s most of the population of its western region were 'encouraged' to emigrate to the Ottoman Empire amidst great suffering and loss of life. The Chechens and Dagestanis of the eastern region, who had resisted the Russians with equal determination, were allowed to remain in their homeland. The reason for this was that the western region, bordering on a Black Sea on which Russia was not permitted to have a navy, was acutely vulnerable to Ottoman or British attack. In the aftermath of the Crimean War, St Petersburg's perception was that Russia was dangerously weak, and Palmerston's England on the offensive worldwide. Palmerston himself commented that 'these half-civilized governments such as those of China, Portugal, Spanish America require a Dressing every eight or ten years to keep them in order', and no one who knew his views on Russia could doubt his sense that she too deserved to belong to this category of states. The Russians were not therefore prepared to leave on this coastline a Sunni population whom they quite rightly believed to be potential allies of the Ottomans in any future war. A British historian of the 'Great Game' (i.e. Anglo-Russian nineteenth-century rivalry in Asia) comments that 'the forcible exile of six hundred thousand Circassians from the Black Sea Coast deprived the Turks and the British of their most valuable potential allies within the Russian Empire.'[18]

The turn of the Chechens (and many other mountain peoples) was to come under Stalin, who accused them of collaborating with Hitler and clearly feared the presence of any suspect minority anywhere near a border. In his mentality and his concern for geopolitics, not to mention his ruthlessness, Stalin was in some ways very much an emperor. Molotov describes him poring over a map of the world, comparing the Soviet Union's geopolitical position to that of its tsarist predecessor.[19] Khrushchev comments that Stalin would have deported the whole Ukrainian people had the numbers involved not daunted even him. Certainly he did deport many smaller peoples at huge cost in lives and suffering.[20] Historians often draw parallels between Stalin, Peter the Great and Ivan the Terrible, sometimes stressing the extent to which the dictator identified with great despots of the past, both Russian and other.[21] But his penchant for geopolitics, massacre and ethnic cleansing is also rather traditionally Caucasian.

Russian expansion in the European western and north-western border-lands partly grew out of a fear for the security of the empire's political and economic heartland. This was particularly true as regards the annexation of Finland in 1808–9. The border of Finland, at that time a Swedish province, ran dangerously close to St Petersburg. On numerous occasions in the eighteenth century Swedish forces had threatened the imperial capital at times when Russia was at war with other powers. It therefore made sense to annex Finland and push back the frontier. At the time most Finns did not regret annexation by Russia since the peace of empire was preferable to being a campaigning ground for Swedish monarchs anxious to revenge the defeat of Poltava, and because in the nineteenth century the tsars allowed Finland a unique degree of autonomy, barely intervening in its internal affairs. They could afford to do this because Russian interests in the country were almost exclusively strategic. Empires that seek to colonize conquered territory with their own farmers or to exploit a native peasantry through an imported aristocracy have little alternative but to employ direct and often brutal methods of rule.

Manipulating a territory's commerce in the interests of the imperial state can often be managed less brutally, though if the intervention causes too much dislocation or damage to local interests the resulting political discontent will probably necessitate the firm imposition of imperial power. In principle, however, a territory held for purely strategic purposes may need to be strongly garrisoned but in other respects can often be allowed great freedom in its internal affairs – unless and until the presence of an imperial garrison itself becomes an intolerable affront to local nationalists.

For most of the nineteenth century the tsars seemed to have understood this point as regards Finland. Urged at one point to reduce the level of Finnish autonomy, Nicholas I responded: 'Leave the Finns in peace. Theirs is the only province in my great realm which during my whole reign has not caused me even a minute of concern or dissatisfaction.'[22] Towards the end of the nineteenth century, however, Petersburg rather forgot the essential reason for its possession of Finland. Attempts to control the Finns more closely, to conscript their sons and to impose Russian laws and language backfired badly. Finland became for the first time a zone of potential rebellion and a source of weakness, all the more dangerous for being so close to the imperial capital. After 1945 the Soviet Union managed its relationship with Finland more intelligently. The acquisition of Finnish Karelia during the Second World War reduced the military vulnerability of Leningrad (St Petersburg). The rest of Finland was allowed formal independence and almost complete internal freedom on the condition that it did nothing to offend Soviet interests and sensitivities, particularly as regards its foreign policy.

The acquisition of the Baltic provinces and Poland also made strategic sense, ensuring for instance that an enemy would have to cross a huge and inhospitable borderland before he could reach the Russian economic and political heartland. There were also important economic reasons for westward expansion. The annexation of Estland and Livonia in 1721 allowed easy direct commerce with the rest of Northern Europe and contributed greatly to the huge expansion of Russian trade in the eighteenth century. Most fundamentally, expansion westward brought millions of new, and by Russian standards rich, subjects under tsarist rule. When Catherine II came to the throne in 1762 Russia's population was still well under 20 million and smaller than that of France. The three Polish partitions in her reign between 1772 and 1795 provided the empress with another 7.5 million subjects,[23] whose fiscal and military contribution to the subsequent struggle with Napoleon was very important. The 'human capital' acquired by Peter the Great through his annexation of the Baltic provinces was much less numerous but in the persons of the Baltic German nobility and professional middle class played an immense role in government and administration, at court and in the armed forces, especially before 1850. One-eighth of all top tsarist officials between 1700 and 1917 came from these two very small groups.[24]

There were very fundamental differences between Russian empire in the European borderlands and in the Asian 'southern rim' – in other words the Caucasus, the Kazakh steppe and Central Asia. Russian rule in Asia can easily be compared with European overseas empire and was an important element in Europe's expansion at the expense of the usually non-Christian and often nomadic world. Russian expansion was based on the use of European techniques and technologies – in other words armies, railways, industry and governmental institutions organized along modern European lines.

IMPERIAL MENTALITIES AND PRIORITIES

It is true that before the era of Peter I ('the Great') the Russian elite's thinking about the steppe, Asia and the non-European world differed considerably from equivalent attitudes in Western Europe. Until near the end of the fifteenth century Russians had been subjects of a non-Christian steppe empire. Even after this empire collapsed, the Russians initially were not always militarily superior to the often formidable Muslim and nomadic peoples who ringed their southern and south-eastern border. Centuries of membership of a Tatar steppe empire had also bred a certain degree of empathy and respect for the ways and values of its diplomacy, warfare and government. Many Muslim and nomad princes and nobles entered the Russian service without initially even being required to convert to Orthodoxy.[25] When the Muscovite dynasty died out in 1598 and years of chaos followed, a converted Tatar prince descended from Genghis Khan became a serious candidate for the Russian throne. Even at the turn of the seventeenth century the Muscovite elite, like the other former subjects of the Tatars, still attached great importance and status to descent from Genghis. Imperial blood combined with the Orthodox faith gave a candidate considerable legitimacy in Russian eyes.[26]

Russian elite mentalities changed with the reign of Peter I. The Westernization of the Russian aristocracy brought with it in time Western attitudes towards nomads and Asiatics. The Russians acquired a European sense of history and progress. Non-Europeans were no longer merely heathen and untrustworthy plunderers: they were now also defined as backward and therefore potential targets for a civilizing mission.[27] More simply but very importantly, Peter's reign made Russia much more powerful, a process which continued under his successors. The sense of overwhelming power and easy victory over the non-European was a key constituent element in European imperialist arrogance: in time the tsarist elites came to share this feeling. The dominant eighteenth- and nineteenth-century Russian elite perspectives on empire in Asia are very familiar to any student of European imperialism, as are the stereotypes through which they were expressed.

Immediately after Russia's initial expansion into the Trans-Caucasus the local tsarist commander, General Tsitsianov, set the tone for Russia's Asiatic empire for most of its later existence. Tsitsianov, himself ultimately of Georgian origin, covered a policy of expansion designed to bring himself personal glory with denunciations of 'Asiatic treachery' against local potentates who opposed him and the 'Persian scum' who backed them.[28] A few years later General Yermolov, Alexander I's viceroy in the Caucasus, justified the widespread use of terror against the native mountain peoples in the following terms: 'Gentleness, in the eyes of Asiatics, is a sign of weakness, and out of pure humanity I am inexorably severe. One execution saves hundreds of Russians from destruction and thousands of Muslims from treason.'[29] Sixty years later another famous military hero and proconsul, General Skobelev, brought the peace of empire to the Turkmen warrior tribes and completed the conquest of Central Asia by the massacre of the entire army that defended Geok Tepe against him. Lord Curzon, the later viceroy of India and no stranger to methods of colonial rule, commented that 'the terrifying effect of such a massacre as Geok Tepe survives for generations.'[30] In the 1890s Russia's attention turned towards expansion in the Far East and brought her into conflict with China and Japan. Attempting in 1897 to justify first the mobilization of a European coalition to turn the Japanese out of Port Arthur and then Russia's own grabbing of the port from China, the foreign minister, Count M.N. Muravyov, claimed that 'history teaches that the Oriental respects strength and might above all else.'[31] In this case, however, the Orientals, namely the Japanese, proved themselves capable of shifting for themselves – dealing Russian imperialism a major blow in 1904–5 and repeating their success against the British Empire in 1941–2.

Most tsarist statesmen also thought in predictably European terms about the civilizing role their country was performing in Asia. Natural resources wasted by the natives must be efficiently exploited, the slothful Asiatic converted to industriousness. Touring the Crimea in 1816, four decades after it had been annexed by his grandmother, Catherine II, the future tsar Nicholas I blamed the province's poverty on the laziness and backwardness of its native Tatar population. 'If the Crimea were not in Tatar hands, it would be completely different, for where there are land-lords and Russian and Little Russian settlers, everything is different. There is grain, spacious gardens. In other words, they take advantage of the wealth of this blessed land.'[32] A century later Count Constantine von der Pahlen, who had led a major tour of inspection in Central Asia, defended the Russian record in the region in terms very familiar to European imperialism. 'The Russian conquest of Turkestan brought about an immense alleviation in the lot of the common man. Slavery was abolished, and capital punishment and the lash done away with, while the staggering relief in the burden of taxation was unique and unparalleled anywhere in the East, British possessions included.'[33] Pahlen's compari-son of Christianity and Islam was also typical[34] of the Russian, and European, imperial view: 'The Christian way of life [was] founded on the free development of the individual and his critical faculties.' Islam was by its nature a source of obscurantism and sloth. One sign of Muslim barbarism was that 'the Mohammedans believe that women, like animals, have no souls, and treat them accordingly.'[35]

Though never doubting the justice and benefit of Russia's imperial civilizing mission, Pahlen was nevertheless full of admiration for many of the nomads Russia had conquered, whom he described as 'these naïve and knightly children of the desert'.[36] Generations of Englishmen and Frenchmen wrote in similar terms about the desert Arabs. For the young officer in particular, colonial campaigning offered adventure and freedom, opportunities for violence and courage in a different, exotic and maybe erotic world. The poet Lermontov empathized with some of the wild, free, courageous Caucasian mountaineers whom he fought.[37] Adventurous young British officers empathized in similar fashion with the Pathan enemy on India's North-West Frontier. Like Lermontov they would have been inclined to despise the conventions of polite society or the life of the humdrum bourgeois in their own country. Such attitudes might or might not have a broader cultural and political significance. Admiration for indigenous peoples could easily accompany doubts about modern bourgeois and industrial society or indeed about democracy.[38] The aristocratic officer might have good reason to have more sympathy for his warrior foe than for the officials of Nicholas I's growing bureau-cracy or the Western European businessmen who were undermining aristocratic values and aristocratic dominance in Russia and Europe respectively.

Given the growing strength of nationalism in nineteenth-century

Europe, it comes as no surprise to discover that European imperialists tended to believe that their own particular brand of empire was best. The British, for instance, prided themselves on Roman standards of justice, Protestant self-discipline and incorruptibility, and the sporting gentleman's sense of fair play. Count Pahlen also argued for the superior virtues – in certain respects – of Russian imperialism. As a Protestant Baltic German aristocrat he was, however, unlikely to sing the praises of Russian national popular characteristics too loudly. Native Russians could be less reticent. Sometimes the Russian claim to be the best imperialists did not add up to much more than the assertion that in their treatment of indigenous peoples the Russians were less cold, less arrogant, less money-grubbing and less evangelizing than other European imperialists. Some Europeans actually agreed with this view in whole or in part.[39] Sometimes, however, the Russian claim to a natural empathy with Asia went deeper than this and had greater significance. Sensitive Russians knew that Europe looked down its nose at Russia and regarded it as only semi-civilized. Lord Curzon for example commented that Russia's conquest of Central Asia was 'a conquest of orientals by orientals'.[40] Most educated Russians bitterly resented such comments but in some cases they caused Russians to think of their part in Europe's civilizing imperial mission in a new light.

The most extreme Russian reaction to European slights was to accept them, in the process celebrating Russia's semi-Asiatic roots, its Tatar heritage, and its separateness from European civilization. This was the essence of so-called Eurasianism, which made some impact on the Russian intelligentsia before 1914 and more after 1917 on the White emigration. Throughout the nineteenth century there had always been a nationalist strain in Russian thinking which stressed Russian uniqueness but this tendency had always emphasized Orthodoxy and Slavdom as the sources of Russian originality. To stress common elements with the Tatars, steppe tradition, even Hinduism and the Confucian Orient was new. To some extent the Russians were merely expressing a fashionable *fin-de-siècle* enthusiasm for the irrational, the exotic and the illiberal. Given Russian intellectual traditions, Russia's geographical position and its ambivalent relationship with Europe, Russians could at a pinch claim these exotic, non-Western cultures and values as part of their own identity. Before 1914 Russian Eurasianism could be very conservative in orientation, stressing for instance Russia's and Asia's common allegiance to autocratic monarchy, an irrational and religious cosmology, and anti-liberal collectivist values.[41] In the context of 1917 and Bolshevik power, however, Eurasian ideas could also merge with belief in the new Russia's revolutionary energy and its potential to destroy Europe's tired bourgeois civilization.

The fruits of Eurasianist scholarship could be impressive and many Eurasianists had a deep and genuine respect for non-European cultures. In the light of current Russian enthusiasm for Eurasianism two points do, however, merit attention. In the first place, before 1914 Eurasianism was very much a minority movement in Russian educated society, most of whose members looked firmly Westwards in both cultural and political terms. Secondly, Eurasianism itself was in many ways a spin-off of Russia's difficult relationship with Europe, its sense of inferiority and rejection. This was very evident in the White emigration, many of whose members were traumatized by the Russian people's rejection of the European elite and its values in 1917, not to mention by the humiliations of life in emigration in Europe, with their cultural compass awry and inherited position in society gone. Behind Eurasian enthusiasm there always lurked a suspicion of Dostoyevsky's famous celebration of Russian imperialism in Asia: 'In Europe we were hangers-on and slaves, whereas in Asia we shall go as masters.'[42]

Dostoyevsky's words say something fundamental about the great differences between Russian imperialism in Asia and in Europe. In Asia on the whole most of the Russian elite felt a sense of superiority and confidence. In the European western borderlands they often felt quite the opposite. Military power and political domination were combined with a sense of vulnerability and cultural inferiority. This was particularly true in the last decades of the tsarist regime. In the eighteenth century, following Peter's lead, there was for generations within the Russian elite an acknowledgement of cultural backwardness and the need to borrow from Europe. This included too, for example, willingness to accept that local government in the Baltic provinces was more advanced and efficient than in Russia and might even profitably be used as a model for future Russian reforms – as indeed to some extent happened with the 1775 reform of Russian provincial government and the 1785 establishment of noble corporate institutions in the Great Russian provinces. Accepting cultural inferiority was easier in the cosmopolitan and aristocratic eighteenth century than in the more nationalist nineteenth century. In any case in the eighteenth century the tsarist state was a triumphant success in war and diplomacy. A sense of security and self-confidence eased the pain of cultural inferiority. After all, in many ways the ancient Romans had accepted their cultural inferiority to Greece and drawn heavily on Hellenism: their enormous pride and self-confidence derived from military and political success made this easily palatable.

The nineteenth-century Russian state was much less successful and felt much more vulnerable. The 1830–1 and 1863–4 Polish insurrections made Russians see Poles as dangerous and inveterate enemies. Defeat in the Crimean War bred a sense of weakness vis-à-vis great power enemies. Stunning Prussian victories in 1866–71 followed by the unification of Germany strengthened this feeling. The aristocracy and middle classes in most of Russia's western borderlands were Poles or Germans: by 1900 these were widely perceived in St Petersburg as actually or potentially disloyal. Considerations of both security and Russian nationalism led to efforts to build up the position of the majority, Orthodox peasantry in the region, who were in modern terminology Ukrainian or Belorussian but whom St Petersburg perceived as Russians. These supposedly loyal, Orthodox and Russian peasants were seen increasingly as the secure foundation of tsarist rule and a guarantee that the western borderlands would remain Russian forever.

St Petersburg became acutely, exaggeratedly conscious of Russian weakness in the region. One result was a swathe of policies designed to boost Russian landowning, the Russian language, the Orthodox Church and peasant economic well-being in the region. Within the Russian heartland government policy towards the peasantry was partly rooted in the conception that a paternalist regime was needed to protect a naïve and vulnerable people against the pressures and temptations of a modern capitalist economy and the wily elites who ran it (noble landowners were by contrast seen as agents of benevolent paternalism). Peasant farms, for instance, could not be sold or mortgaged in order to ensure a basic welfare net and source of subsistence for the rural masses. In the western borderland similar paternalist ideologies and instincts drove policies designed to protect the simple 'Russian' peasant from the better educated, more enterprising and more wily Pole, German and Jew.[43] By 1914 attitudes to the Jews in particular were becoming pathological in some sections of the ruling elite. The 'Jewish threat' became a lightning rod for tensions caused by rapid economic modernization, domestic political instability and external military vulnerability.

The Russian sense of cultural inferiority and weakness in the western borderlands was very dissimilar indeed to the cultural arrogance of West European maritime imperialism. Advocating a range of special privileges and defences for the 'Russian' population of the western borderlands, the former war minister, General Aleksey Kuropatkin, commented that 'ideas of equality and freedom are dangerous for nations weaker in culture and advantageous for those stronger.'[44] This was the language and the policy not of confident imperialism but of post-colonial nationalist governments in South-East Asia and Africa seeking to offset Chinese and Indian economic and cultural dominance.

Behind these differences between Russian imperialism in Europe and in Asia lay one point of fundamental importance. From the perspective of elites and government, the empire in Europe almost always seemed much more important. In part this was a question of culture. The elite felt itself to be European. As Sergey Sazonov, the foreign minister, commented in 1912, 'one must not forget . . . that Russia is a European power, that the state was formed not on the banks of the Black Irtych but on the banks of the Dnieper and of the river Moskva.'[45] Very few of the members of Russia's parliament who heard him make this comment would have disagreed with its thrust or with the minister's sense of Russia's cultural and historical essence.

But much more down-to-earth factors were more important. The western borderlands covered the political and economic heartland of Russian power against its only major threat – which came from Europe. In addition, the western borderlands were much richer and more populous than Russian Asia, and usually made a far greater contribution to the state's treasury and its military power. Above all, this was true of nineteenth- and twentieth-century Ukraine. By 1900 this was the empire's leading agricultural region and the source of the immense cereal exports which were the key to the external trade balance, and therefore to Russia's ability to afford the foreign loans essential to her modernization. In the five decades before 1914 eastern Ukraine also became the centre of the mining and metallurgical industry. A Russian empire that lost Ukraine, as very nearly happened in 1917–18, would cease to be an empire or a great power. In subsequent decades the growth of Siberian heavy industry and of its oil and gas-related economy made Ukraine somewhat less crucial in economic terms to the Soviet Union than it had been to late tsarist Russia. In political and demographic terms, however, its importance was unchanged. By the 1980s, without the large Ukrainian population the Russians would be left almost alone in the Soviet Union with the culturally alien, economically backward but rapidly growing 'Muslim' peoples of the southern rim. Sustaining such an empire might quickly prove neither politically viable nor in the Russians' own interests. In fact, the Ukrainian decision for independence in the autumn of 1991 was followed within days by the disintegration of the Union.

The first 150 years of Russia's empire in Siberia more closely resembled the French empire in Canada than Russian imperialism in any of the regions described so far, though Russian treatment of the indigenous peoples seems to have been worse and the Orthodox Church was much less interested in converting them than was the case with French Catholic missionaries. This was an empire of the wandering trapper, whose *raison d'être* was harvesting furs. Trappers spread thinly over a vast area. The native population was not much thicker on the ground – at the end of the sixteenth century numbering probably only 200,000 in all Siberia. By terror and the taking of hostages the Russians forced the primitive tribes of Siberia to pay both them and the state a heavy tribute in furs. Towards the end of the seventeenth century roughly 100,000 pelts a year reached Moscow as tribute, amounting to one-tenth of the state's total revenue.[46] Though the Russians often treated the indigenous populations with appalling brutality – trade in their women being the runner-up to furs in terms of profitability – in principle they wished to preserve the local population in order to exploit it. To enforce tribute and store its proceeds, forts needed to be built and small garrisons maintained. Some farming was essential in order to keep the garrisons and the traders alive. By 1700 the Russians had come close to exterminating Siberia's fur-bearing animals and the supply of 'soft gold' from the colony was about to decline sharply. Siberia was, however, to develop in other ways very profitable to the Russian economy. By 1913 western Siberia was the most prosperous area of Russian peasant farming in the empire. Of an overall imperial population of almost 164 million, only 10.3 million lived in all Siberia but the Siberians accounted for one-quarter of the purchases of agricultural machinery throughout the empire. West Siberian peasant dairy farmers accounted for 16 per cent of global butter exports and were in the process of capturing the British market when war came in 1914.[47]

Siberia also provides examples of a type of Russian imperial expansion which has no real parallels with West European colonial empires: one might at a pinch make not very precise comparisons with the development of Chinese heavy industry in the Manchurian borderlands, though it needs to be remembered that industrialization here got off to a spectacular start under Japanese colonial rule in the 1930s.[48] Having colonized contiguous regions the Russians (and on occasion also Ukrainians) sometimes turned them into major centres of industry, of crucial importance to the Russian and imperial economy. The first example of this was the metallurgical industry of the Urals, created from the early eighteenth century in areas conquered from, among others, the Bashkirs. By the last quarter of the eighteenth century the Urals iron industry was the biggest in Europe and Russia was the continent's largest producer of iron. A century later the Donbas in eastern Ukraine had become a huge mining and metallurgical centre too, created in a region which had been almost empty even in the 1750s. One hundred years later the west Siberian oil and gas industry became under Brezhnev the leading sector of the Soviet economy and the source of most of its foreign currency earnings. Its development spelled disaster for a number of Siberian native peoples such as the Khanty-Mansi, who had previously been allowed a certain degree of freedom to pursue their traditional culture in vast regions in which few Europeans had ever shown much interest since the extermination of fur-bearing animals.

It is often debated whether expansion and empire benefit a state and its people. Where the Russian people is concerned, a cost–benefit analysis of empire is a difficult exercise and one which, in one form or another, will take up much of this book. It should by now be clear, however, that in the long run the state gained enormously in wealth and power as a result of most, though not all, of its territorial acquisitions. Without these conquests it would not have been a great power. Even today, in a post-imperial era, Siberia – the jewel in Russia's imperial crown – gives Russia the chance to experience the loss of empire and yet remain a great power, something that geography made impossible for the maritime, overseas empires of Britain, France, Spain and the Netherlands. The loss of their overseas possessions doomed these former imperial powers to second-class status or worse. By absorbing Siberia into metropolitan Russia Moscow has the chance, though not the certainty, of avoiding this fate.

PERIPHERAL, LAND EMPIRE

This brings us to the most fundamental geographical distinction between the Russian Empire on the one hand and most modern European empires on the other. The former, with the exception of the unimportant province of Alaska, was land-based: the latter expanded overseas. Some of the distinctions between land and maritime empire are not constant but instead vary according to the development of technology. True oceanic empire was only conceivable with the ship-building and navigational technologies developed in Europe from the fifteenth century. In the nineteenth century steam and the telegraph transformed the grand strategy of maritime empire, though not as fundamentally as the railway revolutionized age-old methods of integrating and exploiting the resources of far-flung land empires. Halford Mackinder's insight into how this shifted the balance of power between land and sea empire was indeed one of the foundations of modern geopolitics.[49] In the contemporary world rocketry and airpower have changed the military balance once again. Modern communications have also made it far easier for emigrants to retain close links with their homelands and to resist integration into the societies where they work and where they live most of their lives.[50]

Some distinctions between land and sea empire have, however, remained more or less constant during most or all of modern history. The key point about seapower is its mobility. No mountains, swamps or rivers impede free movement across the seas, though fleets and amphibious landing forces do, to varying degrees, require bases. In some circumstances victory in one ocean can rather quickly bring the domination of other oceans or even of all the world's seas. Since most international trade in the modern era has been seaborne, the opportunities to monopolize this huge source of wealth or at least to regulate its movement advantageously are obvious. But seapower's mobility makes maritime empire vulnerable. The British lost their North American colonies to a great extent because their lines of communication across the Atlantic were too long and too vulnerable to French attack. By the twentieth century the security of Britain's maritime empire required naval superiority over the Germans, Japanese and Italians in three great seas on either side of the globe. Holding together and defending a Russian empire blessed by secure land-based interior lines of communications was much the easier task.

The medical histories of land and sea empire are also different. A good deal of ink and sentiment has been spent on discussing the relative costs to their subjects of Russian and West European imperialism. If death is the highest cost that empire can impose, disease rather than massacre or exploitation was empire's worst crime. In the Americas and Australasia diseases against which the native populations had no immunity had effects often close to genocide. If William McNeill is right in attributing the arrival in Europe of the Black Death to the Mongols' unification of much of Eurasia, then Europeans too in an earlier era had been the unwitting victims of imperial expansion.[51] On the whole, though smallpox was unknown in most of Siberia before the Russians' arrival,[52] Russian expansion was not accompanied by such extreme medical consequences, especially among the nomads of the steppe region. The Russians expanded within a single ecological system, most of whose population (with the exception of some of the north Siberian peoples) had already built up immunity against the diseases that the Russians brought with them.

The English, Dutch, Spanish, French and Portuguese expanded overseas into what were, for them, new worlds. People of wholly different culture and colour, who had never before imagined each other's existence, suddenly came face to face. The results, both good and bad, were dramatic. The unprecedented integration of the Americas into a European-dominated global economy had enormous long-term consequences. The impact of the New World on European thought and imagination was also profound, playing a role in undermining medieval ways of understanding the cosmos and humanity's role within it. Russia's expansion had no such profound consequences. The Russians were not expanding into a truly new world. As a barrier between continents the Urals were a good deal less impressive than the Atlantic. The native peoples of Siberia were not so different from the tribes of north-eastern European Russia whom the Russians, in their search for fur, had long since discovered and exploited. Indeed, in the case of the Khanty, Voguls and Samoyeds they were the same.[53] The nomads encountered during Russian expansion across the steppe were even more familiar. Not until the Russians collided with the world of the Caucasian mountaineers in the early nineteenth century did they encounter a society that was genuinely new to them and truly fired their imaginations. But even the Caucasian mountaineers were not as astonishing and unexpected an apparition as the societies discovered by the Europeans on first arriving in the Americas.

Geography played an important role in distinguishing the way in which West Europeans and Russians thought about colonization and empire. John Elliott comments that 'crossing that "frightful ocean" (was) an experience that etched itself deep into the consciousness of generations of European migrants.'[54] Once arrived in the New World, the obvious differences in vegetation, climate and animal life convinced the colonist that he or she had embarked on a new life. There are, after all, no kangaroos in Gloucestershire. For the Russian colonist, continuing his ancestors' traditional pattern of movement down the rivers and across the steppe was unlikely to have the same sense of otherness. In today's Russia this lack of a strong traditional sense of distinction between colony and motherland could have important consequences as regards the legitimacy and stability of Russia's post-imperial frontiers.

Geography placed Russia on Europe's periphery. Many consequences flowed from this fact. Peripherality meant that Russia bordered on the Eurasian steppe. Before the balance of power shifted decisively towards sedentary societies in the seventeenth and eighteenth centuries, this made Russia vulnerable to nomadic pressure and invasion. From the 1240s until the second half of the fifteenth century Russia was firstly part of a Mongol near-universal empire, and then a dependency of its successor state, the Golden Horde. In this era Russian eyes were forcibly turned eastwards and the country's isolation from Europe increased. Subsequently the Russian state benefited from the vacuum that followed the Golden Horde's demise and, more basically, from the growing superiority over nomads which a state and army organized on European lines possessed.

England, Spain and Russia, Europe's peripheral powers, became its greatest empires. They could most easily bring Europe's superior techniques and technologies to bear on weaker non-European peoples. The expansion of these three powers was not foreordained. Each had to defeat European rivals before it could launch into successful extra-European expansion. Once the ground had been laid, however, it was much easier to expand on or outside Europe's periphery than at its core. Europe contained rival states of roughly equal sophistication and development. Geography made it easier for coalitions of neighbouring powers to intervene and block the excessive expansion of any would-be empire. It was a great deal harder for European states to stop British expansion in India or Australasia, or Russia's consolidation of its hold on Ukraine or Central Asia. Moreover, when a continental power, first Napoleon's France and then twentieth-century Germany, did aspire to Europe-wide hegemony, the peripheral empires, Britain and Russia, could intervene against it, mobilizing the resources of their extra-European possessions in this cause. Finally, in the post-imperial era, geographical peripherality and its historical and cultural consequences was a factor in making it more difficult for Russian, English and Turkish heirs to empire to come to terms with a new Europe built around a Franco-German 'Carolingian' core.

Partly because it bordered on Europe, Russia's experience of European power and expansion was very different from that of more distant empires in Asia, Africa and the Americas. For the Chinese and Japanese, for instance, European power intruded with dramatic and unexpected effect in the nineteenth century. By then Russia already had three centuries' experience of adapting itself to this reality, one result of which had been a relatively consistent and successful process of borrowing European technologies and ideas. Because their relationship with the West dominated the consciousness of educated Russians it greatly affected their conceptions about their non-Russian subjects, both European and Asian. Geography therefore played its part in making Russians look upon themselves, Europe and empire in ways that differed significantly both from the viewpoints of other European peoples and from the non-European peoples whose lands Europe colonized.

In most peripheral societies in the pre-modern era, institutions and culture were shallower than in the heartlands of the civilizations on which they bordered. Unlike either Byzantium or sixteenth-century West and Central Europe, for example, pre-Petrine Muscovy possessed little by way of secular high culture or vernacular literature. Peripheral societies, partly for this reason, have tended to be adaptable and malleable, absorbing outside influences easily. Sometimes their ability to utilize the technology of neighbouring civilizations has made them formidable conquerors, combining the techniques of more advanced societies with the military virtues of the more primitive periphery. Some Europeans always saw Russians in this light. In the early eighteenth century, for example, they could be viewed as a new and more dangerous form of Turk – as alien, barbarous and terrifying, but much better at adopting Western technology. The astonishing endurance and fortitude of the Russian infantry, the Scythian-style raiding of its Cossack cavalry, remained European stereotypes of Russia for centuries. No doubt they influenced NATO generals, worriedly contemplating the defence of a comfortable materialist civilization against the supposedly tougher and more primitive soldiery of the USSR. In reality, however, cultural, socio-economic and psychological changes in the Soviet Union during the 1970s and 1980s meant that this soldiery was to prove far less formidable than worried Europeans had supposed.

This is just one example of a more general point: geography's influence on the history of Russia's empire was very important but it must not be exaggerated. In most cases what happened in Russians' heads was more significant than where they stood on the map. This is particularly true where mentalities, identities and perceptions of self, Russia, Europe and empire are concerned. The Caucasus inspired the imagination of early nineteenth-century Russians, for example, because in a Romantic age they were increasingly obsessed by a search for national identity.[55] Had the encounter occurred earlier, stupendous mountains and exotic tribesmen would have been seen in the same way as Siberian bog – just one more obstacle to the pursuit of material profit.

Because the Russians were Europe's neighbours they were always more likely to borrow its religion and elements of its culture rather than those of more distant civilizations. But it was not predetermined by geography that they would choose Orthodoxy rather than Catholicism or even Islam. The choice was crucial, and not least for its implications for future relations with Europe. Shared Christianity provided a bridge over which cultural influences travelled. The seventeenth-century Ukrainian Orthodox Church, for instance, was a vital conduit whereby Latin

European modernizing influences reached Moscow. But even before the dramatic programme of Westernization started by Peter I, the relationship with Europe had been one of both attraction and repulsion.

To a great extent, this is true of all non-Western societies in the modern era. All have been forced to Westernize in order to survive, and all have to varying degrees resented this fact and developed nativist, conservative ideologies in response. Russia's relationship with Europe is unique, however. Partly because their indigenous culture was closer to Latin Christianity and was in any case not as rich or deeply rooted as Confucianism or Islam, the Russians proved uniquely successful in adopting Western institutions and values, modernizing their state, and becoming the equal of the European great powers. But precisely because it was more accessible to European influences and subjected to them for far longer, Russian identity was never as secure or as confident as was the case with the older and more alien Confucian, Buddhist or Islamic societies. Perhaps this has had something to do with the peculiar intensity with which modern Russian intellectuals have proclaimed their allegiance to or rejection of the West.[56] Of course, behind all these very complex cultural phenomena the influence of geography cannot be discounted. But so nuanced and intricate a cultural relationship as Russia's links with European civilization is scarcely explicable by the crude measure of geographical determinism.

The fact that Russia was a continuous land empire certainly contributed to Russia's weak sense of a clear divide between colony and motherland, but tsarist policy contributed even more. Crucial to the development of a separate colonial identity in the English-speaking world were self-governing political institutions which allowed that identity to be defined, developed and defended. The Russian government was careful not to allow such institutions to arise. In the second half of the nineteenth century the Siberian autonomist movement put forward claims to a separate Siberian identity rooted in the conditions of frontier life, marriage with the indigenous communities and the absence of nobles or serfdom in Siberian history.[57] The tsarist regime suppressed the movement, put strong constraints on any expression of Siberian identity, and used the Trans-Siberian railway to flood the region with Russian immigrants.

The case of the Cossacks is even more illuminating. Here was a quintessentially frontier society in the sixteenth and seventeenth centuries, fundamentally different from autocratic and serf-owning tsarist Russia. The political and cultural distance between tsarist Moscow and Cossack Zaporozhye was certainly not less than that between colonial Virginia and London. The nineteenth-century Ukrainian poet and nationalist Taras Shevchenko was indeed to mobilize the image of the freedom-loving Cossack as a means to stress Ukraine's distinctiveness, its difference from autocratic and serf-owning Russia. The emergence of a sense of separate Cossack identity rooted in similar anti-tsarist imagery in different political circumstances was quite conceivable. Tsarist policy worked steadily and successfully to avoid any such development. The fact that the Cossack regions were linked to Russia by land made it easier for tsarism to achieve this goal, but did not make either the effort or its success inevitable. To discover the deeper roots of this policy it is necessary to turn from geography to the political traditions of the Russian state, most of which can be traced back to the era before Muscovy began to acquire its empire.

7

The Tsarist State and the Russian People

The history of the Russian Empire is usually taken to have begun in the 1550s. In that decade Tsar Ivan IV ('The Terrible') conquered and annexed the Tatar khanates of Kazan and Astrakhan on the River Volga. These khanates were very far from being the first lands to be swallowed by Moscow's princes in their rise from insignificance to great-power status. They were not even the first territories inhabited by non-Slav and non-Christian peoples who had never previously been subject to a Russian prince. But unlike the quite primitive pagan tribesmen whom Moscow had conquered in the previous two centuries, the khanates of Kazan and Astrakhan were well-organized, sophisticated and powerful Muslim states. They were the first such states to be annexed by Moscow and the first Muslim peoples to come under its rule. Their conquest reversed the previous three hundred years of Russian history, during which the Russian princes had been subjects of a Tatar and latterly Muslim empire. Their annexation opened the way to further imperial expansion into Siberia, across the steppe and to the Caucasus mountains in the south.

Dating Russia's empire from the 1550s therefore makes sense. The aim of this chapter is to investigate the pre-imperial history of the Russian state and people, and to evaluate the influence of institutions, values and traditions established before 1550 on the subsequent history of Russia's empire. Common sense suggests that the political traditions of a state and community will have a big impact on the subsequent history of the empire that they create. So too will the methods by which the empire is initially created – whether for instance by conquest or by a dynastic union such as that which linked Bohemia to the House of Austria or Scotland to England. Even a slight experience of history's twists and turns also, however, suggests that it would be very naïve to reduce all an empire's development to some dominant spirit or tendency in the pre-imperial history of its leading community.

The history of the Austrian and British empires, already considered in previous chapters, supports the argument for common sense. Who can deny the great importance of the fact that the Austrian Empire was a conglomeration of diverse crownlands whose ancient constitutions and identities were preserved because the Habsburg Monarchy was put together by dynastic marriages, not by conquest? The pre-imperial history of these territories and the manner of their consolidation had a huge impact on subsequent Habsburg history without, however, determining everything that came thereafter. There were key turning-points when the empire could have disintegrated or indeed could greatly have increased its long-term power and viability. Even under empire the history of the various crownlands was enormously diverse – Hungary for instance usually following a path that diverged radically from developments elsewhere in the Monarchy. Moreover, the empire of the Counter-Reformation was very different from the enlightened monarchy of Joseph II or the state that struggled in the Habsburgs' last decades against the challenge of nationalism.

Very much the same points can be made about the history of the British Empire. It mattered greatly in the subsequent history of the British Empire that even in 1600 England possessed a powerful parliament, a tradition of local self-government, and a deeply rooted common law. The triumph of these principles over would-be Stuart absolutism in the seventeenth century was also crucial to empire's history. Nowadays, however, even the most naïve and triumphalist Whig historian would shrink from proclaiming the whole history of the British Empire to be the majestic realization of principles of law and democracy immanent in Tudor history and raised to global dominance by England's expansion worldwide. Obviously, a vast swathe of imperial history – including for example most of British government in non-White territories – could scarcely be explained in these terms alone. Even as regards White subjects, the English themselves included, there was a big difference between the Whig eighteenth-century constitution with its powerful monarchy and its aristocratic dominance, and twentieth-century democracy. Indeed, in Chapter 3 of this book it was seen how the shift towards parliamentary domination of the executive within Britain after the 1832 Reform Act had an immediate and major impact on the constitutional and political relationships between Westminster and the White overseas colonies.

In principle one would expect the political traditions of the Muscovite tsardom to have had an even bigger impact on the history of the Russian Empire than English traditions on Britain's imperial history. Oceans divided the English from most of their colonies. From the beginning a clear constitutional and territorial distinction was made between these colonies, and especially the non-White empire, and the Kingdom of England. By contrast the Russian Empire was a consolidated land mass whose rulers' long-term policy was to consolidate their territories into a single homogeneous unit. If law and representative government are the dominant clichés of English political history, autocracy and centralization are their Russian equivalents. Like most clichés, these ones actually embody a great deal of truth. Autocracy and centralization were crucial to the history of Russia's empire. But it would be a vast error and oversimplification to reduce all of Russia's imperial rule over many centuries and across one-sixth of the world's territory to these principles alone.

PEOPLE AND CHURCH BEFORE EMPIRE

By the time the Russian Empire began to be built in the mid-sixteenth century, a Russian people had already existed for many years, possessing a clearly distinct identity both in its own eyes and in those of foreign observers of the Muscovite realm. In origin the Great Russians are a combination of Scandinavian, Slav and Finnic tribes who coalesced into a recognizably distinct community – which one might describe as Muscovite or Great Russian according to taste – between the tenth and sixteenth centuries. The Scandinavian, Viking element was numerically the weakest. Russia differed from England, Ireland and France in never having a sizeable Scandinavian peasant community. The Vikings came as warriors and merchants, never as farmers. They intermarried with Slav elites and by the sixteenth century had long since disappeared as a separate entity. Finnic tribes were more numerous and were the original inhabitants of the Great Russian heartland. Though some Slavs were probably already migrating into this region by the eighth century, the real influx came between 1000 and 1200 AD.[1] The Great Russian people were above all Slav in their language and culture but they were to bear many traces of the Finnic tribes they had absorbed. Vasily Klyuchevsky, most famous of Russia's historians, believed that the high cheekbones, rather dark complexions and thick noses of the Great Russians marked them from other Slavs and were derived from their Finnic ancestors.[2]

The pagan culture of Great Russians drew on Slav, Finnic and

Scandinavian sources. In the eleventh and twelfth centuries a pagan ancestor cult still flourished among the Russian princes, though the dynasty of Rurik had in principle been Christian since 988.[3] Even slower was the penetration of Christianity into the scattered rural population. The villages were not truly conquered by the church until the fourteenth century, at a time when Great Russia was subject to the Mongols. For many centuries afterwards the conquest was far from complete. Christian feasts and beliefs were intertwined with ancient pagan festivals and ways of thinking. Peasant mentalities were conditioned by life in a natural environment whose basic patterns were cyclical. Humans were born, grew up, produced children and died; animals, crops and seasons followed a similar, regular pattern. Nature was all-powerful but it could also be arbitrary and devastating, with disease and the very changeable climate of north-eastern Russia wrecking the people's life. A folk culture repressed by the church but sustained by wandering minstrels combined resignation, attempts to propitiate nature and its forces, and riotous celebration of key moments of the human life-cycle and the agricultural seasons. Abundant rivers and forests, together with tougher types of grain suitable for a northern climate (rye, oats, buckwheat), provided the basis of Russian cuisine. But food and the way it was eaten defined being Russian less than was the case in many other societies, partly because Orthodoxy put no strict taboos on diet. By contrast the bath-house and the drinking of vodka were surrounded by rituals whose pagan origins and significance in Russian culture were evident.[4]

The influence of climate and environment on a people's culture, temperament and psyche cannot be proven, let alone quantified. Historians, not to speak of social scientists, steer clear of making the kind of generalizations for which Montesquieu was famous. But common sense suggests that nature will leave its impact on pre-modern peoples who were so wholly its subjects. The nomad is bound to have different values, dreams and culture from those of the farmer. In the hot desert the Bedouin dreams of grass, water and fountains. In the cold and snow of a Russian winter the sensible peasant spends as much time as he is allowed as close as possible to his stove, which is much the most vital part of his house. In the Russian winter snow is on the ground for five to six months. Summers are very hot. The agricultural seasons are short and hectic. The soil is generally poor, the climate changeable and unreliable. In medieval times settlements were small and scattered. Plots were carved out of forest and swamp; exploited for three or four years, they were then allowed to revert to nature, the peasant moving on to cultivate a new section of the forest.

A people bred in these conditions was likely to differ sharply from, to take but one example, the Chinese peasants south of the Yangtze who were the backbone of another great imperial tradition. Very fertile soils sustained huge concentrated populations engaged in the meticulous, almost craftsmanlike labour of the rice farmer and trained to participate in large-scale irrigation works. Not surprisingly, these factors created attitudes to community, nature and authority which differed sharply from those of the Russian peasant. They also contributed greatly to the strength and solidity of the Chinese Empire, and to the Han Chinese ability to win the allegiance of conquered peoples and to assimilate them. The cultural magnetism of China was rooted not just in an artistic, literary and architectural high culture without rival in the region but also in the clear superiority of its agricultural techniques and technology over those of neighbouring peoples.[5] By contrast, Russian agricultural methods even in 1850 were not merely inferior to those of Baltic peoples, Poles and Finns in the empire's western borderlands but also on the whole not even superior to those of the Volga Tatar peasants whom Russia had ruled since the 1550s. Tatar peasants had little to learn from their Russian peasant neighbours as regards agriculture, let alone hygiene and cleanliness, and this inevitably affected their long-term allegiance to Russian culture or willingness to assimilate.[6] A historian of Russian imperialism in the Far East at the turn of the twentieth century makes even less flattering comparisons between Russian and Chinese peasant farming. 'An agricultural revolution, with the adoption of many new crops by the peasantry, had occurred in China in the eighteenth and nineteenth centuries, whereas Russian peasant husbandry, not long removed from serfdom, was based on primitive medieval rotations and extensive methods contrasting markedly with the more intensive system of the Chinese peasants'.[7] Even if demography had allowed Russians to compete with Chinese for the domination of early twentieth-century Manchuria (which it did not), the Chinese would still have won the competition hands down in terms of agricultural skills and productivity. Inevitably such comparisons did nothing for the prestige of the Russian Empire in oriental eyes.

Vasily Klyuchevsky – free from the constraints that shackle the early twenty-first-century scholar – risked a number of generalizations about the influence of their environment on the character of the Great Russians. The national disinclination to steady, carefully planned work could be ascribed in Klyuchevsky's opinion to a capricious climate which upset any plan and imposed inactivity in some seasons and intense labour in others.[8] Not only are such characterizations of a people often true but in time they become stereotypes, even clichés. Noted by outsiders and believed in by a people itself, they become part of its identity and distinctiveness. In narrower and more purely political terms it is also certainly the case that the whole history of Russian empire bore the impact of the late (seventeenth-century) imposition of a particularly harsh and arbitrary form of serfdom on a people previously used to great freedom and mobility. Although serfdom itself was abolished in 1861 the memories it left behind were still an important factor in the sharp antagonism between Russian elites and masses which destroyed tsarism and empire in 1917.

Even more than by geography and the natural environment, the Russian identity was defined by Orthodox Christianity. By the end of the fourteenth century the church had converted to Orthodoxy a peasantry whose faith had for long been nominal. Henceforth all the great events in the human life-cycle were celebrated with Orthodox rituals, as were the seasons and the harvest. The Orthodox calendar organized the year. The story of Christ's incarnation and resurrection had a great influence on the people's ethical sense and on their understanding of their place in the cosmos. The church's liturgy, music and icons were among the most stirring and beautiful experiences of the people's life. The best evidence of Orthodoxy's capture of the Russian mind is the huge, passionate popular resistance that erupted against changes in the church's rituals and dogmas in the seventeenth century, and which resulted in the breaking away from the church of the so-called Old Believers.

The Orthodox Church was well suited to be the bearer of national identity. It owed allegiance to no foreign head such as the pope. Its sacred language – in other words the language of the liturgy and the scriptures – was Church Slavonic, a form of proto-Russian. In the West, Latin remained the sole language of sacred writing until the Reformation. In the Orthodox Church by contrast, all key religious works were translated from the original Greek into the vernacular. Very few Russians therefore ever learned Greek, and whatever the bonds of shared religion, none doubted that Greeks were foreigners. Indeed, the seventeenth-century revolt of the Old Believers was precisely a reaction against efforts to purify and modernize religious practice on the basis of Greek models. The only Greece that ever meant anything to the Russians was the Byzantine religious heritage and the artistic, architectural and musical culture that sprang from it. Classical Greece was a closed book. A sacred vernacular helped therefore to isolate Russia culturally but it also contributed to the prestige of the Russian language and the self-confidence of the society that spoke it.

By 1500 all the Great Russians were Orthodox. Almost all the tsar's subjects at that time were Orthodox Great Russians. The enemies that surrounded Great Russia, in other words the Muscovite realm, were pagan, Muslim or Latin Christian. The enemies of people, church and ruler were the same – or at least could easily be portrayed as such by the propagandists of the Orthodox tsardom. By 1500 the Moscow dynasty had united almost all the lands of Orthodox Great Russia under its sceptre. From the mid-fifteenth century, the title 'tsar', derived from the name of Caesar, began to be used with increasing frequency by Moscow's ruler, finally entering the coronation service in 1547. Prayers in the liturgy and the bishops' statements made very clear the tsar's position as supreme defender of the orthodox Russian community.

In their desperation to secure help from the West against the Ottomans in 1439 the Byzantines had agreed to reunion with the Latin church. Russians interpreted the eclipse of Byzantium in 1453 as God's punishment for Byzantine apostasy. Russia was now beyond question the champion of the only true faith not only because it was the only remaining independent Orthodox state but also because its faith had proven purer and less prone to error than that of the Greeks. This was the main sense of the doctrine that Moscow was the third Rome, first articulated in the early sixteenth century. Neither this doctrine nor the tsar's adoption of the double-headed eagle and other Byzantine symbols constituted any claim to former Byzantine territory, let alone to Byzantium's traditional ideology of universal empire. But they did represent a big gain in status and self-confidence for both the Russian ruler and the Russian land, together with a total identification of both with the Orthodox cause. In the same period the term 'Holy Russia' – uniting land, people, church and ruler – began to be used to 'express a deeply-felt national spirit'.[9]

The dynasty with which the fate of the Russian people and church was now identified was actually an ancient one. Its ancestor was the semi-mythical Viking chieftain Rurik, forebear of the grand princes of Kiev and Vladimir, and all the horde of minor princelings who ruled most of what we think of today as Ukraine, Belarus (Belorussia) and Russia – known historically as 'Rus' – from the tenth to the fourteenth centuries. Until the fourteenth century the Moscow Rurikid princes were merely one among the many branches of the dynasty – and by no means the most senior and most powerful. Moscow's ascent in the fourteenth century owed much to the fact that its rulers were among the most loyal and diplomatic regional lieutenants of their Mongol khan and overlord, as well as his most effective and 'generous' collectors of taxes. In this period the attention of Moscow's princes was necessarily focused eastwards. Survival depended on the Mongol khan's favour. It entailed learning the language, values and nuances of steppe diplomacy.[10] Some Mongol military, administrative and fiscal techniques were also borrowed.[11]

Inevitably too, luck was crucial to Moscow's rise. A Rurikid prince was expected to divide his patrimony among all his sons. A shadowy unity might prevail for a generation or so under the 'chairmanship' of the senior prince, but in time the division of territory among increasingly distant cousins was bound to lead to the irreversible splintering of the inheritance. Moscow's rise to dominance in Great Russia owed much to the chance that no ruler was survived by more than one male heir for most of the crucial fourteenth century. The civil war of the early fifteenth century was between the many heirs of Grand Prince Dmitry Donskoy (died 1389). Vasily II's victory in the civil war (1420–1440s) over his father's youngest brothers strengthened the principle that the realm was indivisible but did not guarantee it. Only the major changes that occurred in the century preceding the 1550s and the beginning of the empire achieved this. Indeed, if one is searching for political traditions of the Russian state that left their mark on the subsequent history of empire, then it is above all to the hundred years that preceded the conquest of Kazan that one needs to refer.

Between 1450 and 1550 Moscow's rulers grew greatly in strength and status. In 1450 the Golden Horde, heir to the Mongol Empire, still existed and exercised dominion over Russia. The Byzantine Empire also still existed, though greatly weakened, and its monarch remained the leading figure in the Orthodox Christian world. The grand principality of Moscow was just recovering from two decades of civil war. A century later both the Golden Horde and Byzantium had disappeared. Moscow was about to fill the power vacuum in the east left by the Horde's demise. It had already taken first place in the Orthodox world. By assuming the title of tsar, Russia's ruler now reserved for himself a dignity previously allowed by Russians only to the Byzantine monarch and to the Great khans who ruled Genghis Khan's empire and its successor in the steppe, the Golden Horde. In the century before 1550 Moscow acquired a much broader and more grandiose self-image, ideology and ambition. This was reflected too in the ruler's status within his own community. The invasion of Russia between 1450 and 1550 by Byzantine monarchical ideology and symbolism was turning the princely warrior leader of the Muscovite military host into a distant and semi-divine figure way above his subjects' level.[12]

More down-to-earth changes also occurred. Even between the 1470s and 1530s the Muscovite realm more than doubled in size. Partly as a result of annexing so many new territories, something that could genuinely be described as a state had come into existence. The monarch now possessed his own army built around a core of semi-professional infantry musketeers, the so-called *streltsy*, and a much bigger contingent of cavalry who served in his forces in return for grants of land which could be revoked at any time should their service prove unsatisfactory. At the same time, a small, relatively disorganized but nevertheless formidable civil officialdom had developed to raise the tsar's taxes, manage his army and run his foreign policy. The tsar could still not rule effectively over his huge and sparsely populated realm without the support of the major aristocratic families, whose leading members sat in the so-called Boyar Council and advised him on policy. Nevertheless, by the time of the empire's birth in the 1550s the bases of a powerful and centralized absolute monarchy had been created.[13]

This was in large part because the society and political system of most of fifteenth-century Great Russia did not create major obstacles in the way of either autocracy or centralization. As noted in the previous chapter, this was a frontier region whose institutions and territorial boundaries were not deeply rooted. The contrast with the crownlands of St Stephen (Hungary) or St Wenceslas (Bohemia) acquired by the Habsburgs in the 1520s is striking. Most of the lands annexed by Moscow's princes belonged to the Grand Principality of Vladimir and had been ruled as a united territory by a single monarch as late as the twelfth century. Although the Grand Principality had subsequently been divided and redivided among the many branches of the Rurikids, it retained a certain shadowy existence under whichever prince was accepted as 'senior chairman' of the royal clan. Not merely did the various princes all come from ultimately the same family but the military aristocrats who surrounded them had a sense of belonging to some extent to the Grand Principality as a whole, switching allegiance from one prince to another and sometimes having land in more than one princely realm. Since the societies and polities of this region were so similar they were not difficult to unite and homogenize. The region differed from the highly commercialized territories of the Netherlands, Italy or Western

Germany in lacking dense networks of rich, self-governing towns – usually a formidable bulwark against centralization and absolutism. Moreover, the church viewed the whole region as one and usually supported Moscow's drive to unite it politically, though in the long run ecclesiastical autonomy was to be one of the great victims of the absolutist Muscovite state of the seventeenth and eighteenth centuries. Finally, it needs to be mentioned that most of Great Russia was conquered by Moscow rather than acquired by marriage or consent.

The main exception as regards the homogeneity of late medieval Great Russia was the Republic of Novgorod, which was annexed by Tsar Ivan III in the 1470s. Novgorod was the greatest prize of Muscovite expansion before the 1550s: huge in size, relatively populous, and rich through commerce and, above all, furs. Its system of government was much freer and more democratic than in the principalities, though at most times politics was dominated by a patrician oligarchy.[14] In the case of the principalities annexed by Moscow, local political identities were erased, with the local princes and sometimes the boyars (nobles) being absorbed ultimately into the tsar's court or at least into his service.

In Novgorod's case the process of homogenization went far further. The entire landowning aristocracy and merchant elite, including Moscow's own local supporters, was expropriated. The land was given in most cases to the sons of the minor Moscow nobility, who in return owed unconditional service to the tsar. As sometimes happened in the history of empire, Moscow's territorial expansion had an important impact on its domestic constitution and balance of political interests. The huge land fund acquired in the annexed territories allowed the tsar to create his own army and freed him from his previous dependence on semi-voluntary contributions of troops from his relatives and boyars. First practised in Novgorod, the wholesale expropriation of local elites and the creation on their lands of the new military service system was later applied to other provinces, including, under the Ivan IV ('The Terrible'), areas that had long since been part of the Muscovite state. The leading Russian expert on the era sees the treatment of Novgorod as a fundamental break in Russian history of enormous long-term importance. 'The expropriation of the Novgorod upper classes allowed Moscow to concentrate in its hands vast material resources. The power and authority of the monarchy was strengthened. Moscow's violent assault on free Novgorod laid the foundation of the "first empire," and became the point of departure for the development of the imperial system in Russia.'[15]

It is possible to some extent to find imperfect European parallels with Moscow's treatment of Novgorod. In the thirteenth century, for example, the Albigensian Crusade uprooted local elites in south-eastern France and laid the groundwork for later unification of the French kingdom. But the Albigensian Crusade was mounted with the pope's blessing against what was defined as a religious heresy. No such excuses could be found for Moscow's behaviour in Novgorod. In the Habsburg case the obvious parallel is Vienna's destruction of most of the Czech landowning class in the 1620s. Here even more than in the Albigensian case, however, the parallel is poor. The Bohemian aristocracy had actually risen in rebellion against their monarch and deposed him: expropriation was his response after defeating them in war. In any case a core of very wealthy Bohemian families retained their land and remained at the centre of Bohemian politics throughout the empire's existence. Moreover, not merely did the crownland of St Wenceslas survive as a separate entity, it actually continued to be ruled in the traditional manner through local assemblies (estates) dominated by the provinces' aristocracy. Still less does the wholesale expropriation of the Irish landowning class by the English in the sixteenth and seventeenth centuries offer much of a comparison, since it had little effect on the constitution or balance of political forces within England itself. The best parallel with the impact of Ivan III and Ivan IV is probably the policy of China's first emperor, whose uprooting of local elites and drastic homogenization of territories laid the foundations for an imperial centralized rule that lasted for millennia.

TSARIST STATE AND RUSSIAN ELITE: A COMPARATIVE VIEW

The reign of Ivan IV[16] brings out Russia's unique position in comparison to both European and Asian political traditions. The lack of civil or corporate rights of the Russian elite was well illustrated by the rule of a monarch who expropriated land and murdered nobles seemingly at will, without restraint, and in a way that betrayed little logic. On the other hand, Ivan did not – could not – change the basic alliance between crown and military-landowning class that lay at the heart of the Russian polity: all he could do was come close to destroying the polity entirely and leaving it to be gobbled up by predatory neighbours. Out of the chaos created by Ivan came the Time of Troubles, during which government and order disintegrated, the Swedes annexed Russian borderlands and the Poles occupied Moscow. After the election as tsar of a new monarch, Michael Romanov, in 1613 the foreigners were pushed back and the Russian polity was re-established on its old basis, namely as an alliance between the tsar-autocrat and the military-landowning hereditary ruling class. This alliance remained the basis for the polity into the nineteenth century and even to some extent down to 1917.

The military and aristocratic nature of the Russian ruling class sharply distinguished Russia from its Chinese imperial neighbour. In the latter, as we have seen, the military aristocracy had been displaced and destroyed by a non-hereditary civil bureaucratic elite as far back as the Tang era. Moreover, for most of the last millennium the civilian bureaucracy dominated not just politics but also Chinese culture and values. Military values and officers were generally despised by the Chinese political and cultural elite.

Russia was very different. An elite civil bureaucracy with higher education and a sense of corporate identity and power did not exist before tsarism's last century. Even then this bureaucracy was generally detested in Russian society. The traditional ruling class regarded bureaucrats as parvenus and pedants, who had usurped political power from tsar and aristocracy alike. The monarchs needed the bureaucracy in order to rule and modernize their empire effectively, but as the administration grew in size, complexity and self-confidence it became increasingly difficult for them to control – for all the reasons that had long since prevailed in China. Tsars feared the bureaucracy's encroachments on their power, disliked its cumbersome and rule-bound procedures, and denounced the frequent corruption and incompetence of its lower officials. Not even Alexander III or Nicholas II went to Emperor Wanli's lengths, however, though they may at times have dreamed of going on strike against their bureaucrats. Liberal and radical opponents of tsarism had no trouble in hating the bureaucracy, but the latter was also a convenient whipping boy for the loyal or apolitical. It was far easier and more acceptable to vent one's frustration by attacking the bureaucracy than by criticizing the tsar: the latter was the sovereign and the lynchpin of the political system – as in most countries the essential virtue and benevolence of the sovereign could be questioned only by those committed to the state's destruction.

In comparison to nineteenth-century Britain or Germany, Russian bureaucracy was inefficient, very interventionist in economic, cultural and social life, and uncontrolled by a parliament elected by society or its elites. It was also only very partially constrained by the rule of law. In its underground war with the revolutionary movement, for instance, the police regularly violated the elites' civil rights, secretly intercepting and opening the correspondence even of members of the imperial family itself. Not surprisingly, therefore, in Russian literature the bureaucracy is generally a target of satire and contempt, Gogol's work being merely the most famous example. One of Russia's leading literary scholars comments that 'the Russian bureaucracy, an important factor in the life of the state, left almost no trace in Russia's spiritual life: it created neither its own culture, its own ethics, nor even its own ideology.'[17]

In 1721 Peter I drew up a so-called Table of Ranks to formalize the seniority and status of those who served in the new Western-style armed forces and government institutions he had created. According to this table, army and navy officers always outranked civil officials of equivalent grade. It was also much easier for them to acquire noble status than it was for bureaucrats. Highest of all stood the aristocratic Guards officer who automatically gained double promotion should he deign to transfer into a mere line regiment. The provincial landowning noble of the eighteenth and nineteenth century would generally expect to serve as an officer for a few years at least – in the Guards if he could afford it and had the connections, otherwise in a regiment of the line. The Russian nobility had an aristocratic mania for genealogy and took huge pride in the military glory and traditions both of its families and of the state which they had served for centuries. In this respect the Russian elite was far closer to Rome than China and took readily to pan-European models and images of classical military heroism in the eighteenth century. From Peter I onwards male Romanov monarchs identified above all else with their armed forces. By the nineteenth century they were virtually never seen out of uniform, at least when in Russia. But the officer corps of the Guards well into the nineteenth century was a haven not just of aristocracy but of Russian literary and musical high culture as well. In a poor and largely illiterate eighteenth-century provincial society the richer landowners who could afford to send their sons into the Guards were the same people who could pay for a decent education. Not coincidentally, Russian literature was on the whole much kinder to the officer than to the bureaucrat.[18]

The Ottoman Empire had more respect for warriors than mandarin-dominated China but none at all for aristocrats. At the empire's peak from the fifteenth to seventeenth centuries the whole purpose of filling top positions with converted Christian slaves (the *devsirme* system) was to ensure complete dependence on the sultan and an absolute avoidance of a hereditary ruling class with deep roots in society and its own clientele. Even after the collapse of the slave system in the seventeenth century nothing like a hereditary aristocracy developed, which may indeed help to explain the instability of the Ottoman regime's relations with regional elites and its own provincial lieutenants. The last premier of tsarist Russia was a Prince Golitsyn, a member of one of the country's oldest aristocratic families.[19] Fully one-third of the empire's leading civil and military officials in 1894–1914 came from families which had been members of the Russian nobility before 1700, with others coming from aristocratic families rooted in the territories annexed by Peter I and his successors.[20] This was a European, aristocratic pattern of power-holding, far removed from anything typical of the great Muslim and Confucian empires. Moreover, when one takes into account the cultural Westernization of the Russian hereditary ruling class since 1700, its fundamentally European nature becomes more evident than ever.

Nevertheless, the Russian ruling class was a very distinct variation on the European aristocratic theme. To understand why this was the case it is necessary to know something of the early history of the Russian elite. Here we are on ground very well covered by earlier scholars, for the weakness of any feudal tradition in Russia is another of the great – and largely true – clichés of Russian history. In a broad sense the feudal order in Europe encompassed an autonomous international Catholic church not easily controlled by any monarch and usually contrasted by historians with a Byzantine Orthodox Church much more closely under the thumb of the Byzantine emperor in Constantinople. It also included powerful self-governing urban corporations. But the essence of feudalism was rooted in the military-landowning hereditary ruling class and in its relationship with the monarch.[21]

In continental Western Europe, though less in William the Conqueror's Anglo-Norman kingdom, feudalism emerged when royal authority was at its nadir. It was in many ways a system built from below and a response to anarchy and insecurity at local level. The knight's real loyalty lay to his immediate lord, not to his ultimate overlord, a distant king. In this sense feudalism had nothing in common with the system of military service in return for land created by Ivan III of Moscow in the late fifteenth century. The Russian warrior-landowner had no lord but the tsar, whose officials regulated and scrutinized his service closely, in a fashion far closer to the fifteenth-century Ottoman Empire than to feudal Europe. The Russian system of conditional service tenure was created not by a weak monarch but by one whose power was growing rapidly, and the new class of military servitors were a key factor in this growth. Above all and at every level the feudal contract was mutually binding. A right of resistance existed against the monarch who broke his side of the contract. As a result of confrontations between a king and his aristocratic vassals this contract was written down and enshrined in law. The English Magna Carta of 1215 is the most famous example of such a contract but other aristocracies had their equivalents: in an earlier chapter, for example, mention has already been made of the Hungarian Aurea Bulla of 1222. All warrior knights, the king to some extent included, were united by a common ethos and code. Out of this feudal past came among other things an almost obsessive concern with law and historical rights, together with aristocratic representative estates which are the ancestors of modern parliaments. A key point about Russia in 1550 was that it did not have a true equivalent of these representative bodies, let alone a tradition of written law mutually binding on king and subject. This was to matter greatly for the later history of the Russian Empire.

For the historian of empire a comparison between English and Hungarian aristocracy on the one hand and Russia on the other is very significant. Medieval England and Hungary were quintessential feudal lands with strong legal and corporate traditions out of which developed formidable representative institutions at both county and central level. Perhaps more important, these feudal institutions and traditions survived better in England and Hungary than almost anywhere else in Europe. In most of continental Europe in the seventeenth and eighteenth centuries would-be absolute monarchs did much to centralize power in the hands of the dynastic state and its officials, in the process making major inroads into the corporate autonomy, representative institutions and legal rights their subjects had inherited from the feudal era. In England and Hungary too monarchs attempted similar policies but on the whole with little success.

The English aristocracy defeated Stuart absolutism definitively in 1688. It then essentially took over the state and controlled it through an aristocratic parliament and aristocratic ministers for the next two centuries. In Hungary definite victory did not come until 1867 and was even then more equivocal. The Hungarian elite took over their own state but lived in uneasy and distrustful cohabitation with the Habsburg regime in Vienna. In both Britain and Hungary the aristocratic elite came to enjoy considerable legitimacy as defenders of the national cause. In the British case this had much to do with the fact that this elite ruled over what came to be the world's richest, most powerful and most admired country. The Hungarian elite won widespread support above all through its resolute opposition to Habsburg absolutism and centralization during the 1848 Revolution and in the two subsequent decades.

One key to the success of the parliamentary system was that the government was responsible to the political nation. Admittedly even in nineteenth-century Britain, let alone Hungary, this 'political nation' was very far from being the whole people. But the key social, economic and cultural elites could and did feel that they exercised a considerable level of control over the state. In addition, the parliamentary and legal traditions inherited by England and Hungary from feudalism helped even the Hungarians, let alone the English, to co-opt the new elites of a modern, educated and urban society, and to hold their loyalty. By contrast the Russian autocratic regime's denial of secure civil rights or participation in representative institutions to old and new elites certainly contributed to the latter's ambivalence and even alienation vis-à-vis the tsarist government in the last decades before the Revolution. Autocracy allowed a degree of misunderstanding and distrust to develop between the imperial state and its rulers on the one hand, and even basically loyal and conservative social and intellectual elites on the other.

The history of conservative nationalist thought in nineteenth- and early twentieth-century Russia illustrates this point graphically. Slavophilism has been the most significant element in political thinking on the right. It is very important not merely for the role it played before 1917 but also because it resurfaced in the last decades of the Soviet era, when its leading figure was Aleksandr Solzhenitsyn. With the demise of the Soviet Union and of Marxism-Leninism, resurgent conservative nationalism, strongly influenced by the Slavophile tradition, has become a crucial ingredient of contemporary Russian politics. Ironically, in the writings of the current Communist Party leader, Gennady Zyuganov, Slavophilism exerts a much bigger influence than Marx.

The core element in Slavophilism was an attack on modern Western society for its materialism, its individualism and its secularism. The West might in the short run be rich and dynamic but in the longer term in the Slavophiles' view a community needed to be more than just a loose association of anonymous individuals hell-bent on acquiring wealth and restrained by nothing but fear of legal sanctions. The Slavophiles juxtaposed to the West a vision of Russia as an organic community based on mutual obligation, collectivist instincts, and a secure religious sense of the individual's place in God's cosmic order. As a criticism of modern capitalist society this is a rather familiar theme, with obvious links to socialist and conservative doctrines both in nineteenth-century Europe and in the twentieth-century Third World.

Slavophilism from its inception in the 1830s was always a conservative nationalist doctrine, strongly Orthodox and unequivocally monarchist. But its relationship to the tsarist state was ambivalent, and not merely because Nicholas I's censors banned so many of its publications. Nicholas looked askance at the idea of an independent voice claiming to speak in the name of the nation, even if it did so in largely patriotic and conservative terms. After all, the tsar alone was supposed to embody Russia and define its values and interests. Moreover, there was explicit criticism of the regime in the Slavophile idea. Peter I's reforms were seen as having divorced the Westernized state and elites from the Russian land and people. The early Slavophiles came from leading families of the Moscow landowning gentry. Implicitly they claimed to speak for the true Russian land and its values, as distinct from alien St Petersburg with its European manners and architecture and its rule-bound German-style bureaucracy which had interposed itself between Russia's father-tsar and his loyal people. The Slavophiles had a strong sense that the imperial state was not responsive to the values and interests of the Russian land, and that it represented too an alien culture and mentality. There was here more than a touch of the court versus country sentiment which had partly motivated gentry opposition to Charles I of England's authoritarian regime and his suspiciously Catholic and culturally alien court.[22]

In the second half of the nineteenth century the tsarist state and Slavophilism drew closer. The censorship was greatly weakened. Links grew between leading Moscow Slavophiles and prominent figures at court and in the government. But the fact that the state was not in any sense responsible to the political nation was a source of danger right down to 1917. Those who ran the state's foreign policy quite correctly believed that nationalist public opinion, strongly influenced by the intellectual heirs of Slavophilism, failed to understand Russia's weakness or the realities of European great power politics: they therefore attempted to push the state into irresponsible and dangerous policies, above all in the Balkans, which might easily lead to war and defeat. Meanwhile public opinion continued to suspect that foreign policy pursued arcane and sometimes dynastic interests rather than truly Russian ones. The unnecessary and disastrous war with Japan confirmed this suspicion. It burst into flame again during the First World War, when it was widely (though quite wrongly) believed that pro–German and even treasonable factions at court were seeking peace with Germany and were undermining the war effort. This was a key element in the collapse of trust between regime and Russian public (and elite) opinion which led to the overthrow of the dynasty in 1917 and the disintegration of Russia's war effort.

As always with Russian history, however, there are dangers in reading everything backwards from the perspective of 1917. From Peter I's reign until the mid-nineteenth century the tsarist regime and its empire seemed to most observers to be a story of astonishing and dramatic success, which had raised Russia from a despised peripheral land of no significance into a position of almost *primus inter pares* among the continental European great powers. Moreover, in this period Russia appeared to be converging more and more with European political, social and cultural norms. Its French-speaking elites by 1800 shared a European aristocratic culture and values, enjoyed European levels of protection for their property, and lived rather comfortably under an absolute monarchy which in many respects modelled itself on its Hohenzollern and Habsburg neighbours – in the Habsburg case of course on the successful centralized monarchy in Austria and Bohemia rather than on semi-feudal Hungary. If Catherine II's Russia diverged somewhat from European political norms in one direction, George III's England was in its own way just as untypical.

It is true that in 1789 the Russian aristocracy's corporate institutions and civil rights were weaker than in most other European states. The Russian tsar appeared a uniquely powerful and arbitrary ruler. But the tsar could rule in the provinces only through the landowning class, which Paul I described correctly as the state's tax-collector and conscription agency in the villages. Aristocratic groups at court fought for power and its ample rewards, factionalizing and controlling key areas of state officialdom in the process. An 'absolute' monarch who trod too hard on aristocratic interests and sensitivities could pay for his mistake with his life: the eighteenth century witnessed a string of palace coups, spearheaded by the Guards regiments and culminating in the overthrow or murder of monarchs. In the heyday of tsarist Russia from 1700 to the 1850s the Russian variation on the European theme of union between absolute monarchy and privileged aristocracy had some specific and usually unpleasant features. The autocratic monarch and autocratic serf-owner ruled unchecked by law in a manner which could be cruel and barbarous. Not merely, however, was the system's logic deeply rooted in Russian geography and history but it was also extremely effective in the terms in which an eighteenth-century ruler and most eighteenth-century aristocrats measured success.

In a vast, open and sparsely populated plain governed by a very small and imperfect bureaucratic apparatus, serfdom tied the labour force to the land: it therefore made possible labour's exploitation by noble landowner and government tax-collector alike.[23] In the last resort the tsar's army could defend the social order against peasant rebellion. For the provincial nobleman rule by the autocratic tsar was far preferable to its only likely alternative in the seventeenth and eighteenth centuries, namely the state's disintegration amidst anarchic Polish-style battles between aristocratic factions. If the great aristocratic families at court were the major beneficiaries of the tsarist system, the provincial nobility could nevertheless make profitable and prestigious careers in the tsar's military or civil service, with just the chance that merit, luck and imperial favour would bring dazzling riches and rewards, turning an obscure nobleman from the provinces into a wealthy magnate. For the provincial noble this was a far more promising prospect than life as a mere hanger-on of some aristocratic clique. Meanwhile the political stability, coherent policy-making and military power that autocracy usually provided sustained generations of spectacularly successful territorial expansion into fertile and half-empty agricultural regions. As tsarist dominions spread southwards and eastwards, so too did the landholdings of the ruling class. For a nobility whose original Great Russian homeland was seldom very fertile and which in addition divided its estates among its children, the tsardom's huge success as a mechanism for territorial expansion was a key source of its legitimacy.

Vested interest was the central but not the only factor in the alliance of tsar and noble, just as the tsarist regime's success was the main but not the only element in its legitimacy. Tsarism also legitimized itself in elite eyes through the rituals and entertainment of Europe's most sumptuous court, and through gearing its ideology to the changing values and culture of Russia's elites. For an aristocracy there was no great difficulty in identifying with a dynastic state whose history was to such an extent also the history of their own families. In addition, from Peter I's time down to 1917 the Romanovs created a range of military, administrative, educational and honorific institutions and corporations on which they lavished imperial patronage, and which aristocratic families identified with and dominated. At every stage in the public life of the aristocratic male the links of history, patronage and loyalty that bound the elite to the dynastic state were always present: the path led upwards from aristocratic cadet corps to Guards officers' mess, through attendance at court to, perhaps, high government office. At home on the wall hung the gold sword won by grandfather for valour in Russia's defence against Napoleon, and the imperial rescript proclaiming the gratitude of Peter I or Catherine II for earlier ancestors' service to state and dynasty. The cross triumphant over the crescent above the cupola of the family chapel witnessed to ancestors' participation in Orthodox Russia's liberation from the Tatars and thereby the family's role in the very foundation of Russian independence and greatness.[24] Where an individual's ancestry in the male line was not so ancient, glorious or Russian, he could nevertheless submerge himself in the collective memory of the ruling class.

It was only to be expected that a state based on the alliance between crown and aristocracy within the Great Russian heartland should attempt

249

to rule in similar fashion in the non-Russian borderlands. As one early nineteenth-century viceroy noted, government in most non-Russian regions depended on collaboration with the local aristocracy, 'that class which both by our laws and by the nature of things played such an important part in internal administration'.[25] The strategy of alliance with non-Russian aristocracies began with the co-option of Tatar nobles in the fifteenth century and subsequently included, for example, the extremely successful incorporation of the Baltic German nobility and Ukrainian Cossack gentry into the imperial ruling class.

Such incorporation meant access to careers in the imperial service, which both Baltic figures and Ukrainians filled in ever larger numbers – sometimes to the disgust of Russian members of the elite.[26] From the eighteenth-century tsar's perspective, however, the Baltic elite and the Ukrainians were not merely better educated than the Russians, they were also somewhat less likely to be absorbed into Russian aristocratic networks and factions. To local aristocracies tsarist rule brought security of property and status, indeed sometimes their enhancement. The rather new and raw Ukrainian gentry for example acquired the right to enserf the peasantry along with Russian noble status. In the last decades of Swedish rule in the Baltic provinces the crown had confiscated vast swathes of land from the nobility in order to bolster the royal treasury. Under tsarist rule this practice stopped and property rights were far more secure.

In cultural terms absorption into the imperial elite and identification with the tsarist state were not usually difficult for non-Russian elites, though this changed over time. In the fifteenth and sixteenth centuries Muslim and steppe elites could usually enter the Russian ruling class without even needing to convert to Orthodoxy. By the early eighteenth century, however, conversion was essential even to hold one's land, let alone to gain access to court or government office. After Peter's reforms European Catholics and Protestants were easily assimilated into the increasingly cosmopolitan ruling class without any need to convert to Orthodoxy or to absorb specifically Russian cultural values or characteristics. In the last decades of tsarist rule, however, the bureaucratic elites became more ethnically Russian and the state began to identify itself with the Russian population's culture, language and interests. In the process it partly alienated its traditional allies among the non-Russian elites, though this varied from one regional elite to another and was seldom complete. Even where traditional sentiments of aristocratic loyalty to the Romanov state had weakened, fear of social revolution still united the borderlands' aristocracy and the Romanovs.

The same was even more true as regards the landowning class in the empire's Russian core. In the four generations that followed the emancipation of the serfs in 1861 the relationship between the state and the Russian landowning class grew more tense and uncertain. The growing power of the bureaucracy, the impoverishment of many landowners, and the state's commitment to rapid industrialization all served to some degree to alienate sections of the traditional ruling class from the regime. The near-success of extreme social revolution in 1905–6, including the expropriation of much noble land, forced regime and aristocracy back into a close embrace, however. As educated and often very cultured early twentieth-century Europeans, Russian elites often resented the absence of secure civil and political rights in Russia, and saw the frequently blundering and crude tsarist absolute monarchy as an anachronism. A scandal such as the Rasputin affair, with its medieval overtones, increased this sense of shame. But the Revolution of 1905 made it very clear that the Russian landowning nobility would not survive the onset of democracy, whether expressed through arson and riot on their estates or through peasant voting power in a democratically elected parliament. In the eyes of most landowners therefore the tsarist police state acquired a new legitimacy from the events of 1905. When the monarchy fell in 1917 the complete expropriation of the landowning class followed very shortly. Only the victory of military counter-revolution could have saved the Russian aristocracy, as Admiral Horthy and General Franco saved their Hungarian and Spanish peers.[27]

There was a certain historical neatness and logic in the fact that Russia's landowning aristocracy and autocratic regime, intimately connected over the centuries, should disappear at the same time. The term 'autocracy' is often used confusingly in the Russian context and with various meanings. In reality, however, the word ought to imply no more nor less than the obvious fact that the Russian tsar's power was unconstrained by a constitution, by laws or by representative institutions.[28] This was the case in 1550: it remained so in 1850 and even, to a considerable degree, down to 1917. The long-term impact of the autocratic principle on Russia's empire was considerable and can fairly be compared to the ultimate influence of parliamentary government and the rule of law on the British Empire.

To describe Russia's regime as autocratic is not to deny that, especially before 1850, the realities of ruling a vast empire with a small and very inadequate state bureaucracy ensured a great devolution of power to local aristocracies. It is also the case that in some of the regions of the empire conquered by Peter I (ruled 1689–1725) and his successors traditional representative institutions and local laws were allowed to survive, even to flourish, for many generations. The Baltic provinces and Finland provide the best examples of this phenomenon. But the long-term trend, though not always consistent and generally tempered by a pragmatic care for administrative effectiveness and political stability, was towards centralization and homogenization. To varying degrees and at varying speed, the annexed territories were brought more closely under Petersburg's control, their separate political identities and their distinct laws and institutions weakened and often destroyed.

The logic of autocracy had much to do with this. In the first place part of autocracy's *raison d'être* in Great Russia was that it was an extremely effective, not to say ruthless, mechanism for mobilizing the society's human and material resources behind the state's priorities and goals. As Catherine II (ruled 1762–96) noted, once the administrative machinery existed to do so, there was every reason to extend this tried system to outlying provinces in the Baltic region or Ukraine which, relative to Great Russia, were not yet making their full potential contribution in tax and conscripts to the crown's treasury or its armed forces.[29] A similar logic, much less intelligently applied, partly guided Petersburg's efforts to extend its hold on Finland in the empire's last decades.[30]

Administrative standardization usually reduced costs and inefficiencies. It was also politically more acceptable for a regime which had autocracy as its guiding principle. An autocratic tsar, used to the unconstrained exercise of his will, might find the need to conform to local laws and traditions frustrating. This was for example the experience of Alexander I and Nicholas I between 1815 and 1830,[31] having granted the Poles a constitution which, by the European standards of the time, was very liberal. Moreover, even if the monarch could live with semi-constitutional institutions and special laws in parts of the empire's periphery, much of the Russian elite might not be willing to do so. The emperor's subjects in outlying provinces might after all use their laws and freedom to criticize the government's policies or protect its enemies. Especially with the growth of Russian nationalism, it was unacceptable that the tsar's non-Russian subjects should enjoy rights and freedoms which his Russian subjects were denied. Even in the 1760s Russian nobles complained about the Baltic nobility's special status.[32] When Alexander I (ruled 1801–25) granted a constitution to conquered Poland but denied one to a Russian elite flushed with pride after defeating Napoleon, he aroused well-justified rage: this fed into the so-called Decembrist movement which resulted in an attempted coup to overthrow the absolute monarchy in 1825.[33] This underlined the point that so long as Great Russia itself was ruled autocratically and in centralized fashion, it was not easy to sustain indefinitely a more free and law-abiding system of government on the empire's periphery.[34] The autocrat might graciously allow the survival of traditional institutions and freedoms as Peter I and Alexander I did respectively when the Baltic provinces were annexed in 1721 and Finland in 1809. A tsar might even grant a new constitution to a borderland region, as Alexander did to the Poles in 1818. But the autocrat never felt himself bound by any legal contract with his subjects. This after all was autocracy's core meaning. Subjects enjoyed privileges rather than rights. Efforts by the Baltic peoples or Finns to assert that their local privileges were part of the treaties by which their region was incorporated into the Russian Empire were always rejected, even by the most liberal of monarchs.

IMPERIAL STATE – RUSSIAN PEOPLE

In 1550 the Russian state and people were about to create an empire. Four and a half centuries later, at the end of the millennium, they are having to come to terms with suddenly no longer being an empire and having to be a nation. It is often said that a key difficulty in this respect, and one that distinguishes Russians from the core peoples of other European empires, is that they have never previously been a nation, indeed that no Russian nation ever existed before the empire's creation.

In one sense this is obviously true. Russia in 1550 was clearly not a nation in the spirit of 1789 and modern democratic ideals of popular sovereignty and equal citizenship. Even in terms of the alternative ethnic conception of nationality, which stresses solidarity rather than citizenship, there are problems in applying the concept of nation to a society of warrior-aristocrats and peasants, in which not merely did cultures and values diverge widely in some respects but great class antagonism was threatened by the aristocracy's efforts to enserf the peasantry. The basic point, however, is that if Russia was not quite a nation in 1550 it was a great deal nearer to being so than most of the other peoples of Europe, let alone of the world, at that time.[35] The unity of dynasty, church and people which the term 'Holy Russia' implied was by no means a mere slogan or aspiration of propagandists. It is not only Russian historians but also well-qualified Western ones who can describe the movement that expelled the Poles from Moscow and re-established a native polity and dynasty in 1612–13 as one of national liberation.[36] It was not just[37] nationalist nostalgia when Karamzin, the great early nineteenth-century historian, celebrated the solidarity of manners and mentalities in pre-imperial Russia and lamented its subsequent disintegration.

History offers many examples of communities whose sense of solidarity, mutual commitment and collective identity wax and wane over time. In most of contemporary Western Europe and North America, for example, commitment to the nation is weaker than was the case a century ago even in rhetoric, let alone reality: it is hard to imagine a younger generation of today's Americans or Englishmen pouring out their blood in the nation's defence as their ancestors did at Gettysburg and on the Somme. Russia too had a weaker sense of national solidarity in 1914 than in 1550, the blame in this case lying partly at empire's door.

Most obviously, Russians had been the overwhelming majority of the tsar's subjects in 1550. By 1900 they were 44 per cent. The fact that the empire was a single land mass without clear constitutional or territorial borders between peoples made it all the more difficult to define who Russians were or what being a Russian meant. More important, the burdens of sustaining imperial power contributed to weakening the solidarity of the Russian community and its loyalty to the tsarist state. In the end, the Romanovs' empire was brought down in 1917 not by the non-Russian periphery but by a revolt of workers and conscripts in the Russian heartland. A very major immediate cause of revolt was the strain imposed by the First World War, but there were also longer-term reasons for the gradual alienation of the Russian masses from the tsarist state and the social elites which were linked to the demands and burdens of empire.

Even under serfdom Russian peasants had some logical reasons to identify with tsarism and believe that it served their interests at least in part. In periods of anarchy peasant communities suffered badly and the weak went to the wall first. Albeit in a rather Hobbesian sense, the tsarist state was at least a bulwark against anarchy. Marauding bands of rebels, vagrants and bandits were very seldom Robin Hoods. The state also defended the sedentary peasant population against Tatar and nomadic raiders from the steppe, whose main quest was often slaves. The economy and political system of the Tatar Khanate of Crimea in fact partly revolved around raiding into Ukraine and Russia in order to procure slaves for export to the Ottoman Empire and Middle East. The first sugar plantations catering for European demands were to be found in Cyprus and were often based partly on the labour of Russian and Ukrainian slaves captured by the Crimean Tatars' raiding parties.[38] The elimination of the nomadic threat was inconceivable without the intervention of the tsarist regular army: Russia was after all confronting the largest and most formidable concentration of nomadic mounted warriors in the world. Two hundred years after Russia's first collisions with the Bashkirs in the 1550s more than half the regular cavalry regiments of the imperial army were needed to crush a Bashkir rising which occurred on the eve of Russia's intervention in the Seven Years' War (1756–63).[39] Behind the screen provided by the army and the Cossacks Russian peasants colonized vast fertile territories increasingly far from their Muscovite homeland. In 1678, 90 per cent of all Russians lived in the four core Great Russian regions of the tsarist empire – by 1917 less than 50 per cent.[40] As regards security, economic prosperity and demographic growth, the tsarist state did therefore contribute important material benefits to the Russian masses.

There were also less tangible reasons to identify with the regime. The idea of Holy Russia – the trinity of church, tsar and Orthodox people – retained some of its hold on the masses for much of the imperial period. In the last decades of the old regime revolutionary socialists were driven to despair by the seeming strength of Orthodox peasant monarchism.[41] Even peasant Orthodoxy was not, however, an unambiguous source of support for the regime. The seventeenth-century 'Great Schism' had resulted in large-scale defections from the official church. The defectors included many of the most committed members of the Orthodox community, who revolted at attempts to reform the national church and bring it closer to Greek practices. These Old Believers were a key element in the Russian national community. They were also a great potential source of support for a modern Russian nationalism. Their alienation, albeit by the late nineteenth century only partial, from the tsarist regime represented a considerable weakening of tsarism's legitimacy and Russian national solidarity.

The case of the army[42] as a source of mass identification with the tsarist state is even more ambiguous. No doubt the army defended and extended Russian territory, but Russian peasants dreaded conscription into the long-service tsarist regular army that existed from Petrine days until the great military reform of 1874, which – at least in principle – introduced universal short-term military service. Ripped away forever from their families and villages, a large percentage of the new conscripts died from shock and hard treatment even before they reached their regiments. Conditions of service were harsh, the behaviour of officers and NCOs often brutal, and medical services were non-existent before the nineteenth century. And yet, as the French émigré General Langeron commented after decades of service in Russia, this army, whose conditions of service ought to have made it the worst in old-regime Europe, was in many respects probably the best.

Among the explanations for this cited by contemporaries were the unique (for the eighteenth century) ethnic homogeneity of the army and the strong national loyalties of the soldiers. Certainly no observer ever questioned the deep sense of identification of soldiers with their regiments, with some of their commanders, with the Orthodox Church and with the monarchs. The astonishing morale and capacity for self-sacrifice shown by Russian soldiers and sailors on so many occasions is inexplicable unless such factors are invoked. Moreover, although the rank and file of the pre-1874 armed forces were to a considerable extent divorced from civilian society, it is inconceivable that the loyal and often heroic service of literally millions of ordinary Russian men had no impact on the masses' political identity in the eighteenth and nineteenth centuries. Heroes such as Suvorov and Kutuzov, great patriotic dramas such as the 1812 campaign and the defence of Sevastopol, must have left their mark at the time and certainly provided great potential for later exploitation by nationalist politicians and intellectuals.

On the whole, however, there were obvious and powerful reasons for the Russian masses not to identify with tsarism and to regard it as their oppressor. One aspect of empire's burden was serfdom, which reached its furthest and harshest extent in the eighteenth century at precisely the time when Russia was establishing itself definitively as a great power. Until the last quarter of the eighteenth century the Great Russian peasantry bore a much heavier military and fiscal burden than the Ukrainians or Baltic peoples. Muslim peasants even in the Kazan region conquered in the sixteenth century were very seldom enserfed. The dues they paid as so-called 'state peasants' and the obligations they owed were usually much lighter than the poll tax paid by the Russian serf or the labour rent he owed to his master.[43] By the measure of the West European maritime empires it seems astonishing that whereas no Russian noble could own Muslim peasants as serfs, many Tatar nobles – some of whom initially remained Muslim – could own Russian peasants. At least before the mid-nineteenth century the tsarist regime's relationship with the Russian masses had much more in common with the Ottoman elite's treatment of the Turkish peasantry than with the relationship of the core metropolitan population of a European maritime empire to its state. In other respects too the Ottoman parallel fits. With some exceptions, the tsarist empire was usually very tolerant as regards the religion of the non-Orthodox peoples. A crusading spirit and religious proselytism were far less important than in the Habsburg Empire either in Spanish America or in Counter-Reformation Europe. Though there were moments and areas where the tsarist regime backed campaigns of conversion, on the whole these campaigns were brief, often half-hearted and unsuccessful. The religious communities most consistently persecuted were Russian dissenters from the official Orthodox Church, in other words, above all the Old Believers. As with the Shia sects of eastern Anatolia whom Selim I devastated, the Old Believers were persecuted for successive generations since secession from the state's official religion was viewed as both apostasy and treason.

In some ways the position of the Russian masses under tsarist empire actually had more in common with that of the native peoples in European overseas colonies than with these empires' 'master races'. In most European colonies peasants were largely ruled by native village headmen and judged according to some version of customary law. European – and indeed Japanese[44] – officials were usually a rather thin ruling stratum perched on top of native society and unable to penetrate deeply into its life. These officials might admire – even romanticize – the native peasant and warrior and would probably believe that benevolent and paternalistic European rule was essential to their well-being. But they were also certain to be aware of the deep cultural divide between themselves and those they ruled. With such awareness could easily coexist insecurity about indigenous peoples' loyalty and fear of the impact of rumour, government weakness or sudden outbursts of mass hysteria amidst a population conceived as ignorant, gullible and superstitious. This mix of attitudes towards the Russian peasantry was very common with the tsarist elites: one and the same nineteenth-century Russian aristocrat might indeed combine Pushkin's fear of the Russian peasants' capacity for anarchical outbursts – 'senseless and merciless' – with a Slavophile romanticization of the Orthodox peasant and courageous warrior, armed with a patient and self-sacrificing morality, and unswerving in his loyalty to tsar and Russia. Certainly the institutional structure through which St Petersburg governed the Russian territory had much in common with European colonial regimes. Right down to 1917 Russian peasants had their own quite separate system of village and rural parish government and their own courts which operated according to peasant customary law, not the imperial legal code. Peasants elected their own judges and headmen, though usually with an eye to the opinion of the local tsarist police constable and his bosses. The peasantry's major economic asset, namely the village lands, was usually owned collectively by the whole village and periodically redistributed in accordance with the size and needs of individual households.[45]

In the modern era any empire that was to flourish – or indeed even to survive – had to open itself to Western techniques and technologies. These could never easily or wholly be divorced from the values and political ideologies to which they were linked in their European homeland.

In the eighteenth century probably the greatest key to Russian success and Ottoman failure as great powers was the former state's much greater openness to European innovations and to the foreigners who introduced them. It should not be necessary to repeat here that the Muslim peoples of the Balkans and Middle East paid a high price for the Ottomans' failure. The tsarist achievement though considerable was, however, not without cost since in the context of the eighteenth and early nineteenth centuries Westernization could not really penetrate beyond the state apparatus and the social elites. The cultural gap that opened between elites and masses is another of the great clichés of Russian history and was the perpetual lament of the nineteenth-century intelligentsia. The conservative historian Nikolay Karamzin was one of the first to set the terms of this lament at the beginning of the century. 'Until his [i.e. Peter I's] reign all Russians from the plow to the throne, had been alike insofar as they shared certain features of external appearance and of customs. After Peter, the higher classes separated themselves from the lower ones, and the Russian peasant, burgher, and merchant began to treat the Russian gentry as Germans, thus weakening the spirit of brotherly unity binding the estates of the realm'.[46]

To some extent Karamzin was exaggerating. So certainly were later generations of the intelligentsia for whom the split between elite and masses became an obsession. This obsession reflected the radical intelligentsia's acute sense of its own isolation, divorced as it was not just from the masses but also from the bulk of the ruling class, the clergy and the merchantry. In addition, for a group which made passionate commitment to the people's welfare a religion and a source of identity and purpose in life, the sense that this love was unrequited by an unresponsive peasantry was particularly hard to bear. In reality, in Europe as in Russia the basic cleavage in society was between an elite which tried to understand the world in rational and scientific terms and a mass whose thinking was still rooted in magic and religion. Even in France in the second half of the nineteenth century this gap was still significant.[47] Until it was bridged, national solidarity – let alone citizenship – could never be complete.

Although the Russian intelligentsia's concern about the void between elites and masses was an exaggeration, it was not however an illusion. August von Haxthausen, one of the best informed and most level-headed observers of Nicholas I's Russia, remarked that the cultural gap between elites and masses was significantly wider in Russia than in Central and Western Europe.[48] Nor indeed is there any reason to be surprised on this score. At least in Western and Central Europe the 'rationally thinking' elite had to a great extent emerged organically from society and of its own volition. It was not, as in Peter I's Russia, a group initially created at great speed by the state's decree on the basis of explicitly foreign models of thinking, behaviour and even external appearance. Moreover, in most of Western and even Central Europe at any time before 1917 the percentage of 'rationally thinking' people was much greater than in Russia. In part this reflected the impact of Protestantism on mass literacy. In addition, however, it was simply a measure of relative economic and cultural development. The Austrian government began to plan for universal primary education[49] in the last quarter of the eighteenth century; it was to be inconceivable in Russia for at least another hundred years. The relatively low levels of literacy in tsarist society exacerbated the cultural gap between elite and masses: they were an additional reason why the Russian community was more deeply divided and less of a nation in 1914 than it had been in 1550.

UKRAINE AND BELORUSSIA (BELARUS): AMBIGUITIES OF EMPIRE

In the Russian case the relationship between empire and nation contained one additional element of ambiguity which is of huge political importance and which must be traced back to well beyond 1550. Were the Ukrainians and Belorussians entirely separate peoples or merely branches of the Russian nation? For the Ukrainian or Belorussian nationalist the basic problem is that the three peoples share many crucial traditional identity-markers. Russia, Belorussia and Ukraine were all part of Kievan Rus: as the term implies, the political and cultural centre of this Rus world was initially the present capital of Ukraine. One branch of the Kievan ruling dynasty ultimately established itself in Moscow and created the modern Russian tsardom. The Romanovs were the historical heirs to the Moscow Rurikids and could therefore continue their claim to the whole inheritance of Kievan Rus. Orthodoxy united the three peoples, as did its sacred language, Church Slavonic. Historically Tatar and Polish enemies threatened Russians, Ukrainians and Belorussians alike. It was by citing these points that the tsarist state and Russian elite advanced their claim that the three East Slavic Orthodox peoples were in fact a single nation, at least in embryo. The terms of the debate help to explain its frequent rancour. Although Russian and other nationalists in the former Soviet Union clashed, no Russian ever seriously denied, for example, that Latvians or Georgians were separate nations. Nor have many Englishmen denied the very existence of a Scottish nation, while at the same time believing that it formed part too of a broader British identity.

Above all, however, the debate was rancorous because it was and is extremely important. Without Ukraine Russia's survival as an empire and great power would have been unlikely at any time in the last two centuries. As already mentioned, the secession of Ukraine was a crucial factor in the Soviet Union's collapse. A decade after the disintegration of the USSR, the post-Soviet settlement is still far from secure. In both Ukraine and Russia political stability and national identity remain fragile. The question of whether the three East Slavic peoples are wholly separate nations or ought to be joined in some broader unit is still very significant and very controversial.

Whether or not a community is – let alone always has been – a nation is often anything but cut and dry, and depends greatly on definitions. In the Ukrainian case the one clear point relevant to this chapter is that in 1550 it was certainly not predetermined whether Ukraine would or would not ultimately achieve separate nationhood. It is precisely the possibility of many different paths of development that makes a study of Ukrainian history under tsarist and Soviet rule so interesting and important. But the Ukrainian case does bring out the ambiguity of empire both as a concept and a reality. If this is true of empire in general, it is especially so in the Russian and Soviet context.

This chapter opened with the confident assertion that the history of empire in Russia began in the 1550s. A Ukrainian or Belorussian nationalist might well object. Decades before the conquest of Kazan the Muscovite ruler had after all conquered territories now defined as forming part of Belarus and Ukraine. In fact some of these lands were being absorbed even before the last theoretically independent Great Russian principality had been annexed by Moscow. Was the conquest of Ukrainian and Belorussian territory an early example of Russian imperialism or was it rather the regaining and consolidation of national territory? Where does nation end and empire begin both in time and space? It is useful to address these questions if only to deflate the self-confidently dogmatic terms in which the debate over empire and imperialism is sometimes conducted. The pragmatic Muscovite rulers did not of course think in such terms. The key markers of identity in the sixteenth century were religious, dynastic and historical. The language and ethnicity of the masses was not thought politically significant. In any case, sixteenth-century Muscovite rulers expanded their territory and power as and where they could. To justify these acquisitions they could and did claim to be the heirs of Genghis Khan, as well as of the Byzantine emperor and of the grand princes of Kiev and Vladimir.[50] For the ruthless and pragmatic power politicians who ruled Moscow it may not much have mattered how the conquest of a region was legitimized as long as the territories' resources were safely pocketed. The official tsarist claims that Ukraine and Belorussia were not imperial acquisitions but ancient Russian lands, however, did matter greatly as regards subsequent tsarist policy in these regions, and even more as regards Russians' own thinking about the nature of their empire.

8

Tsarist Empire: Power, Strategy, Decline

In 1462 the grand prince of Moscow ruled over 24,000 square kilometres. In 1914 Nicholas II ruled over 13.5 million.[1] The tsarist state was one of the most effective mechanisms for territorial expansion ever known. To many European observers in the nineteenth and early twentieth centuries there appeared something inexorable, remorseless and unstoppable in its advance. Since the absorption of Novgorod in the late fifteenth century territory after territory had been annexed, its separate political identity gradually erased, and its resources mobilized in the cause of tsarist military power and further expansion. The process had moved from the swallowing of the Volga khanates in the 1550s to the conquest of Siberia in the seventeenth century. The core of Ukraine – including Kiev – had been acquired in 1654 and its independence reduced to nothing in the following 150 years. The eighteenth century had seen the acquisition of the strategically and commercially vital Baltic provinces in 1721, Russia's domination of the eastern Baltic region being consolidated by the partition of Poland under Catherine II and Alexander I's conquest of Finland in 1809. The crucial agricultural and mineral resources of southern Ukraine had been acquired after crushing victories over the Ottomans between 1768 and 1792, and by the end of the eighteenth century Russia was the dominant power on the Black Sea. The expansion of Russian power southwards and eastwards in the eighteenth century provided the bases and resources from which the nineteenth-century conquest of the Trans-Caucasus and Central Asia was undertaken.

To be sure, the process of expansion had at times been checked, even reversed, with disaster seemingly staring the Russians in the face. And yet in time, patiently and remorselessly, the process of expansion had revived.

Even in the twelfth century the princes of Great Russia and part of the peasant population had sought to move southwards into the fertile steppe and down the Volga. The Mongols put an end to this process for three centuries but it was renewed with spectacular success. Ivan IV tried to snatch the Baltic provinces in the 1570s and failed, ruining Russia in the process. The state's disintegration followed and in the first years of the seventeenth century, during the so-called Time of Troubles, Russia almost ceased to exist as a political entity. But the state revived, renewed its resources in the seventeenth century, and in the first years of the eighteenth century Peter I seized the prize denied to Ivan the Terrible, the territories we now call Latvia and Estonia.[2] Peter's own plans for expansion into the Trans-Caucasus and Central Asia were far too ambitious for his time and again overstretched Russia's resources, scores of thousands of Russian troops succumbing to disease and climate in Peter's advance along the shore of the Caspian Sea. But his goals were fully achieved in the nineteenth century. In the same way the ambitious war aims against the Ottomans set out by Chancellor Ostermann in 1737, well beyond Russia's means at that time, were all realized by the early nineteenth century.

Determination to check advancing Russian power lay behind the British decision for war in 1854. During the Crimean War Lord Palmerston commented that 'the best and most effectual security for the future peace of Europe would be the severance from Russia of some of the frontier territories acquired by her in later times, Georgia, Circassia, the Crimea, Bessarabia, Poland and Finland ... She could still remain an enormous Power, but far less advantageously posted for aggression on her neighbours.'[3] Russia was defeated in the Crimean War and the 1856 Treaty of Paris humiliated her and greatly weakened her position on the Black Sea. Within fifteen years, however, the treaty had been overthrown and Russia was free to rebuild her Black Sea fleet. Meanwhile Russia was advancing to the conquest of Central Asia, much to the alarm of the British. Between 1891 and 1902 Russia also advanced rapidly in the Far East, for a time seeming likely to emerge as the main winner from the impending disintegration of China.

Defeat and humiliation by Japan, followed by revolution in Russia itself in 1905, seemed to throw into question the very survival of the Russian state and empire. But stability was restored and the years 1907–14 witnessed dramatic economic growth and the rebuilding of Russia's military power. Neither revolution nor the granting of a semi-constitution in 1906 seemed to have changed tsarism's military and expansionist nature. In its 1914 New Year edition, the leading conservative newspaper, *Novoye*

Vremya, wrote of the Russian people's 'still terrible thirst for greatness',[4] a comment which in reality said much more about Russia's elites than about the feelings of the peasant masses whose traditional role it had been to pay the price of empire. If the rapid rebuilding of the army could be seen as a purely defensive measure, it was hard to interpret the very speedy and hugely expensive re-creation of the Baltic fleet's battleship squadrons in similar light. In 1907 the government spent 6.9 million roubles on higher education at a time when a single battleship cost 30 million.[5] By 1914 a complete new squadron of Baltic battleships was already almost finished, with more ships on the way. The purpose of these fleets was to gain Russia prestige, strategic flexibility and international leverage. Plans were afoot to send a squadron to the Mediterranean in order to threaten Constantinople from the west. In the longer run a formidable high seas fleet could hold the balance of naval power between Britain and Germany, giving Russia potential leverage over both. Sir Arthur Nicolson, former British ambassador in Petersburg and subsequently permanent head of the Foreign Office, in 1914 believed that Russia would soon be enormously powerful and that it was essential for Britain to keep her on its side.[6] Theobald von Bethmann-Hollweg, the German chancellor, viewed growing Russian power in similar fashion and feared that within a generation she would be the master of Central Europe.[7] In 1914 Germany launched the First World War partly because it believed that a brief strategic window of opportunity existed, after which Russia would be too powerful to check.

Foreigners who believed in the inherently expansionist nature of tsarist Russia were partly right. In most periods there was both a geopolitical and a domestic political logic behind expansionist policy. Geography almost dictated expansion southwards into the fertile Black Earth steppe and down the rivers to the coastal regions. With Russia firmly established on the coast, there was a clear strategic and economic logic behind attempting to control key 'choke points' of Russian trade, above all at Constantinople. Once acquired, border regions often had their own geopolitical logic, which might point to the need for further expansion: the flourishing of Russia's existing possessions in the Far East might, for instance, depend on the acquisition of a wider defence periphery and greater secure access to food-producing areas.[8]

The alliance between tsar and warrior-landowning nobility which was at the regime's core was a form of joint enterprise traditionally devoted to territorial expansion. Conquests brought the monarchs huge land funds with which they could buy loyalty, legitimacy and support. The nobles could acquire new and fertile estates in the conquered regions by purchase and migration too. Meanwhile, by no means did the crown hand out to its nobles all the lands it conquered. Many remained in the crown's direct possession, together with the peasants who farmed them. Many great empires – for instance Han dynasty China or the Byzantines – had flourished so long as the bulk of the peasant population remained directly under the control of the crown and its officials, and therefore subject to imperial taxation and conscription. When for various reasons peasants and their lands were taken over by aristocratic magnates, the resources needed to sustain the imperial regime dwindled and decline set in.[9] On the other hand, the bureaucratic machine needed to control and tax the peasantry in a vast, pre-modern empire was almost impossible to maintain in efficient working order over the generations. Bureaucrats could easily turn into even more ruthless exploiters of the peasantry than an aristocracy, which at least usually had a long-term interest in its villagers' survival and well-being.

In many ways, from the sixteenth to the nineteenth centuries the Russian tsars had the best of both worlds.[10] There was quite sufficient land and serfs to sustain a powerful and loyal nobility, which itself provided the backbone of local government and officered the tsar's army, court and central elite bureaucracy. By European standards, however, an exceptionally high proportion of the land and peasants remained in the crown's possession. Between 1724 and 1857 the percentage of such peasants – defined by the regime as 'state peasants' – grew from 19 to 45 per cent in the empire's Russian core: by 1857 state peasants considerably outnumbered the nobles' serfs.[11] Russia differed from most of Europe in that the state not merely expropriated the church's lands but also held them for itself rather than letting them fall into aristocratic hands.[12] In the overwhelming majority of cases too, non-Christians in conquered territories were defined as state peasants. In the mid-eighteenth century 90 per cent of the tsar's non-Orthdox subjects in the Volga region were so defined, for example, providing a great and growing source of revenue for the crown.[13]

After the early nineteenth century the acquisition of land to serve the tsar's alliance with the nobility was not such a factor as before, but the prestige and legitimacy achieved by a successful foreign policy remained crucial. This was not unique to Russia. Rule from London by a largely English aristocratic elite was made palatable to nineteenth-century Scots not merely by the material benefits of Union and empire but also by the fact that the United Kingdom was an exceptionally powerful, successful and admired country internationally. Similar legitimacy and prestige accrued in Germany to Prussia and its elites after the dramatic victories of 1866–71 and the sharp rise in Germany's international status that followed.

Between 1854 and 1917 Russia achieved few triumphs in war and diplomacy, above all because she was weaker and more backward than Britain, Germany and the United States. Consciousness of backwardness and failure inevitably weakened the regime's legitimacy in the eyes of Russians and non-Russians alike. A British officer serving briefly in Russia shortly before 1914 recalls the shame felt by his landlady's conscript son at being seen 'in the uniform of the worst army in the world'.[14] Here a sense of Russia's failure as a great power was combined with the belief that the army served the regime rather than the nation, and had indeed been the key to the suppression of popular demands during the 1905 Revolution. In 1907 Russia's prime minister, Pyotr Stolypin, exhorted the Poles to 'take up our point of view, admit that the highest good is to be a Russian citizen, bear the title as proudly as Roman citizens once did.'[15] But it was not at all clear why Poles should take pride in being subjects of a Russia which was more backward than Poland itself, which denied Poles many of a true citizen's rights, and which in addition was generally seen as the least successful and most underdeveloped of the great powers. Stolypin's comparison with Rome in fact merely lent emphasis to Russia's weakness and illegitimacy as an empire in the early twentieth century: after all, Greeks might look down somewhat on Roman culture but they could scarcely deny Rome's power or its military and diplomatic success.

Weak domestic legitimacy and lack of success in war fed off each other in Russia: Nicholas II accepted peace with Japan in autumn 1905 above all for fear of domestic revolution but he did so just as the military situation on land was almost certain to turn sharply in Russia's favour.[16] Defeat by an Asian power drastically reduced the regime's prestige, however, even in conservative and nationalist circles, which itself limited the options and to some extent increased the riskiness of Russian foreign and military policy in the years before 1914, above all because of Russia's need to reassert herself. Those who ran Russian foreign policy in these years were well aware of their empire's weakness and of its need not to lose further legitimacy in nationalist eyes – which meant to some extent listening to the pro-Slav voices in Russia's press and parliament.

Consideration of Russian foreign policy immediately before 1914 is a reminder that what seemed like aggression and expansion to foreigners might in fact be born of a sense of weakness and vulnerability. Indeed, looking at Russian foreign policy over the centuries, vulnerability and weakness were often at least as powerful a factor as an instinct for territorial expansion. Until the eighteenth century Russia was still vulnerable to raiders from the steppe. For most of the period between 1550 and 1917 she was weaker than some of her Western neighbours and fellow great powers. Weakness and expansionism were in any case by no means necessarily at odds with each other: colonizing and fortifying the steppe was the best way to keep raiders from the Russian heartlands: expanding into Central Asia was a sensible way to regain prestige and threaten British India in the aftermath of the Crimean War. Moreover, most Russian colonization was not directed by the state. On the contrary, most colonists were Russian and Ukrainian peasants who before the twentieth century migrated without the state's sanction and usually illegally to the empire's borderlands.

Applying modern Western moral distinctions between expansionism and defence to the pre-twentieth century world makes little sense. In the European system all great powers were bent on increasing their strength in order to secure their interests in an extremely ruthless and competitive world. Territorial expansion was one of the most traditional methods for a nation to shift the balance of power to its own favour. The Hohenzollerns and Habsburgs, though more hampered by geography than the Romanovs, were players in the same game.

So too were the British. It is true, particularly in the nineteenth and twentieth centuries, that British financial and commercial power in certain cases such as Latin America allowed Britain to exercise considerable leverage without direct political and military control. Russia was poorly endowed with such weapons of informal empire. There were strict limits to her ability to subsidize clients outside her borders, let alone to match West European investment and loans. As Prince Baryatinsky, the viceroy of the Caucasus, noted: 'England displays its power with gold. Russia which is poor in gold has to compete with force of arms'.[17] A similar logic was to ensure that Soviet informal empire in Eastern Europe could be sustained only by a permanent threat of military intervention. In tsarist (and Soviet) days Russian exports could seldom compete with those of Western Europe or North America in third markets, which encouraged Petersburg's tendency towards the use of military and political influence to redress the balance. 'Open doors', a favourite Anglo-American watchword in early twentieth-century China, were seldom acceptable to Russia, which had good reason to believe that the rules of international liberal capitalism worked to her disadvantage.[18] As was argued in Chapter 3, however, the British Empire itself was very much more than a mere vehicle for commerce and financial power. The British annexed and colonized more lands than any other European people, the

Russians included. It is naïve to argue that this vast empire was acquired 'in a fit of absent-mindedness', whereas Russian expansion was planned with consistent and Machiavellian single-mindedness by a tiny inner circle of tsarist leaders in Petersburg.

EIGHTEENTH-CENTURY SUCCESS

The core of Russian military power was made up of peasant conscripts hardened by rural life and agricultural labour in the Great Russian climate and soil. Until conscription was extended to the Baltic provinces and Ukraine in the last quarter of the eighteenth century almost all the regular infantry were Great Russians: even subsequently they formed its great majority. In the battles against Frederick II of Prussia in the Seven Years' War Russian infantry gained a reputation throughout Europe for courage, endurance and discipline which it was never to lose. By the second half of the century the cavalry was also much better mounted than in Peter's day and the artillery was on a level with any other in Europe, and capable of developing innovative weapons and tactics. In Catherine's wars Russia's generals succeeded at last in mastering the logistics of moving a large European army across the vast and empty steppe. This enabled them to seize and hold Crimea, the Black Sea coast and the mouths of the Dnieper and the Dniester rivers for the first time. Whereas in 1762 over 40 per cent of the army's 402 most senior officers were non-Russian (three-quarters of these were Baltic Germans), the leading military heroes of Catherine's reign were Russians. Suvorov's troops outfought the armies of the French Revolution in Italy in 1799 but the Russian higher military leadership could not match Napoleon in 1805–7. On the other hand, the Russian army played the biggest role in the allied defeat of Napoleon in 1812–14, in the process gaining great prestige for itself and Russia.

Inevitably, the navy was always very much the junior service in Russia. Nevertheless, the fact that Peter I built his new capital, St Petersburg, on the sea made a navy essential. In the Baltic Sea Russia faced major neighbouring naval powers – first Sweden, then Germany. The overwhelmingly powerful British fleet could also seldom be kept out of the Baltic. When Russia conquered the north shore of the Black Sea in the late nineteenth century, the need for naval power increased. The whole Russian coastline was vulnerable to any fleet that controlled the Black Sea, and the Ottoman sultan was in a position to open the Straits at any time to the British and French navies. As the Russian economy and Russian finances came increasingly to depend on massive grain exports through the Straits the empire's vulnerability to hostile naval powers became more and more acute. For the Russians, the Straits came to have much the same significance as the Channel and the Belgian ports had long possessed for England.

The Russian navy was hampered by having to operate in a number of seas (Baltic, Black Sea, Arctic and Pacific Oceans) with very little chance of concentrating naval forces in any one of them. Even in the age of sail, let alone in the era of the ironclad steamship, navies were at the cutting edge of technology. Conscripting or training skilled seamen was often a problem in peasant Russia. Baltic ports ice-bound for much of the year and wooden hulls liable to rot were other perennial problems. Nevertheless, from its foundation during the Northern War of Peter I against the Swedes the navy developed a tradition of skilled coastal and amphibious warfare, which it was to maintain in the age of the mine and torpedo.

Creating a genuine high-seas fleet with the ability to project power far from Russia's borders was always much more difficult. The costs of such a fleet were enormous and badly strained state finances in the last years of both the tsarist and Soviet regimes. At both these times Russia was making exceptionally great efforts to compete with the world's leading navies. Nor were finance, technology and cadres the only obstacles to sustaining this competition. Russia lacked overseas bases and, especially in tsarist times, was partly dependent on foreign allies when it tried to deploy large naval forces far from home. In Catherine II's reign Russian ocean-going squadrons were sent from the Baltic to the Eastern Mediterranean, where they destroyed the Ottoman fleet and ravaged enemy seaborne communications. But they could never have arrived without British logistical help. Nevertheless, Catherine's reign saw probably the peak of tsarist relative naval power. In 1780 the Russian fleet even played the leading role in forcing the British to accept the rights of neutral shipping during the War of American Independence. At no time in the nineteenth century could Russia have aspired to such a role. In 1905 when the Baltic fleet was sent round the world to its destruction at Tsushima all the weaknesses of Russia as a naval power were evident. The ships could not have reached the Far East without some German and French help. Lack of proper bases en route was one reason why they arrived in a poor condition to fight. In any case, by the time they arrived the main strategic justification for sending them had already disappeared. The Pacific fleet had been destroyed by the Japanese before the Baltic fleet could reinforce it.

Behind the armed forces there already stood in the eighteenth century an almost entirely self-sufficient defence industry and the largest iron industry in Europe. Expansion into the fertile Black Earth zone boosted agricultural production and rural prosperity. Already the most populous as well as much the largest state in Europe by 1800, Russia stood poised on the brink of an explosive nineteenth-century growth in population which would fill the newly conquered lands. Even Catherine II conscripted one million men in the course of her 34-year reign, a figure no other European monarch could match. Faced by the Napoleonic threat, Alexander I conscripted two million men in just 24 years.[19]

In the conditions of the time, a state that could conscript, equip, train and provide officers for armies of this scale had to be formidable, albeit in an often hand-to-mouth way and in a very narrow range of functions. In the first half of the eighteenth century the army itself largely ran the recruitment system and the levying of the poll tax, but after the strengthening of civilian provincial government through the 1775 reform regular civil institutions did the job. For a century after Peter's reign over 80 per cent of tax revenues came from four sources: these were the salt and alcohol levies, the poll tax and the dues paid by state peasants.[20] Over the decades the salt tax lost much of its significance and the state peasants' contributions became more and more important. In the 1750s Russian revenues were only one-fifth of France's,[21] but direct comparisons have their dangers. Russian soldiers were conscripted and regiments to a considerable extent supported themselves or requisitioned supplies. In the Napoleonic era putting a cavalryman in the field, to take a single example, cost far less in Russia than elsewhere in Europe.

At the top level of leadership and coordination of policy the autocratic system of government functioned reasonably well in the first two hundred years of Romanov rule. At a high cost in brutality and exploitation, the alliance between autocrat and serf-owner provided political stability, effective exploitation of human and fiscal resources for military purposes, and relatively coherent and coordinated top-level policy-making. In the eighteenth century the system survived a number of palace coups and some ineffective monarchs. When foreign policy was perceived as too wayward by key members of the court aristocracy, an autocrat's throne and life were in danger. Both Peter III and Paul I were overthrown by palace coups and murdered, partly for this reason. On the whole, however, top-level coordinating institutions worked better in the eighteenth century than in the nineteenth, when government was divided into increasingly large and technically complicated rival ministerial empires. Moreover, eighteenth-century Russia was blessed with two of the ablest monarchs in modern European history, Peter I and Catherine II. Their different styles of rule reflected not just differences in personality and sex but also the considerably more sophisticated and Europeanized nature of the Russian elite by Catherine's time. Catherine also used her more able lovers, above all Potemkin and Orlov, to good political effect. Before the eighteenth century tsars had deliberately married Russian noblewomen from outside the court aristocracy and had used their wives' male relatives as reliable and dependent allies in government and at court. With eighteenth-century tsars marrying foreign princesses this method of building up a monarchical party and manoeuvring amidst court factions became impossible, but Catherine's two great lovers and their networks played a similar and important role.

THE PROBLEM OF POLAND

By the 1780s Russia was undoubtedly a very great power. She was favoured both by her geopolitical position on Europe's periphery and by the contemporary international context. Between 1688 and 1815 Britain and France were inveterate enemies: their rivalry meant they were unlikely to unite against Russia (as happened later in the Crimean War with dire consequences for the security of Russia's coastline) and might indeed compete to woo her. Russia's traditional eastern European rivals – the Ottomans, Sweden and Poland – were in decline. So too, relatively speaking, was France. When French power revived after 1789 at least Russia was a continent removed from Paris. By contrast, not merely were Austria and Prussia in the front line but for most of the period between 1740 and 1854 they were either bitter rivals or very suspicious allies, which made both of them anxious for Russian friendship. In Catherine's reign both Prussia and Austria wooed Russia hard, St Petersburg undoubtedly deriving the more benefit from alliance with Vienna. Catherine's great conquests and their abundant resources seemed to offer wide scope for Russia's future growth and power. Moreover, the regime handled effectively the complicated task of balancing the need to colonize newly conquered regions – often actually with runaway serfs – with the imperative of preserving the serf-based, conservative social order in the Russian heartland. By Catherine's death in 1796 the old threat to social stability in the Russian interior from outbursts of anarchic revolt in the barely controlled southern and eastern frontier lands had largely gone. The Cossacks for instance were now firmly under control and provided invaluable light cavalry for the imperial army. In the early 1780s Catherine appeared as both the arbiter of Central Europe between the Habsburgs and Hohenzollerns, and as the powerful upholder of international maritime law. These were unparalleled achievements for a Russian monarch. If one drew a trajectory of Russian power from Peter I's accession to Catherine's death and continued it onwards into the future, then it was quite realistic to predict in 1796 that the nineteenth century would be Russia's. This prediction seemed confirmed when Napoleon's Grande Armée was destroyed in Russian's vast, inhospitable interior and the Russian army subsequently advanced all the way to Paris. In fact, however, the nineteenth century was to prove much more difficult for the Russian state than the eighteenth.

The first major problem to face St Petersburg after 1815 was Poland, most of which was awarded to Alexander I at the Congress of Vienna. The tsars never found it easy to rule Poland, which was to be a major thorn in their flesh, just as subsequently it was to become a key source of vulnerability for Soviet empire in post-Stalin Eastern Europe. In part the problem for the tsars was that Poland was too big to absorb easily, and its elites were too numerous, too self-confident and too wedded to heroic memories of the old independent Polish Commonwealth, which had after all only finally disappeared in 1795 and which had briefly revived, as the Grand Duchy of Warsaw, under Napoleon. In addition, the Polish and Russian churches and states were age-old enemies and rivals. One major source of rivalry lay in the lands between Poland and Great Russia where the bulk of the population were Belorussian and Ukrainian peasants but the aristocracy was Polish. In the last decades of tsarist empire one of the regime's main objectives was to be the elimination of Polish influence in these border regions and the establishment of their Russian identity.

From Peter I's defeat of the Swedes at Poltava in 1709 until the late 1760s Russia had exercised a considerable degree of indirect control over Poland: it was able to ensure that friendly candidates were elected to the throne, that Polish foreign policy was pro-Russian, that Russian armies could cross Poland en route to campaigns in Germany, and that attempts to strengthen the Polish state and army were blocked. Informal Russian empire was difficult to maintain, however, since Poland bordered on two other great powers, Prussia and Austria, and was the traditional ally and client of France. The Prussians lusted after Polish territory and any revival of French power in Europe was certain to lead to attempts to reassert Polish independence. Nor was the manipulation of Polish factions to serve Russian interests always easy or without risk of a patriotic backlash. Russia's aim in the partitions of Poland was partly to avoid trouble with the German powers and partly to stop the re-emergence of a powerful, reformed Polish state – let alone the pro-French and Pro-Jacobin Poland that raised its head in 1793–5. In addition, there were strategic advantages in pushing Russia's frontier westwards and fiscal ones in acquiring new tax-payers.

In 1815, in line with traditional tsarist policy, Alexander I attempted to base Russian rule in Poland on an alliance with the native aristocracy. Partly to serve Russian prestige in Europe and his own benevolent self-image, Alexander granted the Poles wide autonomy, a powerful elected parliament, and guaranteed civil rights. Just as he encouraged the abolition of serfdom in the Baltic provinces, so too he seems to have regarded Poland as a more advanced and sophisticated region where he could try out reforms which could later be applied in Russia. After 1820, increasingly fearful of revolution, Alexander I adopted a more conservative and authoritarian stance. His successor, Nicholas I, faced an attempted coup by radical officers on ascending the throne in 1825 and was confirmed in his instinctive authoritarianism. A *modus vivendi* between Nicholas I and a nationalist, obstreperous and sometimes radical Polish parliament was never likely. A first Polish revolution was crushed in 1831 and followed by a generation of authoritarian rule. When Alexander II tried to re-create a *modus vivendi* with Polish society in 1856–63 the result was a second Polish insurrection, more dangerous to Russia than the first because it occurred at a time when defeat in the Crimea had exposed Russian weakness to the world. For a time it seemed possible in 1863 that Napoleon III would intervene on the Poles' behalf. This awoke many long-standing Russian nightmares about the strategic threat posed by borderland disaffection and its foreign allies. Two Polish risings destroyed any chance of renewed détente between the regime and Polish elites.[22] Instead an attempt was made to win peasant loyalty by emancipating the serfs of Polish nobles on terms much more generous than could be offered to the serfs of the Russian nobility. A real alliance between tsarism and the Polish peasantry was scarcely possible, however, especially given the opposition of the powerful and nationalist Catholic clergy. As peasants moved to towns and were educated, they began to share nationalist resentment of Russian restrictions on Polish language, freedom and culture. From 1863 to 1914 Russian rule in Poland depended on the memory of failed revolution and its consequences and on the strength of Russian authority and repression. Since an enormous army was anyway maintained in Poland for strategic purposes, holding the country down was not in the short run a great problem. But the nature of tsarist rule in Poland meant that if St Petersburg's authoritarian grasp weakened – in the event for instance of defeat by Austria or Germany – then the region would quickly become ungovernable.

Attempts to 'regain' the borderlands between Poland and Russia led in 1839 to the banning of the Uniate church, in other words of that stream of the Orthodox community which had accepted the Polish-backed compromise whereby the Orthodox liturgy and ritual were preserved but the pope's authority was recognized. Efforts were made to boost peasant agriculture and, on the eve of 1914, to give the Orthodox and therefore supposedly Russian and loyal peasantry a bigger voice in elected local government. Above all, however, large sums and efforts were devoted to reducing Polish landowning in the region and implanting a Russian landowning elite in its place. The policy had some similarities to the manner in which the English went about consolidating their hold on seventeenth- and eighteenth-century Ireland. In the eighteenth century, for instance, the English authorities were convinced that the almost complete expropriation of the Catholic landowning class deprived potential rebellion of its leaders and made revolt impossible unless Ireland was invaded by sizeable French armies.[23]

In comparison to the English in Ireland, Russian policy towards Polish landlords in the Western Borderlands was less ruthless and thorough-going. The number of Polish landowners and the size of their estates in the Western Borderlands were much reduced after 1863 but Poles still remained just over half of all estate-owners in Lithuania and Belorussia at the turn of the twentieth century. Even in Ukraine west of the Dnieper, where the number of small Polish estate-owners was drastically reduced after 1863, Poles still retained most of the medium-sized and big properties.[24] In Ireland by contrast, only 5 per cent of the land was owned by Catholics by 1776.[25] English policy was also more effective: a solid English elite society and culture was established in Ireland and dominated the country for many generations. Despite spending great sums on subsidizing Russian landowning, St Petersburg was on the whole unable to create a sizeable group of landowners willing actually to live on estates in the Western Borderlands and to challenge Polish economic and cultural dominance. In fact, it was probably anachronistic in the second half of the nineteenth century to devote such resources and energy to implanting a landowning elite. In an era of impending mass literacy and urbanization it might well have made more sense even in the relatively backward Western Borderlands to target the children of richer peasants and other emerging middle-class elements. In this region, as in much of Eastern and Central Europe, it was to be these groups that were crucial in the creation of mass national identities.

DILEMMAS OF EMPIRE: 1850–1917

The history of Poland and the Western Borderlands in the nineteenth century showed that the old tsarist policy of basing empire on alliance with local aristocracies was seldom any longer sufficient, might not be desirable, and in certain cases was impossible. Since the old strategy of alliance with aristocracies had served the empire well for centuries, this change was very important. So too was the fact that the tsarist regime never came up with a single coherent new strategy capable of sustaining empire in the modern era.

This was partly because some tsarist statesmen[26] never abandoned the old strategy of alliance with regional aristocracies and religious leaders, which in their view was a much better guarantee of order and loyalty than attempts to woo the peasantry or to Russianize the borderlands.[27] Incoherence was also built into the structure of nineteenth-century tsarist government. There was very inadequate coordination of the policies of the different ministries and the latter often differed considerably over how to govern the non-Russian provinces of the empire. The finance ministry was above all concerned with balancing budgets and encouraging economic development: order and political stability were the highest priority of the interior ministry. It was the much weaker ministry of education that was most concerned with the questions of language, culture and national identity that in the longer term were most decisive for the empire's future. Moreover, in most of the non-Russian borderlands power was exercised by governors-general, who were only very partially under ministerial control and could appeal for support directly to the tsar. These powerful regional semi-viceroys – in the Caucasus there was an actual viceroy – could greatly influence policy in specific regions. In defence of the tsarist regime it does, however, need to be stressed that the Russian empire included a wide range of peoples of very different cultures and levels of socio-economic development. Any attempt to impose a single, 'coherent' strategy on all of them would have been unthinkable and catastrophic. Moreover, it should by now be clear that there was no easy solution to the dilemmas of empire in the modern era. If tsarism floundered, so too did all its imperial rivals.

In chapter 2 of this book, a range of possible responses that imperial regimes might make to the dilemmas of modern empire was outlined. Of these, the most daring was the attempt to create a new, universal – or at least supranational – ideology on which to base imperial rule. This strategy, most nearly approached by Soviet communism, was inconceivable for any monarchical and aristocratic old regime, including tsarist Russia. Sustaining a traditional supranational religion was far more possible, but in this respect Orthodoxy served the tsars poorly since it was essentially a national and not a universal religion. Islam could bind Turk, Arab, Kurd and Bosnian together in common allegiance to the Ottoman sultan. Though by 1900 nationalism was much stronger in most of the Habsburg Empire than in the sultan's Arab or Kurdish domains, nevertheless even Catholicism could play more of a unifying role across ethnic divisions in Austria than was the case with Orthodoxy in Russia.

In principle it might have been possible to strengthen empire by the appeal of the great civilization to which the imperial regime was linked. Together with the economic and military advantages of empire, this might at least have provided some defence against the nationalist challenge. However, though some of the empires studied in this book were better placed than Russia to use the attraction of a great civilization to sustain imperial rule, none[28] of them survived even so. In the tsarist case, the century before 1914 had witnessed a tremendous flowering of Russian literary and musical culture. Not only had the Russian intelligentsia developed a very impressive high culture, but it was also open to people of varying races and religions, and had genuinely cosmopolitan sympathies and outlooks. Drawing inspiration from all the strands of European culture and speaking many languages, the Russian intelligentsia's culture was in some respects genuinely broader than the more national perspective common in the individual cultures of Western Europe. Though Polish and German subjects of the tsar were never likely to defer to Russian culture, the educated classes of Ukraine, Belorussia and the other smaller Christian peoples might well do so, especially if they were allowed to develop their own languages and cultures alongside Russian. Even the late nineteenth and early twentieth-century Muslim reformers, the so-called Jadids, often had considerable respect for the Russian intelligentsia's culture and were inclined to ally with it in order to modernize their own societies.[29] Given the deep antagonism between the tsarist regime and much of the Russian intelligentsia, however, the pull of intelligentsia culture on the non-Russians was not much help to the empire's rulers. If, for example, Ukrainian or Jewish socialists were often drawn to all-imperial revolutionary parties rather than to more narrowly national ones, this was scarcely a gain from the tsar's point of view, though it might subsequently aid the foundation of a socialist empire on tsarism's ruins.

An alternative extreme solution to empire's dilemma was genocide, or at least grand-scale 'ethnic cleansing'. As we have seen, the tsarist regime did 'encourage' the emigration beyond its borders of some of the smaller Caucasian peoples whom it perceived as a threat to Russian security. The rulers of tsarist Russia, meaning both the Romanovs and the aristocracy, were unequivocally European in values and outlook by the nineteenth century, however. They were also sensitive to their reputation in Europe.

To attempt to solve dilemmas of empire through a systematic policy of genocide or ethnic cleansing was beyond the imagination or moral horizon of what was essentially a Victorian ruling class. In their case we are very far removed from the moral worlds of Hitler and Stalin, in which secular totalitarian ideologues could justify, even demand, the extermination of peoples 'standing in history's path'.

It is true, however, that by 1900 anti-semitism was endemic among the Russian ruling elite. It is also the case that by then a combination of intermittent pogroms, legal disabilities and economic misery was encouraging emigration of part of the Jewish population of the Western Borderlands to Western Europe and the United States. But particularly when discussing political persecution and violence, linguistic precision is important. The pogroms were terrible but they were a long way from the systematic ethnic cleansing, let alone genocide, of whole peoples which were to be the strategies of supposedly more civilized European people towards the Jews. Moreover, all recent research emphasizes that the tsarist central government itself did not organize or instigate pogroms, though local authorities sometimes winked at them and more often were slow to stamp on them. Tsarist ministers did not connive in murder and were in any case deeply uneasy at outbreaks of mass violence and very scared that the 'dark people's' uncontrollable propensity for anarchic settling of scores might easily target the ruling classes themselves.[30] On the other hand, it is the case that knowledge of their superiors' frequent antipathy to the Jews could encourage junior officials to believe that failure to stop pogroms would go unpunished, and that during the First World War hundreds of thousands of Jews were expelled by the Russian army from the Western Borderlands with great brutality and for no good military reason.

A third conceivable strategy towards a solution of empire's problems would have been to follow the Austrian path towards some version of multi-ethnic federation. Russian political tradition made such a strategy less likely than in Austria, however. Tsarist centralization had never allowed the empire to develop into an Austrian-style patchwork of crownlands, each retaining a very distinct political identity. Moreover, though the Emperor Franz Joseph was no kind of nationalist, he was by natural inclination a centralizer and an absolutist ruler. In the first years of his reign he attempted to rule in this fashion and failed. Internal opposition and defeat by France and then Prussia forced him to abandon authoritarian and centralized rule and to embark on the road of liberalization and devolution of power to the crownlands. Once he was launched on this path, further moves towards multi-ethnic federalism in

Austria were much less the product of the emperor's wishes than of forces in society that he could no longer control.

No member of the Russian elite looked on Austria's response to multi-ethnic empire as a desirable model to follow. On the contrary, it seemed to them a source of political instability and, above all, military weakness which they must avoid at all costs. Russian military commentators[31] on the wars of 1859 and 1866, for example, stressed the impact of multi-eth-nicity on the supposedly poor morale and fighting capacity of the Habsburg army. They contrasted this with the power of national solidar-ity in the Prussian, Italian and – above all – Russian armies. For them the idea that the Russian Empire was in any sense comparable to polyglot Austria was unthinkable. In military terms these Russian officers had a point. At that time few of the tsar's Muslim subjects were liable to mili-tary service and 90 per cent of the army's intake in 1870, for example, were Russians, Belorussians and Ukrainians. The key point was that for the tsarist elite Belorussians and Ukrainians were beyond any question Russians, albeit Russians speaking a strange dialect and possessing some distinctive, though by no means objectionable or politically dangerous,[32] customs. Indeed, not merely the tsarist elite but virtually all Europeans would have taken it for granted in the 1870s that Ukrainians and Belorussians were far more securely Russian in their national identity and political loyalty than Bavarians were German.

Demography was very important in determining the different responses of the Habsburgs and Romanovs to empire's dilemmas. The Austrian Germans were in no sense a nation and they were also well under a quarter of the empire's total population at the turn of the twentieth century. In these circumstances it was clearly unthinkable to turn the Habsburg Empire into a Germanic nation state. Russia was very different. In the first place – unlike the Germans' situation – all Russians were subjects of the tsar and Russians had a far stronger traditional sense of unity than the various German communities scattered across the Habsburg Empire. Moreover, in 1897 Russians were 44 per cent of the empire's population. If Ukrainians and Belorussians were added, two-thirds of the tsar's sub-jects came from the empire's core nation. In the political thinking of the time, the tsar's Muslim subjects in Asia could largely be discounted from calculations of nationality, since they were perceived to be too backward to play a political role. As regards the small Christian peoples, their fate was seen as indissolubly linked to Russia, since they would not wish to be ruled either by the German kaiser or the Ottoman sultan. In the age of imperialism it was not believed safe or possible for small peoples to main-tain their independence in the borderlands between empires. Moreover, it was also very often believed that these peoples lacked the numbers or resources to develop a true high culture based on their own languages. The Poles were seen as a threat because of their numbers, the strength of their high culture, their memory of statehood and their unshakeable hostility to Russia. But, so it was believed, an empire two-thirds Russian and more than nine-tenths loyal or apolitical could easily find the resources and the will to repress the Poles until such time as the latter accepted the inevitability and the advantages of loyalty to the tsar.

Of course, a great deal hinged on whether the Ukrainians actually were Russian or, to put things more realistically, on whether a people who were bound to become much more literate and much less rural in the process of modernization would come to think of themselves as Russians, as an entirely separate Ukrainian nation, or as some combination of East Slav, Orthodox, Ukrainian and Russian identities and loyalties. On the whole, Russian elites were little bothered by the danger of Ukrainian nationalism in the nineteenth century. Rival elites and the Polish and German high cultures they sustained were seen as the great threat to Russia's hold on the Western Borderlands. It was widely assumed, at least before the Revolution of 1905, that a peasant people would never generate a high culture or political aspirations capable of threatening Russia.

Nevertheless, some nineteenth-century tsarist statesmen were aware of the potential danger of Ukrainian separatism and were determined to nip it in the bud. They focused their attention on the linguistic and cultural foundations of national identity and therefore of subsequent political nationalism. In 1863 General Annenkov, the governor-general of the Kiev region, flatly opposed the publication of the bible in Ukrainian, commenting that by its publication Ukrainian nationalists 'would achieve so to speak the recognition of the independence of the Little Russian language, and then of course they will make claims to autonomy for Little Russia.'[33] Thirteen years later a key government memorandum warned of the dangers of 'various doctrines which superficially contain nothing political and seem to relate only to the sphere of purely academic and artistic interests.' In the long run their danger could be very great. 'Nothing divides people as much as differences in speech and writing. Permitting the creation of a special literature for the common people in the Ukrainian dialect would signify collaborating in the alienation of Ukraine from the rest of Russia.' The memorandum went on to emphasize the very great importance of the Ukrainians to the Russian nation and state: 'To permit the separation . . . of thirteen million Little Russians would be the utmost political carelessness, especially in view of the unifying movement which is going on alongside us among the German tribe.'[34] In the light of such views the tsarist regime did its utmost from 1876 to stop the development of a written Ukrainian language or high culture. Virtually all publication in Ukrainian was banned until the period 1905–14, when revolution, the semi-constitution of 1906 and the partial liberalization of politics allowed the language greater leeway. Even in the so-called Constitutional Era, however, not only the government but also the imperial parliament refused to contemplate any teaching of or in Ukrainian in schools, once again taking a much tougher line over Ukrainian than other languages.[35]

To any Ukrainian nationalist and most democrats, tsarist policy towards Ukraine is of course indefensible. Of present concern, however, is whether or not this policy served the cause of preserving empire. On the debit side it could well be argued that tsarist policy was doomed to failure and to the alienation of the Ukrainian intelligentsia from Russia. One-fifth of all Ukrainians were the subjects not of the tsar but of the Habsburg emperor. Particularly in Austrian Galicia, the Ukrainians were allowed to develop a vernacular high culture, as well as to organize themselves politically and to create a sense of Ukrainian nationhood. In the conditions of pre-1914 Europe nothing could stop Galicia from influencing mentalities and aspirations in Russian Ukraine. St Petersburg should therefore have accepted the emergence of a separate Ukrainian identity, secure in the knowledge that most Ukrainian nationalist intellectuals saw Poland not Russia as their arch-enemy,[36] and most Ukrainians felt far closer to Russian than to German culture. There were very few Russian Ukrainians indeed in 1914 who would have swapped existence within a Russia which allowed them civil and cultural rights with the only geopolitical alternative, namely the protection of Berlin and Vienna.

Comparisons with London's treatment of Scotland also suggest that St Petersburg's efforts to suppress Ukraine's sense of separate identity may well have been unnecessary and counterproductive.[37] In the eighteenth century the cultural distance between London and Edinburgh was roughly similar to that between St Petersburg and Kiev, though the political institutions of the Scottish Kingdom were much more ancient than those of the Ukrainian Hetmanate, which had only come into existence after the overthrow of Polish rule in central Ukraine in the 1640s. Moreover, Scotland had a long history of enmity towards England which had no parallel in Russo-Ukrainian relations. Scottish and Ukrainian elites benefited from incorporation into empires and contributed greatly to the latter's government and culture.[38] It was, however, in the 1840s, precisely when the Scots appeared most satisfied by the Union, that a modern nationalist movement rooted in conceptions of a separate language (barely an issue in Scotland) and ethnicity first appeared in Ukraine. It is hard to believe that the radical and sharply anti-tsarist turn taken by this movement at that time did not owe much to the centralizing, bureaucratic and intrusive despotism of Nicholas I's regime. By contrast, the Scots enjoyed not merely full civil rights but also their own church, law and schools.

Nevertheless, if one accepts the premises of empire it is possible to defend tsarist strategy towards the Ukraine in the regime's last decades. Nineteenth-century Europe offered many examples of initially apolitical cultural movements which in time developed into nationalist and ultimately separatist campaigns. Indeed, some scholars of nationalism see the transition from cultural to political and finally secessionist nationalism as almost an iron law of political science.[39] Undoubtedly the surest way to save an empire was to turn as much as possible of it into a nation, if this could realistically be achieved. Moreover, there are many nations even in contemporary Europe which over time have assimilated peoples culturally and ethnically more distant than Ukrainians were from Russians. It is probably true that the best way peacefully to reconcile most Ukrainian intellectuals to Russian rule in the early twentieth century was to transform the tsarist empire into some fort of federal, socialist republic but it hardly makes sense to condemn Nicholas II for failing to pursue such a policy. Tsarism's opposition to the emergence of a separate Ukrainian identity, its repression of Ukrainian political leaders and organizations, was an important factor in the failure of Ukrainian nationalists to sustain their independence against Soviet pressure in 1918–21.[40] Ukrainian nationalist leaders lacked political experience, there were almost no nationalist organizations in the villages, and a sense of national identity in the peasantry was still usually very weak. An empire of sorts was thereby preserved, which in time even to some extent reconciled some members of the Russian White emigration to the existence of the Soviet regime.

There were good reasons why the last four tsars found it increasingly important to identify their regime with Russian interests, culture and values. During the nineteenth century nationalism in Europe tended to move from the left of the political spectrum towards the right. In part conservative elites sought a popular idea with which to legitimize their own power and combat liberal and socialist opponents. Nationalism had the potential too to reunite societies turned upside-down by mass literacy, migration to cities and work in factories. Disraeli and Bismarck provided models of nationalism's uses to conservative leaders. Russia was a less modern and literate society than Britain and Germany. It also did not have elections and competition for votes between parties. Nevertheless, the regime's leaders were convinced that a degree of public support was essential. Even Alexander III, the supreme embodiment of autocratic power and seeming contempt for public opinion, told his foreign minister that public support for the regime's foreign policy was politically crucial.[41]

Even under a supposedly autocratic regime, there were also pressures from below – in other words from Russian public opinion. A small but sharp illustration of this comes from the world of Russian music. In the mid-nineteenth century patronage from the court was crucial for Russian composers, singers and musicians. Russia's great theatres and opera-houses belonged to the crown and were in fact run by the Ministry of the Imperial Court. It was therefore extremely galling for the rising generation of Russian composers – Mussorgsky, Rimsky-Korsakov and the other members of the 'Mighty Handful' – that the court much pre-ferred to patronize foreign music and paid foreign performers far more than their Russian peers. The campaign to overturn this state of affairs combined individual self-interest and nationalist sentiment among a newly emerging section of the professional middle class in a way very typical of the history of nineteenth-century nationalism.[42]

Of more obvious and general importance is the major shift in the nature of the ruling elite that occurred in the course of the nineteenth century.[43] By 1900 the core of the political elite were long-serving career bureaucrats, overwhelmingly Russian in ethnic origin and much less cosmopolitan in outlook than the aristocratic courtiers of Catherine II or Alexander I. Given nineteenth-century intellectual and political trends, it is not surprising that many of these men believed that the state had a duty to spread the Russian culture and language throughout the empire and to give them a position of pre-eminence in borderlands pre-viously, for example, dominated by Polish, German or Swedish high culture. Nor should one be surprised by a considerable degree of 'big nation' cultural arrogance towards the smaller peoples of empire, whose cultures were seen as having no historical significance. Such arrogance was the European norm at that time. Moreover, even when Russian officials had none of these attitudes, they still might often believe that spreading Russian culture and consolidating a sense of Russian national identity as widely as possible was the surest way to preserve the empire.

It should by now be rather clear why, faced with the dilemmas of modern empire, the main strategy of the tsarist elite was to attempt to turn as much as possible of their empire into something approaching a Russian nation. Given Russia's system of government it is also no surprise that the means used to consolidate the nation had much more in common with aggressive Magyarization than with Westminster's efforts to cajole and persuade the White colonies into some form of Greater British imperial federation.

In one crucial respect, the British and Russians had more in common with each other than either had with the Hungarians. Ruling over many non-European peoples and territories, both the British and the Russians excluded most of them from the project of consolidating an imperial nation. For the British this was nothing new. The overseas colonies had always been constitutionally separate and the English had wholly rejected the idea of assimilating non-Whites. Traditionally, Russia's had been a much more assimilationist empire, a large proportion of the aristocracy being originally of Tatar and nomadic origin. By the nineteenth century, however, the Westernization of Russia's elite had left its mark and willingness to assimilate non-Europeans had declined. The legal concept of 'aliens' (*inorodtsy*) was created in order to define groups who were unassimilable save perhaps in some very distant future and who did not possess the rights and obligations of the tsar's ordinary subjects.[44] In 1900 this category included almost all the indigenous forest, nomadic and Muslim peoples of Russian Asia. Moreover, in practice the regime was not making much effort at this time to integrate even Muslims in Europe into a Russian national community. Even Tatars converted to Christianity were often very dubiously Russian in any cultural sense. Moreover, in the last decades of the old regime not merely were the great majority of Muslims completely immune to conversion but some long-since converted but only superficially Christianized communities were prone to revert to Islam. Meanwhile the tsarist regime was generally suspicious of Muslim reformers who sought to introduce the Russian language and modern subjects into Islamic schools attached to mosques and therefore beyond the government's control. On the whole, St Petersburg preferred in this case to back conservative Islamic forces who sought to protect the isolated and religious identity of the Muslim population. The major technical and political task of bringing the mass of the Muslim peoples into the state's own educational system had not yet been faced.

As regards the Christian minorities, the state was already attempting to use its schools to inculcate the Russian language, identification with Russian culture and to some extent political loyalty. The number of schools had grown enormously in the two decades before 1914 and, had war and revolution not intervened, it was realistic to predict near-universal primary education within a short generation. As a vehicle for russifying the population, however, the educational system had glaring faults. Scattered over an immense area, schools were very difficult for the authorities to control and inspect. Even where they existed – which was rarer in rural Ukraine than in Russia – the village schools were usually rudimentary, three-year, one-class affairs. The teachers were usually women by 1906–17 and even in the Russian villages had limited status and influence among the peasantry. Living in poverty and isolation, they generally shared the intelligentsia's dislike of the tsarist regime. Many of them were socialists and some were revolutionaries. The regime did not trust the teachers, tried to weigh them down with controls, and certainly could not rely on them to conquer the countryside – Russian or non-Russian – for its policies and values. There was a big contrast with the role of schools in cultivating patriotism and imperialism among British or German youth, or with French teachers' sense of mission and status as they set out to conquer France for the nation and the republic.[45]

It is therefore self-evident that in 1914 the tsarist regime was very far from having answers to the dilemmas of empire. On the contrary, as literacy and political awareness spread, the regime's difficulties in managing its multinational empire were bound to increase. The experience of the Revolution of 1905 and the subsequent development of a much freer press and of parliamentary life was increasing the confidence of nationalist intellectuals, making it easier for them to meet and organize, and even to begin to put down some roots in the peasantry in the period just before the First World War.

Nevertheless, in 1914 the non-Russians still posed little immediate threat to the empire's survival. Most of them were still peasants or nomads, not easily mobilized by nationalist intellectuals. Many of the minority peoples felt the need for Russian protection, feared Germans, Poles and Turks more than Russia, or simply accepted the empire's existence as a *fait accompli* in an imperialist age. In any case the core of tsarist power was in the Great Russian heartland and its cities. A regime that held this area and its communications could usually reimpose its authority in the borderlands, as the tsarist regime did in the 1905 Revolution and as the Bolsheviks succeeded in doing after 1917. In the last decades of tsarism, coping with the problems of multi-ethnic empire was an increasingly serious challenge, but the Russian social and political crisis was always a greater threat to the regime.

Russia's crisis had much in common with the difficulties facing other states on Europe's poorer 'Second World' periphery. Middle classes were much smaller, property less secure and politics potentially more radical and violent than in the rich countries of North-Western Europe. In general it makes far more sense to compare Russia to Italy, Spain or Hungary than to Germany, France or Britain. In none of these peripheral countries did democracy or constitutionalism have a smooth ride in the twentieth century. All lived under right-wing authoritarian regimes for a time, and in some cases for decades. Hungary, like Russia, experienced a Bolshevik revolution in 1919. Its Bolshevik regime was overthrown by foreign, in this case Romanian, intervention. It is easier for a foreign army to reach Budapest than Moscow, and Romania had a bigger immediate interest in what regime ruled Hungary than distant France or Britain appeared to have in the overthrow of Russian communism.

In 1914 there was a greater risk of social revolution in Russia than in Hungary, Italy or Spain. Russia was somewhat poorer and, given its size and multinational character, a good deal more complicated to rule. Serfdom and the village commune's traditional control over peasant lives and land had created a more homogeneous peasantry with more collectivist instincts and a greater hostility to the landowning class than was found even in most of Europe's peripheral Second World. The Russian aristocracy was much weaker in terms of both landowning and power than in England or Prussia, but (unlike the case for instance in south or west Germany) it still owned enough land to be a worthwhile target for peasant jacqueries. Peasant egalitarian and collectivist traditions had an impact on labour relations in the cities too. Revolutionary socialism had at least as strong a hold on the Russian working class as anywhere else in Europe. The regime's incoherent but usually repressive labour policy contributed to this but there were also other obstacles – economic, political and cultural – to easy acceptance of capitalism, its values and the foreign or minority (Jewish, Polish, German, Armenian) entrepreneurs and financiers who were often its leading figures.

A key further weakness of the Russian old regime in 1914 was the distrust and alienation felt towards it by large sections of the upper and middle class. As already noted, autocracy proved less successful than Hungarian, Italian or even Spanish semi-liberal regimes at the turn of the twentieth century when it came to uniting the state and the social elites, both old and new. But by the twentieth century Russian society was sufficiently polarized, and both regime and social elites sufficiently vulnerable to revolution, to make liberalization difficult and dangerous. Conservative advisers who warned Nicholas II that only an authoritarian police state could hold this society together and preserve the existence of its propertied elites were by no means necessarily wrong.

Worst of all was the international context, which was much less favourable to Russia than it had been a century before or in the era of Catherine II. The main change was that the Industrial Revoltion, starting in Western Europe and spreading thence to Germany, had tilted the balance of power sharply in Russia's disfavour. In addition, the unification of Germany in 1871 meant that Europe's most powerful military and industrial state was now on Russia's border. Generations of Austro-Prussian rivalry, which had enhanced Russian power and security, came to an end with the signing of the Dual Alliance in 1879. Faced with an unshakeable Germanic bloc in Central Europe, Russia was also challenged by the rapid growth of German influence in the Ottoman Empire and by the rise of Japan, by 1914 a formidable military power adjacent to Russia's vulnerable and sparsely populated Asiatic territory. So long as Russia's rapid economic growth of the three pre-war decades continued and political stability was preserved, the tsarist empire's long-term position as a very great power was assured. In the short run, however, Russia was vulnerable both domestically and internationally. This dangerously destabilizing combination of Russia's present weakness but future power was an important reason why Berlin and Vienna launched a European war in 1914.

The war destroyed the Russian Empire not because the army was defeated but because the home front collapsed. Before the Revolution of 1917 Russia's military record was no worse than that of its Western allies. If the Russian army was on the whole inferior to the German, the same was usually true of the French and British. In 1916 Russia's economic and military performance was often spectacular.[46] The Brusilov offensive inflicted major defeats on the Austrians and Germans, and had a good claim to be the most successful allied offensive of the war before 1918. Meanwhile, against the Ottomans the Russians had done far better than the British, who had been defeated at Gallipoli and in Mesopotamia in 1915. By contrast, the Russian army had defeated the Ottomans in every engagement and were driving deep into Anatolia when revolution came. It came partly because of wartime economic sufferings on the home front but above all because of a complete collapse of faith in the tsarist regime among most Russian elites and the Russian urban masses.

Ironically, in February 1917 the Russians had every likelihood of victory. With British potential at last being realized in military terms in 1916 the pressure on the Germans was becoming overwhelming. German desperation at the prospect of probable defeat had resulted in unrestricted submarine warfare and imminent American intervention. This made eventual allied victory almost certain. Churchill's comment that 'with victory in her grasp she [Russia] fell to earth'[47] was actually correct. Whether the tsarist regime would have survived the inevitable postwar political crisis and what form Russian politics would have taken had the regime fallen after the war is very hard to assess. So too is the nature and long-term stability of any postwar international settlement in which Russia might have participated as a victor.

As the more intelligent conservative ministers had always predicted, however, without the monarchy's legitimacy and the repressive force of its army and police, Russia's socio-economic elites could not survive the onslaught of revolutionary socialism. As already noted, had this process occurred in peacetime before 1914 there is every probability that concerted European military intervention would have ensued, spearheaded by the German army. With the Russian elites also not weakened by war it was very unlikely that a revolutionary socialist regime could have held power for long in the face of domestic and foreign counter-revolution.

In 1917–18 it appeared that the history of empire in Russia was over. All the traditional nightmares of tsarist statesmen were realized. Finland, the Trans-Caucasus, the Baltic provinces and the whole Western Borderlands, including Ukraine, were lost. German domination in Europe loomed. Russia was pushed back to her borders before Peter I made her a great power, in other words more or less to the borders she occupies today. American intervention and allied victory on the Western front ended the prospect of a German Europe and in the process created a great vacuum in Eastern Europe. The victorious Western powers were too far-removed, too exhausted by war and too indifferent to fill that gap themselves, though they did create a *cordon sanitaire* of pro-Western client states to keep Bolshevik Russia safely distant from the European economic and cultural heartland. Beyond that wall, however, the Bolsheviks were able to consolidate their power, move back into Ukraine, Belorussia and the Trans-Caucasus, and re-create an empire in Northern Eurasia.[48]

9

The Soviet Union

THE STATUS OF EMPIRE

Most of the great states discussed in this book were happy to be called empires. The Soviet Union is the exception. Its rulers understood empire and imperialism in Leninist terms,[1] in other words as the last refuge of a capitalist world on the eve of socialist revolution. The Union of Soviet Socialist Republics was the great enemy of this world, the leader of the socialist camp. To call the USSR an empire – to equate it, for example, with tsarist Russia, was seen as a mere propaganda ploy of the capitalist enemy in the Cold War.

Since the Leninist definition of imperialism was rooted in an analysis of modern capitalism, in its terms the Soviet Union cannot be described as an empire. In terms of this book's definition, however, it clearly was one. It was the largest country on earth and contained a huge range of peoples of very varying religion, ethnicity, culture and level of economic development. At its fullest extent between 1945 and 1991 it encompassed all the territories of the Russian Empire with the exception of Finland and most of Poland. It ruled directly over a few provinces that the tsars had never conquered, above all in western Ukraine, much of East Prussia (the Kaliningrad region) and Tuva. More important, it ruled indirectly over a swathe of client states in an outer empire in East-Central Europe. In the nineteenth century some Pan-Slav visionaries had dreamed of an empire of this scale but tsarist Russia had never achieved it, and few tsarist statesmen believed it ever would. In addition, for a time the Soviet Union was the undisputed leader of a great world movement able to call on the active support of Communist parties across the globe. Dostoyevsky in his wilder moods might have anticipated such a scenario but no tsarist statesman ever did.

Neither within the Soviet Union nor in its satellite states was Communist rule ever based on the formal consent of those it governed. The only genuine election in the Soviet era before Gorbachev came to power occurred in the winter of 1917–18 for the so-called Constituent Assembly. In that election the Bolsheviks got one-quarter of the vote. In other words, at that time the party had substantial but by no means majority support. Bolshevik rule was established by force in Central Russia which was then used as a base for the conquest of the tsarist empire's former periphery. In that periphery the Bolsheviks usually had many supporters but more enemies, the bulk of the still largely peasant (though in some cases also nomadic) population often having no very fixed opinion either way but a steady (and historically well-justified) dislike for all forms of government. Communist rule was established wherever Moscow had sufficient force to do so. Once Europe showed no further interest in the Trans-Caucasus, independent Georgia was swallowed by Soviet Russia in 1921 in flagrant violation of Moscow's treaty with Tbilisi. In Finland and the Baltic states, however, local anti-communists were backed by foreign powers and Moscow accepted defeat and recognized these republics. Had the invasion of Poland proved successful in 1920 a Soviet republic would undoubtedly have been set up there. Defeat forced Moscow to accept the limits of its power, at least until new opportunities came in the 1940s. In 1940, as a result of the Ribbentrop-Molotov pact, the Baltic republics, Bessarabia and western Ukraine became Soviet, the local plebiscites supporting these changes being wholly fraudulent. Many states initially rooted in conquest do over the generations acquire the consent of those they govern. This consent may be enthusiastic, resigned or inert. The same might have happened in the Soviet Union. Not until Gorbachev's March 1991 referendum, however, were Moscow's subjects given the chance to consent to membership of the Union. In the nine republics that voted 76.4 per cent of the electorate (of an 80 per cent turnout) confirmed their support for some form of union.[2] By then, however, it was too late and circumstances conspired to tear the USSR apart.

Above all and decisively, its power and its role in the international relations of the twentieth century made the Soviet Union worthy of being called an empire. It played the biggest role in defeating Nazi Germany's bid to dominate Europe. From 1945 to 1991 it was recognized as one of the world's two superpowers. The USSR not merely embodied a great idea, it also spearheaded the major twentieth-century challenge to the liberal capitalist world order, the values it enshrined, and the Anglo-American great power bloc that sustained it. Soviet socialism claimed to be a totally new civilization of universal significance and applicability. It claimed to be the harbinger of the end of history. Here was an empire of truly grandiose impact and ambitions. The aim of this chapter is to compare it to other empires discussed in this book and then to see to what extent the demise of the Soviet Union can be fitted into a broader pattern of the rise and fall of empires.

As with all empires, however, caution is required before generalizing about the Soviet Union. In comparison to most empires the Soviet Union had a short life and was governed through similar institutions and according to similar principles across its entire territory. Nevertheless, there were important differences in the politics of the Soviet Empire both from republic to republic and over time.

Of the fifteen Union republics that existed in 1985, Russia was inevitably in some respects the odd one out. Equal in population to and larger in size than all the other republics combined, Russia was a potential threat both to them and to the all-Union, imperial government.[3] For that reason Russia did not have its own separate Communist Party organization and leadership until the last months of the Soviet Union's existence. In that period the emergence of an autonomous Russian centre of power under Boris Yeltsin was to be crucial to the USSR's demise.

Though in institutional terms the Union republics were uniform, inevitably their very different cultures, economies and histories to some extent influenced how politics was conduced. So too did the personalities of the local leaders and how Moscow viewed the local parties. Politics in Central Asia, for instance, was affected by the traditional strength of clan and tribal loyalties, and by the regional economy's domination by cotton. In the Brezhnev era the Central Asian leaders achieved considerable de facto autonomy by creating tight and often corrupt local patronage networks, controlling the flow of information to Moscow and buying off key figures in the central administration and Brezhnev's own family.

Even within the single Baltic region, to take another example, the politics and political economy of Lithuania differed substantially from those of Latvia and Estonia. The Catholic Church acted as a much more effective focus for Lithuanian nationalism than was the case with the Protestant churches of the other two republics. Even in 1950 Lithuania, unlike Latvia and Estonia, had a large surplus rural population and this contributed to the fact that subsequent Soviet-era industrialization did not entail mass Russian immigration. In the three postwar decades Lithuanian politics was dominated by a single Communist Party boss,

Antanas Snieckus, who had very powerful patrons in Moscow. Snieckus came in time to see himself as the defender of Lithuania's cultural and economic interests against some central policies, however. In Latvia and Estonia Party leaders who attempted to play this role were purged, being replaced by Uncle Toms who, though ethnically native, had spent the interwar years not in independent Latvia or Estonia but in Russia.

Throughout the Soviet period Moscow was committed to preserving the Soviet Union's territorial integrity and the Communist Party's monopoly of power. In *Chto delat'?* (*What Is To Be Done?*),[4] published in 1902, Lenin had outlined the principles which were to legitimize the Party's rule until the collapse of the Soviet Union. Thanks to its grasp of Marx's theories the Party understood the secrets of historical development and the great role that the working class was called on to play in creating communism. The Party therefore had the duty to lead the working class, which itself was the vanguard of all the exploited and oppressed.[5] A further absolute principle of Soviet politics was the centralized and authoritarian control over the whole Communist Party by the top all-Union leadership in Moscow. As early as 1919, when the non-Russian republics were in theory sovereign and independent states, the Eighth Soviet Communist Party Congress established the principle that 'the Central Committees of the Ukrainian, Latvian, Lithuanian Communists ... are completely subordinate to the Central Committee of the all-Russian Communist Party ... [whose decisions] are unconditionally compulsory for all parts of the Party irrespective of their national composition'.[6] The purpose of the Party's rule was the achievement of first socialism (defined partly as the absence of private property) and then the final communist utopia, which represented the end of history.

Whereas the achievement of communism and the role of the Party were absolute fundamentals of Soviet politics, in principle the federal structure of the Soviet state and its institutions were less sacrosanct. These were really tactical devices designed in the first years of Bolshevik power to make the Communist Party's rule effective and acceptable in a multi-national society, and to show the whole world that the Soviet Union was a voluntary federation of equal peoples, not some new version of Russian empire. Nevertheless, the federal structure of the state survived right down to the Gorbachev era, during which time it was to play a crucial role in the collapse of the Soviet Union. According to the Soviet constitution, the USSR was a voluntary federation of Union republics, which retained the right to secede. Within some of these Union republics there were so-called Autonomous Republics and Autonomous Regions, though both in principle and in Soviet practice these had less power than the Union republics themselves. All these units were, however, linked to a specific people and defined as its territorial homeland. The executive, legislative and judicial institutions of the Union republics were the same throughout the Soviet Union, as was their subordination both to the imperial (all-Union) central state institutions in Moscow and, above all, to the hierarchy of Communist Party bodies which stretched from humble rural districts up to the Politburo.

Within this unchanging framework of institutions, ideology and political rules, however, there were very important shifts in Party policy over the decades, not least in Moscow's approach to the national question. In its early years policy was guided in large part by 'gestures of contrition'[7] for previous Russian imperial domination and arrogance. Russian nationalism, denounced as the ideology of tsarism and the White counter-revolution, was defined as the main enemy. The growth of non-Russian languages, cultures and sense of national identity was encouraged. A big effort was put into recruiting non-Russian cadres and, wherever possible, promoting them into top positions in their republics. In Ukraine, for example, by 1930 almost the entire Party and state leadership was Ukrainian, almost all Ukrainians (and many Russians and Jews) were being taught in Ukrainian-language schools and 88 per cent even of factory newspapers were published in Ukrainian.[8] This was a complete contrast to tsarist policy and by 1930 the Ukrainian population had a much stronger sense of national identity than in 1917.

The 1930s witnessed a great reversal. Stalin saw the growing confidence of the non-Russians as a threat to Moscow's power. In addition, top-speed economic development aimed at creating a socialist, modern, industrial and urban society became the overriding priority. A much less hostile view was taken of some aspects of Russian nationalism, which no doubt satisfied the enormous number of working-class and peasant Russians whom Stalin's educational and economic policies were promoting into leadership and managerial positions. Stressing Russian patriotism and linking it to loyalty to the Soviet order was important for Stalin's goal of creating a united, monolithic and isolated society capable of surviving in the increasingly dangerous international environment of the 1930s. The Russians, well over half the total population at that time, constituted the political, territorial and demographic core of the Soviet Union. For obvious reasons, during the Second World War Russian patriotic themes were strongly stressed though Soviet symbols and loyalties still usually took first place in the regime's propaganda and were emphasized more and more as victory over the Germans approached. Nevertheless, by Stalin's death in 1953 the official view of the Russians as leaders, core people and generous patron of the other Soviet peoples of the USSR was firmly established.

This remained true, though usually expressed in less crude terms, in the post-Stalin era. Under Khrushchev and Brezhnev non-Russians again came to dominate office-holding in their own republics. Except for a brief period under Khrushchev, the economy, however, continued to be run in a very centralized, basically Stalinist manner – though without the mass terror which had been one of its essential components in Stalin's time. Moreover, the 1958–9 educational reforms meant that not only higher educational institutions but even high schools in many non-Russian republics operated in Russian. By 1975 only 30 per cent of all books and 19 per cent of textbooks for higher education published in Ukraine were written in Ukrainian.[9] In the post-Stalin decades Ukraine in particular came to occupy a special position and role as the Soviet Union's second republic. Partly because Khrushchev and Brezhnev had served in Ukraine for many years and had numerous clients there, Ukrainians did well in the central Party and government, as well as in the armed forces. But Ukrainian nationalist dissidents were repressed in the 1970s with particular ferocity and the Ukrainian Communist Party leadership was purged in 1970 for trying to defend Ukrainian culture and identity with what Moscow saw as excessive enthusiasm. Russo-Ukrainian solidarity and loyalty to the common Soviet motherland was after all a foundation-stone of the USSR's existence, particularly at a time when birth-rates in the Muslim republics were four times higher than in Russia and the 'yellowing' of the Soviet Union was beginning greatly to worry the Soviet elite.

THE TSARIST LEGACY

The most obvious comparison between the Soviet Union and other great empires is with the empire of the tsars, to which in territorial terms the USSR was the successor. Bolshevik leaders initially saw their seizure of power in Russia as the first step in an imminent world socialist revolution. Lenin understood that the relative backwardness of Russia meant that the forces sustaining capitalism there were weaker than in the other great powers. In his words, Russia was the weakest link in the capitalist chain and therefore the easiest place to start the international socialist revolution. He expected the Russian example, combined with the devastation of the First World War, to bring revolution within the leading capitalist states in the immediate future. The German and Austrian revolutions in November 1918 seemed to confirm this prediction.

Neither Lenin nor most of his colleagues believed that socialism could survive in an isolated Russia standing alone in a world of capitalist powers. The latter would surely have the wit to strangle the infant threat while it was still too weak to resist. Most of the early Bolshevik leaders were not ethnic Russians and were in any case 'internationalist' by ideology. Germany was the geopolitical centre of Europe, the key to the continent's domination. It also had by far the strongest socialist party in Europe. At least in principle, most leading Bolsheviks would have accepted that when revolution came in Germany the latter would become the leading centre of world socialism. It would help backward Russia with the transition to socialism.

In reality, had socialist revolution occurred in Germany there is every probability that the final result would have been great disillusion in Russia. Socialist or not, governments in Germany and Russia would have divergent interests, some of them sharply conflicting. In time the two socialist regimes would have absorbed the different political and cultural traditions of the peoples they ruled: there were after all already very deep differences between Russian and German Social Democracy before 1914. Moreover, Marxist intellectuals, let alone revolutionary Marxists, were never known for their love of compromise or their willingness to smooth over ideological disagreements by pragmatic, self-effacing and emollient behaviour. On the contrary, they were generally strong personalities holding passionate convictions. Previous world religions rooted – as was Marxism – in the tradition of Judaic monotheism had generally split over bitterly contested points of doctrine. These splits usually became territorial, as different doctrines were taken up by rival political factions with distinct regional power bases. In time the rival doctrines and political regimes took on aspects of the local political and cultural tradition. This fate was to befall international communism after the Second World War when communist regimes were established in Beijing and Belgrade, beyond the range of Soviet military power. There is every reason to believe that a similar process would have occurred decades earlier had separate centres of power emerged after 1918 in Moscow and Berlin.

In fact the German revolution was defeated and socialist Russia stood alone. By 1924 it was clear that there would be no European socialist revolution in the near future. The logical response to this was Stalin's doctrine of 'socialism in one country'. In principle this was in no sense an abandonment of the goal of world revolution. It was merely a realistic acknowledgement that this was not an immediate possibility. The immediate task had to be to defend Soviet Russia as the base for future world revolution, and to develop its enormous potential human and material resources. Inevitably, however, to see the overriding immediate goal as the protection and development of a Soviet Russian territorial state existing in a dangerous international environment was to take on many of the traditional foreign policy and geopolitical perspectives of tsarism. Thus in 1921, justifying an aggressive and annexationist policy in the region, Stalin argued that 'the Caucasus is important for the revolution because it is a source of raw materials and food products. And due to its geographical position between Europe and Asia, between Europe and Turkey, its economic and strategic routes are particularly significant'.[10]

Subsequently, as supreme leader, Stalin was very strongly guided in his foreign policy by traditional tsarist perspectives on territorial expansion, geopolitics and power. His leading lieutenant and foreign minister, Molotov, commented later that 'like no one else, Stalin understood the great historical destiny and fateful mission of the Russian people – the destiny about which Dostoyevsky wrote: the heart of Russia, more than that of any other nation, is predestined to be the universal, all-embracing humanitarian union of nations. He believed that once the worldwide communist system had triumphed – and he did everything possible to bring this about – the world's main language, the language of international communication, would be the language of Pushkin and Lenin.' Molotov added that 'my task as minister of foreign affairs was to expand the borders of our fatherland.'[11] This was to assert a traditional imperial view – linking territory, expansion and power – with a crudity which might even have made Nicholas II's ministers shiver.

Inevitably, a regime that defined its mission in these terms came to have great attraction for many Russian nationalists. By 1920–1 it was clear that the Bolsheviks were intent on reuniting as much of the former tsarist empire as they could. This was noted with approval even in some circles of the White emigration. Meanwhile Russia's emergence as the leader of a great world movement also excited some nationalists. Europe's stepchild, widely despised abroad in 1914 as the most backward and barbarous of the great powers, had become the leader and embodiment of progress. In 1921 a delegate to the Tenth Communist Party Congress commented that 'the transformation of Russia from a colony of Europe into the center of a world movement has filled with pride and with a special kind of Russian patriotism the hearts of all those who are connected with the revolution'.[12] Stalin's doctrine of socialism in one country was an optimistic assertion that socialist modernization could be successful in an isolated Russia, that this modernization would take a very different path from that of the capitalist West, and that it would make Russia a much richer and more powerful country. To be modern, power-ful and respected without simply becoming a clone of the West has been for generations the dream of nationalists not just in Russia but every-where outside Western Europe and the United States.

The Revolution could not abolish geography, however. Russia still stood between Germany and Japan. In 1909 the tsarist minister of war, Vladimir Sukhomlinov, had told his French allies that any major threat in the east would hugely reduce Russia's ability to check German expan-sion in Europe.[13] By the 1930s Japan was a much more formidable threat than she had been before 1914.[14] Her economic power was greater. In addition, she ruled all Manchuria by the 1930s and dominated northern China. Before 1914 Japan was very much the junior ally of Great Britain, on whose financial strength she was to some extent dependent. A Russia allied to Britain had little reason to fear Japanese aggression. In the 1930s Soviet Russia was not Britain's ally. Moreover Japan was no longer in any sense dependent on Britain, whose relative international power had declined. The economic depression of the 1930s had radicalized Japanese politics and increased Japan's appetite for territorial expansion in Asia. The sparsely populated Russian Far East had briefly come under Japanese military occupation after the Revolution. In the 1930s it was under threat from Japanese armies deployed nearby on the other side of the long Korean and Manchurian border. This threat became most acute in 1938–9 just as the crisis in Europe also came to a peak. Countless border 'incidents' and two major battles occurred between Soviet and Japanese troops. Hitler hoped that Japanese forces would strike north into Siberia as German armies swept eastwards towards Moscow. Had this happened, the threat to the Soviet Union's existence would have been very great. In fact, desperate above all for oil, the Japanese opted to strike southwards against the European colonies in South-East Asia, in the process bring-ing the United States into the war and greatly reducing the likelihood of German victory.

Significant as the Japanese threat was to the Soviet Union, the German one was always much greater. There were more Germans than Japanese, the German economy was more developed, and Germany could find many potential allies against the USSR among the small states of East-Central Europe. In addition, the centres of Soviet power – the Moscow and Leningrad regions and Ukraine – were much closer and more vulnerable to German armies than to the Japanese. In fact even the new Urals-West Siberian industrial region developed in the 1930s was mar-ginally closer to Berlin than to Tokyo.

German power, a terrible threat to Russia before 1914, was an even worse danger in the 1930s. The Versailles Treaty had created a power vacuum of small states in East-Central Europe, incapable of defending themselves and in general very anti-communist. The British and French proved unwilling and unable to stop Hitler from moving into this vacuum in the 1930s. Before 1914 it was unclear whether Germany's expansionist ambitions were predominantly land-based and a threat to Russia, or rooted in commercial and maritime rivalry with Britain. In the 1930s Hitler's writings and Nazi ideology left no room for doubt on this score. The German leader would always have been happy to strike a deal with London and admired the British Empire, which he saw as a bulwark of Aryan domination of the globe. The 'Jewish-Bolshevik' regime was Hitler's great enemy, *Lebensraum* in the east the basis for his vision of Germany's unassailable future power. The Soviet leadership had always deeply feared a coalition of capitalist powers bent on the destruction of the homeland of socialism. Given Moscow's commitment to international revolution and its perception of international relations as a zero-sum-game between capitalism and socialism, this fear of capitalist encroachment was wholly reasonable. In the context it made sense to see the Munich Agreement as Anglo-French consent to German expansion eastwards.

In principle Stalin, faced with the German threat, had the same options as Nicholas II. He could seek to deter and if necessary defeat this threat in alliance with the French and British. Alternatively, he could seek to deflect German expansion westwards, hoping that the Germans, French and British would check, weaken and exhaust each other. Meanwhile Russia could increase her relative power by devoting herself to the development of her immense resources. In 1939, after failing to come to terms with the West European allies, Stalin opted for deflection: in other words he made the opposite choice to that of Nicholas II.

It could well be argued that Russia's rulers made the wrong choice both before 1914 and in 1939. Tsarist policy did not deter Germany and in 1917 Russia disintegrated under the strains of war. Out of the First World War came the Russian Civil War, the famines and the Stalinist dictatorship. Millions died. Out of the First World War there also emerged an extremely unstable international order in Europe, Hitler, and the terrible security dilemma facing Moscow in the late 1930s. In 1939 the British, the French and most German generals believed there would be a stalemate on the Western front. Stalin gambled on such a stalemate and lost. The Germans defeated France within six weeks and were then in a position to mobilize the entire continent's resources for war with

Russia. This was a repetition of the Napoleonic threat of 1811–12. It was the nightmare that tsarist statesmen had sought to avoid in 1914. Like Alexander I in 1812 Stalin stood against all continental Europe in 1941 and ultimately won but at a horrendous cost to the Soviet peoples. Looking back at the foreign policy of tsarist and Soviet leaders between 1906 and 1941 it is certainly possible to argue that grievous mistakes were made. Above all, however, what is striking are the hugely difficult dilemmas of Russian security in this period and the tragically high stakes for which Russian leaders were playing.

Victory over Germany and Japan transformed international relations. For Russian foreign policy a basic continuity exists from the 1890s to 1945. The overriding issue was the challenge of Germany and, to a lesser extent, Japan. Victory in 1945 eliminated the German and Japanese military threat to Russia for the remainder of the Soviet period. Though in the perception of Soviet leaders the United States more than filled that gap, in reality Soviet security was never again under the same level of military threat as it had been in the 1930s or before 1914. The American leadership was less aggressive and more rational than William II, let alone Hitler. The existence of nuclear weapons made war far more risky and far less likely to result in anything that could sensibly be called victory.

Nevertheless, in a more fundamental sense the basic Russian dilemma of imperial security continued unabated after 1945. Russia was still locked into competition with Western rivals richer and – at least in economic terms – more powerful than herself. Partly because nuclear weapons made the uninhibited use of military strength too dangerous, economics came to the forefront of global rivalry and power politics. In 1981, for example, Brezhnev commented that, 'as we know, the decisive sector of the competition with capitalism is the economy and economic policy'.[15] Moreover, the Soviet regime did not just inherit the tsarist intelligentsia's chip on the shoulder about the West, it also turned it into dogma. Soviet communism was defined against Western capitalism. Soviet ideology promised that communism would triumph over capitalism and linked the regime's legitimacy explicitly to this promise. In the immediate post-revolutionary years Lenin and his comrades expected this triumph in the very near future. At worst, even in the 1920s, it was seen as a matter of one generation. Under Stalin huge sacrifices were justified by the call not just to create socialism but also to overcome traditional Russian backwardness and overtake the Western enemy.[16] In his 1961 Communist Party Programme[17] Khrushchev promised explicitly that within the lifetime of adult Soviet citizens the Soviet Union would have overtaken the West and achieved 'Communism', in other words a society based on material wealth and abundance. Even if the balance between military, economic and ideological factors of power had changed somewhat since tsarist days, the security and survival of the Soviet Empire still revolved crucially around competition with the West.

Modern Russian history's main underlying dynamic from the seventeenth century to the Gorbachev era can be seen as three great cycles of modernization, each of them initiated from above by the state and each of them designed to allow Russia to compete with the great powers of the West.

The first great cycle might loosely be called 'catching up with Louis XIV', though it began with an attempt to match the military power and administrative efficiency of Sweden rather than of the much more distant Bourbons, who even in 1700 were still beyond Russia's horizon. Being a great European power in the era of absolutism was tsarism's overriding goal in this cycle of modernization, the triumph over Napoleon the final evidence of success. One result of the victories of 1812–14 was the conservative regime of Nicholas I: victory legitimizes a society's institutions and traditions. It gives social elites and political leaders little incentive to sacrifice their interests and inherited values in the cause of reform. A Russian noble elite and a tsarist regime whose international security and prestige seemed safe had no incentive to engage in destabilizing, radical changes. Meanwhile, however, the underlying realities of international power were changing in Russia's disfavour because of the uneven spread of the Industrial Revolution from west to east in Europe. Defeat in the Crimean War brought this reality home to Russia's rulers, created a willingness for reform within the upper classes, and allowed a younger generation of reformist bureaucrats frustrated by Nicholas I to take power.[18] This resulted in the launching under Alexander II of the second great cycle of modernization from above, Russia's effort to catch up with the West in the era of the Industrial Revolution.

This era began in the 1850s and ended in the 1970s. Stalin's victory over Germany in 1945 symbolized success in this cycle as surely as Alexander I's victory over Napoleon had done in the first. Brezhnev's conservative and increasingly gerontocratic regime had many similarities with that of Nicholas I, some of which had their roots in a parallel sense of secure international status and power. Regiments paraded, medals multiplied on the rulers' chests and the memories of wartime triumphs were invoked by an aging leadership – much as had been the case under Nicholas. In the last two decades Western historians have gone some way towards rehabilitating Nicholas I's regime, stressing the great constraints under which it operated and the often intelligent way in which it created the foundations for Russia's later modernization. It will be interesting to see whether future historians are able partially to rehabilitate the Brezhnev-era leadership, showing for instance that some of its members had a more realistic sense of Soviet vulnerability than their successors. Just as under Nicholas I, a younger generation of the ruling bureaucracy under Brezhnev watched its gerontocratic bosses in frustration, partly because they understood better than the gerontocracy that changes in the international economy were shifting the balance of power against Russia. Their chance came under Gorbachev in the third great cycle of modernization, whose initial underlying motive was to ensure that the Soviet Union remained a truly great modern power in the era of the microchip and the computer.

Parallels between tsarist and Soviet dilemmas of empire are not hard to find. The most frequently remarked are the similarities between Peter I and Stalin, both of whom used despotic methods to mobilize people and resources in the cause of economic modernization and military power. Though partly true the comparison does, however, ignore the fact that Peter's reign greatly increased Russia's openness to Western ideas and immigrants whereas the logic of Stalin's policy was the creation of an autarchic, monolithic and xenophobic society as far as possible closed to all outside influences. By no means coincidentally, key targets of Stalin's postwar terror were the old intelligentsia with its pre-Soviet culture and memory, supposedly cosmopolitan Jews, the elites of the newly annexed Baltic and Galician regions, and even wretched former prisoners of war, who had enjoyed a glimpse of Hitler's paradise.

In some ways a better parallel is between the eras of Alexander II and Mikhail Gorbachev, who launched the second and third great cycles of modernization respectively. Similarities are to a considerable extent rooted in parallels in the global ideological and economic context in which the Russian leaders operated. In the 1850s and 1860s liberalism was the dominant European creed in both economics and politics.[19] In the 1980s neo-liberalism once again ruled the roost under Ronald Reagan and Margaret Thatcher. In both eras liberal principles were associated with prosperity, progress and power.

Not coincidentally, Alexander II and Gorbachev were – by Russian standards – liberal modernizers. Among the key elements of their reforms were greater respect for the rule of law, much greater freedom of expression, and the liberation of the people's economic potential from the shackles of serfdom and the command economy. Alexander and

Gorbachev quickly encountered some of the dilemmas of the liberal modernizer in the Russian and Soviet imperial context. It was much easier to license critical voices to undermine the intellectual defences of conservative vested interests than to silence these radical voices when, from the regime's point of view, they went too far. Within a decade of the demise of Nicholas I small but influential sections of the intelligentsia were calling for the overthrow not just of the monarchy but also of private property and marriage. Very soon after launching his reforms, Gorbachev was confronted with demands for the end of communism and the dissolution of the Soviet Union. Both Alexander and Gorbachev accepted the need for partial introduction of capitalist principles but neither leader had much interest in or sympathy for liberal economic values and both deeply feared their impact on political stability: as a result both leaders put heavy constraints on the development of a free market in land and labour. Political stability both before the 1860s and in the 1980s had depended in part on the ability of an authoritarian regime to create a climate of fear, inertia and public disinterest in politics. Reform from above undermined this and threatened the regime's survival, above all in the non-Russian western borderland, where the state's rule was less legitimate than in its Muscovite heartland. Alexander's reforms quickly led to revolution in Poland. The Soviet regime dominated a much larger informal empire than the tsarist one in East-Central Europe. In addition, by the 1980s the non-Russian peoples of the Soviet Union were much more literate and urban than had been the case in the 1860s, and therefore often more susceptible to nationalism. The revolts that occurred in East-Central Europe and in the non-Russian republics of the Soviet Union played a crucial role in the USSR's destruction.

If one stands well back from the details and side-roads of Russian and Soviet history one can actually see important continuities in the relationship between the state and the social elites. The American historian Edward Keenan[20] is for instance quite right to draw parallels between the sixteenth-century Muscovite polity and Stalin's USSR. The two regimes sought to maintain xenophobic, closed and monolithic societies, rooted in ideological certainties, and both employed extraordinary levels of arbitrary and destructive terror against the social elites. Slowly under tsarism and much more rapidly in the Soviet era, the elites had their revenge. The tsarist nobility by the later nineteenth century enjoyed absolute security for their property and considerable protection for their persons. The Soviet elite quickly ended Stalin's terror after his death and, under Brezhnev, enjoyed greater security of tenure as regards their jobs. Both elites came more and more to hanker too after Western rights and freedoms. To varying degrees modernization and competition with the West required opening Russia up to Western ideas. Russian and Soviet elites thereby acquired some Western values and mentalities. They also acquired the ability to make comparisons with the West, which generally taught them that Western elites enjoyed wealth, rights and freedoms denied to their Russian peers. Much of the political history of imperial Russia revolves around efforts to merge Western liberal principles with authoritrian tsarist traditions of government. The great difficulties this caused played a crucial role in the collapse of tsarist Russia. To anyone familiar with the problems of late tsarist history it was not at all surprising that Gorbachev's attempts to introduce more or less overnight to Soviet politics wholly alien Western principles of law and democracy led to the collapse of the Soviet system of government and the disintegration of the Soviet Union. To an extent Gorbachev and the Soviet elite were victims of their own ignorance of Russian history. The Soviet regime had proclaimed itself to be the harbinger of a new world era in world history. It had denied its continuity with the tsarist past and propagated an extremely distorted version of Russian history. Had it better understood the recurring dilemmas of imperial rule in Russia, the 1980s elite should have predicted many of the dangers it was to encounter in the era of perestroika.

Nevertheless, it would be entirely wrong to deny that enormous differences existed between the tsarist and Soviet regimes and the empires they governed. A brief look at the institutions of the Soviet regime makes this clear. The core of the Soviet polity was the Communist Party. The permanent officials in the Party's various secretariats and departments were the nation's ruling elite. At the top they devised policy. At lower levels they attempted to ensure its implementation and in theory coordinated the work of all the other bureaucratic organizations through which the Soviet Union was governed. Tsarist government had no similar super-bureaucracy. Still less did it have any equivalent to the Party's other main function, which was to act as a mass organization of millions of members designed to spread communism's inspiration among the masses and act as a recruiting agent for future elites. Tsarist bureaucracy and its penetration of society was small-scale by communist standards.

This was partly because the tsarist economy was largely in private hands. In 1914 the state owned 8.3 per cent of the empire's wealth and 10 per cent of its industry.[21] The contrast between the tsarist economy, especially in its last decades, and Soviet state ownership of all factories, farms and shops is immense. To be sure, there was a tradition of state encouragement of economic modernization, best embodied in tsarism's last decades by Sergey Witte. But the tsarist regime could only encourage Russia's economic development within the context of private ownership of Russia's assets and of a global capitalist economy on which Russia's commercial and financial prosperity depended. There was a world of difference between this and running the centrally planned and state-owned Soviet economy.

Neither did tsarist Russia have any parallels to the third institutional pillar of the Soviet regime, namely the federal system. Like almost all traditional empires it ruled to some extent through local aristocracies and in some non-Russian areas it allowed local institutions of government to survive for a time. But the Soviet regime actually created new native elites and institutions, organized them into a uniform federal system, and in theory built the entire Soviet system of government on federal principles, even guaranteeing republics the constitutional right to secede. Much of Soviet federalism was a sham for most of the Soviet era but it was never a complete sham and at times, especially in the 1920s and under Gorbachev, it was a vastly important political reality. Soviet federal institutions and principles not merely owed nothing to the tsarist past but had in fact explicitly been created in order to show that the Soviet regime rejected the nationalist ideology and centralizing tendencies of its tsarist predecessors.

In general it is important to remember how much effort the Soviet regime put into obliterating the Russian past and destroying the traditional sources of Russian identity. The first people to be deported en masse by the Soviet regime were the Don and Kuban Cossacks, in other words ethnic Russians, who on the whole had supported the White cause during the Civil War. In later decades the regime was to deport a number of other peoples, in this case non-Russians, with equal or even greater brutality. In many cases, of which the Chechens and the Crimean Tatars are the best examples, deportation and its horrors actually strengthened a sense of national identity and solidarity. By contrast a separate Cossack identity was effectively destroyed, partly because Russian-speaking Cossacks deported from their villages and mixed with other Slavic elements in the Stalinist city or camp had fewer cultural defences against Sovietization than Muslim Chechens or Tatars. It is true that during the Second World War and afterwards the Soviet regime manufactured ersatz Cossack traditions, dance troupes and even military units. These had a roughly similar link to authentic Cossackdom as the tartan-wearing German consort of Queen Victoria had to the clans who charged at

Culloden. The failure of any genuine Cossack units and traditions to re-emerge in the wake of the Soviet Union's collapse underlined the extent to which any authentic Cossack identity had been broken.[22]

Still more thorough was the obliteration of the core element in traditional Russian political loyalty and identity, namely the monarchy and the Romanov dynasty. No monarch or member of the dynasty since the mid-eighteenth century was allowed a favourable portrait in print or on screen in Soviet times. All the male Romanovs on whom the Soviet regime could lay its hands in 1917–19 were killed, as were a number of the females. As regards Nicholas II, his wife and children, the regime went to great lengths to destroy every remnant of their corpses and to hide whatever remained. In the 1970s it blew up the house in which the family had been killed. By the 1980s the Romanov family was about as real to ordinary Russians as the Sheriff of Nottingham, Robin Hood's villainous enemy, was to the ordinary Englishman.

Unlike the Romanovs the Orthodox Church could not be wholly obliterated though thousands of clergy were killed in the first years of the new regime, and even more in the 1930s. A third assault on clergy and churches occurred under Khrushchev, who retained a degree of communist fervour and therefore saw the church as an ideological enemy to be uprooted. Under the much less ideologically motivated Brezhnev, church closures more or less ceased but it remained true that overt belief was extremely ill-advised for anyone with aspirations to get on in the Soviet world and that any organized effort to educate children in religion outside the home was strictly punished. During and after the Second World War the church was allowed an open organized existence but a strictly circumscribed one in which loyalty to the Soviet regime had to be loudly proclaimed and its political goals served. Interestingly, and here there were parallels with tsarism, the Orthodox Church was used as an agent of Sovietization in the western regions of Ukraine annexed in 1945.

The tsarist ideological trinity of 'Orthodoxy, Autocracy, Nationality' could be expressed in less abstract terms as the union of church, monarch and loyal peasant people. In principle one might have expected a socialist regime to treat the peasantry more kindly than the priesthood or the Romanovs. After all, for most Russian radicals the *narod* – in other words the peasantry and its communal institutions – had been the essence of Russianness in cultural terms, and the key object of political loyalty and devotion. Neither Marx nor mainstream European Marxism had much time for the peasants, however, whom Engels in a memorable phrase once called the highest form of animal in the farmyard. In the 1920s during the New Economic Policy era the regime did nevertheless come to a *modus vivendi* with the peasantry. This was destroyed by Stalinist collectivization, which shattered the foundations of Russian rural society for good. The peasantry's religion-based culture was uprooted, most of its more enterprising elements deported and its incentive to work destroyed, along with the cottage industries that had flourished in tsarist days and had sustained rural skills and traditions. On top of this came the vast suffering of the Second World War, borne very disproportionately by the peasantry, and the incentives of any modernizing society, greatly increased by Soviet collective farm conditions, for young people with ambition and initiative to leave the countryside. Rural Russia of the 1980s was the supreme example of the Soviet regime's success in obliterating everything worthwhile in traditional culture and putting nothing credible in its place. In most modern societies the countryside and the farmer embody myths and images that are an important element in national identity. But for the Soviet regime peasants were backward and therefore alien to a Soviet identity which was above all else modern and rooted in the conquest of nature.

From the 1930s the Soviet regime did take over much of the military-patriotic tradition of tsarist Russia. Above all this was because of the growing external threat to the USSR. Not surprisingly, the invocation of traditional Russian military patriotism and pride reached its height in 1941 with Hitler at the gates of Moscow, and even in the postwar era the link to this aspect of the tsarist past was never dropped, though in the Soviet Russian pantheon it took a very second place to the glorification of Soviet military patriotism in the Second World War. Nevertheless distant rulers such as Alexander Nevsky and Peter I were forgiven their royal blood, later military commanders their noble origins. In fighting Russia's enemies they had served the interests of the Russian people and also, so it was usually stressed from Stalin's time, of the other Soviet peoples as well. The latter, like Russian workers and peasants, had suffered under tsarist oppression but they had been spared the worse fate of Ottoman or German rule. Their life had become linked to that of the world's most progressive people, subsequently the founders of the world's first socialist society.

The other great pre-revolutionary legacy that contributed to Russian identity in the Soviet era was cultural. Before 1917 educated Russians had taken great pride in their country's literary and musical heritage. By identifying with it they felt and were Russian. By definition the barely literate peasantry could not share this identity. Mass education and literacy, achieved in the 1930s, changed this situation. After wavering with 'progressive', 'proletarian' and modernist art and culture, the Stalinist cultural counter-revolution in the 1930s[23] restored classical literature and music to their pedestal. The classics became central in the system of mass Russian-language education and gave all Russians a common and very healthy source of identity and pride. As usual in the Soviet era, Soviet and Russian identities were not sharply demarcated. All Soviet citizens were encouraged to take pride in Pushkin, for the prestige of an imperial people's high culture helps to legitimize the polity and to consolidate its peoples' unity – which is not for one minute to deny that this high culture may be of immense richness and value to all those who imbibe it.

In the Soviet case the hold of Russian high culture was enhanced by the fact that anyone in the USSR with ambitions for a successful career required fluency in Russian. The latter was the language of the Party and central state organs, including the so-called all-Union ministries and committees (e.g. Gosplan – the State Planning Commission) which ran the key sectors of the economy. It was also the language of much of republican government, including all communications with the centre. Higher education in most republics was dominated by Russian. Especially in the Slav 'sister republics' of Ukraine and Belorussia education too was increasingly Russian after 1959. By 1974 even in Ukraine only 60 per cent of pupils were enrolled in Ukrainian-language schools:[24] the majority of urban Ukrainians were by then taught in Russian with parents often agreeing with the Soviet authorities that this best served their children's future careers.

In some major contemporary multi-ethnic countries – India and Indonesia for example – the language of government has very deliberately not been that of the majority people, in these cases Hindi or Javanese. The Soviet Union was quite different. Russian was unequivocally the language of state and of the all-Union elite. From the 1930s it was often portrayed not just as an imperial lingua franca but as the medium of progress, high culture and modernity. Russian was the language of the manager, of the skilled worker, of social mobility and of the future. This helped Russians to feel that they were the bearers of progress and civilization, as well as power, especially in the non-European and less developed regions of the Soviet Union. Other languages, though no doubt beautiful and comforting to their native speakers, were defined as ethnic – with connotations often of folklore and the village.[25] Though Baltic peoples and even Georgians might always scoff at the Russian language's civilizing pretensions, in most other republics they were widely accepted so long as the Soviet regime retained some of its legitimacy. In some republics, not just Slav Belorussia and Ukraine but also Kazakhstan, the very widespread use of Russian did contribute to a common sense of Soviet identity. The obvious link between a Soviet identity and the language of Pushkin no doubt also helped to legitimize the USSR in Russian eyes. Non-Russian nationalists, however, especially Ukrainians, inevitably associated the USSR with cultural Russification, with a threat to their own identities, and with a typical imperial contempt for the status of their own language and culture.

If the Russian language, high culture and military tradition were key elements in Soviet identity, so too were other features which had no links to the tsarist past. To some extent they were merely the everyday experience of Soviet life, a life that by the 1970s the majority of Russians lived in an urban block of flats rather than a peasant hut. Soviet meant modern and urban: it also meant a life lived under 'real socialism'. Work in a Soviet office or factory had a tempo, a pattern and habits of survival different from those of either a traditional peasant or a modern capitalist society. A childhood and adolescence passed in Soviet schools and in the Party youth organizations, the Pioneers and Komsomol, left their distinctive marks and memories, on Russian and non-Russian alike, which obviously set them apart from pre-revolutionary Russians. So did successive Soviet generations' experience of Stalin's terror and crash educational courses of the 1930s, of the sacrifices and patriotic uplift of the 1940s, or of Khrushchev's denunciation of Stalin and its impact. There certainly was such a thing as a Soviet identity, though it differed greatly between classes and generations, let alone between nationalities, as regards both its strength and, in part, content.

The term 'Soviet identity' is in fact a little ambiguous. On the one hand it can mean little more than the sharing of certain characteristics and attitudes bred by life in the Soviet Union. On the other it can mean a sense of positive identification with the Soviet Union and loyalty to the Soviet regime. Russian peasants in the 1920s and the rapidly growing Central Asian rural population of the 1980s were not very Soviet in either sense. The younger generation of the Moscow middle class by 1980, by contrast, might seem very recognizably Soviet to Western eyes without themselves feeling much loyalty to the Soviet regime, its values or institutions. On the other hand the generation that had witnessed the building of an urban, industrial society under Stalin might much more wholeheartedly identify with the Soviet regime, especially if they were beneficiaries of the great opportunities this period offered to ambitious young people of worker and peasant origins. In addition, this generation had also participated in the regime's most unequivocal triumph, victory in the Second World War. Inevitably, however, all generalizations about identity hide the many complexities of individual cases: there are many examples from the Soviet era of individuals whose sense of Soviet identity was very ambivalent and whose loyalty to Soviet values changed greatly over the decades.[26]

At the core of a strong sense of Soviet identity there had to be, however, a number of shared beliefs, assumptions and understandings. Every modern society has used its school system to inculcate these assumptions, partly through the story told in history lessons about the country's past. Certainly this was true of all Europe before 1939. In the Soviet case the story was told with an unusual number of conscious omissions and in a way that was very different from the history taught before 1917. The Soviet version was saccharine, populist and Russia-centred: the Russian people had committed no wrongs and were the victims of oppression. All history's sins were to be laid on the shoulders of tsars and nobles. Peasant colonists in alien lands brought with them only culture and progress. All that was best in Russian educated society had formed part of a radical and then socialist tradition, of which the Bolsheviks were the only legitimate heirs. Russian history was therefore uniquely progressive, even before the Russian masses and intelligentsia joined together to create the world's first socialist society, thereby becoming mankind's vanguard and model. This society was the most modern, just, equal and powerful in the world. It was a story of unique success whose benefits existed for all Soviet citizens to share and all foreigners to admire.

The trouble with this story was that from the late 1950s it was beginning to lose credibility, a process that began with Khrushchev's denunciation of Stalin in 1956. So young a society and identity as the Soviet one took risks when it denounced the man who had laid so many of its foundations and led the USSR for most of its existence. In addition, as the Soviet elite became better educated and more able to make comparisons with the outside world, the increasing failure of the USSR to match Western economic growth was bound to have an impact on its faith in its own regime and ideology.

As faith in the Soviet version of modernity waned, its receding left gaps which were sometimes filled by elements of the old Russian identity. Some of these elements, such as tsarist military traditions and respect for pre-revolutionary literary culture, had already been partly incorporated into the Soviet pantheon, though they could be developed in ways much less acceptable to the Soviet regime. So too could anti-semitism, a very unlovable tsarist tradition, which Stalin had begun to exploit in vicious style in the years immediately before his death and on which the Brezhnev regime played after 1967. Other ideologically more difficult elements (for the Soviet regime) in the tsarist heritage were belief in Orthodoxy and nostalgia for the culture and values of peasant Russia. This lay at the roots of the so-called 'village prose' trend in Russian literature, which was very influential in the last three decades of the USSR's existence. For a number of reasons the Soviet regime compromised with this school of writers. Brezhnev appears to have seen their glorification of the village as lending legitimacy to his own programme of pouring investment into Russian agriculture. In addition, though the values of village prose writers were rather far from Soviet modernizing triumphalism, they were at least nationalist and often anti-Western and anti-liberal. Nevertheless, the regime's attempts to co-opt this strain in Russian nationalism were never whole-hearted or entirely successful. Village prose writers received medals and public esteem but the regime did nothing to reverse collectivization or to restore the Orthodox Church to its traditional position as the moral guide to society.[27]

Sometimes Russian nationalists could evolve into outspoken opponents of the regime. In the tsarist era the early Slavophiles had seen the imperial state as alien to the Russian land's interests and values. A Soviet regime which legitimized itself by Marxist ideology and undermined the Russian church and peasantry could very easily be portrayed in these terms – much more easily indeed than the late tsarist order of Alexander III and Nicholas II which went out of its way to portray itself as Russian to the core. In the person of Alexander Solzhenitsyn were combined Slavophile, religious, environmentalist and cultural values which predated the Soviet era and which the Soviet regime had tried to uproot. The survival of Solzhenitsyn, victim of the Gulag, to bear witness to the regime's crimes and to sustain values it had tried to destroy was a sign that the Soviet regime had not succeeded in uprooting the old Russian identity entirely, partly because for all their scale and horror Stalin's purges had not destroyed the whole educated class of tsarist Russia and its traditions. Under Gorbachev, as the failure of the regime's project of socialist modernity and the crimes committed in its creation became public knowledge, many Russians abandoned their commitment to a Soviet identity. This was an important reason for the regime's collapse. With the regime the empire too fell.

THE BRITISH AND SOVIET EMPIRES COMPARED

In comparing the Soviet Union to the British Empire, or indeed to modern European maritime imperialism in general, it is important to make clear distinctions between empires' structures on the one hand and the basic values and principles they sustain on the other. There was a great and obvious difference between Soviet authoritarian socialism and British liberalism and capitalism. A world dominated by the Soviet Union would run on very different principles and uphold very different political and moral values from those informing one in which British power predominated. At its most interesting and important, the clash of empires is also a competition between different civilizations and ideals. That is one reason why the study of empires can seldom be value-free. Certainly no comparison between British and Soviet empire can be.

Yet in some ways British and Soviet imperial ideologies were not so dissimilar, at least if the comparison is on the basis of the nineteenth and twentieth centuries. Both were products of the eighteenth-century Enlightenment with its faith in progress and its belief that the world will get happier as people become richer and more rational. These were both modern empires devoted to the idea of 'improvement'. Macaulay shared with Lenin a pristine optimism about progress based exclusively on Western principles: neither had any sympathy for cultural relativism or for native traditions. Neither doubted that education, rationality and economic development could be achieved by all mankind regardless of race, and that their benefits would be unequivocal.

In time the optimism of Macaulay and the early Victorian Utilitarian imperialists was tempered by a number of factors. It was challenged by racialist doctrines arguing the ineradicable inferiority of the non-White, and by Romantics and cultural relativists, who argued for the preservation of as much as possible of native customs and drew strength from the development of anthropology in twentieth-century universities.[28] Of course, commitment to improvement was also always constrained by limited finances and by the pragmatic caution of colonial bureaucrats, who feared that too enthusiastic policies of modernization would antagonize native interests and lead to political instability. Soviet nationalities policy was also constrained by finance and by political caution. Under Brezhnev, the regime in fact pursued a conservative policy of *Quieta non movere*, for instance allowing corrupt Central Asian elites great leeway to run their own republics and retreating from suggestions to reduce the status of the Union republics in the new 1977 Soviet constitution. Because of the nature of Marxist-Leninist ideology and its role in the

Soviet political system, however, conservative or relativist conceptions could never be advanced in public. In any case the impact of world war and of declining power weakened British liberal optimism decades before Soviet man began to turn pessimist in the 1970s. In the post-1945 era it was the United States rather than Britain which best matched undiluted Soviet faith in progress and modernity.

Nevertheless, the Soviet and British empires can both be seen as part of a global process of modernization whose origins lie in the seventeenth-century Scientific Revolution, in the eighteenth-century Enlightenment and in the nineteenth-century Industrial Revolution. This process encompassed first Europe's elites and its cities, then European rural society, and finally ever greater sections of the world beyond the seas. In the Soviet case the collectivization of Russian and Ukrainian agriculture and the incorporation of Slavic and rural society into the dominant urban Soviet culture was as much a part of this process as the campaign to bring literacy to Central Asia or abolish the wearing of the veil. Parallels may be found in British imperial history. The destruction of Gaelic culture and society in the Scottish Highlands was part of the same process of modernization under the aegis of metropolican power as that which brought railways to India and began the transformation of the Third World. As was the case with Russian and Ukrainian peasant society, the destruction of Scottish Gaeldom, carried out with the enthusiastic support of the Scottish Lowlands, was actually more complete than modernization's impact on peripheral regions of the empire.

The Soviet regime was, however, much more thoroughgoing in its commitment to modernization than the British ever were in their non-White colonies. The Soviet government, for example, achieved universal literacy and middle-school education even in Central Asia, something far beyond British aspirations in India or Africa. Even by 1939 two-thirds of Kazakh women were literate.[29] By the 1950s rates of literacy in Soviet Central Asia were far higher than in the Muslim states of the Middle East. By the 1970s the percentage of 'Muslims' and Russians in Soviet institutions of higher education was equal. A Western expert who certainly could not be accused of pro-Soviet bias commented in the early 1980s that 'the Soviet educational record in Central Asia is as good as humanly possible given the objective circumstances and the low starting point'.[30] The assault on indigenous religious and cultural traditions was also much more intense than in the British empire. In 1924, for instance, the Russian Republic's criminal code was extended to Central Asia without any modifications to accommodate local custom. By 1927 all the Islamic courts had gone.[31] Also much greater was the level of economic investment. To find any parallel to Soviet industrial development outside Russia one would probably need to look not to Western imperialism but to Japanese policy in Manchuria and Korea.[32] Like the Soviet regime, the Japanese did to some extent conceive of their empire as an integrated whole. They industrialized Manchuria and Korea in an effort to increase Japan's economic power. To a certain extent too the Japanese were operating within a single racial and cultural region (at least until their conquest of South-East Asia in the Second World War) and the empire was therefore somewhat more homogeneous and integrated than the British one. Nevertheless, the gap between metropolis and colonized periphery was far more obvious in the Japanese Empire than in the Soviet Union. Non-Japanese were always openly and unequivocally second-class citizens in the Japanese Empire. The colonies were ruled by Japanese bureaucrats and generals. No non-Japanese held any post of significance in Tokyo. The contrast with the native domination of offices in the Soviet republics and with non-Russian membership of the Politburo is very striking.

This leads to the critical question of the relationship between Moscow and non-Russian elites in the Soviet Union. The basic principle, not always observed under Stalin or even afterwards, was that both Union and Autonomous republics were the homelands of a specific people, the so-called titular nation, which had a right to dominate office-holding in its republic and to protect its culture within the republic's territory. Especially after the Stalin era, it was usually easier to protect the native language and culture in a Union republic than in an Autonomous one. The Volga Tatars, for instance, had been the cultural leaders of Russia's Muslims in 1914. Because it was a principle that Union republics must be on the USSR's periphery the Tatars, surrounded by Russia, received only Autonomous status. This was one reason why by 1985 they had fallen behind some of the other Muslim peoples as regards access to higher education and publications in their own language. More books were published in Tatar in 1913 than in the year of Brezhnev's death.[33]

By the Brezhnev era natives held the great majority of key positions in republics, though loyal (and generally Russian) agents of Moscow headed military and often security agencies, and sometimes even held key posts in the appointments bureaux of the Communist Party. The first major ethnic conflicts encountered by Gorbachev were the 1986 riots in Alma-Ata when Moscow removed the native First Secretary of Kazakhstan and appointed a Russian in his place. By that time such a move was seen *inter alia* as a break with tradition and an insult to the native people.

The extent of the republican leaders' power differed over time and between regions. They were always bound by the discipline of the highly centralized and hierarchical Soviet Communist Party and could be removed by Moscow at any time for any reason. The centrally planned economy and budgets were also tightly controlled from Moscow, and no sources of truly autonomous republican finance existed. The core of the economy, including its military, high technology and energy sectors, was run by so-called all-Union ministries, organized on ultra-centralized principles, dominated often by Russian managers and often with a largely Russian workforce, and operating solely in the Russian language. In Ukraine, for example, these all-Union ministries owned 85 per cent of all industrial stock on the eve of the Soviet Union's collapse.[34] In every republic, Russia included, the all-Union status of these enterprises allowed them to devastate the local environment and public health, while local authorities stood by helplessly. On the other hand the republican leaders enjoyed high status, great powers of patronage, and a considerable input into certain policies, above all in the cultural sphere. As already noted, the republican First Secretary's power also depended in part on his personal relationship with the tiny circle of key power-holders in Moscow's Politburo. From the centre's perspective both the Soviet system's legitimacy and the effective and tactful exercise of power in the republics required one to work in large part through native elites. The latter had to be given some leeway above all in the cultural sphere. But they also had to be watched in order to ensure that central policies were implemented and no encouragement was given to local nationalism. In the early 1930s and again at the end of the decade Stalin massacred the republican elites – though it bears mention that he treated Russian cadres no more gently. In the post-Stalin era there was a constantly recurring tension between the centre and some republican leaderships which tried to defend native cultural or economic interests against central policies and priorities. Nevertheless, until Gorbachev's accession to power the federal system appeared to function tolerably from the centre's perspective.

In comparative imperial terms Soviet federalism was a species of indirect rule. Natives ruled their own territories under central supervision, and to some extent under the watchful eye of Moscow's non-native local agents. In the British Empire the White colonies enjoyed a level of self-government far beyond that of Soviet republics. Even before 1914 they were to a great extent independent states, with London retaining the major say only in foreign and defence policy. Efforts to create some form of all-imperial cabinet or parliament failed, above all because the colonies would not give up their independence.

In the non-White colonies indirect rule was far less sweeping and worked very differently. In the sense that the British used the term, it meant an alliance with native dynasties, aristocracies and tribal leaderships. These were allowed great though varying autonomy to run their domestic affairs, the British always controlling external and military matters, and having the power to intervene decisively on any issue that greatly concerned them. Although the occasional native prince might be a modernizer, the ruler of Mysore in the 1930s for example doing much to create an Indian aircraft industry, the basic tendency of British indirect rule was conservative. In India for instance the practice of indirect rule was much praised by British officials who believed that the Mutiny of 1857 had been caused by incautious modernizing British policies which had offended conservative Indian interests and values. In the 1930s the princes were still seen by the British as very useful allies in blocking the calls of Congress for democracy and Indian home rule.[35]

Together with the other Western empires, the British also, however, relied on the collaboration of new indigenous middle classes which the imperial power had itself educated along Western lines and which it needed to staff all but the key positions in the various government offices and in the economy. To a great degree colonial nationalism was at least initially rooted in the frustration of a European-educated class which was denied access to senior bureaucratic positions in its own country, let alone the democratic rights which the British, French and Dutch proclaimed as their own national heritage. The so-called 'law of colonial ingratitude' meant basically that it was those groups which the colonial power itself had created which would in time be the cause of its overthrow. Unlike the native aristocracy this new middle class was not usually tied to pre-colonial regional identities. It saw itself as belonging to the colony as a whole and dreamed of turning the colony into a nation and itself controlling the levers of power and patronage. By creating colonial frontiers, separate administrations and a new native middle class the Western empires laid the foundations of new nations, which might but more usually did not coincide with historic territorial or ethnic entities.

To what extent were there parallels here with Soviet federalism? As was the case with some of the colonies of the European maritime empires, some Soviet republics were in fact well-established nations in 1917. This was true of the Georgians and Armenians, though the Soviet Armenian Republic was not the traditional homeland of most people of Armenian descent. The Baltic peoples had established their claim to be nations by 1917. Ukrainian nationalists were still striving for this against strong Russian opposition.

Only in Central Asia therefore can one really say that the Soviet authorities created new nations in a way comparable to the practice of Europeans in Africa. Even in Central Asia, however, the new republics' borders were not simply lines where rival colonial powers bumped into each other, or where statesmen in Europe divided territories into spheres of interest. Soviet ethnographers worked hard to delineate borders, usually putting the greatest emphasis on language but taking into account other factors such as economic viability. Different peoples could, however, have very different key markers of identity. 'In the case of the steppe nomads . . . "national awareness" or "tribal self-identity" were considered so strong as to make any other criteria practically useless. Linguistic, cultural and religious differences among the Kazakhs, Kirgiz and Turkmen might be negligible, but their clan genealogies were so clearly drawn and so vigorously upheld that most ethnographers had no choice but to follow.'[36]

In the settled core of Central Asia, creating nations was more complicated since bilingualism was very common, local loyalties were strong, and identity was defined more by occupation than by language or ethnicity. The Soviet regime has frequently been accused of dividing up Central Asia in order to avoid the creation of a single, great pan-Turkic or pan-Islamic republic. No doubt Moscow did oppose the emergence of such an entity but it is certainly not true that pan-Turkic or pan-Islamic ideas had wide support among the region's masses at the time. Moreover, in trying to create ethnically defined nations in Central Asia the Bolsheviks were only applying the principle they upheld throughout the Soviet Union. A consistent application of the pan-Turk or pan-Islamic principle would also after all have pointed to the creation of a single East Slav or Orthodox republic out of Russia, Ukraine and Belorussia – which in the circumstances of the early 1920s, when part of Ukraine had been lost to Poland and Belorussian national consciousness was very weak, might not have been a hopeless undertaking. A recent British expert on Soviet efforts to create nations and borders comments that 'while it was a somewhat artificial process to construct national groups in Central Asia, the task was approached in a thoroughly scientific manner.'[37]

As in the maritime empires Soviet federalism did contribute to the development of new nations by defining borders, creating territorial institutions, and providing republics with many of the trappings of statehood. In the Central Asia of the 1980s for example, native elites and middle classes with a real sense of national identity existed to a far greater degree than sixty years before, though regional and clan loyalties still often remained very strong. Even in Ukraine, where ethnic identity and intelligentsia-led nationalism had deeper roots, the Soviet era as a whole helped to strengthen a sense of Ukrainian nationhood. Under Soviet rule all of present-day Ukraine came together for the first time as a single territory with its own institutions and symbols. Purges, Russian immigration, Soviet educational policy and the famine of 1932–3 took a heavy toll, but even so there was more of a Ukrainian sense of national identity in 1991 than there had been in 1914. On the other hand, in no Soviet republic was a non-Russian elite allowed to use its language and history in a free and unequivocal policy of nation-building. In all cases creating a national identity and patriotism was constrained by the demands of the higher Soviet identity and loyalty, as interpreted and monitored by the central Party and state authorities.

It is a moot point whether in time the 'law of colonial ingratitude' would have operated in the Soviet Union as well, leading to its destruction at the hands of native elites and non-Russian identities which the regime itself had partly created. In the Brezhnev era there were signs of this. By the 1970s nationalism was clearly growing even in the Central Asian intelligentsia, let alone in the European republics. By 1982 there was a sharp divide between the Russian or at least Slavic imperial elite in Moscow and republican elites more and more dominated by natives. Tensions between the two elites were evident, and resulted in a number of spectacular purges of republican leaderships in Gorbachev's early years. Native elites growing in self-confidence were certain to mount increasing challenges to central allocation of a shrinking budgetary cake. By the early 1980s the leading German expert on the Soviet nationalities rightly remarked that 'the political price for preserving the empire is rising'.[38] It was possible to foresee a future parallel with British India in its last decades, when the price of placating Indian elites and Indian nationalism was London's abandonment of the financial, economic and military arrangements that had made India valuable to Britain in the first place.[39] It was even easier to see powerful long-term reasons for the Russians to abandon direct responsibility for Central Asia's growing and alien population and its economic problems. In fact, however, the centre of the empire, in other words Moscow, imploded in 1991, imposing a premature independence even on Central Asian leaders who felt unprepared for it.

In general, however, it is important to remember the very significant differences between the Soviet and the more typically colonial relationship between the central imperial government and native elites.

In the first place, natives dominated positions in Soviet republics to an extent that was never true in any entire British colony. Even the handful of key Russians who were Moscow's eyes and ears in a republic often 'went native' under Brezhnev, joining the local elites in denying Moscow accurate information as to local events. Moscow's native allies were always members of a new middle class, never a co-opted aristocracy. Especially in the 1920s they were often eager allies of the Soviet regime in a process of socio-economic modernization and nation-building which had limited parallels in the British Empire at least until the last years of colonial rule. On the other hand, these elites were then subjected to devastating purges and executions which also had no parallels in peacetime in twentieth-century British, French or Dutch imperial history. Within republics Russians did enjoy some advantages: they could almost always speak their own language at work and educate their children in it. Urban natives might not have access even to middle education in their native language in their own republic and certainly would not do so if they lived outside it. Even in Central Asia, however, where Russians provided the great majority of the skilled workers, managers and engineers, the situation was not a typical colonial one. By the 1980s natives predominated in universities and had priority for government jobs.

In the first years of Communist rule in Central Asia the local governments (i.e. soviets) had great power and Moscow's control was weak. 'The Soviets were for the most part overwhelmingly Russian in composition and often exhibited a hostility to the local population which can only be described as straightforward racism.'[40] In tsarist days foreigners had frequently noted that Russian peasants and soldiers lacked a typically European sense of racial arrogance and superiority, largely because their level of wealth and education was generally little superior to the native peoples.[41] On the other hand, skilled workers and the lower middle class had a more typically colonial mentality. The subsequent Soviet stress on the Russians' role as 'elder brothers' among the Soviet peoples encouraged this attitude, though the Soviet educational system in time created a society in which the cultural gap between Russian and native was far narrower than in most European colonies. There is in any case a distinction between elder brothers and the more typically paternal metaphor employed in other European empires to describe the relationship between White rulers and the non-Whites they ruled.

There were obvious parallels between the Russian-dominated soviets in early Soviet Asia and White-dominated assemblies in many of the European overseas colonies. Very soon, however, Moscow imposed its rule on the local soviets, turning them into rubber-stamp bodies like their Russian equivalents while at the same time insisting on the recruitment of natives into positions of influence in Party and government bodies. Since subsequently no section of the Soviet population enjoyed democratic rights there was no chance of a colon-dominated local assembly or a powerful colon lobby in an imperial parliament from which native representatives were excluded. Nor, with the very partial exception of the Jews in the 1920s, was Soviet rule based on collaboration with indigenous minorities within republics. In the European colonies by contrast minorities such as the Chinese in Malaysia, Christians in Indonesia or Asian economic elites in Africa might be crucial allies of the imperial power. A key distinction was that the Soviet Union had no autonomous economic sphere so there was no chance for ethnic minorities to exercise economic power, as they so often did in European colonies. In the Soviet Union all power was political and within republics this was exercised overtly by titular nations.

The biggest difference between the Soviet Union and the British Empire was, however, that its rulers conceived of the USSR as a single country and sought to create a Soviet people united by common customs, loyalties and ideals. This was quite different from the dominant British conception of empire in which constitutional law and geography sharply divided the metropolitan nation from its dependent overseas colonies. In the Soviet case a clearly defined Russian nation did not exist, did not possess genuine self-governing national institutions, and certainly did not control the imperial state. The latter was run by an imperial Party elite, largely Russian in ethnicity but Soviet in loyalty. Probably few of them distinguished between Russian and Soviet even in their private thoughts, seeing the Soviet Union as embodying all that was best in Russian culture and history, and as deserving the loyalty of all Russian patriots.

In a sense their empire was closer to Rome than to Britain. Their ruling elite was more willing to assimilate non-Whites than Britain was at any time in its imperial history. The role of the Russian language and Russian high culture had Latin and Roman parallels; moreover, the Soviet imperial identity was above all a question of political loyalty, at least external ideological conformity and acceptance of the Party's behavioural norms. Natives could become Soviet (or Roman) in a way they could never become British, at least so long as the British Empire existed. Nevertheless, the parallels with Rome should not be pushed too far. In the last two centuries of the Roman Empire's existence most emperors and most of the Senatorial elite were not even of Italian let alone Roman origin.[42] It is very hard to imagine the overwhelmingly Russian-dominated imperial elite of the late Soviet era[43] developing in this direction. Moreover, the Roman Empire was sustained in part by the splendour and prestige of its Graeco-Roman high culture. Had socialist modernity fulfilled its promise, a Soviet empire might also have been sustained by a vibrant, rich, imperial high culture. To uphold an empire's prestige requires more than Pushkin, an excellent metro system and a few Stalinist skyscrapers dotting its capital's skyline. This is particularly true if, quite unlike Rome, the empire is locked in competition with a rival state and civilization which appear far more successful than its own. In fact, the Russo-Soviet intelligentsia of Moscow and Leningrad was in many ways deeply impressive in its culture, but by the 1980s most of its leaders had themselves lost faith in the Soviet system.

Exotic comparisons with the ancient world do in any case obscure the extent to which Soviet history fits into the framework of modern European imperialism, in other words into a process in which most of the world was ruled by Europeans in the name of modernizing principles defined in Europe. Colonization was a key element in making the new world European. In Russia most colonization of Asia and the steppe occurred in tsarist days but by no means all. In 1926 8.6 per cent of Russians lived outside the borders of the Russian republic, which had grown to 17.8 per cent by 1959. Most of these emigrants lived in cities, the great exception being the farmer-colonists who flooded into northern Kazakhstan under Khrushchev in the 1950s. Khrushchev's Virgin Lands scheme of the 1950s in which 1.5 million Slavs colonized northern Kazakhstan, turning the Kazakhs into a minority in their own republic, was the last gasp of Europe's territorial expansion at the expense of non-Christian Asia. To force this policy through over the protests even of the Kazakh Communist Party, Khrushchev had to purge the Kazakh elite and put in European leaders, one of whom was his client Leonid Brezhnev.

In the 1930s Stalin's policy of overnight collectivization, geared in part to a strategy of crash industrialization, killed one-third of the Kazakh population and perhaps 5 million Ukrainian peasants.[44] In the Soviet era the cotton monoculture economy imposed on Central Asia was vastly extended in comparison to tsarist times and its workforce was compelled to enter collective and state farms. The cotton crop grew from 2.2 million tons in 1940 to 9.1 million in 1980 under constant prodding from Moscow.[45] Raw cotton was still, however, transported in colonial style to textile factories in the Russian heartland. Partly because Soviet-style modernization was pushed more determinedly than in the European empires, its ecological consequences were more devastating. Among the most lasting monuments to Soviet empire outside Russia are Chernobyl and the disappearing Aral Sea. Finally, in demographic terms too the rise and fall of Russo-Soviet empire fits a broader pattern. In 1800 20 per cent of the world population was of European descent. By 2050 the figure will probably be nearer 5 per cent.[46] One hundred years ago a famous Russian scientist predicted that the Russian population would peak at 600 million.[47] In fact the Slav population grew relatively to the Muslim population of the Soviet Union until 1959 and then went into sharp decline, Soviet demographic patterns subsequently reflecting common distinctions between First and Third World. Even in the 1970s 'Muslim' births in the Soviet Union exceeded Russian ones. Since demography has always been one key to imperial power and consolidation, the sharp decline in Russian fertility and the rapid growth of the least Soviet element of the population were harbingers of troubles to come. Today the Third World's growing population knocks on Russia's southern border, as the Maghreb's numbers scare the Southern Europeans and Americans fear an influx across the Rio Grande.

OTTOMAN, HABSBURG AND SOVIET EMPIRES COMPARED

The comparison between the Soviet and British empires goes to the heart of political debate in the Cold War era and in the territories of the former Soviet Union. If indeed the USSR was merely one variant on the common theme of modern European imperialism, then its ideological claims in the Cold War were very hollow. The Soviet Union's disintegration was necessary and inevitable in an anti-imperialist era and fulfilled the requirements of the United Nations Charter, which promised self-determination to nations. The Soviet-British comparison therefore entails contentious and politically explosive questions.

By contrast, comparison between the Soviet and Ottoman empires is the sort of arcane study left to scholarly freaks. In one sense this comparison is indeed a little strange. The Soviet Union was a twentieth-century phenomenon, linked to conceptions of materialism, science and rationality. There are obvious problems in comparing such an empire with a pre-modern polity rooted in a fundamentally different religious conception of human existence. The Ottomans certainly had a sense of imperial civilizing mission. They too wanted to settle the nomad and bring rational high Islamic belief and culture to primitive and heretical peoples who had thus far failed to see the light.[48] But secularization and materialism, foundations of modern Western and Soviet culture, were anathema to the Ottomans and to all Muslim empires.

Nevertheless, from one angle there are important similarities between Soviet communism and Islamic empire. Both movements became rooted in Europe's borderlands and both were in a sense European heresies. Depending on one's viewpoint, Islam was either the heir to the Judaic and Christian monotheistic tradition or one of this tradition's many heresies. Exactly the same could be said of Soviet communism's relationship to the European liberal tradition whose roots lay in the radical Enlightenment. Marx saw communism as the final realization of freedom, rationality and material abundance, whose achievement had been the goal of the French *philosophes*, of Hegel and of the British political economists. Communism's enemies saw it as a perversion of truly liberal and enlightened ideals.

Islam and Soviet communism were the greatest external challenges that Latin Christian civilization has thus far faced. Both movements were universalist religions, open to all humans regardless of sex, class or ethnicity. They offered a new understanding and purpose to human existence. Their message was deeply inspiring to millions of people and it was designed in both cases to transform most aspects of human existence. The new doctrines legitimized rulers and systems of government but they also had big social and cultural implications. In the Soviet Union, for instance, communist ideology was the basis for a totally new way of running a modern economy. Both Islam and (in principle) Soviet communism had their own style of architecture and urban planning. The two ideologies left their distinct mark on the relations between men and women. Both movements' sense that they represented a new era in world history was reflected in the new names their adherents gave their children. Public behaviour and rituals under both Soviet communism and Islam were in many ways sharply different from what had existed before these movements' eruptions. The beliefs, institutions, values and behaviour linked to this religion and ideology offered the possibility of uniting, mobilizing and inspiring a great community of people in a wide territory in a manner that overlay and outweighed the significance of ethnic differences, without necessarily needing to uproot these ethnicities or deny their legitimate role in domestic and cultural life. These were in other words potentially splendid ideologies of empire.

One obvious difference between Islamic and Soviet empire was that the latter's existence was so fleeting – a matter indeed of a single lifetime. In part this just reflects the overall rate of change in the modern world, with rapid change in technology and mentalities undermining any but the most flexible of political systems. An additional reason may be that in one sense Soviet ideology was not nearly totalitarian enough. There were powerful human emotional and religious yearnings to which Marxism-Leninism had no response. Because Soviet ideology was materialist and this-worldly, for instance, it had limited answers to human yearnings for immortality, and was far too easily disproved by the evidence of one's own eyes. Despite Marx's predictions it was clear in 1910, let alone in 1980 (though less so in 1935), that European capitalism had not made a small group of people rich and the bulk of the population wretchedly poor and ripe for revolution. Nor did Leninist predictions about the inevitability of war between the capitalist powers and the resulting global triumph of socialism look very convincing by 1985, when Gorbachev came to power and initiated a necessary process of radical rethinking of the Leninist doctrines that had previously underpinned Soviet foreign policy. The message and comfort that Islam provided spoke more directly to the individual heart and was less easily falsified. Marxism, even Soviet Marxism-Leninism, was too dry and intellectual for its own good. High Islamic thought could match Marxism in these respects but Islam also had room for a more populist, emotional and sensual strain, best embodied in the Sufis and Dervishes. Though early Soviet propaganda in posters and films was sometimes brilliant, on the whole – not surprisingly, given their ideology – the Fascists were more effective in their appeal to the emotional, sensual and irrational elements in the individual and mass psyche.

Though it sounds banal to say that Islam is a religion and Marxism an ideology, the distinction is in fact an important one. What matters most to Islam is correct belief, a life lived in accordance with this belief, and humanity's relationship to God. Economics and politics are not unimportant to Islam but they are of secondary importance. Despite centuries of Islamic monarchy, for instance, there is nothing in Islamic belief that says that monarchy is the best form of rule for a Muslim people. Moreover, by the time the Ottomans established their empire in the fifteenth century, Islamic civilization had already existed for three-quarters of a millennium. Correct Islamic belief and the legitimate laws and customs of a Muslim society were already very deeply rooted. No Muslim ruler would dare to challenge these beliefs or to overstep the boundary that circumscribed the legitimate realm of political action. If he did so, he would not long survive. In response to the totalitarian strivings of Communist regimes, Western scholars stressed the concept of civil society, in other words of a large sphere of thought and activity protected by law from the state's intrusion. Though the Ottoman conception of the good society was never democratic or liberal, it has in many ways always encompassed the belief in society's autonomy vis-à-vis the state.[49] As we have seen, to a very great extent the Ottoman rulers believed that in an Islamic society matters of belief, family, justice, culture and education should be left to the religious leaders of the Muslim communities. It therefore made very good sense to allow non-Muslim communities – in other words the large Christian and Jewish minorities – a similar autonomy in these matters. A crucial element in sustaining the millet system was precisely that in Ottoman thought and practice huge areas of social life were not politicized.

In all these respects the Soviet regime could not have been more different. The Bolsheviks themselves created the first socialist society. They therefore had to define its contours – including the relationship between the political, social and cultural spheres. Marx was a materialist philosopher. It is above all in his view economic relationships that determine historical developments. Though in this sense Lenin was every inch a Marxist, the main emphasis and originality in his thinking was political. It revolved around how best to gain and sustain power, above all in specifically Russian conditions, and how to use that power to create a socialist and thereafter a communist society – the latter being the ultimate goal and stage of human development. Unlike the case in Islamic empire, economics and politics were the absolute core of Marxist-Leninist ideology. This ideology would find it hard to accept that any area of society or culture was autonomous, non-political or free from the state's intervention. The whole purpose of the Leninist state was after all to transform traditional society and culture in order to create a modern, socialist community. Beliefs, family life, justice, culture and education – which the Ottoman regime had happily resigned to the Christian and Jewish millets – were crucial to the Soviet project of socialist modernization. They must be determined by the Leninist state. That state might allow non-Russian republican leaderships in the Soviet Union to run their local variant of socialist modernization through the idiom of the local language and to preserve those elements of the local culture that were not in conflict with the regime's overall goals. This was the meaning of the slogan 'national in form, socialist in context', which defined and legitimized Soviet policy towards the non-Russian minorities. But the Soviet regime could never accept some modernized version of the Ottoman millet or the Ottoman conception of institutional multi-culturalism. The Bolsheviks had before their eyes the vision of a single, huge, integrated, industrialized, socialist society. If national autonomy or culture in any serious way cut across the achievement of this goal it would be sacrificed to the higher good. Since the republican political leaderships who controlled all aspects of social, cultural and educational policy were members of the extremely centralized and hierarchical all-Union Communist Party, Moscow would have no difficulty in imposing on them its discipline and priorities. When republican Communist elites sought to protest or mitigate Stalin's near-genocidal policy of collectivization, for example, they were savagely purged.

In one crucial respect, however, the Soviet and Ottoman empires were very similar, much more similar than either of them was to the modern European maritime empires. The British, French and Dutch nation states ruled their empires, and their governments were responsible in political terms to metropolitan national electorates whose interests and values they existed to serve. The Soviet and Ottoman empires worked very differently, above all as regards the imperial ruling elite's relationship with the people of the empire's core.

The Russian and Turkish peoples were not permitted for most of the imperial era to elect genuine representatives. Nor was the imperial ruling elite in any sense responsible to the empire's core people. Instead the elite pursued its own interests and those of the empire, as the elite itself defined them. Members of the imperial elite might or might not be drawn from the core people and empathize with its culture and interests. This varied over time. The early Bolshevik top elite, for instance, were very often Jewish or Polish in ethnic origin[50] and comopolitan in culture. In politics they were 'Marxist-internationalist' and very hostile to the traditional elements of Russian political identity and values. By the end of the Brezhnev era the elite was far more Russian in ethnic origin,[51] partly as a result of the enormous social mobility that marked the Stalinist era. But senior Party officials had decades of experience in the Party-state apparatus and lived a privileged existence quite literally fenced off from normal Russian society. They were more remote from their community than the political elite in a Western society partly because they had no need to seek election and partly because privileged lifestyles under socialism were never entirely legitimate and were therefore best hidden. In its heyday the Ottoman elite, very often non-Turkish in ethnic origin and of mixed Islamic, Arabic and Persian culture, were even more remote from the ordinary Turk. Ottoman court Turkish was incomprehensible to the Anatolian peasant and the imperial elite used the term 'Turk' as synonymous with 'boor' or 'yokel'.

In the last decades of both the Soviet and Ottoman empires it is true that very many Russians and Turks did see the empire as 'their own'. Increasingly the two empires recruited their cadres from the core people and both empires could be seen as defending Turkish and Russian interests from outside enemies, and as making Russians and Turks major players in global great-power politics. Nevertheless, the relationship of core people and empire was always equivocal. Ordinary Russians could have strong legitimate doubts whether their empire truly served their interests by propping up Communist regimes in East–Central Europe by subsidized Russian oil and gas, or by devoting immense sums to challenging the United States in the fields of arms, space exploration or aid to international communist revolution. Indeed, for many Russians the idea that they lived in an empire was unacceptable precisely because, true to Marxism–Leninism, they believed that empire benefited a metropolitan people whereas the Soviet 'empire' seemed only to impose sacrifices on Russia. Ordinary Turks had even more reason to feel that they were empire's victims not its beneficiaries. The burden of taxation and conscription fell much more disproportionately on impoverished Anatolians than it did on the Great Russians, and it was by no means clear what interest a Turkish peasant had in protecting Ottoman rule in the Christian Balkans or the Arab provinces.

In the Habsburg Empire too, the relationship between the Austrian Germans and the Habsburg state was very ambivalent, and never more so than in the empire's last decades. To a greater extent than the Turks in 1914 and a far greater extent than the Russians under Soviet rule, the Austrian Germans were a very diverse group of different communities, not a single people, let alone a politically conscious nation. Clearly the Habsburg state was in no sense responsible to this non-people. On the other hand German was the internal language of the officer corps and the central bureaucracy, and both of these groups were German both (usually) in ethnic origin and in culture. German elites on the whole found it easier to identify with this state than Hungarians, Czechs or most other peoples of the Monarchy. Many Austrian Germans saw the empire as a vehicle for giving them a major cultural and political role in the world. As with the Russian attitude to the Soviet Union, the Austrian-German relationship with the Habsburg Empire was ambivalent and varied over time and between classes and regions. The comparison is in fact a rich and fascinating one.

As regards the state's relations with non-German peoples, Austrian practice and, still more, the ideas of the Austro-Marxists cast an unfavourable light on the Soviet era. The Austro-Marxists had bitter experience of what happened when politics revolved around battles between peoples over culture, language, education and the control of territorial units. They understood that these conflicts gained full rein under democracy and could destroy any hopes for its development, let alone for an advance to socialism. This was the logic behind their scheme for 'national universities', which were designed along the millet's lines to allow autonomy to the various peoples in cultural, linguistic and educational matters.

Whether Austrian practice or the Austro-Marxists' ideas could actually have contained national discord within acceptable limits is a moot point. What is certain is that the Soviet decision to reject the Austro-Marxist model and adopt a federal one in the long run proved fatal to the Soviet Union. The federal model, especially in the form it took, was by no means the only and inevitable option. Before 1917 it was in fact explicitly rejected by the Bolsheviks, who saw it as a threat to the unity of their party and a means to make national differences more rigid and enduring. Instead the Bolsheviks said they intended to allow peoples the right to secession but to retain a unitary state in any country they ruled. Once in power, however, they proved very unwilling to let peoples secede. In some cases, where a people was surrounded on all sides by Russia, this was barely feasible anyway. Since the Bolsheviks in these early years needed support in non-Russian regions, opposed Russian nationalism and were very anxious to offer the world an example of socialist equality of peoples they more or less stumbled into federalism. Both Lenin and Stalin became convinced that this was the best practical solution to the nationalities problem. Nevertheless the decision in 1922–4 to create a federation of republics each in principle equal to Russia and possessing the theoretical right to secede owed much to Lenin. Here is one of the many examples cited in this book where circumstances and individual personalities had a fateful impact on the rise and fall of empires.

At least in Austria most of the territorial units ('crownlands') cut across simple ethnic boundaries. They therefore to some extent not only bolstered but also confused nationalist politics. The federal republics created by Moscow were, however, specifically designed to be national territories in which a single nation expressed its ethnic and cultural identity, and dominated government office. In constitutional theory and in symbolism these were much closer to being sovereign states than were Austria's crownlands. They were also given the constitutional right to secede. Given the fact that all the republics had initially been brought into the Union by force, and that this process had occurred within living memory, there was every chance that if political freedom was allowed the Union as constituted would disintegrate. In fact the Soviet federal constitution worked only because it was in part mere façade. Real power lay not with state institutions but with the Communist Party, which was a centralized and Moscow-dominated institution. Even the degree of autonomy allowed to republics in the 1920s might in some cases, had it continued, have led to demands for even greater freedom from Moscow. Certainly it would have required Moscow to compromise fundamentally with the republics over the allocation of resources and the definition of long-term goals and strategies. It was partly to avoid this necessity that Stalin reversed the nationalities policy of the 1920s and wiped out the non-Russian elites that the regime itself had created and cultivated. Though after his death there was no repetition of this huge-scale savagery, fear and an inertia bred partly by memories of terror were crucial to holding the Soviet Union together and negating the federal system's in-built risk of disintegration. When Gorbachev liberalized Soviet politics and proclaimed adherence to the rule of law, the inherent vulnerability of Soviet federalism became evident and played a big role in the USSR's destruction.

Austrian history does, however, offer a hint that the complete disintegration of the Soviet Union in 1991 was not inevitable, and that empires can to some extent transform themselves into multi-ethnic, democratic federations. The Habsburg Empire was initially very much the empire of an ideology, namely the Catholic Counter-Reformation. That ideology bound the empire together and gave it its identity. In the name of that ideology the Spanish and Austrian Habsburgs in the sixteenth century tried to reconquer Europe for Catholicism. The attempt failed and by the mid-eighteenth-century it was becoming clear in Vienna that Counter-Reformation principles were an obstacle to the empire's modernization and the state's power. Under Maria Theresa and Joseph II (from 1740 to 1790) these principles were therefore largely abandoned and political, economic and cultural reforms were introduced rooted in the principles of the North European and largely Protestant Enlightenment. In other words the Habsburgs were borrowing what were basically their enemies' principles in order to survive as a modern society and a great power. In 1914 the Habsburg Empire was still a Catholic polity and Counter-Reformation principles still meant something for the dynasty, let alone for large sections of the peasantry. But in politics and economics it was liberalism that dominated the empire's practices, as did the rule of law and a vibrant if acrimonious multi-culturalism.

For the Slav and Central Asian republics of the Soviet Union a similar evolution was in principle conceivable under Gorbachev. It appears to be the direction in which he himself was hoping to lead the Union by 1991. A common Soviet identity had at least as much resonance as a common Habsburg identity possessed in 1914. The Soviet Union had been a closed society for many decades: outside influences were to a far greater extent excluded than in the Habsburg case. The unique and all-pervading Soviet political and economic system had put its very powerful stamp on society. For better or worse the Soviet Union was much less under external threat than Austria-Hungary, and therefore much less likely to disintegrate under the grievous strains of war. Even more than in the Habsburg case there were enormous advantages in possessing a united imperial economic space given the degree to which the socialist system had tightly integrated all the republics into a single economy. Many factors contributed to Moscow's inability to save at least part of the federal union: these included the role of circumstances and personalities, the many shallowly buried skeletons of Soviet history, and the appalling complications of managing simultaneously a triple transition from authoritarianism to democracy, from a command economy to the market, and from empire to a genuine multinational federation.

In one crucial way the decline and dissolution of the Soviet Union was fundamentally different from the Habsburg experience. There was no world war. The causes of the First World War and even of the Habsburg decision to go to war in 1914 are very complicated and much debated. They cannot simply be reduced to a sense of imperial decline relative to great power rivals and to a consciousness that history seemed to be turning its back on the values and classes that underpinned the conservative, dynastic, aristocratic Habsburg elite and the empire it ruled. Nevertheless, these factors certainly mattered greatly in Vienna in 1914 and they had potential parallels in 1980s Moscow. The Soviet Union was losing the competition with international capitalism and the political and cultural values with which the latter was associated. There was little prospect of this process being reversed peacefully and many obvious dangers to the regime's legitimacy and long-term survival if it were not. Given the immense resources poured into its armed forces by the Soviet regime and the strongly geopolitical and military cast of mind of its leaders, was there not some logic in trying military means to end the spiral of decline vis-à-vis the capitalist enemy?

There were in fact a number of good reasons not to adopt such a strategy. In the first place, until the late 1970s Soviet decline vis-à-vis the West was not self-evident. Vietnam had seemingly devastated American willpower, the Soviet Union was making advances in the Third World, and the dramatic rise in oil prices after 1973 appeared both a threat to Western capitalism and a glorious opportunity for the Soviet Union to reap immense profits from its energy exports, thereby avoiding any need for destabilizing market reforms. Other factors were also crucial, not least the mentality of the ruling elite. Brezhnev's gerontocracy was far too complacent, old and comfortable to risk everything on a conflict with the West. The younger generation of reformers who came to power with Gorbachev were imbued with a genuinely humane vision of socialism and in any event clearly believed in the possibility of the Soviet Union's reform and revitalization. Their enemies, who for instance led the putsch in 1991, were generally less humane but as the events of 1991 themselves showed they were cautious bureaucrats without the stomach or the ruthlessness for a successful coup, let alone for the awesome level of brinkmanship which could have unleashed a third world war. The basic point of course was that the dangers of war in the nuclear age were known to be immeasurably greater than they had seemed in 1914. In that year it had been possible, albeit mistaken, to believe in a quick war and a victory which would strengthen both an empire's international weight and the position of its ruling elites. Facing NATO and living in a world of nuclear weapons, only a deeply evil and irresponsible leadership could have risked the Austrian option even had they understood the extent or the irreversibility of imperial decline, and seen no possible domestic strategy for its containment. At least for the moment, the existence of weapons of mass destruction is one of the key reasons why the traditional competition between empires in the form of all-out war is out of date.

THE DECLINE AND FALL OF THE SOVIET EMPIRE

When contemplating the causes of the decline and fall of empires, it is useful to divide these causes into two basic categories, the first external and the second domestic. Within the first category come geopolitics and the international context in which an empire is operating. The relative power of an empire and its rivals, the skill with which that power is used – in other words issues of military and diplomatic leadership – are all aspects of this external category. Domestic factors include an empire's system of government, its ability to mobilize resources and its handling of relations between the imperial centre and its key lieutenants in a wide imperial periphery. In this category too come ideology and culture, for these are issues that greatly affect an empire's legitimacy and cohesion. Crucial too are the nature and strength of the domestic challenges to empire: traditionally these were most often the difficulties of distance, space and communications, and in the modern era, above all the threat of nationalism. In reality of course these two categories overlap: a state's external power, for example, depends on its economic weight and on the magnetic force of its ideology and culture. Nevertheless, it clarifies the initial discussion of an empire's fall to think in terms of these two categories.

In the Soviet case the most basic reason for empire's decline was that the Union set itself Herculean tasks in the external sphere and difficult ones domestically. Internally the basic task was to create a viable political community out of an enormous mixture of peoples from varying cultures, religions and races. This feat had to be achieved in a world in which nationalism and popular sovereignty were very powerful ideologies, and in which universal literacy and rapid economic development were essential to the Soviet state's legitimacy and survival. The Soviet Union could not in other words exist in the traditional manner of empire, in which largely illiterate and static peoples could live together in a great polity without necessarily being brought into close connection by economic links and without suffering undue interference from an imperial government which confined itself to demanding loyalty and a sufficient tribute to sustain an emperor's dignity and his military might. All modern empires to some extent faced the acute dilemmas of combining imperial order with the challenges of modernization. Because it was both an empire and the would-be flagship of socialist modernity, the Soviet Union confronted this dilemma in the sharpest possible form.

Nevertheless, there are dangers in taking its demise for granted. The word and label 'empire' invite this mistake since to contemporary ears they signify both illegitimacy and inevitable disintegration. As noted earlier in this book, however, some empires have evolved and survived, and others might have done so. Austria-Hungary by 1914 was on the way to becoming a multi-ethnic federation, and China in the 1990s has evolved most of the way from empire to nation state. India and Indonesia are vast multi-ethnic countries which so far have survived the nationalist challenges which many believe made the collapse of the Soviet Union certain.

In comparison to Indonesia and India, however, the Soviet Union did bear the historical stigma of empire. Unlike India it had not evolved flexible and tested institutions and political cadres used to managing multi-ethnicity by compromise, open bargaining and semi-democratic means. In 1989–91 it was having to evolve these institutions and methods overnight, in the midst of severe economic crisis, and in a political system whose rules and conventions were being destroyed week by week. In addition, seven decades of centralized and tyrannical rule had stored up deep resentments and left many skeletons shallowly buried. *Glasnost* and then democratization brought all these resentments and skeletons to the surface. The sudden shocking admission that communism had failed was a terrible blow to Soviet patriotism and a Soviet identity which had been rooted in a vision of a common, successful socialist modernity. The central government had been exceptionally successful in mobilizing the population's meagre resources for imperial purposes, in other words the global competition for power and prestige. Given the chance, the population was bound to demand that its needs come first. It might easily be persuaded that throwing off the omniverous imperial state was the key to a better life. Republican leaders too were certain to want to seize control over local assets. In most of the republics anti-centrist feeling was bound also to be anti-Russian. The central Soviet regime was dominated by Russians, spoke Russian, glorified Russia's role as elder brother in the creation of socialism, and inhibited the free expression of non-Russian nationalism. In addition, seven decades of Soviet rule followed centuries of tsarist empire. In the eyes of much of the non-Russian intelligentsia the link between the two empires seemed very clear.

Externally the Soviet Union set itself the goal of overthrowing international capitalism. Until 1945 it was the only state in the world with this objective. Subsequently it acquired some allies, though in time the world's other communist states became more a liability than an asset. Before the First World War Russia's foreign minister, Sergey Sazonov, had commented[52] that, given Russia's weakness in Asia and her immense border with China, it was vital to her interests to have a weak neighbour to her south. Ironically communism both strengthened and united China, at least for a time, and provided ideological sources of conflict with Russia additional to those that history, geopolitics and culture already supplied in abundance. The confrontation with China in the Soviet Union's last three decades further worsened the external challenge facing Moscow.

But the basic difficulty always remained the self-imposed task of overthrowing global capitalism. This was a hugely ambitious goal for any single country to set itself, let alone one that by tradition was economically much more backward than Western Europe. The fact that in the Cold War the Soviet Union proclaimed this goal and in its foreign policy seemed to pursue it enabled a vastly powerful coalition of capitalist states to be mobilized and sustained against Moscow. The result was a great overstraining of Soviet economic resources, poured fruitlessly into competition with a much richer enemy. Because the state's ideology tied the regime's legitimacy so closely to successful competition with capitalism, the domestic consequences of Soviet communism's failure to achieve its external goals were always likely to be very severe. The ideology might perhaps be jettisoned or radically revised, and the Soviet territorial union might, at least in part, be reformed and preserved on a new basis. But the transition was found to be very difficult and crisis-ridden: it was sure to require time and careful management.

The most basic reason for the decline and fall of the Soviet Union was therefore extremely simple. At the core of this empire was an ideology that failed. Marxism-Leninism created an economic system that proved less efficient than capitalism. Its predictions about the economic collapse of capitalism and of unending war between the major capitalist states proved wrong, at least between 1945 and 1991. Partly for this reason Soviet ideology and the Soviet political and economic system lost credibility and legitimacy in the eyes both of significant parts of the population and of the ruling elite. Other ideologies such as nationalism and Western individualism and capitalism began to fill the void as Soviet self-confidence evaporated. When the regime came to its final crisis in 1991 it had remarkably few truly committed supporters willing to suffer, act resolutely, and if necessary kill in its defence.

Although the failure of ideology was the single most important factor in the collapse of the Soviet regime, it was not the only factor. Nor does it fully explain why the collapse of the Communist regime resulted too in the disintegration of the Soviet state and territorial union. A number of other factors, some of them common to the decline and fall of empires, were also important.

Empires thrive on fear of external enemies. They are one of its main *raisons d'être*. When the British drove the French from North America in the Seven Years' War (1756–63), the American colonists lost the need for British imperial protection: the declaration of American independence came thirteen years after the Treaty of Paris had ratified the expulsion of France from Canada. The Hungarian elites too had accepted the Habsburgs partly for fear of Russia and to some extent lost interest in the empire after Russia's seeming eclipse as a threat in 1918. Gorbachev's sane and deeply laudable new thinking in foreign policy destroyed any sense of a Western threat to Soviet security. Old Soviet military leaders, deployed on television in 1989–91 to defend the Union's necessity in terms of defence and security, could conjure up no threat more terrifying than the Japanese wish to recover the Kurile Islands. This was not a danger likely to reconcile Latvians to Soviet power. Given the failure of communist ideology and of the communist economy only the German threat could legitimate Soviet rule in East-Central Europe. Brandt's Ostpolitik helped to defuse this sense of threat but so too did the whole internal development of West Germany since 1945, and indeed the mere passage of time, memory and generations.

The informal empire in East-Central Europe proved to be a classic case of overstretch. By the mid-1980s this region was more of a liability than an asset to the Soviet Union. To sustain this dominion required continuing economic subsidies (at least so long as world energy prices remained high) and the threat of periodic Soviet invasions to sustain illegitimate local regimes. In particular the rise of Solidarity and the crisis of 1980–81 faced Moscow with the daunting prospect of military intervention to sustain its hold on Poland, the largest and most anti-Russian of its satellite states. The great difficulty was how to disengage from East-Central Europe without doing fatal damage to Moscow's ideological legitimacy within the USSR or its relations with some of the Union's non-Russian republics, whose own aspirations for independence would certainly be fuelled by any humiliating Soviet withdrawal from East-Central Europe. This dilemma was greatly complicated by the fact that Moscow had over-stretched itself territorially even within the borders of the USSR itself. Above all the territories annexed by Stalin in 1945 – the Baltic republics, western Ukraine and Bessarabia (western Moldova) – were millstones around Moscow's neck. Indeed, it is quite conceivable that had Stalin not annexed these regions most or even possibly all of the Soviet Union might have survived Gorbachev's era intact, at least for a time.

The Baltic republics were small, with a combined population of barely seven million, but they proved very important. Their native populations had enjoyed independence between the wars and had a strong sense of national identity and of the illegitimacy of Soviet rule. This was compounded by bitter memories of mass deportations and executions after 1945; by a correct belief that independent Baltic republics had enjoyed Scandinavian living standards and could do so again freed from Soviet rule; by resentment – in Latvia and Estonia – at mass Russian immigration which made Latvians, for example, a minority in their own capital city. The moment a Soviet regime genuinely liberalized, strong opposition to Soviet rule was bound to surface in the Baltic republics. By 1989 it was possible to mobilize over two million people in these republics in demonstrations against the Ribbentrop-Molotov 1939 pact which had handed the Baltic peoples over to Stalin: this was a huge percentage of the adult native population. The Baltic Popular Fronts were an inspiration to nationalists throughout the USSR both organizationally and by their attacks on the legitimacy of Soviet power. The Baltic peoples could not be crushed without slaughter and serious damage to détente with the West, which was the core of Gorbachev's foreign policy and of his strategy of switching resources from defence to the consumer economy. When thirteen Lithuanians were killed in January 1991 Western opinion was far more outraged than by the much larger number of deaths in Baku during Soviet military action in the previous year. The Baltic peoples were Europeans, their annexation had never been recognized by the Western powers, and they had a certain claim on the Western conscience.

Still more serious were the consequences of western Ukraine's annexation and the forced exchange of population between Poland and the Soviet Ukraine after the Second World War. The Baltic peoples were a serious embarrassment but the Soviet Union would easily survive their secession. It would not survive the secession of Ukraine, which would leave Russia virtually alone in a Union with Central Asian Muslim states very different from her in culture and certain in the longer run to be a major economic and political liability. West Ukraine had always been and remained the heartland of Ukrainian nationalism. Before 1939 the greatest enemy of West Ukrainian nationalism had, however, been the local and historically dominant Polish community. After 1946 there were few Poles left in Ukraine and even fewer Ukrainians in Poland. There was therefore much less of a basis for mutual discord. The Soviet Empire became the great enemy of Poles and Ukrainians alike. Far-sighted opponents of Soviet rule in both communities put imagination and effort into ending the history of Polish-Ukrainian antagonism.[53]

In 1914 Peter Durnovo[54] had warned Nicholas II against annexing Galicia, stressing that this would greatly contribute to the threat that Ukrainian nationalism posed to the Russian Empire. Stalin would have been wise to heed such warnings. No doubt he believed that he was removing an irredentist threat to Soviet Ukraine and that his policemen were more than capable of crushing nationalism in the annexed region. In the short run he was correct. The dangers of Stalin's annexation only became clear under the conditions of democratization introduced by Gorbachev, when a Ukrainian nationalist movement rooted above all in Galicia played a key role in Ukraine's secession from the Soviet Union. As noted earlier, there were parallels here with British policy in South Africa. In 1899–1902 the British started and won a war to annex the Transvaal and Orange Free State. They did so in large part to remove an irredentist threat to their control of the Cape Colony, whose White majority were Boers, and thereby to all South Africa, which was a key economic and strategic asset to their empire. Subsequently, however, the liberal government that came to power in 1905 allowed colon (i.e. White) democracy in the South African Federation, to which the two annexed Boer republics were attached. The result in the long run was to hand all South Africa over to the Boer nationalists whom Britain initially conquered and annexed.

In the last years of the Soviet Union Ukraine witnessed not just an important anti-Soviet nationalist movement but also the defection to the nationalist camp of crucial elements of the republic's Communist elite, headed by First Secretary Leonid Kravchuk. The size and ethnic diversity of an empire always makes the relationship between the centre and its regional lieutenants vital and politically fragile. The centre needs to pursue a policy of carrot and stick. It must control its lieutenants' appointment and dismissal, and provide them with protection, legitimacy and resources. This the Soviet regime traditionally did. Republican first secretaries knew that their survival and their ability to pursue successful policies depended on the centre's support and on the budgetary resources it controlled. They shared its Marxist-Leninist legitimacy and enjoyed office and high status under the protection of its security forces.

All this was undermined by Gorbachev's reforms. The failure of economic reform combined with *glasnost's* revelations about the Soviet past destroyed the legitimacy of communism and Moscow. Democratic principles, introduced partially for the all-Union ballot in March 1989 and much more fully in the republican March 1990 elections, made the republican leaders' survival dependent not on the Central Party authorities in Moscow, as in the past, but on their own local electorates. The Lithuanian Communist leadership under Algirdas Brazauskas was the first to understand the implications of democratic reform and split from the CPSU in 1989: other Party leaders followed suit, finding in nationalism an alternative legitimacy far more acceptable to most republican electorates in the conditions of 1990–91. With Moscow powerless, the economy collapsing and the tax base shrinking, republican leaders had every incentive to seize control of local assets in order to cement their hold over clients and increase their chances of satisfying the electorate's needs. The immense percentage of local assets controlled by the all-Union ministries made this both personally tempting and politically essential to republican elites.

Of course, many elements in this process – for example the scramble to seize state property – were unique to the Soviet case, but Judith Brown, for instance, analyses the disintegration of the Mogul empire in eighteenth-century India in terms very familiar to anyone who watched the breakdown of Moscow's relationship with its republican lieutenants.[55] Carrot and stick is not after all a particularly sophisticated or socialist concept. Nor does it take much wit to realize that regional leaders will not hand over resources to an imperial centre unless they are coerced or persuaded into doing so, unless they receive something substantial in return, or unless their local power-base is too weak to sustain them without central support. In the 1990s it transpired that in most republics the federal system had allowed republican leaderships the means to independent survival so long as they adapted to the challenges and opportunities of *perestroika* with sufficient speed and wit. After the collapse of the Soviet Union nine of the fifteen newly independent states were ruled by the previous republican leaders for much or all of the 1990s.

This suggests that the collapse of the Soviet Union was scarcely a simple or unequivocal triumph for democracy. Nevertheless, democratization, albeit limited, did contribute greatly to the Soviet Union's disintegration. The March 1990 elections brought to power autonomous republican governments which were legitimate in terms of Soviet law and could claim that law's support for their demand to secede. In a way even more important was the impact of democracy in the Russian Republic. Most empires survive partly because they can force the people of the empire's core to make sacrifices in the imperial cause. From the advent of mass democracy in the 1880s British statesmen had juggled the conflicting fiscal requirements of metropolitan social welfare and imperial defence.[56] They had periodically bemoaned the electorate's opposition to conscription. The Portuguese Empire survived a little longer than others in the late twentieth century partly because Portugal was not a democracy and the people did not therefore need to be asked whether they wished to pay taxes or see their sons conscripted in the empire's cause. But the burden of empire's defence contributed greatly to revolution in metropolitan Portugal in 1974.

Russia in 1988–91 has hints of both British and Portuguese experience. When the authorities tried in 1990 to mobilize the Russian North Caucasus military district's reservists for peace-keeping operations in the imperial periphery, the reservists refused to answer the call and the state was too weak to enforce it. Yeltsin's ability to mobilize great resentment in Russia against the central Soviet regime and elite owed much to the people's demand for resources to be spent on its own welfare rather than (as they saw it) on subsidizing other republics and sustaining the imperial ambitions of a superpower. In 1917 tsarism had been overthrown in part by a popular revolt against the burdens of empire, in this case the awful costs of continuing a First World War whose logic meant little to a semi-literate people. In 1991 too, Russian resentment against the exorbitant burdens of empire contributed greatly to the Soviet Union's demise.

The obvious danger of comparative history is, however, to push comparison too far. There was much in the collapse of the Soviet Union that was extraordinary, even unique, by the standard of other empires' disintegration. That helps to explain why so few experts anticipated its demise. Most empires collapse above all because they are defeated or gravely weakened in war. The former was the fate of the Ottomans and Habsburgs, the latter of the British and, still more, French and Dutch in post-1945 South-East Asia. When Andry Amalrik made his famous prediction that the Soviet Union would not survive beyond 1984 he based his prophecy in part on the consequences of a future war with China. In fact, with the exception of the very limited[57] conflict in Afghanistan, war was not a factor in the USSR's collapse. On the other hand, what mattered crucially in the Soviet case was that the end of empire coincided with and hugely complicated the dismantling of the communist political and economic systems. Nevertheless, invoking the perils of transition is far from a complete explanation of the Soviet Union's collapse. In the years between 1985 and 1991 chance, misunderstanding, personalities and circumstances played significant roles.

As in all revolutions, in 1985–91 history speeded up. New actors and movements leaped onto the stage. Events crowded in on each other at dizzying speed. Exhausted and bewildered leaders were unable to comprehend, let alone control events. Actions set off trains of unexpected consequences. At the time even well-informed commentators found it very difficult to understand what was happening, let alone to predict future developments. In retrospect attempts have been made to explain the chaotic train of events, sometimes with the help of some of the key actors themselves. Not all these attempted clarifications are convincing. Chaos is often a truer picture than clarity.

Through all this turbulent final period, however, one factor does stand out and that is Mikhail Gorbachev's personality. Radical reform was not inevitable in 1985. If the ruling gerontocracy had been as wholly selfish as it was often portrayed, the obvious need for change could still have been subordinated to petty, short-term personal interests. Even when a strategy of radical reform was adopted, it did not need to take the path chosen by Gorbachev. Apart from Moscow and its satellites, the world's two leading communist states in the 1980s were China and Yugoslavia. Their leaderships opted for very different strategies from Gorbachev's. It is plausible to argue that Yury Andropov, had he lived, would have chosen the Chinese path of gradual economic reform guided by the authoritarian rule of the Communist Party bureaucracy. There were good reasons why a Chinese strategy might not have worked so well in Russia. Stalin had destroyed the peasantry, above all in the Slav republics. Agricultural production could not be raised simply by removing controls on peasant enterprise in Chinese fashion. The creation of free economic zones was complicated by the multinational nature of the Soviet population and by the federal system. Economic autonomy might be 'misused' for nationalist goals once the centre weakened its hold over outlying regions. Russia had no Chinese-style diaspora to invest in its economy, and so long as the Cold War continued Western governments would strongly discourage massive outside investment. It is also asserted, though never proved, that the Soviet bureaucracy would have put up far more ferocious opposition to any changes than their Chinese counterparts and therefore had to be undermined by radical political reform before anything substantial could be done to improve the economy. Nevertheless, something close to the Chinese strategy could certainly have been attempted in the Soviet Union and could scarcely have failed in more spectacular manner than the economic policy actually adopted by Gorbachev.

Authoritarian economic reform might have been linked to an attempt to ground the regime more firmly in Russian nationalism. Slobodan Milošević's strategy has been a catastrophe for the Serbs but thus far a personal success: he is the only Communist leader in East-Central Europe to have held on to power throughout the last decade and has enriched himself and his family in the process. Once again, there were good reasons why a Milošević-style strategy might not have worked so 'well' in Russia. It was much easier for a Serb nationalist leader to find targets for Serb nationalist anger than would have been the corresponding case in Russia. Albanians, Croats and the federal government all fitted the bill well. Politics had in any case been more open in Yugoslavia than in the Soviet Union for many years. The population was more used to being mobilized for political causes and the struggle between the various Yugoslav nations was much more out in the open. For this reason too it would have been harder to mobilize mass Russian nationalism since the Russian population was politically much more inert. In addition, the Soviet regime had come much closer to co-opting Russian nationalism than was the case in Yugoslavia, where Tito had spent much time and ingenuity trying to keep the Serbs in their place. The fact that a 'Serbian strategy', or indeed a 'Chinese' one, might not have been so effective in Russia was no guarantee that it would not be tried. There were many members of the Soviet political elite of that time whom one could imagine attempting such a strategy.

Gorbachev and his circle came, however, from the pro-Western section of the Russian intelligentsia. They sought to draw closer to Western social democracy and liberalism rather than to the Chinese authoritarian political model or to Serbian-style ethnic nationalism. Even given the basic goals of Gorbachev and his circle, however, the need to prioritize political rather than economic reform in 1987–90 was not self-evident. The certainty of effective bureaucratic opposition to any economic reform strategy could not be taken for granted: much of the *nomenklatura* was after all subsequently to take to privatization with alacrity. No doubt it paid a radical reformer to create some additional institutional base of power and legitimacy for himself, in order to secure himself against a repeat of the Communist oligarchs' coup which had overthrown Khrushchev. Creating a basically subservient all-Union parliament in 1989 and getting it to elect Gorbachev as head of state was one thing, however: proceeding in 1990 to far more genuinely democratic elections in the republics, thereby in many cases handing legitimate power to anti-Soviet nationalists, was quite another, and obviously far more risky. Within the programme of economic reform itself there were major contradictions and shortcomings. The Soviet leader showed dazzling tactical skill and self-confidence in pushing reform past the Party elite. He seems also to have been excessively confident about the stability and legitimacy of the Communist regime. All these points can only be explained, in part anyway, by Gorbachev's biography. The same is true of his handling of Yeltsin, whose relationship with Gorbachev was crucial in Russia's destruction of the Soviet Union. It remains deeply interesting why the General Secretary of the Communist Party of the USSR should have pursued policies which put Party and Union at such obvious risk and why he drew back from using the degree of force required to keep the Soviet Union together.

This book began with an explanation of the enormous role played by Qinshihuangdi, the first Chinese emperor, in founding the Chinese imperial tradition. It is not inappropriate to conclude this chapter by stressing how much the last Soviet emperor, Mikhail Gorbachev, contributed – for better or for worse – to the ending of the Soviet tradition of empire.

Part Four

AFTER EMPIRE

IO

After Empire

The aftermath of empire is a huge subject. Empires have not just existed over the millennia: all of them have also ultimately collapsed. The aftermaths of empire therefore span every era and every continent. From one angle, the whole of European history from the fall of the Roman Empire in the fifth century could be viewed as empire's aftermath. Much of that history has revolved around trying to ensure security, stability and economic cooperation among the multitude of conflicting peoples and princes left behind in empire's wake. This story has already been told in Chapter 2, however, and will not be repeated here.

Considered in the twentieth century alone, the aftermath of empire could still be an immensely wide-ranging subject. In the cultural sphere it could, for example, encompass a vast array of issues from the long-term impact of empire on the psyche of Third World intelligentsias to more light-hearted studies of Indian, Chinese and Vietnamese restaurants in Europe. The aim of this chapter on the twentieth century is more modest. The focus is above all political, and sticks largely to the empires already covered in Parts Two and Three – the Habsburg, Ottoman, British and Russo-Soviet empires, in a comparison of the impact of empire's demise on the former peoples of these empires, on the states that emerged from their ruins, and on international order. Even this task is enormous in scope and full of pitfalls. The end of empire and the process of decolonization had many differences even within a single empire, as this chapter makes clear. Comparisons across the many territories of a range of empires are hugely complicated.

In the present author's view any attempt to define all-encompassing and scientific laws governing empire's aftermath would be foolish, and a more modest desire to spot some patterns across empires and to use comparisons to sharpen understanding of individual cases is far more sensible and rewarding. Even given this limited ambition one must remain on one's guard. In a comparison of the aftermath of one regime that collapsed in 1918 and another that fell in 1991 it may well be not so much the specifics of empire and its fall that one is comparing as the differing nature of the international order and of the ideologies, states and forces that sustain it. Equally, not everything that happens to either the former metropolitan or subject peoples after an empire's collapse is necessarily a legacy of empire.

AFTER THE HABSBURGS

The Habsburg Empire collapsed after four years of total war in 1918. The experience of war had some impact on what followed. War veterans played a brutal role in the Hungarian counter-revolution and, grouped together in the Heimwehr, in Austrian politics of the 1920s and of the 1930s. Wars create military heroes who can go on to become political leaders in the post-imperial world. Miklos Horthy, Hungary's most distinguished senior officer in the Habsburg wartime armed forces, was his country's ruler from 1922 to 1944. The disintegration of the empire in 1918 was accompanied by very little violence or bloodshed in its Austrian half. Parliamentary institutions and universal male suffrage under the late empire had created legitimate national and regional leaders to whom power was transferred peacefully. Hungary's parliament, in which neither the non-Hungarians nor the Magyar masses were represented, could not so easily create legitimate post-imperial leaders or smooth the transfer of power to them. That is one reason why the collapse of the empire in the Hungarian Kingdom was followed by much greater violence than in Austria.

Nevertheless, the Austrian Germans were traumatized by the collapse of empire. Even the Austrian half of the former empire had spread over 180,000 square miles and contained 30 million people. The new Austrian Republic had 6.5 million citizens in 50,000 square miles. Austria-Hungary had been a great power in terms of both politics and culture. Imperial Vienna was a superb, multi-national, culturally vibrant capital. Republican Vienna was no longer the hub and meeting-place for much of Eastern and Central Europe. Austria counted for almost nothing in world affairs. Indeed, as the events of 1919–20 showed, it could easily be pushed around and dictated to not just by the victorious allied great powers but even by the Czechs. To be Austrian before 1914 meant to have an imperial identity, to feel that one counted in the world. Particularly for Austrian elites, it was difficult to come to terms with life in a state that would make no impact on history.

Memories of imperial grandeur inevitably detracted from the new republic's legitimacy and were a factor in the support for the idea of unity with a new Great Germany. Hitler's Great German empire, however, imposed huge suffering on the Austrians and taught them the price of empire and the cost of playing a leading role in world affairs. In 1946 the President of the reconstituted Austrian Republic, Karl Renner, spoke for his people: 'We never again want to be held within a great power or any kind of empire . . . We want to live for ourselves and seek only that in the world.'[1] Not only the memory of war and defeat but also the existence of a threatening Soviet bloc only 30 miles from Vienna reinforced this feeling. Living for oneself in cosy, neutral, parochial little Austria meant abdicating responsibility for world affairs and sinking into a sweet life of cake with plenty of cream. Even staging Expo '95 in Vienna was too great an international burden to contemplate for a public worried by rising house prices and traffic congestion.[2]

The problem in 1918 was not just that republican Austria had been suddenly demoted from imperial status but also that it was in no sense a nation. The new Austria was not even all the core German lands of the old empire since the 3.5 million Germans of the Bohemian Sudetenland had been swallowed by Czechoslovakia. In fact, as was said at the time, the new Austria was just those bits of the old empire that no one else wanted. Indeed, the Austrian Germans did not much want the new state themselves. The traditional objects of their loyalty were the Habsburg Empire as a whole, their province, and German cultural pride and identity. The dynastic empire was irretrievably lost, though nostalgia for it long remained powerful. Provincial loyalty led many Tyrolese to prefer to live as a unit under the despised Italians rather than partition Tyrol and join its northern half to Austria.[3] Left free to choose, the Vorarlberg would probably have opted for union with Switzerland. Meanwhile the bulk of the Austrian electorate would have supported amalgamation with Germany. Since this option would have increased Germany's power and territory it was vetoed by the allies. The new Austria was not therefore sustained by the legitimacy that springs from democratic self-determination.

In these circumstances it is not at all surprising that many Austrians welcomed the Anschluss in 1938. Rule from Berlin over the next seven years reinforced a sense of Austrian identity among sections of the population but if the Second World War had ended in anything other than an unconditional allied victory, Austria would have followed Bavaria's footsteps as a very distinct but also very German province. In 1945, however, asserting a strongly separate Austrian identity was a means not merely to avoid partition or Soviet rule, but also to shed all responsibility for the Nazi regime and its evils,[4] particularly useful given Hitler's 'Austrian' ancestry and childhood. Decades of peace and prosperity, not to mention the mere passage of time, helped to legitimize the second republic. Membership of the European Union from 1994 in principle offered the possibility of preserving a separate Austrian identity, combining with the Germans without falling under their rule, while broadening horizons and taking some responsibility for European and world affairs.

Unlike post-1945 Austria, the interwar republic could not acquire legitimacy and prosperity through economic development. In part this was because it had great trouble adapting to the collapse of the single Habsburg economic space. A market of 51 million in 1918 was suddenly reduced to 6.5 million. Before 1914 Austrian industry and Hungarian agriculture had a mutually beneficial symbiotic relationship, Viennese finance served the whole empire, and the capital drew its coal and many of its consumer goods from Bohemia. Given the prosperity of post-1945 Austria, interwar complaints that the republic was non-viable in economic terms look strange today. There is no doubt that these complaints were often politically motivated and were used to justify the demand for union with Germany, about which Austrian business was in fact always much less enthusiastic than liberal and socialist political leaders and publicists.[5] Unlike the case after 1945, however, the interwar Austrian Republic had to survive in a world economy increasingly dominated by protective tariffs and national autarchy. All the successor states to the Habsburgs followed this line to varying degrees even in the 1920s. With the great depression these tendencies were redoubled and economic crisis threatened the legitimacy of all the states in the region.

Given the already weak legitimacy of Austria's republican regime it is not surprising that party politics, already bitter in the 1920s, became much more so in the following decades. For socialists the Austrian patriotism proclaimed by Dolfuss and his supporters was merely a cover for authoritarian rule and reactionary policies. The brief civil war between the Dolfuss regime and the socialists in February 1934 further hardened party hatreds. Five months later Dolfuss himself was murdered in an attempted coup by the Austrian Nazis. There was never much chance of a united Austrian front against Hitler. In part the bitterness of Austrian party politics was a reflection of economic crisis, of the republic's basic illegitimacy, and of the vicious ideological divisions in European politics as a whole during the 1930s. In addition, in comparison to pre-1914 Austria there was no sovereign imperial state and bureaucracy to mediate and if necessary suppress party conflict.

In one sense the position of the Hungarians, the other 'ruling people' of the old empire, was a good deal better than that of the Austrians after 1918. There was never any doubt about the strength of Hungarian national identity or the legitimacy of the independent Hungarian state. This state had, however, came into existence amidst social revolution, Bolshevik dictatorship, foreign military intervention, and counter-revolutionary terror. Inevitably, Admiral Horthy's regime was hated and feared by many Hungarians.

Once this regime was established in 1920, however, it was very unlikely to be overthrown by domestic social revolution. The biggest issue in Hungarian politics in the next two decades became the revision of the post-1918 territorial settlement. The Treaty of Trianon reduced Hungary from a country of 109,000 square miles and 20.9 million people (1910) to just over 35,000 square miles and 7.6 million citizens in 1920.[6] The settlement was not 'fair' in ethnic terms. Even in border regions concentrated areas of Hungarian settlement were handed over to the Slovaks, Romanians and Serbs. Given demographic patterns in the region, however, no adjustment of borders, however fair, could have avoided the creation of large national minorities in all the successor states to the Habsburg empire. Nor would the most painstaking concern for fairness have reconciled the Hungarians to the break-up of the historical and multinational Hungarian Kingdom of St Stephen. Not surprisingly, opposition to Trianon was strongest among the Hungarian elites: the bulk of the often very poor and disenfranchised rural population had more pressing everyday concerns. Of the three million Hungarians whom the peace treaty left outside the new state's borders, 424,000 had returned to Hungary by December 1924.[7] The majority of these were from the upper and middle classes and they formed an influential nationalist and revisionist lobby. The Hungarian elites believed that historic rights not ethnicity legitimized state boundaries. In any case they had no respect for democracy, majorities and the counting of heads: nor did it cross their minds that Romanians, let alone Slovaks, could be their equals.

Nevertheless, nationalism and revisionism were far from being purely elite concerns: in the late 1930s, at least in the towns, they enjoyed mass support.[8] The old Hungarian aristocratic elite were far from enthusiastic allies of Hitler, whose regime they viewed with moral revulsion as well as social contempt. Once Germany showed itself willing and able to overthrow the Versailles–Trianon settlement in the late 1930s, however, no Hungarian government could have stood aside, particularly once the British and French had proven unwilling to defend that settlement themselves. If before 1938 the Hungarians had not themselves challenged the settlement overtly, this was a result of weakness, financial as well as military and political. In the fifteen years after 1918 Hungary was very dependent on foreign loans, above all from France. These came on condition that Budapest refrain from propaganda against the territorial status quo.[9]

The two other main successor-states to the Habsburgs were Yugoslavia and Czechoslovakia. Both were new multinational countries containing peoples whose loyalty to the state was conditional at best. Of these peoples the most dangerous were the Sudeten Germans because they lived on the German–Czech border and might receive support for secession from what remained even after 1918 Europe's potentially most powerful state, namely Germany. Since Germany was a key loser from the Versailles peace settlement and never accepted the legitimacy of its new eastern borders, the threat to the new Czechoslovak state was evident from the moment of its birth.

Where attitudes to Slavs were concerned, much of the German electorate in the Sudetenland was no less arrogant than the Hungarian elites and rather less reticent about allying wholeheartedly with Hitler. Nevertheless, the Sudeten Germans had some reason to feel the victims of injustice. The right of self-determination, proclaimed from the rooftops by the allies in 1918, had been denied to them as to the Austrians. Whereas historical Hungary, the crown of St Stephen, was carved up in the name of self-determination and the rights of peoples, the opposite principle was applied to the Sudetenland. Historical Bohemia, the crown of St Wenceslas, to whose territorial integrity the Czechs were passionately committed, was preserved in the teeth of the Sudetenlanders' desire to unite with Austria or merge into an all-German state. Allied determination not to permit the territorial expansion of Germany and to give the new Czechoslovakia defensible borders played a big role in this seeming injustice. Sudeten industry suffered greatly from the disintegration of its former Habsburg market, rather more so than was the case in the Czech regions of Bohemia and Moravia. With the 1930s economic crisis this became a burning issue. So too did German claims that the Czech government was less generous to them than to Czechs as regards subsidies to industry and relief for the unemployed.

In these complaints there was some justice[10] but more exaggeration. In comparison to most imperial peoples' fate after the collapse of empire the Germans were treated well in Czechoslovakia. They enjoyed citizenship and full civil and political rights. They controlled their own state schools and their own elected local governments and from 1926 German parties always formed part of the ruling coalition in Prague. Before the Depression and, above all, before Hitler came to power, the great majority of Sudeten Germans were unenthusiastic about Czechoslovakia but they were reconciled to its existence and to the need and possibility to adapt themselves to its laws and political institutions, under which they enjoyed considerable de facto autonomy. Czechoslovakia could only be destroyed from outside, as indeed was the case with Yugoslavia. The latter was much less democratic and less law–abiding than Czechoslovakia and most Croats regarded the Karageorgević regime without affection. Nevertheless, by the late 1930s a wary *modus vivendi* between the nationalities existed. Internal ethnic divisions weakened both Yugoslavia and Czechoslovakia against external aggression but there was no chance of either state disintegrating spontaneously from within.

The origins of the disaster that struck the former Habsburg lands between 1938 and 1945 lay in internal German political developments after 1918 and in the overall geopolitics of the European continent. Germany was not permanently divided or weakened in 1918 and the victorious allies proved unwilling and unable to defend the territorial settlement they had imposed at the end of the First World War.

Nevertheless, the collapse of the Habsburg Empire and its consequences played a big role in enabling Hitler to destroy Europe. The successor states to the Habsburgs were too weak and too divided to put up any effective resistance to Hitler when Nazi Germany moved into the region over which the Habsburgs had ruled for so long. Had the empire still existed, its leaders would have fought Hitler tooth and nail. The one force with which the Habsburgs could never compromise was pan-German nationalism, whose programme entailed the unification of the empire's German-speaking core provinces in a state ruled from Berlin. Confronted with a direct pan-German challenge the Habsburgs would have faced the disloyalty of one section of their German subjects, but they would have been in a far better position than the republic of the 1930s to mobilize and unite the other Catholic, socialist and patriotic Austrian sections of the German community against Hitler. They would also have enjoyed the absolute and unhesitating support of their Slav subjects, and above all the Czechs, in this struggle. Preserving Central Europe from pan-German nationalist dominion was after all the most basic function of the Habsburg Empire in Czech eyes and a key source of the empire's legitimacy. Nor would the confrontation with Nazi Germany have been purely political and strategic. Hitler hated the Habsburgs and all they stood for, and the loathing was reciprocated by the Archduke Otto. The dynasty and those who advised it had lived before 1918 in a different moral universe from the world created by Hitler and his henchmen.

For the peoples of the former Monarchy the consequences of the empire's collapse became evident only after 1938. They were subjected first to a German and then to a Russo-Soviet empire. Both empires imposed high costs with few benefits on the region. The Russo-German struggle to dominate Europe brought huge suffering and devastation to the former Habsburg lands, partly because it unleashed a number of vicious local conflicts between the region's peoples. One consequence was ethnic cleansing on a stupendous scale in Poland, in the Balkans and for the former empire's German subjects. Of the latter, when the Second World War began roughly five million lived outside the Austrian Republic but in the other successor states to the Habsburgs. By 1946 the great majority of them had fled, died or been expelled.[11]

The greatest victims of all were the Jews, very often the most imperially-minded and loyal of all the Habsburgs' subjects. The empire's collapse brought them great and immediate problems. Other former Habsburg subjects had their own home-lands: the Jews did not. Even in Hungary, where many of them had assimilated and become Magyar patriots before 1914, they became targets for ultra-nationalists and scapegoats for all the miseries of the interwar era. Elsewhere in the former empire, even in democratic Czechoslovakia, the fact that the Jews were very often German-speaking and linked in the public mind to the imperial regime contributed to their unpopularity. They were an imperial relic in a world of bitter, paranoid and inward-looking rival nationalisms. They were also simply much too prominent in the economy for their own safety. Hugh Seton-Watson has noted dispassionately that 'the industry of Poland, Rumania and Hungary in 1918 was mostly in the hands of the Jews, who also dominated banking ... the free professions were filled, in proportions ranging from a quarter to two-thirds, with Jews.'[12] The result was deep unpopularity and various forms of restriction on Jewish education and employment. Even for most of the region's anti-semites however, Hitler's Final Solution to the Jewish question was beyond the imagination.

AFTER THE OTTOMANS

The collapse of the Ottoman Empire occurred over a much longer period than the fall of Austria-Hungary. In the five decades before 1918 the Habsburgs lost no territory: they gained Bosnia-Herzegovina. By 1914 the Habsburg Empire was generally taken to be weaker than the leading European states – Germany, Britain, France and Russia – but it was still unequivocally a great power. The Ottoman situation was very different. Though the empire still existed in 1914, the decline in its power had been evident to all ever since the disastrous war with Russia of 1768–74. Since then further wars with Russia had almost all ended in defeat and major loss of territory. In the nineteenth century France and Britain had absorbed the sultan's main North African territories. In 1912 his former Balkan subjects had defeated him in war and virtually expelled the Ottomans from Europe. In the case of Austria the crisis caused by empire's collapse broke suddenly and dramatically in 1918. By then the equivalent Ottoman crisis had lasted for more than a century. Its core was the fate of Constantinople, the Straits and the Balkans – which European statesmen had long since dubbed 'the Eastern Question'. Throughout the nineteenth century this question had been one of the great perennial issues of European power politics and the cause of a number of wars and acute crises.

In another sense too the Austrian and Ottoman empires were very different. The Habsburg Empire was really a single geopolitical unit formed around the Danube basin. This whole region was crucial to the European balance of power and, above all, to the twentieth-century competition between Germany and Russia for hegemony in Europe. By contrast, the Ottoman Empire stretched from the North Caucasus to Algeria. It can best be seen as (at least) four distinct though of course connected geopolitical zones. These were the North Caucasus and Crimea; the Balkans; the Arab provinces; and Anatolia, in other words the future Turkish Republic. The empire's 'Far West', in other words most of North Africa, was in fact really a separate fifth zone and most of it had long since been lost by 1914.

The first zone, Crimea and the North Caucasus, was absorbed by the Russian Empire between 1774 and the 1860s. It therefore disappeared from international view and became a Russian domestic issue. With the collapse of the Soviet Union, Crimea and the North Caucasus became once again major international questions, though ones best analysed later in this chapter in the context of the post-Soviet crisis. Nevertheless, today's problems in the Crimea and North Caucasus are to a small degree post–Ottoman as well as post–Soviet. Islam is central to the identity both of the Crimean Tatars and of most of the peoples of the North Caucasus, above all in the way that they define themselves against the Russians. One element[13] – not by any means the most important – in the current instability in Crimea and the North Caucasus is part of the wider tension between the 'Christian' and 'Islamic' worlds which stretches along a borderline from Central Asia to the Maghreb. Given the right circumstances, Turkish economic and even conceivably quiet military support for the Crimean Tatars or some of the peoples of the North Caucasus cannot be entirely ruled out.

Much more familiar to the Western observer is the second major zone, namely the Balkans. The expulsion of the Ottoman Empire from this region had dramatic consequences for Europe. No empire replaced Ottoman rule in the Balkans, at least until 1945 when the Soviet Union came to dominate much of the region. The main successors to the Ottomans in the region were a handful of small independent nations – the Serbs, Greeks, Bulgarians and Romanians. Their rivalry, above all over Macedonia, was a cause of instability and heightened nationalist emotion throughout the region. More dangerously, the Balkans became a key zone of competition between the great powers, above all Austria and Russia. Both powers had key political, economic and strategic interests in the region. Both sought Balkan clients. Great power and local rivalries became entwined and in 1914 involved all Europe in a horrendous war. Decades of instability and further conflict ensued until, after 1945, both Europe as a whole and the Balkans in particular achieved – at a great price in terms of wasted lives and resources – a sort of stability in the Soviet-American stand-off usually called the Cold War. When this period ended in 1991 some unfinished business resumed in the Balkans. This is not for one moment to suggest that the fall of Yugoslavia and the subsequent bloodshed and ethnic cleansing was the direct, let alone inevitable, result of the Ottoman expulsion from the Balkans. Nevertheless, the Muslim Albanians, Bosnians and Kosovars are among the very last leftovers of Ottoman rule in the region. In what is now a sea of Christian peoples they are defined to a great extent by their Islamic religion and Ottoman cultural heritage. It is unreasonable to expect Turkey to be indifferent to these peoples' fate, though foolish to believe that its limited resources will enable it to play more than a small role.

The third major geopolitical zone of the Ottoman Empire consisted of the Arab provinces. Lying on or adjacent to the south-eastern shore of the Mediterranean, though stretching as far as the Persian Gulf, these provinces had a certain geographical unity. In cultural terms they were both Islamic and Arab. Almost all of them also came under British and French imperial rule, sometimes before the Ottomans' final collapse in 1918 and sometimes after.

Because in this region one empire's rule was succeeded by that of others, the immediate consequence of the Ottomans' collapse was not chaos or instability. The British and French could impose the 'peace of empire' on their dominions, maintain their clients in power, and rule out any wars between the new, and in theory sometimes independent, states into which the former Ottoman Empire was divided. Since in much of the region even uninhabited territory often concealed vast oil wealth, an empire's ability to control boundary disputes was needed. Within a long generation, in other words by the 1950s, British and French imperial power was fading fast throughout the region, however. At this point the consequences of empire's collapse became evident, though this had much less to do with the Ottoman heritage than with British and French policy in the region.

In comparison to the Habsburg Empire, the Ottoman economy was far less of a single integrated unit. The empire's disintegration therefore mattered much less, in the Arab provinces merely reinforcing an existing European economic domination. But the territorial carve-up did for example store up serious problems as regards the management of rivers and waters, above all between Turkey, Syria and Iraq. It also left immense oil wealth in the hands of the Gulf emirates, which could not defend themselves against their neighbours. Most of the new countries carved out of the Ottoman Empire had very little ethnic or historical legitimacy. Their borders reflected above all British and French geopolitical interests and the bargains struck between London and Paris. The Kurds found themselves divided between four countries. Iraq had a Shia majority but has been ruled throughout its existence by Sunnis, who were initially British clients. The Greater Lebanon created by France on behalf of its Maronite Christian clients ensured conflict in the longer term between its Christian and Muslim communities. Most of these states before the 1950s were ruled by rich, small oligarchies whose members were partly Western in culture. When British and French protection was removed these oligarchies were very vulnerable in the face of anti–Western feeling and the demands of a rapidly growing, educated and new urban 'middle class' of officers, officials and unemployed ex–students.[14]

Worst off were the two territories subject to European colonization. In Algeria European colons who numbered over one million by the 1950s lorded it for 130 years over a much more numerous native population. Empire ended in a war which resulted in the flight of the entire European community and the death of much of the native population. In 1917 the British decided for a variety of reasons to encourage and protect the development of a national territory for the (initially mostly European) Jews in Palestine. Within two decades they had got very cold feet about this project because of the damage it was doing to Britain's cause in the Arab world. Since the Arab Middle East was perceived as crucial to Britain's global geopolitical interests, an attempt was made to backpeddle. By 1945–7 the British position in Palestine was hopelessly compromised by the need to balance Britain's determination to maintain its standing in the Arab world and London's dependence on the United States, whose president was a strong supporter of the Jewish cause. Very inadequate resources to sustain the role of imperial policeman added to gnawings of conscience given the tragedy that had just befallen Europe's Jews made the British dilemma all the worse. The result was the abandonment of the British Mandate in 1948, immediate war between the Israelis and the Arabs, and deep and lasting instability throughout the region.

The fourth geopolitical zone of the Ottoman Empire was Anatolia, in other words modern Turkey. By 1914 Turkish nationalism had spread widely among educated Turks who now often saw Anatolia as their true homeland rather than the Ottoman Islamic empire as a whole, which did not mean that they wished to be rid of the empire or did not feel considerable allegiance to it as well. By 1918, however, the empire was irretrievably lost, which drew an exclusive loyalty to and concentration on Anatolia and the Turkish national cause. Mobilizing the Anatolian peasant masses behind this cause was very difficult, however. Peasant horizons were narrow and local. If they identified with anything beyond the local it was with Islam and the Ottoman dynasty, not with the new-fangled Turkish nation dreamed up by the intellectuals of Constantinople in the two decades before 1914 and given meat by the struggles with Christian Balkan nationalists in the faraway borderland of Macedonia. Moreover, by 1918 the Ottoman conscript army had been at war almost continuously for seven years. Even for the very tough and courageous Anatolian peasantry enough was enough. Like the Austrians after 1945, they wanted a quiet life. Even Turkish elites were exhausted by war and demoralized by defeat in 1918.

The one factor that made possible a rebirth of Turkish nationalism was the allied invasion of the Anatolian homeland in 1919–21 and the plans for its partition. Eastern Anatolia was to form an Armenian protectorate, the west to fall to Greece. The Armenians and Greeks were not just Christians and therefore enemies of Islam; during the previous generation they had also often been embroiled with their Turkish and Kurdish neighbours in Anatolia in any number of local disputes. Nothing contributes more to peasant nationalism than a foreign army occupying its villages. During the First World War the Russians had conquered much of eastern Anatolia amidst bitter fighting which, as usually happened in that part of the world, involved the spoliation and massacre of local civilians as well. In the eastern province of Van, for example, 60 per cent of the Muslim population is reckoned to have died during and immediately after the war.[15] In May 1919 the Greek army landed at Smyrna (Izmir), to be greeted as liberators by the large Greek community of the region. In the circumstances the murder, plunder or at least terrorization of much of the local Turkish population was inevitable. It was not too difficult to mobilize Turkish Anatolian elites against an ancestral enemy which sought to annex and partition their homeland. Local notables helped to mobilize the peasantry.[16] For the Turkish and Kurdish masses the war was proclaimed as a struggle for Islam and village against the brutal, irreligious invader. No play was made with republicanism: on the contrary, the sultan was to be rescued from allied captivity.

Nevertheless, the Anatolian war of 1919–22 laid the basis for the Turkish republican nation state and its definitive break with the imperial past. There were good reasons for Turkish elites to break with empire. For almost 150 years before 1920 empire had brought defeat after defeat. The multi-ethnic empire had to an ever-increasing degree been dominated economically by its Christian minorities and dictated to by the Christian great powers. Enver's dream of 'empire renewed' in the Caucasus and Central Asia on a Pan-Turkic basis had proved a dangerous and costly illusion during the First World War. In 1919–22 the sultan himself, the supreme symbol of the Ottoman heritage, had become a seemingly willing and subservient tool of allied plans to destroy Turkey.

Realism too argued for a shift to an exclusively non-imperial Turkish nationalism. By supreme courage and effort the Turks might just regain control of their homeland and the British, French and Italians might just acquiesce in this. Neither Turkish resources nor allied patience would allow any move towards empire's restoration. The Turkish leader in the war of independence, Mustapha Kemal (Atatürk), was a supreme realist. He was also an experienced general, well capable of calculating the realities of power. Reflecting on Woodrow Wilson's advocacy of national self-determination, he commented: 'Poor Wilson, he did not understand that lines that cannot be defended by the bayonet, by force, by honour and dignity, cannot be defended on any other principle.'[17] This was to revert to Bismarck's belief in blood and iron, a fully justified and realistic view in the Middle East of 1919–22. Kemal was determined to keep

Turkish dreams within a territory he could conquer, defend and consolidate. As was bound to be the case, his vision of Turkish republican nationalism drew immense prestige and legitimacy from the fact that Kemal won the war of independence and liberated Turkish national soil from the Christian powers and the Greeks. Generations of defeat had ended with resounding victory. The republic was blessed. It was sustained too by the enormous personal charisma of its founder, Kemal, the victor over the British at Gallipoli in 1915 and now Turkey's George Washington.

The Austrian Republic was founded in defeat, in a sense of illegitimacy; it was weakened by a conviction among much of the elite that little Austria could never achieve anything worthwhile on its own. Nostaliga for empire was widespread. An alternative to the old empire, namely Greater Germany, beckoned from the north. Republican Turkey was different. Pan-Turkic dreams were discredited and discarded. The Ottoman memory 'meant endless defeat, retreat and suffering.' By contrast 'nationalism and the national state meant success, victory and the beginning of a new life.' The empire was identified with backwardness and weakness, the nation with modernity and pride. The result was 'not only a renunciation of empire; there was a positive revulsion.'[18] At the same time, however, the largely Turkish officers, officials and professionals who had been trained to rule an empire now formed the backbone of the new republican state.

Unlike the other losers of the First World War the Turkish Republic accepted the territorial status quo. In the single case where it did harbour ambitions for territory beyond its border, the Alexandretta district of northern Syria, it waited quietly for events to turn in Turkey's favour, which happened in 1939 when the French ceded the district in order to buy Turkish goodwill in the coming world war. Domestically the republican regime was in many ways Jacobin, even Bolshevik. A line was drawn across the past. The monarchy was abolished, Islam disestablished, and the traditional script replaced by the Latin alphabet. The new Turkish identity was to be secular, resolutely modern, and rooted in a state-imposed official doctrine about Turkish history, the glories of the Turkish language and the origins of the Turkish race. Though an almost Stalinist monolithic allegiance to these doctrines was demanded of scholars and political leaders, the Kemalist vision of modernity was essentially Western: unlike the Soviet regime, it offered no universal alternative vision of modernity, merely a Turkish variation on the Western model of

a middle-class and capitalist society. The creation of a true Turkish bourgeoisie was a key aim of the regime, and the survivors of the old Christian
and Jewish merchant class on Turkish soil were squeezed out. In particular, the 1942 wealth tax was used against minority business and resulted
very often in the latter's takeover by local Turkish notables well connected
to the republican regime.[19]

Pressure on the small non-Muslim minorities was all part of a nationalist project to create a monolithic Turkish nation. Minorities and ethnic
divisions had weakened the old empire and allowed foreign intervention.
The new republican nation would avoid this fate. There would be one
nation, speaking one language, educated in state schools to share one
culture and loyalty. The many Muslims whose families had fled to
Anatolia as refugees from the Balkans, Crimea or the Caucasus adapted
to this regime without difficulty. They continued to use their own language in private, sometimes retained some degree of identification with
their ancestral traditions, but had no qualms about their primary identity
as Turks.

With the Kurds, the one large, indigenous non-Turkish people in
Anatolia, matters were more complicated. The republican regime was
fully Jacobin in its refusal to accept a separate Kurdish historical and cultural identity. In its eyes the Kurds were a backward and isolated branch
of the Turkish race whose culture had unfortunately been somewhat cor-
rupted over the centuries by Persian influences. The Turkish state would
restore their true Turkish identity to them but in appropriate modern
form. Many Kurds did in fact become modern Turks through the process
of assimilation, education and urbanization. A considerable proportion
of the Kurds were Alevis, i.e. religious dissidents; they attached more
importance to religion than to ethnicity, identified with their fellow
Alevis and shared their loyalty to the republican regime. On the other
hand, in the remote south-east of Anatolia a strong sense of a separate
Kurdish identity did develop in the twentieth century, partly because the
interwar Kemalist regime lacked the resources or cadres to establish an
effective educational system in this region and inculcate a Turkish identity, myths and language into the local population. By the post-1950 era,
when the state began to be in a position to mount such a programme, a
sense of Kurdish separateness had already taken root and the attempt to
destroy it encountered great opposition. In the end, multi-ethnicity, one
of empire's bugbears, returned to haunt a nation which thought that it
had shed all aspects of its imperial legacy.

By the 1950s other elements of the Ottoman past were also beginning
to impinge powerfully on Turkish public life. Kemalist Turkey had a

much smaller intelligentsia and a far smaller working class than Stalin's USSR. Nor did Kemalism ever possess the same terrifying messianic force as Marxism–Leninism in its heyday. The Kemalist regime, unlike Stalin, never destroyed and transformed the village and its mentality. Deep in the life, values and world-view of the Turkish village was Islam. With mass rural immigration into the cities there also came peasant religion. With the arrival of democracy in 1950 mass values and aspirations could not simply be ignored by the state. Not surprisingly, much of the new, urban mass electorate did not share the elite's secular and Western values. Apart from anything else, they encountered more of the pitfalls and far fewer of the benefits of Western-style modernity. The post-Kemalist state did to a considerable extent adapt itself to the new reality. After 1950 Islam was accepted as a component of the Turkish identity and the state began to spend a large slice of its revenues in support of religion. There remains, however, a very wide gap between the heirs of Kemal on the one hand and the Islamic political parties on the other as regards the role of Islam in Turkish family and cultural life, not to mention in the state's foreign policy and Turkey's alignment with the Western or Muslim worlds. One result of this split is a more pluralist debate about the late Ottoman era and its politics. The Ottoman effort, above all under Abdul Hamid II, to retain Islam as a key element in the life and legitimacy of the state again has its public defenders.[20]

Cyprus was another imperial legacy that returned to trouble Ankara from the 1950s. The island had been conquered by the Ottomans in 1571. It was de facto ceded to the British in 1878. London's interest in the island was as a military base, and this became very important to the British during the Cold War when they were ejected from the southern shore of the Mediterranean. In 1878 roughly one-quarter of the Cypriot population was Turkish, by 1960 rather less than one-fifth. Much of the Turkish elite left the island with the coming of British rule. True to Kemalist tradition, the Turkish government remained mute about Cyprus so long as British imperial rule prevailed. By 1960, however, the British were preparing to pull out from everywhere but their two sovereign base territories on the island.

During the 1950s a Greek-Cypriot nationalist movement had attempted to achieve union (*enosis*) between Cyprus and Greece by a campaign of terror. Turkish Cypriots were a disproportionate element in the British Cypriot police and frequent targets for terrorists. London was happy to bring Ankara into Cypriot affairs in order to balance Athens and ease its own partial retreat from responsibility for the island. In 1959–60 the British, Greek and Turkish governments agreed a constitution for independent Cyprus. This embodied a guaranteed share in power for the Turkish minority together with autonomy for their townships and protection of their cultural rights. As is often the way with such compromises, the system of government that resulted was unwieldy and prey to many mutual vetoes. In 1963 the Greek–Cypriot leadership attempted radically to modify the constitution. The mass of Greek Cypriots in any case believed that the island belonged to them by historical and majority right. Political tension exploded into widespread pogroms against the Turks. By 1964 half the Turkish population had concentrated into an area which constituted only 1.6 per cent of the island's territory[21] but was run by the Cypriot Turks' own local administration. Neither Britain, a guarantor of the 1960 constitution, nor the United States did anything to reverse this situation. In subsequent years low-level violence continued, with many more Turks than Greeks as its victims. In 1974 the Greek military regime in Athens, desperate for prestige, backed a coup in Cyprus which deposed Archbishop Makarios, the island's Greek Cypriot ruler, and proclaimed union with Greece. Again, the British, the Americans and the international community did nothing. Athens refused to budge. The Turkish government invoked its rights as guarantor of the 1960 constitution and invaded Cyprus.

As a result of Turkish military intervention 37 per cent of the island came under Turkish Cypriot control. Somewhere between 140,000 and 200,000 Greeks fled the new Turkish enclave in northern Cyprus. Tens of thousands of Turks fled in the other direction.[22] The de facto partition of the island remains unresolved and unrecognized by the international community more than a quarter of a century later. It remains too one of the key sources of conflict between Turkey and Greece, which could quite easily spill over into war, and which contributes to the tension throughout the Balkans and the eastern Mediterranean.

Cyprus is a classic example of post-Ottoman and post-imperial conflict, postponed but not resolved by the intervening period of British imperial rule. It was a reminder of what so often happened in the past when the Ottoman Empire receded. It was a foretaste of what was to come in the Balkans at the end of the Cold War.

The history of ethnic cleansing began with the Ottoman Empire's retreat in the late eighteenth century. By 1914 many millions of Muslims from the Balkans, Crimea and the North Caucasus had taken refuge in Ottoman territory or died in the conflicts that engulfed these regions when Ottoman rule ended. Where they could, the Ottomans resorted to wholesale massacre of Christian civilians in the attempt to suppress rebellion and sustain their empire. The process reached a crescendo between 1914 and 1922 with the Armenian genocide (estimated at up to one-and-a-half million deaths), the death of perhaps two million or more Anatolian Muslims,[23] and the forced population exchange at the end of the 1919–22 war which saw 1.5 million Greeks uprooted from Asia and 500,000 Turks from Europe.

Even then the process was not over. The events in Cyprus in the 1960s and 1970s are not the only link between the terrible years of ethnic cleansing during the Ottoman Empire's collapse and the tactic's return to Europe in the 1990s. In 1870 there were perhaps as many Muslims as Orthodox Christians within the borders of present-day Bulgaria. By 1920 a mere 14 per cent of the population was Muslim. Nevertheless, a further 100,000 Muslims left Bulgaria in 1934–9, and 155,000 more were expelled in 1950–51. As the Bulgarian Communist regime approached its final crisis, persecution of Muslims was stepped up, and 370,000 fled Bulgaria in 1989.[24] Neither in Cyprus nor in Bulgaria were expulsion and flight accompanied by mass murder on the scale of the 1990s. On the other hand, even the 1990s do not remotely reach the level of genocidal horror of some episodes in the decline and fall of the Ottoman Empire. Only ignorance of history and lack of imagination allowed Europeans to be taken so wholly unawares by ethnic cleansing in the Balkans of the 1990s. The precedents were clear and appalling.

AFTER THE BRITISH

The end of empire was much less traumatic for the British than for the Turks or the Austrians, or indeed for the French. It was not accompanied by revolution or civil war in the UK. Britain's traditional political institutions – parliamentary government and constitutional monarchy – were untouched. Britain was not flooded by White settlers in overseas colonies ethnically cleansed in the course of their liberation from imperial rule. Decolonization entailed some humiliations, of which the fiasco at Suez in 1956 was probably the worst, but Britain suffered no equivalent of Dien Bien Phu, let alone of defeat in a world war. The 1950s and 1960s were decades of rising prosperity, full employment and the benefits of the new welfare state: life for the ordinary man and woman was much more comfortable than it had been in the era when Britain was the world's leading imperial power. The end of empire did not even in the short term require the Englishman, unlike the Turk or Austrian, to think afresh about what it meant to be English and how to identify with the British state.

An English nation had existed well before the British Empire was created. Shakespeare, the vernacular Bible, the Spanish Armada, and the seventeenth-century consolidation of parliamentary monarchy were key elements in the creation of this nation and of its political identity. The late nineteenth-century advocates of imperial federation, Arthur Seeley and his followers, had dreamed of developing a 'Greater British' nation and identity but they had never succeeded. Very few Englishmen thought of Australia, let alone Nigeria, in the same way as they thought of Kent. The strength of emotional identification with English soil was totally different from the commitment to overseas empire. In constitutional terms the United Kingdom and the overseas empire were always sharply distinct. The loss of empire therefore had minimal constitutional implications for Britain. For most British people the impact of two victorious wars was far greater than the loss of empire. Victory legitimizes institutions and a community's established ways. It had this effect in post-1945 Britain too. The retreat from empire was for the most part presented to the public as the culmination of Britain's long-held commitment to democracy and self-government, in other words as a satisfactory conclusion to a well-executed mission of trusteeship. There was just enough truth in this, and just enough dignity and mutual goodwill in Britain's retreat from most of its colonies, to make the myth acceptable. For a time too the Commonwealth was a fig-leaf to hide Britain's declining status, as was perhaps the pomp and circumstance that continued to surround the monarchy.

Of course Britain's diplomatic, military and political elites understood and experienced a sense of declining status and shrinking horizons. In this sense they were more like the Austrians than the Turks, for whom the loss of empire was almost a liberation. But the gloom and partial loss of confidence that affected sections of the governing elite had as much to do with Britain's relative economic decline in comparison to the rest of Europe as it did with the loss of empire. If empire's loss mattered before 1960, in the 1970s and 1980s economic decline was a much more burning issue. In any case Britain's loss of status was far less dramatic than Austria's. As a victor in 1945, Britain was one of the 'big three' though admittedly the junior member of the triumvirate. For more than a decade after 1945 it was much richer than devastated continental Europe. It retained a global role and influence for at least two decades after 1945. It was the key US ally in the Cold War and this overshadowed the loss of empire, contributed to a continuing British sense of global mission, and reinforced the wartime sense of unity with the Americans, a sense which went beyond a mere military alliance of convenience. The British brokered the 1954 Geneva peace in Indochina and defeated the communist insurgency in Malaya. Suez was a shock but it was really the economic crises and the radical shift in morals and culture in the 1960s that marked a clear break with the past.

Empire's loss had greater implications for the United Kingdom and a British identity than it had for England and the English. An English empire had existed for a hundred years before the Anglo-Scottish Union of 1707. Access to England's colonial trade was one factor in the Scottish desire for union. Under the Union Scottish west-coast industry and the Scottish aristocracy and professional middle-class had benefited greatly from empire. The British state as a whole and in particular specific institutions such as the monarchy and the armed forces gained additional lustre and prestige from the association with empire. At least as important, however, was that Britain had been the richest and most powerful state in the world, that it – almost uniquely in 1850 – lived under a liberal constitutional order, and that it was widely admired and envied. Declining Scottish enthusiasm for the Union after 1965 was linked to the reduced significance of these factors quite as much as to the loss of empire.

All Western Europe now had liberal-democratic governments and the European Union offered the prospect of linking a separate Scottish state and identity to a larger unit which would provide a wide market, a sense of security, and an alternative to isolation. The discovery of North Sea oil, 'Scottish oil', for a time encouraged the belief that Scotland could manage the economics of independence without difficulty. The decline in religious commitment weakened the sense of the Protestant British Union's separation from a Papist Europe. Nor in any case was Scotland unique. In much of Western Europe peoples long subsumed in supposed 'nation states' began to assert their separate identity and even sometimes a claim to statehood: the Flemish, Catalans, Basques and Bretons all belonged to this group. Since Scotland was an ancient kingdom and had always retained under the Union both many distinct institutions and its own cultural identity it is in no way surprising that it should conform to this common West European trend. The devolution of power to an elected Scottish assembly may encourage or may divert the Scottish desire for independence. In global terms it matters little either way. The United Kingdom was a strategic alliance to create a great power. Whatever the Scots do, that great power is dead. The main *raison d'être* of the United Kingdom is therefore finished. Democratic institutions and habits are too deeply entrenched in mainland Britain for Scottish independence to be accompanied by violence. The English are quite capable of accepting the

Union's ending psychologically. A certain Anglo-Scottish mutual sourness is about the worst one could expect. Moreover, independence within the European Union is a rather different matter from the glories of Bannockburn, though political rhetoric may no doubt sometimes suggest otherwise. What the impact of the Union's ending might be in Ulster is an interesting point: the Protestant settlement there was after all more Scots than English.

Ireland is a bigger and more complex issue from the perspective of empire. The end of empire in the 26-county Irish Free State (and later Republic) was accompanied by a rapid decline in the size of the Anglo-Irish, Protestant minority. This was 10 per cent of the overall population in 1911, 7 per cent in 1926 and 3.5 per cent by 1981.[25] During the war of independence and the subsequent civil war a very small number of Protestant civilians were murdered, while a considerably larger number felt intimidated or in some cases had their property or business destroyed. Overall, perhaps 1,400 people lost their lives on both sides during the war of independence. The number of deaths in the subsequent civil war in the Free State and in ethnic conflict between Catholics and Protestants in Northern Ireland was also very small when compared to the awful bloodshed and the ethnic cleansing which accompanied the demise of the other empires, though of course Ireland's population was also small. During the Algerian war of independence, for example, the French killed perhaps 140,000 Algerians and the Nationalist FLN about a further 100,000 of their own Muslim people.[26]

Nevertheless, within the republican movement and the republican elite the Civil War of 1922–3 was fought with great viciousness. The IRA assassinated Members of Parliament and judges, the government responding with 'breathtakingly draconian measures'. 'Summary executions without trial, on the basis of arbitrary reprisal, were carried out by ex-comrades.'[27] Given this history, the strength of democracy and political stability in independent Ireland was remarkable. The new Ireland was unequivocally Catholic and nationalist. Protestants might well find it hard to identify with this Irish nation. But the Irish state bent over backwards not to discriminate against Protestants and there was little ethnic cleansing even during the war, let alone after 1921: less indeed than occurred in Belfast where the victims were the Catholic community.

Even more remarkably, the republican elite, which had fought against each other so bitterly in the Civil War, was subsequently for the most part reconciled to parliamentary democracy. De Valera's supporters, the defeated side in the Civil War, entered Parliament as the Fianna Fail Party in 1927 and gained power in the 1933 elections. When they lost the 1948 elections it was taken as self-evident that they would resign power into the hands of the victors of the Civil War and their heirs, Fine Gael. One explanation for this remarkable development might be that by 1914 constitutional government, civil rights and democracy had put down roots in Ireland. From this perspective the wars of 1919–23 were an aberration, the return to constitutional politics a reassertion of the Irish norm. David Fitzpatrick comments that 'Irish democracy remained firmly derivative from its detested British prototype.'[28] Another line of argument, not necessarily contradictory, stresses that post-1921 Ireland had a large middle class, a much larger community of educated, property-owning peasant-farmers, not many workers or agricultural labourers, and a very powerful Catholic Church that was identified strongly with Irishness and the new national state. The strength of Irish democracy is therefore unsurprising. The British themselves had bought out the old and formerly dominant landowning aristocracy, whose continued existence might easily have been a spur to rural radicalism.[29]

Though in the circumstances admirably stable and democratic, the new Ireland was also, however, very parochial. In rejecting the British Empire and losing much of the old Anglo-Irish elite, the Republic also lost its window on the world. Among the great benefits of membership of the European Union was that it encouraged not just economic development but also broader perspectives which were not encumbered by imperial memories or by the traditional Irish obsession with England. This made it easier to come to terms with Irish history and to build a more constructive relationship with the English, not least over the question of Ulster. With a post-imperial government in London increasingly seeing Ulster as a burden rather than a strategic asset, the road was open to compromise.

For the historian of empire, and perhaps above all for the Russianist, Ulster is one of the most important and most fascinating questions in British imperial history. As with the Russians, Germans, Austrians and Turks, here is empire within Europe, in the borderland of the dominant imperial people itself. During the imperial era, here as in many other cases, this dominant people colonized its borderland without however destroying or completely expelling the native population. When empire falls, will the colonized region be incorporated into the newly independent 'native' state? Will the descendants of the settlers be ethnically cleansed? Will they set up an independent state of their own? Or will they remain part of the metropolitan nation state, now shorn of its empire? What will the relationship be between the descendants of the settlers and the native people in the borderland? How will this affect the relations between the old metropolitan state and its newly independent former colonized neighbours? These were burning questions in the ex-Ottoman Balkans, and in post-Habsburg and post-Hohenzollern Central Europe. They are crucial to the future of post-Soviet Northern Eurasia.

From a Russian perspective a number of points stand out clearly as regards Ulster. As empire in Ireland reached its crisis in 1906–23 the Ulster Protestants were enormously proud of being British and had a deep sense of superiority over the Catholic population. 'For Irish Unionists, being "British" was a shorthand for remaining part of God's chosen people, with all the spiritual and material privileges that this conferred.'[30] No doubt this fact seems self-evident to most historians of Britain and of other imperial peoples. It is very far from being self-evident in contemporary Russia and the Russian diaspora, however; both pride and its absence are important factors in the behaviour of imperial peoples stranded, actually or potentially, in new nation states dominated by 'natives'.

British parliamentary liberalism and later democracy also had a big impact on the way that the Ulster, and Irish, question evolved. They limited the imperial government's ability to dominate the Irish agenda or retard the development of national and regional consciousness. The Loyal Orange Institution, crucial to the Ulster Protestant identity, dates back to 1795, in other words to a world still far from democracy but already possessing parliamentary institutions and some civil rights. In the nineteenth century democratic politics in both Ireland and Ulster, together with freedom of speech and publication, allowed communities to organize themselves, to select their own leaders, and to define, articulate and defend their own interests and identities. In Ireland Protestants and Catholics to a considerable extent defined these identities against each other and in terms of their relationship to England. An open society and democratic struggle between political parties encouraged the sharpening of these identities and their mobilization for political purposes.

From London's perspective in 1900 Irish political development since 1850 was in many ways encouraging. The revolutionary and violent tradition in Irish politics had to a great extent been sidelined. Constitutional nationalism was dominant. Home Rule if it came would satisfy most constitutional nationalists for a time at least, though the Unionists' argument that it would merely whet Irish appetites and put key levers of power and patronage in nationalist hands also had its point. The future of a Home Rule Ireland in 1900 was no more certain than that of present-day Scotland with its new autonomous parliament. One certainty from London's perspective was that if Ireland was to enjoy Home Rule it would be much safer if Ulster remained within Ireland as England's Trojan Horse. The threat of Ulster's secession backed by London's power ought to be sufficient to keep a Home Rule administration in line. But the rulers in London were not the Emperor Francis Joseph in 1867 or the Soviet Politburo, calculating imperial interests and denying a voice to their subjects, and not least to the diasporas. In London Irish and Ulster MPs had a considerable voice. They could exploit party political rivalry in Britain itself, sometimes even holding the balance of power. Nor was membership of a democratic polity any obstacle to organizing their local community to use or threaten violence as a means of bending parliament to their will. Indeed, in the absence of a police state the process was much easier. By 1914 the interaction of party political conflict in London and the mobilization – even arming – of rival communities in Ireland was threatening the breakdown of the constitution, civil war in Ireland, violence in some British cities, and the paralysis of the British government at a time of supreme crisis in Europe. Interestingly, when the British ambassador in Petersburg spoke to the tsar and his foreign minister in the spring of 1914, the discussion centred on the impact of domestic revolutionary crisis on the foreign policy not of Russia but of the United Kingdom.[31]

The British Empire did not collapse all at once. Even when India was lost in 1947 great importance was still attached to imperial possessions in the Middle East, Africa and South-East Asia. Partly this was for economic reasons. Commodity exports from the colonies were crucial dollar-earners for Britain. In the immediate postwar era it was not at all clear that the world would experience decades of economic growth and a return to something like the Victorian free-trading system. If on the contrary the global economy repeated its interwar history then not just colonial commodities but also imperial economic blocs might be crucial. This possibility lingered in some British minds into the 1950s. The major military commitment in Malaya during the 1950s owed something to the importance London attached to Malayan tin and rubber, though it was also linked to a determination to check the advance of communism in the context of war in Korea, Mao's triumph in China and conflict in Vietnam.

London hoped to retain much of its global influence despite the loss of formal empire. In the immediate post-1945 years it hoped that the Commonwealth would be a vehicle for this influence. The White Commonwealth had after all provided vast assistance to Britain during the war despite having no formal obligation to do so. But the war had revealed clearly American pre-eminence within the anglophone camp and in the Cold War global competition the White Commonwealth countries dealt separately with Washington and looked to it for leadership. For Britain too the relationship with the United States and American commitment to security in Europe took precedence over all other considerations. London was gratified that India agreed to join the Commonwealth after independence but the war that promptly broke out with its fellow Commonwealth member and neighbour, Pakistan, showed the limits of solidarity within a no-longer White Commonwealth. In the 1960s India became an ally of the Soviet Union and Pakistan a client of Washington. In Malaya British influence lasted longer. During the confrontation with Indonesia in the early 1960s Britain honoured its commitment under the 1957 defence agreement and provided valuable assistance.

Informal empire, however, usually requires greater resources than direct rule. There is no native tax-base on which to draw. There is competition on an equal basis with other countries as regards economic aid, military assistance, trade concessions and forms of cultural 'imperialism' such as subsidized places at metropolitan universities for students from the ex-colonies. Former colonial subjects are no longer constrained by political power in their choice of outside assistance or goods. By the late 1960s an increasingly poor Britain was no longer able or willing to compete. Willingness was a factor. Partly for reasons of prestige the French subsidized many of their former African colonies, and deployed troops to protect their borders in emergencies and even sometimes to prop up their rulers against internal unrest. The British quickly washed their hands of Africa and in 1969 withdrew too from 'east of Suez', with the partial exception of the small emirates of the Arabian Gulf.

The legacy of British empire in its former colonies is a huge and complicated subject, not least because this empire was so enormous and so diverse. To compare post-independence Ireland to post-colonial Africa, for example, is almost an insult to all concerned. Levels of wealth and literacy differed hugely, as did the length of imperial rule and the speed with which colonized peoples and their elites were forced to come to terms with dramatic changes in culture and values. The ancient roots of national identity in Ireland and their consolidation in nineteenth-century schools and Victorian semi-democratic politics bear no resemblance to the history of African peoples under British colonial rule.

Nevertheless, some common features of the British imperial heritage do exist and provide a basis for cautious comparison. The international borders bequeathed by empire are a political problem, partly because they frequently divide peoples between many states or cut across natural trade routes. In addition, so long as the imperial power existed it provided for security against external foes: its successors in a small colony might prove unable to do so. A classic example of the latter problem is the Iraqi invasion of Kuwait in 1990: the division of the Kurds between four states is an obvious example of the former. It is, however, to the point that even the Kurds are not demanding unification in a single country. To do so would incite the wrath of all the neighbouring states and of all the international community. It would also require agreement or civil war between the many groups and factions into which the Kurds are divided in these four successor states to Middle Eastern empire. Given their usual lack of ethnic and historical legitimacy, it is the survival of almost all the colonial-era borders that is most surprising. These borders were most artificial in Africa: nevertheless, not until the establishment of Eritrean independence in 1993 were post-colonial borders infringed and a new state created on the African continent. Nor in today's world are wars between existing states over borders or national irredenta frequent. Of the 86 violent conflicts recorded by the UN between 1989 and 1997 only three involved war between states: the rest were wars within states and were usually caused by inter-ethnic and inter-communal conflict.[32]

Post-colonial borders often play a role in encouraging these conflicts. The imperial power frequently created colonial states on a much bigger territorial scale than the native peoples wanted or could create for themselves. This was particularly true in enormous and sparsely populated Africa, which one scholar reckons had 7,000 separate political units in the immediate pre-colonial era.[33] The colonial states often therefore contained many peoples and had no historical legitimacy in native eyes. Sometimes the British destroyed native kingdoms in the process of creating their empire: they did this for instance in nineteenth-century Kandy and Burma. Even where British rule neither destroyed nor delegitimized a native dynasty, a historical kingdom and its royal house might be a source of regional rather than national loyalty in the post-colonial era and therefore a cause of fear and jealousy to the rulers of the new and often barely legitimate state. Sometimes, however, the British both protected the traditional rulers and united them into viable federations to which independence was subsequently granted. The two leading examples of this are

Malaya and the United Arab Emirates. In the British Empire this worked only where the imperial power had a cosy relationship with native dynasties, where the emergence of radical nationalism did not delegitimize empire's clients, and where the rulers shared religion and ethnicity with their subjects. In the French and Dutch empires, however, King Mohammed V of Morocco and Sultan Hamengkubuwana IX of Yogyakarta were rare but brilliant examples of native monarchs who legitimized their dynasties by timing to perfection the abandonment of the colonial power and their adherence to the national cause.

An empire brought external resources to the government of colonies. This did not mean subsidies from London: financial self-sufficiency was Holy Writ in the British colonial empire. But it did mean British-officered bureaucracies, armies and police forces. It was not easy for natives to identify with the colonial state and its alien and often racially very arrogant officials. On the other hand the British-officered bureaucracy, army and police provided a backbone for the colonial state. The British officials by the twentieth century were usually honest, incorruptible and fair according to their (admittedly often blinkered and self-serving) lights. They generally stood outside and above native factions, and ethnic groups and interests. The colonial state could to some extent mediate between native peoples and interests. It could also usually deter or repress inter-communal violence, so long as its authority was not undermined and local hatreds enflamed by the prospect of imminent decolonization.

Inevitably it was harder for a native bureaucracy and army to fulfil this role once the British had gone. Army and bureaucracy could not stand outside and above society in the former colonial manner. To some extent they were bound to be taken over by groups within society who sought to use them for their own private and sectional interests. This was particularly dangerous in multi-ethnic societies with a weak sense of overall national identity, little experience of citizenship and strong local loyalties. Patron–client relations, kinship links and local solidarity were not just often deeply embedded in a people's culture and values, but also offered some security in a very uncertain world where the state provided no effective welfare net, the rule of law barely applied, and the government was viewed as a source of jobs and patronage rather than as an impartial mediator in society.

On the whole the situation was more stable in India than in Pakistan, let alone most of Africa. The Indian state was historically more legitimate. The British had ruled an all-Indian state for generations. The bureaucracy and army were formidable, deep-rooted institutions with a strong *esprit de corps*. By the time independence came in 1947 there were many senior Indian officers and officials to whom power could safely be passed. In Africa the colonial state and its institutions were never as legitimate, deep-rooted or effective as this. British rule had been much more short-lived and in most cases, when it began, the Africans who were governed had been less literate and sophisticated than, for example, Bengali society at the commencement of the British Raj in the eighteenth century. When British rule ended in Africa there was seldom an equivalent of the Indian Civil Service to which power could be handed, let alone of a Congress Party with decades of political experience in a parliamentary system and a strong commitment to supra-ethnic Indian unity and identity.

The British Empire contained three major diaspora peoples, of whom the British themselves were one. The temperate lands which they colonized en masse – Canada, New Zealand, Australia and the United States – after empire's demise became largely anglophone, White-dominated nation states. These 'new Britains', above all of course the United States, were the basis for the pre-eminence of the English language and of basically British political values and institutions worldwide at the end of the second millennium AD. 'Decolonization' in Australasia and Canada caused no real problems since London had long reconciled itself to their possible eventual independence. The continued existence of pockets of indigenous peoples and their claims to lost lands and rights were an embarrassment to these White post-colonial societies but not a major one. In Australia, Canada and the United States most native peoples had been too marginalized and decimated to make a major impact on White society. A far more significant impediment to nation-building in Canada were the Quebecois. A conquered European people with their own national territory were much more difficult to integrate into an anglophone nation than other immigrants from Europe who came voluntarily to anglophone colonies, had no ancestral territorial claims in the new world, and in varying degrees were happy to assimilate to anglophone culture, while at the same time of course contributing to the creation of new-world anglophone national identities which were different from the British.

As is generally the case with the end of empire, the main potential problems for the dominant imperial people came neither in territories that they had swamped with colonists, nor in lands they had left uncolonized and ruled through bureaucrats, soldiers and merchants alone. It was a middle range of territories with sizeable White settler communities but large native majorities whose decolonization was likely to cause most trouble to London. Above all this meant South Africa and Southern Rhodesia (Zimbabwe). From London's perspective matters were both simplified and complicated by the well-established tradition of granting self-government to sizeable White communities. This allowed the White South Africans and Rhodesians to ride roughshod over native interests. It also allowed these White minorities to proclaim their independence from Britain, de jure in South Africa and de facto in Southern Rhodesia. In most ways South African independence was a vast relief for the British. Having contributed greatly to the creation of a wealthy (by African standards) but also extremely racist and unjust society, London could avoid any opprobrium or responsibility for the consequences. Since in 1965 Rhodesia was still a crown colony, it was not so easy to evade any responsibility for its future. In comparison to the French or Portuguese, however, the British escaped very lightly from their African empire. They had the good sense not to attempt to hold this empire in the face of serious native resistance. They also never pretended to integrate African, or other, colonies into the British nation state. That is one important reason why unlike not only the French and the Portuguese but also the Turks and the Germans, post-imperial Britain was not faced by an influx of 'overseas British' fleeing the consequences of empire's collapse.

The other two diaspora peoples in the British Empire were the Indians and the Chinese. They spread widely, though not as widely as the British, partly because they were excluded from most of the self-governing White dominions. The mass of overseas Indians and Chinese were often labourers in plantations or mines, work which the indigenous peasantry shunned: they provided too a mass of peddlers and shopkeepers. Their elite was initially mostly composed of merchants, though some of these later moved into finance and industry. British colonial officialdom often disliked the Chinese or Indian businessman, just as it also often preferred the Bedouin warrior to the Jew. Bureaucratic and military paternalism perceived in native princes, soldiers and peasants both a sort of Romantic communion of values and a *raison d'être* for paternalistic rule. Nevertheless, the empire provided protection, some privileges and many advantages for diaspora business elites. Like the Jews in the Habsburg Empire, the Chinese elite in the Malay Peninsula and Singapore assimilated the dominant imperial language and high culture, in this case English. So long as the empire existed it would have been even more inconceivable for a member of the Chinese elite to become Malayan rather than English than it was for a member of the Jewish business elite to become Czech rather than German. Even after empire's demise the world's dominant international language and cosmopolitan culture was more attractive than becoming a Malay, even if the Malays themselves had been willing to offer full assimilation.

As with the Jews in post-imperial Central and Eastern Europe, the Indians and Chinese were often deeply unpopular with the indigenous peoples in whose lands they lived.[34] Sometimes there were specific reasons for this. In Ceylon, for example, tea plantations with Tamil labour imported from India had been created by the British partly on land expropriated from the Sinhalese peasantry. Not surprisingly, after independence the determination to get this land back added to other causes of anti-Tamil feeling. Uniquely, in 1964 the Indian government agreed on the repatriation of 525,000 labourers over the next 15 years, in return for which a further 300,000 were to be granted Sri Lankan citizenship.[35]

Popular resentment of the Chinese trader and money-lender, 'relentless creditors of the native peasantry',[36] was very reminiscent of attitudes to Jews in East-Central Europe. Above all, the Indians and Chinese were resented because of their enormous economic power: in the Indian case this applied primarily in Burma and East Africa, both of which were opened up to Indian businessmen under British rule. In Uganda and Burma the Indians were driven out after independence. In South-East Asia the Chinese had deeper roots, though their numbers and economic power had grown enormously under European imperial rule. Even in the 1980s it was estimated that in Indonesia between 70 per cent and 75 per cent of private domestic capital was owned by Chinese, who constituted less than 3 per cent of the population. In Malaysia Chinese made up 35 per cent of the population but owned 85 per cent of private domestic capital.[37] In Malaysia the Chinese were subjected to a major pogrom in 1969 and to a range of discriminatory policies whose declared aim was to reduce inequalities of wealth between the Malay and Chinese communities. In Indonesia the period of instability between 1959 and 1968 saw terrible pogroms against the Chinese, though these did occur in the context of massive overall violence, the great majority of whose victims were native Indonesians. The fall of the Suharto regime brought further anti-Chinese pogroms, which included the mass rape of Chinese women.[38]

The position of the Chinese in South-East Asia was not made any easier by local fears of the potential power of China in the region, and claims made by Beijing on the allegiance of the overseas Chinese. When China went communist in 1948 and the Cold War engulfed the region matters worsened. In addition, however, one has to take into account the emergence in this period of modern indigenous nationalism in the region. Often raw, resentful, insecure and in the process of self-definition, this new nationalism found a satisfactory target in ex-imperial diaspora peoples. Maybe the experience of colonial rule deepened the insecurity: free from colonial rule and blessed by an ancient monarchy and a secure cultural identity, the Thais proved much more confident and generous in the treatment of the Chinese than was true of their neighbours.

Nevertheless, the attitude of the Malays or Fijians to the Chinese and Indian communities respectively was almost inevitably hostile. Under imperial rule, when native peoples had no control over immigration the British had encouraged the mass immigration of outsiders who not merely in some cases dominated the economy but also in the Fijian case came very close to turning native peoples into a minority in their own lands. This raises not just practical problems about inter-communal relations in the post-imperial era but also more theoretical issues as well. Are the rights of immigrants, especially if they become a numerical majority, to be equal or even superior to those of a native people whose only homeland this is? On the whole the predominant Western answer is that democracy and equal civil rights for all must prevail. That is an easier position for former colonizing peoples to take than it is for those whom they have colonized. Nor does it easily accord with the deep fear and resentment in Western society of levels of immigration far lower than those that brought the Chinese to Malaya or the Indians to Fiji in colonial times.

So long as empire appeared permanent and the British had no thought of decolonization, they not merely protected but also often favoured minorities. The Indian and Chinese diasporas made a huge contribution to the empire's economy, above all to its modern, commercial and export sectors. Some indigenous minorities made a disproportionate contribution to empire's administration and military power, sometimes because they had (or were perceived by the British to have) particular skills or qualities such as literacy or valour, sometimes because they were seen as more loyal than the local majority people. It is in the nature of empires to play divide-and-rule at least to some extent, just as it is also natural for minorities to look to the imperial power for protection against potentially dominant local peoples who may be ancestral rivals. The British did not create religious, ethnic and historical differences among their subjects: in most cases they could not have erased them even had they tried. But the practice of imperial rule did sometimes sharpen ethnic and communal differences and tensions. So too inevitably did the approach of decolonization, which often caused local majorities to clamour to regain full control of 'their' country and government, and minorities to fear exclusion.

The onset of decolonization somewhat changed British perceptions and priorities. The main aim now was to avoid chaos, which would be bad for British prestige and self-esteem and would offend British officials' real sense of responsibility for the peoples and territories they governed. A stable successor regime had to be found which would as far as possible protect Britain's remaining strategic and economic interests, and would not go over to the Soviet side in the Cold War. Stability, British interests and even perhaps democracy all pointed towards doing a deal with the dominant local people and its elites. Pushing a defence of minority rights or interests too strongly would merely annoy the majority and harm British interests. It might also possibly require a long-term British commitment to the minority's defence, which contradicted one of the key aims of decolonization, which was precisely a reduction in Britain's worldwide commitments. In any case Britain's own constitution, an inevitable model for British officials, contained no bill of rights, no guarantees for minorities and no proportional representation.

To partition a colony between its peoples would probably infuriate the majority and would reverse a long tradition of trying to create large, economically viable and defensible units. It might well create terrible precedents for other colonies. Moreover, even if the geographical distribution of peoples made partition conceivable, it could very easily degenerate into hideous ethnic cleansing. A further basic point was that the closer decolonization came, the less room for manoeuvre the British possessed. Native officials and soldiers could not be expected automatically to obey the orders of a departing imperial regime if faced by the opposition of their own people and of their own future political masters. In 1946–7 a major reason for getting out of India quickly was awareness that the Indian bureaucracy and army were no longer wholly reliable weapons in British hands given Britain's imminent departure and spiralling inter-ethnic and inter-communal tensions.

The history of decolonization in South Asia illustrates many of these general points but it also showed how very different the process was from colony to colony. The British had lost Burma to the Japanese in the Second World War. They returned in 1945 anxious to restore the economy by a period of direct rule and to pay their debts to minority peoples who had often helped them greatly against the Japanese. It quickly became clear, however, that the Burmese majority and its elites controlled most of the levers of power. To dislodge them would only have been possible by the sort of military conquest which the Dutch attempted (and failed to achieve) in Indonesia between 1945 and 1949. Except in Malaya, where they had majority support, the British never attempted this kind of military effort after 1945. Burma was certainly not worth such an investment. The colony was essentially abandoned without any effective safeguards for minority rights and without there even being a stable Burmese government to which power could be ceded. Civil war was the immediate and inevitable result. The armed struggle of some of the minorities against the government in Rangoon continues to this day.

The fate of India was far more important to British interests and British prestige. By 1945–7 London would have preferred to hand over power to an undivided Indian successor state. The Congress Party was regarded as the best available guarantor of stability and was trusted to have an at least relatively favourable attitude post-independence to Britain and her inter-ests. The Congress would certainly oppose the Communist Party, stamp on social revolution in the countryside, and keep its distance from Moscow. Having previously looked on the princely states as a possible counterforce to the Congress the British now abandoned them – in terms of *Realpolitik* quite rightly, since the largely Muslim princes and landed aristocracies were losing ground with every year as industrial and com-mercial development, a growing Hindu middle class, and the beginnings of mass electoral politics bit into their power. But neither London nor the Congress could impose Indian unity on the Muslim League once the latter had gained the support of the elites in the Muslim majority provinces. By 1946 London was in any case anxious to cut its commit-ments and be gone. Since it would no longer be ruling India it was wholly unprepared to commit scores of thousands of troops and vast (and in 1946 non-existent) financial resources to imposing and policing a settlement. Competitive democratic party politics and the mobilization of religious and communal feeling to gain support in elections greatly worsened tension between Hindus and Muslims in 1946–7. Impending British departure further heightened the tension. The sudden need to draw a new state frontier through territories that were historically united and lived in by Hindus, Muslims and Sikhs caused massacre and ethnic cleans-ing in Punjab on a vast scale.

Partition on religious and communal lines not only resulted in great immediate suffering but also created a new Pakistani state which was never viable in its post-independence form. Nearly a thousand miles of Indian territory separated East and West Pakistan. Islam was never likely to suffice to hold this state together in the face of geography and of the state's domination by the Punjab and its elite. East Bengal's revolt against rule by an alien Punjabi state resulted in further massacres, war between India and Pakistan, and Bangladeshi (i.e. East Bengali) independence in 1971. Meanwhile, predictably, amidst the bitterness of communal violence and partition in 1947, conflict erupted between Pakistan and India over possession of the border province of Kashmir. The province's status remains in dispute to this day and is a key factor in the acute hostility of India and Pakistan, both of which are now armed with nuclear weapons. In both Pakistan and India domestic party politics and fears for domestic political stability feed into aggressive foreign and defence policies which could easily escalate into renewed war.

Decolonization in Ceylon (Sri Lanka) was far more peaceful and orderly than in India or in Burma. There was no inter-communal violence, no whisper of partition and not even a very fervent independence movement. For eight years after independence Ceylon was run by established Sinhalese elites who dominated the United National Party and achieved a *modus vivendi* with their Tamil peers from the north of the island. Within Ceylon there were roughly seven Sinhalese for every two Tamils in these years. The traditional centre of Tamil settlement was in the north. Before the Europeans arrived Ceylon consisted of three kingdoms, the northern one being Tamil and the other two Sinhalese. The island was finally united by the British in 1815.

Upon independence the Tamils inevitably feared Sinhalese domination. The Sinhalese often felt that this was their moment to reclaim the island for themselves. They believed, not wrongly, that the British had recruited a disproportionate number of Tamils into government service and that Tamils had an unfair share of middle-class jobs and places in higher education. Indeed, even in 1969 Tamils had half of all the places in university medical faculties and only slightly fewer in engineering departments.[39] Since the nineteenth century Buddhist Sinhalese scholars have increasingly stressed that the whole island really belongs to the Sinhalese alone. Despite the fact that most Tamils had inhabited Ceylon for centuries they were defined as latecomers and as colonists. From Ireland to Bohemia, Cyprus and Fiji this is a familiar theme of nationalist 'intellectuals', even sometimes of very civilized and perceptive ones such as the first president of Czechoslovakia, Thomas Masaryk.[40] Ceylon was almost unique as a country where followers of Theravada Buddhism were a large majority of the population. Buddhist monks stressed the fusion of Sinhalese ethnicity and culture, Theravada Buddhism and their sacred territory, the whole island of Ceylon. If Tamils feared Sinhalese domination, Sinhalese nationalists saw themselves as a threatened minority in a Hindu–dominated region.

Politics within the Sinhalese community became competitive and democratic from the early 1950s. In 1956 the Sri Lanka Freedom Party won the elections on a programme of Sinhalese nationalism, which insisted among other things that Sinhalese should be the sole language of government. Inevitably this radicalized Tamil opinion. SLFP policy caused Tamil protests in parliament, anti–Tamil pogroms, and a competition between the two Sinhalese parties for the mass nationalist vote. When S.W.R.D. Bandaranaike, the SLFP leader, tried to retreat from confrontation with the Tamils he was assassinated by extremist nationalists in his own camp. A subsequent effort by the United National Party to restore a *modus vivendi* with the Tamils after the victory in the 1965 elections also ended after violent Sinhalese riots and protests. The Tamil Tigers, the main Tamil armed resistance movement, was founded in 1976. By the early 1980s Tamil terrorism and the equally brutal response of Sri Lanka's overwhelmingly Sinhalese army had brought about a guerrilla war which killed 40,000 people in the north–eastern region of Sri Lanka alone in the years between 1987 and 1993.

Comparisons between the end of empire in India and in Ceylon are an unhappy reminder that although mayhem during decolonization may lead to decades of subsequent violence and instability, its absence is no guarantee of later inter–ethnic peace. The history of Sri Lanka since independence is also a reminder that one cannot blame the imperial era and its heritage for all subsequent ills. A political system that allows one party, and therefore one people, undiluted power is extremely dangerous in any multinational society. Though conflict between peoples might have been less exacerbated and more repressed under empire's rule, it was also to some extent the product of a process of modernization which began before the end of Britain's empire and continued after it. In most traditional societies different peoples can live in the countryside in relatively close proximity without having much to do with each other. Modern communications, trade and urbanization reduce this isolation. In post–independence Sri Lanka as in nineteenth–century Bohemia modernization has also meant mass education and battles over language and jobs, above all government jobs. In Sri Lanka 87 per cent literacy by 1981 made this a burning issue. There was acute competition for jobs among a newly literate younger generation in a country where half of all those in employment were paid by the state. Young men with some education but not too much proved excellent terrorists, especially when engaged in a desperate and fruitless struggle for government jobs. Young

Sinhalese terrorists moved between armed revolutionary Trotskyism and radical anti-Tamil nationalism with disconcerting ease. Behind the radicalism and the inter-ethnic violence there also to some extent lay other problems common to the Third World, whether or not the countries concerned had passed through a period of imperial rule. These problems included poverty, very rapid population growth, and horrendous mismanagement of the economy by governments determined to use the country's wealth to buy clients, hang on to power and satisfy personal ends.

AFTER THE SOVIET UNION

This book was completed eight years after the collapse of the Soviet Union. Eight years after the fall of the Habsburg Empire Europe was rejoicing in the 'spirit of Locarno'. The Treaty of Locarno, signed in 1925, seemed to have put an end both to post-1918 international instability and to the rivalries that had caused the Great War in the first place. Meanwhile the European economy was recovering quickly, thanks in large part to American prosperity, buoyed by the ultra-expansionist, optimistic and profit-hungry mood of Wall Street. There were still four years to the crash and four more to Hitler's accession to power. The Second World War and the extermination of the Jews were still further over the horizon.

Eight years after the collapse of the Ottoman Empire the Balkans were quiet and so too were the former Ottoman territories in Asia and Africa: in the latter case British and French imperial rule still had two decades to run. Eight years after independence was granted to India, the core of Britain's empire, the Suez crisis had not yet occurred and nor had dramatic decline in British economic power. Within the subcontinent the united state of West and East Pakistan, created in defiance of all geopolitical and ethnic logic, still had another sixteen years of life. Except for Africa, eight years after independence came to most of Britain's colonies they were still ruled by elites from the colonial era, usually anglophone, often European in culture and generally able to secure inter-ethnic peace by quiet deals with elites of minority communities. The age of true mass politics and of populist nationalism was still to come.

In the post-imperial Soviet context these are still therefore very early days. There will be many surprises in the future. Nevertheless, the first years of independence are always important both for what does happen during this time and what does not. Not merely are millions of lives uplifted or destroyed in these years but events often cast a very long shadow. At the beginning of the twenty-first century, for example, we have still not escaped the consequences of the partition of Palestine and Kashmir in 1947–8.

In the last eight years we have seen significant violence in six of the fifteen former Soviet republics. These are Moldova, Tajikistan, the three Trans-Caucasian republics (Georgia, Armenia and Azerbaijan), and Russia itself. Often this violence has been limited to relatively small regions and sections of the population. By the standards of other collapsing empires the bloodshed has been remarkably small. We have seen no equivalent of the violence that killed or expelled the great majority of Muslims from much of the Ottoman Empire, and most Christians from the rest. The end of the Russian Empire was not accompanied by world war, as was the case with the Habsburgs, Romanovs and Hitler's Reich. We have not seen bloodshed to match India's partition, let alone the wars in Vietnam and Algeria which brought the end of the French Empire. It is important to ask why not.

The most crucial reason was that in the Soviet case it was Russia itself that played a key role in empire's destruction. This does not mean that in 1990–1 the majority of the Russian people wished to destroy the Soviet Union. They were merely unwilling to make sacrifices to preserve it and anxious to secure for themselves a better deal within it. Nor even were Boris Yeltsin and his associates opposed in principle to the Union's survival. But their struggle with the all-Union government, their determination to take over its power and its assets, were key factors in the empire's collapse in 1991. Yeltsin was also the great obstacle which defeated the August 1991 coup, whose main aim was to save the empire. Subsequently Yeltsin took the lead in the December 1991 Belovezhe negotiations with Ukraine and Belorussia (Belarus) which led to the Union's dissolution. There are no true precedents for this among other empires, though the Portuguese metropolitan revolution of 1974 which led quickly to independence for the colonies is perhaps the best parallel. In the Portuguese case, however, as in that of the French and Dutch after 1945, independence was preceded by many years of bitter warfare precisely because the metropolitan state was determined to maintain empire. Even the British fought long rearguard police actions, even a limited war in Malaya, either to postpone independence or to ensure that it came on terms acceptable to them. Other states launched world wars to retain or regain empire. Meanwhile Yeltsin's Russia dismantled the Soviet Empire, forcing independence on states such as Belorussia and the five Central Asian republics whose elites and populations had recently made clear their desire for the Union to continue. In the March 1991 referendum carried out in nine of the fifteen Soviet republics (admittedly with some confusion due to the asking of more than one question) 76.4 per cent of the voters favoured the Union's preservation on an 80 per cent turnout, which included very big majorities in Belorussia and Central Asia. Not surprisingly, independence donated by Moscow only nine months later came as a shock.

The policies of Yeltsin's Russia are also one reason for another great puzzle, namely the relative quiescence of the 25 million Russians who suddenly found themselves minorities in foreign states upon the Soviet Union's collapse. In the British and French cases far smaller communities of Ulster Protestants and *pieds noirs* (French settlers in Algeria) had fought a similar fate bitterly and in Ulster's case with success. Like many Muslim minorities in Europe the *pieds noirs* had not merely opposed the end of empire with guns in their hands but suffered almost complete extinction as a community as its result. In the post-Soviet case almost no Russian civilians were killed or ethnically cleansed from any of the fourteen other republics of the former USSR. Ironically, by far the highest Russian civilian casualties were the thousands of Russians in Grozny killed by the Russian army and airforce during the campaigns to crush Chechnya's bid for independence. But in most of the ex-Soviet republics the Russians became second-class citizens, indeed in Latvia and Estonia the majority of them initially became not citizens at all, but merely residents. Moreover, as with the Germans in interwar Bohemia, the sectors of the economy in which most Russians worked – generally heavy industry and very often defence-related – were those hardest-hit by the collapse of the Union and the subsequent economic depression. Faced with these challenges and in some cases fearing native hostility, many Russians emigrated back to Russia, above all from Central Asia and from the younger, professional sections of the Russian population. But at the end of 1999 more than 90 per cent of Russians remained in the fourteen independent republics, and only in Moldova did a Russian community engage in a successful bid for secession.

One reason for the Russian diaspora's quiescence was that they received no encouragement to intransigence from Yeltsin's Moscow, in sharp contrast to British Conservative support of Ulster Unionism before 1914, or to Paris's backing for the *pieds noirs*. Before the collapse of the Union Yeltsin allied himself to the other reformist republican leaderships and opposed the all-Union government in the name of democracy and self-determination. In January 1991, in the dramatic days when Moscow launched its crackdown in the Baltic republics, Yeltsin flew to the region to sign pacts with the pro-independence governments, an extremely significant political gesture. After the collapse of the Soviet Union at the end of 1991 the situation changed. By 1993 political realities within Russia made it impossible for any leader to ignore the plight of the Russian diaspora, and in particular the denial of citizenship to most Russians in Latvia and Estonia. This issue was seized on by the Russian Communist and nationalist opponents of Yeltsin, and could be used all the more successfully because of his role in the collapse of the Union and the creation of the diaspora in the first place. In the December 1993 paraliamentary elections the party of the ultra-nationalist Zhirinovsky won 22.9 per cent of the vote on a platform which stressed, among other things, defence of the Russian diaspora. Zhirinovsky himself, born in Kazakhstan and very anti-Muslim, was 'the authentic voice of the poor colonist, the miserable scion of the ruling nation who nursed resentment against all around him – whether in Algeria, South Africa or Kazakhstan.'[41] In fact Zhirinovsky and his party were to prove rather ephemeral and lightweight, but their demands that the diaspora be defended were to be adopted by the political mainstream. Already moving towards a rhetorical support for the diaspora, Yeltsin was confirmed in this policy by the elections. In 1994 he issued so-called 'Fundamental Guidelines' for Russian support of the diaspora, setting out a range of policies to sustain the Russian language, culture, schools and media in the 'Near Abroad', which was Moscow's term for the former Soviet Union.

Though this programme was proclaimed with a great flourish, almost nothing was done, even as regards cheap and politically innocuous measures such as ensuring access to Russian television. Moscow was not prepared to take any practical steps to help the diaspora. Russian troops were withdrawn from the Baltic republics by 1994, despite earlier rhetoric that their removal depended on the Baltic peoples making concessions to the local Russian community. Neither was there any equivalent step to Hitler's efforts to finance, arm and radicalize pan-German forces in Austria and the Sudentenland in the 1930s. Nor did Moscow respond aggressively when developments within neighbouring republics gave it an opening to intervene. Of all the Russian-majority areas lost in 1991 Crimea means most to Russians, partly because of its beauty and its place in Russian literature, but above all because of the huge Russian losses in the two great sieges of Sevastopol in 1854–5 and during the Second World War. The fact that Crimea was part of the Russian Republic until 1954, and was then handed over to Ukraine by Khrushchev in an almost

off-hand gesture, adds to the resentment. In 1994 a secessionist movement gained power in Crimea, securing a large though not very committed majority at the polls and seeking reunion with Russia. Yeltsin's
regime refused to have anything to do with the secessionist government
in Simferopol, which was one reason why it collapsed so quickly and so
ignominiously. Quizzed by a Western journalist about the chances of
resurgent Russian imperialism, the Crimean prime minister, Yevgeny
Saburov, commented: 'Do you think Russia will pay our bills? There's
about as much chance of the United States doing so . . . Since 1991 Russia
has pursued an isolationist policy without any serious concern for the
position of Russians outside Russia's borders. There's been some talk, but
that's all. This so-called Russian imperialism now exists only in the pages
of your newspapers.'[42]

'Paying the bills' was indeed one cause for Russian reticence. Beset by
economic and financial crisis, and dependent on IMF loans, Russia like
interwar Hungary was constrained to hide its resentment of the post-
imperial settlement. By 1995 any lingering dreams of forward policy in
the Near Abroad were wrecked by the Russian army's debacle in
Chechnya. Russia was exposed to all as extremely weak not only in
financial but also now in military terms. The reality of what warfare
meant both to young conscripts and to civilian victims of bombardment
was evident every day in the terrifying television coverage of Grozny: this
was a great disincentive to imperialist dreams. In any case, once the Soviet
Union had disintegrated into independent states recognized by the international community, attempts by Moscow to mobilize the Russian diaspora, still more to challenge sovereign borders, were bound to be very
costly. They would inevitably infuriate all the republican governments, as
well as the entire international community – for which the sanctity of
borders was an absolute principle. Since Moscow itself was proclaiming
this principle in relation to the Chechens, Tatars and other minorities
within the Russian Federation, it would also expose Russia to international ridicule and domestic destabilization. In any case Yeltsin and his
ministers were not seriously interested in changing borders or aiding the
diaspora. They had other much more pressing priorities within Russia.
Economic stabilization and reintegration into the world economy was
one such priority, and would clearly be threatened by adventures or even
instability in the Near Abroad. Yeltsin's governments were far too
divided, obsessed by factional struggles and by the often corrupt pursuit
of personal interest to worry much about policy, as distinct from politically convenient rhetoric, towards the Russian diaspora.

In other former empires a diaspora might have done much more on its own behalf to ensure that its voice was heard. The Russian diaspora, however, consisted of people inured over the centuries to powerless obedience to government, and traditionally denied the possibility of articulating their own interests and choosing leaders to defend them. In the Soviet Union there were no equivalents to the autonomous civic groups, the free press or the parliamentary institutions that had, for example, allowed Ulster Unionists to exert such a formidable political influence. Competitive party politics, allowing different nationalist movements to mobilize mass support and feed off each other's radicalism, had no place in the Soviet Union. Russians in the non-Russian republics of the Union did not even possess their own, theoretically autonomous, territorial institutions, unlike the indigenous minorities: in the Gorbachev era many of these small peoples used such local government institutions to stake out claims for real autonomy and defend their group interests. The closest the Russians outside Russia came to possessing such institutions were the big factories in which they worked; these so-called all-Union factories, subordinated directly to ministries in Moscow, very often had Russian managers and a largely Russian workforce. With their own community housing, schools and cultural institutions, they were in many ways a world unto themselves. With the collapse of the Soviet Union, however, the link with Moscow was cut, and the factories them-selves were crippled by economic collapse and in no position to rally Russians against republican governments.

Before August 1991 it had in fact made perfectly good sense for the Russian diaspora to leave the Union's defence largely to the government in Moscow. The central authorities had immense military and police forces at their disposal, and it hardly seemed likely that these would stand aside while the Union disintegrated. In addition, the March 1991 refer-endum seemed to show that in the republics in which the Russian dias-pora was largely concentrated neither the indigenous population nor most of the republican elites wanted independence. In the Baltic republics, where this clearly was the case, much of the Russian popula-tion believed it would benefit from the economic prosperity to be expected from independence; for furthermore, before the Union's col-lapse the Baltic popular fronts needed Russian support and at that time never advocated the exclusion from citizenship of most of the Russian community which was to occur later in independent Latvia and Estonia. In Latvia and Estonia, as elsewhere in the Soviet Union, matters moved with dramatic speed after August 1991, and the diaspora's position was transformed before it had the time to react to events. Once independent republics existed, any overt secessionist or even nationalist Russian movement would be strongly discouraged, not to say repressed, by the new regimes. In any case Russians would always be in a minority in these states. In some republics, above all in Central Asia, democracy barely existed or soon disappeared. Russians therefore had little chance to organize politically in order to defend their interests. In Latvia and Estonia, on the other hand, where democracy was strongest, lack of citizenship deprived most Russians of the vote. In these circumstances possibilities of successful collective action were limited and individuals had to decide for themselves whether to come to terms with the new order or to emigrate to the Russian Federation, formed in December 1991 after the collapse of the Soviet Union.

Mobilizing the Russian diaspora for effective political action was also complicated by other deeper factors. Russian nationalism and Russians' sense of their own national identity in the 1990s were confused. For obvious historical reasons a Russian political identity could never be built around French or English conceptions of citizenship, political participation or civil rights. Nor, however, was Russia's a typical East European ethnic nationalism, born out of a small people's resentment of empire and its determination to preserve a threatened language, culture and separate national existence. For centuries Russia had contained many peoples. A great high culture based on the Russian language had been created. This culture had always been cosmopolitan and imperial. The worldwide power and prestige of both the imperial state and the imperial high culture had become part of Russian pride and of what it meant to be a Russian. So too had the knowledge that many people not of Russian ethnic origin shared this pride and identity to varying degrees. The imperial state itself had played a much bigger and more autonomous role in defining national identity than could be the case in the West.

As we have seen, even in 1914 the Russians were not really a nation. The cultural gap between elite and peasantry was too wide, and the argument within educated society about what institutions, values and symbols truly defined Russianness was too bitter. Creating a stable Russian identity was complicated in the twentieth century by the fact that tsarist and Soviet imperial visions were often in conflict: a Soviet identity could not simply be built on tsarist foundations. After three generations of Communist rule a Soviet Russian identity was consolidating itself by the 1970s. This identity was, however, then directly challenged under Gorbachev by growing public awareness of the Soviet system's complete failure to compete in economic terms with the West, and by new revelations of the awful crimes committed in the past by the regime in order to create this failed vision of modernity. Partly for this reason, when conservative bureaucrats and managers tried to mobilize the Russian diaspora in a number of so-called 'international fronts' to defend the Communist regime and the Soviet Union they could seldom arouse any enthusiasm. Widespread hopes for a better life in a post-Soviet world of independent republics were shattered by economic collapse after 1991. Nostalgia for the old Soviet order blossomed even more in the Russian diaspora than in Russia itself. By then, however, the dissolution of the Union was irreversible fact. Even those who most regretted the Soviet Union's collapse often understood that its restoration was impossible.

Creating a post-Soviet sense of Russian identity in the diaspora was not easy. A sense of common Soviet values and loyalties had united many people who were not ethnically Russian. Many of these people spoke Russian as their first language and had a strong admiration for Alexander Pushkin and the Russian cultural heritage. That did not necessarily make them Russians in the narrow political sense. It did not guarantee, for instance, that they would sympathize with efforts to revive elements of the pre-Soviet identity, whether in the form of Orthodoxy, Cossack organizations or nostalgia for the tsarist military tradition. Even less did it mean that they would feel loyalty to the post-Soviet Russian state, its symbols or its leaders. That state's performance in the 1990s did little to earn it admiration or legitimacy. Least of all had Yeltsin and his government earned the loyalty of the Russian diaspora, whom he had cast adrift in 1991 and abandoned ever since then. In any case, in certain areas, the coal-mining Donbas region of east Ukraine for example, local loyalty and identity was stronger than any feeling for either the new Ukrainian or the new Russian state. Since all national politicians were widely detested and all states and their capital cities were commonly perceived as leeches and exploiters, this regional identity was all the stronger. The confused sense of post-Soviet Russian identity had often very down-to-earth consequences. In Ukraine for example Russian nationalism and Soviet loyalty had sharply conflicting agendas. The nationalist wish for regions of east and south Ukraine, for example Crimea, to secede and join Russia was anathema to the largely russophone Ukrainian Communist Party. Secession would inflame Ukrainian nationalism, weaken and divide Ukraine's Russian-speaking population, and make any restoration of a Russo-Ukrainian federation inconceivable forever.

Matters were further confused by the fact that the Russian Federation itself was only four-fifths Russian and faced a number of strong nationalist movements within its non-Russian and non-Christian minorities.

The Russian state could not afford to define itself in exclusively Russian ethnic terms for fear of the effects on Tatars, Bashkirs, Yakuts and a string of North Caucasian native peoples. General Alexander Lebed, presidential candidate in the 1996 elections, asked: 'What is a national policy in Russia? 132 nations and peoples, Orthodoxy, Catholicism, Muslims, Buddhists, Jews, a mass of sects. What can unite and hold together this huge, multi-lingual, multi-ethnic mass? What strings must one pluck in so varied human souls in order to get these people to live together peacefully without coercion, in order not to destroy one another? The national question in Russia is not finished.'[43] Having shed an empire, Russia in other words had still not quite become a nation. Given the multinational reality of the Russian Federation this was true in fact. It was even more so as regards the mentality of Russian elites, who were wholly unused to thinking of their country in narrow ethnic terms.

There was a big difference between the Russian people's experience of empire's collapse and the German experience after 1945. The Germans had been crushingly defeated in a long-drawn-out war during which they had suffered immensely. Enemy armies occupied Germany. They forced the Germans to confront the Nazi regime's crimes. Subsequently there came dramatic economic recovery and an unprecedented level of prosperity. In the Soviet case empire's end came unexpectedly, in peacetime, almost overnight and with minimal foreign intervention. It was therefore very difficult to comprehend. Emil Payin, himself a key figure in Moscow's policy towards the Russian diaspora, comments that 'this makes the process of the overall collapse of a once powerful state completely incomprehensible to the man in the street and makes it even more difficult for Russian minorities to adapt to the idea that their life in a foreign ethnic milieu will never be the same. Some Russians still entertain the hope that some wonderful day everything will be back as it was and the single state will reappear.'[44]

In some ways Russian popular attitudes in the 1990s were rather similar to those of Austrians after 1945. The population had had enough of empires, enough of sacrificing itself in the name of History and great causes. The Second Austrian republic won its people's loyalty above all through the prosperity it provided. A post-imperial Russia could certainly do the same. If Russia experienced an economic boom to match Europe's of the 1950s and 1960s then the democratic institutions, national borders and state institutions of the Russian Federation would gain great legitimacy in the hearts of a people exhausted by generations of sacrifice and privation, and devoted almost exclusively to the pursuit of private ends and a higher standard of living. Nationalist and communist intellectuals would still hover on the margins of politics, but the core of the Russian elite would concentrate on becoming rich, which is indeed what they are already doing. Economic collapse and disillusionment with Western capitalism, coming on top of the end of empire and the failure of Soviet socialism, has created a poisonous atmosphere among political elites and deepened public alienation. In part ordinary people are too busy surviving to care about politics, but cynicism and disillusionment go well beyond this. In Soviet times the population could not be uninvolved in politics or public affairs in a manner typical of a traditional peasant society. On the contrary, they were constantly being mobilized for meetings, demonstrations and collective declarations of commitment to socialist ideals – all of which by the Brezhnev era were a hollow and cynical pretence in the eyes of even half-intelligent participants. They were also told that the path to successful modernity led through political belief and collective action. Now democracy too seems a regime of pompous verbiage and broken promises, covering a reality of corruption, gross and illegitimate inequality, mass poverty and crime.

As regards their impact on the metropolitan people, the collapse of the British and Soviet empires are barely comparable. It is true that British elites were also to an extent disoriented by victory in war followed by a sharp decline in relative power and status. But to get the full measure of a comparison with the Soviet Union one would have to imagine the overnight collapse of the British Empire at a time when it had seemed stable, the simultaneous secession of Scotland (Ukraine) and Wales (Belarus), the disintegration both of the monarchy and of parliamentary government, and an economic crisis much worse than the great depression of the 1930s. Nor are comparisons with Turkey any more appropriate. More than a century of decline and defeat had bred a certain weariness of empire, not to mention a sense that collapse was more than possible. In any case disintegration followed defeat in war, whose verdict was clear-cut. For a brief period there did follow within Turkish society a conflict between Ottoman-Muslim-imperial and Turkish nationalist identities and commitments. Moreover, the bulk of the population longed only for a private life and bare material satisfaction.

In the Turkish case, however, everything was transformed by the fact that empire's collapse was immediately followed by the attempt of ancient enemies to invade and annex the nation's homeland itself. Against such a threat Turkish nationalism was able to coalesce and find both unity and heroic leadership. If the Americans seized Moscow, and the Poles, Chinese and Turks proceeded to carve up the rest of Russia, the Russian elites and population might respond in similar fashion. But the 1990s have not offered Russian nationalism anything like so obvious a target against which to unify or define itself. Partly as a result, the end of empire in Russia has brought nothing like the Turkish experience of reinvigoration and rebirth, for which many of its opponents hoped so ardently in 1988–91. On the other hand, not only the lack of obvious external enemies and aggressors but also the confused, contradictory and inchoate state of present-day Russian nationalism have contributed greatly to an ending of empire which, so far, has been much less terrible than either earlier imperial precedents or the nature of the Soviet regime might have led one to expect.

The behaviour of Russia and the Russians is beyond question the most important factor in the peculiar history of the collapse and the immediate aftermath of the Soviet Empire. However, other factors did also contribute to the empire's relatively peaceful demise. Above all, the federal system, which played so big a role in the collapse of the USSR, also helped to ensure that the end of empire was in most cases relatively smooth and non-violent. Under Soviet federalism the fifteen union republics had a range of governmental institutions staffed largely by well-educated native cadres. They also had clearly defined borders. The March 1990 elections had given the reality of democratic legitimacy to some republican governments and a veneer to others. In no case in 1991 was power in a republic seized by force or armed rebellion. In all cases independence was ceded by Moscow in December 1991 to the legally established government which also generally exercised full effective control throughout the republic's territory. The sudden last-minute demarcation of borders between newly constituted political units, so fatal in the Indian case in 1946–7, was avoided. The republican bureaucracies would inevitably face many problems in adapting to an independent post-socialist world. Nevertheless, the strength of institutions and the number of well-trained officials were usually much superior to the norm in most of the Middle East or Africa on the eve of independence.

Soviet federalism could not, however, ensure a peaceful transition to independence in all republics. It is time to look at individual cases, comparing them both to each other and to examples drawn from the collapse of other empires.

Moldova is a small republic placed between Ukraine and Romania at the south-western tip of the former Soviet Union. It is divided by the River Dniester into a smaller eastern region (Trans-Dniestria) and a much larger western one (Moldova proper). Trans-Dniestria has been under tsarist and then Soviet rule for the last two centuries but the rest of Moldova was part of Romania from 1918 to 1940. In 1989, 14 per cent of the population were Ukrainian and 13 per cent were Russian, though as was usual in the Soviet Union many Ukrainians living outside their own republic spoke Russian as their first language and identified themselves with the Russians, though they did so as part of a common Soviet identity rather than a Russian one. In Southern Moldova 150,000 Gagauz, Orthodox in religion but ethnically Turkish, were a reminder that this region had once been Ottoman and that even after generations of war and ethnic cleansing South-Eastern Europe defied neat division into homogenous nations defined by language, religion and culture. Nevertheless, the Romanians of Moldova have their own distinct identity, partly because of Slav influence but more because they were not part of the Romanian Kingdom in the nineteenth century in the period when a national identity was being sculpted by the newly independent Romanian state. Whether in the end Moldova will retain its independence or merge with Romania depends on future circumstances. Things could go either way. Since international borders are not changed easily, the best guess at present is that circumstances and inertia will combine to keep Moldova separate.

As elsewhere in the Soviet Union, Gorbachev's rule encouraged the growth of ethnic nationalism in Moldova and undermined the ruling Communist oligarchy. The majority Romanian community in 1989 made Romanian the state language, restored the Latin script and subsequently adopted the same flag and anthem as the Romanian Republic. This drew furious protests from the Slav minority, which dominated most towns but had its main stronghold in Trans-Dniestria. By the time Moldova declared its independence after the failure of the August 1991 coup, Trans-Dniestria had already de facto seceded, with strong support from the central authorities in Moscow. The core of the Slav secessionist movement were Trans-Dniestria's big defence and heavy industrial factories, all of them directly subordinated to all-Union industrial ministries. Crucial support also came from the local Soviet military garrison.

The parallels with Ulster and Turkish Cyprus are obvious. As empire collapses, the descendants of metropolitan settlers in a border province secede and rejoin their original homeland, which was once the empire's core and is now a nation state. The fact that Slavs in Trans-Dniestria were reacting partly to the threat of union (*enosis*) with Romania makes the Greek and Irish parallels all the more obvious. Nevertheless, these parallels are not as clear-cut as they seem. There was a very specific post-Soviet element in the story. As was generally true of the republican opposition movements that sprang up under Gorbachev, the Moldovan Popular Front combined nationalist intellectuals and more pragmatic elements from the Communist Party apparatus. Factionalism within that apparatus was crucial to the whole story of independence and its aftermath. In the Moldovan case the Bessarabian faction of the Communist elite, which had been permanently excluded from top office by Trans-Dniestrians, seized the opportunity to grab power. In response the Trans-Dniestrian Communist elite launched a regional secessionist movement. The result was the de facto partition of Moldova and low-level violence, which erupted into a serious war along the Dniester in 1992, killing 1,000 people on the Moldovan side alone and causing 30,000 refugees to flee their homes.

To date there has been no further ethnic cleansing but also no real move to end partition. Both the Slav minority in Moldova and – much more – the 40 per cent of the Trans-Dniestrian population who are Romanian face a range of discriminatory policies. Renewed violence and ethnic cleansing is therefore a real possibility. Meanwhile, as in most of the former Soviet Union, the alliance between the nationalist cultural intelligentsia and reformist Communist elites partly broke down in Moldova once Moscow was defeated. Power is held by the old *nomenklatura*, indeed at the top level by precisely the same individuals who dominated the Moldovan Communist Party in the two years before independence. On the other hand, also very typically of the former Soviet Union, the nationalist intelligentsia 'are prominently represented in most of Moldava's key cultural and educational institutions. One of the main sources of support for pan-Romaniaist parties comes from university professors and school teachers, and one should not underestimate the power of educators to shape the political sensibilities of Moldova's future voters.'[45]

Towards the other, eastern end of the Russian Republic's southern border lie the five Central Asian republics, Kazakhstan, Uzbekistan, Kyrgyzstan, Turkmenistan and Tajikistan. Their problems after 1991 were often very similar to those of former European colonies in the Third World. They were the poorest of the Soviet republics, with far the highest birth-rates and therefore a growing pool of impatient young men competing for an inadequate quantity of irrigated land and a limited number of urban jobs and dwellings. Impatient and frustrated young men are the usual carriers of political violence. In the Central Asian case an obvious future target might be Russians with superior jobs and housing in the cities. Much of Central Asia depends greatly on a single export commodity, cotton: again this is a rather familiar post-colonial situation. Abundant oil, gas and minerals offer the prospect of future wealth to Turkmenistan, Kazakhstan and Uzbekistan. Foreign investment needs to be attracted by political stability, tolerable levels of corruption, some degree of confidence in binding contracts and legal arrangements, and the means to export oil and gas through secure pipelines. None of this can be taken for granted in the region. Nor is a flood of oil money any guarantee of political stability, as the last shah of Iran discovered. Big dollar export earnings greatly raise the political stakes, offering wealth to those who control key government positions. Oil-rich provinces, particularly if they already possess a distinct identity of their own, can be very hard for central government to control. In countries whose elites are not checked by democracy or the rule of law, and do not feel any strong sense of nationhood or commitment to their own people, revenues from oil, gas and minerals can simply disappear into the private foreign bank accounts of a small, ultra-rich and largely expatriate clique. Not merely do the mass of the population not benefit but the local economy can easily be wrecked by fluctuating export earnings and currencies. Any public sense of political morality, honesty or patriotism is ruined. Nigeria offers awful examples of this danger but it is not unique.

The Central Asian republics were by tradition Islamic, though religion's hold was always greater by far in the cities and the settled Fergana Valley than among the Kazakh, Kyrgyz and Turkmen nomads. In the Soviet era Islam lost ground though on the whole not as much as was the case with the Christian religions. Independence brought strong signs of Islamic resurgence. The native former Communist elite who ruled the now independent states recognized that Islam was an important part of many people's lives and was essential to the creation of post-Soviet national identity. But they feared greatly lest Islamic fundamentalism, on the march in so much of the region to their south, should escape their control. In the event of the native ex-imperial elite's inability to manage mounting socio-economic crisis this could happen in the future, particularly in the event of splits within the elite.

As in most of the ex-colonial Third World, the Central Asian sense of national identity is weak. These are new nations created by Soviet decree. Since their creation in the 1920s a sense of nationhood has often developed among the elites but local loyalties remain very strong, particularly among the mass of the population. Only in Uzbekistan has there been any true tradition of statehood. But the Uzbek republic was really built on the foundations of the former emirate of Bukhara, to which the territories of the former khanate of Khiva and parts of tsarist Turkestan were attached in the 1920s when Uzbekistan was created. Rivalries between the key cities and regions of Uzbekistan are veiled but remain fierce. Among the former nomads of Kazakhstan, Kyrgyzstan and Turkmenistan matters are worse. At best in pre-Russian times the many clans and tribes of these peoples had united temporarily in military confederations when faced by pressing external threats. The immense area of Kazakhstan, 16 million people in a territory as big as Western Europe, and the mountains and valleys of Kyrgyzstan contribute to this localism. As is often the case in Africa,[46] it is by no means always clear in Central Asia whether one is confronting ancient clan and tribal communities, regional interest groups or political patron-client factions. In reality the three often overlap.

In these circumstances maintaining effective government and balancing regions is never easy. It often becomes harder as foreign investment pours into a few provinces rich in energy or minerals but not into others. Regions and their elites compete to capture central government. In a post-colonial situation, with regimes anxious to strengthen national identity and cultural intelligentsias only too happy to serve the nationalist cause, some factions within the elite compete to be the best nationalists. 'When a predominantly russified, urban, and northern Kyrgyz elite gained power during the transition from Communist rule, its most vulnerable flank lay exposed not to the Russians and Uzbeks but to Kyrgyz leaders who were willing to outbid them as defenders of ethnic Kyrgyz interests.'[47] In states with often large Russian and Uzbek minorities, competition between factions of the majority community's elite to be the best nationalists could have dire consequences. At independence almost 40 per cent of Kazakhstan's population was Russian,[48] much of it concentrated in northern provinces bordering on Russia where they were a large majority. The border itself had no historical, economic or geographical logic. Most Russian soldiers would be very unwilling indeed to fight Ukrainians. The Russian state would pay an exceptionally heavy price in terms of Western anger for any military intervention in Latvia or Estonia, whatever the circumstances. But the Russian army would have few qualms about intervening in Kazakhstan should conflict within the Kazakh elite lead to the eruption of trouble between Russians and Kazakhs in the north.

For the moment, however, inter-ethnic peace and political stability reigns in most of Central Asia. Unlike the case in much of the post-colonial world, civilian rulers in the region do not need to fear military coups. The Communist era taught strict subordination of the armed forces to civil power. In any case, in most of Central Asia native republican military units barely exist. There was no separate colonial army in the Soviet Union, as there was in the West European maritime empires, for a post-imperial regime to inherit. Since there was also no war of independence there are no ex-guerrilla armies either. The region is still dominated by former members of the old Communist Party elite, overwhelmingly of native origin, transformed now into state functionaries, and subordinated to presidents whose personal authority and charisma have been greatly boosted since independence. Needless to say, none of these people had any of the training in the values and procedures of democracy that Irish or even Indian politicians gained under British rule, or Czechs and Slovenes under Austria. In 1999 three of the five republics had been ruled without interruption by their former Communist leaders. With political stability so dependent on individual lives and no rules yet established for the succession, the dangers of presidential power are obvious. So far, however, only temporarily in Tajikistan has the old elite lost power and authority collapsed. The result there in 1992 was a civil war which pitted the old Communist establishment, backed by certain regions and by the Uzbek minority, against anti-Communist, Islamic and regional forces opposed to the central government. A few months of war killed between 50,000 and 100,000 people and created half a million or more refugees from a population of 5.1 million.[49] The Communist elite won but it has never achieved complete control throughout the republic and intermittent violence continues together with mass poverty and much feuding within the ruling factions. For the other republics' leaders events in Tajikistan were both excuse and reason to concentrate power very closely in their own hands.

In contrast to Central Asia, the end of empire threw much of the Caucasus region into immediate and violent conflict. In most of the small autonomous republics north of the mountain range, which remained part of the Russian Federation, the native Communist elite hung on to power. Rarely loveable let alone democratic, they made their bow to nationalism but were at heart cool, pragmatic political realists. Because of its history, however, Chechnya was always likely to be the odd man out in the region. Having fought the tsars throughout the 1840s and 1850s, then risen against Soviet rule in 1920–1, the Chechens had been deported en masse to Central Asia by Stalin, losing perhaps half their population in the process. Returning to their native region during Khrushchev's rule, they nurtured the rock-hard anti-imperial nationalism which one might expect of a community with such a history. When the empire collapsed they made their bid for independence from Russia. In 1994 Moscow met their challenge head-on, its invasion of Chechnya unleashing the bloodiest war so far in the Caucasus region. The war revealed the extraordinary inefficiency, corruption and lack of fighting spirit of the Russian army. It left behind lasting violence and instability in Chechnya, which threatened to spill over into neighbouring Dagestan, wrecking the very precarious balance which kept that territory's thirty-three small peoples more or less at peace with each other. As this book went to press, a second Russo-Chechen war was being fought.

South of the Caucasus Mountains only Armenia enjoyed any degree of political stability. The term is strictly relative since in the 1990s the Armenians also experienced great impoverishment, massive emigration and a war with Azerbaijan – the only example so far of war between, as distinct from within, the former Union republics of the USSR. The cause of the war was typically post-imperial. When delineating republican frontiers Moscow had given the Armenian-majority enclave of Nagorno-Karabakh to Azerbaijan. No Armenian had ever accepted this as just but so long as the empire's power remained firm and invincible they had recognized realities. When Gorbachev began to undermine the police state and allow political debate, the Nagorno-Karabakh issue returned to the agenda. Like most peoples, let alone peoples undergoing a post-imperial national revival, the Azeris refused to cede territory. They too had a defensible case for holding Nagorno-Karabakh, which also had great symbolic importance for Azeri nationalists. The Armenians won the war partly because Nagorno-Karabakh's militia was far more committed to the struggle than any of the motley levies fielded by the Azeris. In addition, Armenian nationalism has far deeper and older roots, and much greater emotional force, than is the case in Azerbaijan, which as a nation is a purely twentieth-century and partly Soviet creation. By contrast, the Armenians, not unlike the Jews, are an ancient people whose sense of national identity has been enormously strengthened by modern memories of genocide.

As with most of the conflicts in the former Soviet Union, a ceasefire but no true peace reigns between Armenia and Azerbaijan. Twenty per cent of Azerbaijan remains under Armenian occupation. Quite apart from thousands of military casualties, hundreds of thousands of Armenians and Azeri civilians have fled each other's republics. Hundreds have been massacred. This is not quite the Punjab or the Indo-Pakistan war of 1947–8; given the numbers involved it could not be. The parallels are obvious, however, as is the long shadow this war could throw over the whole region's prospects for stability and security. After experimenting very unsuccessfully with rule by the anti-Communist, nationalist intelligentsia, Azerbaijan is now once again under the thumb of Heider Aliev, the republic's wily, long-serving Communist Party boss in the Brezhnev era. Similar developments have occurred in neighbouring Georgia, which the rule of the nationalist intelligentsia reduced to even greater chaos. Edvard Shevardnadze, Gorbachev's foreign minister and Brezhnev's viceroy in Georgia, returned to power in 1992 and has ruled ever since. Not surprisingly, experienced Communist officials often prove much more realistic politicians than intellectuals conditioned by the Soviet system to a passionate defence of their peoples' cultural rights but denied any training in politics or government.

Georgia is an unusual case in the Soviet context. In 1990 the nationalist intelligentsia came to power unaided, defeating the Communist Party in the elections and pushing it into opposition. This had much to do with the fact that the Communist Party was discredited by its role in the brutal suppression of a demonstration in Tbilisi in April 1989, during which a number of women and children were killed. The victors in the 1990 elections, however, lacked political experience, unity or restraint. The result was small-scale civil war between political factions and their armed gangs of supporters, some of the militias really being more criminal *condottieri* than genuine political groups. In addition, violence erupted between the Georgians and the small Abkhaz and Ossetian peoples in the republic's northern borderland. Both the Abkhaz and the Ossetians had their own small autonomous territories within Georgia during the Soviet era. They always looked to Moscow for protection from the Georgians and, with Russian help, enjoyed considerable control over local jobs and promotions within their own districts. The prospect of the Union's collapse and their unilateral subordination to a Georgian nation-state filled them with horror – a very familiar story among minorities when empire dissolves. The threat made by Gamsakhurdia, first president of independent Georgia, to abolish the two minorities' autonomous institutions was a powerful incentive to radicalism. The Abkhaz in particular injected real life into their autonomous institutions and successfully seceded from Georgia. In 1993 they defeated the Georgian army, partly because the latter lacked professional military cadres (like most of the post-Soviet republics) but also because the Abkhaz received help from Russia and from their Muslim neighbours north of the Caucasus. Two hundred thousand Georgians fled Abkhazia. They remain refugees.

★

Apart from the Caucasus, Tajikistan and Moldova, the only other republic to see major political violence since the collapse of the Soviet Union
has been Russia. Most of this violence occurred in the North Caucasus,
which is part of the Russian Federation, during the Chechen wars. In
addition, however, there was a brief but bloody armed conflict between
Yeltsin and the opposition on the streets of Moscow in October 1993.
The casualties of this battle numbered in tens, rather than thousands as in
Chechnya. But this war within the political elite and in Russia's capital
had ominous possible consequences and said much about the bitterness
and danger of Russian high politics.

In part this was merely a struggle for power between ambitious politicians in a society where law meant little and the Soviet constitution, still
in force, was almost unworkable in the absence of the former flywheel
of government, the Communist Party's institutions. The contenders in
the battle for power were mostly former allies in the struggle against
Gorbachev. In post-Soviet Russia power might be not just a means in
itself or a way to control policy, but a source of great personal wealth. In
addition, however, government and parliament clashed furiously over
economic policy, the opposition seeing Prime Minister Gaidar's 'shock
therapy' as leading to the destruction of Russian manufacturing industry
and the impoverishment of the population. Much of the opposition
hated Yeltsin above all for destroying the empire and undermining
Russian power. Some of them dreamed of restoration, as indeed the
Communists, Russia's strongest party, still do.

Moscow of the 1990s sometimes bore a smell of interwar Vienna. The
gun battles of October 1993 had some resemblance to the vicious four-
day civil war in Vienna in February 1934 when hatred between parties
reached its peak, Heimwehr military veterans strutted like Moscow's
afgantsy (veterans of the Afghan war), and political violence flared against
a background of dramatic economic collapse. Austrian and Russian elites
shared an intense nostalgia for empire's power, status and significance.
Many were thoroughly disorientated by its loss. Alexander Lebed commented on the Soviet Union's collapse that 'whoever doesn't regret its
ruin has no heart but whoever thinks it will be possible to restore it in its
old form has no brains. There is something to regret: to be the Citizen
of a Great Power, albeit with many failings but nevertheless Great, or of
an impoverished "developing" country – there is quite a difference.'[50]

Lebed is a very realistic and pragmatic Russian nationalist. Other
nationalists are often much more paranoid, and the circumstances of the
1990s gave them some reason to be so. The nationalist intelligentsia had
long since tended to see their pro-Western intellectual opponents as not

just misguided but also as traitors to Russia. It was a long-established canon of nationalist thinking that Western ideas were inappropriate to Russia, that their import into Russian government would destroy imperial power, and that the consequence would be domination of the world by Western civilization, Russia's moral destruction, and its reduction to the status of a colony. In 1988 the ultra-nationalist organization Pamyat (Memory) declared: 'We are being transformed into a technically backward power, on a level with India and Brazil.'[51] By 1993, and even more by 2000, this comment did not seem fanciful.

The liberalizing regime of Gorbachev, dominated by representatives of the pro-Western camp, had indeed – for better or worse – contributed greatly to the empire's destruction. Under Yeltsin, more radically pro-Western reformers had presided over the spectacular collapse of the economy, which by the end of the 1990s was dominated by exporters of energy and primary materials, and by a business-cum-political elite whose level of wealth and corruption cast the Brezhnev era wholly into the shade. Christopher Clapham, doyen of British experts on Third World politics, makes a comparison between types of corruption which is relevant to Soviet and post-Soviet politics. In an economy largely closed to international capitalism, corruption usually means 'the redistribution and exchange of benefits within the community rather than the siphoning of resources from it.' By contrast, corruption linked to the export of energy or minerals, 'extractive corruption, is often on a large scale, rests on the manipulation of state power, and maintains the lifestyle of a privileged class of state employees and their confederates.'[52] Brezhnev's Soviet Union was not an entirely closed economy, least of all for the Communist elite, who had access to a range of Western consumer goods. The new post-Soviet elite has, however, been able to turn many of the resources that used to sustain a superpower into its own private property. It has used the unlimited right to foreign travel and foreign bank accounts, never possessed by the Communist elite, to transfer much of this wealth abroad in order to secure for itself the lifestyle of the Western ultra-rich. This is an elite in Latin American or Nigerian style.

In the view of the early 1990s reformers, economics would ultimately determine politics and even morals. Marxist instincts were buttressed by deference to state-of-the-art, orthodox Anglo-American social science wisdom. With private property established, the iron laws of capitalism would sooner rather than later turn Russia into a flourishing modern economy along Western lines. Perhaps the prophets of liberal orthdoxy will be proved right. Perhaps the cultural and educational level of the Russian people, together with Russia's tradition of statehood, will rescue it from Third World status. For most countries, however, escape from the Third World has proved extremely difficult. Those few that have succeeded, almost all of them in East and South-East Asia, have done so under the rule of formidable dirigiste bureaucracies totally unlike the disintegrating state apparatus and corrupt political-cum-business-cum-criminal elite of the Russia of the 1990s. Given present-day Russian realities it is in many ways surprising that paranoid nationalism has not made more of an impact on Russian politics. Its failure to do so may owe much to the fact that the Soviet model of political economy, which embodied to perfection the principles of autarchy and Russia's separate path to modernity, only recently collapsed in ruins after imposing huge costs on the Russian people.

Thus far the only part of the former Soviet Union to have made a relative success of the transition to capitalism are the Baltic republics, with the Estonians in the lead and the Latvians not far behind. There are many reasons for their superior performance but history and culture are very important. Like the Poles and Hungarians but unlike any of the other ex-Soviet peoples, the Baltic peoples rejected the Soviet past totally and were determined to reassert their European identity and to rejoin Europe at top speed. The relative success and better prospects of the Baltic economies are the key reason why the Russian minority, though dissatisfied, remains in the republics. Rates of emigration are much lower than among the Russians of Central Asia. The relationship between Baltic peoples and Russians is quite different from the usual post-imperial one. The Baltic peoples combine deep resentment of Soviet imperial rule with an old-fashioned North European Protestant disdain for backward, sloppy Slavs. Particularly at present, with Russian pride at a low ebb, the Russians feel no sense of superiority whatsoever vis-à-vis their former colony, though by the end of the 1990s the Russian communities were beginning to regain their voices as the shock of 1991 wore off and the Soviet heritage of political quiescence faded into history. Democracy was beginning to teach lessons as to how a community could mobilize to defend its interests.

Both the reality and the self-image of the Baltic peoples as peace-loving, law-abiding, sober Europeans are an important constraint. Given the realities of Soviet rule in the Baltic between 1945 and 1991, and the many contemporary reasons for inter-ethnic hostility, the almost complete lack of violence in the independent republics is remarkable. Membership, actual and desired, of European institutions has also been important. European pressure has toned down some of the more extreme policies towards the Russian minority such as the tiny Latvian proposed quota for annual naturalization of non-citizens and the Estonian intention to deny work permits to certain sections of the Russian community. Membership of the European Union, if it comes, will allow the EU to make a major contribution to peaceful inter-ethnic relations in the Baltic and overall European security. Unrestricted rights of residence and employment throughout the EU for all Russians living in the Baltic republics would be a relatively inexpensive policy given the small numbers involved – the total Russian community in the three republics was only 1.7 million in 1989[53] – but also a wise one. Inter-ethnic relations in the Baltic may not always remain peaceful, they have the potential to cause major problems between Russia and the West, and statesmanlike action by the EU to reduce the possibility of future trouble would be valuable to Baltic peoples and Russia alike. Between 1945 and 1991 the West's policy towards the Baltic republics was unheroic, albeit unavoidable. The EU has not always shown a willingness to look beyond butter mountains to the great questions of European security. Now is the time and opportunity to change.

In comparison to Ukraine and Kazakhstan, the two republics with the biggest Russian minorities, the Baltic peoples' treatment of the Russians has been ungenerous. Though Kazakh and Ukrainian have been declared state languages, and their role in education and government service is being enhanced, restrictions on the use of Russian are much less severe than in the Baltic republics. The Baltic peoples could well argue, however, that political rights have real meaning in their case, since their republics are genuine democracies, whereas Kazakhstan (though much less Ukraine) has an authoritarian presidential regime covered by a very thin democratic veneer. Moreover, very understandably in the historical circumstances, whatever the law or President Nazarbayev may say, Kazakhstan's state is now dominated almost entirely by Kazakhs who are determined to ensure that privatization places most of the republic's assets in Kazakh (i.e. their) and not Russian-minority hands.

The Baltic peoples' justification for their treatment of the Russian minority rests on the argument that the Baltic republics' legal status was different from that of any other non-Russian peoples subject to Soviet rule. In 1940 the three republics were internationally recognized independent states and members of the League of Nations. Their annexation by Moscow was in breach of international law and was never recognized by the Western powers. The post-1991 republics are the successors to the states illegally annexed in 1940 and therefore recognize as citizens only those people who were citizens in 1940 or their descendants. Anyone else residing in the republics is an immigrant, with a right perhaps to residence but no automatic claim on citizenship. Behind these legal arguments lies bitter resentment at the fact that in 1939 Latvians were 75.5 per cent of their republic's population and Estonians 90 per cent. By 1989 the figures were 51.8 per cent and 64.7 per cent.[54] Wartime losses, together with executions and deportations carried out by the Soviet regime, played some part in this shift but the key factor was massive Slav immigration. As usual with empires, under Soviet rule indigenous people lost control over immigration into their native lands.

Albeit to varying degrees, empire always entails the subjection of the native people to alien rulers, alien cultures and values: modern empire's assumption is usually that these values and culture are superior to those of the indigenous population. The end of empire generally brings a backlash, with natives reasserting ownership of territory and the value of their own language, culture and traditions. This backlash is divided and confused when indigenous elites recognize that the empire did to some extent embody modernity, progress or at least superior wealth and power, and that in these terms it was an advance on native tradition.

The Baltic peoples have no such sense, quite rightly believing that Soviet socialism brought not just alien rule and great repression but also externally imposed backwardness, which deprived the Baltic peoples of the near-Scandinavian living standards they enjoyed in the 1930s. The swollen nationalist emotions of a people liberated from empire can be a real problem for ethnic minorities in a newly independent state, especially if they are not indigenous, historic minorities but a people who immigrated under colonial rule. Even the Sinhalese, scarcely models of ethnic tolerance, do not deny the right of the centuries-old Tamil communities to continue to exist in northern Sri Lanka – so long as they accept the pre-eminence of Sinhalese language and culture, and Sinhalese dominance of public office. They do reject the right of residence of nineteenth-century Tamil immigrants and, as we have seen, have successfully negotiated with the Indian government for the repatriation of most of them.

The Russians' fate in the Baltic republics is vastly superior to that of the Turks and Muslims when the Ottoman Empire receded. It is worth reiterating that there have been no massacres and no ethnic cleansing in the Baltic republics. In comparison to Czech treatment of Germans between the wars the Baltic peoples have been relatively ungenerous in their policies on citizenship, language and education. However, the role of the Sudeten Germans in undermining Czechoslovakia and supporting

Hitler in the 1930s led after 1945 to the brutal ethnic cleansing of the entire German community, including of course many Germans who loathed the Nazis and had been loyal to Czechoslovakia to the end. The English minority in post-independence Ireland enjoyed full political and civil rights (as did the much larger Irish minority in Britain) but they were subject to the laws and prejudices of a republic which strongly asserted its Catholic and Gaelic identity, convinced that this justly reflected the fact that Catholic Gaels were the island's original inhabitants, that they were a majority, and that the reassertion of their identity was a belated recognition of the wrongs they had suffered under imperial rule. Greek Cypriots had almost identical assumptions to those of the Irish Catholics. Unlike the Irish they did have the chance to preserve the unity of their island so long as they were prepared to tolerate a share in power and considerable autonomy for the ex-imperial Turkish minority. They proved unwilling to do so and the result was Turkish invasion and partition.

In many ways, the most interesting comparison to the Russians' situation in the Baltic Republics is the fate of the Chinese and Indian diasporas in parts of the former British Empire. Between the 1830s and 1876, for example, 453,000 Indian indentured labourers were 'imported' into Mauritius, 238,000 into British Guiana and 143,000 into Trinidad. After independence the result was often bitter conflict with the indigenous, or in the West Indian case African, population. These Indians were employed in colonial plantation agriculture, a sort of British equivalent of the Moscow-run all-Union industries which directed factories and deployed labour across the Soviet Union. The 61,000 Indians 'imported' into Fiji were in absolute terms no great number but the indigenous Fijian population was also small. After independence the almost equal numbers of Indians and Fijians became a source of great tensions, given democracy's stress on the counting of heads and the rights of majorities. The indigenous population, and particularly its elites, believed that they had the right to unrestricted rule over their ancestral homeland. They feared both the loss of political control and the island's over-population. Some called for the repatriation to India of part of the population at the expense of Britain, the former imperial power which had initially brought them to Fiji. In these circumstances, stable, mutually tolerant, democratic politics was almost impossible.[55]

The Chinese community in Malaya was only 35 per cent of the overall population, and had older roots and a far richer and more confident elite than the Fijian Indians. Nevertheless, the feeling of the Malay majority that the territory was theirs by historical right and that the Chinese had an alternative homeland of their own went very deep. Tunku Abdul Rahman, the first post-independence prime minister of Malaya, was a member of one of the Malay royal houses and an absolutely quintessential traditional, colonial-era notable, willing to tolerate minorities and to strike behind-the-scenes compromises with their elites. Anything further from a populist nationalist would be hard to imagine. Yet to keep in tune with his constituency, in the run-up to independence even he had sometimes to stress the historical rights of the Malays, as against British plans to create a new-fangled multi-ethnic Malayan territorial identity: 'with regard to the proposal ... that independence should be handed over to the "Malayans", who are these "Malayans"? This country was received from the Malays and to the Malays it ought to be returned. What is called "Malayans", it is not yet certain who they are; therefore let the Malays alone settle who they are.'[56] After independence Malaya was rather more generous to the Chinese as regards language[57] and citizenship than the Balts were towards the Russians. As regards the political rights accruing to citizens, however, these do not amount to a great deal more in Malaya than in Kazakhstan. The domination of the state and political power by and for ethnic Malays was part of Malaya's unwritten constitution from the start. After the 1969 anti-Chinese pogroms it was codified and strengthened by the decision of the national Consultative Council to ban public or parliamentary discussion of issues concerning language, citizenship and Malay political predominance.[58] Both the Malays and the Fijians would have applauded the statement in the 1989 Latvian declaration of sovereignty that Latvia was the 'only place on earth where the Latvian nation can fully exercise its right to statehood and develop without hindrance the Latvian language, national culture and economy.'[59]

It is much less easy to make post-imperial comparisons for the two remaining former Soviet republics, Belarus and Ukraine. Belarusian independence is to a great extent an accident of history. The republic has no meaningful tradition of statehood and a weak sense of national identity. In language and culture it is close to Russia. Its Soviet identity was reinforced by its great suffering during the Second World War, and by the late but relatively successful (by Soviet standards) industrialization of the 1960s and 1970s. Belorussians voted to preserve the Union in March 1991 and any chance for an independent Belarus to legitimize itself quickly was wrecked by the subsequent collapse of the economy. In 1994, in relatively free and fair elections, the population elected as president Alexander Lukashenka, a junior Communist Party bureaucrat and the chairman of a state farm. Lukashenka, a good public speaker, ran on a populist, anti-corruption ticket against the Communist establishment's candidate and has all the political sophistication and commitment to democracy that one might expect in the circumstances. He has become an advocate of reunion with Russia and a number of agreements to this effect have been drawn up between the two republics. In principle, a Russian Federation broad enough to accommodate the far more alien Tatars, Bashkirs and Yakuts could be expected to have no trouble in finding a place for a distinct Belorussian identity. However, having once achieved independence, the minority but vocal nationalist intelligentsia would be outraged to lose it, and therefore troublesome for Russia to absorb. And there are further major obstacles to reunion. Once states have separated, putting them together again is a complicated task. The petty ambitions of ruling elites can be a problem. Whether Lukashenka would really want to become merely the president of one of Russia's autonomous republics is a moot point, as is the Russian elite's willingness to offer him something better. It is also debatable whether it is in Russia's interests to reabsorb a poorer republic whose economy remains entirely unreconstructed and Soviet.

Ukraine, with its population of 52 million, is a much more complicated and more important problem. The relationship of Ukraine with Russia is unique. The whole history of the Ottoman, Habsburg and British empires offers no valid parallels. In some regions of Ukraine, above all Galicia, Volhynia and Kiev, a sense of national identity is vastly stronger than in Belarus. The great majority of Ukrainians would reject the status of a mere autonomous republic in Russia out of hand. In any case, bread and butter issues are crucial for most of the population in a time of extreme economic crisis and deprivation. A key Ukrainian problem is that the various regions of this very large country have sharply different histories and identities. This comes on top of the general post-Soviet weakening of the state's power and the strengthening of local political and business elites, some of which are closely tied to criminals. In addition, the Donetsk-Lugansk (Luhansk) region, containing 16 per cent of the total population, is probably Europe's largest industrial rust belt.

Conflicts between regional centres of power do not mean that Ukraine is about to disintegrate but they do make coherent, let alone radical, economic policy-making very difficult. In a Western country with a vibrant civil society and an autonomous private economy this would not much matter. Ukraine is not a Western capitalist society and requires an effective state and radical economic policy changes if it is to have any chance of becoming one. So far the level of inter-ethnic peace and toler-ance in the republic has been impressive. In the unlikely event that a coalition of regional elites from central and western Ukraine came to power in Kiev in alliance with the nationalist intelligentsia, grabbed all the state's patronage and favours for themselves, and tried to impose nationalist policies in language, education and foreign policy, then polit-ical stability in Ukraine would be threatened. The same would be true in the also unlikely event that a coalition of eastern elites excluded the central and western power-holders and began, in Belarusian style, to negotiate some form of reunion with Russia. But probably the greatest threat to Ukrainian security and independence would come quite simply if Ukraine's economy continued to decline, and Russia experienced dra-matic economic recovery. In eastern Ukraine identities are fluid and loyalty to any state is weak. The large votes for independence in the December 1991 referendum were driven by hopes of prosperity once the all-consuming central government and its supposedly insatiable imperial appetites were removed. These hopes have been shattered. If Russia were willing and able to hold out convincing prospects of a much better life then eastern Ukraine's allegiance to Kiev would slip and Europe would have a major crisis on its hands. This is not an immediate or even likely prospect given the current state of the Russian economy.

Inevitably, peace and political stability in Northern Eurasia (i.e. the whole of the former Soviet Union) will depend greatly on what happens to the region's economies. More than anything else, however, the region's economics will depend on its politics. The post-Soviet economic crisis is also, and very significantly, a post-imperial one. The potentially very difficult problems of managing irrigation and access to water among the newly independent republics of Central Asia have parallels in post-Ottoman Turkey, Syria and Iraq. The more general parallel is, however, with the problems faced by Central Europe in coming to terms with the collapse of the single Habsburg economic space. The Soviet case is, however, much worse than the Habsburg one for the obvious reason that the USSR had a near-autarchic, socialist economic system planned from Moscow in an extremely centralized fashion and designed as a single eco-nomic unit. The disintegration of this unit into a patchwork of econom-ically irrational national units comes on top of the 'normal' problems of transition from a socialist to a capitalist economy and is bound to cause chaos. Efforts to achieve a partial and sensible economic reintegration of some at least of these units are now stymied not just by nationalist opposition but also by the fact that the process of economic reform has moved much faster in some republics than in others. In any case, in most republics memories of empire and fears of renewed Russian expansionism make voluntary economic reintegration very difficult.

There is already quite a heated debate in the West about economic policy in post-Soviet Russia, and the role of Western advice in the formulation of that policy. 'Who lost Russia?' will become a much hotter issue should the Russian economy continue to stagnate and, still more, should Russia collapse or become a threat to Western security. Russia's post-Soviet economic crisis was not simply post-imperial in the sense of having to come to terms with the collapse of the integrated Soviet economy. Great space and great military power are of the essence both of empire and of Russia's current economic problems. Of the socialist states only China could remotely match Russia in size. Comparisons with Poland, let alone the tiny Czech and Hungarian republics, tucked snugly into Central Europe, can be very misleading. The economy of the world's largest state was run with very little regard to the true price of fuel and transport. Attempts to apply a true price to a Russian-scale economy planned in this way were certain to cause chaos. In all circumstances and even in capitalist economies transforming defence industries to meet the demands of the very different civilian market is difficult. The Soviet Union was a military superpower with a very weak civilian industrial sector. The collapse of the defence industry, almost inevitable in the post-Soviet and post-Cold War context, meant the collapse of Soviet industry as a whole, or at least of its high-technology core. Even in purely economic terms, therefore, Russia's imperial heritage greatly worsened the already huge difficulties faced by any socialist economy's transition to capitalism.

The political heritage of empire was worse. The Poles, Hungarians and Czechs rejoiced in the end of empire and saw it as a means to realize their true identity by returning to Europe. Russia's relationship to Europe was always much more equivocal. The Soviet empire was to some extent Russian and its ending must always therefore seem at best a mixed blessing to Russians, especially when combined with a situation in which 25 million Russians found themselves outside Russia, sometimes in territories such as Crimea and northern Kazakhstan which no Russian saw as alien, imperial land. The political economy of 'shock therapy' in Russia never added up. For economic reasons the process was bound to be much lengthier and more painful than in Poland or Hungary. In political terms it needed to succeed more quickly and more unequivocally because history ensured that it would seem less legitimate to Russians than to Poles, Czechs or Hungarians.

Some scholars[60] have compared the contemporary politics of Northern Eurasia to medieval Europe. The king is weak, his barons are strong. They control the regions. No state bureaucracy capable of defending the public interest functions. But power at court, winning the factional politics that prevails there, is essential to the baron's well-being. It provides the lucrative patronage, monopolies and offices which are essential, among other things, to preserving his local base against his many rivals in the region who will ravage his land and steal his cattle at the first opportunity. Less exotic comparisons exist with parts of the contemporary Third World. Again, the state is weak. It pursues no public good. But it is a formidable source of patronage and its laws and licences grant control over resources to factions that conquer it, and are a major hindrance to their rivals. In an energy or minerals export economy the state can be a vastly profitable business, standing like a toll-gate between foreign companies and a country's outflow of oil, gas, gold and minerals. The ordinary subject has little allegiance to the state, or to a distant medieval king. Neither can offer patronage or security in an extremely hostile and uncertain world. The local lord, the local Third World notable and his patron–client network, may offer just this. His ability to do so is sometimes cited[61] as a key reason for the surprising degree of political stability in the Third World and the absence of social revolution.

The post-Soviet parallels are obvious. The collective farm's chairman and the factory manager are the local notables. They provide some security, above all some employment, in a dangerous, bewildering world in which socialism has died and Western-style capitalism has not really arrived, or rather has arrived but only in its grossest and least productive manifestations. Meanwhile the state does not even always pay its own employees, let alone provide security for the ordinary citizen. The chairman and the factory manager, minor local potentates, may well have a political boss in the regional centre as patron and protector. By contemporary Western standards the feudal baron was an arch-criminal running a sort of protection racket. So may the regional boss be: certainly he may well have links to the criminal world. But to condemn every ex-Soviet boss as a criminal would be very unfair. A key theme of this chapter has been that these ex-Communist notables usually proved much less destructive in the 1990s than political leaders drawn from the nationalist intelligentsia. The history of empire and its aftermath elsewhere makes this no surprise. Hugh Seton-Watson emphasized the disastrous, destructive influence of the nationalist intelligentsia in interwar Central Europe.[62] In the post-imperial Third World the replacement of colonial-era notables by nationalist and populist political leaders allied to a nationalist intelligentsia and mobilizing mass passions has frequently resulted in tragedy – in Sri Lanka, to take only one example. At present in the former Soviet Empire the notables are firmly in the saddle but everywhere new states are having to seek legitimacy in nationalism. Defeated in the political arena, the nationalist intelligentsia dominate centres of education and culture. In the longer run that could well be dangerous.

Meanwhile the rule of the notables is very often the rule of monopoly, linked to political influence and sometimes sustained by the gun. It is not a milieu in which law, control or predictability can flourish, or in which a modern capitalist economy can easily grow. There is a precedent in history for overcoming the rule of the barons. It was called royal absolutism and flourished in early modern Europe. The king created an authoritarian bureaucratic regime, backed it with a professional army, and as far as possible pursued an autarchic and mercantilist economic policy. In time he began to mobilize mass nationalism to boost the population's loyalty to the central state. It is not likely that the US Congress, the IMF or the world's human rights lobbies would much appreciate some aspects of this answer to dilemmas of contemporary post-Soviet politics. General Pinochet is not the most attractive of models in the best of circumstances. Given the dire history of despotism in the ex-Soviet region and the history too of Third World 'strongmen' who have reduced their state and country to a swamp of misery and corruption, the Pinochet model for Russia looks particularly unappetizing. The current extent of chaos and corruption in the armed forces suggests that a Russian Pinochet could turn into something closer to a Mobutu.

After all the high hopes of the Gorbachev era it is deeply depressing to be talking about the Third World, let alone Mobutu. On the other hand, as this chapter makes clear, the end of empire in the past has caused disaster on a scale far surpassing anything that has yet struck the Russo-Ukrainian core of the old Soviet Union. Thus far we have actually been rather fortunate as regards the consequences of this empire's collapse. Of course our luck may not last. Many of the former Soviet republics are fragile and could implode. Neighbours, including Russia itself, could be sucked into the chaos. Russia itself could collapse into banditry and lasting impoverishment. A worst-case scenario sees Russia as a sort of Nigeria, its vast potential resources squandered by the weakness of the state, the gross corruption of the elite, and the total collapse of any sense of patriotism or public service in the population.

Such a Russia would combine the worst mixing of Soviet bureaucratic morals and the nastiest aspects of global capitalism. A Russian Nigeria, armed with nuclear weapons and with a public opinion bitterly anti-elite and anti-Western, would obviously be a danger to the world. But actually Russia is not Nigeria, not in other words a former colony only artificially stuck together in the twentieth century from disparate peoples with no common history. Russian national identity is at present confused but it has deep roots and an immense cultural tradition to draw on. It has too a great tradition of statehood, often despotic but nevertheless formidable in its ability to unite people and mobilize resources in a very harsh international environment in which Russia has almost always been competing with richer rivals. It also still has a population that is very well educated by any Third World standard. In the longer run a people with these assets and traditions should not hover near the frontiers of the Third World and probably will not do so. But the road to recovery will probably be slow and certainly painful. Even in a best-case scenario some of the methods used to restore an effective Russian state will be unpalatable. The day when Russians will enjoy even semi-First-World levels of prosperity and security seems long distant. A strong possibility exists that it will never come.

Simply because Russia and its former empire are fated by geography to live side by side, the post-imperial relationship between them is a more important and more dangerous matter than in the case of Europe's maritime empires. Once direct rule over the empire was lost, Russia found it very difficult to compete with the West for indirect influence in its former republics because its economy was too weak. Other former imperial powers faced the same conundrum after empire's end, for informal empire actually requires greater resources and greater superiority to rival powers than is the case when 'fair competition' can be avoided by the exercise of political control. Tsarist Russia in its last century was also usually unable to compete economically with the European powers in the territories just beyond its borders and was therefore driven to assert direct political control over neighbouring regions and markets in order to protect its interests. The same realities drive today's Russia to use its geographical position, its military power and its control over oil and gas pipelines to make up for economic weakness in its struggle to defend its interests in its former empire. Because, unlike the metropolises of the Western maritime empires, Russia is not separated by oceans from most of its former colonies, it cannot be indifferent to instability in neighbouring territories and former Soviet republics inevitably fear a rebirth of Russian power and expansionism. By contrast, maritime empires could leave civil war and banditry in their wake without needing to fear that bandits would cross their borders or kidnap their citizens. The wars in Chechnya have in part to be understood in the light of this reality.

For any European with a sense of history the obvious and terrifying possible parallel with Russia today is Hitler's Germany. A string of small political groups have put forward ideas very similar to Hitler's. Zhirinovsky sometimes sounds like Hitler though, when it comes to voting in parliament, under Yeltsin his party usually acted as the president's poodles. The Communist Party, at present Russia's most popular political movement, and its leader Gennady Zyuganov, are not born-again Social Democrats like their fellow Polish and Hungarian former Communists and they have a great deal of nostalgia for empire. Meanwhile Russia remains potentially much the most powerful state in the ex-Soviet region and was the great loser from the 1991 territorial settlement. In that sense the parallels with post-First World War Germany are obvious. The states of East-Central Europe were much too weak to stop a resurgent Germany from moving into the vacuum left by the Versailles settlement. The same could be the case in contemporary Northern Eurasia.

But today's international context is very different from interwar Europe. The global forces that would oppose a renewed Russian bid for empire are much stronger than the European great powers that stood in Hitler's path. Their resources overwhelmed the USSR in the Cold War. For the foreseeable future Russia will be much weaker than Brezhnev's Soviet Union. Of course, the possible future challenges to global order outlined in Chapter 2 could alter the international context: Islam, China, a crash of 1929 proportions or fierce ecological pressures. A truly Islamic or Chinese challenge to the present global order would give Russia more room to manoeuvre with Washington and the IMF but would also almost certainly align Russia with the West. Despite the current popularity of Eurasian ideas in Russia, bred by the same anti-Western frustration that fuelled such ideas among the White emigration, Russia is by tradition and culture far closer to Europe than to Muslim or Confucian Asia. A real spread of Islamic fundamentalism along Russia's southern border and into its own Muslim minorities would be a big challenge to Russian security. In the same way, a common rhetorical and even diplomatic front with China against American global hegemony is one thing, an alliance with China to challenge the global order quite another. Russia is far too weak for such a policy. In any case it has a long border with China and now remains the only European country that still possesses substantial and sparsely populated territory which the Chinese consider to have been stolen from themselves. With the Russian population predicted to shrink dramatically in the next decades, the threat to its East Asian possessions could become more and more severe. This could for instance result in policies designed to lure the diaspora back to Russia. Certainly, the last thing Russia should welcome is Chinese domination in East Asia. As regards true global financial or ecological disaster, the most obvious point is that the weak would go to the wall. At present Russia is weak. It is hard to imagine that the rather tired nationalist and imperialist ideas rediscovered by today's Russians from the pre-1914 era would provide sufficient inspiration for Russians to mount a challenge to the global order, let alone to mobilize foreign supporters.

Above all, the geopolitics of AD 2000 is very different from that of the 1930s. If one accepted Hitler's premises, there was a ghastly logic to his actions. Germany's annexation of Austria and Czechoslovakia before 1939 did greatly increase its power. Together with skilful use of modern military technology these conquests did help Hitler to defeat France in 1940 at a very low cost to Germany. The Germans did then acquire great additional power through their ability to mobilize the resources of the whole of conquered Europe behind their war effort. This did allow Hitler, in alliance with Japan, to make a realistic bid to dominate Eurasia, though the challenge was a difficult one and arrogant miscalculation of Soviet potential contributed to disaster. No such logic could support a Russian attempt to pursue a Hitlerian strategy in today's world.

The reason goes to the heart of this book. The Soviet Union was the last of the great old empires. It was a modernized, perfected version of empire, suitable to the twentieth century. It had empire's traditional obsession with territory, autarchy and the mobilization of all available resources for military power. It deported and punished whole peoples in true imperial style. It harnessed one of the great twentieth-century ideologies to empire's cause, in the process mobilizing the power of religion and massive social mobility and girding itself against the great enemy of modern empire, which is nationalism. The Soviet Union was a perfect modern empire and a complete disaster. It was so partly because the Marxist-Leninist ideology on which it was founded was deeply flawed, and partly because it survived into an era in which even a modernized variant of empire was redundant. It played empire's game – international power politics – and lost decisively against Cold War enemies who outmatched it in military power and enjoyed a vastly richer and freer life as well. The lesson of Soviet history is that empire does not pay in today's world, even in terms of its own narrow priorities of power. The idea that Russia will become great again by regaining responsibility for the fate of scores of millions of ex-Soviet Muslim subjects or by intervening in a collapsing Ukraine to regain Crimea or Kharkov is a total nonsense. At the very most such a policy might reassure anxious Russian generals that they will be militarily superior to Turkey in AD 2050. That is neither a grandiose imperial vision nor an achievement worthy of Russia's history or of the enormous past suffering of its people. The basic present-day reality is that the Soviet Union showed that the idea of empire is now bankrupt and did so at the price of shattering the Russian people for at least one post-imperial generation and probably more.

Conclusion

'Empire' is a powerful and dangerous word. It has a rich and ambiguous history. It has strong polemical connotations now as in the past. The emotions it arouses when applied to the former Soviet Union help to make the concept of empire important for a Russianist. But they are also a warning to tread with caution and an open eye. It may by now be possible for historians (British ones anyway) to study the British Empire without feeling the need to attack or defend it on moral grounds. Only ten years after the collapse of the Soviet Union this is still not so easy for historians of Russia.

Nowadays it is polite to call a state an empire only when it is safely dead and beyond resurrection. To the twenty-first-century mind empire sins against both democracy and modernity: it is both wicked and redundant. As applied to the Soviet Union this verdict makes much sense. The Soviet Union was an empire. It was based on authoritarian, anti-democratic principles and it repressed and exploited its subjects, non-Russian and Russian. Under Lenin and, even more, Stalin the level of repression was massive. Moreover, whatever the strengths of this modernized empire when confronted by Hitler, by the 1980s it was redundant. Its repression of individual creativity and its attempt to seal the Soviet peoples off from the outside world were important sources of weakness. When radical reform came under Gorbachev the heritage of empire and the bitterness it had aroused were one reason why the Soviet Union did not evolve towards a multi-ethnic federation based on consent and mutual compromise among its many peoples.

But a simple condemnation of both empire and the Soviet Union is neither the whole truth nor very interesting. What after all is the point

413

in driving one more nail into the coffin of the Soviet Union? In any case, the tale of empire's wickedness and redundancy, contrasted to the morality and modernity of the democratic nation, is much too simple. In its time empire was often a force for peace, prosperity and the exchange of ideas across much of the globe. It sustained great cultures and civilizations. From its origins in the savage repression of the Vendée and revolutionary France's attempted conquest of Europe the history of the would-be democratic nation has sometimes been very chequered. White democratic nationalism in Europe's colonies of settlement generally far outdid aristocratic and bureaucratic empire in its devastation of indigenous peoples.

Of course, empire too has many sins to its name, though some of them in my view are in part wrongly addressed. If, for example, one were to choose the British Empire and concentrate on its worst aspects, the slave trade and the Opium War with China would come near the top of the list. In a sense these were aspects of empire: perhaps more significantly, however, they were also precursors of globalization. Europeans looted Africa for slaves and forced opium on the Chinese in order to create a global trading network from which they derived huge profits. They took no responsibility for ruling either Africa or China at that time. In comparison to the slave trade or the enforced commerce in opium, British rule in India or West Africa at the beginning of the twentieth century was both more unequivocally imperial and often possessed a genuine sense of responsibility and ethics.

The democratic nation, imbued with almost religious sanctity in 1789 and by later Romantic nationalists, does not even any longer necessarily seem more modern than empire. In the era of multi-culturalism, globalization and the European Union, aspects of the Holy Roman Empire or of the Habsburg Monarchy in 1900 actually appear more appropriate than the Jacobin nation or the frenzied ethnic nationalism that devastated Europe in the first half of the twentieth century and could easily repeat its triumph in the huge, multi-ethnic polities of twenty-first-century Asia. The victory of nationalism over empire in the Habsburg and Ottoman lands had devastating consequences. So far in the former Soviet Union we have, by historical standards, been very lucky. But these are still early days.

In the past empires drew their power from a number of sources. Michael Mann divides these into military, political, economic and ideological elements of power.[1] In my book we have seen plentiful evidence of all four. Most empires base their strength on a mix of these factors, though the balance between them differs from empire to empire and indeed over time even within a single empire. The Mongol Empire was the embodiment of military power. In the Chinese tradition of empire it is probably the strength of Confucianism and of Chinese high culture that is most remarkable. The decline of the Soviet Union probably owed more to the failure of its ideology – in which for example its economic system was rooted – than to any other factor. The economic and financial power of the British Empire stands out in comparison to the great military and dynastic land empires of history. In the maintenance of the Habsburg Empire it is perhaps politics and diplomacy that were most significant, though one would need to distinguish between the empire of the seventeenth century, armed with the ideological force of the Counter-Reformation, and the nineteenth-century empire on the defensive against rival great powers and domestic nationalism. The study of the rise and fall of empires convinces me, however, that to Michael Mann's four sources of power we must add demography and geography. The Ottoman Empire had too few Muslims and, even more, too few Turks to extend and consolidate its hold on the Balkans. The immense population sustained by the rice culture of southern China was an enormously important factor in the reconquest of northern China (and Manchuria) from nomadic invaders, and the consolidation of Chinese civilization throughout most of East Asia. The colonization of new worlds by Britain's surplus population was obviously a crucial element in the domination of the globe by the English language, culture and political values at the end of the second millennium. As sources of power demography and geography are often linked: China's population depended fundamentally on the possibility of rice farming. But geography is also a vastly important independent factor in the rise and fall of empires. This was evident in would-be universal empire's survival in East Asia and disappearance in Western Europe. It was evident in the expansion of Europe's peripheral powers from the sixteenth century. It was vital too in the Americans' ability to create a state of continental size by the last quarter of the nineteenth century, and then to use this continental base as a springboard for global power. Confined at the centre of Europe, Germany's bid for world power and empire faced far greater obstacles. If the word 'geography' can be extended to include ecology, then a combination of geographical and demographic factors at present seems the likeliest development to shatter today's American-led global order and to bring a return to an era of devastating conflict.

The relative importance of the main sources of power has changed over time. In comparison to the millennium before 1500, for example, military power appears somewhat less important in AD 2000 and economic power rather more so. Traditionally, the nomadic warrior of the steppe was the terror and the conqueror of great sedentary societies. In the twentieth century, however, military power appears to a considerable extent to depend on economic strength. The high-technology weapons that devastated Iraq with minimal loss to Western forces seemed to confirm the lesson of two world wars that in the end technology and economic power win. The Western victory in the Cold War seemed to contain the same lesson. For the moment it seems unlikely that power will shift fundamentally back towards armed force, even if we come to face urban nomads armed with pocket weapons of mass destruction in the anonymous mega-cities of the twenty-first century.

Where other sources of power are concerned the situation is less clear-cut. Since it is less easy to coerce people to obey, persuading them by the power of ideology and its propagandists may be more important than in the past. As Fukuyama notes, the hegemony of democracy as a political idea and (less securely) of liberal and free-trading principles in economics are very important factors in American power. They are scarcely more important, however, than the hold of Confucianism or of the imperial system of examinations on elites under most Chinese imperial dynasties. Politics, in other words mobilizing and targeting resources in the cause of power, is more difficult in contemporary democracies than often used to be the case, but certainly not less important. Modern communications have made geography less crucial in some respects but it does still appear to be true that global power requires a state to be continental in scale. As noted in Chapter 2, it is partly for this reason that the European Union exists and faces rather familiar problems of modern empire.

Demography also remains very significant. If, for example, the Russian population continues to shrink, that will have major implications for Russia's hold on its Far Eastern possessions and perhaps for its policy towards the Russian diaspora. In the longer term, the prospect that people of European descent may well be less than ten per cent of the world's population by 2050 must have important implications for the balance of global power between not just states but also cultures and values. Whether or not Asian middle classes are conquered by American values becomes an important issue. Multi-culturalism, multi-ethnicity and relatively generous immigration policies are themselves in one sense elements in the global power and ideological attraction of the United States. As has usually been the case with empires, however, questions of external power and domestic politics are closely connected. How will the United States cope with problems of domestic multi-ethnicity and multi-culturalism, and what impact will this have on its ability and its willingness to project its power globally?

In this book I have steered well clear of providing too rigorous and 'scientific' a definition of empire. Like Maurice Duverger,[2] I strongly suspect that such a definition would prove unusable. I have raced across eras and empires scattering generalizations as I pass in a way that will enrage some historians. Nevertheless I am too much of a historian to reduce the whole history of empire to a series of formulas – scientifically 'rigorous' and 'objective' and politically correct – even if I thought the task were possible. Empire is a fine subject, peopled by leopards and other creatures of the wild. To reduce all this to definitions and formulas is to turn the leopard into a pussycat, and even then into an incomplete but misshapen pussycat with three legs and no tail.

During my research I have looked at many empires as well as at a number of present-day states which, though not truly imperial, nevertheless face some of empire's dilemmas and share some of its characteristics. In my opinion this helps to put empire into perspective, to bring out some of its key elements, and to question some of the teleology that creeps into the study of empire if one approaches it with Western assumptions and on the basis of European history alone. But I have on the whole confined systematic comparison to the period from the sixteenth century when Russia first became an empire, and I have largely restricted myself to empires that were not just modern Russia's contemporaries but also its rivals. It seems to me that empires operating at the same time and within the same international system of states face many similar dilemmas and offer the best basis for comparative history. In comparing empire's aftermaths I have also mostly kept to the twentieth century and to the empires about which I wrote in detail in earlier chapters.

The fact that this book is written by a historian of Russia inevitably influences the questions it raises and the manner in which it approaches its subject. A Russian crazy mirror held up to the object of one's lifetime study and affection could easily be regarded by historians of empire as an alien invasion of sacred territory. A historian of the British Empire, for example, might well feel that the relative weakness of Russia in financial and commercial terms means that these elements of power do not get proper recognition in my chapter on Britain. Historians of the Ottoman Empire might have cause for even greater indignation. For generations they have suffered the condescension of Western historians about Ottoman failure and decline, and about the domination of the Ottoman

Empire by the Western powers. At last they have established the case that decline was not continuous from 1600 until 1918, and that the empire's peoples were not mere objects of Western power, walk-on players in an act directed from abroad. Now along belatedly comes a Russianist and the old song about decline rings out again.

In general, however, comparative history can never replace the work of specialists. It can merely shed light from unexpected angles and ask strange questions. No one sensible is likely to regard the author of this book as the last word on the British and Ottoman empires. As regards the Ottoman Empire, however, it does seem to me that the comparison with Russia is an important one, at least for the historian of Russia. Perhaps this is merely an excuse for self-indulgence: the historian of tsarist Russia gets so used to Western historians' analyses of Russia's backwardness, wickedness and failure that it is a relief to make comparisons that work in Russia's favour. As usual, the poor rob the poorer with greatest success. Certainly, for the period 1700–1914 the comparison is in Russia's favour as regards the most essential element of empire, which is power. I believe this did have much to do with exceptionally able Russian leaders and generals between 1689 and 1796. But it had more to do with other factors, most of which were beyond the Ottomans' control. These included crucially our old friend geopolitics: there were far fewer obstacles to Russian advance than was the case with the Ottomans, who had reached the geographical, demographic and logistic limits to possible expansion by 1700. In addition, precisely because the Ottoman state had been so very much more powerful and successful than Russia before 1600 it was much less inclined to radical change and the wholesale borrowing of Western values and models. In its heyday the Ottoman administration had been more efficient and just than the alliance between monarch and aristocratic serf-owner which was the core of both the Habsburg and Romanov polities. But in pre-modern conditions a bureaucratic machine of this sophistication was difficult to sustain over the generations.

The poor Russianist must in any case be allowed to savour imperial Russia's success since its consequences quickly turned sour. The triumph of Peter's and Catherine's Russia was based on a tightening of serfdom and the Westernization of the Russian elites, which in the long run contributed to undermining the solidarity of Russian society, with dire results in 1917. The autocratic and despotic state, with its formidable capacity to mobilize resources despite ruling a poor society in a very difficult geographical environment, was the essential element in Russia's emergence as a great European power. But power was bought at very high cost. Here the comparison with the Habsburg state at least in its last half-century is an important one. In terms of external power the tsarist state was more formidable and successful at mobilizing resources from its society. But this was partly because the Habsburgs coped with the domestic dilemmas of managing multi-ethnicity in a modernizing society in a manner that was more civilized and potentially more successful than the Romanovs'. Here one goes to the core of empire's dilemma in the modern era. The demands of external power and of civilized management of multi-ethnicity pulled hard in opposite directions. The Habsburgs were worthy precursors of the European Union but they lived in a more vicious international environment in which the weak went to the wall and those who drove them there were praised for Darwinian vigour and masculinity.

The Russian Empire was a hybrid. It combined aspects of modern European empire and of the tradition of autocratic land empire which stretches back to antiquity. It was an important part of the expansion of Europe but itself was in many ways a peripheral and backward economy and society, more similar to some of Britain's non-White colonies than to Britain itself, and even in 1900 well behind China in terms of agricultural techniques and productivity. The tsarist empire was in fact many empires. Its various regions differed greatly. In some regions comparison with European overseas empire makes sense, in other cases it is entirely inappropriate. Sometimes a Russian perspective does yield what seem to me to be interesting and unusual comparisons: for instance it throws a sharp and unusual light on the relationship between London, Ulster and the Catholic Irish. On the other hand, there are many elements in the tsarist empire that were *sui generis*. It is, for example, hard to find easy parallels with the role of the Urals – colonized territory but centre of Russian heavy industry in both the eighteenth and twentieth centuries – in other empires. Moreover, though the fates of Ukraine and Scotland can usefully be compared, in terms of population, agriculture, heavy industry and strategic position Ukraine was more important to the Russian and Soviet empires than Scotland was to the great Victorian world empire ruled from London.

The rise and fall of the Russian and Soviet empires were owed to many factors but the international context was of immense importance. Russia and then the Soviet Union operated within an international system in which they were usually weaker than some at least of their rivals. The extent and nature of this relative weakness differed over time. Under Peter I and Catherine II the gap closed considerably, and for a time indeed Russia was even regarded as the leading military power at least of Eastern and Central Europe. In the first half of the nineteenth century the Industrial Revolution tilted the balance of power sharply back towards Western Europe and then Germany. Under Stalin and in Khrushchev's early years Russia appeared once again to be overtaking most of its great power rivals, only once again to be left stranded in the age of the computer and the microchip.

But it was not just deep economic factors that determined Russia's relative standing among the great powers. A huge amount also depended on political rivalries and alliances within the great power club. In the eighteenth century Russia had a relatively easy ride because she was able to exploit British rivalry with France and, more importantly, Austrian rivalry with Prussia. Disaster came in the Crimean War because for the first time ever the British and French were united in a war against Russia, which made her coastline very vulnerable to allied landings. From 1879 the Austro-German alliance posed an even greater threat, since the potential enemy was well placed to invade the empire's political and economic heartland. Western historians argued for decades whether constitutional democracy or Bolshevism was the more logical fate for tsarist Russia and whether revolution would have come had there not been a war. For reasons made clear in this book, it seems to me that in 1914 neither stable, constitutional democracy nor Bolshevism was Russia's likeliest fate. Whether had no war occurred there would have been a socialist revolution is impossible to say, though it is hard to imagine the autocratic monarchical regime surviving for many more decades into the twentieth century. What seems to me almost certain is that in peacetime the great powers would never have allowed Russia to secede from 'Europe', repudiate its debts and set itself up as the headquarters of world revolution. In alliance with anti-Bolshevik forces in a peacetime Russia, and spearheaded by the Prussian army, it seems to me certain that international intervention would have had the means and the will to nip Bolshevism in the bud.

The enormous importance of the international context did not cease with the Revolution of 1917. Ultimately the main reason for the collapse of the Soviet Union was not the absolute failure of the socialist experiment but rather its relative failure as measured against Russia's capitalist rivals. The most basic reason for this failure was the inefficiency of state socialism when compared to capitalism, at least as the latter emerged after the Second World War under American leadership. Also hugely important, however, was the fact that all the major capitalist states hung together against the Soviet Union under American leadership. The contrast with 1933–45 was fundamental and, from the Soviet perspective, fatal.

In the post-Soviet era the fate of the Russian people and those of the other former Soviet republics depends above all on the peoples themselves and their rulers. As Chapter 10 made clear, the obstacles to peace and progress are so formidable that we should be surprised not that things have been bad but rather that they have not been much worse. The Ottoman, Habsburg and even British empires collapsed amidst much more bloodshed and horror than we have yet seen in the former Soviet Union. That has something to do with the fact that the end of the Soviet Union came in peacetime and without obvious foreign intervention or threat. It owed much to the existence of Soviet republics with legitimate governments and clear borders. Gorbachev's policies contributed hugely to the break-up of the Soviet Union but they also helped greatly to ensure that this would occur in a relatively smooth and legal manner. The fact that Yeltsin's Russia actually contributed to the Union's break-up and undermined the forces that opposed it was also of immense significance. The Russian people had suffered so much in the cause of communism and empire that they were totally unwilling to suffer further in defence of either. But coping with empire's aftermath on top of the more 'normal' problems of political and economic recovery from communism imposed immense burdens on Russians and non-Russians alike. One reason why the collapse of the Soviet Union was relatively peaceful was that the various peoples of the Union had no tradition or experience of democratic politics. The various nationalities were therefore much more difficult to mobilize against each other than in Yugoslavia, let alone in early twentieth-century Ireland. In this respect, for example, the contrast between the Russian diaspora on the one hand and Ulster Protestants or *pieds noirs* was very important. At present, as was often the case in the immediate aftermath of other empires, colonial era notables (i.e. Communist Party leaders) still rule most of the former Soviet Union. In general this is a cause of stability though also sometimes of stagnation and corruption. But if other post-imperial situations, and events in the Caucasus after 1991, are a guide, the general replacement of the notables by more populist and nationalist leaders would be a very mixed blessing.

The process of 'transition' is very far from completed in the former Soviet Union. It may never be 'completed' in large areas, which could remain poor, violent and unstable for decades. Salvation will certainly not come from the IMF, the World Bank or any other outside force. On the other hand, so long as the global economy does not suffer some spectacular disaster like the 1930s, capitalism and democracy will remain the dominant models to which mankind, and the former Soviet peoples too, will aspire for the near future. There are at present far stronger obstacles in the path of Russian revanchism than faced Hitler in the 1930s. But in the longer run Russia's fate will depend greatly on the overall stability of the present American-led global order, on whether it can offer Russia the chance to be more than a Second World exporter of energy and raw materials, and on whether Russians will be willing and able to take the chances that do become available.

I have dedicated this book to members of my own family whom I describe as children, and victims, of empire. The main purpose of this book, however, is to show that this description fits the Russian people as a whole.

Notes

PREFACE

1. A term borrowed from M. Mann, *The Soruces of Social Power*, 2 vols, Cambridge University Press, 1986.

CHAPTER 1.   EMPIRE: A WORD AND ITS MEANINGS

1. H. Grimal, 'L'évolution du concept d'empire en Grande Bretagne', ch. xiii, pp. 337–64, in M. Duverger (ed.), *Le Concept d'Empire*, Presses Universitaires de France, Paris, 1980, p. 352.
2. J.A. Hobson, *Imperialism. A Study*, Unwin Hyman, London, 1988 [1902], p. 3.
3. M. Mann, *Sources*.
4. P. Veyne, 'L'Empire romain', ch. v, pp. 121–9, in Duverger (ed.), *Concept*, p. 123.
5. R. Folz, *The Concept of Empire in Western Europe from the Fifth to the Fourteenth Century*, Greenwood Press, Westport, 1969, p. 4.
6. G. Fowden, *Empire to Commonwealth. Consequences of Monotheism in Late Antiquity*, Princeton University Press, 1993, pp. 106–7.
7. Toynbee considers these comparisons on a number of occasions but his main discussion of universal states and empires is in *A Study of History*, vol. vii, Oxford University Press, London, 1954: see in particular pp. 415–20.
8. Fowden, *Empire*, p. 6.
9. A. Miguel, 'L'Empire arabo-musulman (septième–treizième siècle)', ch. viii, pp. 203–204, in Duverger, *Concept*, pp. 221–2.
10. See e.g. C. Mackerras, *China's Minorities. Integration and Modernisation in the Twentieth Century*, Oxford University Press, Hong Kong, 1994, pp. 141–2. Above all see D.C. Gladney, *Muslim Chinese. Ethnic Nationalism in the People's Republic*, Harvard University Press, MA, 1991.
11. A. Hitler, *Mein Kampf*, trans. R. Manheim, Pimlico Press, London, 1993, pp. 3, 401, 557.
12. Otto von Habsburg, *Die Reichsidee. Geschichte und Zukunft einer übernationalen Ordnung*, Amalthea Verlag, Vienna, 1986, pp. 7, 28, 41, 74.
13. Folz, *Concept*, p. 17.
14. Quoted by A. Pagden, *Lords of all the World*, Yale University Press, New Haven, 1995, p. 14.
15. See J. Robertson, 'Gibbon's Roman Empire as a universal monarchy: *The Decline and Fall* and the imperial idea in early modern Europe', pp. 247–70, in R. McKitterick and R. Quinault, *Edward Gibbon and Empire*, Cambridge University Press, 1997.

16. *The Federalist Papers*, ed. C. Rossiter, Penguin, New York, p. 33.
17. Baron de Montesquieu, *Deux Opuscules de Montesquieu. Réflexions sur la Monarchie Universelle en Europe*, J. Rowan, Paris, 1891, p. 19.
18. A. Smith, *An Inquiry into the Nature and Causes of the Wealth of Nations*. Oxford University Press, Oxford, 1993, Book IV.
19. Hobson, *Imperialism*, pp. 67, 71, 106.
20. J. Schumpeter, *Imperialism (and) Social Classes*, Meridian Books, New York, 1955 [1951], pp. 65–8, 75–6, 92.
21. Lord Milner, *The Nation and the Empire. Being a Collection of Speeches and Addresses*, Constable, London, 1913, pp. 464–5.
22. Milner, *Nation*, p. 463.
23. J.R. Seeley, *The Expansion of England*, Macmillan, London, 1885, pp. 16, 75.
24. Lord Rosebery, *Questions of Empire*, London, 1900, pp. 6, 36.
25. Seeley, *Expansion*, pp. 46, 51, 75.
26. Milner, *Nation*, pp. 152, 290.
27. Rosebery quoted by Hobson, *Imperialism*, p. 234 and Rosebery, *Questions*, p. 37.
28. Quotations are from D.K. Fieldhouse, *The West and the Third World*, Blackwell, Oxford, 1999, p. 44.
29. V.I. Lenin, *Imperialism, the Highest Stage of Capitalism*.
30. His major work is *The Modern World-System*, 3 vols, Academic Press, San Diego, 1989 [1974].
31. E.M. Said, *Orientalism. Western Conceptions of the East*, Penguin, London, 1985.
32. J. Tomlinson, *Cultural Imperialism*, Pinter Publishers, London, 1991, p. 173.
33. M.W. Doyle, *Empires*, Cornell University Press, Ithaca, 1991.
34. S.M. Eisenstadt, *The Political Systems of Empires*, Transaction Books, London, 1992.
35. E. Gibbon, *History of the Decline and Fall of the Roman Empire*, ed. J.P. Bury, London, 1909–14.
36. R. Macmullen, *Corruption and the Decline of Rome*, Yale University Press, New Haven, 1988.
37. A.H.M. Jones, *The Later Roman Empire, 284–602. A Social, Economic and Administrative Survey*, 2 vols, Johns Hopkins University Press, Baltimore, 1992.
38. P. Kennedy, *The Rise and Fall of the Great Powers: Economic Change and Military Conflict from 1500 to 2000*, New York, 1988.

CHAPTER 2.   POWER AND EMPIRE IN THE GLOBAL CONTEXT

1. D. Bodde, 'The State and Empire of Ch'in', ch. 1, pp. 20ff., in D. Twitchett and M. Loewe (eds), *The Cambridge History of China*, vol. 1: *The Ch'in and Han Empires 221 BC–AD 220*, Cambridge University Press, 1986, here p. 60.
2. P. Garnsey and R. Saller, *The Roman Empire. Economy, Society and Culture*, Berkeley, 1987, p. 7.
3. F. Dikötter, *The Discourse of Race in Modern China*, Hurst, London, 1992.
4. S. Harrell, 'Introduction. Civilising Projects and the Reaction to Them', in S. Harrell (ed.), *Cultural Encounters on China's Ethnic Frontiers*, University of Washington Press, Seattle, 1994, p. 26.
5. For example, Hainan. See F. Chongyi and D.S.G. Goodman, 'Hainan: communal politics and the struggle for identity', ch. 5, pp. 53–92, in D.S.G. Goodman (ed.), *China's Provinces in Reform*, Routledge, London, 1997.
6. Norma Diamond, 'Defining the Miao. Ming, Qing and Contemporary Views', pp. 92–116, in Harrell (ed.), *Cultural Encounters*, here pp. 101–4.
7. Garnsey and Saller, *The Roman Empire*, p. 20. B.W. Jones, *The Emperor Domitian*, Routledge, London, 1992, p. 109 cites the same figure though he notes that the direct comparison is with the twelfth-century Song dynasty.
8. Garnsey and Saller, p. 26; 101–04; A. Lintott, *Imperium Romanum. Politics and Administration*, Routledge, London, 1993, p. 54.

9.   R. Huang, *1587. A Year of No Significance. The Ming Dynasty in Decline*, Yale University Press, New Haven, 1981, p. 75.

10. B.S. Bartlett, *Monarchs and Ministers, The Grand Council in Mid Ching China 1723–1820*, California University Press, Berkeley, 1991, pp. 64, 134.

11. Bodde, 'The State and Empire of Ch'in', pp. 56–7.

12. S.E. Finer, *The History of Government*, vol. 1: *Ancient Monarchies and Empires*, Oxford University Press, 1997, pp. 472–3.

13. Montesquieu, in *Deux Opuscules de Montesquieu*, Paris, 1891, p. 11.

14. R. Bonney, 'The Eighteenth Century. II. The Struggle for Great Power Status and the End of the Old Fiscal Regime', ch. 11, pp. 315ff., in Bonney (ed.), *Economic Systems and State Finance*, Clarendon Press, Oxford, 1995, here pp. 352–7, 380.

15. C. Mackerras, *China's Minorities. Integration and Modernisation in the Twentieth Century*, Oxford University Press, Hong Kong, 1994, p. 250.

16. C. Blunden and M. Elvin, *Cultural Atlas of China*, Phaidon, Oxford, 1983, p. 37.

17. On Israel see A. Hastings, *The Construction of Nationhood*, Cambridge University Press, 1997.

18. L.J. Moser, *The Chinese Mosaic. The Peoples and Provinces of China*, Westview, Boulder, 1985, p. 136.

19. C. Tilly, *Coercion, Capital and European States AD 990–1992*, Blackwell, Cambridge, MA, 1994, p. 15.

20. See e.g. P.J. Taylor, *The Way the Modern World Works*, Wiley, Chichester, 1996, especially pp. 55–7. These are perennial weaknesses of the so-called 'World Systems' school.

21. J. Osterhammel, *Colonialism*, Marcus Wiener, Princeton, 1997, p. 42.

22. A.J. Toynbee, *A Study of History. Abridgement of Volumes I–VI by D.C. Somervell*, Oxford University Press, 1946, p. 95.

23. R. Giradet, *L'Idée Coloniale en France de 1871 à 1962*, La Table Ronde, Paris, 1972, p. 28.

24. R. Szporluk, *Communism and Nationalism. Karl Marx versus Friedrich List*, Oxford University Press, 1988, p. 107.

25. W.D. Puleston, *Mahan, The Life and Work of Captain Alfred Thayer Mahan*, Jonathan Cape, London, 1939, p. 129.

26. Seeley, *The Expansion of England*, Macmillan, London, 1885, p. 46.

27. P. Griffith, *The Art of War in Revolutionary France. 1789–1802*, Greenhill Books, London, 1998, p. 29.

28. J. Mayall, *Nationalism and International Society*, Cambridge University Press, 1990, p. 46.

29. A.T. Mahan, *The Interest of America in Sea Power. Present and Future*, Sampson Low, London, 1897, p. 235.

30. A point made in H.W. Weigert et al. (eds), *Principles of Political Geography*, Appleton-Century-Crofts, New York, 1957, pp. 5–11.

31. Szporluk, *Communism and Nationalism*, p. 82.

32. W.R. Taylor, *Cavalier and Yankee*, Oxford University Press, New York, 1993.

33. B. Anderson, *Imagined Communities*, Verso, London, 1991.

34. See part 2 and especially chs 11–14 in A. Offer, *The First World War. An Agrarian Interpretation*, Clarendon Press, Oxford, 1989.

35. G.W. Gallagher, *The Confederate War*, Harvard University Press, Cambridge, MA, 1977, p. 289.

36. K. Burk, *Britain, America and the Sinews of War, 1914–1918*, Allen & Unwin, Boston, 1985, pp. 10, 88 takes the crisis very seriously; N. Ferguson, *The Pity of War*, Penguin, 1998, ch. 9 does not.

37. H.J. Mackinder, *Democratic Ideals and Reality*, Holt, New York, 1942, pp. 149–50.

38. Interestingly, the Japanese, who borrowed the German constitution, fell victim in 1941 to just the same inability to coordinate civil and military policy. Pearl Harbor was a brilliant military and disastrous political move.

39. P. Liberman, *Does Conquest Pay? The Exploitation of Occupied Industrial Societies*, Princeton University Press, 1996, pp. 40, 49.
40. Osternammel, *Colonialism*, p. 102. on e.g. literacy in the Dutch East Indies.
41. F. Furedi, *Colonial Wars and the Politics of Third World Nationalism*, I.B. Taurus, London, 1994, p. 108.
42. Weigert, *Principles*, p. 172.
43. V. Larionov, 'Why the Wehrmacht Didn't Win in 1941', in J.L. Wieczynski, *Operation Barbarossa*, Charles Schlacks Publisher, Salt Lake City, 1993, p. 208.
44. J.B. Nye, *Bound to Lead. The Changing Nature of American Power*, Basic Books, New York, 1991, p. 91.
45. F. Fukuyama, *The End of History and the Last Man*, Penguin, London, 1992.
46. Z. Brzezinski, *The Grand Chessboard*, Basic Books, New York, 1997, p. 27.
47. S.P. Huntington, *The Clash of Civilizations and the Remaking of World Order*, Touchstone Books, London, 1997.
48. Finer, *History of Government*, vol. 1, p. 8.
49. D.A. Low, *Eclipse of Empire*, Cambridge University Press, 1991, pp. 156–7.
50. In the 1950s Congress ran almost all state governments, by 1987 only 12 out of 25. Increasingly, President's Rule was used not to protect the state but to help the central Congress leaders' local clients.
51. Ishtiaq Ahmed, *State, Nation and Ethnicity in Contemporary South Asia*, Pinter, London, 1996, p. 92.
52. Ibid., p. 95.
53. M. Chadda, *Ethnicity, Security and Separatism in India*, Columbia University Press, New York, 1997, p. 169.
54. Quoted on p. 101 of S. Corbridge, 'Federalism, Hindu Nationalism and Mythologies of Governance in Modern India', pp. 101–27 in G. Smith (ed.), *Federalism. The Multi-Ethnic Challenge*, Longman, London, 1995.
55. P. Kratoska and P. Burton, 'Nationalism and Modernist Reform', ch. 5 in N. Tarling (ed.), *The Cambridge History of South-East Asia*, vol. 2: *The Nineteenth and Twentieth Centuries*, Cambridge University Press, 1992, p. 275.
56. 60.4 per cent of Indonesia's population lived in Java in 1971. Much of the population of western Java is Sundanese. M.C. Ricklefs, *A History of Modern Indonesia since c. 1300*, Stanford University Press, 1993, p. 281.
57. P. Liddle, *Leadership and Culture in Indonesian Politics*, Allen & Unwin, Sydney, 1996, p. 66.
58. Ibid., p. 67. Kratoska and Batson, 'Nationalism', p. 305.
59. For this figure and an analysis of the massacres in Bali, see ch. 11 of G. Robinson, *The Dark Side of Paradise. Political Violence in Bali*, Cornell University Press, Ithaca, 1995.
60. Liddle, *Leadership and Culture*, p. 253.
61. Whatever I know on the Holy Roman Empire's last centuries is owed to Professor Rudolph Vierhaus of the Max Planck Institute in Göttingen, who was my adviser for an earlier book comparing European aristocracies. His *Germany in the Age of Absolutism*, Cambridge University Press, 1988 is a fine introduction to the empire's significance in the last period of its existence.

CHAPTER 3.   THE BRITISH EMPIRE

1. See, above all, chapter 1 of Rory Miller, *Britain and Latin America*, Longman, London, 1993.
2. Quoted in M. Beloff, *Imperial Sunset*, vol. 1, *Britain's Liberal Empire, 1897–1921*, Alfred A. Knopf, New York, 1970, p. 98. Luke Trainor argues that celebrations of monarchical loyalty in the late nineteenth century were contentious: see L. Trainor, *British Imperialism and Australian Nationalism*, Cambridge University Press, 1994, e.g. ch. 6. British veneration of the monarchy was greater in the 1900s than in the 1870s and 1880s.

3. See e.g. D. Omissi, *The Sepoy and the Raj 1860–1940*, Macmillan, London, 1994, pp. 107ff.

4. This is the core of J.M. Ward's argument in *Colonial Self-Government. The British Experience 1759–1856*, Macmillan, London, 1976.

5. No serious effort was made in the Cromwellian era to convert the Irish, who were regarded as irredeemable. A little thought was given to the wholesale expropriation and expulsion of peasants as well as landlords and their resettlement in the west but land without labour would have been valueless to the new Protestant gentry and the importation of sufficient numbers of English farmers and labourers to replace the Irish was inconceivable. See e.g. N. Canny, 'The Marginal Kingdom. Ireland as a Problem in the First British Empire', in B. Bailyn and P.D. Morgan (eds), *Strangers Within the Realm*, University of North Carolina, Chapel Hill, 1991, pp. 59–61.

6. For instance, the creeping southwards movement of Protestant farmers in Armagh, but e.g. in north Wexford the strength of the 1798 Catholic rebellion owed much to exceptionally high levels of Protestant settlement. R.E. Forster, *Modern Ireland 1600–1972*, London, 1988, pp. 275–9. Even in Longford, not an area of particularly heavy Protestant settlement, landlords traditionally preferred Protestant tenant farmers both for political reasons and because they were seen as more efficient. Liam Kennedy, *Colonialism, Religion and Nationalism in Ireland*, Queen's University Press, Belfast, ch. 1.

7. In 1765 the Company was formally invested with the post of *diwan*, collector of revenues, for the Mogul provinces of Bengal, Bihar and Orissa: see e.g. P. Lawson, *The East India Company*, Longman, Marlo, 1993, p. 105.

8. Barbara L. Solow, Introduction, p. 1 in B.L. Solow (ed.), *Slavery and the Rise of the Atlantic System*, Cambridge University Press, 1991.

9. B.L. Solow, ch. 1: 'Slavery and Colonisation', in Solow (ed.), *Slavery*.

10. P.D. Curtin, *The Rise and Fall of the Plantation Complex. Essays in Atlantic History*, Cambridge University Press, 1990, p. 26.

11. The single most direct comparison between North American slaves and Russian serfs is P. Kolchin, *Unfree Labor. American Slavery and Russian Serfdom*, Harvard University Press, Cambridge, MA, 1987.

12. This is a paraphrase of p. 72 of B. Porter, *The Lion's Share. A Short History of British Imperialism 1850–1983*, Longman, Harlow, 1984.

13. J. Kendle, *Ireland and the Federal Solution. The Debate over the United Kingdom Constitution, 1870–1921*, McGill-Queens University Press, Kingston, 1989, p. 21.

14. T.R. Metcalf, *Ideologies of the Raj*, Cambridge University Press, 1994, p. 33.

15. A. Offer, *The First World War: An Agrarian Interpretation*, Oxford University Press, 1989, p. 95.

16. H.J. Mackinder, *Britain and the British Seas*, Heinemann, London, 1902, p. 343.

17. Mackinder, *Democratic Ideals*, pp. 141, 146.

18. Seeley, *Expansion*, p. 263.

19. L. Stone, Introduction, p. 6 in Stone (ed.), *The Imperial State at War. Britain from 1689 to 1815*, Routledge, London, 1994.

20. R. Bonney, 'The Eighteenth Century. II. The Struggle for Great Power Status and the End of the Old Fiscal Regime', pp. 320–1, 329, 332, 378, 380 in Bonney (ed.), *Economic Systems and State Finance*, Clarendon Press, Oxford, 1995.

21. P.J. Cain and A.G. Hopkins, *British Imperialism: Innovation and Expansion, 1688–1914*, Longman, Harlow, 1993, vol. 1, p. 283.

22. Porter, *Lion's Share*, p. 235.

23. General Essame calls the Australians 'the most formidable infantry on either side of the whole war, outclassing all others in courage, ingenuity, endurance, initiative and skill with their weapons', P. Young (ed.), *History of the First World War*, BPC, Paulton, 1971, vol. 7, p. 2949.

24. J. Darwin, *The End of Empire*, Oxford, 1991, p. 62 comments that British commitment to Europe was essential if the Americans were to be drawn in too.

25. S.J. Connolly, *Religion, Law and Power. The Making of Protestant Ireland 1660–1760*, Oxford University Press, 1992, pp. 249–50.
26. See e.g. Prince L.H. von Pückler-Muskau, *Tour in England, Ireland and France in the Years 1826, 1827, 1828 and 1829*, Zurich, 1940, pp. 67–8, 74–6. Also e.g. D.M. Wallace, *Russia*, Vintage Books, New York, 1961, pp. 156–8 for a portrait of the English-style magnate in Russia.
27. Quoted in D.A. Low, *Eclipse of Empire*, Cambridge University Press, 1991, p. 4.
28. On the police and repression see e.g. David Arnold, *Police Power and Colonial Rule. Madras 1859–1947*, Oxford University Press, Delhi, 1986, especially ch. 6 and Conclusion.
29. Seeley, *Expansion*, pp. 219–45.
30. I owe this insight to Professor Christopher Bayly who also helped me to avoid many errors in writing this chapter.
31. A.L. Friedberg, *The Weary Titan. Britain and the Experience of Relative Decline 1895–1905*, Princeton University Press, 1988, pp. 238, 263.
32. J. Tomes, *Balfour and Foreign Policy*, Cambridge University Press, 1997, pp. 36–9, 173, 197.
33. J.H. Elliott, Introduction, p. 4 in N. Canny and A. Pagden (eds), *Colonial Identity in the Atlantic World 1500–1800*, Princeton University Press, 1987.
34. Smith, *The Wealth of Nations*, Oxford University Press, 1993, pp. 362–3.
35. Kendle, *Ireland*, p. 108.
36. Beloff, *Imperial Sunset*, p. 315.
37. K. Neilson, *Britain and the Last Tsar. British Policy and Russia, 1894–1917*, Oxford University Press, 1996, pp. 24, 33, 123.
38. Sir C.P. Lucas, *Greater Rome and Greater Britain*, Clarendon Press, Oxford, 1912, pp. 98–99.
39. R.J. Popplewell, *Intelligence and Imperial Defence. British Intelligence and the Defence of the Indian Empire*, Frank Cass, London, 1995, p. 90.
40. Popplewell, *Intelligence*, pp. 27, 65.
41. Metcalf, *Ideologies*, p. 223.
42. A. Offer, 'Pacific Rim Societies. Asian Labour and White Nationalism', pp. 233–4, in J. Eddy and D. Schreuder (eds), *The Rise of Colonial Nationalism*, Allen & Unwin, Sydney, 1988.
43. Trainor, *British Imperialism*, p. 16.
44. Lucas, *Greater Rome*, pp. 93–101.
45. P. Liberman, *Does Conquest Pay? The Exploitation of Occupied Industrial Societies*, Princeton University Press, 1996, p. 109.
46. This paragraph is owed almost entirely to L. Colley, *Britons. Forging the Nation, 1707–1837*, Yale University Press, New Haven, 1992 and L. Greenfeld, *Nationalism: Five Roads to Modernity*, Harvard University Press, Cambridge, MA, 1992.
47. This point (and many others in this paragraph) is derived from L. Kennedy, *Colonialism*, ch. 8.

CHAPTER 4.   THE OTTOMAN EMPIRE

1. H. Inalcik and D. Quataert, *An Economic and Social History of the Ottoman Empire 1300–1914*, Cambridge University Press, 1995, p. 782.
2. Inalcik and Quataert, *Economic*, pp. 79, 776–7.
3. C. von der Goltz, 'Stärke und Schwäche des türkischen Reiches', *Deutsche Rundschau*, vol. LXXXXIII, October/December, 1897, p. 105.
4. In 1481 the Ottoman Empire covered 335,000 square miles, 178,400 in Asia and 156,600 in Europe. By 1566 the empire's total size was 877,800 square miles, of which 462,700 were in Asia, 224,100 in Europe, and 191,000 in Africa. See p. 133 in D.E. Pitcher, *An Historical Geography of the Ottoman Empire*, E.J. Brill, Leiden, 1972.
5. J.M. Landau, *Pan-Turkism. From Irredentism to Cooperation*, Hurst, London, 1995, p. 52.
6. M.S. Hanioglu, *The Young Turks in Opposition*, Oxford University Press, 1995, makes this point well in both Introduction and text. On these points I benefited greatly from a talk given by

Professor H. Unal entitled 'The Emergence of Turkish Nationalism and the Destruction of the Ottoman Empire: A Study of the Rise of Young Turk Nationalism and its Implications', presented at a conference at the Austrian Cultural Institute in London on 28 November 1998 on 'The Decline of Empires'.

7. C.V. Findley, *Bureaucratic Reform in the Ottoman Empire. The Sublime Porte 1789–1922*, Princeton University Press, 1980, p. 229.

8. Von der Goltz, 'Stärke', p. 111.

9. S. Deringil, *The Well-Protected Domains. Ideology and the Legitimation of Power in the Ottoman Empire*, I.B. Taurus, London, 1998, p. 65.

10. Inalcik and Quataert, *Economic*, p. 714.

11. Bonney (ed.), *Economic Systems*, p. 368.

12. R. Owen, *The Middle East in the World Economy 1800–1914*, I.B. Taurus, London, 1993, pp. 59–60.

13. C. Imber, 'Ideals and Legitimation in early Ottoman Empire', in M. Kunt and C. Woodhead (eds), *Suleyman the Magnificent and His Age*, Longman, London, 1995, p. 148.

14. M.E. Yapp, *The Making of the Modern Near East, 1792–1923*, Longman, London, 1987, pp. 131–5. G. Veinstein, 'Les provinces balkaniques (1606–1774)', p. 304, in R. Mantran (ed.), *Histoire de l'Empire Ottoman*, Fayard, Paris, 1989.

15. Andrew Hess, *The Forgotten Frontier*, University of Chicago Press, 1978.

16. H. Kayagli, *Arabs and Young Turks. Ottomanism, Arabism and Islamism in the Ottoman Empire, 1908–1918*, University of California Press, Berkeley, 1997, p. 15 and ch. 5.

17. I owe this point to Valentin Mandache, who is currently a PhD student at LSE working on Moldovan identity.

18. B. Braude and B. Lewis, *Christians and Jews in the Ottoman Empire. The Functioning of a Plural Society*, Holmes & Meier, New York, 2 vols, 1982; here vol. 1, pp. 9–10.

19. See e.g. chs 2, 3, 4 of Braude and Lewis, *Christians and Jews*.

20. See e.g. ch. 6 of J. Salt, *Imperialism, Evangelism and the Ottoman Armenians 1878–1896*, Frank Cass, London, 1993.

21. J. McCarthy, *The Ottoman Turks*, Longman, Harlow, pp. 330, 333, 336–7, 338–41.

22. Yapp, *Making*, pp. 134–6.

23. C. Issawi, 'The Transformation of the Economic Position of the Millets in the Nineteenth Century', in Braude and Lewis, *Christians and Jews*, pp. 262–4, 271.

24. Owen, *Middle East*, chs 8, 9.

25. Yapp, *Making*, pp. 134–6.

26. Findley, *Bureaucratic Reform*, p. 230.

27. Feroz Ahmed, 'The late Ottoman Empire', ch. 1, here in M. Kent (ed.) *The Great Powers and the End of the Ottoman Empire*, Frank Cass, London, 1996, p. 22.

28. The debate about genocide is, quite rightly, hugely charged and contentious. Although V.N. Dadrian fails to put the horrific events of 1915–16 in their context, the evidence he presents from German, Austrian and Turkish sources in my view leads inescapably to the conclusion that the extermination of the Armenians was actually planned by a clique within the Young Turk leadership and executed by the sinister 'Special Organization' (Teskilat Mahsusa) of the army. See in particular V.N. Dadrian, *The History of the Armenian Genocide*, Berghahn, Oxford, 1995, chs 11, 14, 19.

29. Deringil, *Well-Protected*, p. 170.

CHAPTER 5.   THE HABSBURG EMPIRE

1. F.A.J. Szabo, *Kaunitz and Enlightened Absolutism 1753–1780*, Cambridge University Press, 1994, p. 76.

2. J.P. Bled, *Franz Joseph*, Blackwell, Oxford, 1994, p. 152.

Notes

3. G.E. Rothenberg, 'The Habsburg Army in the First World War 1914–1918', pp. 289–300; here p. 291 in B.K. Kiraly and N.F. Dreisziger (eds), *War and Society in East Central Europe*, vol. XIX, Columbia University Press, 1985.

4. A. Sked, *The Decline and Fall of the Habsburg Empire 1815–1918*, Longman, London, 1989, pp. 179–80.

5. Bled, *Franz Joseph*, p. 39.

6. R.J.W. Evans, *The Making of the Habsburg Monarchy 1551–1700*, Oxford University Press, 1979, p. 24.

7. C. Ingrao, *The Habsburg Monarchy 1618–1815*, Cambridge University Press, 1994, p. 191.

8. D. Beales, *Joseph II*, vol. 1, *In the Shadow of Maria Theresa*, Cambridge University Press, 1987, p. 50.

9. C. Duffy, *The Army of Maria Theresa. The Armed Forces of Imperial Austria, 1740–1780*, Terence Wise, London, 1990, p. 8.

10. Ingrao, *Habsburg Monarchy*, pp. 97, 216, 219.

11. Ingrao, *Habsburg Monarchy*, p. 20.

12. T. Kletecka, 'Aussenpolitische Vorstellungen von Parteien und Gruppen in Cisleithanien', pp. 399–458, in *Die Habsburgermonarchie 1848–1918* (henceforth *HM*), Österreichischer Akademie der Wissenschaften, vol. VI, *Die Habsburgmonarchie im System der Internationalen Beziehungen*, vol. I, Vienna, 1989, p. 442.

13. Both the last quotations are from G. Wawro, *The Austro-Prussian War. Austria's War with Prussia and Italy in 1866*, Cambridge University Press, 1996, pp. 24, 38.

14. J.C. Allmayer-Beck, 'Die Bewaffnete Macht in Staat und Gesellschaft', in *HM*, vol. V, *Die Bewaffnete Macht*, 1987, pp. 30–1.

15. P. Schimert, 'The Hungarian Nobility in the Seventeenth and Eighteenth Centuries', ch. 7 in H.M. Scott (ed.), *The European Nobilities*, vol. 2, *Northern, Central and Eastern Europe*, Longman, London, 1995, p. 147.

16. V. Preis, 'The System of Estates in the Austrian Hereditary Lands and in the Holy Roman Empire: A Comparison', in R.J. Evans and T.V. Thomas (eds.), *Crown, Church and Estates. Central European Politics in the Sixteenth and Seventeenth Centuries*, St Martin's Press, New York, 1991, p. 12.

17. See A. Alcock, 'Trentino and Tyrol. From Austrian Crownland to European Region', in S. Dunn and T.G. Fraser, *Europe and Ethnicity. World War I and Contemporary Ethnic Conflict*, Routledge, London, 1996, p. 70.

18. N. Der Bagdasarian, *The Austro-German Rapprochement, 1870–1879*, Associated University Press, Madison, 1976, p. 45.

19. A point I owe to Valentin Mandache.

20. F. Gottas, 'Die Deutschen in Ungarn', in *HM*, vol. III, pt 1, *Die Völker des Reiches*, 1980, pp. 340–410, here p. 342.

21. H. Mommsen, *Die Sozialdemokratie und die Nationalitätenfrage im Habsburgischen Vielvölkerstaat*, Europa Verlag, Vienna, 1963, p. 26.

22. B. Sutter, 'Die politische und Rechtliche Stellung der Deutschen in Österreich 1848 bis 1918', in *HM*, vol. III, pt 1, *Völker*, p. 244.

23. Bagdasarian, *Austro-German Rapprochement*, pp. 101–3.

24. Most of these statistics are drawn from pt V, ch. 1 of O. Jaszi, *The Dissolution of the Habsburg Monarchy*, University of Chicago Press, 1977. For the Czechs see pp. 506–7 and 511 of J. Kiralka and R.J. Crampton, 'Die Tschechen', in *HM*, vol. III, pt 1, *Völker*.

25. B. Sutter, 'Die politische und rechtliche Stellung der Deutschen in Österreich 1848 bis 1918', in *HM*, vol. III, pt 1, *Völker*, p. 166.

26. J.W. Bower, *Culture and Political Crisis in Vienna: Christian Socialism in Power 1897–1918*, University of Chicago Press, 1995, p. 121.

27. P. Kulemann, *Am Beispiel des Austro-Marxismus*, Junius Verlag, Hamburg, 1979, p. 133.

28. N. Leser, *Zwischen Reformismus und Bolschewismus*, Hermann Bühlaus, Vienna, 1985, p. 97.

29. R.A. Kann, *The Multinational Empire. Nationalism and National Reform in the Habsburg Monarchy 1848–1918*, Octagon Books, New York, 2 vols, here vol. 2, p. 159.

30. Jaszi, *Dissolution*, p. 295.

31. J. Komlos, *The Habsburg Monarchy as a Customs Union: Economic Development in Austria-Hungary in the Nineteenth Century*, Princeton University Press, 1983, p. 163.

32. A.C. Janos, *The Politics of Backwardness in Hungary 1825–1945*, Princeton University Press, 1982, p. 163.

33. Quoted on p. 11 of J. Frankel, 'Assimilation and the Jews in Nineteenth-Century Europe: towards a new historiography?', in J. Frankel and S.J. Zipperstein (eds.), *Assimilation and Community: the Jews in Nineteenth-Century Europe*, Cambridge University Press, 1992.

34. I. Deak, 'The Fall of Austria-Hungary. Peace, Stability and Legitimacy', ch. 4 in G. Lundestad (ed.), *The Fall of Great Powers. Peace, Stability and Legitimacy*, Scandinavian University Press, Oslo, 1994, p. 89.

CHAPTER 6. THE RUSSIAN EMPIRE: REGIONS, PEOPLES, GEOPOLITICS

1. Toynbee, *A Study of History*, Abridgement of Volumes I–VI by D.C. Somervell, Oxford, 1946, pp. 69–95.

2. Baron de Montesquieu, *The Spirit of the Laws*, trans. T. Nugent, New York, 1949, pp. 221–73.

3. H.J. Mackinder, *Democratic Ideals and Reality*, Holt, New York, 1942, pp. 29–34, 50, 86–94.

4. J. Abu-Lughod, *Before European Hegemony. The World System AD 1250–1350*, Oxford University Press, New York, 1989.

5. D. Kirby, *Northern Europe in the Early Modern Period. The Baltic War 1492–1772*, Longman, London, 1990, pp. 27, 77, 80.

6. R.E. Jones, *The Emancipation of the Russian Nobility, 1762–1785*, Princeton University Press 1973, p. 182.

7. W.H. Parker, *An Historical Geography of Russia*, London, 1968, p. 20. The classic statement about the environment's influence on Russian history is to be found in the third and fourth lectures of V.O. Klyuchevsky, *Sochineniya. Kurs russkoy istorii*, Moscow, 1956, vol. 1, pp. 45–72.

8. Parker, *Historical Geography*, p. 20.

9. D. Morgan, *The Mongols*, Cambridge, MA, 1986, p. 91.

10. E.I. Druzhinina, *Severno e Prichernomore 1775–1800g*, Moscow, 1959, p. 50 states that in the mid-1770s the Zaporozhye Host had less than 60,000 members and covered an area of 8 million desyatinas.

11. E.I. Druzhinina, *Yuzhnaya Ukraina v periode krizisa feodalisma 1825–1860gg*, Nauka, Moscow, 1981, pp. 41–42. Of a total 21 million desyatinas, half belonged to 6,000 landowners, about two-thirds of whom were nobles or enjoyed equivalent rights.

12. P. Herlihy, *Odessa. A History 1794–1914*, Harvard University Press, Cambridge, 1986, p. 13.

13. M. Khodarkovsky, *Where two Worlds Met*, Cornell University Press, Ithaca, 1992, p. 234.

14. M.B. Olcott, *The Kazakhs*, Hoover, Stanford, 1987, p. 86.

15. A. Lambert, *The Crimean War. Britain's Grand Strategy against Russia 1853–1856*, Macmillan, 1990, passim.

16. Count K.K. Pahlen, a Senator inspecting Central Asia, rejoiced that 300 million roubles worth of cotton was supplied by Turkestan to Russian mills in 1908–9, all of which would previously have been imported from the United States. R.A. Pierce (ed.), *Mission to Turkestan. Being the Memoirs of Count K.K. Pahlen*, Oxford University Press, London, 1964, p. 91. See H. Carrere d' Encausse, *Islam and the Russian Empire. Reform and revolution in Central Asia*, I.B. Taurus, London, 1988, p. 41 for statistics on the growth of cotton production.

17. Statistics from p. 26 of N.K. Gvosdev, 'Alliance or Absorption: Imperial Perspectives and Policies toward Georgia 1760–1819', PhD, Oxford University, 1995.

18. The two quotations are from David Gillard, *The Struggle for Asia 1828–1914*, London, 1977, pp. 98–9, 104.

19. *Molotov Remembers. Inside Kremlin Politics. Conversations with Felix Chuev*, Ivan R. Dee, Chicago, 1995, pp. 8–10.

20. See A.M. Nekrich, *The Punished Peoples. The deportation and fate of Soviet minorities at the end of the Second World War*, W.W. Norton, New York, 1978.

21. Most famously, R.C. Tucker, *Stalin in Power. The Revolution from Above 1928–41*, Norton, New York, 1990, especially pp. 50–65.

22. T. Polvinen, *Imperial Borderland. Bobrikov and the Attempted Russification of Finland 1898–1904*, Duke University Press, Chapel Hill, 1995, p. 22.

23. E.C. Thaden, *Russia's Western Borderlands 1710–1870*, Princeton University Press, 1984, p. 32.

24. E. Amburger, *Geschichte der Behordenorganisation Russlands von Peter dem Grossen bis 1917*, Leiden, 1966, pp. 502–19.

25. On this see e.g. a very thorough and well-documented study by Craig Kennedy, 'The Juchids of Muscovy: A Study of Personal Ties between Émigré Tatar Dynasts and the Muscovite Grand Princes in the Fifteenth and Sixteenth centuries', PhD, Harvard University, 1994.

26. R.G. Skrynnikov, *Tretii Rim*, Saint Petersburg, 1994, p. 151.

27. Y. Slezkine, *Arctic Mirrors. Russia and the Small Peoples of the North*, Cornell University Press, Ithaca, 1994, ch. 2 is good on this shift in Russian perception.

28. A.L. Altstadt, *The Azerbaijani Turks. Power and Identity under Russian Rule*, Stanford University Press, ch. 2, 1992, p. 17.

29. M. Gammer, *Muslim Resistance to the Tsar. Shamil and the Conquest of Chechnia and Daghestan*, Frank Cass, London, 1994, p. 151.

30. G.N. Curzon, *Russia in Central Asia in 1889 and the Anglo-Russian Question*, Frank Cass, London, 1967, p. 386.

31. D. Schimmelpenninck van der Oye, 'Ex Oriente Lux. Ideologies of Empire and Russia's Far East, 1893–1904,' PhD, Yale University, 1997, p. 249.

32. R.S. Wortman, *Scenarios of Power. Myth and Ceremony in Russian Monarchy*, Princeton University Press, 1995, p. 258.

33. R.A. Pierce (ed.), *Mission to Turkestan. Being the Memoirs of Count K.K. Pahlen*, Oxford University Press, London, 1964, p. 156.

34. See e.g. my comments on V.P. Cherevansky, the only expert on Central Asia appointed to Nicholas II's State Council between 1894 and 1914: *Russia's Rulers under the Old Regime*, Yale University Press, New Haven, 1989, pp. 200–1.

35. Both quotations from R.A. Pierce (ed.), *Mission to Turkestan*, pp. 42, 51.

36. Ibid., p. 152.

37. On this issue see S. Layton, *Russian Literature and Empire. The Conquest of the Caucasus from Pushkin to Tolstoy*, Cambridge University Press, 1994, ch. 8.

38. John Mackenzie writes of 'the powerful critique of home culture – particularly its industrialism – that lies at the centre of so many representations of the attractions of other life-styles', in J.M. Mackenzie, *Orientalism. History, Theory and the Arts*, Manchester University Press, 1995, p. 21.

39. See e.g. R.K.I. Quested, *'Matey' Imperialists. The Tsarist Russians in Manchuria 1895–1917*, University of Hong Kong Press, 1982, pp. 123–29.

40. Curzon, *Russia*, p. 392.

41. David Schimmelpenninck's thesis, cited in note 31 above, is a fine source on this. For further works on Eurasianism see Bibliography.

42. Cited for instance most appropriately on the opening page of Milan Hauner's very thoughtful *What is Asia to Us? Russia's Asian Heartland Yesterday and Today*, Routledge, London, 1992.

43. See in particular H. Rogger, *Jewish Policies and Right-Wing Politics in Imperial Russia*, London, 1986, ch. 2.

44. T.R. Weeks, *Nation and State in Late Imperial Russia*, N. Illinois University Press, De Kalb, 1996, p. 31. See also Kuropatkin's entry in his diary on his visit to the Baltic provinces in 1903: *Dnevnik A.N. Kuropatkina*, Nizhpoligraph, N. Novgorod, 1923, p. 7.

45. *Stenograficheskiy otchot Gosudarstvennoy Dumy*, 3 sozyv, 5 sessiya, col. 2170.

46. W.B. Lincoln, *The Conquest of a Continent. Siberia and the Russians*, Random House, London, 1994, p. 86; J. Forsyth, *A History of the Peoples of Siberia. Russia's North Asian Colony 1581–1990*, Cambridge University Press, 1992, p. 40.

47. L.M. Goryushkin, 'Migration, settlement and the rural economy of Siberia, 1861–1914', pp. 140–55, in A. Wood (ed.), *The History of Siberia. From Russian Conquest to Revolution*, Routledge, London, 1991, pp. 144–49.

48. On Japanese economic policy in Manchuria see e.g. W.G. Beasley, *Japanese Imperialism 1894–1945*, Clarendon Press, Oxford, 1987, ch. 3.

49. H. Mackinder, 'The Geographical Pivot of History', *The Geographical Journal*, vol. XXIII, no. 4, 1904. Most of the article is reprinted in R.E. Kasperson and J.V. Minghi (eds), *The Structure of Political Geography*, Chicago, 1969, ch. 14.

50. See e.g. W.H. McNeill, 'Introductory Historical Commentary', in G. Lundestad (ed.), *The Fall of Great Powers. Peace, Stability, and Legitimacy*, Scandinavian University Press, Oslo, 1994, pp. 1–21.

51. W.H. McNeill, *Plagues and Peoples*, Blackwell, New York, 1977, ch. 4.

52. A.W. Crosby, *Ecological Imperialism: The Biological Expansion of Europe*, Cambridge University Press, 1986, p. 38. Forsyth, *History*, somewhat corrects Crosby on the small impact of disease on the Siberian forest peoples; see p. 58 for his comment on smallpox.

53. J. Martin, *Treasure of the Land of Darkness. The Fur Trade and its Significance for Medieval Russia*, Cambridge University Press, 1986, pp. 142–3.

54. J.H. Elliott, 'Introduction: Colonial Identity in the Atlantic World', pp. 3–14 (here p. 4) in N. Canny and A. Pagden (eds), *Colonial Identity in the Atlantic World 1500–1800*, Princeton University Press, Cambridge, MA, 1987.

55. Layton, *Russian Literature and Empire*.

56. The introduction and first chapter of Tim McDaniel's thoughtful *The Agony of the Russian Idea*, Princeton University Press, 1996 is a source of many insights on this matter. So too is my personal experience of having lived for many years in a Confucian society and having observed the relationship between indigenous culture, Western influence and Japanese nationalism.

57. W. Faust, *Russlands Goldener Boden. Der sibirische Regionalismus in der zweiten Hälfte des 19 Jahrhunderts*, Cologne, 1980; S. Watrous, 'The Regionalist Conception of Siberia, 1860–1920', ch. 7, pp. 113–32, in G. Diment and Y. Slezkine (eds), *Between Heaven and Hell. The Myth of Siberia in Russian Culture*, St Martin's Press, New York, 1993.

CHAPTER 7. THE TSARIST STATE AND THE RUSSIAN PEOPLE

1. S. Franklin, J. Shepard, *The Emergence of Rus 750–1200*, London, 1996, pp. 71–4, 332–3.

2. Klyuchevsky, *Kurs*, vol. 1, lecture xvii, p. 297.

3. C.J. Halperin, 'The Russian Land and the Russian Tsar. The Emergence of Muscovite Ideology, 1350–1408', *Forschungen zur osteuropäischen Geschichte*, vol. 23, 1976, pp. 20–1.

4. R. Milner-Gulland, *The Russians*, Oxford, 1997, pp. 23–32.

5. E.g. Colin Mackerras singles out 'the Han method of agriculture' as crucial to the expansion and consolidation of the Chinese empire, *China's Minorities. Integration and Modernisation in the Twentieth Century*, Oxford University Press, Hong Kong, 1994, p. 24.

6. A. Kappeler, *Russlands Erste Nationalitäten. Das Zarenreich und die Völker der Mittleren Wolga vom 16. bis 19 Jahrhundert*, Bohlen Verlag, Cologne, 1982, e.g. pp. 425, 446, 475–6.

7. R.K.I. Quested, *'Matey' Imperialists*, 1982, p. 11.

8. Klychevsky, *Kurs*, pp. 313–15.
9. Milner-Gulland, *Russians*, p. 111.
10. E.L. Keenan, 'Moscovy and Kazan: Some Introductory Remarks on the Patterns of Steppe Diplomacy', *Slavic Review*, vol. 26, 1967, pp. 548–58.
11. See e.g. ch. 2 of D. Ostrowski, *Muscovy and the Mongols*, Cambridge University Press, 1998, pp. 36ff.
12. On the evolution of ritual and ideology see ch. 1 of R. Wortman, *Scenarios of Power, Myth and Ceremony in Russian Monarchy*, Princeton University Press, vol. 1, 1995, pp. 13ff. and 'Ceremony and Empire in the Evolution of Russian Monarchy', in C. Evtuhov, B. Gasparov, A. Ospovat, M. von Hagen (eds), *Kazan, Moscow, St Petersburg. Multiple Faces of the Russian Empire*, OGI, Moscow, 1997, pp. 23ff.; also M. Cherniavsky, 'Khan or Basileus: An Aspect of Russian Medieval Political Theory', *Journal of the History of Ideas*, vol. 20, 1959, pp. 459–76.
13. On the evolution of the Russian ruling elite, institutions of government and state officialdom, see ch 1 of D. Lieven, *Russia's Rulers*; the footnotes discuss the relevant bibliography.
14. On Novgorod and its fate see e.g. R.G. Skrynnikov, *Tragediya Novgoroda*, Moscow, 1994, and for a recent discussion of its significance in English: H. Birnbaum, 'Did the 1478 Annexation of Novgorod by Muscovy Fundamentally Change the Course of Russian History?', in L. Hughes (ed.), *New Perspectives on Muscovite History*, London, 1993.
15. R.G. Skrynnikov, *Tretiy Rim*, pp. 53, 186.
16. The best place to start when investigating Ivan IV's reign and personality is R. Hellie (ed.), 'Ivan the Terrible. A Quatercentenary Celebration of His Death', *Russian History*, Winter 1987 edition, whose many articles present conflicting views on a highly controversial subject.
17. Yu M. Lotman, *Besedy o russkoy kul'ture. Byt i traditsii russkogo dvoryanstva (XVIII-nachalo XIX veka)*, St Petersburg, 1994, p. 27. For a fuller discussion of these issues see D. Lieven, *Nicholas II*, John Murray, London, 1993, ch. 5.
18. Lotman, *Besedy*, especially pp. 9–43.
19. E. Amburger, *Geschichte*, p. 519.
20. Lieven, *Russia's Rulers*, ch. 2.
21. Above all, see M. Bloch, *Feudal Society*, Phoenix Books, University of Chicago Press, Chicago, 2 vols, 1964.
22. Michael Hughes makes this point well in his 'Independent Gentlemen: the Social Position of the Moscow Slavophiles and Its Impact on their Political Thought', *Slavonic and East European Review*, 1993, p. 71. For a further comment on sources on the Slavophiles see Bibliography.
23. R. Hellie, *Enserfment and Military Change in Muscovy*, University of Chicago Press, 1971 remains the seminal work in English on serfdom's origins.
24. My uncle Leonid Lieven, for example, would recall as a small child staying in the country estate of his aunt, a Princess Gargarin, and having explained to him the symbolism of cross over crescent and its testimony to the Gagarins' participation in Dmitry Donskoy's victory over the Tatars at Kulikovo Field in 1380.
25. A.L.H. Rhinelander, *Prince Michael Vorontsov; Viceroy to the Tsar.* McGill-Queen's University Press, Montreal, 1990, p. 67.
26. Immortalized by General Yermolov's witty request to Alexander I to be promoted to a German. This was in the Napoleonic era when foreigners and non-Russian subjects of the tsar packed the senior ranks of the army. Their presence was all the more galling since in the previous era, that of Catherine II, top positions were generally held by Russians (e.g. Rumyantsev, Suvorov, Panin), who had led the imperial army to some of the greatest victories in its history.
27. I spell out these points in greater detail in my 'The Aristocracy and the Gentry', in E. Acton, V.I. Cherniaev, W.G. Rosenberg (eds.), *Critical Companion to the Russian Revolution*, Arnold, London, 1997, pt VI, pp. 481–9.

28. On Russia's pre-1905 'constitution' see M. Szeftel, 'The Form of Government of the Russian Empire prior to the Constitutional Reforms of 1905–06', in J.S. Curtis, *Essays in Russian and Soviet History*, Columbia University Press, New York, 1962.

29. See e.g. Z.E. Kohut, *Russian Centralism and Ukrainian Autonomy*, Harvard University Press, Cambridge, 1988, pp. 104ff.

30. E.g. one important initial element in this policy was an entirely misguided effort to impose conscription in Finland: given the country's size, even the successful imposition of this policy would have brought Russia minimal benefit.

31. On Alexander's thinking, see e.g. J. Hartley, 'The "Constitutions" of Finland and Poland in the Reign of Alexander I: Blueprints for Reform in Russia?', in M. Branch, J. Hartley and A. Maczak (eds), *Finland and Poland in the Russian Empire*, School of Slavic and East European Studies, London, 1993, pp. 41–60.

32. See e.g. I. de Madariaga, *Russia in the Age of Catherine the Great*, Weidenfield & Nicolson, London, 1981, pp. 172–3.

33. Alexander's granting of a constitution to Poland at first raised Russian radicals' hopes of a similar measure for Russia: and the subsequent disappointment and sense of humiliation was all the greater: see e.g. V.I. Semevsky, *Politicheskiya i obshchestvennyya idei Dekabristov*, St Petersburg, 1909, e.g. pp. 262–4, 502.

34. It is to the point that Alexander I, who toyed constantly with schemes for constitutional reform, also contemplated plans for a high degree of decentralization.

35. See e.g. the discussion in G.H.N. Seton-Watson, *Nations and States*, Westview, Boulder, 1977 for an example of the author's characteristic breadth of comparison, insight and robust common sense.

36. M. Perrie, *Pretenders and Popular Monarchism in Early Modern Russia*, Cambridge University Press 1995, p. 208.

37. Though nationalist and Romantic nostalgia did certainly play a role. See e.g. Paul Bushkovich's comment that Peter I did not inherit an organic religious culture little affected by Western influence (pp. 176–9) and his earlier analysis of the evolution of the Russian elite's religion and worldview in the two pre-Petrine centuries: *Religion and Society in Russia. The Sixteenth and Seventeenth Centuries*, Oxford University Press, 1992.

38. Curtin, *Rise and Fall of the Plantation Complex*, ch 1.

39. W.C. Fuller, *Strategy and Power in Russia 1600–1914*, Free Press, New York, 1992, ch. 3, pp. 95–7.

40. P. Kolstoe, *Russians in the Former Soviet Republics*, Hurst, London, 1995, p. 15.

41. For a sceptical view of the myth see D. Field, *Rebels in the Name of the Tsar*, Houghton Mifflin, Boston, 1976. For background on this issue e.g. M. Cherniavsky, *Tsar and People. Studies in Russian Myths*, Yale University Press, New Haven, 1961, and M. Perrie, *Pretenders and Popular Monarchism*, 1995.

42. On the army, its morale and ethnic homogeneity see Fuller, *Strategy*, especially ch. 3 and C. Duffy, *Russia's Military Way to the West. Origins and Nature of Russian Military Power*, Routledge & Kegan Paul, London, 1981. He cites the comment of the Military Commission of 1762–3: 'The strength of the army consists in, most basic of all, the existence of common language, religion, customs and blood' (p. 126).

43. According to incomplete statistics e.g. in 1678 Muslim Tatar landlords owned c. 15,000 Russian serfs in the region of the former Kazan khanate: Kappeler, *Russlands erste Nationalitäten*, p. 217.

44. One comes across colonial parallels to Russian rural administration in most colonies, some of them far beyond the Russian specialist's usual horizon: see e.g. M.R. Peattie, *Nan'yo. The Rise and Fall of the Japanese in Micronesia 1885–1945*, University of Hawaii Press, Honolulu, 1988, pp. 71–7.

45. The best introduction to this is an article by Boris Mironov, 'The Russian Peasant Commune after the Reforms of the 1860s', in B. Eklof and S.P. Frank (eds), *The World of the Russian Peasant. Post-Emancipation Culture and Society*, Unwin Hyman, London, 1990, pp. 7–43. Even the English language secondary literature on the Russian peasantry is by now enormous.

46. The quotation is from N.V. Riasanovsky, *The Image of Peter the Great in Russian History and Thought*, Oxford University Press, 1985, p. 27.
47. An idea of it may be obtained from E. Weber, *Peasants into Frenchmen. The Modernization of Rural France, 1870–1914*, Stanford University Press, 1976.
48. A. von Haxthausen, *The Russian Empire. Its Peoples, Institutions and Resources*, trans. R. Faire, F. Cass, London, 2 vols, 1968; here vol. 2, p. 185.
49. In 1781 universal primary education became obligatory in Austria though in some crownlands decades passed before law became fact: G.B. Cohen, *Education and Middle Class Society in Imperial Austria 1848–1918*, Purdue University Press, W. LaFayette, 1996, p. 15.
50. Edward Keenan denies that Moscow's sixteenth-century rulers had any interest in Ukraine or the Kievan heritage: 'On Certain Mythical Beliefs and Russian Behaviour', ch. 1 in S.F. Starr (ed.), *The Legacy of History in Russia and the New States of Eurasia*, Armonk, 1994, a view denounced by Ostrowski, *Muscovy and the Mongols*, ch. 8. The comparativist throws up his hands in despair when faced with such disagreements, though in this case the disagreement is of little significance as regards the present book's argument.

CHAPTER 8.   TSARIST EMPIRE: POWER, STRATEGY, DECLINE

1. Figures cited, for example, by Orest Subtelny, *Ukraine. A history*, University of Toronto Press, 1988, p. 173.
2. Actually not all Latvia. Courland, in other words southern Latvia, was dominated indirectly by Russia in the eighteenth century but only formally annexed as a result of Poland's partition.
3. Quoted by P.B. Henze, 'Circassian Resistance to Russia', in M.B. Broxup (ed.), *The North Caucasus Barrier*, Hurst, New York, 1992, pp. 62–111 (here p. 80).
4. *Novoye Vremya*, no. 13580, 1/4 January 1914, p. 2.
5. K.F. Shatsillo, *Russkiy imperializm i razvitiye flota*, Moscow, 1968, p. 210.
6. K. Neilson, *Britain and the Last Tsar*, Oxford University Press, 1995, especially ch. 11.
7. K. Jarausch, *The Enigmatic Chancellor*, Yale University Press, New Haven, 1972, ch. 5. Niall Ferguson cites Bethmann's famous comment in 1914 that 'the future belongs to Russia, which grows and grows and weighs upon us as an ever heavier nightmare', in *The Pity of War*, Allen Lane, London, 1998, p. 98.
8. J. Le Donne, *The Russian Empire and the World. 1700–1917. The Geopolitics of Expansionism and Containment*, Oxford University Press, 1997, ch. 9; see especially p. 222.
9. This is a major theme of S. Eisenstadt, *The Political Systems of Empires*, Transaction Publications, London, 1992.
10. Eisenstadt's criticism of tsarist Russia's failure to sustain an autonomous peasantry outside aristocratic control is therefore a little wide of the mark. See p. 209 of his essay in A. Motyl (ed.), *Thinking Theoretically about Soviet Nationalities*, Columbia University Press, New York, 1992.
11. See M. Bagger, 'The role of the Baltic in Russian Foreign Policy, 1721–1773', in H. Ragsdale (ed.), *Imperial Russian Foreign Policy*, Cambridge University Press, 1993, pp. 68–9.
12. See my *Aristocracy in Europe, 1815–1914*, Macmillan, London, 1992, chs 1 and 2.
13. Kappeler, *Russlands erste Nationalitäten*, p. 332.
14. J. Connell, *Wavell: Soldier and Scholar*, London, 1964, p. 67.
15. Weeks, *Nation and State*, p. 146.
16. John Westwood, for example, makes these points in *Russia Against Japan*, London, 1986, pp. 163ff.
17. Gillard, *Struggle for Asia*, pp. 102–3.
18. D. Spring, 'Russian Imperialism in Asia in 1914', *Cahiers du Monde Russe et Soviétique*, vol. XX, 1979 is good on this specific point. D. Geyer, *Russian Imperialism*, Leamington Spa, 1987 is the best general source on the implications of Russian financial, commercial and economic weakness.

19. J.P. Le Donne, *Absolutism and Ruling Class*, Oxford University Press, 1991, p. 274.

20. Ibid., p. 144.

21. Fuller, *Strategy and Power*, p. 105.

22. With the very partial exception of a few great families of aristocratic magnates.

23. S.J. Connolly, *Religion, Law and Power. The Making of Protestant Ireland 1660–1760*, Oxford University Press, 1992, especially ch. 6.

24. Witold Rodkiewicz, 'Russian Nationality Policy in the Western Provinces of the Empire during the Reign of Nicholas II, 1894–1905', PhD, Harvard University, 1996, pp. 205ff. The argument in this paragraph is based on Dr Rodkiewicz's excellent thesis.

25. R.F. Foster, *Modern Ireland 1600–1972*, London, 1998, p. 210.

26. The most important figure in this group was the highly intelligent Nikolay Bunge, who served as minister of finance and chairman of the Committee of Ministers. The key document on Bunge's views is available in English as G.E. Snow, 'The Years 1881–1894' in *Russia: A Memorandum Found in the Papers of N.Kh. Bunge. A Translation and Commentary*, Philadelphia, 1981. A new and intelligent biography was published in Moscow by Rosspen in 1998: written by V.L. Stepanov, it is entitled *N.Kh. Bunge. Sud'ba reformatora*. One of the great advantages of the collapse of the USSR is that balanced work is now being produced in Russia on tsarist statesmen and policies, based on archival research. One of Bunge's main disciples was Anatoly Kulomzin, whose memorandum of 1905 on the failings of nationality policy is discussed in my *Russia's Rulers*, pp. 250–4.

27. Rodkiewicz establishes the lines of division over policy in the Western Borderlands on pp. 11–12 of *Russian Nationality Policy*. He then illustrates excellently how these divisions expressed themselves in detail across a range of policies.

28. One might perhaps cite the Chinese case as an exception. By the twentieth century, however, the Han Chinese were more than the bearers of a great civilization. At least potentially, they were far closer to being a nation than any group which constituted 90 per cent of the population of any of the other empires considered in this book.

29. A key figure here was Ismail Bey Gaspirali (Gasprinsky), the Crimean Tatar educationalist and reformer, who was one of the earliest and most influential advocates of introducing the Russian language and study of the natural and social sciences into Muslim schools. A.W. Fisher for example discusses Gaspirali in his book *The Crimean Tatars*, Hoover Institution Press, Stanford, 1978, pp. 99ff. For a further discussion of sources on Muslim reformism, see Bibliography.

30. The key work here is J.D. Klier and S. Lambroza (eds), *Pogroms*, Cambridge University Press, 1992. Honourable mention should also be made of H. Rogger, *Jewish Policies and Right-Wing Politics in Imperial Russia*, Macmillan, London, 1998, especially ch. 2.

31. I owe this insight entirely to Gudrun Persson and her excellent thesis entitled 'The Russian Army and Foreign Wars 1859–1871', PhD, London University, 1999. On this issue see above all ch. 4.2.1, pp. 84–90.

32. On Russian traditional attitudes to Ukrainian distinctiveness, see above all an article by Paul Bushkovich, 'The Ukraine in Russian Culture. 1790–1860', *Jahrbücher für Geschichte Osteuropas*, vol. 39, no. 3, 1991, pp. 339–62.

33. Rodkiewicz, 'Russian Nationality Policy', p. 329.

34. D. Saunders, 'Russia's Ukrainian Policy (1847–1905): A Demographic Approach', *European History Quarterly*, vol. 25, no. 2, 1995, pp. 181–208: here pp. 185–7.

35. See in particular Olga Andriewsky, 'The Politics of National Identity. The Ukrainian Question in Russia 1904–1912', PhD, Harvard University, pp. 211ff. This was admittedly the Third Duma, dominated by the Russian property-owning and professional elites.

36. I am grateful for a gentle reminder on this point from Professor Roman Szporluk of Harvard University after reading my comments in D. Lieven, 'Russian, Imperial and Soviet Identities', *Transactions of the Royal Historical Society*, 6th Series, vol. 8, 1998, pp. 253–69.

37. Stephen Velychenko for instance argues this in 'Empire Loyalism and Minority Nationalism in Great Britain and Imperial Russia, 1707–1914: Institutions, Laws and Nationality in Scotland and Ukraine', *Comparative Studies in Society and History*, vol. 39, no. 3, 1997, pp. 413–41.

38. For example, compare Linda Colley, *Britons. Forging the Nation 1707–1837*, Yale University Press, New Haven, 1992 and D. Saunders, *The Ukrainian Impact on Russian Culture 1750–1850*, Edmonton, 1985.

39. For example, Miloslav Hroch, *Social Preconditions for National Revival in Europe*, Cambridge University Press, 1985.

40. For example, B. Kravchenko, *Social Change and National Consciousness in Twentieth-Century Ukraine*, Macmillan, London, 1985, ch. 1 makes crucial points about the weakness of the Ukrainian intelligentsia in 1914. I.I. Rudnytsky, *Essays in Modern Ukrainian History*, Cambridge, 1987 also quite rightly comments (p. 32) that tsarist Russia provided Ukrainians with a very poor training in self-government.

41. A.F. Rotstein (ed.), *Dnevnik V.N. Lamzdorfa, 1886–1890*, Moscow, 1926, p. 36.

42. R.C. Ridenour, *Nationalism, Modernism and Personal Rivalry in nineteenth-century Russia*, UMI Research Press, 1981 is the source for this paragraph.

43. On the pre-1825 elite see above all an outstanding article by John Le Donne, 'Ruling Families in the Russian Political Order', *Cahiers du Monde Russe et Soviétique*, vol. XXVIII, nos 3–4, July-December 1987, pp. 233–58 and 295–322. On Nicholas II's elite see my *Russian Rulers*.

44. Quite unjustifiably the Jews were also redefined as aliens in the late nineteenth century.

45. On Russian teachers and the educational system the best places to start are: B. Eklof, *Russian Peasant Schools: Officialdom, Village Culture, and Popular Pedagogy, 1861–1914*, University of California Press, Berkeley, 1987; Scott Seregny (among other good pieces), 'Power and Discourse in Russian Elementary education', *Jahrbücher für Geschichte Osteuropas*, vol. 47, no. 2, 1999, pp. 161–86 and 'Teachers, politics and the Peasant Community in Russia, 1895–1918', in B. Eklof (ed.), *School and Society in Tsarist and Soviet Russia*, Macmillan, Houndmills, 1993. An excellent British study is Thomas Darlington, *Special Reports on Educational Subjects, Vol. 23. Education in Russia*, London, 1909.

46. See e.g. Ferguson, *Pity of War*. 'Russia ... in terms of increased output, had the most successful war economy', ch. 9, p. 263.

47. W.S. Churchill, *The World Crisis, 1911–1918*, Four Square Books, London, 1964, p. 776.

48. I set out my views on these issues in greater detail in my chapter 'Russia, Europe and World War I' in E. Acton, V.I. Cherniaev and W. Rosenberg, *Critical Companion to the Russian Revolution 1914–1921*, Arnold, London, 1997, pp. 37ff.

CHAPTER 9. THE SOVIET UNION

1. The key text here is Lenin's *Imperialism, the Highest Stage of Capitalism*. The text I use comes from *V.I. Lenin. Selected Works in Three Volumes*, Progress Publishers, Moscow, 1977, pp. 634–731.

2. See e.g. V. Tishkov, *Ethnicity, Nationalism and Conflict in and after the Soviet Union*, Sage, London, 1997, pp. 50–51.

3. The obvious parallel is imperial Germany between 1871 and 1918, where no imperial chancellor could rule effectively unless he was also prime minister of Prussia, which was by far the largest and most powerful of the federated German states.

4. *What Is To Be Done?*, in *Lenin. Selected Works*, pp. 92–241.

5. A key development here was Lenin's adaptation of Marx to the Russian and therefore largely peasant context. See in particular *Two Tactics of Social-Democracy in the Democratic Revolution*, in *Lenin. Selected Works*, pp. 425–527.

6. Cited e.g. on p. 137 of M. Rywkin, *Moscow's Muslim Challenge*, M.E. Sharpe, New York, 1982.

7. A term used by Yuri Slezkine on p. 419 of his 'The USSR as a Communal Apartment, or How a Socialist State Promoted Ethnic Particularism', *Slavic Review*, vol. 53, no. 2, 1994, pp. 414–52.

8. See e.g. B. Krawchenko, *Social Change and National Consciousness in Twentieth-Century Ukraine*, Macmillan, Houndmills, 1985, p. 129. The figure for newspapers dates from 1933.

9. Krawchenko, *Social Change*, p. 238.

10. H. Carrere d'Encausse, *The Great Challenge. Nationalism and the Bolshevik state, 1917–1930*, Holmes & Meier, New York, 1992, p. 121.

11. *Molotov Remembers*, pp. 8, 188.

12. F.C. Barghoorn, *Soviet Russian Nationalism*, Greenwood, Westport, 1956, p. 29.

13. His comment was recorded by the French military attaché in Russia and is cited in D. Lieven, *Russia and the Origin of the First World War*, Macmillan, London, 1983, p. 10.

14. Anthony Eden records Stalin's comment in 1935 that Russia's position was worse than in 1914. 'Stalin said he considered it basically worse because in 1913 there was one potential aggressor, Germany, and now there were two, Germany and Japan.' Quoted by R. Tucker, *Stalin in Power. The Revolution from Above 1928–1941*, W.W. Norton, New York, 1990, p. 343.

15. P. Dibb, *The Soviet Union. The Incomplete Superpower*, Macmillan, London, 1988, p. 70.

16. The key quotation, cited in every work on Stalin, gives his ruminations on Russia's backwardness, on the humiliations this caused her from a string of foreign enemies over the ages, and on the need to end this backwardness at breakneck speed in order to avoid future disasters. Ronald Suny e.g. cites this comment on p. 235 of his *The Soviet Experiment*, Oxford University Press, 1998.

17. There is an English translation of the programme between pp. 445 and 589 of *The Road to Communism. Documents of the 22nd Congress of the Communist Party of the Soviet Union*, Foreign Languages Publishing House, Moscow, 1961.

18. W. B. Lincoln, *In the Vanguard of Reform: Russia's Enlightened Bureaucrats, 1825–1861*, De Kalb, Northern Illinois University Press, 1982 is an excellent social and intellectual history of the origins of Alexander II's reforms. Nothing yet matches it on the prehistory of Gorbachev's reform team.

19. E.J. Hobsbawm, *The Age of Capital*, London, 1975 is splendid on this era's assumptions and principles.

20. See E. Keenan, 'Muscovite Political Folkways', *Russian Review*, 45, 1986, pp. 115–81.

21. O. Crisp, *Studies in the Russian Economy before 1914*, Macmillan, London, 1976, p. 51. Roughly 10 per cent of industry was owned by the state.

22. Much of this is borrowed from my brother, Anatol Lieven. See his *Chechnya. Tombstone of Russian Power*, Yale University Press, New Haven, 1998, ch. 6.

23. S. Fitzpatrick, 'Culture and Politics under Stalin: A Reappraisal', *Slavic Review*, June 1976, vol. 35, no. 2, pp. 211–32.

24. B. Krawchenko, *Social Change*, pp. 230–1.

25. These points are very well brought out e.g. by Sergey Kondrashev in his thesis on Soviet Tatarstan: 'Nationalism and the Drive for Sovereignty in Tatarstan 1988–92, Origins and Development,' PhD, Manchester University, 1995, especially ch. 2.

26. A very interesting example being Snieckus, the Lithuanian leader referred to previously in this chapter. See e.g. A. Shtromas, 'The Baltic states as Soviet Republics: Tensions and Contradictions', ch. 4, pp. 86ff in G. Smith (ed.), *The Baltic States. The National Self-determination of Estonia, Latvia and Lithuania*, Macmillan, Houndmills, 1991, here pp. 99ff.

27. This paragraph owes much to Y.M. Brudny, *Reinventing Russia. Russian Nationalism and the Soviet State 1958–1991*, Harvard University Press, Cambridge, MA, 1998.

28. For a discussion of anthropology's relationship with the Soviet regime see Y. Slezkine, *Arctic Mirrors*.

29. D.M. Crowe, 'The Kazakhs and Kazakhstan: the struggle for Ethnic Identity and Nationhood', *Nationalities Papers*, vol. 26, no. 3, 1998, p. 403.

30. Rywkin, *Moscow's Muslim Challenge*, pp. 104–8.

31. Carrere d'Encausse, *Great Challenge*, pp. 164–6.

32. P. Liberman, *Does Conquest Pay? The Exploitation of Occupied Industrial Societies*, Princeton University Press, 1996 chs 6 and 7 on Japanese and Soviet empire, though admittedly the latter concerns East-Central Europe rather than the non-Russian republics of the USSR.

33. Simon, *Nationalism*, p. 328.

34. I. Prizel, 'Ukraine between proto-democracy and "soft" authoritarianism', in K. Dawisha and B. Parrott (eds), *Democratic Change and Authoritarian Reactions in Russia, Ukraine, Belarus and Moldova*, Cambridge University Press, 1997, p. 345.

35. On the princely states, the realities of indirect rule, and British hopes for federalism see Ian Copland, *The Princes of India in the Endgame of Empire*, Cambridge University Press, 1997.

36. Slezkine, 'USSR as a communal Apartment', p. 429.

37. J. Smith, *The Bolsheviks and the National Question 1917–23*, Macmillan, Houndmills, 1999, p. 84.

38. Simon, *Nationalism*, p. 8.

39. I owe this insight to P.J. Cain and A.G. Hopkins, *British Imperialism. Crisis and Deconstruction. 1914–1990*, vol. 2, London, 1993, ch. 8 and B.R. Tomlinson, *The Political Economy of the Raj, 1914–1947. The Economics of Decolonization in India*, London, 1979.

40. Smith, *Bolsheviks*, p. 93.

41. A range of foreign comments on this theme are cited by e.g. Quested, *'Matey' Imperialists*, pp. 13–16.

42. Well over half the Senators came from outside Italy by the early third century: e.g. Garnsey and Saller, *Roman Empire*, p. 123.

43. Robert Service calls Gorbachev's Politburo 'virtually a Slavic men's club': *A History of Twentieth-Century Russia*, Allen Lane, London, 1997, p. 456.

44. The numbers are still disputed and uncertain in the Ukrainian case. On the Kazakhs see e.g. M.B. Olcott, 'The Collectivization Drive in Kazakhstan', *Russian Review*, vol. 40, no. 2, 1981, pp. 122–42. See also Sue Davis and Stephen Sobol's statistics, 'The importance of Being Ethnic: Minorities in Post-Soviet states – the Case of Russians in Kazakhstan', *Nationalities Papers*, vol. 26, no. 3, 1998.

45. J. Critchlow, *Nationalism in Uzbekistan*, Westview, Boulder, 1991, p. 63.

46. D.A. Low, *Eclipse of Empire*, Cambridge University Press, 1991, pp. 6–7.

47. M. Hauner, *What is Asia to us? Russia's Asian Heartland Yesterday and Today*, Routledge, London, 1992, p. 152: The scientist was D.I. Mendeleyev.

48. See e.g. the comments of S. Deringhi, *The Well-Protected Domains. Ideology and the Legitimisation of Power in the Ottoman Empire 1876–1909*, I.B. Taurus, London, 1998, ch. 3.

49. M. Yapp calls the Ottoman state minimal government in an armed bazaar (*The Making of the Modern East 1792–1923*, Longman, London, 1987, p. 36). This is not quite what Hegel had in mind when he thought of a civil society embodied in the law-abiding burghers of a German city and their civic institutions and pride!

50. Trotsky, Zinoviev, Kamenev and Sverdlov were Jewish, Stalin was Georgian and Dzerzhinsky was Polish. Apart of course from Lenin, Nikolay Bukharin was the only Russian of almost equivalent status in 1917–21.

51. Gorbachev's Politburo in early 1988 was the most Russian in Soviet history. Edvard Shevardnadze was its only non-Slav full member.

52. In a conversation with the British counsellor in St Petersburg in 1912; PRO, FO 371, 1468, no. 29844, p. 452.

53. I owe this insight to conversations with Professor Roman Szporluk and an excellent talk given at LSE by Dr Tim Snyder, both of Harvard University.

54. See T. Riha (ed.), *Readings in Russian Civilisation*, Chicago University Press, 1964.

55. J. Brown, *Modern India. The Origins of an Asian Democracy*, Oxford University Press, 1994, pp. 38–9.

56. A.L. Friedberg, *The Weary Titan. Britain and the Experience of Relative Decline 1895–1905*, Princeton University Press, 1988, especially ch. 3.

57. See e.g. Mark Galeotti, *Afghanistan. The Soviet Union's Last War*, Frank Cass, London, 1995.

CHAPTER 10.   AFTER EMPIRE

1. G. Stourzh, *Vom Reich zur Republic. Studien zur Österreichsbewusstein im 20 Jahrhundert*, Ed. Atelier, Vienna, 1990, pp. 64–7.
2. G. Brook-Shepherd, *The Austrians. A Thousand Year Odyssey*, HarperCollins, London, 1997, p. 445.
3. The Tyrolese Diet in Innsbruck actually offered all Tyrol to Italy. A. Alcock, 'Trentino and Tyrol. From Austrian Crownland to European Region', in S. Dunn and T.G. Fraser (eds), *Europe and Ethnicity. World War I and Contemporary Ethnic Conflict*, Routledge, London, 1996, p. 70.
4. A. Pelinka, *Zur Österreichischen Identität. Zwischen deutscher Vereinigung und Mitteleuropa*, Uerberreuther, Vienna, 1990, pp. 17–18.
5. F. Mathis, 'Wirtschaft oder Politik? Zu den "wirtschaftlichen" Motiven einer politischen Vereinigung zwischen 1918 und 1938', in M. Gehler, R.F. Schmidt, H.-H. Brandt, R. Steininger (eds), *Ungleiche Partner? Österreich und Deutchland in 19. and 20. Jh.*, Franz Steiner Verlag, Stuttgart, 1996, pp. 428–33.
6. R. Pearson, 'Hungary: a state truncated, a nation dismembered', in Dunn and Fraser, *Europe and Ethnicity*, pp. 88–9.
7. R. Brubaker, *Nationalism Reframed. Nationhood and the national question in the New Europe*, Cambridge University Press, 1996, pp. 156–8.
8. E.g. in the May 1939 elections, despite (in the towns) universal male suffrage and a secret ballot, 'in "Red Budapest" the radical right-wing parties outpolled the Social Democrats by a two-to one margin': T. Sakmyster, *Hungary's Admiral on Horseback ... Miklos Horthy, 1918–1944*, Columbia University Press, New York/Boulder, 1994, p. 232.
9. E.g. the crucial 1931 French loan: J.K. Hoensch, *A History of Modern Hungary 1867–1986*, Longman, London, 1988.
10. Both Hugh Seton-Watson and Elizabeth Wiskemann were (quite rightly) much more sympathetic to the Czech than the Sudetan case in the late 1930s but the former agreed that Prague was somewhat more generous to Czech than Sudeten industry in the Depression and the latter conceded that the government erred badly in giving road-repair and other relief work to Czechs in areas of high German unemployment. E. Wiskemann, *Czechs and Germans. A Study of the Struggle in the Historic Provinces of Bohemia and Moravia*, Macmillan, London, 1967, p. 193; H. Seton-Watson, *Eastern Europe between the Wars, 1918–1941*, Cambridge University Press, 1945, pp. 280–1.
11. Brubaker, *Nationalism Reframed*, p. 165.
12. Seton-Watson, *Eastern Europe*, pp. 291–2.
13. One element but not the most important one in either case. Huntingdon's *Clash of Civilizations* has a kernel of truth but greatly simplifies the range of conflicts in the contemporary world and their causes. The basic Crimean Tatar identity is national and not Islamic. Its politically most important elements are strong attachment to the homeland and bitter historical memories of suffering and deportation. Moreover, the Crimean issue involves much more than Tatars and entwines deeply in Ukrainian and Russian politics. On all these issues see an excellent thesis on Crimea by Gwendolyn Sasse, London University, 1999. The basic identities in the North Caucasus are also national rather than religious, even as regards the Chechens: on this see A. Lieven, *Chechnya. Tombstone of Russian Power*.
14. See e.g. the many excellent essays in M.J. Cohen and M. Kolinsky (eds), *Demise of the British Empire in the Middle East*, Frank Cass, London, 1998. The pressures of a mass, literate and increasingly urban society on political systems run by and for Arab notables is a key theme e.g. in M.E. Yapp, *The Near East since the First World War*, Longman, London, 1991.

15. H. Poulton, *Top Hat, Grey Wolf and Crescent. Turkish Nationalism and the Turkish Republic*, Hurst, London, 1997, p. 89.

16. The peasantry of central Anatolia, untouched by foreign armies, was not at all enthusiastic about conscription into Kemal's army: see e.g. F. Ahmad, 'The political economy of Kemalism', in A. Kazancigil and E. Ozbudun, *Atatürk. Founder of a Modern State*, Hurst, London, 1997, p. 155.

17. H. Poulton, *Top Hat, Grey Wolf and Crescent*, p. 93.

18. B. Lewis, 'The Ottoman Empire and its Aftermath', *The Journal of Contemporary History*, 1980, vol. 15, pp. 27–36 (here p. 32).

19. E.J. Zurcher, *Turkey. A Modern History*, I.B. Tauris, London, 1994, p. 208.

20. Deringil, *Well Protected Domains*.

21. V. Calotychos (ed.), *Cyprus and its People*, Westview, Boulder, 1998: Calotychos, ch. 1, p. 7.

22. The figures for the Greeks are disputed. V. Calotychos, a Greek source, writes that 170,000–200,000 Greeks fled their homeland in northern Cyprus: see V. Calotychos (ed.), *Cyprus and its People*, p. 7. C.H. Dodd, a generally more pro-Turkish source, puts the figure at 140,000–160,000. See C. Dodd (ed.), *Cyprus. The Need for New Perspectives*, Eothen Press, Huntingdon, 1999, p. 10.

23. Zurcher, *Turkey*, p. 170 cites 2.5 million dead.

24. Over 150,000 of these refugees returned within a year, however. Brubaker, *Nationalism Reframed*, pp. 152–55.

25. Statistics from R.B. McDowell, *Crisis and Decline. The Fate of the Southern Unionists*, Lilliput Press, Dublin, 1997, pp. 163–4. Professor McDowell also provides a fair analysis of the reasons for the decline in Protestant numbers.

26. L. Kennedy, *Colonialism*, p. 193.

27. Foster, *Modern Ireland*, pp. 511–13.

28. D. Fitzpatrick, *The Two Irelands 1912–1939*, Oxford University Press, 1998, p. 150.

29. Bill Kissane, 'The Not-So Amazing case of Irish Democracy', *Irish Political Studies*, 10, 1995, pp. 43–68.

30. Fitzpatrick, *Two Irelands*, p. 25.

31. On 31 March 1914, for instance, Sir George Buchanan reported Sazonov's acute anxiety about Britain's position in any conflict with Germany: 'this preoccupation has notably increased since the Ulster question has entered on an acute stage. During the past fortnight he has repeatedly spoken to me of the anxiety with which the various phases of the present crisis are being followed by the Russian Government and the Russian public, and he has expressed his apprehension lest internal dissensions and disaffection in the army might so weaken England's position as to render her voice of no account in the councils of the nations.' *British Documents on Foreign Affairs: Reports and Papers from the Foreign Office Confidential Print* (eds K. Bourne and D.C. Watt), Part 1, Series A. Russia, 1859–1914 (ed. D. Lieven), vol. 6, p. 379.

32. Chadda, *Ethnicity*, pp. x–xi.

33. A. Clayton, *Frontiersmen. Warfare in Africa since 1950*, UCL Press, London, 1999, p. 1.

34. The comparison with Jews is now traditional, and was made for instance even in an essay written by the King of Siam. In her splendid book on the Chinese diaspora, *Sons of the Yellow Emperor*, Mandarin, London, 1991, Lynn Pan entitles one chapter 'The Jews of the East'.

35. Ishtiaq Ahmed, *State, Nation and Ethnicity*, p. 250.

36. Wang Gungwu, *Community and Nation. China, South-east Asia and Australia*, Allen & Unwin, St Leonards, 1992, p. 31.

37. *Cambridge History of South-East Asia*, ch. 8: N. Owen, 'Economic and Social Change', here pp. 496–97.

38. 1,188 people are reckoned to have lost their lives in the 13–14 May 1998 pogrom in Jakarta: see E. Aspinall, 'Opposition and Elite Conflict in the fall of Soeharto', p. 138 and the comment p. 217, G.A. Aditjondro, 'A New Regime, A More Consolidated Oligarchy, and a Deeply

Divided Anti-Soeharto Movement' which suggests that one section of the army high command instigated these rapes, in G. Forrester and R.J. May (eds), *The Fall of Soeharto*, Crawford Hurst, Bathurst, 1999.

39.   Ishtiaq Ahmed, *State, Nation and Ethnicity*, p. 253 gives figures of 50 and 48.3 per cent respectively for Tamils in 1969. By 1988 the pattern of colonial employment had been fully reversed: the Sinhalese were 74 per cent of the population but held 85 per cent of all government jobs. My discussion of Sri Lanka is based above all on Ahmed's excellent book.

40.   Thomas Masaryk described the Germans of the Sudetenland as 'emigrants and colonists' on first returning to Czechoslovakia in 1918: Wiskemann, *Czechs and Germans*, p. 123. The Germans had lived in the region for many centuries.

41.   J. Devlin, *Slavophiles and Commissars. Enemies of Democracy in Modern Russia*, Macmillan, Houndmills, 1999, p. 50.

42.   A. Lieven, *Ukraine and Russia. A Fraternal Rivalry*, US Institute of Peace, Washington, 1999, p. 116.

43.   A. Lebed, *Za derzhavu obidno*, Moscow, 1995, p. 437.

44.   E. Payin, 'The Disintegration of the Empire and the Fate of the Imperial Minority', ch. 2, pp. 21–36, in V. Shlapentokh et al. (eds), *The New Russian Diaspora. Russian Minorities in the Former Soviet Republics*, M.E. Sharpe, Armonk, 1994, p. 35.

45.   C. King, *Post-Soviet Moldova. A Borderland in Transition*, Center for Romanian Studies, Iasi, 1997, p. 32.

46.   B. Davidson, *The Black Man's Burden*, James Currey, London, 1992, for example pp. 184–5.

47.   E. Huskey, 'Kyrgyzstan: the fate of political liberalism', in K. Dawisha and B. Parrot, *Conflict, cleavage and change in Central Asia and the Caucasus*, Cambridge University Press, 1997, ch. 7, p. 248.

48.   G. Gleason, *The Central Asian States. Discovering Independence*, Westview, Boulder, 1997, p. 83.

49.   M. Atkin, 'Thwarted democratisation in Tajikistan', in Dawisha and Parrott, *Conflict, cleavage and change*, ch. 5, p. 278.

50.   Lebed, *Za derzhavu*, pp. 409–10.

51.   Devlin, *Slavophiles*, p. 36.

52.   C. Clapham, *Third World Politics. An Introduction*, Routledge, London, 1988.

53.   Statistics on the size and distribution of the Russians in the USSR are neatly set out in the appendix (pp. 134–6) of N. Melvin, *Russians Beyond Russia. The Politics of National Identity*, Royal Institute of International Affairs, London, 1995.

54.   Statistics from G. Smith, A. Aasland, R. Mole, 'Statehood, Ethnic Relations and Citizenship', ch. 6 in G. Smith (ed.), *The Baltic States. The National Self-Determination of Estonia, Latvia and Lithuania*, Macmillan, Houndmills, 1996, p. 182.

55.   The statistics are from V. Lal, *Fiji. Coups in Paradise*, Zed Books, London, 1990, ch. 2, p. 19.

56.   T.N. Harper, *The End of Empire and the Making of Malaya*, Cambridge University Press, 1999, p. 322.

57.   The role of English in Malaya confused the issue: see Wang Gungwu's splendid 'Malaysia: Contending Elites', ch. 13, pp. 197–215 in his *Community and Nation*, Allen & Unwin, Sydney, 1992.

58.   *Cambridge History of South-East Asia*, ch. 7: Yong Mun Cheong, 'The Political Structures of the Independent States', p. 429.

59.   Smith et al., 'Statehood, Ethnic Relations and citizenship', in Smith (ed.), *The Baltic States*, p. 190.

60.   See e.g. Anatol Lieven, *Ukraine*, pp. 87ff. and V. Shlapentokh, 'Early Feudalism – The Best Parallel for Contemporary Russia', *Europe-Asia Studies*, vol. 48, no. 3, 1996, pp. 398–411.

61.   E.g. Clapham, *Third World Politics*, ch. 3: anyone who reads this book will realize my great debt to Professor Clapham.

62.   Seton-Watson, *Eastern Europe*, e.g. p. 306.

CONCLUSION

1.   M. Mann, *The Sources of Social Power.*
2.   M. Duverger (ed.), *Le Concept d'Empire*, pp. 6–7.

Bibliography

This bibliography is by no means intended to list all the books I have read about empire, let alone all those I should have read to cover this subject in a truly full and scholarly manner. It is designed to help people who have the inclination to interest themselves in empire, empires and Russia, and who have some leisure to devote to the subject. The bibliography gives preference to works in English, and after that to books in French and German. After twenty-five years in the field I have inevitably read a great deal in Russian but I have refrained from citing these works in most cases since the great majority of those who read this book will not know the Russian language. I have also confined my bibliography, with very few exceptions, to books: to include academic articles relating to empire would make it immensely long and indigestible.

INTRODUCTORY AND CHAPTER 1. EMPIRE: A WORD AND ITS MEANINGS

The best place to start the comparative study of empire is M. Duverger (ed.), *Le Concept d'Empire*, Presses Universitaires de France, Paris, 1980; this book contains many excellent essays on various empires and a range of understandings of what empire means. The editor, Maurice Duverger, believes that the term's core meaning is more appropriate to the great land empires from antiquity to the Soviet era than to the West European maritime empires. Michael Doyle on the other hand defines empire as the relationship between societies of the centre and the periphery, and is therefore most concerned precisely with the maritime European empires and their antecedents in the ancient world: *Empires*, Cornell University Press, Ithaca, 1986. Shmuel Eisenstadt, *The Political Systems of Empires*, Transaction Publishers, New Brunswick, 1992 is an extremely scholarly study whose main focus is on the great land empires, though the author believes that many early modern European and many modern maritime empires do also qualify as imperial within his definition of the term. Readers may well find Eisenstadt's social science terminology rather hard to follow. A useful short cut is to read his piece 'Empires' in David L. Sills, *International Encyclopaedia of the Social Sciences*, vol. 5, pp. 41–8, Macmillan, New York, 1968. Sir Ernest Barker's essay 'Empire' in the 1911 edition of the *Encyclopaedia Britannica* is also very useful.

Bibliography

Many works look a little more narrowly at the history of the concept of empire and imperialism. G. Miles, 'Roman and Modern Imperialism', *Comparative Studies in Society and History*, vol. 32, 1990 is a good introduction to this topic. R. Folz, *The Concept of Empire in Western Europe from the Fifth to the Fourteenth Century*, Greenwood Press, Westport, 1969 and J. Muldoon, *Empire and Order. The Concept of Empire*, Macmillan, Houndmills, 1999 are surveys of how the meanings of the word 'empire' evolved in medieval Europe. Anthony Pagden, *Lords of all the World*, Yale University Press, New Haven, 1995 covers ideas and ideologies of empire from the origins of the Spanish, French and English transoceanic empires down to 1800. Otto von Habsburg, *Die Reichsidee. Geschichte und Zukunft einer übernationalen Ordnung*, Amalthea Verlag, Vienna, 1986 is interesting as an attempt to link a concept of empire foreign to the anglophone world to contemporary European developments.

The best introduction to twentieth-century concepts of empire and imperialism is W.M. Mommsen, *Theories of Imperialism*, Weidenfeld, London, 1980. E.R.J. Owen and R.B. Sutcliffe (eds), *Studies in the Theory of Imperialism*, Longman, London, 1972 contains many useful essays. Particular attention should be paid to an article by R. Robinson and J. Gallagher entitled 'The Imperialism of Free trade', *Economic History Review*, vi, 1953. A. Brewer, *Marxist Theories of Imperialism. A Critical Survey*, Routledge, London, 1980 is a brief but thorough introduction to this topic.

Over the centuries a number of major works have become part of the history of the concept of empire. I have read by no means all of them. Key books of the modern era (some in many editions) which I have read and recommend are: Baron de Montesquieu, *Réflexions sur la monarchie universelle en Europe*; Abbé Raynal, *L'Anti-colonialisme au XVIIIème Siècle*, Presses Universitaires, Paris, 1951; Adam Smith, *An Inquiry into the Nature and Causes of the Wealth of Nations*; J.A. Hobson, *Imperialism. A Study*; J. Schumpeter, *Imperialism and Social Classes*, Blackwell, Oxford, 1951; A.T. Mahan, *The Influence of Sea Power upon History*, 1892 and his much less well-known *The Interest of America in Sea Power. Present and Future*, Sampson Low, London, 1897; J.R. Seeley, *The Expansion of England*, Macmillan, London, 1885; R. Hilferding (ed. T. Bottomore), *Finance Capital: A Study of the Latest Phase of Capitalist Development*, Routledge, London, 1951; V. Lenin, *Imperialism, the Highest Stage of Capitalism*; A. Hitler, *Mein Kampf*; H.J. Mackinder, 'The Geographical Pivot of History', *Geographical Journal*, 23, 1904 and *Democratic Ideals and Reality: A Study in the Politics of Reconstruction*, Constable, London, 1919; A.J. Toynbee, *A Study of History*, above all vol. VII, Oxford University Press, London, 1954; F. Fanon, *The Wretched of the Earth*, MacGibbon & Kee, London, 1965; K. Wittfogel, *Oriental Despotism: A Comparative Study of Total Power*, Yale University Press, New Haven, 1957; I. Wallerstein, *The Modern World System*, 3 vols, Academic Press, San Diego, 1974; Edward Said, *Orientalism. Western Conceptions of the East*, Penguin, Harmondsworth, 1985. Failure to follow the immense literature spawned by the ideas of Fanon and, even more, Said is a gap in this book. While by no means belittling the great contribution made to the study of empire by some of Said's insights, I (and I suspect a great many historians) sympathize with some of the criticisms made by J.M. Mackenzie in *Orientalism. History, Theory and the Arts*, Manchester University Press, 1995.

A vast literature exists on most of these authors and their ideas. Part of this (e.g. on Lenin and his concept of imperialism) I shall cover in the context of individual empires and their traditions. Worth noting here, however, is R. McKitterick and R. Quinault (eds), *Edward Gibbon and Empire*, Cambridge University Press, 1997 which is a useful insight into the differing conceptions of empire over the ages. Brendan O'Leary, *The Asiatic Mode of Production*, Basil Blackwell, Oxford, 1989 is a very interesting book and *inter alia* a convincing critique of Wittfogel.

Studies of the rise and fall of empires are a genre all on their own. I have only sampled Edward Gibbon's *History of the Decline and Fall of the Roman Empire*. Quite apart from studies of the decline and fall of individual empires, to be noted later, a number of key works attempt to tackle the question of why empires decline in general. The best-known recent attempt to tackle this question was Paul Kennedy's *The Rise and Fall of the Great Powers*, Unwin Hyman, London, 1988, which made a big impact on an American public opinion very concerned about the seeming decline of US power and competitiveness in the 1980s. G. Lundestad (ed.), *The Fall of Great Powers*, Oxford/Scandinavian University Press, Oxford, 1994 contains a wide range of essays both of a general and a comparative nature and on individual empires' decline. So does the very useful K. Barkey and M. von Hagen (eds), *After Empire*, Westview, Boulder, 1997. A Demandt (ed.), *Das Ende der Weltreiche*, C.H. Beck, Munich, 1997 has some very good essays comparing the fall of empires from ancient Persia to the Soviet Union. C. Cipolla, *The Economic Decline of Empires*, London, 1970 is narrower but also useful. J. Snyder, *Myths of Empire*, Cornell University Press, Ithaca, 1991 attempts to generalize about the foreign policy and expansionist tendencies of empire by linking them to domestic politics. C.A. Kupchan, *The Vulnerability of Empire*, Cornell University Press, Ithaca, 1994 also compares the foreign policies of modern empires. G.R. Urban (ed.), *End of Empire. The Demise of the Soviet Union*, American University Press, Washington, 1993 is actually far more than a study of the collapse of the USSR. It is really a general discussion about empires, ideology and civilization: it consists of interviews with Otto von Habsburg, Hugh Trevor-Roper, Elie Kedourie and others, and the interviews were conducted with all George Urban's skill at getting people to talk briefly but with great insight.

Many works that do not concentrate explicitly on the fate of empires are nevertheless crucial to this theme. Michael Mann, *The Sources of Social Power*, Cambridge University Press, 1986 (especially the first volume) probably heads this category of books: he divides power into four categories – military, economic, ideological and economic – and discusses the balance between these four types of power both in general and in a range of specific ancient and medieval polities, including the key empires of the pre-modern world. This is an exceptionally thoughtful book though anyone comparing Mann's work to my own will note a number of important differences: for instance, I count geography and demography as crucial independent factors of power.

Among other works of social science very important to anyone trying to understand the history of empire are two books by R. Gilpin: *War, Change and World Politics*, Cambridge University Press, 1981 and *The Political Economy of International Relations*, Princeton University Press, 1987. P. Liberman, *Does Conquest Pay? The Exploitation of Occupied Industrial Societies*, Princeton University Press, 1996 is a very useful reminder that traditional military imperialism can have its logic even in our age. I.S. Lustick, *Unsettled States: Disputed Lands*, Cornell University Press, Ithaca, 1993 looks in particular at the places of Ireland and Algeria in the British and French polities but brings out very well how subjective and contingent is the distinction between nation state and empire. So too from a rather different angle does A. Buchanan, *Secession. The Morality of Political Divorce from Fort Sumter to Lithuania and Quebec*, Westview, Boulder, 1991.

The general literature can be divided up between a number of themes relevant to empire. One is colonization. The place to start here is the admirably clear and comprehensive work by J. Osterhammel entitled *Colonialism*, Marcus Wiener/Ian Randle, Princeton and Kingston, 1997. M. Ferro, *Colonization*, Routledge, London, 1997 is also useful on this issue. Colonization merges easily into the history of migration, yet another vast topic. Apart from works on specific examples of colonization and migration, see for a general study of modern migration, Wang Gungwu (ed.), *Global History and Migrations*, Westview, Boulder, 1997. D.K. Fieldhouse, *The West and the Third World*, Blackwell, Oxford, 1999 is a very impressive attempt to sum up all aspects of the historical relationship between the Developed and Third worlds, going well beyond simply colonization and also well beyond mere concepts and into detailed comparative history.

The history of empire is very closely connected to a range of subjects such as war and government which themselves possess vast bibliographies. Even a very meagre political scientist like myself has inevitably read and benefited from a great number of works on government which I cannot list here. If the student of empire is to use one book on this subject as a bible, however, then it has to be the three volumes of S.E. Finer, *The History of Government*, Oxford University Press, 1997. Finer covers many of the key imperial political systems in detail but there is also a clarity and common sense to his immensely scholarly volumes which puts empire sharply into perspective against a range of other types of polity. I never found any single work to match Finer on the subject of war but nevertheless learned a great deal from J. Keegan, *A History of Warfare*, Hutchinson, London, 1993: P. Paret (ed.), *Makers of Modern Strategy from Machiavelli to the Nuclear Age*, Clarendon Press, Oxford, 1990: M. van Creveld, *The Transformation of War*, The Free Press, New York, 1991.

As regards geopolitics, Mahan, Mackinder and Wallerstein have already been mentioned. Two biographies of Mahan and Mackinder are well worth reading: W.H. Parker, *Mackinder. Geography as an Aid to Statecraft*, Clarendon Press, Oxford, 1982 and W.D. Puleston, *Mahan. The Life and Work of Captain Alfred Thayer Mahan*, Jonathan Cape, London, 1939. Geopolitics is something of an obsession of mine and I can list only a few of the key works I have enjoyed. Geoffrey Parker, *Geopolitics. Past, Present and Future*, Pinter, London, 1998 is a brief, fair survey of the topic and G.O. Tuathail, S. Dalby and P. Routledge, *The Geopolitics Reader*, Routledge, London, 1998 is a useful introduction to key texts. Other books worth more than the passing mention I can make in this bibliography are: D. Hooson (ed.), *Geography and National Identity*, Blackwell, Oxford, 1994; P.J. Taylor, *Political Geography. World-Economy, Nation-State and Locality*, Longman, Harlow, 1989; H.W. Weigert, V. Stefansson and R.E. Harrison (eds), *New Compass of the World*, George Harrap, London, 1949. J.N. Pieterse, *Empire and Emancipation*, Pluto Press, London, 1989 is a basically sympathetic criticism of the Wallerstein school for excessive stress on economic factors of power and domination.

Nationalism, empire's nemesis, has an immense and rapidly growing literature. Interest is partly due to the resurgence of nationalism in Western Europe from the 1960s onwards and to its role in the collapse of the Soviet Union. A vast academic industry is now devoted to the subject. As with government, I can only note a number of key works which have influenced my thinking in this book. These include A.D. Smith, *The Ethnic Origins of Nations*, London, 1986: A. Hastings, *The Construction of Nationhood*, Cambridge University Press, 1997; J.A. Armstrong, *Nations before Nationalism*, University of North Carolina Press, Chapel Hill, 1982 – all of which stress the deep roots and historical origins of nationalism. In different ways and to different degrees their opponents underline that

448

the nation and nationalism are products of mass literacy, wide markets, urban anomie and other aspects of modernity: see above all E. Gellner, *Nations and Nationalism*, Oxford University Press, 1989; I see Benedict Anderson's *Imagined Communities*, Verso, London, 1991 as a basically modernist text though instant categorization of this sort does no justice to a subtle and very interesting book. J.A. Hall (ed.), *The State of the Nation. Ernest Gellner and the Theory of Nationalism*, Cambridge University Press, 1998 is a remarkable collection of essays, worthy of Gellner himself. E. Kedourie (ed.), *Nationalism in Asia and Africa*, NAL Books, London, 1970 is useful to the student of empire. As will be evident from my own book, I doubt whether there is such a thing as nationalism: English, British, Czech, Russian, Soviet, Indonesian and Chinese nationalism – to take but a handful of extreme examples – are similar to the extent that they are doctrines and emotions capable of consolidating political communities but the content, origins and sources of these various nationalisms are vastly different. As regards nationalism and the European maritime empires, it is important to read James Mayall, *Nationalism and International Society*, Cambridge University Press, 1990.

A number of other works of social science deserve a mention. They include J.H. Kautsky, *The Politics of Aristocratic Empires*, University of North Carolina Press, 1982 and R. Niebuhr, *Nations and Empires. Recurring Patterns in the Political Order*, Faber & Faber, London, n.d.; R.G. Wesson, *The Imperial Order*, University of California Press, Berkeley, 1967. Theda Skocpol, *States and Social Revolution*, Cambridge University Press, 1979 was important because it turned the attention of social scientists to the significance of war, power and the international context – factors which it had been unfashionable to consider. A still very important book for anyone wishing to understand the dilemmas of traditional rulers in modernizing societies is S.P. Huntington, *Political Order in Changing Societies*, Yale University Press, New Haven, 1968. For insights into monarchical autocracy and its psychology the diary of the last Shah of Iran's Minister of the Imperial Court, Asadollah Alam, *The Shah and I*, I.B. Tauris, London, 1991 is a shrewd source. So is R. Kapuszinski, *The Emperor and Shah of Shahs*, Picador, London, 1994.

CHAPTER 2.   POWER AND EMPIRE IN THE GLOBAL CONTEXT

Chapter 2 covers much of the world's history from the foundation of the Roman and Chinese empires to the present day. It is based on wide reading over the last three decades: obviously it is impossible to do more here than cite a few key texts for the chapter's main sections.

When I began this book I knew nothing about Chinese or Roman empire. An excellent starting-point was two atlases produced by Facts on File, New York and Oxford: T. Cornell and J. Matthews, *Atlas of the Roman World*, 1990 edition, and C. Blunden and M. Elvin, *Cultural Atlas of China*, 1983. The maps are outstanding and so is the text in both cases. (In fact the whole series is a godsend to anyone coming afresh to the study of empire). Mark Elvin, *The Pattern of the Chinese Past*, Stanford University Press, 1973, chapter 1 is a thoughtful attempt to discuss the problem of size in pre-modern empire and to relate this to empire's longevity (Michael Mann also tackles this issue in volume 1 of his *Sources of Social Power*). Arthur Waldron, *The Great Wall of China*, Cambridge, 1990 is very readable and thoughtful. On the crucial relationship with the northern steppe frontier and its warrior nomads see: T.J. Barfield, *The Perilous Frontier. Nomadic Empires and China, 221 B.C. to A.D. 1757*, Blackwell, Oxford, 1992 and S. Jagshid and V.J. Symons, *Peace, War and Trade along the Great Wall*, Indiana University Press, Indianapolis, 1989. As regards general histories of China, I progressed from J.K. Fairbank, *China: A New History*, Harvard University Press, Cambridge, 1992 to Jonathan Spence, *The Search for Modern China*, London, 1990, thence to Zhangyuan Fu, *Autocratic Tradition and Chinese Politics*, Cambridge University Press, 1993, and from there (via a number of other works) to the many excellent volumes of the *Cambridge History of China*, my single biggest investment in books in the course of this project. I owe an immense amount to the richly detailed and comprehensive chapters of this splendid series.

These works were the basis for a somewhat more detailed study of imperial power in China, which itself provides a benchmark against which to measure all subsequent imperial systems of autocratic and bureaucratic rule. B.S. Bartlett, *Monarchs and Ministers. The Grand Council in mid Ch'ing China. 1723–1820*, Berkeley, 1991 is, I think, the most scholarly and fascinating book I have ever read on the workings of monarchical absolutism and authoritarian bureaucracy in any society. It inspired me to make two expeditions to China to inspect the Forbidden City and to cover the walls of my house with portraits of the Qing emperors. R. Huang, *1587. A Year of No Significance. The Ming Dynasty in Decline*, Yale University Press, New Haven, 1981 and S.H. Tsai, *The Eunuchs in the Ming Dynasty*, SUNY Press, Albany, 1996 also made a great contribution to my knowledge of imperial court politics. S. Naquin and E.S. Rawski, *Chinese Society in the Eighteenth Century*, Yale University Press, New Haven, 1987 was an excellent background against which to concentrate on imperial politics. P.A. Kuhn, *Soulstealers. The Chinese Sorcery Scare of 1768*, Harvard University Press, Cambridge, MA provides a fascinating angle on dilemmas of alien rule in China. P.K. Crossley, *The Manchus*, Blackwell, 1997 brings the surprised European (and Russian) student of empire nose-to-nose with a people (or were they really a people?) who conquered an empire and in the process lost their own identity.

As regards multi-ethnicity, another crucial aspect of empire, L.J. Moser, *The Chinese Mosaic. The People and Provinces of China*, Westview, Boulder, 1985 is splendid in its detail and complexity, above all as regards the endless groups within the Han Chinese population. L. Dittmer and S.S. Kim (eds), *China's Quest for National Identity*, Cornell University Press, Ithaca, 1993 in particular contains a fascinating discussion (chapter 4 by A. Watson) of the creation of all-imperial rituals in pre-modern China. J. Unger (ed.), *Chinese Nationalism*, M.E. Sharpe, Armonk, 1996, especially chapter 1 by James Townsend, was also useful to me, as was F. Dikotter, *The Discourse of Race in Modern China*, Hurst, London, 1992, which is a good counterpart to Western empires' stance on race and assimilation. E.H. Schafer, *The Vermilion Bird. T'ang Images of the South*, University of California Press, Berkeley, 1967 is in a way a comment about the diversity of China, the process of assimilation and colonization, and the creation of an imperial community. It is a good contrast to cultural encounters in the building of other empires and a reminder of the blurred line between empire and nation.

On the minorities proper, I read C. Mackerras, *China's Minorities. Integration and Modernisation in the Twentieth Century*, Oxford University Press, Hong Kong, 1994: S. Harrell (ed.), *Cultural Encounters on China's Ethnic Frontier*, University of Washington Press, Seattle, 1994: D.C. Gladney, *Muslim Chinese. Ethnic Nationalism in the People's Republic*, Harvard University Press, Cambridge, 1991; F. Thierry, 'Empire and Minority in China', in G. Chaliand (ed.), *Minority Peoples in the Age of Nation States*, London, 1989.

450

D.S.G. Goodman and G. Segal, *China Deconstructs*, London, 1994 was a useful warning to a naïve Russianist like myself why contemporary China was actually unlikely to 'deconstruct', as the Soviet Union had just done.

I have read rather less on Rome than on China. My two main standbys were P. Garnsey and R. Saller, *The Roman Empire. Economy, Society and Culture*, California University Press, Berkeley, 1987 and A. Lintott, *Imperium Romanum. Politics and Administration*, Routledge, London, 1993. *The Oxford Classical Dictionary*, 3rd edition, Oxford University Press, 1996 was hugely valuable. So too were the two volumes edited by John Wacher, *The Roman World*, Routledge, London, 1987. A.H.M. Jones, *The Later Roman Empire. 284–602*, Johns Hopkins University Press, 2 vols, Baltimore, 1964 provided answers to many questions that bothered me and M. Grant, *The Fall of the Roman Empire*, London, 1990 was an excellent layman's guide to the debate on the fall of the Roman Empire in the West. I was barely able to follow up the leads provided by Michael Grant save through the general literature but R. Macmullan, *Corruption and the Decline of Rome*, Yale University Press, New Haven, 1988 ought to be required reading for any student of the Brezhnev era and Edward Luttwak, *The Grand Strategy of the Roman Empire*, Johns Hopkins University Press, 1976, fed my liking for geopolitics and grand strategy.

Garth Fowden, *Empire to Commonwealth. Consequences of Monotheism in Late Antiquity*, Princeton University Press, 1993 is a very important book for the student of empire, linking questions of geography, ideology and power in an exceptionally thought-provoking way. I came to the study of Byzantine empire full of determination to illustrate the power of ideology by showing how religious dissent undermined much of the Byzantine Empire's willingness to resist the seventh-century Islamic offensive: W.E. Kaegi, *Byzantium and the Early Islamic Conquests*, Cambridge University Press, 1992 sent me away suitably abashed with a true historian and scholar's warning that the sources do not actually substantiate this traditional interpretation of early Arab successes against the Byzantines. J. Herrin, *The Formation of Christendom*, Princeton University Press, 1987 is an excellent guide to the development of Christianity as an ideology of empire and to the split between Latin and Byzantine Europe. My main sources on the Byzantine Empire were volume 4, parts 1 and 2 of *The Cambridge Medieval History: The Byzantine Empire*, edited by J.M. Hussey, Cambridge, 1966: R. Browning, *The Byzantine Empire*, the Catholic University of America Press, Washington, 1992; J.F. Haldon, *Byzantium in the Seventh Century*, Cambridge University Press, 1990 and W. Treadgold, *The Byzantine Revival. 780–842*, Stanford University Press, 1988.

The development of the European system of international relations is an immense subject. A good introduction is A. Watson, *The Evolution of International Society*, Routledge, London, 1992. Narrower but still useful is E. Luard, *The Balance of Power*, Macmillan, Houndmills, 1992. On the evolution of the European state, C. Tilly, *Coercion, Capital and European States. AD 990–1990*, Blackwell, London, 1994 is splendid in its sweep, its clarity and its lack of teleology. B.M. Downing, *The Military Revolution and Political Change. Origins of Autocracy and Democracy in Early Modern Europe*, Princeton University Press, 1992 relates political and military development in a very interesting and (to me) convincing manner. T. Ertman, *Birth of the Leviathan. Building States and Regimes in Medieval and Early Modern Europe*, Cambridge University Press, 1997 is also very interesting on comparative bureaucratic and constitutional development. For all its age, P. Anderson, *Lineages of the Absolutist State*, New Left Books, London, 1974 retains its sparkle. Three books (at least) by W.H. McNeill are crucial to my story of empire: *The Pursuit of Power*, University of

Chicago Press, 1982; *Europe's Steppe Frontier*, University of Chicago Press, 1964; *Plagues and Peoples*, Doubleday, Garden City, 1976. The history of Europe's rise needs to be set against a wider global background. The best way I know to do this is to read J. Abu-Lughod, *Before European Hegemony. The World System A.D. 1250–1350*, New York, 1989 and K.N. Chaudhuri, *Asia Before Europe. Economy and Civilisation of the Indian Ocean from the Rise of Islam to 1750*, Cambridge University Press, 1990. On the peasant base which sustained the military and fiscal burdens of empire T. Scott (ed.), *The Peasantries of Europe. From the Fourteenth to the Nineteenth Centuries*, Longman, London, 1998 is the most up-to-date comparative study. The articles on the Russian and Ottoman peasantries by Edgar Melton and Fikret Adanir are particularly useful.

On the origins of Eastern Europe's relative backwardness there are important essays in D. Chirot (ed.), *The Origins of Backwardness in Eastern Europe*, California University Press, Berkeley, 1989. Larry Woolf, *Inventing Eastern Europe. The Map of Civilisation in the Mind of the Enlightenment*, Stanford University Press, 1994 approaches the same basic issue from a very different and interesting angle. On this issue see also chapter 1 of G. Schöpflin, *Politics in Eastern Europe*, Oxford University Press, 1993. On another peripheral region, also crucial to Russia, see the two volumes by David Kirby, *Northern Europe in the Early Modern Period. The Baltic World 1492–1772*, Longman, London, 1990 and *The Baltic World 1772–1993*, Longman, London, 1995.

The literature on European power politics and inter-state relations from the fifteenth to the twentieth century is so immense that one needs to be very selective. The surveys on which I most relied were: R. Bonney, *The European Dynastic States 1494–1660*, Oxford University Press, 1991: D. McKay and H.M. Scott (eds), *The Rise of the Great Powers 1648–1815*, Longman, London, 1983; P.M. Schroeder, *The Transformation of European Politics 1763–1848*, Clarendon Press, Oxford, 1994; A.J.P. Taylor, *The Struggle for Mastery in Europe 1848–1918*, Oxford University Press, 1954. S. Woolf, *Napoleon's Integration of Europe*, Routledge, London, 1991; D. Gates, *The Napoleonic Wars 1803–1815*, Arnold, London, 1997; M. Broers, *Europe under Napoleon*, Arnold, London, 1996; C.J. Esdale, *The Wars of Napoleon*, Longman, London, 1995 are useful guides to the closest Europe came to re-creating a pan-continental empire between the fall of Rome and the rise of the European Union. On the origins of the First World War, see the individual volumes of the Macmillan series listed under the different empires. The two volumes by E.J. Hobsbawm, *The Age of Capital*, Weidenfeld, London, 1975 and *The Age of Empire*, Weidenfeld, London, 1987 cover much more than inter-state relations and are essential reading.

There is a vast literature on the sinews of power of the European states. Above all, this means the development of European armies and fleets. But it also means economic, financial and fiscal systems. On the latter (apart from works listed under individual empires) see above all R. Bonney (ed.), *Economic Systems and State Finance*, Clarendon Press, Oxford, 1995 and R. Bonney (ed.), *The Rise of the Fiscal State in Europe c. 1200–1815*, Clarendon Press, Oxford, 1999. The latter is particularly useful for Russianists because it contains a short but irreplaceable chapter on the fiscal history of Russia by Richard Hellie. S. Pollard, *Peaceful Conquest. The Industrialisation of Europe 1760–1970*, Oxford University Press, 1981 and R. Sylla and G. Toniolo (eds), *Patterns of European Industrialisation. The Nineteenth Century*, Routledge, London, 1991 provide crucial background information on the relative economic power and patterns of development of Europe's regions and states.

452

Bibliography

Perhaps the best place to start on armed forces is G. Parker, *The Military Revolution*, Cambridge University Press, 1988. Next comes C. Rogers (ed.), *The Military Revolution Debate*, Westview, Boulder, 1995. F. Tallett, *War and Society in Early Modern Europe 1495–1715*, Routledge, London, 1992 carries the story on and J. Black, *European Warfare 1650–1815*, Longman, London, 1994 takes it down to the defeat of Napoleon. The great work on mid-nineteenth-century warfare is Michael Howard, *The Franco-Prussian War*, Collier Books, London, 1969. As with many other books in the series, *The Cambridge Illustrated History of Warfare*, edited by Geoffrey Parker, Cambridge University Press, 1995 is not only very attractively produced and illustrated but also has an excellent text.

On the First World War, Niall Ferguson, *The Pity of War*, Penguin, London, 1998 is particularly good on the finance and economics of war; David Stevenson, *The First World War and International Politics*, Clarendon Press, Oxford, 1988 is excellent on the war's diplomacy; A.R. Millett and W. Murray (eds), *Military Effectiveness*, volume 1: *The First World War*, Allen & Unwin, London, 1988 is the best general military survey (though sadly lacking a chapter on Austria); Norman Stone, *The Eastern Front. 1914–1918*, Hodder & Stoughton, London, 1975 is essential reading on a crucial aspect of the war which usually merits a chapter in English-language books; Avner Offer, *The First World War. An Agrarian Interpretation*, Clarendon Press, Oxford, 1989 is, as always with this author, original and very thought-provoking. H.C. Meyer, *Mitteleuropa in German Thought and Action. 1815–1945*, The Hague, 1955 is important for possible scenarios had Germany won the war. So too is O.S. Fedyshyn, *Germany's Drive to the East and the Ukrainian Revolution, 1917–1918*, Rutgers University Press, 1971.

On the interwar order and its breakdown probably the best short-cut is to read P. Bell, *The Origins of the Second World War in Europe*, Longman, London, 1996 and Akira Iriye, *The Origins of the Second World War in Asia and the Pacific*, Longman, London, 1987. Then read D.C. Watt, *How War Came*, Mandarin, London, 1990. On the war itself, R. Overy, *Why the Allies Won*, Allen Lane, London, 1995 asks useful questions. R.A. Parker, *The Second World War*, Oxford University Press, 1989 is a good single-volume survey. Volume 4 of *Germany and the Second World War. The Attack on the Soviet Union*, edited by Horst Boog et al., Clarendon Press, Oxford, 1998 is crucial to an understanding of Germany's motives and plans, as well as the first year of the Soviet-German war. This volume alone is over 1,300 pages and isn't light reading. It is, even so, excellent value.

The Cold War also has an immense literature. On its origins, I like D. Reynolds, *The Origins of the Cold War in Europe*, Yale University Press, New Haven, 1994. J.L. Gaddis, *We Now Know. Rethinking Cold War History*, Clarendon Press, Oxford, 1997 is an exciting survey of the war's first two decades; R. Garthoff, *Detente and Confrontation: Soviet-American Relations from Nixon to Reagan*, Brookings Institution, Washington, 1985 and R. Garthoff, *The Great Transition; American-Soviet Relations and the End of the Cold War*, Brookings Institution, Washington, 1994 continue the story until the war's end. George Kennan's important analysis of Soviet goals and methods is reprinted as chapter 12 in F.J. Fleron, E.P. Hoffmann and R.F. Laird, *Soviet Foreign Policy. Classic and Contemporary Issues*, de Gruyter, New York, 1991.

On the European maritime empires the place to start is G.V. Scammell, *The First Imperial Age. European Overseas Expansion c. 1400–1715*, HarperCollins, London, 1989. J.H. Parry, *The Establishment of the European Hegemony 1415–1715*, Harper Torchbook, New York, 1961 remains a classic. J.D. Tracy (ed.), *The Political Economy of Merchant Empires. State Power and World Trade*, Cambridge University Press, 1991 contains many important essays, as does J.D. Tracy (ed.), *The Rise of Merchant Empires. Long-distance Trade in the Early Modern World*, Cambridge University Press, 1990. G. Raudzens, *Empires, Europe and Globalization. 1492–1788*, Sutton Publishing, Stroud, 1999 takes the story to the French Revolution. D.C. Coleman (ed.), *Revisions in Mercantilism*, Methuen, London, 1969 is an important book and was my introduction to this subject.

The expansion of the maritime empires was inevitably closely linked to seapower: a useful book on this subject is R. Harding, *Seapower and Naval Warfare 1650–1830*, UCL Press, London, 1999. D.B. Ralston, *Importing the European Army. The Introduction of European Military Techniques and Institutions into the Extra-European World 1600–1914*, University of Chicago Press, 1996 was particularly useful for me because it brought together Russian, Ottoman and maritime empires' experience. Disease and ecology are crucial issues in the history of empire: on this see above all A.W. Crosby, *Ecological Imperialism: The Biological Expansion of Europe. 900–1900*, Cambridge University Press, 1986; I owe a great debt to this splendid book. N.D. Cook, *Born to Die. Disease and New World Conquest 1492–1650*, Cambridge University Press, 1998 is also of exceptional interest. On the clash of cultures which early European imperialism set off, see A. Pagden, *European Encounters with the New World*, Yale University Press, New Haven, 1993 and S.B. Schwartz (ed.), *Implicit Understandings*, Cambridge University Press, 1994.

Slavery and the slave trade are major issues in European imperial history. The Russianist approaches them best through M.L. Bush (ed.), *Serfdom and Slavery*, Longman, London, 1996 and P. Kolchin, *Unfree Labor. American Slavery and Russian Serfdom*, Harvard University Press, Cambridge, MA, 1987. On the slave trade the best starting-point is the survey by H.S. Klein, *The Atlantic Slave Trade*, Cambridge University Press, 1999. An important and very useful book is P.D. Curtin, *The Rise and Fall of the Plantation Complex. Essays in Atlantic History*, Cambridge University Press, 1990. There are many good articles in B. Solow (ed.), *Slavery and the Rise of the Atlantic System*, Cambridge University Press, 1991.

The main comparative study of modern colonial empire from start to finish is D.K. Fieldhouse, *The Colonial Empires. A Comparative Survey from the Eighteenth Century*, Macmillan, Houndmills, 1982. A key book on the development of empire in the nineteenth century is D.R. Headrick, *The Tools of Empire. Technology and European Imperialism in the Nineteenth Century*, Oxford University Press, 1981. This shows how technology vastly increased the difference in power between Western and colonized peoples during the nineteenth century. Another important work is R. Szporluk, *Communism and Nationalism. Karl Marx against Friedrich List*, Oxford University Press, 1988: this helps to explain the intellectual bases of late nineteenth-century protectionism. W.L. Langer, *The Diplomacy of Imperialism*, Alfred A. Knopf, New York, 1951 remains well worth reading.

On the Spanish colonial empire the best introduction is chapter 1 of J.H. Elliott, *Spain and its World*, Yale University Press, New Haven, 1989. Alternatively, there is J. Lynch, *Spain 1516–1598. From Nation State to World Empire*, Oxford University Press, 1991. L. Bethell (ed.), *Colonial Spanish America*, Cambridge University Press, 1987 is very useful, as is chapter 1, by J. Lynch, of L. Bethell (ed.), *The Independence of Latin America*, Cambridge University Press, 1987. Two very interesting books on the impact on metropolitan Spain of the loss of empire are: M.P. Costelloe, *Responses to Revolution. Imperial Spain and the Spanish American Revolutions, 1810–1840*, Cambridge University Press, 1986; S. Balfour, *The End of the Spanish Empire 1898–1923*, Clarendon Press, Oxford, 1997. The loss of the last colonies in the late nineteenth century caused far more frenzy, partly because empire by then was much more fashionable and highly rated than it had been just after 1815.

On the early Portuguese empire see, S. Subrahmanyam, *The Portuguese Empire in Asia 1500–1700*, Longman, London, 1993 and A. Russell-Wood, *A World on the Move. The Portuguese in Africa, Asia and America 1415–1808*, St Martin's Press, New York, 1992. On the brief and rather insignificant German overseas empire, see W.O. Henderson, *The German Colonial Empire*, Frank Cass, London, 1993. On the much more important French empire see: R. Aldrich, *Greater France. A History of French Overseas Expansion*, Macmillan, Houndmills, 1996 and R. Giradet, *L'Idée Coloniale en France de 1871 à 1962*, La Table Ronde, Paris, 1972. R.F. Betts, *Uncertain Dimensions. Western Overseas Empires in the Twentieth Century*, Oxford University Press, 1985 is a study of the French and British empires. I. Lustick, *State-Building Failure in British Ireland and French Algeria*, Institute for International Studies, Berkeley, 1985 is a very interesting, explicit comparison between two major disasters of British and French empire. It is essential reading for anyone concerned with the role of settlers in European colonies and with the ambiguous definitions of empire and nation. I will list literature on the East Indies separately: a key book, however, on the early Dutch trading empire is C.R. Boxer, *The Dutch Seaborne Empire 1600–1800*, Penguin, London, 1990.

On the Japanese empire there is W.G. Beasley, *Japanese Imperialism. 1894–1945*, Clarendon Press, Oxford, 1987; R.H. Myers and M.R. Peattie (eds); *The Japanese Colonial Empire, 1895–1945*, Princeton University Press, 1984; M.R. Peattie, *Nan'yo. The Rise and Fall of the Japanese in Micronesia 1885–1945*, University of Hawaii Press, Honolulu. Chapter 12 of volume 5 of *The Cambridge History of Japan. The Nineteenth Century*, ed. M.B. Jansen, Cambridge University Press, 1989 and chapters 5 and 6 of volume 6, *The Twentieth Century*, ed. M.B. Jansen, 1988 are comprehensive surveys of Japan as an imperial power. D. Colman, *The Nature and Origins of Japanese Imperialism*, Routledge, London, 1992 is also a significant book for the comparative study of empires.

My discussion of the United States partly takes me back to classes many years ago with Dr Jonathan Steinberg at Cambridge. Two very good books on American ideology and identity are: E. Foner, *The Story of American Freedom*, Picador, London, 1999 and S.M. Lipset, *American Exceptionalism*, Norton, London, 1997. J.B. Nye, *Bound to Lead. The Changing Nature of American Power*, Basic Books, New York, 1991 presents the case for continuing American power very convincingly: D.W. White, *The American Century. The Rise and Decline of the United States as a World Power*, Yale University Press, New Haven, 1996 puts the opposite point of view. The domination of American ideals and ideology worldwide is a very major part of American power: on this, Francis Fukuyama, *The End of History and the Last Man*, Penguin, London, 1992 is required reading. Conflicting views of American global influence, which are linked too to attitudes to domestic political strategies, are found in: Z. Brzezinski, *The Grand Chessboard*, Basic Books, New York, 1997 and S.P. Huntington, *The Clash of Civilizations and the Remaking of World Order*, Touchstone Books, London, 1997. The story of the native American population is told well in J. Wilson, *The Earth Shall Weep*, Picador, London, 1998. A. Starkey, *European and Native American Warfare 1675–1815*, UCL Press, London, 1998 is far more than military history narrowly defined and is a very useful insight into native resistance and the tactics of forest warfare.

G.W. Gallagher, *The Confederate War*, Harvard University Press, Cambridge, MA, 1997 to my mind says everything there is to say about Confederate nationalism and the South's war effort. D. Gilpin Faust, *The Creation of Confederate Nationalism*, Louisiana State University Press, Baton Rouge, 1988 and W.R. Taylor, *Cavalier and Yankee*, Oxford University Press, New York, 1961 are also very interesting. So are some collections of essays on the war: e.g. G.S. Boritt (ed.), *Why the Confederacy Lost*, Oxford University Press, 1992. I am less convinced by the argument in R.E. Beringer, H. Hattaway, A. Jones, W.N. Still, *Why the South Lost the Civil War*, University of Georgia Press, Athens, 1986. It is very important to put the Civil War in its international context. B.H. Reid, *The Origins of the American Civil War*, Longman, London, 1996 does this well. K. Bourne, *Britain and the Balance of Power in North America. 1815–1908*, Longman, London, 1967 gives fascinating insights into possible British strategies. Note too the discussion in W. Baumgart, *The Crimean War 1853–1856*, Arnold, London, 1999, chapter 5 on the possibilities of European conflict spreading to North America. Wars and revolutions are often most truthfully as well as most entertainingly told as a narrative: see J. McPherson, *Battle Cry of Freedom*, Oxford University Press, 1998.

On ethnic and other nationalisms in India, see as background: H. Kulke and D. Rothermund, *A History of India*, Routledge, London, 1986 and P.R. Brass, *The Politics of India since Independence. The New Cambridge History of India*, vol. IV.1, Cambridge University Press, 1990; M. Chadda, *Ethnicity, Security and Separatism in India*, Columbia University Press, New York, 1997 and Ishtiaq Ahmed, *State, Nation and Ethnicity in Contemporary South Asia*, Pinter, London, 1996. On the origins, specific natures and development of national identities in South-East Asia see *The Cambridge History of Southeast Asia. Volume 1: From early Times to c. 1800*; Volume 2, *The Nineteenth and Twentieth Centuries*, ed. N. Tarling, Cambridge University Press, 1992. Also B. Anderson, *The Spectre of Comparisons. Nationalism, Southeast Asia and the World*, Verso, London, 1998. On Indonesia alone, see M.C. Ricklefs, *A History of Modern Indonesia since c. 1300*, Stanford University Press, 1993; P. Liddle, *Leadership and Culture in Indonesian Politics*, Allen & Unwin, Sydney, 1996; G. Robinson, *The Dark Side of Paradise. Political Violence in Bali*, Cornell University Press, Ithaca, 1995. I learned an immense amount from all these books.

On the European Union, see P. Gowan and P. Anderson (eds), *The Question of Europe*, Verso, London, 1997; W. Wallace, *Regional Integration: the West European Experience*, Washington, 1994; R. Bideleux et al. (eds), *European Integration and Disintegration. East and West*, Routledge, London, 1996; H. Miall, *Shaping the New Europe*, Pinter, London, 1993.

CHAPTER 3.   THE BRITISH EMPIRE

The literature on the British Empire is immense and often of very high quality. P.J. Marshall (ed.), *The Cambridge Illustrated History of the British Empire*, Cambridge University Press, 1996 is the best one-volume history: it upholds the reputation of the series for attractive layout combined with first-rate scholarship. Peter Marshall's book only starts in 1783, however. Anyone wanting a single volume covering the empire's entire history should turn to T.O. Lloyd, *The British Empire 1558–1983*, Oxford University Press, 1984. There are two excellent one-volume histories of the empire in the nineteenth and twentieth centuries: R. Hyam, *Britain's Imperial Century 1815–1914*, Macmillan, Houndmills, 1993; B. Porter, *The Lion's Share. A Short History of British Imperialism 1850–1983*, Longman, Harlow, 1984. Looming behind these works is the new multi-volume history of the empire whose first two volumes have already appeared: *The Oxford*

Bibliography

History of the British Empire. Volume 1: The Origins of Empire, ed. N. Canny; Volume 2: The Eighteenth Century, ed. P. Marshall; both volumes Oxford University Press, 1998. The last three volumes in the series, including the exceptionally useful R. Winks (ed.), Historiography, Oxford University Press, 1999 were published after my book was completed.

P.J. Cain and A.G. Hopkins, British Imperialism. Volume 1: Innovation and Expansion. 1688–1914; Volume 2: Crisis and Decolonisation 1914–1990, Longman, Harlow, 1993 is a splendid tour de force: it stresses the crucial role of finance and financial interests in British imperialism. There are also two excellent general histories of the empire covering short but vital periods: C. Bayly, Imperial Meridian. The British Empire and the World 1780–1830, Longman, London, 1989; M. Beloff, Imperial Sunset. Volume 1: Britain's Liberal Empire. 1897–1921, Alfred A. Knopf, New York, 1970. A.P. Thornton, The Imperial Idea and its Enemies, Macmillan, London, 1959 remains a very useful book.

On the empire as great power, the key volume to consult for the long eighteenth century is L. Stone (ed.), The Imperial State at War. Britain from 1689 to 1815, Routledge, 1994. J. Brewer, The Sinews of Power, Unwin Hyman, London, 1989 is excellent on the fiscal system and the formidable nature of the state that ran it. The Royal Navy was the most impressive element in British power in the nineteenth century: A. Lambert, The Last Sailing Battlefleet. Maintaining Naval Mastery 1815–1850, Conway, London, 1991; D.K. Brown, Warrior to Dreadnought. Warship Development 1860–1905, Chatham Publishing, London, 1997. In both cases scholarship is combined with splendid illustrations.

By the end of the century Britain was, relatively speaking, losing power. On this see: A.L. Friedberg, The Weary Titan. Britain and the Experience of Relative Decline 1895–1905, Princeton University Press, 1988. I.R. Smith, The Origins of the South African War 1899–1902, Longman, London, 1996 is very useful as an insight into British policy-making and thinking in this era. E.H.H. Green, The Crisis of Conservatism. The Politics, Economics and Ideology of the British Conservative Party 1880–1914, Routledge, London, 1996 is relevant for a student of empire because at this time imperial problems (above all, Ireland) impinged mightily on domestic British politics. The best short history of declining British power in the twentieth century is D. Reynolds, Britannia Overruled. British Policy and World Power in the Twentieth Century, Longman, London, 1991. A. Orde, The Eclipse of Great Britain. The United States and British Imperial Decline 1895–1956, Macmillan, Houndmills, 1996 traces the crucial relationship with the United States. C. Thorne, Allies of a Kind, London, 1978 and W.R. Louis, The United States and the Decolonisation of the British Empire 1941–1945, Clarendon Press, Oxford, 1977 cover key moments of the Anglo-American relationship in more detail. R. Parker, Chamberlain and Appeasement, Macmillan, Houndmills, 1993 is an excellent study of the dilemmas of receding power and the illusions of a particular era, people and ruling class: its narrow focus (by the standard of most of the books I have read on empire) and its concentration in part on a single individual gives it vividness and immediacy. The best books on decolonization are by John Darwin: The End of the British Empire, Blackwell, Oxford, 1991: Britain and Decolonisation, Macmillan, Houndmills, 1988.

On empire and Britain L. Colley, Britons. Forging the Nation. 1707–1837, Yale University Press, New Haven, 1992 is outstanding. M. Hechter, Internal Colonialism. The Celtic Fringe in British National Development 1536–1966, Routledge, London, 1975 argues a case for relative deprivation and underdevelopment. In my view this is countered effectively by

457

D. McCrone, *Understanding Scotland. The Sociology of a Stateless Nation*, Routledge, London, 1992: this told me rather more about Scottish national identity than other books in principle more exclusively devoted to this topic. T.M. Devine, *Clanship to Crofters' War. The Social Transformation of the Scottish Highlands*, Manchester University Press, 1994 is good on the impact on Gaelic society of the newly industrialized Lowlands and of British power. Hugh Kearney, *The British Isles. A History of Four Nations*, Cambridge University Press, 1989 is excellent on the waxing and waning of complementary and rival identities in the British Isles. On this see also A. Grant and K.J. Stringer (eds), *Uniting the Kingdom. The Making of British History*, London, 1995.

There are now many good histories of modern Ireland. On the whole at present the Republican historians are in retreat: this is partly a reaction to events in Northern Ireland and partly too perhaps a response to their previous domination (Trinity College Dublin excluded!) of the telling of Irish history in the Republic. G. Boyce and Alan O'Day (eds), *The Making of Modern Irish History*, Routledge, London, 1996 is a round-up of revisionist interpretations of Irish history. I loved R. Foster, *Modern Ireland 1600–1972*, London, 1988 though it is sometimes roundly denounced in the Nationalist camp: I lack the knowledge to judge either way. L. Kennedy, *Colonialism, Religion and Nationalism in Ireland*, Queen's University Press, Belfast, 1996 has some excellent essays which put Irish history in European perspective. S.J. Connolly, *Religion, Law and Power. The Making of Protestant Ireland 1660–1760*, Oxford University Press, 1992 is fascinating for someone like myself who is interested in the creation and maintenance of colonial elites in alien societies. J. Kendle, *Ireland and the Federal Solution. The Debate over the United Kingdom Constitution 1870–1921*, McGill-Queen's University Press, Kingston, 1989 strikes an immediate chord with anyone interested in the history of the Russo-Soviet and Austrian empires.

V.G. Kiernan has an interesting article entitled 'The Emergence of a Nation' in C. Philpin (ed.), *Nationalism and Popular Protest in Ireland*, Cambridge University Press, 1987 and Nicholas Canny contributed 'The Marginal Kingdom: Ireland as a Problem in the First British Empire' to B. Bailyn and P.D. Morgan (eds), *Strangers within the Realm*, University of North Carolina Press, Chapel Hill, 1991. Historians of the eighteenth-century empire are more inclined to include Ireland than those who study the nineteenth-century empire, at which point Ireland was part of the United Kingdom.

On Britain in the Americas R. Middleton, *Colonial America. A History 1588–1776*, Blackwell, Oxford, 1992 and A. McFarlane, *The British in the Americas 1480–1815*, Longman, London, 1994 are good surveys. Canada set the trend for colonial self-government though political development in the English metropolis had a more important influence on dominion self-government even than events in Canada. On this see: G. Martin, *Britain and the Origins of Canadian Confederation 1837–67*, Macmillan, Houndmills, 1995 and J.M. Ward, *Colonial Self-Government. The British Experience 1759–1856*, Macmillan, London, 1976. On Australia see: M. Clark, *A History of Australia*, Pimlico, London, 1995; G. Blainey, *The Tyranny of Distance*, Macmillan, London, 1968; L. Trainor, *British Imperialism and Australian Nationalism*, Cambridge University Press, 1994. Trainor's book on the emergence of an Australian identity ties in well with J. Eddy and D. Schreuder (eds), *The Rise of Colonial Nationalism*, Allen & Unwin, Sydney, 1988, which is an excellent study of the development of a strong though ambivalent sense of British, White but also colonial identity in the Dominions. As regards the victims of these new nations, the indigenous populations, I have barely scratched the surface of the literature. H. Reynolds, *The Other Side of the Frontier*, Penguin, Ringwood, 1990 covers aboriginal resistance in Australia and James Belich, *The Victorian Interpretation of Racial Conflict. The Maori, the British and the New Zealand Wars*, McGill-Queen's University Press, Montreal, 1986, is a splendid story and much more besides.

On India Judith Brown, *Modern India. The Origins of an Asian Democracy*, Oxford University Press, 1994 is excellent: its introductory comments about the end of the Mogul empire should make any Sovietologist prick up his or her ears at similarities to the collapse of the USSR. Her book is best read alongside S. Sarkar, *Modern India 1885–1947*, Macmillan, Houndmills, 1983 whose perspective is much more anti-British. As regards the creation of British India Christopher Bayly, *Indian Society and the Making of the British Empire*, Cambridge University Press, 1988 and P. Lawson, *The East India Company*, Longman, London, 1993 were my guides. On the last decades of British rule B.R. Tomlinson, *The Political Economy of the Raj, 1914–1947. The Economics of Decolonization in India*, London, 1979 is excellent. On the forces of order/repression I recommend D. Arnold, *Police Power and Colonial Rule. Madras 1859–1947*, Oxford University Press, Delhi, 1986 and D. Omissi, *The Sepoy and the Raj. The Indian Army 1860–1940*, Macmillan, London, 1994. I. Copeland, *The Princes of India in the Endgame of Empire*, Cambridge University Press, 1997 is an absorbing study in the politics of indirect rule. T.R. Metcalf, *Ideologies of the Raj*, Cambridge University Press, 1994 is essential reading. D.A. Low, *Eclipse of Empire*, Cambridge University Press, 1991 is useful both for his study of the end of the Indian empire and for his comparisons between British and Dutch colonial policies in the twentieth century.

I finished my attempt to understand the British Empire by reading Sir Charles Lucas, *Greater Rome and Greater Britain*, Clarendon Press, Oxford, 1912.

CHAPTER 4.   THE OTTOMAN EMPIRE

The literature on the Ottoman Empire is smaller and sometimes of lower quality than is the case with the British Empire. There is one very good general history: R. Mantran (ed.), *Histoire de L'Empire Ottoman*, Fayard, Paris, 1989. By now the two-volume history by S.S. Shaw, *History of the Ottoman Empire and Modern Turkey*, Cambridge University Press, 1976 is really beginning to feel its age. H. Inalcik and D. Quataert, *An Economic and Social History of the Ottoman Empire 1300–1914*, Cambridge University Press, 1994 is splendid. It is well supplemented by R. Owen, *The Middle East in the World Economy 1800–1914*, I.B. Tauris, 1993. J. McCarthy, *The Ottoman Turks*, Longman, Harlow, 1996 is a useful introduction to Ottoman life and culture, though pitched on the whole to a first-year undergraduate readership. D.E. Pitcher, *An Historical Geography of the Ottoman Empire*, E.J. Brill, Leiden, 1972 is rather disappointing but the Facts on File series again comes up trumps with F. Robinson, *Atlas of the Islamic World since 1500*, New York, 1992. E. Gellner, *Muslim Society*, Cambridge University Press, 1995 and P.S. Khoury and J. Kostiner (eds), *Tribes and State Formation in the Middle East*, University of California Press, Berkeley, 1990 are very useful as background and for purposes of comparison.

There are some very good general books in English on specific periods of Ottoman history. C. Kafadar, *Between Two Worlds. The Construction of the Ottoman State*, University of California Press, Berkeley, 1995 is much the best book on the early Ottoman realm. H. Inalcik, *The Ottoman Empire. The Classical Age 1300–1600*, Phoenix, London, 1994 is also excellent and takes the story down to the end of Suleyman the Magnificent's age. M. Kunt and C. Woodhead (eds), *Suleyman the Magnificent and His Age*, Longman,

London, 1995 contains some useful essays. N. Itzkowitz, *Ottoman Empire and Islamic Tradition*, Chicago University Press, 1980 is a splendid but very short introduction to the whole period down to the catastrophic defeat of the Ottomans by Catherine II's Russia. F. Ahmad, *The Making of Modern Turkey*, London, 1993 and E.J. Zurcher, *Turkey. A Modern History*, London, 1994 take the story from the beginning of the nineteenth century to the present day. Since both Zurcher and Ahmad are concerned with Republican Turkey and its origins they inevitably do not pay much attention to the rest of the empire and there is a risk of getting a rather unbalanced overall picture. By contrast M.E. Yapp, *The Making of the Modern Near East 1792–1923*, Longman, London, 1987 is concerned with the whole Ottoman region.

There are many good studies of specific regions of the empire in the Ottoman era. I have been able to read only some of them. They include: P.F. Sugar, *Southeastern Europe under Ottoman Rule 1354–1804*, University of Washington Press, Seattle, 1993; M. Winter, *Egyptian Society under Ottoman Rule*, Routledge, London, 1992; B. Lewis, *Istanbul and the Civilisation of the Ottoman Empire*, University of Oklahoma Press, Norman, 1989; F. Adanir, 'Tradition and Rural Change in Southeastern Europe during Ottoman Rule', in D. Chirot (ed.), *The Origins of Backwardness in Eastern Europe*, University of California Press, Berkeley, 1989; E. Akarli, *The Long Peace. Ottoman Lebanon 1861–1920*, I.B. Tauris, London, 1993; D.Z. Khoury, *State and Provincial Society in the Ottoman Empire. Mosul 1540–1834*, Cambridge University Press, 1997; D. Ze'evi, *An Ottoman Century. The District of Jerusalem in the 1600s*, SUNY Press, Albany, 1996.

On the peoples of the empire, the millet system and the challenge of nationalism the only place to start is B. Braude and B. Lewis, *Christians and Jews in the Ottoman Empire. The Functioning of a Plural Society*, 2 vols, Holmes & Meier, New York, 1982. This is a splendid and enormously useful book. Its only disadvantage is that it is a collection of essays rather than an integrated history and therefore suffers from many gaps. S.S. Shaw has written a very useful history of the Jewish millet: *The Jews of the Ottoman Empire and the Turkish Republic*, Macmillan, Houndmills, 1991.

On the Ottoman Empire as a great power there are a number of useful works, some of them very recently published: R. Murphey, *Ottoman Warfare 1500–1700*, UCL Press, London, 1999; G. Agoston, 'Ottoman warfare in Europe 1453–1826', in J. Black (ed.), *European Warfare 1453–1815*, Macmillan, Houndmills, 1999; A. Hess, *The Forgotten Frontier*, University of Chicago Press, 1978; M.S. Anderson, *The Eastern Question. 1774–1923. A Study in International Relations*, Macmillan, London, 1966; M. Kent (ed.), *The Great Powers and the End of the Ottoman Empire*, Frank Cass, London, 1996; F. Anscombe, *The Ottoman Gulf. The Creation of Kuwait, Saudi Arabia and Qatar*, Columbia University Press, New York, 1997; U. Trumpener, *Germany and the Ottoman Empire, 1914–1918*, Princeton University Press, 1968. Bernard Lewis, *The Muslim Discovery of Europe*, Norton, New York, 1982 also really belongs here since receptivity to European innovations was crucial to the preservation of the empire's power and security.

On the politics of the dynasty, of the court and of succession to the throne L.P. Pierce, *The Imperial Harem. Women and Sovereignty in the Ottoman Empire*, Oxford University Press, 1993 is splendid. There are fascinating contrasts with dynastic politics in mono-gomous Christian monarchies or with China, where one woman might bear the monarch many sons (something not allowed in the Ottoman harem). On administration see: D.M. Kunt, *The Sultan's Servants. The Transformation of Ottoman Provincial Government 1550–1650*, Columbia University Press, New York, 1983; K. Barkey, *Bandits and*

Bureaucrats. The Ottoman Route to State Centralization, Cornell University Press, Ithaca, 1994: I do wonder, however, whether Barkey does not rather play down the costs to the Ottoman military-fiscal machine's effectiveness of the *modus vivendi* reached with provincial bandit chiefs in the seventeenth century. The tsars would never have tolerated such compromises. On the reformed administration of the empire's last period, see: C.V. Findley, *Bureaucratic Reform in the Ottoman Empire. The Sublime Porte 1789–1922*, Princeton University Press, 1980; R.H. Davison, *Reform in the Ottoman Empire 1856–1876*, Princeton University Press, 1963.

The article by Colmar von der Goltz, 'Stärke und Schwäche des türkischen Reiches', *Deutsche Rundschau*, LXXXXIII, October/December 1897 is an excellent introduction to discussion of the weaknesses of the late Ottoman Empire. S. Deringil, *The Well-Protected Domains. Ideology and the Legitimation of Power in the Ottoman Empire*, I.B. Tauris, London, 1998 is a good study of the ideological bases of Abdul Hamid's regime. M.S. Hanioglu, *The Young Turks in Opposition*, Oxford University Press, 1995 and J.M. Landau, *Pan-Turkism. From Irredentism to Cooperation*, Hurst, London, 1995 look at ideological alternatives. Three key books study the situation in the Arab provinces: R. Khalidi et al. (eds), *The Origins of Arab Nationalism*, Columbia University Press, New York, 1991; E. Tauber, *The Emergence of the Arab Movements*, Frank Cass, London, 2 vols, 1993; H. Kayagli, *Arabs and Young Turks. Ottomanism, Arabism and Islamism in the Ottoman Empire 1908–1918*, University of California Press, Berkeley, 1997. The consensus of these books, to put things crudely, is that Arab nationalism was not yet a threat to the empire in the absence of war and might well never have become one. On the Armenian issue see in particular: J. Salt, *Imperialism, Evangelism and the Ottoman Armenians 1878–1896*, Frank Cass, London, 1993. On the genocide itself V.N. Dardrian, *The History of the Armenian Genocide*, Berghahn, London, 1995 is more a judicial indictment than a work of history. It fails to explain the very good reasons for acute Turkish paranoia about the threat of Anatolia's dismemberment: but the book's evidence of deliberate genocide seems to me convincing and its scholarly credentials sound. M.J. Somakian, *Empires in Conflict. Armenia and the Great Powers 1895–1920*, I.B. Tauris, London, 1995 though also (and justly) condemnatory, is better on the genocide's awful international context.

CHAPTER 5.   THE HABSBURG EMPIRE

There are a number of splendid general histories of the Habsburg Empire. The only one to cover the entire period is J. Berenger, *A History of the Habsburg Monarchy 1278–1700*, Longman, London, 1994 and *A History of the Habsburg Empire 1700–1918*, Longman, London, 1997. The first volume is particularly valuable because there is no comparable book in English on the first centuries of the dynasty. C. Ingrao, *The Habsburg Monarchy 1618–1815*, Cambridge University Press, 1994 covers the dynasty's central period excellently. A. Sked, *The Decline and Fall of the Habsburg Empire 1815–1914*, Longman, London, 1989 takes the story to the end in fine style, in my view very rightly stressing that there was nothing whatsoever inevitable about the empire's final collapse.

R.J.W. Evans, *The Making of the Habsburg Monarchy 1551–1700*, Oxford University Press, Oxford, 1979 is a brilliant and beautifully written book. It is invaluable to anyone trying to compare empires, perhaps above all because of its discussion of Habsburg ideology. As regards the period 1848–1918 the multi-volume *Die Habsburger Monarchie 1848–1918*, produced by the Austrian Academy of sciences, is superb and was vastly useful to me. I made particular use of volume 3 part 1, *Die Völker des Reiches*, published in 1980 and of volume 5, *Die Bewaffnete Macht*, published in 1987. The only reason I did not have to make more use of volume 6, *Die Habsburgermonarchie im System der Internationalen Beziehungen*, published in 1989 was that its main article on Habsburg foreign policy was written by Roy Bridge, whose *From Sadowa to Sarajevo*, Routledge, London, 1972 is available in English. See also his excellent *The Habsburg Monarchy among the Great Powers 1815–1918*, Berg, Oxford, 1990.

Richard Evans and T.V. Thomas (eds), *Crown, Church and Estates. Central European Politics in the Sixteenth and Seventeenth Centuries*, St Martin's Press, New York, 1991 goes to the core of the early Habsburg system of rule. Its transformation in the eighteenth century is covered well by P.G.M. Dickson, *Finance and Government under Maria Theresa 1740–1780*, 2 vols, Oxford University Press, 1987 and F.A.J. Szabo, *Kaunitz and Enlightened Absolutism 1753–1780*, Cambridge University Press, 1994. The ambiguities of the term 'Austria' in this era are explained by Greta Klingenstein, 'The meanings of "Austria" and "Austrian" in the eighteenth century', in R. Oresko, G.C. Gibbs and H.M. Scott (eds), *Royal and Republican Sovereignty in Early Modern Europe*, Cambridge University Press, 1997. H.M. Scott (ed.), *The European Nobilities. Volume 2: Northern, Central and Eastern Europe*, Longman, London, 1995 contains two good chapters on the nobilities of Austria-Bohemia and Hungary, who were the Monarchy's pillars for much of its existence: chapter 5 by J. van Horn Melton, 'The Nobility in the Bohemian and Austrian Lands, 1620–1780' and chapter 7 by Peter Schimert, 'The Hungarian Nobility in the Seventeenth and Eighteenth Centuries'.

Much of the empire's politics in its last decades revolved around the nationalities issue and I discuss this literature below. O. Jaszi, *The Dissolution of the Habsburg Monarchy*, University of Chicago Press, 1977 was originally published seventy years ago by a scholar who had played a prominent role in pre-1914 Hungarian radical politics. Some of Jaszi's judgements seem wrong in the light of later scholarship but the book still repays reading. G.B. Cohen, *Education and Middle-Class Society in Imperial Austria 1848–1918*, Purdue University Press, West Lafayette, 1996 is valuable. M. Cornwall (ed.), *The Last Years of Austria-Hungary*, University of Exeter Press, 1990 has some useful pieces. Mass politics in the Monarchy's German core during its last decades are excellently covered by J.W. Boyer, *Political Radicalism in Late Imperial Vienna: Origins of the Christian Social Movement 1848–1897*, University of Chicago Press, 1981 and J.W. Boyer, *Culture and Political Crisis in Vienna: Christian Socialism in Power, 1897–1918*, University of Chicago Press, 1995. Quite apart from being extremely interesting in themselves, these volumes force any Russianist to ask why the tsarist regime took such a different path in labour relations and democratization and whether the Austrian strategy was possible in Russia. On economic development see: D.F. Good, *The Economic Rise of the Habsburg Empire 1750–1914*, California University Press, Berkeley, 1984 and J. Komlos, *The Habsburg Monarchy as a Customs Union: Economic Development in Austria-Hungary in the Nineteenth Century*, Princeton University Press, 1983.

On questions of war, power and international relations there is a large literature of varying quality. What seem to me to be the key works essential to any student of the subject are: C. Duffy, *The Army of Maria Theresa. The Armed Forces of Imperial Austria, 1740–1780*, Terence Wise, Doncaster, 1990; G. Rothenburg, *The Austrian Military Border in Croatia 1522–1747*, University of Illinois Press, Urbana, 1960; G. Rothenburg, *The Military Border in Croatia, 1740–1881*, University of Chicago Press, 1966; *Napoleon's Great*

Bibliography

Adversary: The Archduke Charles and the Austrian Army, 1792–1814, Batsford, London, 1982, and *The Army of Francis Joseph*, Purdue University Press, West Lafayette, 1976; G. Wawro, *The Austro-Prussian War. Austria's War with Prussia and Italy in 1866*, Cambridge University Press, 1996; F. Deak, *Beyond Nationalism. A Social and Political History of the Habsburg Officer Corps 1848–1918*, Oxford University Press, 1990; L. Sondhaus, *The Naval Policy of Austria–Hungary 1867–1918*, Purdue University Press, West Lafayette, 1994; N. der Bagdasarian, *The Austro-German Rapprochement, 1870–1879*, Associated University Presses, Madison, 1976; S.R. Williamson, *Austria-Hungary and the Origins of the First World War*, Macmillan, London, 1991; B.K. Kiraly and N.F. Dreisziger (eds), *War and Society in East-Central Europe*, vol. XIX, Columbia University Press, New York, 1985.

There are a number of good biographies of Habsburg monarchs: R.J.W. Evans, *Rudolph II and His World*, Thames & Hudson, London, 1977; J.P. Spielman, *Leopold I of Austria*, Thames & Hudson, London, 1977; C. Ingrao, *In Quest and Crisis. Emperor Joseph I and the Habsburg Monarchy*, Purdue University Press, West Lafayette, 1979; D. Beales, *Joseph II. Volume 1: In the Shadow of Maria Theresa*, Cambridge University Press, 1987; T.C.W. Blanning, *Joseph II*, Longman, Harlow, 1994; S. Beller, *Francis Joseph*, Longman, Harlow, 1996; J.P. Bled, *Franz Joseph*, Blackwell, Oxford, 1994. R.A. Kann, *Dynasty, Politics and Culture*, Columbia University Press, Boulder, 1991 has valuable pieces on Franz Joseph and Franz Ferdinand. A. Wheatcroft, *The Habsburgs*, London, 1995 is a good history of the dynasty.

As regards the nationalities, Hungary probably deserves to come first, P.F. Sugar, P. Hanak, T. Frank (eds), *A History of Hungary*, Indiana University Press, Bloomington, 1994 covers the country's whole history. J.K. Hoensch, *A History of Modern Hungary 1867–1986*, Longman, London, 1988 takes in just the post-1867 compromise era. A.C. Janos, *The Politics of Backwardness in Hungary 1825–1945*, Princeton University Press, 1982 is thoughtful and thought-provoking, even if his main theme that Hungary's was a politics primarily of backwardness doesn't always convince. E.H. Balazs, *Hungary and the Habsburgs 1765–1800*, CEU Press, Budapest, 1997 covers an important period well. There is a good chapter on the Hungarians (as well as ones on the Austrians and Czechs) in M. Teich, R. Porter (eds), *The National Question in Europe in Historical Context*, Cambridge University Press, 1993.

On the Austrian Germans see above all: G. Stourzh, *Von Reich zur Republik. Studien zur Österreichsbewusstein im 20 Jahrhundert*, Ed. Atelier, Vienna, 1990: G. Brook-Shepherd, *The Austrians. A Thousand-Year Odyssey*, HarperCollins, London, 1997. On the Jews see: W.O. McCagg, *A History of the Habsburg Jews 1670–1918*, Indiana University Press, Bloomington, 1992 and J. Frankel and S.J. Zipperstein (eds), *Assimilation and Community. The Jews in Nineteenth-Century Europe*, Cambridge University Press, 1992. My main source on the various nations and the mechanisms set up to manage their demands was volume 3, part 1 of *Die Habsburgermonarchie* (cited above). In addition, R.A. Kann, *The Multinational Empire. Nationalism and National Reform in the Habsburg Monarchy 1848–1918*, 2 vols, Octagon Books, New York, 1970 is immensely scholarly and useful. U. Ra'anon et al. (eds), *State and Nation in Multi-Ethnic Societies*, Manchester University Press, 1991 has useful articles on Austro-Marxism. On the latter see also: H. Mommsen, *Die Sozialdemokratie und die Nationalitätenfrage im Habsburgischen Vielvölkerreich*, Europa Verlag, Vienna, 1963; P. Kulemann, *Am Beispiel des Austro-Marxismus*, Junius Verlag, Hamburg, 1979; N. Leser, *Zwischen Reformismus und Bolschewismus*, Hermann Buhlaus, Vienna, 1985.

R.L. Rudolph and D.F. Good (eds), *Nationalism and Empire. The Habsburg Monarchy and the Soviet Union*, St Martin's Press, New York, 1992 is a valuable attempt to compare the two empires' handling of minority ethnic nationalism, though the contributions are of very varying quality. Claudio Magris, *Danube*, Collins Harvill, London, 1997 is a monument to a lingering sense of Habsburg identity.

CHAPTER 6.   THE RUSSIAN EMPIRE: REGIONS, PEOPLES, GEOPOLITICS

CHAPTER 7.   THE TSARIST STATE AND THE RUSSIAN PEOPLE

CHAPTER 8.   TSARIST EMPIRE: POWER, STRATEGY, DECLINE

The literature on empire as regards tsarist Russia is on the whole not as full or of as uniformly high quality as it should be, given empire's importance in Russian history and the significance of Russia in international relations. A. Kappeler, *Russland als Vielvölkerreich*, Berg, Munich, 1993 is a study of the multi-national population, and of the mechanisms and ideologies developed by the tsars to rule and exploit it. It is a superb book, with nothing remotely to match it in English. It is very unfortunate that this book is still only accessible to scholars able to read German, an ability no longer to be taken for granted among British and American Russianists. The closest English-language equivalent to Kappeler is M. Rywkin (ed.), *Russian Colonial Expansion to 1917*, London, 1988 but this is a small though useful book, made up of a number of brief outline essays, and nowhere near as comprehensive as Kappeler's work. C. Evtuhov, B. Gasparov, A. Ospovat, and M. von Hagen (eds), *Kazan, Moscow, St Petersburg. Multiple Faces of the Russian Empire*, OGI, Moscow, 1997 contains some interesting pieces on imperial topics but it too is not remotely a substitute for a book such as Kappeler's.

One key aspect of modern empire is multi-ethnicity, the other is power. Amazingly, there are no general works on tsarist foreign policy in English. The closest one comes to this is D. Mackenzie, *Imperial Dreams. Harsh Realities. Tsarist Foreign policy 1815–1917*, Harcourt Brace, Fort Worth, 1994. This is a useful short survey for undergraduates. An older collection of essays edited by I. Lederer, *Russian Foreign Policy. Essays in Historical Perspective*, Yale University Press, New Haven, 1962 is by now rather dated though still interesting in parts. The scholar with Russian can fall back on the usually very thorough volumes on foreign policy being produced by the Institute of Russian History of the Russian Academy of Science: *Istoriya vneshney politiki Rossii* (A history of Russia's foreign policy), published in Moscow by Mezhdunarodnyye otnosheniya. Obviously, however, these are of no use to the normal Western scholar of international relations or to a broader Western audience. There are a number of good books on individual problems of tsarist foreign policy: D.M. Goldfrank, *The Origins of the Crimean War*, Longman, London, 1994 and B. Jelavich, *Russia's Balkan Entanglements 1806–1914*, Cambridge University Press, 1991. As regards both key aspects of empire, in other words both power and the management of multi-ethnicity, the student in search of a comprehensive survey who lacks Russian or German still does best to rely on Hugh Seton-Watson, *The Russian Empire 1801–1917*, Oxford University Press, 1967. Hugh was the supervisor of my doctorate and a scholar for whom I had the utmost respect and affection. He was also a modest man and would have been most surprised to discover that his was still the last word for most anglo-phone scholars on what he saw as the central, crucial aspects of Russian history.

Apart from Seton-Watson's book, the student of tsarist foreign policy should consult Hugh Ragsdale (ed.), *Imperial Russian Foreign Policy*, Cambridge University Press, 1993. The book is a collection of (usually very good) chapters on disparate subjects, not a coherent synthesis on foreign policy. But the two excellent chapters by Al Rieber provide both a framework for thinking about perennial questions of tsarist foreign policy and a survey of the existing literature on the subject. Next one should turn to W.H. Parker, *An Historical Geography of Russia*, University of London Press, London, 1968, an exceptionally useful book. Mark Bassin has written a number of articles on Russian geopolitics: see e.g. 'Russia between Europe and Asia: the Ideological Construction of Geographical Space', *Slavic Review*, vol. 50, no. 1, 1991: 'Turner, Solov'ev and the "Frontier Hypothesis"; The Nationalist Signification of Open Space', *Journal of Modern History*, 65, September 1993. His *Imperial Visions. Nationalist Imagination and Geographical Expansion in the Russian Far East. 1840–1865*, Cambridge University Press, 1999 came out after my book went to press. On geography see also: C. Goehrke, 'Geographische Grundlagen der russischen Geschichte', *Jahrbücher für Geschichte Osteuropas*, New Series, vol. 18, no. 2, 1970. John LeDonne, *The Russian Empire and the World. 1700–1917. The Geopolitics of Expansionism and Containment*, Oxford University Press, 1997 is idiosyncratic, a touch determinist but original and interesting.

D. Geyer, *Russian Imperialism. The Interaction of Domestic and Foreign Policy 1860–1914*, Berg, Leamington Spa, 1987 was an attempt to integrate late-tsarist Russia into then fashionable German scholarship on imperialism and the domestic roots of foreign policy. The result was a very intelligent and interesting book, though in my view the German model of the primacy of domestic factors in the making of foreign policy (*Primat der Innenpolitik*) derived from the Hohenzollern Kaiserreich is only very partially correct when applied to imperial Germany, and greatly distorts the reality of most foreign policy decision-making in late-imperial Russia. This is a major theme of my *Russia and the Origins of the First World War*, Macmillan, London, 1983. It is a source of partial though friendly disagreement with the leading American scholar in the field of late imperial foreign policy, David MacDonald: see his *United Government and Foreign Policy in Russia, 1900–1914*, Harvard University Press, Cambridge, MA, 1992, a very good book based on a fine doctoral dissertation; its stress on the domestic roots of foreign policy seems to me to be partly true as regards Russia's involvement in the war with Japan but much less so of 1914. As regards Russian financial and economic relations with the West, see R. Girault, *Emprunts russes et investissements français en Russie 1887–1914*, Paris, 1973; Susan McCaffray, *The Politics of Industrialisation in Tsarist Russia*, Northern Illinois University Press, De Kalb, 1996; J.P. McKay, *Pioneers for Profit. Foreign Entrepreneurship and Russian Industrialisation 1885–1913*, Chicago University Press, 1970.

The most far-ranging study of Russian empire is Ariel Cohen, *Russian Imperialism. Development and Crisis*, Praeger, Westport, 1996. This is very different from my book in that it is a work of social science rather than of comparative history: its focus is almost exclusively on Russia and even then it concentrates much more on the Soviet than the tsarist period. Cohen's differs from my approach both in his concept of empire and as regards many of his judgements on Russian and Soviet imperialism. Nevertheless this is a valuable and interesting work, which opens up many questions.

Probably the best-studied aspect of tsarist empire by anglophone scholars is the army.

Bibliography

Pride of place here goes to a superb book by William Fuller, *Strategy and Power in Russia: 1600–1914*, Free Press, New York, 1992. The book has not had the impact it deserves in the field partly because 'defence studies' have been ghettoized and are unfashionable, even politically suspect, among the majority of American Russianists. A blend of immense but unpretentious scholarship, and written with clarity and style, this deserves to be one of the first books to be read by anyone coming fresh to Russian history.

Apart from Fuller's book there are a number of other first-class works in English on the imperial army: J. Keep, *Soldiers of the Tsar. Army and Society in Russia 1462–1874*, Clarendon Press, Oxford, 1985; C. Duffy, *Russia's Military Way to the West. Origins and Nature of Russian Military Power 1700–1800*, Routledge, London, 1981; C. Duffy, *Eagles Over The Alps*, The Emperor's Press, Chicago, 1999; F.W. Kagan, *The Military Reforms of Nicholas I. The Origins of the Modern Russian Army*, Macmillan, Houndmills, 1999; J.S. Curtiss, *The Russian Army under Nicholas I. 1825–1855*, Duke University Press, Durham, 1965; B. Menning, *Bayonets before Bullets: The Imperial Russian Army, 1861–1914*, Indiana University Press, Indianapolis, 1992; D.A. Rich, *The Tsar's Colonels*, Harvard University Press, Cambridge, 1998; W. Fuller, *Civil-Military Conflict in Imperial Russia 1881–1914*, Princeton University Press, Princeton, 1985. D. Beyrau, *Militär und Gesellschaft in vorrevolutionären Russland*, Bohlau Verlag, Cologne, 1984. In addition, one of the key Russian works on the armed forces, L.G. Beskrovny, *The Russian Army and Fleet in the Nineteenth Century*, Academic International Press, Gulf Breeze, 1996 is available in English translation.

Inevitably, the navy, very much the junior partner within the Russian military establishment, has received a great deal less attention from Western scholars. The best English-language history is D.W. Mitchell, *A History of Russian and Soviet Sea Power*, André Deutsch, London, 1974. J.N. Westwood, *Russian Naval Construction 1905–1945*, Macmillan, Houndmills, 1994 is actually a much broader study than its title suggests. Where the navy is concerned, however, there really is no alternative to Russian-language sources. The place to start is: F.N. Gromov (ed.), *Tri veka rossiyskogo flota* (three centuries of the Russian navy), 3 vols, Logos, St Petersburg, 1996. On the other hand, a number of general works on wars do make a major contribution to understanding the nature and limitations of Russian power: see e.g. W. Baumgart, *The Crimean War 1853–1856*, Arnold, 1999 and J.N. Westwood, *Russia against Japan*, Macmillan, London, 1986.

Many good books are now appearing on various regions and peoples of the tsarist empire and the government's policy towards them. Given the likely opening in time of many republican and regional archives, this excellent development seems certain to continue. Interest in nationalism and the non-Russians has in any case grown exponentially in recent years in line with general trends in academia, which themselves owed much to the disintegration of the Soviet Union.

On tsarist policy in the western borderlands, the empire's key strategic and economic non-Russian region, see: E. Thaden, *Russia's Western Borderlands 1710–1870*, Princeton University Press, 1984; E. Thaden, *Russification in the Baltic Provinces and Finland*, Princeton University Press, 1984; T. Weeks, *Nation and State in Late Imperial Russia*, Northern Illinois University Press, De Kalb, 1996. On tsarist policy in Finland see also T. Polvinen, *Imperial Borderland. Bobrikov and the Attempted Russification of Finland*, Duke University Press, Durham, NC, 1995.

On Ukraine, one should start with Orest Subtelny, *Ukraine. A History*, Toronto University Press, 1988, which is excellent and balanced. P.R. Magosci, *A History of*

Ukraine, University of Washington Press, Seattle, 1996 is another general history. On Ukraine within the empire two key works are: Z. Kohut, *Russian Centralism and Ukrainian Autonomy*, Harvard University Press, Cambridge, 1988 and D. Saunders, *The Ukrainian Impact on Russian Culture 1750–1850*, Edmonton, 1988. P.J. Potichnyi et al. (eds), *Ukraine and Russia in their Historical Encounter*, Edmonton, 1992 has some good essays. On the key Ukrainian cities see P. Herlihy, *Odessa. A History 1794–1914*, Harvard University Press, Cambridge, MA, 1986; M.F. Hamm, *Kiev. A Portrait 1800–1917*, Princeton University Press, 1993. A.F. Markovits and F.E. Sysysn (eds), *Nation-Building and the Politics of Nationalism. Essays on Austrian Galicia*, Harvard University Press, Cambridge, MA, 1982 does not really belong in a section on tsarist Ukraine but the book, and especially chapter 1, is crucial to an understanding of later Ukrainian history. Most of B. Krawchenko, *Social Change and National Consciousness in Twentieth-Century Ukraine*, Macmillan, Houndmills, 1992 is about developments in Soviet Ukraine but its first chapter is an excellent summary of Ukrainian development to 1914 and is essential to an understanding of the failure of Ukraine to achieve statehood in 1917–21.

On the Jews and Russian policy towards them see: J. Klier, *Russia Gathers its Jews. The Origins of the 'Jewish Question' in Russia 1772–1825*, Northern Illinois University Press, De Kalb, 1986; J. Klier, *Imperial Russia's Jewish Question. 1855–1881*, Cambridge University Press, Cambridge, MA 1995; H. Rogger, *Jewish Policies and Right-Wing Politics in Imperial Russia*, Macmillan, Houndmills, 1986; H.D. Lowe, *Antisemitismus und reaktionäre Utopie*, Hamburg, 1978; J. Klier and S. Lambroza (eds), *Pogroms. Anti-Jewish Violence in Modern Russian History*, Cambridge University Press, 1992.

There is a very useful series on the non-Russian peoples of the tsarist empire and the Soviet Union published by the Hoover Institution of Stanford University: A.W. Fisher, *The Crimean Tatars*, 1978; A.-A. Rorlich, *The Volga Tatars*, 1986; A. Plakans, *The Latvians*, 1995; T. Raun, *Estonia and the Estonians*, 1991; M.B. Olcott, *The Kazakhs*, 1987. On the very important German communities in the empire see the series *Deutsche Geschichte im Osten Europas*: Gerd von Pistohlkors, *Baltische Länder*; G. Stricker, *Russland*; this series is published by Siedler Verlag and its volumes carry no date though both these volumes are very recent. R. Suny, *The Making of the Georgian Nation*, Indiana University Press, Bloomington, 1994 is the great source on Georgia.

On Russia in Asia the place to start is the excellent and imaginative M. Hauner, *What Is Asia To Us? Russia's Asian Heartland Yesterday and Today*, Routledge, London, 1992. C.P. March, *Eastern Destiny. Russia in Asia and the North Pacific*, Praeger, Westport, 1996 is a useful introductory survey. S. Kotkin and D. Wolff (eds), *Rediscovering Russia in Asia. Siberia and the Russian Far East*, M.E. Sharpe, Armonk, 1995, has some good contributions on imperial topics; so too does an older collection of essays edited by W. Vucinich, *Russia and Asia*, Stanford University Press, 1972. S.G. Marks, *Road To Power. The Trans-Siberian Railroad and the Colonization of Asian Russia, 1850–1917*, London, 1991 is a useful book on the creation of the empire's key link through Asia, though perhaps a touch too critical given the urgency to build the railway because of the acute vulnerability of Russia's Far East and given too the scarcity of resources. On relations with China, see: S. Paine, *Imperial Rivals. China, Russia and Their Disputed Frontier*, M.E. Sharpe, Armonk, 1996. In the last years of the tsarist regime relations with Japan also loomed large. On this see I. Nish, *The Origins of the Russo-Japanese War*, Longman, London, 1985 and B.A. Romanov, *Russia in Manchuria 1892–1906*, Ann Arbor, 1952. R.K.I. Quested, *'Matey' Imperialists. The Tsarist Russians in Manchuria 1895–1917*, University of Hong Kong

Press, Hong Kong, 1982 is a key book on tsarist empire, providing major insights into not just policy in Manchuria but also into Russian attitudes to non-European peoples.

W.B. Lincoln, *The Conquest of a Continent. Siberia and the Russians*, Random House, London, 1994 is a well-written introduction to Siberian history. V.L. Mote, *Siberia. Worlds Apart*, Westview, Boulder, 1998 and J.L. Stephan, *The Russian Far East*, Stanford University Press, 1994 are both most concerned with post-1917 history but contain useful information on their regions for the tsarist period too. A. Wood (ed.) *The History of Siberia from Russian Conquest to Revolution*, Routledge, London, 1991 has some very good chapters on the administration and development of Siberia, the penal system, and the Alaskan settlement. On the native peoples a good introduction is the comprehensive and admirable study by J. Forsyth, *A History of the Peoples of Siberia. Russia's North Asian Colony 1581–1990*, Cambridge University Press, 1992. Then read a very good book by Y. Slezkine, *Arctic Mirrors. Russia and the Small Peoples of the North*, Cornell University Press, Ithaca, 1994 which is interesting on not just how the Russians viewed the native peoples but also how they viewed themselves; and W. Faust, *Russlands Goldener Boden. Der sibirische Regionalismus in der zweiten Hälfte des 19 Jahrhunderts*, Bohlau Verlag, Cologne 1980, in which Siberian regionalism is interestingly compared to the emergence of Creole national identity in the West European maritime colonies.

On nomadism, with particular reference to the nomadic peoples of the Russian Empire, see: A.M. Khazanov, *Nomads and the Outside World*, Wisconsin University Press, Madison, 1994. On the tsarist state and nomadism (in this particular case the Kalmyks) see the very interesting Michael Khodarkovsky, *Where Two Worlds Met*, Cornell University Press, Ithaca, 1992. On the conquest and 'pacification' of the Bashkir: A. Donnelly, *The Russian Conquest of Bashkiria 1552–1740. A Case Study in Imperialism*, Yale University Press, New Haven, 1968. On the conquest and rule of the Volga Tatars: A. Kappeler, *Russlands erste Nationalitäten. Das Zarenreich und die Völker der Mittleren Volga vom 16 bis 19 Jahrhundert*, Bohlau Verlag, Cologne, 1982. On the conquest of the North Caucasus, M. Gammer, *Muslim Resistance to the Tsar. Shamil and the Conquest of Chechnia and Daghestan*, Frank Cass, London, 1994; M.B. Broxup (ed.), *The North Caucasus Barrier*, New York, 1992; R. Traho, 'Circassians', *Central Asian Survey*, vol. 10, nos 1/2, 1991. On the Kazakhs, *Nationalities Papers*, vol. 28, no. 3, 1998: *Focus on Kazakstan*, eds D.M. Crowe, Zh. Dzhunusova, S. Sabol; much of this concerns Soviet and independent Kazakhstan but there are also good historical pieces. On Russian rule in Central Asia see: R.A. Pierce, *Russian Central Asia 1867–1917*, University of California Press, Berkeley, 1960; S. Becker, *Russia's Protectorates in Central Asia. Bukhara and Khiva 1865–1924*, Harvard University Press, Cambridge, 1968. On Russian migration there is the classic book by D. Treadgold, *The Great Siberian Migration*, Princeton University Press, 1957.

For insights into the mentality of top tsarist officials in Asia see e.g. R.A. Pierce (ed.), *Mission to Turkestan. Being the Memoirs of Count K.K. Pahlen*, Oxford University Press, 1964; A. Rhinelander, *Prince Michael Vorontsov. Viceroy to the Tsar*, McGill-Queen's University Press, Montreal, 1990 and D. Mackenzie, *The Lion of Tashkent. The Career of General M.G. Cherniaev*, University of Georgia Press, Athens, 1974. Two recent works in English take up some of the themes and approaches linked to Edward Said's works and the debate on post-colonialism: S. Layton, *Russian Literature and Empire. The Conquest of the Caucasus from Pushkin to Tolstoy*, Cambridge University Press, 1994: D.R. Brower and E. Lazzerini, *Russia's Orient. Imperial Borderlands and Peoples 1700–1917*, Indiana University Press, Bloomington, 1997. These are both valuable and well-written books. There are

Bibliography

useful articles too on empire in J. Burbank and D.L. Ransel (eds), *Imperial Russia: New Histories for the Empire*, Indiana University Press, Bloomington, 1998. On the international context of nineteenth-century Russia's expansion in Asia, i.e. the so-called Great Game, see D. Gillard, *The Struggle for Asia 1828–1914*, Longman, London, 1977.

On Russian nationalism, Russian identity and tsarist imperial ideology, Geoffrey Hosking, *Russia, People and Empire*, HarperCollins, London, 1997 is the best starting-point. An article by myself entitled 'Russian, Imperial and Soviet Identities', *Transactions of the Royal Historical Society*, 6th series, vol. 8, 1998 contains many footnotes referring to articles on this subject. R. Milner-Gulland, *The Russians*, Blackwell, Oxford, 1995 is a good introduction to the origins of Russian ethnicity and identity. J. Pelenski, *Russia and Kazan: Conquest and Imperial Ideology (1438–1560s)*, Mouton, Paris/The Hague, 1974 is an important book. So is R.S. Wortman, *Scenarios of Power. Myth and Ceremony in Russian Monarchy*, vol. 1, Princeton University Press, 1995, which discusses imperial ceremonies and values, and thereby the ideology of the state and its ruling elites. Yu. M. Lotman, *Besedy o russkoy kulture. Byt i traditsii russkogo dvoryanstva: XVIII–nachale XIX veka* (Discussions on Russian culture. Life and traditions of the Russian nobility: 18th–early 19th century), St Petersburg, 1994 is very good on some of these issues but so far available only in German not English translation. On the development of national identity and nationalism see: H. Rogger, *National Consciousness in Eighteenth-Century Russia*, Harvard University Press, Cambridge, 1960; T. Martin, *Romantics, Reformers, Reactionaries. Russian Conservative Thought and Politics in the Reign of Alexander I*, Northern Illinois University Press, De Kalb, 1997; N.V. Riasanovsky, *The Image of Peter the Great in Russian History and Thought*, Oxford University Press, 1985; A. Walicki, *The Slavophile Controversy*, Oxford University Press, 1975; E.C. Thaden, *Conservative Nationalism in Nineteenth-Century Russia*, University of Washington Press, Seattle, 1964; R. Pipes, *Struve: Liberal on the Right, 1905–1944*, Harvard University Press, Cambridge, MA, 1980.

Many other books, frequently covering specific periods or aspects of Russian history, have an important bearing on the development of Russian statehood, power, empire and identity: it is not easy to choose between them. The following I would consider essential reading for a beginner in the field: S. Franklin and J. Shepard, *The Emergence of Rus 750–1200*, Longman, London, 1996; R.O. Crummey, *The Formation of Muscovy 1304–1613*, Longman, London, 1987; C.J. Halperin, *Russia and the Golden Horde. The Mongol Impact on Russian History*, I.B. Tauris, London, 1985; D. Ostrowski, *Muscovy and the Mongols*, Cambridge University Press, Cambridge, 1995; N.S. Kollmann, *Kinship and Politics. The Making of the Muscovite Political System 1345–1547*, Stanford University Press, 1987; R. Hellie, *Enserfment and Military Change in Muscovy*, University of Chicago Press, 1971; V.A. Kivelson, *Autocracy in the Russian Provinces. The Muscovite Gentry and Political Culture in the Seventeenth Century*, Stanford University Press, 1996; P. Bushkovitch, *Religion and Society in Russia. The Sixteenth and Seventeenth Centuries*, Oxford University Press, 1992.

For Peter I and after: L. Hughes, *Russia in the Age of Peter the Great*, Yale University Press, New Haven, 1998; I. de Madariaga, *Russia in the Age of Catherine the Great*, Weidenfeld, London, 1981; N. Riasanovsky, *The Parting of the Ways. Government and Educated Society in Russia 1801–1855*, Clarendon Press, Oxford, 1976; D. Saunders, *Russia in the Age of Reaction and Reform 1801–1881*, Longman, London, 1992; W.B. Lincoln. *In the Vanguard of Reform. Russia's Enlightened Bureaucrats 1825–1861*, Northern Illinois University Press, De Kalb, 1981; P. Gatrell, *The Tsarist Economy. 1850–1914*, Batsford, London, 1986; O. Crisp, *Studies in the Russian Economy before 1914*, Macmillan, London,

1976; B. Eklof, J. Bushnell, L. Zakharova (eds), *Russia's Great Reforms*, Indiana University Press, Bloomington, 1994; D. Lieven, *Nicholas II*, John Murray, London, 1993; G. Hosking, *The Russian Constitutional Experiment: Government and Duma 1907–1914*, Cambridge University Press, 1973; R. Pipes, *The Russian Revolution 1899–1919*, Harvill, London, 1990; E. Acton, V. Cherniaev, W. Rosenberg (eds), *Critical Dictionary to the Russian Revolution 1914–1921*, Arnold, London, 1997. At present the most popular book in Britain on the revolution is Orlando Figes, *A People's Tragedy. The Russian Revolution 1891–1924*, Jonathan Cape, London, 1996: very well written and excellent in its introduction of elements of biography into the narrative, Figes's book seems to me to exaggerate the regime's room for manoeuvre before 1914 and very much to underestimate the significance of the geopolitical context in which Russia was operating. These are key obsessions in many of my books on the era and my opinions should therefore be taken with a pinch of salt. Figes's first book, *Peasant Russia, Civil War: The Volga Countryside in Revolution (1917–1921)*, Cambridge University Press, 1989 is one of the best monographs on the revolutionary period written in the last twenty-five years.

Last but definitely not least, there are a number of PhD dissertations on both tsarist and Soviet history; among those which have helped me greatly with this book and richly deserve publication are: O. Andriewsky, 'The Politics of National Identity: The Ukrainian Question in Russia 1904–1912', Harvard University, 1991; N.K. Gvosdev, 'Alliance or Absorption: Imperial Perspectives and Policies toward Georgia 1760–1819', Oxford University, 1995; S. Kondrashev, 'Nationalism and the Drive for Sovereignty in Tatarstan 1988–92. Origins and Development', University of Manchester, 1993;' W. Rodkiewicz, 'Russian Nationality Policy in the Western Provinces of the Empire during the Reign of Nicholas II, 1894–1905, Harvard University, 1996; Gwendolyn Sasse, 'State and Nation-Building in Post-Soviet Ukraine. The Case of Crimea', London University, 1999; David Schimmelpenninck van der Oye, 'Ex Oriente Lux. Ideologies of Empire and Russia's Far East 1893–1904', Yale University, 1997, A. Zelkina, 'The History of the Naqshbandi Sufi Brotherhood in the North Caucasus. Its Impact on the Religious, Social and Political Life of the Area in the First Half of the Nineteenth Century,' Oxford University, 1996.

CHAPTER 9. THE SOVIET UNION

The potential English-language bibliography on empire in the Soviet period is far greater than for late tsarist Russia. Western historians of Russia from 1861 to 1917 have concentrated very heavily on the Revolution of 1917 and its causes, to an extent that can impose a strong teleology and sometimes unbalances our view of tsarist society. In addition, after the 1960s the dominant trend was to study 'history from below' rather than the story of 'kings and battles', and the international geopolitical, diplomatic and military context which to a considerable extent determined what happened in Russia was often ignored. This tendency among Western historians rather confirmed a bias supported by the Soviet regime: Soviet Russia was one of the rare European countries to have no monuments to the dead of 1914–17. The revolution was glorified, the war forgotten: rather conveniently, since the Bolsheviks had played a very important role in undermining the war effort and 'Soviet Patriotism' would have found too close a study of the war an embarrassment. After 1945 by contrast a large industry grew up in the West devoted to the study of Soviet power. The USSR was now the key adversary. If internal aspects of empire, meaning above all the nationalities question, drew less attention than Soviet foreign and military policy, nevertheless the multi-national composition of the Soviet Union was always understood to be one of its most important and vulnerable elements and much attention was devoted to it. In this bibliography I will do no more than list some of the most essential works on empire in the Soviet era. It should be remembered that some of the key surveys of non-Russian peoples' histories have already been noted in connection with the tsarist period.

The obvious place to start a study of Soviet foreign policy is the collection of key articles in F.J. Fleron, E.P. Hoffmann and R.F. Laird (eds), *Classic Issues in Soviet Foreign Policy: From Lenin To Brezhnev*, Aldine de Gruyter, New York, 1991 and *Contemporary Issues in Soviet Foreign Policy*, Aldine de Gruyter, New York, 1991. The sister volume, E.P. Hoffmann and R. Laird (eds), *The Soviet Polity in the Modern Era*, Aldine de Gruyter, New York, 1984 will also be useful.

General surveys of Soviet foreign policy and its ideological bases include: G.L. Bondarevsky, *Documents on Soviet Foreign Policy*, Frank Cass, London, 1995; G. Gorodetsky, *Soviet Foreign Policy. A Retrospective*, Frank Cass, London, 1994; M. Light, *The Soviet Theory of International Relations*, Wheatsheaf, 1988; A. Lynch, *Soviet Study of International Relations*, Cambridge University Press, 1987; N. Malcolm, *Soviet Political Scientists and American Politics*, Macmillan, London, 1984; I. Neumann, *Russia and the Idea of Europe: A Study in Identity and International Relations*, Routledge, London, 1995; J. Nogee and R. Donaldson, *Soviet Foreign Policy since World War II*, Pergamon, New York, 1988; A. Ulam, *Expansion and Coexistence: Soviet Foreign Policy 1917–73*, Praeger, New York, 1974. P. Dibb, *The Soviet Union: the Incomplete Superpower*, Macmillan, London, 1988 is a very good attempt to sum up all the strengths and weaknesses of the Soviet Union as Gorbachev came to power, stressing the weaknesses and at times using the concept of empire. If I had to recommend one book on the late USSR as an empire I would choose Dibb.

On specific periods of Soviet foreign policy see: G. Kennan, *Russia and the West under Lenin and Stalin*, Little, Brown, Boston, 1961; K. McDermott and J. Agnew, *The Comintern: a History of International Communism from Lenin to Stalin*, Macmillan, Houndmills, 1996; S. White, *The Origins of Detente: the Genoa Conference and Soviet-Western Relations 1921–1922*, Cambridge University Press, 1985; M. Beloff, *Foreign Policy of Soviet Russia*, Oxford University Press, London, 2 vols., 1974; J. Haslam, *The Soviet Union and the Struggle for Collective Security in Europe 1933–1939*, Macmillan, London, 1984; K. Dawisha, *The Kremlin and the Prague Spring*, University of California Press, Berkeley, 1985; R. Garthoff, *Detente and Confrontation: Soviet-American Relations from Nixon to Reagan*, Brookings Institution, Washington, 1985; R. Garthoff, *The Great Transition: American-Soviet Relations and the End of the Cold War*, Brookings Institution, Washington, 1994.

On the Soviet armed forces, military history and the defence industries see e.g.: M. von Hagen, *Soldiers in the Proletarian Dictatorship: The Red Army and the Soviet Socialist State 1917–1930*, Cornell University Press, Ithaca, 1990; J. Erickson, *The Soviet High Command*, Macmillan, London, 1962; D.M. Glantz, *Stumbling Colossus. The Red Army on the Eve of the World War*, Kansas University Press, Lawrence, 1998; H. Shukman (ed.), *Stalin's Generals*, Weidenfeld, London, 1993; M. Harrison, *Accounting for War. Soviet Production, Employment and the Defence Burden 1940–1945*, Cambridge University Press, 1990; and T.J. Colton, *Commissars, Commanders, and Civilian Authority*, Harvard University Press,

Cambridge, MA, 1979 was the best book on the politics of the armed forces to be published in the Soviet era. M. Galeotti, *Afghanistan. The Soviet Union's Last War*, Frank Cass, London, 1995 is a cool and balanced account of the war's impact, with an admirable avoidance of hyperbole. See also C. Gaddy, *The Price of the Past. Russia's Struggle with the Legacy of a Militarised Economy*, Brookings Institution, Washington, 1996.

On multi-ethnicity and its management there are a number of good general surveys both for the whole Soviet period and for specific periods. The best overall guide is G. Simon, *Nationalism and Policy towards the Nationalities in the Soviet Union*, Westview, Boulder, 1991. Then see R. Suny, *The Revenge of the Past*, Stanford University Press, 1993; compare it to the very different interpretation of B. Nahaylo and V. Swoboda, *Soviet Disunion*, Hamish Hamilton, London, 1990. R. Pipes, *The Formation of the Soviet Union*, Harvard University Press, Cambridge, MA, 1954 is still very useful on the early period; so is J. Smith, *The Bolsheviks and the National Question 1917–23*, Macmillan, Houndmills, 1999; these two books have very different perspectives and come to often opposite judgements about Bolshevik policy. H. Carrère d'Encausse, *The Great Challenge. Nationalism and the Bolshevik State 1917–1930*, Holmes & Meier, New York, 1992 and Y. Slezkine, 'The USSR as a Communal Apartment, or How a Socialist State Promoted Ethnic Particularism', *Slavic Review*, vol. 53, no. 2, 1994 are also good and sharply differing interpretations. See also V. Tishkov, *Ethnicity, Nationalism and Conflict in and after the Soviet Union*, Sage, London, 1997 and L. Hadja and M. Beissinger (eds), *The Nationalities Factor in Soviet Politics and Society*, Westview, Boulder, 1990.

On Russian identity and Russian nationalism in the Soviet era see: F.C. Barghoorn, *Soviet Russian Nationalism*, Oxford University Press, 1956; J. Dunlop, *The Faces of Contemporary Russian Nationalism*, Princeton University Press, 1983; Y.M. Brudny, *Reinventing Russia. Russian Nationalism and the Soviet State 1958–1991*, Harvard University Press, Cambridge, MA, 1998; J. Dunlop, *The Rise of Russia and the Fall of the Soviet Union*, Princeton University Press, 1993. On the creation and nature of the Soviet identity see: S. Fitzpatrick, *Everyday Stalinism*, Oxford University Press, 1999; S. Kotkin, *Magnetic Mountain. Stalinism as a Civilisation*, University of California Press, Berkeley, 1995; V. Dunham, *In Stalin's Time. Middle-class Values in Soviet Fiction*, Duke University Press, Durham, 1991. For an authentic voice of High Stalinism brilliantly recorded see: *Molotov Remembers. Inside Kremlin Politics. Conversations with Felix Chuev*, Ivan Dee, Chicago, 1993. For a useful comparison between Stalinism and German Nazism see: I. Kershaw and M. Lewin (eds), *Stalinism and Nazism. Dictatorships in Comparison*, Cambridge University Press, 1997. T. McDaniel, *The Agony of the Russian Idea*, Princeton University Press, 1996 traces a core element (Russia's uniqueness and global mission) in Russian nationalist thinking from tsarist through Soviet to post-Soviet times; this is an important book with great significance for students of contemporary Russia. H. Hardeman, *Coming to Terms with the Soviet Regime*, Northern Illinois University Press, De Kalb, 1994 is particularly interesting given the current vogue for Eurasianism in Russia: it traces similar currents in the early years of the White emigration.

Much of the basic literature on the non-Russian peoples has already been listed in the section on Chapters 6–8. Similarly, many of the books in this section are also key reading for the post-imperial section (Chapter 10). On the Baltic republics see also: R. Misiunas and R. Taagapera, *The Baltic States. Years of Dependence 1940–1980*, Hurst, London, 1983; A. Lieven, *The Baltic Revolution*, Yale University Press, New Haven, 1993; R. Karklins, *Ethnopolitics and Transition to Democracy. The Collapse of the USSR and Latvia*, Brookings

Institution, Washington, DC, 1994; G. Smith (ed.), *The Baltic States. The National Self-Determination of Estonia, Latvia and Lithuania*, Macmillan, Houndmills, 1996. A. Shtromas, 'Prospects for Restoring the Baltic States' Independence: A View on the Prerequisites and Possibilities of their Realisation', *Journal of Baltic Studies*, vol. XVII, no. 3, 1986 was a very perceptive prophecy of events to come.

On Soviet and post-Soviet Ukraine see: J. Mace, *Communism and the Dilemmas of National Liberation. National Communism in the Soviet Ukraine 1918–1933*, Harvard University Press, Cambridge, MA, 1983; R. Conquest, *The Harvest of Sorrow*, Arrow Books, London, 1986; D. Marples, *Stalinism in Ukraine in the 1940s*, Alberta University Press, Calgary, 1972; A. Wilson, *Ukrainian Nationalism. A Minority Faith*, Cambridge University Press, 1997; S. Velychenko, *Shaping Identity in Eastern Europe and Russia. Soviet-Russian and Polish Accounts of Ukrainian History 1914–1991*, St Martin's Press, New York, 1993; A. Lieven, *Ukraine and Russia. A Fraternal Rivalry*, United States Institute for Peace Studies, Washington, 1999.

On the Muslim peoples of the Soviet south, S. Akiner, *Islamic Peoples of the Soviet Union*, London, 1986 is a very useful work of reference. M. Rywkin, *Moscow's Muslim Challenge*, New York, 1982 was probably the most balanced assessment of the state of the Central Asian republics at the death of Brezhnev. B.F. Manz (ed.), *Central Asia in Historical Perspective*, Westview, Boulder, 1994 contains many good essays on the region's history including a very useful introduction by the editor. V. Naumkin, *State, Religion and Society in Central Asia*, Reading, 1993 also has good pieces, including an outstanding essay by L. Chvyr, 'Central Asian Tajiks: Self-Identification and Ethnic Identity', which brings out all the complexity and ambiguity of ethnic and national markers in this part of the world. J. Critchlow, *Nationalism in Uzbekistan*, Westview, Boulder, 1991 is a good study of the most important of the Central Asian republics on the eve of independence. B. Rumer, *Soviet Central Asia. A Tragic Experiment*, Unwin Hyman, London, 1989 is a study of the failure of Soviet-style modernization in the region. Since 1991 there have been a number of general surveys of Central Asian political development. Inevitably all such studies risk rapid obsolescence. Nevertheless, some of these studies (especially those with a strong historical tilt) are very useful: see e.g. Y. Kulchik, A. Fadin, V. Sergeev, *Central Asia after the Empire*, Pluto Press, London, 1994; Y. Roi, *Muslim Eurasia. Conflicting Legacies*, Frank Cass, London, 1995; T. Atabaki and J. O'Kane, *Post-Soviet Central Asia*, I.B. Tauris, London, 1998. See also G. Gleason, *The Central Asian States. Discovering Independence*, Westview, Boulder, 1997.

On the Caucasus region before and after 1991, see: R. Gachechiladze, *The New Georgia: Space, Society, Politics*, UCL Press, London, 1995, a very useful book with a geographer's eye on Georgian history, culture and contemporary dilemmas; S. Goldenberg, *Pride of Small Nations. The Caucasus and Post-Soviet Disorder*, London, 1994; A. Lieven, *Chechnya. Tombstone of Russian Power*, Yale University Press, New Haven, 1998, an excellent book not just on the conflict and the region but also, and in many ways more importantly, on the collapse of Russia as a great power after 1991. A.M. Nekrich, *The Punished Peoples. The Deportation and Fate of Soviet Minorities at the End of the Second World War*, New York, 1978 is largely about the deportation and subsequent fate of the small peoples of the North Caucasus. R.G. Suny, *Looking Toward Ararat. Armenia in Modern History*, Indiana University Press, Bloomington, 1993, covers tsarist and Soviet Armenian history; so does the excellent history edited by R.G. Hovanissian *The Armenian People. From Ancient to Modern Times*, St Martin's Press, New York, 1997. On the geopolitics and international relations of the region see J.F. Wright, S. Goldenberg and R. Schofield (eds), *Transcaucasian Boundaries*, UCL Press, London, 1996.

On the collapse of the USSR much the best book is J. Hough, *Democratisation and Revolution in the USSR 1985–1991*, Brookings Institution, Washington, DC, 1997: it asks some very shrewd questions and provides many plausible answers: above all, it expresses a well-justified wonderment at the way the USSR was allowed to collapse. Archie Brown, *The Gorbachev Factor*, Oxford University Press, 1996 is a skilful and determined defence of Gorbachev. A. Dallin and G. Lapidus (eds), *The Soviet System in Crisis. A Reader*, Westview, Boulder, 1991 is particularly interesting; it gathers all the best-known names in Sovietology and is a record of what they believed was happening at a time when *perestroika* was still in progress. It is in part a memorial to just how confusing events often seemed at that time. W. Odom, *The Collapse of the Soviet Military*, Yale University Press, New Haven, 1998 is the best explanation of the army's failure to save the Union. I have read two useful comparisons of late-Communist Russia and China: M. Pei, *From Reform to Revolution. The Demise of Communism in China and the Soviet Union*, Harvard University Press, Cambridge, 1994 and P. Nolan, *China's Rise, Russia's Fall. Politics, Economics and Planning in the Transition from Stalinism*, Macmillan, Houndmills, 1995. R. Thomas, *Serbia under Milosević*, Hurst, London, 1999 and T. Judah, *Serbs. History, Myth and the Destruction of Yugoslavia*, Yale University Press, New Haven, 1997 were my main sources on the collapse of Yugoslavia though I also benefited from the wisdom of Dejan Jović, one of the LSE's many excellent PhD students.

There are a number of books devoted to comparisons of empire's collapse in the Soviet Union and elsewhere. Apart from the volumes already listed which are edited by Barkey and von Hagen, by Lundestad, and by Demandt, there is a volume in a series on post-Soviet Northern Eurasia entitled *The End of Empire? The Transformation of the USSR in Comparative Perspective*, ed. K. Dawisha and B. Parrott, M.E. Sharpe, Armonk, 1997. R. Brubaker, *Nationalism Reframed. Nationhood and the National Question in the New Europe*, Cambridge University Press, 1996 is a valuable comparison of present-day Northern Eurasia with post-imperial interwar Central Europe.

CHAPTER 10.   AFTER EMPIRE

As regards post-Soviet Northern Eurasia, the period since the collapse of the USSR is so short and so unstable that true scholarship devoted entirely to post-Soviet politics is very difficult. On Russian politics since 1991, R. Sakwa, *Russian Politics and Society*, Routledge, London, 1996 and L. Shevtsova, *Yeltsin's Russia. Myths and Reality*, Carnegie, Washington, 1999 are probably the best introductions. L. Buszynski, *Russian Foreign Policy after the Cold War*, Praeger, Westport, 1996 is useful on Russian foreign policy and N. Malcolm, A. Pravda and M. Light, *Internal Factors in Russian Foreign Policy*, Oxford University Press, 1996 is valuable on the link between domestic and foreign policy. The same is true as regards Judith Devlin's book on post-Soviet Russian authoritarian political groups, *Slavophiles and Commissars. Enemies of Democracy in Modern Russia*, Macmillan, Houndmills, 1999.

There are a number of useful books already on the post-1991 Russian diaspora. They include: P. Kolstoe, *Russians in the Former Soviet Republics*, Hurst, London, 1995; C. King and N. Melvin (eds), *Nations Abroad. Diaspora Politics and International Relations in the Former Soviet Union*, Westview, Boulder, 1998; V. Shlapentokh, M. Sendich, E. Payin

Bibliography

(eds), *The New Russian Diaspora. Russian Minorities in the Former Soviet Republics*, M.E. Sharpe, Armonk, 1994. Books on individual post-Soviet countries are covered in the section on Chapter 9. As regards collections on all the post-Soviet states the best to date are: K. Dawisha and B. Parrott (eds), *Conflict, Cleavage and Change in Central Asia and the Caucasus*, Cambridge University Press, 1997; K. Dawisha and B. Parrott, *Democratic Changes and Authoritarian Reactions in Russia, Ukraine, Belarus and Moldova*, Cambridge University Press, 1997; I. Bremmer and R. Taras (eds), *Nations and Politics in the Soviet Successor States*, Cambridge University Press, 1996; G. Smith et al. (eds), *Nation-Building in the Post-Soviet Borderlands*, Cambridge University Press, 1998.

The best starting-point as regards the impact of the loss of empire on the former imperial metropolitan states and peoples is the collection of splendid essays in *The Journal of Contemporary History*, vol. 15, no. 3, 1980. The key books on post-imperial Austria and Hungary have already been listed, as has Brubaker's comparison between post-Habsburg and post-Hohenzollern Central Europe and today's former USSR. My only addition to the list is a shrewd and even at times amusing book by Thomas Sakmyster, *Hungary's Admiral on Horseback*, Columbia University Press, New York, 1994. Hugh Seton-Watson, *Eastern Europe between the Wars 1918–1941*, Cambridge University Press, 1945 is probably still the best book on ethnic politics and its link with international relations in the region. Another even older book by Elizabeth Wiskemann, *Czechs and Germans. A Study of the Struggle in the Historic Provinces of Bohemia and Moravia*, reprinted by Macmillan, London, 1967 is also still very valuable. There are a number of other more recent accounts of the crucial Czech-German relationship in interwar Czechoslovakia: see V.S. Mamatey and R. Luza (eds), *A History of the Czechoslovak Republic 1918–1948*, Princeton University Press, 1973; S. Dunn and T.G. Fraser (eds), *Europe and Ethnicity. World War 1 and Contemporary Ethnic Conflict*, London, 1996 contains many essays on post-Habsburg Europe.

Much of the literature on post-imperial Britain and her former colonies has been listed already: this is also true for works on Britain itself. The only additions here are a sharp collection of essays edited by Bernard Crick, *National Identities. The Constitution of the United Kingdom*, Blackwell, Oxford, 1991 and three very interesting new books on independent Ireland: E. O'Halpin, *Defending Ireland. The Irish State and its Enemies since 1922*, Oxford University Press, 1999; D. Fitzpatrick, *The Two Irelands 1912–1939*, Oxford University Press, 1998; R.B. McDowell, *Crisis and Decline. The Fate of the Southern Unionists*, Lilliput Press, Dublin, 1997.

On the overseas empire, in addition to books relating to South and South-East Asia that I have already discussed, a number of works on the Chinese and Indian diasporas should be mentioned: these include Wang Gungwu, *Community and Nation. China, South-East Asia and Australia*, Allen & Unwin, St Leonards, 1992; Lynn Pan, *Sons of the Yellow Emperor*, Mandarin, London, 1991; V. Lal, *Coups in Paradise*, Zed Books, London, 1990; and R.S. Milne, *Politics in Ethnically Bi-Polar States*, UBC Press, Vancouver, 1981. T.N. Harper, *The End of Empire and the Making of Malaya*, Cambridge University Press, 1999 is new and stimulating.

On post-imperial Africa I have not even scratched the surface: I have read and greatly enjoyed (if one can use such a word for what is so often a tragic story): A. Clayton, *Frontiersmen. Warfare in Africa since 1950*, UCL Press, London, 1999; B. Davidson, *The Black Man's Burden*, James Currey, Oxford, 1992: A. Horne, *A Savage War for Peace. 1954–1962*, Macmillan, London, 1977; J. Iliffe, *Africans. The History of a Continent*, Cambridge

University Press, 1995; N. McQueen, *The Decolonisation of Portuguese Africa*, Longman, London, 1997; E. Osaghae, *Crippled Giant. Nigeria since Independence*, Hurst, London, 1999; A. Wilson, *African Decolonisation*, Arnold, London, 1994. I started my reading on decolonization with R.F. Holland, *European Decolonisation*, Macmillan, Houndmills, 1985. Since then I have benefited from reading on colonial emergencies F. Furedi, *Colonial Wars and the Politics of Third World Nationalism*, I.B. Tauris, London, 1997 and R.F. Holland (ed.), *Emergencies and Disorder in the European Empires After 1945*, Frank Cass, London, 1994. C. Clapham, *Third World Politics. An Introduction*, Routledge, London, 1988 has been my guide and inspiration throughout my work on this book's last chapter.

Finally, on post-Ottoman issues see: L.C. Brown (ed.), *Imperial Legacy. The Ottoman Imprint on the Balkans and the Middle East*, Columbia University Press, New York, 1996; A. Kazancigil and E. Ozbudun (eds), *Atatürk. Founder of a Modern State*, Hurst, London, 1997; H. Poulton, *Top Hat, Grey Wolf and Crescent. Turkish Nationalism and the Turkish Republic*, Hurst, London, 1997; D. Fromkin, *A Peace to End All Peace. Creating the Modern Middle East 1914–1922*, Penguin, London, 1991; C.H. Dodd (ed.), *Cyprus. The Need for New Perspectives*, Eothen Press, Huntingdon, 1999; V. Calotychos (ed.), *Cyprus and its People*, Westview, Boulder, 1998. Michael Llewellyn-Smith, *Ionian Visions. Greece in Asia Minor 1919–1922*, Hurst, London, 1998 is excellent and very readable. A. Mango, *Atatürk*, John Murray, London, 1999 is the best biography yet of the founder of the Turkish Republic.

Index

Index